A TRAVELER'S COMPANION

A TRAVELER'S COMPANION

A COLLECTION FROM
HARPER'S MAGAZINE

GALLERY BOOKS
An Imprint of W. H. Smith Publishers Inc.
112 Madison Avenue
New York City 10016

This volume first published in 1991 by
Reed International Books Limited
Michelin House, 81 Fulham Road, London SW3 6RB

This edition published in 1991 by Gallery Books
an imprint of W. H. Smith Publishers Inc.
112 Madison Avenue, New York 10016

ISBN 0 - 8317 - 4260 - 7

Printed in Great Britain by The Bath Press, Avon.

CONTENTS

STREET LIFE IN INDIA

STREET LIFE IN INDIA.

BY EDWIN LORD WEEKS.

I.

I WAS agreeably disappointed in finding Bombay to be not the Oriental Liverpool I had imagined, but the proper and fitting threshold of India, an index, or rather an illustrated catalogue, of all Eastern races. Perhaps the most interesting spots in which to study the mixed and cosmopolitan character of the population are the stables for the sale of Arab horses. As it is still early in the day, the regulation time for "chota hazri" being somewhere about sunrise, we shall have time to take them in on the way down to the bazars, in which we shall probably lose ourselves, as the geography of Bombay is uncommonly bewildering at first. The "shigram" is waiting at the door, and the advantages of an early start in this climate are unquestionable. The "shigram," or "palkee gharry," is a vehicle found throughout the length and breadth of India; it is an oblong black box on four wheels. Inside there are two seats facing each other; a door on each side, sometimes sliding in grooves, sometimes made to swing outward in the usual manner. The windows are fitted with sliding blinds, and when all are closed but one, it makes a capital travelling studio. Our route lies along a broad suburban sort of avenue, to a square adorned with a bronze statue of Jamsetjee Jeejeebhoy, the great Parsee banker, and turning sharply to the left, we halt at the entrance of the largest of these Arab stables. Within the gate are lofty thatched sheds, and in the deep shadow are groups of the slender, swarthy natives of southern Arabia in striped mantles, with silk "kafeeyas," or tasselled handkerchiefs, twisted about their heads, looking much as they do in the cafés of Cairo, and drinking thick Mocha from the same kind of little cups. Their horses struck me as being much shorter-bodied than the horses of Africa or Syria, and had a larger average of chestnuts or bays among them. They are brought by sea from the ports of Arabia and the Persian Gulf. Another stable was chiefly tenanted by Persians, stalwart fellows with ruddy, sunburnt faces, stiff black mustaches, and shaven foreheads, showing a bluish patch below the rim of their round black or drab felt caps. They wear pale blue or green cotton kuftans, belted in at the waist, and hanging down over loose wide trousers of dark blue drill. Those who are not exercising or rubbing down their horses, many of which are still suffering from the effects of the sea-voyage and in poor condition, are asleep, stretched out in the shade, on their chests or on benches, or lounging amid a picturesque litter of camp baggage, pans, kettles, coffee-pots, and boxes, with well-worn prayer rugs spread over them. Others are busy over their water-pipes, or "kalians"; others, again, pounding coffee in a mortar, or winnowing grain with graceful movements. They are, however, none too busy to gather behind me and to make confidential remarks in Persian to each other, as I jot down a few impressions of color on small panels. To get a better point of view, and keep out of the way of a large and belligerent ram, I am obliged to place my camp-stool against a post to which several fluffy white Persian kittens are tethered by strings; they soon get wound up around the legs of the camp-stool, and make themselves so generally uncomfortable that another change of base becomes necessary, and this time I get within range of a large and inquisitive monkey, whose chain is just long enough to enable him to play havoc with palette and brushes, while my attention is distracted by the ram, which is kicking up a cloud of dust in the rear. One morning, a few days later, when making the round of these stables with a distinguished officer who had been in command of the com-

missary department in the Afghan war, my companion was recognized by an old Beloochee chief, robed in white, with a vast spotless turban, hair and beard dyed blue-black, and his long locks hanging down each side of his face and mingling with his beard. This gentleman had furnished all the horses for the campaign, and together they had sat under a tree—the English chief and the Beloochee—and counted out into little piles whole lakhs of rupees as the horses were trotted up for inspection.

India is never silent; whether in city or jungle one is always surrounded by vigorous and sometimes obtrusive animal life, and in writing of the every-day life of the country one should never lose sight of the relation which exists between it and that of the people. It is really one of the great attractions of India, provided always that one does not object to living for a while on terms of daily intimacy with the animal kingdom. With us in the West animal life is banished from our cities, or exists only in a state of bondage, and it is daily becoming more difficult to get within rifle-shot of any wild creature. But on entering one of the crowded and primitive old cities of India one cannot help wondering to whom all these animals belong, and why this bullock is blocking up the narrow street, or ruminating in the front doorway of a fine house. But we are not long in finding out that these animals have quite as much right to their share of the street as we have. For the most part, all these beasts, save the monkeys, are gentle and well-behaved, rarely presuming on their privileges; and their placid confidence in human nature shows that their trust has never been betrayed. Many incidents in the *Arabian Nights*, which even after a long familiarity with the Moslem East may have seemed to belong to the domain of pure fantasy, become to the observer in India simple illustrations of every-day life, such as the story of Cogia Hassam, whose turban was snatched from his head by a kite, and even the history of King Beder, who was transformed into a bird. But to understand why these things are, let us look at them for a moment with the eyes of a Brahmin, and all will be made clear. Modern science has not superseded the Brahmin's creed; he absorbs it, and it agrees with what he already knows. He does not care to inquire further, for his

convictions are deeply rooted. He believes in the transmigration of souls, as
did the Indian or Aryan contemporaries
of Plato. All these creatures were people once like ourselves, but they inhabit
for a time these animal shapes. So, too,
may we. "The Brahmin who has stolen
gold shall pass a thousand times through
the bodies of spiders, of serpents, of aquatic animals, of evil vampires." "The
murderer of a Brahmin passes into the
body of a dog, a hog, or an ass, a camel
or bull, a wild beast, or a Tchandala (a
mixed caste, the lowest of all), according
to the gravity of his crime." But all
of them are not necessarily criminals:
the uncouth and bald-headed adjutant
standing on one leg on yonder roof, apparently asleep, but keenly watching the
square below out of one half-closed eye,
was doubtless a usurious "Bunia"; and
as for the crows and birds of prey, one
has not far to look for their human prototypes in any country.

From the Arab stables it is but a short
step to the Copper Bazar, a most animated
centre of life and movement. We have
not yet been long enough ashore to have
become accustomed to the vivid colors of
the costumes, the splendid sunlight and
depths of shadow in the streets, and that
mingling of the beautiful with the quaint
and grotesque which emphasizes the contrast with what we have left. Against
the dimly remembered and sombre background of Europe, with the hopeless melancholy of its autumn landscape, its sad-
colored garments in harmony with the
leaden skies, is displayed the splendor of
the tropics—a new nature, young and
lusty, where there is no suggestion of decay. We enter at once into another atmosphere and a more joyous life, which
finds its outward expression in the huge
and quaintly fashioned turbans of crimson and scarlet with flashes of gold, in
vests of gold brocade and shawls of daintily tinted silks, in the swinging skirts and
floating draperies of the women, the flashing of the sunlight on the piled-up copper
jars deftly posed on their heads, and the
musical jingle of bracelets and massive
silver trinkets. For here the streets have
not the sadness of all Mohammedan cities,
which is due to the absence of women's
faces. Above all, this sentiment of the
far South is felt in the rich, mellow greens
of the foliage, to which the humid air of
the coast lends a velvety softness not seen

further inland. It is all color. Even
the odd little native carriages, or "hack-
eries," which take the place of "Hansom
cabs" with the Hindoos, are curtained with
Indian red, orange, and dull blue; a long,
narrow awning, to protect the driver from
the vertical sunbeams, stretches from the
roof, and, supported by an upright stick
planted in the yoke, reaches almost to the
horns of the fast-trotting little bullocks,
and even they are blanketed with Joseph's
coat of many hues.

We are now in the Copper Bazar, and
the "gharry wallah" reins up in "the
thick of the throng," and close to the
shop which is unconsciously most picturesque. It is a long range of old wooden
houses, whitewashed, and with dark beams,
wide eaves shading the upper stories,
which, except for the many windows, are
very like the old Moorish buildings in the
"Bibrambla" at Granada. The gleaming copper-ware is displayed in the cav-
ernous shops of the lower story, which
are separated from each other by stout
posts with carved wooden brackets supporting the horizontal beam above, and
protected from the sun by old and tattered awnings. Piles of huge brazen and
copper vessels are ranged in front; some
with the iridescent glitter of new metal,
the rough surfaces showing each stroke
of the hammer; others with the dull and
oxidized tones of old bronze. But the
sun beats down on the flat roof of the carriage, and the stuffy interior, with but one
window left open, soon becomes like the
hottest cell of a Turkish bath; and, as the
sun is getting well up, we seek the shade
of a narrow street close by, where there is
a fascinating row of fruit stalls, with huge
bunches of plantains gleaming yellow under the canvas awnings, and piles of man-
goes, guavas, and custard-apples. On the
shady side of the street the houses are
high and imposing; the upper portions
project well over the lower floors, and are
supported on stout teak-wood pillars which
have elaborately carved brackets projecting diagonally outward from their capitals to the sculptured horizontal beams
above. Here the crowd is so dense that
although I have stationed a servant close
to the window to keep the people from
forming a compact ring about the gharry,
he is obliged to call in the aid of a native
policeman; and yet, if we are on foot, we
may wend our way through the press
without coming in contact with a single

person. Long practice, combined with hereditary instinct, has taught them to avoid with unerring precision the touch of another's garments. Those who belong to the higher castes would have penances and numberless purifications to undergo should they by chance be contaminated by those of lower grades, while the latter are equally careful to avoid touching their superiors. Even the humpbacked cows which wander about at their will seem to have inherited the same instinct.

White prevails in the costumes. They wear tightly fitting gowns or "kuftans," or sometimes short jackets of white cotton or transparent muslin, which are fastened over the left breast, and instead of trousers a long strip of white cloth, edged with red, and so fastened at the waist as to fall in graceful folds below the knee. There is also a great deal of primitive nudity, particularly among the coolies and watercarriers, the polished bronze of whose backs shines as if it had been rubbed with oil. But the most striking feature of all is the bewildering and endless variety of the turbans, both in form and in color. I have never passed a day in Bombay without noting several new shapes, for here one may encounter people from every province of India, Persia, and central Asia. Many peculiar forms are worn by the Indian Mussulman as well as by the various Hindoo castes. As we had cast covetous eyes upon these turbans, and determined to carry away as many as possible, visits to the various shops where they are made formed amusing incidents in our afternoon drives. Each caste or order has its own hatter, who generally keeps no stock in trade, but expects his clients to bring their own cloth; and, first wetting the material, he winds it into shape, and fashions it with consummate skill over a form like a barber's block. Yards upon yards of crimson silk or cloth go to the making of one of these imposing structures, such as are worn by certain Mahratta castes, with pleated folds crossing and overlying each other, and sometimes forming, as it were, little points or horns, tipped with cloth of gold.

Having passed the morning among the bazars, we usually devoted ourselves during the heat of the day to the study of such models as could be found, and to the pleasing contemplation of snake charmers; of ferocious combats between the mongoose and the whipsnake, to the utter annihilation of the latter; the feats of jugglers; and the unwilling performances of highly educated but reluctant monkeys. In the late afternoon, when the sun gets low, the victoria provided by our Parsee landlord draws up under the portico, and we spend the remaining hours before dinner in driving about among the "old clothes" shops, looking for costumes and bric-à-brac, and then along the shady roads away from the city. A favorite route led us by painted and many-windowed villas of wealthy Parsees; past "high-walled gardens, green and old"; under the slender and slanting stems of tall cocoa-palms, which lean over the street at every angle; along dusty roads, where we used to meet droves of blue-gray buffaloes, and groups of laughing Hindoo girls carrying their brazen jars; and so toward the charming suburb of Malabar Hill, where are all the handsome "bungalows" of wealthy foreign residents, buried in luxurious and wellkept shrubbery. The road winds along the base of the promontory which juts out into the sea at right angles to the longer peninsula, and under the temple walls of Mahaluxmee, where it skirts the shore. It is a purple sea, breaking lazily on black volcanic rocks. A few cocoapalms on a distant cliff are bending before the strong sea-breeze, which is yet so soft that it is like a caress. The road widens, and there are seats placed near the water. We pass the residence of the Rao of Cutch, gay with glazed galleries and colored awnings. Many servants and attendants are standing about the gates, and also a crowd of grotesque fakirs, who expect to be fed and sent on their way rejoicing. Here we wind slowly upward past the "Towers of Silence," where the Parsees lay their dead. A few vultures are sailing above. Then a point is reached where we may look off over the wide expanse of the bay, far to seaward, and down over dark cliffs half hidden by thickets of wild date-trees —rich green tangles, with the gray limbs of some forest giant protruding in places over a green, billowy sea of cocoa-nut groves—along the curving silver line of the beach below, to the long peninsula of Bombay, beyond which can be seen, distant and faint, the ridges of the Western Ghauts. And if the roseate haze which veils the horizon lifts a little we may discern the outline of the fairy isle of Elephanta, far out in the bay.

After leaving this point the road winds past many bungalows, which stand well back behind high hedges, among flowering trees and bright pastures. Everything suggests indolence and luxury.

nine members of the household, and see that they get their necessary exercise, for the Christian dog, like his master, is prone to fall into lazy habits in this climate. A little further on, if we leave the road

BULLOCK FEEDING IN THE STREET.

Further on we pass the grounds of the Gymkana, where young men and girls are strolling about in tennis costume. Here we meet the "dog boy," a Hindoo urchin, leading dogs of various sizes in leash. His office is to look after the ca-

and turn down a narrow lane which winds past old carved houses, and down long flights of stone steps, we are again in primitive India. This is the sacred tank which reflects the temples of Walkeswar. Dark banyans and tangles of brighter green hang over the worn steps of the margin, and, together with white walls and weather-stained pyramidal spires, are mirrored in the water below. In the shrines above you may see the stone bull decked with yellow flowers and daubed with red-ochre. Crowds of pilgrims and fakirs jostle each other on the wet pavement. Some of these fakirs are painted and decorated with such elaborate grotesqueness that the audience of a Paris circus would greet them with wild delight. On reaching the carriage again there is still time to drive to the "Fort" and hear the band play. A rather steep descent under high cliffs winds down to the shore of the "Back Bay," where are moored a number of quaintly carved, high-sterned, and la-teen-sailed galleys in the shallow water. This is the beginning of the fashionable promenade, the "Allée des Acacias" of Bombay. But what drive in Europe has such a decorative background? Where, except at an opera ball, could one see such mingling of varied costumes and

BIRD-HOUSE IN A PUBLIC SQUARE.

races; and where else could one find more show of luxury and pomp among the equipages which crowd the roadway? It is all doubly interesting because of the meeting of East and West, of England and "Young India," and the old conservatism which is slowly putting off its stiffness and taking unto itself new ways. For these contrasts are more marked here than elsewhere. Here is the correct, properly appointed victoria, which might be in Hyde Park but for the liveried Indian footmen behind; here the dog-cart and trimly varnished trap, with a cockney "tiger" born in Houndsditch. Now comes a ponderous family chariot containing an entire Parsee household, a portly and pompous old gentleman—perhaps a banker, whose rotund person is clad in white, and his spectacled face surmounted by a tall, mitre-like cap of black oil-cloth. His large-eyed ladies are decked with loose silken shawls, very self-asserting in color, pale blue and lilac and salmon-color being favorite tints. The Parsee face has something of the Persian and a little of the Jewish character— large eyes, prominent nose and chin, clipped mustache, and mutton-chop whiskers. Indeed, if you should meet this gentleman in Regent Street, clothed by a West End tailor, you would swear that he was an Englishman with a slight strain of foreign blood; but his visiting card, if not his accent, will betray him every time, for he is always Jamsetjee or Ruttonjee. Now we meet a huge and lumbering barouche drawn by four splendid horses. Syces run in front, and the statuesque servants are in gorgeous liveries of scarlet and gold. Inside sits a Rajput prince, with his ministers or some of his numerous brothers—a "sixteen-gun man," to use a Bombay term, referring to the number of guns with which a Rajah is saluted, according to his rank; and galloping behind, in a cloud of dust, is a group of black-bearded Indian lancers, erect and soldierly, in neat uniforms of Karkee drill, gold-fringed turbans, with clanking "tulwars" and scarlet pennons fluttering from the tips of their lances. Next is a dog-cart behind a fast trotter; two young Persians, "gommeux" from the city of Ispahan, with tall black caps and well-cut coats from the best Bombay tailor, are perched up in the front. Just behind them is an Arab "sheik," riding a long-tailed white horse, wearing the camel's-hair mantle and striped yellow "kafeeya" of his race.

A rather handsome man, with a Rajput turban and English-cut garments, who is intent on driving two horses tandem from the top of a lofty two-wheeled trap, is pointed out as the Rajah of Nagpore. Other carriages of more modest pretensions contain Mussulman or Hindoo merchants, wearing their curiously shaped caste turbans. A golden glow from the setting sun is thrown on the wall of towering and swaying cocoa-nut palms which borders the drive on the landward side. Here the road takes a turn inward and crosses the railway, which does not seem to be a disfigurement. Green fields fenced in by low white rails lie between the tracks and the sea. The several stations between this point and Colaba, where the Bombay, Baroda, and Central India has its terminus, are graceful low stone buildings, with open and pillared loggias wreathed in trailing vines which harmonize with the landscape. We may get down here and continue our promenade along the sea on foot. Passing between posts, we enter upon a gravelled path, with seats at intervals, which runs close to the rocky shore. Groups of well-dressed people of many races are sauntering along. Here and there a Parsee in white, with tall black mitre, is perched on a rock, book in hand, idly turning over the leaves, his lips moving as if repeating a prayer, while he gazes steadily at the setting sun, which now sinks, a dim red ball, behind the purple rim of the Arabian Gulf. For the Parsees are the last survivors of the worshippers of fire and of the sun. Just beyond, a Mussulman, with grave dignity of demeanor, spreads a shawl upon the grass, and begins the usual genuflections and prostrations; but here he faces the setting sun, for Mecca lies far to the westward.

The short, golden twilight is over, and darkness is coming on, but the drive home through the Hindoo city is always amusing at night, and as the tall houses have a lower floor or deep veranda, quite open to the street, and the upper stories have their many and complicated shutters thrown wide open, we get the benefit of all the illumination. The street is *en fête*. We can see all the people inside, and feel as if they had taken us into their confidence. Brown-skinned Brahmin gentlemen, innocent of shirts, but wearing wide-spreading and elaborately wound crimson turbans, are lolling out of the windows; others are going to bed under their porches; and the low-posted native bedstead, covered with a criss-cross arrangement of hempen cords, which all day has stood up against the front of the house, is now brought into play. Some are already asleep, and, stretched out on their low "charpies," as they are called, have the uncanny look of corpses in winding-sheets. At many of the upper windows are "Nautch-girls"—moon-faced beauties, brown and buxom, with gazelle eyes, and glittering with trinkets. Some of the shops below are still open, and lit by the flickering flames of tall brass lamps of quaint design. Down a narrow side street, as we drive past, we get a glimpse of a wedding procession, accompanied by a din of tomtoms, glaring torches, fireworks, and an all-pervading smell of gunpowder.

II.

We have chosen Ahmedabad as the first resting-place in our progress north, and are soon *en route*, being fortunate enough to secure a roomy compartment in the evening mail-train. As the night wind blows in at the open windows with the spicy fragrance of the wooded country through which we are passing, we feel a sense of relief at escaping from the melting nights of Bombay. The morning light reveals a park-like country with broad-spreading trees, here and there a dusty road with lumbering bullock carts waiting for the train to pass; everything in the carriage is coated with a layer of the same fine dust. A slender tree overhanging the track nearly breaks down with the weight of a dozen large monkeys, which are chasing each other up and down, quite regardless of the passing train. These monkeys, or rather apes, are greenish gray in color, with long tails, and their black faces are framed with a fringe of snow-white beard in startling contrast. Their collective expression is grotesquely mournful. All along this line of railway they seem to outnumber the human inhabitants.

To an amateur of new impressions there is no amusement more fascinating than to wander aimlessly about and lose himself in the mazes of a new Oriental city. One knows beforehand what to expect of Venice, of Cairo, of Damascus, and one may be sure of sitting down to just such a table d'hôte and with the same menu as in Paris. But Ahmedabad is like the city of a dream, as it has never been made familiar to us by painters or described in guide-books. It does not matter where one goes, every street shows us something strange, and as one seldom meets a European, the Anglo-Indian considering it "infra dig" to be seen on foot in the streets of a native city, one might fancy himself in Bagdad in the golden prime of good Haroun-al-Raschid. This narrow street, which leads us to the "Manik Chouk," or principal avenue, is lined on each side with ancient houses of carved teak-wood. Bombay has prepared us in a measure for the street architecture of Guzerat; but here the type exists in its purity. These houses are often carved all over, up to the broad eaves. There are brackets with female figures like caryatides; the sculptured heads of horses and elephants, rich with detail, ornament the ends of projecting beams. Wherever there is a surface of stuccoed wall, it is decorated with painted processions in fresco, wherein elephants and horses, princes, soldiers, and fakirs, are depicted with vivid colors, but rude in drawing and often laughably grotesque. Many of these houses are painted in arabesque, but the colors on most of them have faded or have been washed away, so that only a few patches of blue and orange remain in the interstices of the awnings, which, with the gray tones of the old wood, make an agreeable harmony of color. As the sun is just up, the people are opening their doors and windows, and standing up their beds against the walls; some are performing their toilet operations in full view of the street, and gossiping with their neighbors as they squat in their doorways. A whole row of them are brushing their teeth with wooden sticks in unison over the gutter. Brown babies of all sizes are playing in the doorways among the chickens and kids. Here is a house carved like a jewel-box, the heavy door is sumptuously wrought with cross-beams, ornamented with projecting metallic bosses. While we are lost in admiration it suddenly opens, and a couple of cows rush madly out and clatter down the steps of the portico: cows in this country do not object to going up and down stairs. We are not to suppose, however, that this is a barn; it only happens that

THE BRIDAL PROCESSION.

the cows, in coming from their quarters behind, are obliged to traverse the lower floor of the family mansion.

There are occasional bird-houses raised on tall posts. One was a curiously carved octagonal structure which stood in a crowded square; the pillar supporting it was raised on a gayly painted pedestal, surrounded on the top by a fence of wire netting. It had a ladder raised up when not in use, and little baskets or trays hung from the house above, containing food for passing birds. These aerial restaurants are usually monopolized by the ubiquitous crow. The principal avenue, or rather boulevard, called the "Manik Chouk," is crowded at this early hour with country people, as it is market-day. They are already spreading their awnings, which are like square sails with a post at the intersection of two diagonals, so that they can be planted at any angle. They shelter groups of women and baskets of tropical fruits—plantains and bananas, custard-apples, guavas, and many strange varieties. There are stands for the sale of cheap jewelry, clothing, and European wares, piles of pottery, and water jars of every shape. Everywhere one notices the pungent aromatic odor of guavas. It is the prevailing odor of Ahmedabad just now. Across the avenue towers an imposing triumphal arch, or rather a series of three arches, forming a superb background for the variegated crowd. This is the "Tin Darvaja," or "three gateways." It is of cream-colored stone, built in the usual style of Ahmedabad mosques. Between each arch projects a buttress, reaching nearly to the top, and sculptured after the manner of the minarets. Out of a narrow lane a procession emerges from the shadow of a great gateway, with prolonged and shrill tooting of horns and beating of drums. They are bringing home the bride in a carriage the like of which was never seen out of India. Two great white oxen yoked together advance with stately tread drawing the carriage. Their branching horns are nearly hidden by silver rings, the massive headstalls are of the same glittering metal, and they are covered by scarlet robes reaching nearly to the ground. The bulky pole of the carriage is covered with cloth of the same color, and the yoke is of copper, with a row of silver bells tinkling below it. But the carriage itself is gorgeous, and with a dome of heavy gold embroidery

glittering like Benares brass, and bordering its base, as well as around the red awning which shelters the driver, hang double rows of crimson silk tassels. The wheels have an elaborate system of copper brakes, as complicated as the rigging of a "three-decker." Even the leather bellows-like arrangement under the carriage is bestarred with painted flowers. The multitude of small bells tinkle as it moves along, and through the scarlet curtains we see the bride, with round young face. half hidden by heavy jewelry. We recognized at once the inspiration of Edwin Arnold's picture in "The Light of Asia":

> "....while the prince
> Came forth in painted car, which two steers drew,
> Snow-white, with swinging dewlaps, and huge humps
> Wrinkled against the carved and lacquered yoke."

Having sent to find out the owner of this wedding carriage, we were told that it was the property of two young Hindoos who had just inherited a large estate from their father. They kindly sent it to the bungalow, driver and all, excepting the bride, to be used as a model. We called afterward to thank them, and were shown into a teak-wood mansion, and up stairs to a drawing-room quite English in character, with engravings of the Queen and Prince Consort, European furniture, and crystal chandelier swathed in muslin. They were young men of twenty or thereabouts, and spoke very fair English. We were then shown the stables, across the street, where several vehicles of the same description, more or less elaborate, were ranged in order. They were probably an important source of revenue to the owners, as they are in great demand for fashionable weddings.

The bungalow is not placed at an impossible distance from the city, as in most places, but within easy walking distance of many interesting spots. Close to it is the "Queen's Mosque," one of the most attractive monuments of the city; and a little further on is another mosque, to which we were attracted in passing by the play of sunlight and shadow in the court, seen through the half-open gate. There was a sheet of water reflecting the shadowed marble façade with dark arches, and the dazzling white of a sunlit wall, above which rose the time-worn domes of an ancient tomb in the adjoining garden; large earthen pots with flowering shrubs stood about the tank. Being hospitably received by the venerable mollah, or priest,

AT THE FOOT OF THE TOWER.

in charge, I chose a shady corner near where he sat, in the checkered shadow of a fig-tree, while he smoked a primitive hubble-bubble, or drowsed and nodded over his Koran. A few loungers were asleep or bathing in the tank, and breaking the broad white reflection with long azure ripples. It was a drowsy place, enlivened only by the monotonous murmur of the hubble-bubble and occasional piercing cries from the flocks of sleek green parrots which flitted about among the trees. After the last bather had lain down in the shade, some young monkeys appeared in the tree-tops, and swinging themselves down into the court, advanced toward the water, looking furtively behind them; but catching sight of an old one, they scampered away out of sight, while he walked to the steps with dignified deliberation, and first taking a drink, performed his ablutions much as the people had done just before; then he seated himself on the broken cornice of a wall to meditate and hunt for fleas. The little ones then came out from their hiding-places, and each in turn, according to size,

went through the same performance. These monkeys are the street buffoons of Ahmedabad.

On another occasion, having decided to paint the entrance of the "Jumma Musjid," or Great Mosque, the shigram was brought to anchor in the middle of the street, and in front of the chosen spot. I am deep in the study of relative values, when a large monkey, springing from a roof on the other side, comes down with a tremendous thump on the roof of the carriage, and, using it like the spring-board of a gymnasium, bounces off again, to land on a low tiled roof under the mosque wall. Seeing a good opportunity to try a new "extra rapid" plate, I get out with my camera, and cautiously approaching, succeed in getting a shot. Now the "gharry wallah," who is deeply interested, also gets down, and taking a banana, holds it up to the eaves, and the monkey, after many precautions, reaches down and takes it from his hand. This enables me to get a second plate. While the fruit sellers are intent on my proceedings, another monkey makes a sudden and victorious raid on a basket of guavas, to the huge delight of the by-standers, who join in a loud laugh at the expense of the victim.

III.

But the head centre of all monkeydom is the holy city of Muttra, or Mathura, a sort of supplementary Benares, on the river Jumna. Here we find another species, the same, I think, from which the organ-grinder generally selects his partner. The principal care in life of the citizens is to protect themselves and their property from the depredations of this privileged class, for, as they are sacred—and what animal is not in Hindoo-land ?—they cannot be killed or molested in any manner. On the day of our arrival, having engaged a shigram, we took the usual long drive from the dâk bungalow to the city. We stopped at the steps leading up to the gateway of the principal mosque, which was faced with beautiful glazed tiles, the colors of which were still fresh and brilliant, although the whole pile showed many signs of neglect and decay. There were two tall "minars," crowned with graceful domed pavilions, quite covered with the same artistic tile-work. As it was necessary to get some idea of the geography of the town, we lost no time in ascending one of these towers, up a narrow winding stair, over dust and débris, disturbing hundreds of pigeons. When we looked down from the topmost gallery over the expanse of flat-roofed houses and sculptured pyramids of temples, the central figure in the foreground below was a woman in skirt and bodice, but without the usual long shawl or "chuddah," standing alone upon a house-top, and, to judge from her gestures, in great distress. On the next roof, perhaps ten feet away, across the narrow street, a group of monkeys were chattering in great excitement over her silken shawl, which had been captured by the chief. After examining it with rapt attention, he threw it suddenly over his head, and raising one corner, peered out at the others, mimicking the motions of some photographer whom he had seen at work. Then, to the visible despair of the woman, he started off in a series of flying leaps, dragging the shawl after him, closely pursued by the rest of the gang, who were wild to get hold of it and do likewise. Soon it was torn to shreds, and as the captor tripped and got entangled in the fluttering folds, he was quickly overhauled by his pursuers, and every one of them got a strip of the plunder.

Every window in the town is barred with lattices, as not even the highest is out of their reach, for they could give points to the best gymnast that ever swung on a trapeze. Along the underside of the highest balconies they follow one another in single file, leaping past intervening brackets, or with one bound they clear the street, and swinging from the pendent branches of a banyan-tree, in they go at some small opening left for a moment unguarded, lured by the sight of a bowl of milk on the sill; and when they are chased out again at the point of the broomstick, they go and console themselves among the stalls of the fruit sellers in the bazar. But their chief field of action is along the "ghâts," where stone steps descend to the fast-flowing Jumna. Here at intervals are octagonal stone towers separating the different bathing-places, often surmounted by domes resting on slender columns. A tall sculptured tower of red sandstone rises straight from the brink among a group of time-worn temples. This tower seems to be tenanted only by monkeys. There still remain a few stone gargoyles, but the animated gargoyles are even more interesting. At a small square window sits a mother monkey with her infant, which at once suggests a caricature of the Madonna della Seggiola; near the base of the tower squat small urchins provided with large shallow baskets of what seem to be dried pease. At a sign from the passer, they scatter handfuls over the pavement, which is at once covered and nearly hidden by a struggling mass of monkeys.

In the early morning hours these steps are crowded with bathers and women filling their sparkling copper jars with water; the varied colors of the costumes, the fantastic architecture, the dense foliage and drooping branches of the great banyans which overhang the water, are all mirrored in the swiftly moving current. One of the ghâts is set apart for the women who come to bathe, and here is an ever-shifting kaleidoscope of vivid color. The eye is caught by the shimmer of silk and gold, as they throw off their shining draperies and reveal their lovely outlines and the satin lustre of their amber-brown skins. Sometimes a sudden shriek goes up from among the fair bathers, as some enterprising monkey is seen scaling up to

ALONG THE GHÂTS.

the wide eaves of a temple, dragging after him an embroidered "chuddah." Then there is a great hubbub and babel of tongues, and the monkey police appear on the scene. The chief business of these men is to keep a watchful eye on the little demons; they are armed with long white wands, which are only used to intimidate the transgressor, but it would seem without much success. Their usual plan, since the shawl is always high out of reach, is to place a bit of fruit or some other tempting bait on a lower terrace, and then to steal around to the rear, while the monkey is expected to forget the shawl in his eagerness to seize the new plunder; but I have seen him cautiously descend, dragging the shawl after him, secure the fruit, and then make good his escape, without losing any of his booty, to some eminence whence he could safely deride with hideous grimaces his baffled pursuers. A frequent object of cupidity is the small, glittering brass pot which every Hindoo carries for drinking purposes, and which is sometimes filled with sour milk, or some other succulent dainty. The successful robber retires to the roof of some shrine just above the heads of the crowd, nonchalantly devours the contents of the pot, and then, forgetting all about it, down it falls from his careless hand on the head of some unlucky wight below. One morning an unusual commotion arose among the monkey population as an elephant passed along the narrow street just above the steps. The excitement was intense, particularly among the smaller fry, who followed along from roof to roof, peeping out from behind the openings at the colossus with the eager curiosity of small boys. A most moving incident was a fight nearly to the death between two rival patriarchs, and I am sure that we could not have felt more breathless interest at our first bull-fight in Granada. One would have expected much preliminary chattering and mutual vituperation; but no; the combatants went at it with the quiet determination of two veteran pugilists. At first there was considerable excitement among the others as they all rushed down to take part in the fray; but the monkey police used their sticks to good advantage in keeping them back, and then tried to separate the principals; touch them they dared not. All the crowd came down and formed a ring on the steps; some threw water on the combatants, but it was of no use. They

clinched, tugged, and wrestled; the fur flew; they both fell into the water, and crawled out nearly drowned, and so weakened by loss of blood that they could hardly stand; and at last they dragged themselves wearily up the steps, and limped down the main street, followed by all the by-standers.

Notwithstanding the prominent part played by the monkeys in the little dramas of street life, they do not seem to be often cultivated as pets, for the reason that the popular mind, with the patient resignation of fatalism, has long since learned to endure them as necessary evils, and in places like Muttra, where they are held in exceptional veneration, they enjoy all the privileges of town paupers, including immunity from labor. But throughout India people will make pets of any animals which can be induced to contribute to their entertainment. We noticed in Delhi that the average small boy, as well as children of a larger growth, exhibited a particular fondness for a certain little bird of ashen plumage and black crest. This was the famous bulbul of which Hafiz has much to say, and some Western poets also who have sentimentalized about the Vale of Cashmere without even having seen it. He is usually tethered by a string attached to his leg, and sits upon his owner's finger, or hops about on his arm; sometimes too he adorns a tall perch in front of the doorway. A lady at the hotel remarked that "it was touching to see how fond these poor people were of their little birds." The mystery was soon solved. Returning from a drive one afternoon, we passed the colossal gateway of the great mosque, and saw that the broad and towering flight of steps before the principal entrance was covered with scattered groups of people, all intent on some occupation of absorbing interest. So vast and imposing was the architectural background that the crowd of little figures suggested one of Martin's weird pictures of the Judgment Day. Some great religious ceremony was evidently going on. So we got out, deeply impressed, to obtain a nearer view, when, behold, in the centre of each little group was a pair of these birds in mortal combat; and they fought as pluckily as the bravest of game fowl, and breathless was the interest shown by every spectator, whether street urchin or shawled and turbaned merchant.

In front of almost every shop in the

bazars of Lahore and Amritsar hang dome-shaped cages of bamboo. Often two or three hang in a row from the daintily carved balconies or highest terraces of the houses, and they are covered with scarlet or party-colored curtains to keep out the

of well-dressed natives at the review on Jubilee Day at Lahore I observed many who had brought their partridges with them in cages, carefully curtained to exclude the sun and dust, perhaps with the thought that if the interest of the specta-

THE SUCCESSFUL ROBBER.

sun. In each of these cages is a sturdy red-legged partridge, loved and prized for his pugnacious qualities. When the merchant takes his morning stroll, and sits down on the bench which runs along the front of each shop to gossip with his neighbor, he produces his tame partridge from the folds of his shawl, and lets him run about, or plays with him in the pauses of conversation. Among the dense crowd

cle flagged, they might get up a little private circus of their own. There was also the man who always goes about accompanied by his pet ram. On this occasion the animal had been carefully washed and combed in honor of the day, his horns gilded, and he was arrayed in his gala blanket of scarlet cloth, thickly wadded, which, as the sun was rather hot, seemed quite superfluous.

FROM THE HEBRID ISLES

THE SMOOTHING OF THE HAND.*

ST. MARTIN'S CROSS.
From a Photograph by Valentine and Sons, Dundee.

GLAD am I that wherever and whenever I listen intently I can hear the looms of Nature weaving Beauty and Music. But some of the most beautiful things are learned otherwise —by hazard, in the Way of Pain, or at the Gate of Sorrow.

I learned two things on the day when I saw Sheumas McIan dead upon the heather. He of whom I speak was the son of Ian McIan Alltnalee, but was known throughout the home straths and the countries beyond as Sheumas Dhu, Black James, or, to render the subtler meaning implied in this instance, James the Dark One. I had wondered occasionally at the designation, because Sheumas, if not exactly fair, was certainly not dark. But the name was given to him, as I learned later, because, as commonly rumored, he knew that which he should not have known.

I had been spending some weeks with Alasdair McIan and his wife Silis (who was my foster-sister), at their farm of Ardoch, high in a remote hill country. One night we were sitting before the peats, listening to the wind crying amid the corries, though, ominously as it seemed to us, there was not a breath in the rowan-tree that grew in the sun's-way by the house. Silis had been singing, but silence had come upon us. In the warm glow from the fire we saw each others' faces. There the silence lay, strangely still and beauti-

ful, as snow in moonlight. Silis's song was one of the *Dana Spioradail*, known in Gaelic as the Rune of the Looms. I cannot recall it, nor have I ever heard or in any way encountered it again.

It had a lovely refrain, I know not whether its own or added by Silis. I have heard her chant it to other runes and songs. Now, when too late, my regret is deep that I did not take from her lips more of those sorrowful strange songs or chants, with their ancient Celtic melodies, so full of haunting sweet melancholy, which she loved so well. It was with this refrain that, after a long stillness, she startled us that October night. I remember the sudden light in the eyes of Alasdair McIan, and the beat at my heart, when, like rain in a wood, her voice fell unawares upon us out of the silence:

*Oh! oh! ohrone, arone! Oh! oh! mo ghraidh,
    mo chridhe!*
    *Oh! oh! mo ghraidh, mo chridhe!**

The wail, and the sudden break in the second line, had always upon me an effect of inexpressible pathos. Often that sad wind-song has been in my ears, when I have been thinking of many things that are passed and are passing.

I know not what made Silis so abruptly begin to sing, and with that wailing couplet only, or why she lapsed at once into silence again. Indeed, my remembrance of the incident at all is due to the circumstance that shortly after Silis had turned her face to the peats again, a knock came to the door, and then Sheumas Dhu entered.

"Why do you sing that lament, Silis, sister of my father?" he asked, after he had seated himself beside me, and spread his thin hands against the peat glow, so that the flame seemed to enter within the flesh.

Silis turned to her nephew, and looked at him, as I thought, questioningly. But she did not speak. He, too, said nothing more, either forgetful of his question, or content with what he had learned or failed to learn through her silence.

The wind had come down from the corries before Sheumas rose to go. He said he was not returning to Alltnalee,

* The first piece in this selection of short tales and episodes is not Hebridean, but belongs to Argyll. Its localization, however, is accidental and non-essential, and it might as well have been set by the Waters of Uist as by the Hills of Arrochar.

* Pronounce mogh-rāy, mogh-rēe (my heart's delight: *lit.*, my dear one, my heart).

but was going upon the hill, for a big herd of deer had come over the ridge of Mel-Mòr. Sheumas, though skilled in all hill and forest craft, was not a sure shot, as was his kinsman and my host, Alasdair McIan.

"You will need help," I remember Alasdair Ardoch saying, mockingly, adding, "*Co dhiubh is fhearr let mise thoir sealladh na fàileadh dhiubh?*"—that is to say, Whether would you rather me to deprive them of sight or smell?

This is a familiar saying among the old sportsmen in my country, where it is believed that a few favored individuals have the power to deprive deer of either sight or smell, as the occasion suggests.

"*Dhuit ciàr nan carn!*—the gloom of the rocks be upon you!" replied Sheumas, sullenly; "mayhap the hour is come when the red stag will sniff at my nostrils."

With that dark saying he went. None of us saw him again alive.

Was it a prophecy? I have often wondered. Or had he any vague premonition?

It was three days after this, and shortly after sunrise, that, on crossing the south slope of Mel-Mòr with Alasdair Ardoch, we came suddenly upon the body of Sheumas, half submerged in a purple billow of heather. It did not, at the moment, occur to me that he was dead. I had not known that his prolonged absence had been noted, or that he had been searched for. As a matter of fact, he must have died immediately before our approach, for his limbs were still loose, and he lay as a sleeper lies.

Alasdair kneeled and raised his kinsman's head. When it lay upon the purple tussock, the warmth and glow from the sunlit ling gave a fugitive deceptive light to the pale face. I know not whether the sun can have any chemic action upon the dead. But it seemed to me that a dream rose to the face of Sheumas, like one of those submarine flowers that are said to rise at times and be visible for a moment in the hollow of a wave. The dream, the light, waned; and there was a great stillness and white peace where the trouble had been. "It is the Smoothing of the Hand," said Alasdair McIan, in a hushed voice.

Often I had heard this lovely phrase in the Western Isles, but always as applied to sleep. When a fretful child suddenly falls into quietude and deep slumber, an isles-woman will say that it is because of the Smoothing of the Hand. It is always a profound sleep, and there are some who hold it almost as a sacred thing, and never to be disturbed.

So, thinking only of this, I whispered to my friend to come away; that Sheumas was dead weary with hunting upon the hills; that he would awake in due time.

McIan looked at me, hesitated, and said nothing. I saw him glance around. A few yards away, beside a great bowlder in the heather, a small rowan stood, flickering its featherlike shadows across the white wool of a ewe resting underneath. He moved thitherward slowly, plucked a branch heavy with scarlet berries, and then, having returned, laid it across the breast of his kinsman.

I knew now what was that passing of the trouble in the face of Sheumas Dhu, what that sudden light was, that calming of the sea, that ineffable quietude. It was the Smoothing of the Hand.

THE WHITE FEVER.

ONE night, before the peats, I was told this thing by old Cairstine Macdonald, in the isle of Benbecula. It is in her words that I give it:

In the spring of the year that my boy Tormaid died, the moon-daisies were as thick as a woven shroud over the place where Giorsal, the daughter of Ian, the son of Ian MacLeod of Baille 'n Bad-a-sgailich, slept night and day.*

All that March the cormorants screamed, famished. There were few fish in the sea, and no kelp-weed was washed up by the high tides. In the island and in the near isles, ay, and far north through the mainland, the blight lay. Many sickened. I knew young mothers who had no milk. There are green mounds in Carnan kirk-yard that will be telling you of what this meant. Here and there are little green mounds, each that soft and round you might cuddle it in your arm under your

* *Baille 'n Bad-a-sgailich :* the Farm of the Shadowy Clump of Trees. *Cairstine,* or *Cairistine,* is the Gaelic for *Christina,* as *Tormaid* is for Norman, and *Giorsal* for Grace. "The quiet havens" is the beautiful island phrase for graves. Here, also, a swift and fatal consumption that falls upon the doomed is called "The White Fever." By "the mainland," Harris and the Lewis are meant.

plaidie. They call these bit graves "the wee lammies."

Tormaid sickened. A bad day was that for him when he came home, weary with the sea, and drenched to the skin, because of a gale that caught him and his mates off Barra Head. When the March winds tore down the Minch, and leaped out from over the Cuchullins, and came west, and lay against our homes, where the peats were sodden and there was little food, the minister told me that my laddie would be in the quiet havens before long. This was because of the white fever. It was of that Giorsal waned, and went out like a thin flame in sunlight.

The son of my man (years ago weary no more) said little ever. He ate nothing almost, even of the next to nothing we had. At nights he couldna sleep because of the cough. The coming of May lifted him awhile. I hoped he would see the autumn; and that if he did, and the herring came, and the harvest was had, and what wi' this and what wi' that, he would forget his Giorsal that lay i' the mools in the quiet place yonder. Maybe then, I thought, the sorrow would go, and take its shadow with it.

One gloaming he came in with all the whiteness of his wasted body in his face.

His heart was out of its shell: and mine, too, at the sight of him.*

This was in the season of the hanging of the dog's mouth.

"What is it, Tormaid-a-ghaolach?" I asked, with the sob that was in my throat.

"*Thraisg mo chridhe,*" he muttered (my heart is parched). Then, feeling the asking in my eye, he said, "I have seen her."

I knew he meant Giorsal. My heart sank. But I wore my nails into the palms of my hands. Then I said this thing, that is an old saying in the isles: "Those who are in the quiet havens hear neither the wind nor the sea." He was so weak he could not lie down in the bed. He was in the big chair before the peats, with his feet on a *claar*.

When the wind was still I read him the Word. A little warm milk was all he would take. I could hear the blood

* *A cochall a' chridhe*: his heart out of its shell— a phrase often used to express sudden derangement from any shock. The ensuing phrase means the month from the 15th of July to the 15th of August. *Mios crochaidh nan con*, so called as it is supposed to be the hottest if not the most waterless month in the isles. The word *claar*, used below, is the name given a small wooden tub, into which the potatoes are turned when boiled.

BARRA HEAD, OUTER HEBRIDES.
From a photograph by G. W. Wilson and Co., Aberdeen.

in his lungs sobbing like the ebb-tide in the sea-weed. This was the thing that he said to me:

"She came to me, like a gray mist, beyond the dike of the green place, near the road. The face of her was gray as a gray dawn, but the voice was hers, though I heard it under a wave, so dull and far was it. And these are her words to me, and mine to her—and the first speaking was mine, for the silence wore me:

Am bheil thu' falbh,
  O mo ghraidh?

  B'idh mi falbh,
    Mùirnean!

C'uin a thilleas tu,
  O mo ghraidh?

  Cha till mi an rathad so;
  Tha an't ait e cumhann—
    O mùirnean, mùirnean!
  B'idh mi falbh an drùgh
  Am tigh Pharais,
    Mùirnean!

Sèol dhomh an rathad,
  Mo ghraidh!

  Thig an so, Mùirnean-mo,
    Thig an so!

Are you going,
  My dear one?

  Yea, now I am going,
    Dearest.

When will you come again,
  My dear one?

  I will not return this way;
  The place is narrow—
    O my darling!
  I will be going to Paradise,
    Dear, my dear one!

Show me the way,
  Heart of my heart!

  Come hither, dearest, come hither,
    Come with me!

And then I saw that it was a mist, and that I was alone. But now this night it is that I feel the breath on the soles of my feet."

And with that I knew there was no hope. "*Ma tha sin an dàn!*.... if that be ordained," was all that rose to my lips. It was that night he died. I fell asleep in the second hour. When I woke in the gray dawn, his face was grayer than that and more cold.

FROM IONA.
THE SEA-WITCH OF EARRAID.

ONE day this summer I sailed with Phadruic Macrae and Ivor McLean, boatmen of Iona, along the southwestern reach of the Ross of Mull.

The whole coast of the Ross is indescribably wild and desolate. From Feenafort (Fhionn-phort), opposite Balliemore of Icolmkill, to the hamlet of Earraid Light-house, it were hardly exaggeration to say that the whole tract is uninhabited by man and unenlivened by any green thing. It is the haunt of the cormorant and the seal.

No one who has not visited this region can realize its barrenness. Its one beauty is the faint bloom which lies upon it in the sunlight—a bloom which becomes as the glow of an inner flame when the sun westers without cloud or mist. This is from the ruddy hue of the granite, of which all that wilderness is wrought.

It is a land tortured by the sea, scourged by the sea wind. A myriad lochs, fiords, inlets, passages, serrate its broken frontiers. Innumerable islets and reefs, fanged like ravenous wolves, sentinel every shallow, lurk in every strait. He must be a skilled boatman who would take the Sound of Earraid and penetrate the reaches of the Ross.

There are many days in the months of peace, as the islanders call the period from Easter till the autumnal equinox, when Earraid and the rest of Ross seem under a spell. It is the spell of beauty. Then the yellow light of the sun is upon the tumbled masses and precipitous shelves and ledges, ruddy petals or leaves of that vast Flower of Granite. Across it the cloud shadows trail their purple elongations, their scythe-sweep curves, and abrupt evanishing floodings of warm dusk. From wet bowlder to bowlder, from crag to shelly crag, from fissure to fissure, the sea ceaselessly weaves a girdle of foam. When the wide luminous stretch of waters beyond—green near the land, and further out all of a living blue, interspersed with wide alleys of amethyst—is white with the sea-horses, there is such a laughter of surge and splash all the way from Slugan-dubh to the Rudha-nam-Maol-Mòra, or to the tide-swept promontory of the Sgeireig-a'-Bhochdaidh, that, looking inland, one sees through a rainbow-shimmering veil of ever-flying spray.

But the sun spell is even more fugitive upon the face of this wild land than the spell of beauty upon a woman. So runs one of our proverbs: as the falling of the wave, as the fading of the leaf, so is the beauty of a woman, unless — ah, that *unless*, and the indiscoverable fount of

IONA—CATHEDRAL AND ST ORAN'S CHAPEL.
Drawn from a photograph by Valentine and Sons, Dundee.

joy that can only be come upon by haz-ard once in life, and thereafter only in dreams, and the Land of the Rainbow that is never reached, and the green sea-doors of Tir-na-thonn, that open now no more to any wandering wave!

It was from Ivor McLean, on that day, I heard the strange tale of his kinsman Murdoch, the tale of "The Ninth Wave"; and from him also, though at another time, that white-light episode of the Fes-tival of the Birds. It was Phadruic, however, who told me of the Sea-witch of Earraid.

"Yes," he said, "I have heard of the *uisge-each*" (the sea-beast, sea-kelpie, or water-horse), "but I have never seen it with the eyes. My father and my brother knew of it. But this thing I know, and that is what we call *an-cailleach-uisge*" (the siren or water-witch); "the *cailliach*, mind you, not the *mhaighdeann-mhàra*" (the mermaid), "who means no harm. May she hear my saying it! The cail-liach is old and clad in weeds, but her voice is young, and she always sits so that the light is in the eyes of the be-holder. She seems to him young also,

and fair. She has two familiars in the form of seals, one black as the grave, and the other white as the shroud that is in the grave; and these sometimes upset a boat, if the sailor laughs at the uisge-cailliach's song.

"A man netted one of those seals, more than a hundred years ago, with his her-ring-trawl, and dragged it into the boat; but the other seal tore at the net so sav-agely, with its head and paws over the bows, that it was clear no net would long avail. The man heard them crying and screaming, and then talking low and muttering, like women in a frenzy. In his fear he cast the nets adrift, all but a small portion that was caught in the thwarts. Afterwards, in this portion, he found a tress of woman's hair. And that is just so: to the stones be it said.

"The grandson of this man, Tòmais McNair, is still living, a shepherd on Eilean-Uamhain, beyond Lunga in the Cairnburg Isles. A few years ago, off

Callachan Point, he saw the two seals, and heard, though he did not see, the cailliach. And that which I tell you, Christ's Cross before me, is a true thing."

THE SIGHT.

The "vision," or second-sight, is commoner in the Western Isles than in the Highlands: now at least, when all things sacred to the Celtic race, from the ancient language to the last lingering Be'althainn (Beltané*) and Samh'in rites, are smiled at by the gentle and mocked by the vulgar. One day will come when men will

For we of the passing race see this thing: that in a day to come the sheep-runs shall not be in the isles and the Highlands only —for we see the forests moving south, and there will be lack, then, not of deer and of sheep, but of hunters and shepherds.

What follows is only a memento of what was told me last summer by a fisherman of Iona. If I were to write all I know on good authority about what is called second-sight, it would be a volume and not a few pages I should want. The "sight" has been a reality to me al-

THE HERDSMAN, STAFFA.
From a photograph by Valentine and Sons, Dundee.

be sorrier for what is irrevocably lost than ever a nation mourned for a lapsed dominion. It is a bitter cruel thing that strangers must rule the hearts and brains, as well as the poor fortunes, of the mountaineers and islanders. But in doing their best to thrust Celtic life, Celtic speech, Celtic thought, into the sea, they are working a sore hurt for themselves that they shall lament in the day of adversity.

* *Beltane* is the 1st of May; *Sav'un*, the Fire of Peace, on Halloween (31st October). Thus the phrase: "*o Bhealltainn gu Samhuinn* (from May day to Hallowmas day).

most from the cradle, for my Highland nurse had the faculty, and I have the memory of more than one of her trances.

But now I am writing about Iona, though that is but a "summer isle" for me, who am more long-time familiar with the wilder and remoter Hebrides.

There is an old man on the island named Daibhidh (David) Macarthur.* It was Ivor McLean, my boatman friend, who took me to him. He is a fine old

* As there are several Macarthurs on Iona, I may say that the old man I allude to is not so named. Out of courtesy I disguise his name.

COAST OF IONA—THE SIGHT.
From a photograph by Valentine and Sons, Dundee.

man, though "heavy" a little; with years, perhaps, for his head is white as the crest of a wave. He is one of the very few Ionians, perhaps of the two or three at most, who do not speak any English.

"No," he told me, "he had never had the sight himself. Ivor was wrong in saying that he had."

This, I imagine, was shyness, or, rather, that innate reticence of the Celt in all profoundly intimate and spiritual matters; for, from what Ivor told me, I am convinced that old Macarthur was intermittently, or at least had more than once proved himself, a seer.

But he admitted that his wife had "it."

We were seated on an old upturned boat on the rocky little promontory, where, in olden days, the innumerable dead who were brought to the sacred soil of Iona were first laid. For a time Macarthur spoke slowly about this and that; then, abruptly and without preamble, he told me this:

The Christmas before last, Mary, his wife, had seen a man who was not on the island. "And that is true, by St. Martin's Cross," he added.

They were sitting before the fire, when, after a long silence, Macarthur looked up to see his wife staring into the shadow in the ingle. He thought she was brooding over the barren womb that had been her life-long sorrow, and now in her old age had become a strange and gnawing grief, and so he turned his gaze upon the red coals again.

But suddenly she exclaimed, "*C'ait am bheil thu dol?*" (Where are you going?).

Her husband looked up, but saw no one in the room beside themselves.

"What has come to you?" he asked. "What do you see?"

But she took no notice.

"*C'uine tha thu' falbh?*" (When are you going?) she asked, with the same strained voice and frozen eyes. And then, once again, "*C'uine thig thu rithisd?*" (When will you come again?). And with that she bowed her head, and the thin backs of the hands upon her knees were wet with falling tears.

And for the fourth of an hour she would say nothing except moan, "*Tha an amhuinn domhain; tha an amhuinn domhain: fuar, fuar; domhain, domhain.*"* (Deep, deep is the river; cold and deep; cold and deep!).

* Pronounce Ha aun ah-ween do'-inn; fēw-ar, fēw-ar; do'inn, do'inn.

And the man she saw, added Macarthur, was her nephew, Luthais, in Cape Breton, of Nova Scotia, who, as they learned before Easter, was drowned that Christmas-tide. He was the last of his mother's race, and had been the foster-child of Mary.

CELTIC RUNES.

THE RUNE OF THE SEVEN WINDS.

It was in the Isle of Skye that I first heard in the Gaelic both of the following runes, though this was years ago. Since then I have heard "The Reading of the Spirit" (with slight variations, twice or thrice, and fragmentarily oftener). So recently as last summer I was told it almost as it stands, so far south and inland—that is, for the West Highlands—as a hill shealing on the north side of Loch Goil, in Argyll. True, the man who told it was an islesman by birth and connections, though I doubt if he had heard it in the west, for certain Gaelic words which he interpolated in his narrative, given as recited to him by an old woman named Macgibbon, now dead, were those not of a "deasach" (West-Highlander), but of a "tuathach" (North-Highlander).

But as, in the first instance, each was linked with a narrative, I give both with the Skye setting.

One of the sea-bends of that island—with Rum, the grandest of the Inner Hebrides—is called Loch Staffin. Often have I lain upon the lofty basaltic cliffs of the Kilt Rock, and on wild days listened to the appalling crash and roar of the seas upon the narrow bowlder-strewn shores beneath, and to the screaming of the wind up the gullies and ravines which slice these precipices. It was on one of these days, but after a great storm, and when the sun was unclouded, though the wind still came with a long swaying rush from the sea, that I heard the Rune of the Seven Winds. As I lay on the thyme and short ling, with a whistle of driven air through the spires of the heather about me, I felt the salt against my face at times, and often the spray from a sheer torrent close by, blown backward by the force of the gale. From the Kilt Rock itself came a strange flutelike, or, rather, oboe-sobbing of the wind as it struck against and raced up and across and in and out the ribbed and serrated cliff.

In the original the lines were occasionally rhymed, and in a longer and more chantlike measure; but I will give the shorter version here, as perhaps more indicative of the impression conveyed to the Gaelic Celt.

The first four winds are the *Gaoth tuath* (the North Wind), *Gaoth 'n ear* (the East Wind), *Gaoth deas* (the South Wind), and *Gaoth 'niar* (the West Wind). The three others are the Breaths of the Grave, of the Depths of the Sea (or Oblivion), and of the Future.

In the first couplet the North Wind is alluded to as the breath of the pole-star. A more literal rendering of the original of the second would be,

> *By the wild strained voice on the summits,*
> *When the feet of the dead folk are knowing*
> *   The sound of its flowing.*

This is in allusion to the ancient Celtic custom of burying the dead with their feet to the east. It is believed that the Wind of the Resurrection will come from the east, and so the righteous dead will be awakened by its breath across the world. From this has come the tradition that the dead know whenever the east wind blows, and that in this way tidings reach them of the two worlds, that which they have left and that beyond the grave, or "the sleep." In the Outer Hebrides it is commonly believed that those about to die soon can feel "the breath on the soles of the feet." In the third couplet a little expansion would again be more explicit, e. g.:

> *By the high blithe cry on the rivers,*
> *On the straths and the glens and the máchar,*
> *   Where the Heat-star moveth.*

The *máchar* is any flat (generally a sandy, or at any rate sea-margining, plain), and the Heat-star is supposed to be the source of the moist south or southwest wind. The West Wind, again, blows from the Land of Rainbows, a poetic isles-idiom for the seaward west.

I.

By the Voice in the corries
When the Pole-star breatheth:

By the Voice on the summits
The dead feet know:

By the soft wet cry
When the Heat-star troubleth:

By the plaining and moaning
Of the Sigh of the Rainbows:

GYLEN CASTLE.
From a photograph by G. W. Wilson and Co., Aberdeen.

By the four white winds of the world,
Whose father the golden Sun is,

Whose mother the wheeling Moon is,
The North and the South and the East and the
   West:

By the four good winds of the world,
That Man knoweth,
That One dreadeth,
That God blesseth—

    Be all well
      On mountain and moorland and lea,
    On loch-face and lochan and river,
    On shore and shallow and sea!

II.

By the Voice of the Hollow
Where the worm dwelleth:

By the Voice of the Hollow
Where the sea-wave stirs not:

By the Voice of the Hollow
That Sun hath not seen yet:
By the three dark winds of the world;
The chill dull breath of the Grave,
The breath from the depths of the Sea,
The breath of To-morrow:

By the white and dark winds of the world,
The four and the three that are seven,
That Man knoweth,
That One dreadeth,
That God blesseth—

    Be all well
      On mountain and moorland and lea,
    On loch-face and lochan and river,
    On shore and shallow and sea!

Were this an old rune the tenth line would probably have run, "Whose *mother* the golden Sun is," for with the ancient Celts the sun was feminine. I do not know, but surmise that the line "That One dreadeth" is in allusion to an old Celtic saying that at the last day the Evil One will be scourged out of the world

   "By the white and dark winds....
   The four and the three that are seven."

THE RUNE OF THE READING OF THE SPIRIT.

There could hardly be any place more romantic than the spot where for the second of three times I heard this rune, or rather a more circumstantial and annotated variant.

In September of last year I was ferried across the Sound of Kerrera by an old boatman who was proud of three things —that he had known old Dr. Norman Macleod, "the Queen's Norman," besides "Dr. Donald, worthy man," and other Macleods known to this unworthy member of Clan Leod; that he had seen and shaken hands with Mr. Gladstone; and that he knew Professor Blackie, and had heard him sing "Fear-a-bhata."

That afternoon I went with my friend, a peasant farmer near the south end of

THE KILT ROCK, LOCH STAFFIN, SKYE.
From a photograph by Valentine and Sons, Dundee.

stronghold was built; of Fionn and Fianna, the Fingalians; of the coming and going of Ossian in his blind old age; of beautiful Malvina; of the galleys of the Fomorians; of the songs and the singers and all the beautiful things of "the old ancient long ago."

But what I heard was this. My friend told me some other short runes, and sang one or two *orain spioradail*, among them my famous namesake's "Farewell to Fiunary," a song dear to every native of Lorne and Morven, from Oban and the south isles to Arisaig and Ardnamurchan. But this only has remained with me:

"You know that my mother's people are Skye folk. It was from the mother of my mother that I heard what you call the Rune of the Reading of the Spirit, though I never heard it called anything but old Eilidh's *Sian*. She lived near the Hart o' Corry. You know the part? Ay, true, it is wild land—wild even for the wilderness o' Skye. Old mother Eilidh had 'the sight' at times, and whenever she wished she could find out the lines o' life. It was magic, they say. Who am I to know? This is true, she knew much that no one else knew. When my mother's cousin, Fergus MacEwan, who was mate of a sloop that sailed between Stornoway and Ardrossan, came to see her—and that was in the year before my mother was married, and when she was courted by Fergus, though she was never for giving her life to him, for even then she loved my father, poor fisherman of Ulva though he was (though heir, through his father's brother, to this crofter-farm on Kerrera here)—when Fergus came to see her, because of the gloom that was upon his spirit, she foretold all. At first she could 'see' poorly. But one wild afternoon, when the Cuchullins were black with cloud-smoke, she bade him meet her in that lonely savage glen they call the Loat o' Corry. He was loath to go, for he feared the place. But he went. He told

Kerrera, and lay down in the grassy, bowldered wilderness beneath the cliff on which stands the romantic ruin of Gylen Castle. The tide called in a loud insistent whisper, rising to a hoarse gurgle, from the sound. The soft wind that came from the mountains of Mull was honey-sweet with heather smell. The bleating of the ewes and lambs, the screaming of a few gulls, the clear repetitive song of a yellowhammer—nothing else was audible. At times, it is true, like a deep sigh, the suspiration of the open sea rose and fell among the islands. Faint echoes of that sigh came round Gylen headland and up Kyle-gylen. It was an hour wherein to dream of the Sons of Morven, who had landed here often, long before the ancient

all to my mother before he went away next dawn, with the heart in him broken, and his hope as dead as a herring in a net.

"Mother Eilidh came to him out of the dusk in that wuthering place just like a drifting mist, as he said. She gave him no greeting, but was by his side in silence. Before he knew what she was doing she had the soles of her feet upon his, and her hands folding his, and her eyes burned against his like hot coals against ash. He felt shudders come over him, and a wind blew up and down his back; and he grew giddy, and heard the roaring of the tides in his ears. Then he was quiet. Her voice was very far away when she said this thing, but he remembered every word of it:

"By that which dwells within thee,	(the soul)
By the lamps that shine upon me,	(the eyes)
By the white light I see litten	
From the brain now sleeping stilly,	(the light on the brow)
By the silence in the hollows,	(the ears)
By the wind that slow subsideth,	(the slacking breath)
By the life-tide slowly ebbing,	
By the deith-tide slowly rising,	(the pulsing blood)
By the slowly waning warmth,	
By the chill that slowly groweth,	
By the dusk that slowly creepeth,	
By the darkness near thee,	
By the darkness round thee,	(swoon, or trance)
By the darkness o'er thee—	
O'er thee, round thee, on thee—	
By the one that standeth	
At thy side and waiteth	(the soul)
Dumb and deaf and blindly,	
By the one that moveth,	
Bendeth, riseth, watcheth,	(the phantom)
By the dim Grave-Spell upon thee,	
By the Silence thou hast wedded. . . .	

    May the way thy feet are treading,
    May the tangled lines now crookèd,
    Clear as moonlight lie before me!

LOAT O' CORRY, FROM HART O' CORRY.
Drawn from a photograph by G. W. Wilson and Co., Aberdeen.

" Oh! oh! ohrone, ochrone! green the branches bonnie:
Oh! oh! ohrone, ochrone! red the blood-drop berries:
Achrone, arone, arone, arone, I see the green-clad Lady,
She walks the road that's wet with tears, with rustling sorrows shady. . . .
Oh! oh! mo ghraidh.

"Then it was that a great calm came upon Fergus, though he felt like a drowned man, or as one who stood by his own body, but speechless, and feeling no blowing of wind through his shadow-frame.

"For, indeed, though the body lived, he was already of the company of the silent. What was that *caiodh*, that wailing lamentation, sad as the *Cumha fir Arais*, which followed Eilidh's incantation, her spell upon 'the way' before him, that it and all the trailed lines of his life should be clear as moonlight before her? ' *Oh! oh! ohrone, ochrone! red the blood-drop berries;*' did not these mean no fruit of the quicken-tree, but the falling drops from the maimed tree that was himself? And was not the green-clad lady, she who comes singing low, the sprouting of the green grass that is the hair of the earth? And was not the road, gleaming wet with ruts and pools all of tears, and overhung by dark rustling plumes of sorrow, the road that the soul traverses in the dark hour? And did not all this mean that the Grave Spell was already upon him, and that the Silence was to be his?[*]

"But what thing it was she saw, Eilidh would not say. Darkly she dreamed awhile, then leaned forward and kissed his breast. He felt the sob in her heart throb into his.

"Dazed, and knowing that she had seen more than she had dreamed of seeing, and that his hour was striding over the rocky wilderness in that wild Isle of Skye, he did not know she was gone, till a shuddering fear of the silence and the gloom told him he was alone."

[*] (1) *Caiodh* (a wailing lament) is a difficult word to pronounce. The Irish *keen* will help the foreigner with *Kae-yh* or *Kae-yhn*. (2) The *Cumha fir Arais* (pronounce *Kav'ah feer Arooss*) means the lament of the Man of Aros, *i. e.*, the chieftain. Aros Castle, on the great island of Mull, overlooking the sound, was one of the strongholds of Macdonald, Lord of the Isles. (3) The quicken (rowan, mountain-ash, and other names) is a sacred tree with the Celtic peoples, and its branches can either waive away or compel supernatural influences. (4) The green-clad Lady is the Cailleach-nam-Sliabhain, the Siren of the Hill-Sides, to see whom portends death or disaster. When she is heard singing, that portends death soon for the hearer. The grass is that which grows quick and green above the dead. The dark hour is the hour of death, *i. e.*, the first hour after death.

Coll MacColl (he that was my Kerrera friend) stopped here, just as a breeze will suddenly stop in a corrie, so that the rowan berries on the side of a quicken will sway this way and that, while the long thin leaves on the other will be as still as the stones underneath, where their shadows sleep.

I asked him at last if Eilidh's second-sight had proved true. He looked at me for a moment, as though vaguely surprised I should ask so foolish a thing.

"No sleep came to Fergus that night," he resumed, quietly, as though no other words were needed, "and at daybreak he rose and left the cot of his kinsman, Andrew MacEwan. In the gray dawn he saw my mother, and told her all. Then she wished him farewell, and bade him come again when next the *Sunbeam* should be coming to Portree, or other port in Skye; for she did not believe that her mother had seen speedy death, or death at all, but perhaps only a time of sorrow, and even that she had done this thing to send Fergus away, for she too had her eyes on Robert MacColl, that was my father.

"'And so you will come again, Fergus my friend,' she said; and added, 'and perhaps then you will be telling me of a Sunbeam ashore, as well as that you sail from Ardrossan to the far-away islands!'

"He stared at her as one who hears ill. Then he took her hand in his, and let it go suddenly again. With one arm he rubbed the rough Uist cap he held in his left hand; then he brushed off the wet mist that was gray on his thick black beard.

"'You are not well, Fearghas-mo-charaid,' my mother said, and gently. When she saw the staring pain in his eyes, she added, with a low sob, 'My heart is sore for you!'

"'It is nothing. *Tha mi dubhachas*' (I have the gloom). And with that he turned away, and she saw him no more, that day or any day of all the days to come."

"And what thing happened, Coll?"

"They kept it from her, and she did not know it for long. It was this: Fer-

THE OLD MAN OF STORR.
From a photograph by G. W. Wilson and Co., Aberdeen.

gus MacEwan did not sail far that morning. He was ill, he said, and was put ashore. That night Aulay Macaulay saw him moving about in that frightful place of the Storr Rock, moaning and muttering. He would have spoken to him, but he saw him begin to leap about the pinnacled rocks like a goat, and at last run up to The Old Man of Storr and beat it with his clinched fists, blaspheming with wild words; and he feared Fergus was mad, and he slipped from shadow to shadow, till he fled openly. But in the morning Aulay and his brother Finlay went back to look for Fergus. At first they thought he had been drowned, or had fallen into one of the fissures. But from a *balachan*, a 'bit laddie,' as they would call him in the town over the way [Oban], they heard that a man had pushed off that morning in John Macpherson's boat, that lay about a mile and a half from the Storr, and had sailed north along the coast.

"Well, it was three days before he was found—stone-dead. If you know the Quiraing you will know the great Needle Rock. Only a bird can climb it, as the saying goes. Half-way up, Finlay Macaulay and a man of the neighborhood saw his body as though it were glued to the rock. It was windless weather, or he would have been blown away like a drifted leaf. They had to jerk the body down with net-poles. God save us the dark hour of Fergus, that died like a wild beast!"

A LOST RUNE.

There is a strange Shetland rune, or incantation rather, of which I had occasionally heard lines, but only once was favored with orally *in extenso*. Some time ago, however, I came across a practically identical version of it in an interesting volume called *Scenes and Stories of the North of Scotland*, by John Sinclair. Though familiar with the Shetland Isles, Mr. Sinclair was unable to obtain this old *sian* from more than one source, and all his inquiries failed to elucidate one or two obscure lines. Since then I have tried to get these dubious lines explained by Shetlanders, not without partial success: indeed, I might have succeeded wholly were I not handicapped by lack of knowledge at first hand of the Shetland dialect.

Now, however, I am able also to reconstruct the fugitive lines of its Celtic equivalent, though unfortunately this is not without its own obscurities. In Shetland the lines are uttered as a spell to send "The Guid-folk" about their business; that is, they are pronounced by one who has for the time being no longer need of supernatural aid or advice, and wishes to get quit of his or her uncanny servants.

Here is this old-world Scoto-Scandinavian charm, as given by Mr. Sinclair:

Da twal, da twal aposells,
Da eleven, da eleven evengelists,
Da ten, da ten commanders,
Da nine, da brazen sheeners,
Da eicht, da holy waters,
Da seven starns i' da heavens,
Da six creation mornins,
Da five, da tumblers o' my bools,
Da four, da gospel-makers,
Da tree triddle trivers,
Da twa lily-white boys dat clothe demsells in green, boys,
Da ane, da ane, dat walks alon—
      An' now yese a' gang hame, boys.

Here the most obscure lines are the eighth and tenth ; though the fourth, fifth, eleventh, and twelfth are as puzzling, if not—to a Southerner—so impossible. In the remote place where I write, I have not Mr. Sinclair's book within reach, and I forget what guesses he made for the fourth and fifth; but my informant corroborated the statement made to Mr. Sinclair that "da tree triddle trivers" (almost pure Norwegian) meant "the three treadle-workers"—that is, "the spinners"; in other words, the three Fates. Again, this is corroborated by the equivalent line in the Celtic variant. In the version given by my informant the fourth line was not "Da nine, da brazen sheeners," but

      "Da nine, da blazing shiners"—

that is, the Northern Lights, or Aurora Borealis—a Northern phenomenon which profoundly impressed both the Scandinavian and the Celtic imagination. Again, "Da eicht, da holy waters," was given to me as—

      "Da eicht, da holy writers."

The Celtic variant, however, here bears out "waters." In this variant, moreover, the preceding (fourth) line is wholly different from either "blazing shiners" or "brazen sheeners" (lamps, presumably). The mysterious Celtic "By the Five who pass at death" may be as obscure as "Da five, da tumblers o' my bools," but at least does not sound gibberish. Again, the last lines vary materially. The Shetlandic two lily-white boys

are probably "sprites." I do not know what meaning Shetlanders may attach to the twelfth line. My informant said "the ane" was Satan.

I will now give the Celtic incantation:

By the twelve white apostles,
By the eleven evangelists,
And by the ten holy commandments,
By the Nine Angels,
By the Flowing of the Eight Rivers,
By the seven stars of the World,
By the six Days of Creation,
By the Five who pass at death,
By the four Gospels,
By the three who weave and sever,
By the two white Beings clad in green,
And by the Lonely Spirit (*Spioraid aonarach*)—
      To the mountain hollow!
      To the hill hollow!
      To the hollow i' the hill!

The allusions in the first, second, third, and seventh lines, to the Pleiades in the sixth line, and to the Fates in the tenth line are plain enough.

"The Five who pass at death" is, I take it, an allusion to a very ancient, obscure, and rare Celtic legend: that an hour before dawn, on the day we die, five shadowy beings come out of the darkness, look at us, beckon, and vanish. These are the Shadows of those of our race who have crossed the frontier of death: the Shadow of our own soul; the Shadow of the grave; the Shadow of what shall be; and the Shadow of the Unmentionable and the Unknown.

I am not sure what the eleventh line means. Possibly the two white beings are the Soul and the Body. Possibly the allusion is to the twin brothers Life and Death. The mention of the color-epithet "green" is congruous, for green is at once the sacred, the mystic, and the demoniac color. The "guid-folk" of the hills are clad in green; the *Bandruidh* or *Cailleach*, that fatal siren of the hill-side, is always seen in a green robe; "Black Donald" himself, when he appears to mortal vision, is always "a tall gaunt stranger clad in green"; the road to Paradise that leads out of the Valley of the Shadow of Death is "an upland way of shining green"; the souls of the blest are visible in raiment a green as pale as the leaves of the lime when the sun shines through them; and the Spirit of God is sometimes revealed as "a green gloom tremulous with golden light."

Nor, again, am I sure as to the meaning of the twelfth line. Possibly the allusion is to the Holy Ghost; though the usual

Spioraid Naomh could have been used more readily and as impressively as *Spioraid Aonanarach*, or *Aonarach*. *Aonanarach* can mean "desolate" or "deserted" as well as "solitary" or "lonely." Probably, therefore, the "Spioraid aonanarach" is the Prince of Darkness. The line was also repeated to me with the terminal *aonaranachd;* and so would run, "The one that goeth in loneliness." This is obviously translatable variously. Were the allusion to God, probably the line would run, "And by Himself that is forever alone" (*i. e.*, above and beyond all). Allusively God is almost invariably spoken of as *E-Fein*, "Himself." To some the Gaelic words would have a sombre significance, as though indicative of the Evil Spirit, who, moreover, is supposed to be liege lord of all human seeming though non-human creatures, such as the guid-folk, the wood-dwellers, the wave-haunters, and the like. It has been suggested to me that "the one that goeth in loneliness," or "the one that walketh alone," is no other than the Wandering Jew. On some of the far Hebrides, "By the lonely one!" (meaning either Judas or the Wandering Jew) is still used exclamatorily. Many of the oaths in use among the isles and Western Highlands are either what the Scots call "papistical" or are distinctly pagan. "By Mary" is common; and (in South Uist and Barra) "By the Rood," "By the Book," "By the Blood," "By the Sun," and "Son of Mary." Here and there in the Outer Hebrides may be heard "By the Great Sabbath"; and "By Those of Old" (the ancient pagan deities; the Tuatha-Da-Danann). Occasionally one hears "By the Hill" (though this may be in allusion to Calvary, and not, as I take it, to the Bheinn-an-Bealthein, the Hill of the Fire-Altar); "By the Voices," *i. e.*, Wind and Sea (or Tide); "By the Wind"; and, quite frequently, "By the Stones." "The Stones" are the Druidical granite or other slabs, remnants of pagan temples, many of which, singly or in groups, are to be found in Scotland; most notably at Stennis in Orkney, in the west of the Isle of Arran, and at Callernish on Loch Roag, on the Atlantic coast of Lewis, of the Outer Hebrides. There are few stranger survivals of pagan days extant than the Gaelic phrase so often heard in the west and northwest: "I am going to the Stones," or "I have been at the Stones,"

instead of "I am going to—or have been at—Church." Conjecturally, but almost certainly, this is a visible link in the nigh invisible chain connecting us with "our ancestral selves" in the days of Druidic worship, "*ann o shean*" (in the existence of old), as Ossian says somewhere.

As to the "nine angels" of the fourth line, I have not been able to ascertain from any one, or from any book, who the nine angels are, why nine in number, or what their mission is or was. I have myself heard the phrase used once only, and then not as an oath (though "By the Nine Angels" is a Uistean oath), but in some such way as, "No one will know that thing till he sees what the Deep hides, or what lies beyond the stars, or hears what the Nine Angels whisper to each other." Elsewhere[*] I have quoted a Hebridean rune in which occurs the invocation:

> *Crois nan naoi aingeal leam*
> *'O mhullach mo chinn*
> *Gu craican mo bhonn!*

(The cross of the Nine Angels be about me, From the top of my head To the soles of my feet!)

Since I wrote this, it has occurred to me that possibly "the Nine Angels" may be the "nine angelic orders." Or again, it may be a half-pagan, half-Christian confusion with the nine Muses. In this connection, it is strange that the old Greek *Aoede* ("Song"), the third of the three original Muses, so closely resembles the Celtic *Aed* or *Aodh* (also *Aidh;* variant of *Aoidh*).

It is possible that the allusion to the eight rivers, in the fifth line, is purely Celtic. I remember having heard in my childhood that the Fountain of Living Water in the centre of Paradise is fed by eight great rivers. Four of these flow eternally, respectively from the east, the south, the west, and the north. Of the other four, two flow into the Fountain of Living Water from below, namely, the river of human tears and the river of human hopes; and two forever descend in rainbow-dews, the river of Peace, that is the benediction of God, and the river of Beauty, that is the *anail nan speur*, the breath of the skies—the loveliness that is pain, *an acain Pharais*, "the moan of heaven," and the loveliness that is a chant of joy, *Seinn Pharais*.

[*] In *Pharais: A Romance of the Isles.*

DAYS AND NIGHTS WITH A CARAVAN

THE ADVANCE-GUARD OF A HOMEWARD-BOUND GĀRFLA

WESTWARD from the green valley of the Nile to where the blue waves of the Atlantic curl in on its sands, stretches the vast orange-yellow belt of the Great Desert, the "Sahra" of the Arabs. Although partly walled in from the Mediterranean on the north by the classic Atlas, along the coast of Tripoli its sea of gold blends green with the sapphire of the Middle Sea.

The port of Tripoli, low-lying and white, shimmering under a hot African sun in her setting of palm-gardens, is the natural gateway to the Sahara, the focus of the three great caravan routes which stretch away south. The Sahara is not a deserted tract of level sand. Its sun-scorched surface of sand-hills and oases, mountain ranges and plateaus, greater in area by some half-million miles than the United States and Alaska

combined, is peopled by three to four millions of Berbers, Arabs, and Blacks, with a few Turkish garrisons in the north. By way of Ghadames, Ghat, and Murzuk, through the Fezzan to Lake Tchad, go the caravan trails, and then far away south again—south to that country called Sudan, Land of the Blacks. Here its teeming millions form the great negro states of Bambara, Timbuctoo, and Hausaland in the west; Bornu and Baghermi around Lake Tchad; Wadai, Darfur, and Kordufan in the east, extending from Abyssinia to the Gulf of Guinea.

Of these trails, their trade and the men who escort the heavily loaded gārflas (caravans), little enough has been said; still less of the innumerable dangers which constantly beset them as they creep their way across the burning, desolate wastes on their long journeys to the great trade marts of the Sudan: Timbuctoo, Kano, Kannem, Bornu, and Wadai.

Southwest from Tripoli twenty days' journey as the camel travels, on the direct route from Tripoli to Timbuctoo, lies the little sun-baked town of Ghadames, which has figured largely in the history of the caravan trade with the interior. From Ghadames also runs the route to the Sudan by way of Ghat; so, by reason of her location, Ghadames erected fonduks (caravansaries) and became a stopping-place for gārflas; and her merchants, pioneers of the gārfla trade.

Many years ago they established themselves in the town of Tripoli, with agents at Ghat and the big trading posts in the far Sudan. To these, gārflas conveyed periodically large consignments of goods, which were exchanged for ivory, ostrich feathers, and gold-dust, to be sold in Tripoli and eventually, in the form of finished products, to enhance the wealth and display of Europe. Through their superior intelligence and honesty, the merchants of Ghadames enjoyed for many years a monopoly of the trade which they had created.

But the Tripoli merchants could not indefinitely withhold their hands from a trade within their grasp, and upon which, to a great extent, the commercial prosperity of their own city depended. However, it was not until some thirty years ago that they seriously entered into competition with the Ghadamsi. At times large profits are reaped, but frequently enormous losses are entailed — not so much through the rise and fall of the European market as through the dangers *en route*, in which attacks and pillage by desert robbers, and reprisals to make good losses incurred by tribal warfare, play no small part. The merchants who fit out a gārfla must stand all losses, consequently great care is given to the selection of both the camels which carry the valuable merchandise and the men who accompany them.

The tall and swift riding-camel known as the mehari is seldom met with in northern Tripoli. The finest male draught-camels, the jamal, costing from $50 to $60 apiece, with a carrying capacity of about three hundredweight, are used for transport. From consumption or the effects of the long strain, scores often die by the way and many others at the end of the "voyage." The wages of the men for conducting a return cargo are sometimes as high as five thousand dollars. Not only must the gārfla sheiks have great courage and endurance, but must be trustworthy traders, and shrewd diplomats of no small calibre. Many of the Sultans and chiefs, particularly the Touaregs, through whose territories lie the gārfla routes, exact not only homage but tribute from the gārfla sheiks. To bring this tribute within a reasonable sum and

RAIS MOHAMMED GAWAHJE, LEADER OF THE CARAVAN

FONDUK-EL-TAJURA, THE FIRST HALTING-PLACE

secure a safe-conduct requires extraordinary skill and tact. The opportunities for dishonesty afforded the gārfla men are many, and occasionally men and goods are never heard from again.

Groaning, grunting, wheezing, and bubbling, the last camel of the caravan was loaded. His driver, a Black from Hausa, took an extra hitch in a rope; in silhouette against the lurid afterglow the camel moved through the Tripoli fonduk gate, a hair-mattress on stilts.

With my own Arabs I brought up the rear. Another long shadow merged itself into those of my horses and men, and a keen-eyed, well-armed Arab, Rais Mohammed Gawahje, leader of the caravan, b'slaamed to my Arabs and rode on. No fiery barb carried this man of the desert, but a pattering little donkey. Soon he was lost among the camels and the dust.

Passing through the suburb of Sciara-el-Sciut we were well into the oasis of Tripoli; not the typical pictured oasis with a spring and a few feathered palms, but an oasis extending a five-mile tongue of date-palms along the coast at the edge of the desert. Under their protecting shade are gardens and the wells by which they are irrigated. In this oasis lies the town of Tripoli. Beyond this oasis the Turks object to any stranger passing, lest he may be robbed or killed by scattered tribes which the Turkish garrisons cannot well control. Permission granted, safety over part of my route was doubly secure, for Hadji Mufta the Arab had spoken to his friend Gawahje, and I was assured of all the hospitality and protection which these nomads could offer— that is, after we had broken bread together. Mohammed Gawahje was among the most trusted of these leaders, having at times conveyed large sums of money along the dangerous coast routes to Bengazi.

The make-up of this gārfla, as is usual with those bound for the interior, had required months of preparation, and was composed of many smaller ones, which had delayed their time of departure in order to take advantage of the protection afforded by numerical strength. In its heavy loads were packed the heterogeneous goods generally taken, consisting of cotton and wool, cloth, waste silk, yarn, box rings, beads, amber, paper, sugar, drugs, and tea, of which British cotton goods formed more than fifty per cent. of the value. Besides these it carried some native products. Every autumn caravans arrive from the interior and return with dried dates; for, among the tribes of the Fezzan, Tripoli dates form the chief article of diet, and, in the oases of the desert, dates chopped with straw are used as fodder.

So one August night I found myself a part of a Saharan gärfla, one of the vertebræ of a monster sand-snake which wormed its way through the oasis of Tripoli toward the Great Desert. The distorted shape of the moon bulged over the horizon through a silent forest of palm groves; the transitional moment between twilight and moonlight passed, the dew had already begun to cool the night, and the gärfla had struck its gait.

Across the moonlit roadway the long shadows of the date-palms lifted and wriggled over the dun-colored camels and their heavy loads, over trudging little donkeys, goats, and sheep, over the swarthy figures of men. Some were heavily covered in their brown baracans, some half naked, a law unto themselves, its power vested in their crooked knives, knobbed clubs, and long flintlocks, whose silvered trimmings caught the moon-glint as in the distance they scintillated away like scattered fireflies.

Silently the great snake moved on, save as some hungry camel snatched at the cactus hedge and gurgled a defiant protest as its driver belabored it about the head; or as the oboes and tom-toms in barbaric strains broke the stillness of the night. Then, to ease the march or soothe the restless animals, the gärfla men from time to time would take up the wild peculiar chant, with its emphasized second beat, and the songs of brave deeds in love or war would echo through the palm groves far off on the desert sauds. We passed Maläha, a chott (dried lake) where salt is obtained. About midnight the gärfla halted.

"Fonduk-el-Tajura," remarked one of our men. "Here we make our first halt." Serving as places of rest and protection and in some cases supply-depots, the importance of fonduks to gärflas and the trade is inestimable. These plain, walled, rectangular enclosures are often surrounded by the palm and olive gardens

SAND-BILLOWS OF THE GREAT DESERT

of the keeper, who may supply fresh fruits, vegetables, and other domestic products. Fonduk-el-Tajura was typical of those found throughout North Africa. The impatient beasts, hungry and eager to seek relief from their heavy loads, tried to jam through the single portal wide enough for but one camel and its burden. All was dust and confusion. Amid yells, curses, and "hike hikes," the drivers sought to extricate their animals or save the goods from being torn from the loads. The interior of the fonduk was a square open enclosure bordered by a covered arcade as a protection for the men in the rainy season. When all were in, the heavy doors were closed and barred against marauders. All about me the great beasts were dropping to the earth, remonstrating and groaning as vigorously as when they were loaded. The packs taken off, their saddles were carefully removed and scoured with sand, for the hump must be kept clean, healthy, and free from saddle-sores. Arabs declare that the camel feeds on his hump, and it is a

A Gārfla In Camp

fact that when near the limit of his endurance the hump seems to furnish nourishment by gradually being absorbed into his system, sometimes disappearing altogether; consequently, to the Arab, the hump is the barometer of the camel's condition.

The camels were soon given their green fodder, which, at fonduks, generally consists of fōoa (madder-top roots) or barley, the ksūb (guinea corn), or bishna (millet), while that cheapest and almost indispensable food, the date, finds its way to the mouths of men and beasts. The mainstay of the gārfla men is dried dates and bread made with guinea corn. On long voyages the day's fare is often consumed on the march, and halts at such times are made only to rest and feed the camels. At fonduks or oases longer stops are made; there groups of men may be seen squatting about a big wooden bowl of bazine or coos-coos, their national dishes, made chiefly of cereals.

The quick-moving form of Gawahje appeared here and there with the manner of a man used to command, and after he had brought informal order out of the confusion, I had an opportunity to meet my host. Under the portal of the fonduk a charcoal fire glowed red in an earthen Arab stove. About it in the candle-light we seated ourselves—Rais Gawahje, the fonduk-keeper, my dragoman El-Ouachi, and myself. To Gawahje my dragoman presented my gifts, seven okes of sugar cones and fifteen pounds of green tea. Some of the tea was immediately brewed and mixed half with sugar and a touch of mint. We drank the syrupy liquid and broke bread together, and then Gawahje inquired after my health.

From my bed on the single stone seat at the side of the entrance I looked through an open door across the passageway to the only room of the place, used as a prayer-chamber, in which was the kibleh.* In the dim light of the oil-lamp indistinct forms of several devout Moslems knelt or prostrated themselves before Allah, droning their prayers. Out in the fonduk enclosure all was quiet now save for the peaceful chewing of cuds, or an occasional sound as a camel swallowed or a cricket chirped. The moonbeams shooting their silvery shafts lit up portions of the farther wall.

* The sacred niche which indicates the direction of Mecca.

The soft breath of the silent night blew gently from the south through the feathered tops of the date-palms, and pulling my blanket over me I feel asleep.

A low cry from outside awakened me and pandemonium broke loose among the dogs. Cautiously drawing aside a small panel covering a peep-hole, the keeper, after a brief conversation, satisfied himself that all was well, and as the heavy doors swung open, another caravan entered. The first beasts came through like a maelstrom. Half awake in the semi-darkness I dodged the swing of a long neck as one of the vicious brutes attempted to bite me in passing, while several Arabs dragged aside a badly crushed comrade.

Invariably the desert thief lurks about the fonduks in the small hours of the morning, watching an opportunity to prey on any belated traveller as he approaches, or to rob the fonduk. With the help of a companion he scales the wall outside, and by a rope drops noiselessly down in some dark corner of the square enclosure, or near a corner he scrapes a hole in the wall large enough for him to pass through. This is not difficult. A quart or two of vinegar occasionally applied not only assists in disintegrating the wall of sun-dried bricks, but renders his work noiseless as he digs with his knife. Inside he sneaks among the men and camels, keeping always in the shadow, stealing here a baracan, there a gun or whatever it may be, and frequently, unobserved, retreats as he entered.

After a scant three hours' sleep a lantern flashed in my face, Gawahje passed and the fonduk was soon astir. The camels once more took up their heavy burdens and passed out. The last to leave was Gawahje. At the entrance he and the keeper kept tally of his animals, after which he paid the fonduk fee of ten paras, or two cents per head for camels and donkeys and a nominal sum for goats and sheep. The charge for my horses was twenty paras apiece.

The gardens had long since disappeared, and the lanelike roads lost themselves in the sand which carpeted the palm groves through which we now travelled. The night dew which nourishes the desert's scattered plant life lay heavy jewelled on bent blades of rank grass and sand-lilies. The date-palms through violet

SAHARA—AN OASIS AMONG THE DUNES

GRAND MOSQUE OF OUARGLA, IN THE DESERT OF SAHARA

ground mists showed indistinct and soft-ened against the brilliant rose-dawn of day. They ended, and suddenly in the orange-gold of the morning sunlight the sand billows of the mighty Sahara rolled away south over the horizon.

For days we travelled over these hills of sand, sometimes wind-blown into all kinds of queer wave formations and shapes, sometimes over endless level reaches; obliterated by the shifting sand, great sections of the gârfla routes are mere directions, the only guides the sun and the stars. Through regions where grows the tall rank grass, and in oases, the routes are traceable by hard-packed sand. In the dry season at times they pass over stony wadees (dried river-beds) contain-ing only rippling heat-waves. In the rainy season these wadees are transform-ed to roaring torrents and often sweep away men and beasts at the fords. Through deep defiles the trails worm their way to high plateaus, where above the sand level they wriggle along in parallel camel-paths with their innumerable con-nections. Up over the rocky mountain-ous routes, among the parched thorny shrubs, patches of halfa, and poisonous

milk-plants, they become very much worn, sometimes to a depth of ten or twelve feet below the level of the ground, where they interlace like the bewildering paths of a maze.

During the season of the warm rains, which sink into the porous surface until they are arrested at no great depth, vast subterranean sheets of water are formed, which could almost anywhere be brought to the surface by sinking artesian wells. Many streams flow inland, where they are lost in the sand or the salt lakes. At this time whole sections of the parched desert seem almost overnight to have changed to another land. Mountains and valleys blossom, and the banks of the wadees seem afire with the flaming oleander. By these streams or springs are the oases where date-palms and gardens are plant-ed, and Arab houses, fonduks, or towns are built which determine the course of the caravan routes. At intervals are wells for the use of the gârfla. A great danger lies in missing these wells. One very hot summer some men nearly reach-ed the gardens of Tripoli, but could go no farther. When found they could only say, "ma! ma!" (water). It was given them, and they drank, and died straightway.

I watched our gärfla wind around or zigzag over the hills of sand, breaking and linking itself together again as it crawled its slow pace of three miles an hour. It marched in irregular order, characteristic of the Arabs, stringing out for miles, but closing in together for protection against attack as night approached. The Arab usually refrains from riding the jamal, for every pound of weight and its adjustment on these great beasts must be considered; and even an Arab has to ride a jamal but an hour or two to appreciate the luxury of walking.

Through the most dangerous districts the men were distributed the length of the caravan, with a strong rear-guard—for it is from this point that an attack by an enemy is most feared. As the sun gets high, most of the men muffle themselves in their heavy woollen baracans to keep out the heat, and transfer their long flintlocks from across their shoulders to the packs of the animals. Between eleven and three o'clock occurs the midday rest. Tents are rarely if ever carried by gärflas. Instead the camels are unloaded and lie down; the men repose under a tentlike covering, using their baracans propped up a few feet with a stick, war-club, or gun. Under these in the suffocating heat their owners snatch the only rest of the day, for, generally speaking, they travel twenty-one hours out of the twenty-four.

We moved south. Passing caravans became scarce. A dust-cloud would appear in the distance, grow large, and a caravan of Bedouins, those nomads of the desert, in all their barbaric paraphernalia would pass by, eying us suspiciously with unslung guns, calling to their savage wolf-hounds or holding them in leash in order to avoid a conflict with our gärfla dogs. For many of their tribal

wars and feuds have started under less provocation than a dog-fight.

Sometimes I would ride forward with my dragoman, anticipating a longer rest by reaching a fonduk several hours ahead of the slowly moving gärfla. On one of these occasions, as we ascended a sand-hill, the advance-guard of a homeward-

HADJI ALI, KEEPER OF THE FONDUK

bound gärfla suddenly loomed up before us. Eleven months before, they had started from the great trade mart of Kano, the first caravan to arrive from there for two years, owing to the general insecurity of the roads. Three months they had held over at Zinder and a month at both Aïr and Ghat. It took us all the afternoon to ride by the twelve hundred and twenty camels. They carried a thousand loads of Sudan skins from the famous dye-pits of Kano, destined to find their way to New York for the manufacture of gloves and shoes; two hundred loads of ostrich feathers, and ten loads of ivory, besides odd lots of rhinoceros horns, gum arabic, and wax, valued altogether at over two hundred and five thousand dollars. Ostrich eggs, worked leather, and basket-work dangled from the loads. Here and there the skin of a leopard or cheetah, shot on the way, was thrown across a pack or hung from the shoulders of some big negro. Black women there were, too, slaves or concubines for some of the rich town Moors or Turks. As the gärfla neared Tripoli runners would be sent ahead, and there would be great rejoicing among the men who had waited several years for the arrival of their goods.

I well remember one day in mid-August; the mercury stood at 155 degrees in the sun. I do not know what it registered in the shade, for there was none save our own shadows. As the sun wore round behind us I shifted the broad band of my woollen cholera-belt to my back, and cast my own shadow to protect as far as possible the neck and head of my horse, for the poor beast was suffering terribly from the heat.

All day we rode in this furnace, and the brave fellows trudged barefooted in the scorching sand. At intervals I heard a rumble like distant thunder, which proved to be only the soughing of the gibli (southeast wind) through the vent in the top of my sun-helmet. Strange as is the fascination of the desert, yet one feels its monotony keenly; he notices with avaricious interest anything which will relieve him from the intense heat overhead and the everlasting wriggling heat-waves of the sun-glare underneath. So for hours at a time I watched the formation of camel footprints in the sand. Sometimes the feet of the great beasts would kick over the shining dung-beetles, the black scarabeus, or would scuff through and destroy the beautiful point-lace patterns of the lizard tracks, left by their toy-like designers as they scurried away and mysteriously disappeared beneath the sand. As the afternoon wore on I would doze in my saddle, to wake up with a jump as I jammed against a jamal, or the muzzled mouth of a "biter" swung sharply against my head.

Tall, sun-tanned Arabs, and big negroes black as ebony, formed the escort of the gärfla. Many of the latter first saw Tripoli when they were driven up from the Sudan under the crack of the slave-whip. Rarely complaining in the intense heat, they moved forward, long guns slung across their backs and often native fans in their hands. Usually the men go barefooted; sometimes over stretches of soft sand they wear broad-soled desert slippers, and on rocky ground sandals are worn. Most of the Blacks have their tribal marks, a certain number of deep slashes across the cheeks and temples, made by their parents with sharp stones when they were children. As one Black trudged along beside me his splendid calf muscles played underneath three stripes cut in the black skin.

Early one morning I had ridden some miles in advance of the gärfla. Save for the soft scuff of my horse's hoofs and the stretching of my leather trappings, a great silence hung over the untrammelled sand-hillocks, and their blue-pervaded, mysterious shadows lengthened. A rounded top here and there broke the silver moon as it mellowed toward the horizon. Suddenly my horse shied, nearly unseating me. Instinctively I searched the sky-line of hilltops. Had it not been for the black spot of a head I might not have noticed the gray baracaned figure of a desert thief who, in his sleep, rolled out of his sandy lair. Startled, he sat bolt upright, and for a second stared blankly at me. He reached for his long gun which lay by his side, but I covered him with my revolver and there he sat until out of range and sight. The fellow had been left by his comrades, who were probably in the vicinity. This trick of burrowing under the sand beside the course of an oncoming gärfla is often resorted to. As the gärfla passes, the thieves rise out of the earth, make a quick onslaught, and then rapidly retire, taking with them what booty they can lay hands on, and frequently stampeding some of the camels.

Occasionally these vultures also resort to the tactics of a sneak-thief, and choose a time at night when a fast-moving caravan overtakes a slower one. During the confusion caused by the mixing-up of men and animals in passing, the thief falls in from the rear and naturally is taken by either party to be a member of the other gärfla. Then, pilfering anything he can seize from the loads, he falls back to the rear and drops out of sight behind a sand-hill.

Lightly blowing in the face of the south-bound gārflas, there springs from the southeast a gentle wind, the gibli, which playfully twirls little eddying whiffs of sand into miniature whirlwinds. In this manner it may blow for days, evaporating the water in the goatskin bags, and sometimes terminating in a terrible sand-storm. Then, when the jamal, craning their long necks, sniff high in the air and utter a peculiar cry, the gārfla men know well the ominous signs; far off on the horizon, creeping higher and higher, the sky of blue retreats before a sky of brass.

To the hoarse cries and curses of the men as they try to hobble the fore legs of the excited camels are added uncanny guttural groanings of the jamal, the braying of the asses, and the pitiful bleating of goats and sheep. High in the air great flames of sand reach out, then the lurid sand-cloud, completely covering the sky, comes down upon the gārfla. In the confusion some of the water-bags are broken and the precious liquid disappears in the sand. Turning tail and driving down before the blast go some of the unhobbled camels, maybe carrying a driver with them, never to be heard of again.

In the deep-yellow gloom the gārfla, back to the storm, lies huddled together; the men, wrapped up completely in their baracans on the leeward side of the camels, hug close to the goatskins of water. The whole air is surcharged with suffocating heat and fine powdered sand-dust, which finds its way even as far as Malta and Sicily. It penetrates everywhere, inflames the eyes, and cracks the skin of the already parched tongues and throats of the gārfla men. The torment at times is indescribable, and some poor devil, like the camels, will run maddened into the hurricane.

The sand-storm lasts from a few hours to six or seven days, and during it the men lie thus, occasionally digging themselves to the surface as they become partially covered with sand. Frequently all the remaining water dries up. At such times camels are often sacrificed for the sake of the greenish water which may be obtained from the honeycomb cells of

the reticulum, a mature camel yielding about five or six quarts; and, strange as it may seem, this water is cooler than that carried in goatskins. The storm over, a surviving gārfla of emaciated men and animals staggers on to the nearest oasis or town, over plains which before were sand-hills, and sand-hills which now are plains.

The first stop of any length made by the gārflas on their southward march is at Murzuk with its eleven thousand inhabitants, that desolate capital of the Fezzan—Murzuk the horror of Turkish exiles, where a man is fortunate if the deadly climate takes away only his senses of smell and taste. Here a thorough rest is given to camels and men. Fresh supplies are obtained, the gaps in the ranks filled out, and again the wearisome march is resumed. Some fifteen hundred miles south of the coast they pass over the undefined boundary-line of Tripoli through the dangerous country of the Touaregs and the Damerghous.

From time immemorial, slaves suffering inconceivable torments have been brought across the Sahara from the Sudan, for those regions extending from Abyssinia to the Gulf of Guinea have furnished an almost inexhaustible supply. Particularly from the Central Sudan the slave-trader has gathered in his human harvest to the chief depots of Timbuctoo in the west and Kuka in the east.

You will find an occasional Arab who will tell you of a route heretofore unmentioned, a secret route known only to the Senusi, a large fraternity of Moslems located in Tripoli who make proselyting wars and expeditions from Wadai to their capital. Along this route never less than fifteen caravans cross the desert every year, which bring about ten thousand slaves alive to tell the tale; and they estimate that forty thousand victims fall on the march. Once on the secret route you cannot lose your way, for it is lined with human bones. Many of these slaves were formerly embarked for Turkey, and there seems to be little doubt that slaves are still conveyed to Canea and Salonica, Constantinople and Smyrna.

Arriving late one night at a fonduk we found the place already so crowded that when our gārfla was in, men and animals were literally jammed together. The filth and vermin in the place, not to mention the sickening odors, disturbed not the sons of Allah. The great doors were bolted; I slept outside under the olive-trees with my men in the gardens of Hadji Ali, the keeper, preferring the external annoyance of thieves. They disturbed us twice during the night, and a white wolf-hound entered my camp under the direction of his master, getting away with a pair of my men's desert slippers. To make up much-needed rest I delayed my start next morning to some five hours behind the gārfla.

As the sun rose high, I found Hadji Ali seated outside the fonduk adjusting a new flint in his pistol. This done, he gazed long at the weapon, and his wrinkled, scarred old face softened as when a man looks upon a thing he loves. Many journeys across the Sahra with the gārfla had sapped his wiry arms of their youthful strength, and the ugly scar over his left eye was a trophy of his last voyage three years before, which had nearly landed him in the fields of the blessed. Under the shade of an olive-tree Hadji Ali told me the story.

"You must know, Arbi [master], that we were a gārfla thirteen thousand camels strong, proceeding north to Tripoli from Kano, which was many months behind us. The escort and transport were principally men of Aïr and their animals. Three years before, Sadek, one of their chiefs, was slain by Moussa, a brother of the Sultan of Damerghou. Two years after, the slayer in turn was killed by the men of Aïr.

"As we entered the country of the Damerghous our guards were doubly watchful and our camels tied one to the other. All through the wild country, when in camp, we formed a square with the animals, the men and guards being inside. We were strong and not afraid, and did not intend to pay either tribute or homage for passing through the territory. It was at the end of the dry months, and some of the wells contained no water. We were all weak and suffering, and a number of our men had the sleeping-sickness. We made haste to reach the wells of Farok, not two days'

journey from Damerghou itself. We had almost reached them when narrow ravines obliged us to fall one behind the other. Suddenly from ambush the men of Damerghou furiously attacked us in great numbers. The character of the country prevented us from bringing our men together. We fought hard and well, but Allah willed. Two hundred and ten were killed on both sides, amongst whom were twelve Tripolitans, some of them being among the most famous gārfla leaders of Tripoli. Twelve thousand camel-loads of guinea corn destined for Aïr, one thousand camel-loads of ostrich feathers, ivory, Sudan skins, and mixed goods, with the entire transport, fell into the hands of the Damerghous.

"Near the end of the fight, Arbi, a big man, broke through my guard with his two-edged sword. It was night when I came to myself and I had been stripped of everything. With great effort I reached the wells of Farok. Near where I fell I found half buried in the sand my pistol with its charge unfired—but that is another story."

The total value of these goods lost, including the animals of burden, amounted to more than $800,000, and the wells of Farok, where the capture occurred, lie in an air-line about 1905 kilometres southwest of Tripoli.

The opening of new routes southward and deflection of trade in that direction still lessen the prospect of inducing it to return to the shores of Tripoli, and except as regards Wadai and part of the Sudan the bulk of the trade may be said now to be lost to Tripoli. Tribal feuds on caravan routes unexpectedly change favorable aspects and disconcert traders.

Long before the royal caravan of the Queen of Sheba, with its heavy embroidered trappings, brought gifts to Solomon; long before that Semitic nomad Abraham came out of Ur—caravans had crept their patient, steady way across the hot sands and deserts of the East. But the days of the Tripoli caravan trade are numbered, and the single wire of telegraph line which has already found its way to Murzuk is but the forerunner to herald the coming of the iron horse into the land of the gārfla.

CAIRO IN 1890

"**I** LOVE the Arabian language for three reasons : because I am an Arab myself; because the Koran is in Arabic ; because Arabic is the language of Paradise." This hadith, or saying, of Mohammed might be put upon the banner of the old university of Cairo, El Azhar, that is, the Splendid. El Azhar was founded in the tenth century, when Cairo itself was hardly more than a name. In its unmoved attachment to the beliefs of its founders, to their old enthusiasms, their methods. and hates, El Azhar has opposed an inflexible front to the advance of European ideas, sending out year after year its hundreds of pupils to all parts of Egypt and to Nubia, to the Soudan and to Morocco, to Turkey, Arabia, and Syria, to India and Ceylon, and to the borders of Persia, believing that so long as it could keep the education of the young in its grasp, the reign of the Prophet was secure. It is to-day the most important Mohammedan college in the world; for though it has no longer the twenty thousand students who crowded its courts in the thirteenth and fourteenth centuries, there is still an annual attendance of from seven to ten thousand; by some authorities the number is given as twelve thousand.

The twelve thousand have no academic groves; they have not even one tree. There is nothing sequestered about El Azhar; it is near the bazars in the old part of the town, where the houses are crowded together like wasps' nests. One sees nothing of it as one approaches save the minarets above, and, in the narrow, crowded lane, an outer portal. Here the visitor must show his permit, and put on the mosque shoes, for El Azhar was once a mosque, and is now mosque and university combined. After the shoes are on he steps over the low bar, and finds himself within the porch, which is a marvel as it stands, with its fretwork, carved stones, faded reds, and those old plaques of inscription which excite one's curiosity so desperately, and which no dragoman can ever translate, no matter in how many languages he can complacently ask, "You satisfi?" One soon learns something of the older tongue; hieroglyphics are not difficult; any one with eyes can discover after a while that the A of the ancient Egyptians is, often, a bird who bears a strong resemblance to a pigeon; that their L is a lion; and that the name of the builder of the Great Pyramid, for instance, is represented by a design which looks like two freshly hatched chickens, a foot-ball, and a horned lizard (speaking, of course, respectfully of them all). But one can never find out the meaning of the tantalizing characters, so many thousand years nearer our own day, which confront us, surrounded by arabesques, over old Cairo gateways, across the fronts of the street fountains, or inscribed in faded gilt on the crumbling walls of mosques. It is probable that they are Kufic, and one would hardly demand, I suppose, that an English guide should read black-letter? But who can be reasonable in the land of Aladdin's lamp?

The porch leads to the large central court, which is open to the sky, the breeze, and the birds; and this last is not merely a possibility, for birds of all kinds are numerous in Egypt, and unmolested. On the pavement of this court, squatting in groups, are hundreds of the turbaned

PORCH OF EL AZHAR.

After a photograph by Sebah, Cairo.

students, some studying aloud, some reading aloud (it is always aloud), some listening to a professor (who also squats), some eating their frugal meals, some mending their clothes, and some merely chatting. These groups are so many and so close together that often the visitor can make the circuit of the place only on its outskirts; he cannot cross. There is generally a carrier of drinking-water making his rounds amid the serried ranks. "For whoever is thirsty, here is water from God," he chants. One is almost afraid to put down the melodious phrase, for the street cries of Cairo have become as trite as the *Ranz des Vaches* of Switzerland. Still, some of them are so imaginative and quaint that they should be rescued from triteness and made classic. Here is one which is chanted by the seller of vegetables—the best beans, it should be explained, come from Embebeh, beyond Boulak—"Help, O Embebeh, help! The beans of Embebeh are better than almonds. Oh-h, how *sweet* are the little sons of the river!" (This last phrase makes poetical allusion to the soaking in Nile water which is required before the beans can be cooked.) Certain famous baked beans nearer home also require preliminary soaking. Let us imagine a huckster calling out in Boston streets, as he pursues his way: "Help, O Beverly, help! The beans of Beverly are better than peaches. Oh-h, how *sweet* are the little sons of Cochituate!"

The central court of the Splendid is surrounded by colonnades, whose walls are now undergoing repairs; but the propping beams do not appear to disturb either the pupils or teachers. On the east side is the sanctuary, which is also a school-room, but a covered one; it is a large, low-ceilinged hall, covering an area of thirty-six hundred square yards; by day its light is dusky; by night it is illuminated by twelve hundred twinkling little lamps suspended from the ceiling by bronze chains. The roof is supported by three hundred and eighty antique columns of marble and granite placed in irregular ranges; there are so many of these pillars that to be among them is like standing in a grove. The pavement is smoothly covered with straw matting; and here also are assembled throngs of pupils—some studying, some reciting, some asleep. I paid many visits to El Azhar, moving about quietly with my venerable

little dragoman, whom I had selected for an unusual accomplishment—silence. One day I came upon an arithmetic class; the professor, a thin, ardent-eyed man of forty, was squatted upon a beautiful Turkish rug at the base of a granite column; his class of boys, numbering thirty, were squatted in a half-circle facing him, their slates on the matting before them. The professor had a small blackboard which he had propped up so that all could see it, and there on its surface I saw inscribed that enemy of my own youth, a sum in fractions—three-eighths of seven-ninths of twelve-twentieths of ten thirty-fifths, and so on; evidently the terrible thing is as savage as ever! The professor grew excited; he harangued his pupils; he did the sum over and over, rubbing out and rewriting his ferocious conundrum with a bit of chalk. Slender Arabian hands tried the sum furtively on the little slates; but no one had accomplished the task when, afraid of being remarked, I at last turned away. The outfit of a well-provided student at El Azhar consists of a rug, a low desk like a small portfolio easel, a Koran, a slate, an inkstand, and an earthen dish. Instruction is free, and boys are admitted at the early age of eight years. The majority of the pupils do not remain after their twelfth or fourteenth year; a large number, however, pursue their studies much longer, and old students return from time to time to obtain further instruction, so that it is not uncommon to see a gray-bearded pupil studying by the side of a child who might be his grandson. To me it seemed that two-thirds of the students were men between thirty and forty years of age; but this may have been because one noticed them more, as collegians so mature are an unusual sight for American eyes.

All the pupils bow as they study, with a motion like that of the bowing porcelain mandarins. The custom is attributed to the necessity for bending the head whenever the name of Allah is encountered; as the first text-book is always the Koran, children have found it easier to bow at regular intervals with an even motion, than to watch for the numerous repetitions of the name. The habit thus formed in childhood remains, and one often sees old merchants in the bazars reading for their own entertainment, and bowing themselves to and fro as they read. I have even beheld young men, smartly

STUDENTS IN THE OUTER COURT, EL AZHAR.

After a photograph by Abdullah Frères, Cairo.

dressed in full European attire, who, lost in the interest of a newspaper, had forgotten themselves for the moment, and were bending to and fro unconsciously at the door of a French café. A nation that enjoys the rocking-chair ought to understand this. Some of the students of El Azhar have rooms outside, but many of them possess no other shelter than these two courts, where they sleep upon their rugs spread over the matting or pavement. Food can be brought in at pleasure, but those two Oriental time-consumers, pipes and coffee, are not allowed within the precincts. In one of the porches barbers are established; there is generally a row of students undergoing the process of head-shaving. The fierce fanatical blind pupils, so often described in the past by travellers, are no longer there; the porter can show only their empty school-room. Blindness is prevalent in Egypt; no doubt the sunshine of the long summer has something to do with it, but another cause is the neglected condition of young children. There is no belief so firmly established in the minds of Egyptian mothers as the superstition that the child who is clean and well dressed will inevitably attract the dreaded evil-eye, and suffer ever afterward from the effects of the malign glance. I have seen women who evidently belonged to the upper ranks of the middle class—women dressed in silk, with gold ornaments, and a following servant—who were accompanied by a poor baby of two or three years of age, so dirty, so squalid and neglected, that any one unacquainted with the country would have supposed it to be the child of a beggar.

In addition to the bowing motion, instruction at El Azhar is aided by a mnemonic system, the rules of grammar, and other lessons also, being given in rhyme. I suppose our public schools are above devices of this sort; but there are some of us among the elders who still fly mentally, when the subject of English history comes up, to that useful poem beginning "First, William the Norman"; and I have heard of the rules for the use of shall and will being properly remembered only when set to the tune of "Scotland's burning!" Surely any tune—even "Man the Life-boat"—would become valuable if it could clear up the bogs of the subjunctive.

It must be mentioned that El Azhar did not invent its mnemonics; it has inherited them from the past. All the mediæval universities made use of the system.

The central court is surrounded on three sides by chambers, one of which belongs to each country and to each Egyptian province represented at the college. These sombre apartments are filled with oddly shaped wardrobes, which are assigned to the students for their clothes. There is a legend connected with these rooms: At dusk a man whose heart is pure is sometimes permitted to see the elves who come at that hour to play games in the inner court under the columns; here they run races, they chase each other over the matting, they climb the pillars, and indulge in a thousand antics. The little creatures are said to live in the wardrobes, and each student occasionally places a few flowers within, to avert from himself the danger that comes from their too great love of tricks. There are other inhabitants of these rooms who also indulge in tricks. These are little animals which I took to be ferrets; twice I had a glimpse of a disappearing tail, like a dark flash, as I crossed a threshold.

In beginning his education the first task for a boy is to commit the Koran to memory. As he learns a portion he is taught to read and to write those paragraphs; in this way he goes through the entire volume. Grammar comes next; at El Azhar the word includes logic, rhetoric, composition, versification, elocution, and other branches. Then follows law, secular and religious. But the law, like the logic, like all the instruction, is founded exclusively upon the Koran. As there is no inquiry into anything new, the precepts have naturally taken a fixed shape; the rules were long ago established, and they have never been altered; the student of 1890 receives the information given to the student of 1490, and no more. But it is this very fact which makes El Azhar interesting to the looker on; it is a living relic, a survival in the nineteenth century of the university of the fourteenth and fifteenth. It is true that when we think of those great colleges of the past, the picture which rises in the mind is not one of turbaned, seated figures in flowing robes; it is rather of aggressive, agile youths, with small braggadocio caps perched on their long locks, their slender waists outlined in the shortest of jackets,

BEFORE THE SACRED NICHE.

After a photograph by Sebah, Cairo.

and their long legs encased in the tightest
of parti-colored hose. But this is because
the great painters of the past have given
immortality to these astonishing scholars
of their own lands by putting them upon
their canvases. They confined themselves
to their own lands too, unfortunately for
us; they did not set sail, with their colors
and brushes, upon Homer's "misty deep."
It would be interesting to see what Pintu-
ricchio would have made of El Azhar; or
how Gentile da Fabriano would have
copied the crowded outer court.

The president of El Azhar occupies, in
native estimation, a position of the highest authority. Napoleon, recognizing this
power, requested the aid of his influence
in inducing Cairo to surrender in 1798.
The sheykh complied; and a month later
the wonderful Frenchman, in full Oriental costume, visited the university in state,
and listened to a recitation from the Koran.

Now that modern schools have been established by the government in addition
to the excellent and energetic mission
seminaries maintained by the English,
the Americans, the Germans, and the
French, one wonders whether this venerable Arabian college will modify its ten-
ets, or shrink to a shadow and disappear.
There are hopeful souls who prophesy the
former; but I do not agree with them.
Let us aid the American schools by all the
means in our power. But as for El Azhar, may it fade (as fade it must) with its
ancient legends draped untouched about it.

All who visit Cairo see the Assiout
ware—pottery made of red and black
earth, and turned on a wheel; it comes
from Assiout, 230 miles up the Nile, and
the simple forms of the vases and jugs,
the rose-water stoups and narrow-necked
perfume-throwers, are often very graceful. Assiout ware is offered for sale in
the streets, but the itinerant venders are
sent out by a dealer in the bazars, and the
fatality which makes it happen that the
vender has two black stoups and one red
jug when you wish for one black stoup
and two red jugs sent us to headquarters. But the crowded booth did not contain our heart's desire, and as we still lingered, making ourselves, I dare say, too
pressing for the Oriental ease of the proprietor, it was at last suggested that Mustapha might perhaps go to the store-room
for more? (the interrogation point meaning baksheesh.) Seizing the opportunity,

we asked permission to accompany the
messenger. No one objecting—as the natives consider all strangers more or less
mad—we were soon following our guide
through a dusky passageway behind the
shop, the darkness lit by the gleam of his
white teeth as he turned, every now and
then, to give us an encouraging smile
and a wink of his one eye, over his shoulder. At length—still in the dark—we arrived at a stairway, and ascending, found
ourselves in a second-story court, which
was roofed over with matting. This court
was surrounded by chambers fitted with
rough sliding fronts: almost all of the
fronts were at the moment thrown up, as
a window is thrown up and held by its
pulleys. In one of these rooms we found
Assiout ware in all its varieties; but we
made a slow choice. We were evidently in
a lodging-house of native Cairo; all the
chambers save this one store-room appeared to be occupied as bachelors' apartments. The two rooms nearest us belonged to El Azhar students, so Mustapha said: he could speak no English,
but he imparted the information in Arabic to our dragoman. Seeing that we
were more interested in the general scene
than in his red jugs, Mustapha left the
Assiout ware to its fate, and lighting a
cigarette, seated himself on the railing
with a disengaged air, as much as to say:
"Two more mad women! But it's nothing to me." One of the students was
evidently an ascetic; his room contained
piles of books and pamphlets, and almost
nothing else; his one rug was spread out
close to the front in order to get the light,
and placed upon it we saw his open inkstand, his pens, and a page of freshly
copied manuscript. When we asked where
he was, Mustapha replied that he had gone
down to the fountain to wash himself, so
that he could say his prayers. The second chamber belonged to a student of another disposition; this extravagant young
man had three rugs; clothes hung from
pegs upon his walls, and he possessed an
extra pair of lemon-colored slippers; in
addition we saw cups and saucers upon a
shelf. Only two books were visible, and
these were put away in a corner; instead
of books he had flowers; the whole place
was adorned with them; pots containing
plants in full bloom were standing on the
floor round the walls of his largely exposed abode, and were also drawn up in
two rows in the passageway outside, where

he himself, sitting on a mat, was sewing. His blossoms were so gay that involuntarily we smiled. Whereupon he smiled too, and gave us a salam. Opposite the rooms of the students there was a large chamber, almost entirely filled with white hue, that it resembled vegetation of some sort—a colossal cabbage. Directly behind him, also on the threshold, squatted a large gray baboon, whose countenance expressed a fixed misanthropy. Every now and then this creature, who was secured by a

AN EGYPTIAN DANCING GIRL.

bales, like small cotton bales; in a niche between these high piles, an old man, kneeling at the threshold, was washing something in a large earthen-ware tub of a pink tint. His body was bare from the waist upward, and as he bent over his task, his short chest, with all the ribs clearly visible, his long brown back with the vertebræ of the spine standing out, and his lean seesawing arms, looked skeleton-like, while his head, supported on a small wizened throat, was adorned with such an enormous bobbing turban, dark green in long loose cord, ascended slowly to the top of the bales and came down on the other side, facing his master. He then looked deeply into the tub for several minutes, touched the water carefully with his small black hand, withdrew it, and inspected the palm, and then returned gravely, and by the same roundabout way over the bales, to resume his position at the door-sill, looking as if he could not understand the folly of such unnecessary and silly toil.

In another chamber a large very black

negro, dressed in pure white, was seated upon the floor, with his feet stretched out in front of him, his hands placed stiffly on his knees, his eyes staring straight before him. He was motionless; he seemed hardly to breathe.

"What is he doing?" I said to the dragoman.

"He? Oh, he *berry* good man; he pray."

In a chamber next to the negro two grave old Arabs were playing chess. They were perched upon one of those Cairo settees which look like square chicken-coops. One often sees these seats in the streets, placed for messengers and porters, and for some time I took them for actual chicken - coops, and wondered why they were always empty. Chickens might well have inhabited the one used by the chess-players, for the central court upon which all these chambers opened was covered with a layer of rubbish and dirt several inches thick, which contained many of their feathers.

The same day we made search for the Khan of Kait Bey. No dragoman knows where it is. The best way, indeed, to see the old quarters is to select from a map the name of a street as remote as possible from the usual thoroughfares beloved by these tasselled guides, and then demand to be conducted thither. We did this in connection with the Khan of Kait Bey. But when we had achieved the distinction of finding it, we discovered that it was impossible to see it. The winding street is so narrow, and so constantly crowded with two opposed streams of traffic, that your donkey cannot pause to give you a chance to inspect the portion which is close to your eyes, and there is no spot where you can get a view in perspective of the whole. So you pass up the lane, turn, and come down again; and, if conscientious, you repeat the process, obtaining for all your pains only a confused impression of horizontal plaques and panels, with ruined walls tottering above them, and squalid shops below. There is a fine arched gateway adorned with pendentives; that, on account of its size, you can see; it leads into the khan proper, where were once the chambers for the travelling merchants and the stalls for their beasts; but all this is now a ruin. One of the best authorities on Saracenic art has announced that this khan is adorned with more varieties of exquisite arabesques than any single building in Cairo. This may be true.

But to appreciate the truth of the statement one needs wings or a ladder. The word ladder opens the subject of the two ways of looking at architecture—in detail or as a whole. The natural power of the eye has more to do with this than is acknowledged. If one can distinctly see, without effort and aid, a whole façade at a glance, with the general effect of its proportions, the style of its ornament, the lights and shadows, the outline of the top against the sky, one is more interested in this than in the small traceries, for instance, over one especial window. There are those of us who remember the English cathedrals by their great towers rising in the gray air, with the birds flying about them. There are others who, never having clearly seen this vision—for no opera-glass can give the whole—recall, for their share of the pleasure, the details of the carvings over the porches, or of the old tombs within. It is simply the far-sighted and the near-sighted view. Another authority, a master who has had many disciples, has (of late years at least) devoted himself principally to the near-sighted view. In his maroon-colored Tracts on Venice he has given us a minute account of the features of the small faces of the capitals of the columns of the Doge's palace (all these ofs express the minuteness of it); but when we stand on the pavement below the palace—and naturally we cannot stand in mid-air—we find that it is impossible to follow him: I speak of the old capitals, some of which are still untouched. The solution lies in the ladder. And Ruskin, as regards his later writings, may be called the ladder critic. The poet Longfellow, arriving in Verona during one of his Italian journeys, learned that Ruskin was also there, and not finding him at the hotel, went out in search of his friend. After a while he came upon him at the Tombs of the Scaligers. Here, high in the air, at the top of a long ladder, with a servant keeping watch below, was a small figure. It was Ruskin, who, nose to nose with them, was making a careful drawing of some of the delicate terminal ornaments of those splendid Gothic structures. One does not object to the careful drawings any more than to the descriptions of the little faces at Venice. They are good in their way. But one wishes to put upon record the suggestion that architectural beauty as viewed from a ladder, inch by inch, is not the only aspect of that beauty; nor is it, for a large number of us, the most important aspect. A man who is somewhat deaf, if talking about a symphony, will naturally dwell upon the strains which he has heard—that is, the louder portions; but he ought not therefore to assume that the softer notes are insignificant.

On the 31st of January, 1890, we took part in a horse-race. It was a long race of great violence, and the horses engaged in it were disgracefully thin and weak. "Very Mohammedan that," some one comments. The race was Mohammedan from one point of view, for it was connected with the dervishes, Mohammedans of fanatical creed. The dervishes, however, remained in their monasteries—with their fanaticism; the race was made by Christians, who, crowded into rattling carriages, flew in a body from the square of Sultan Hassan through the long, winding lanes that lead toward old Cairo at a speed which endangered everybody's life, with wheels grating against each other, coachmen standing up and yelling like demons, whip-lashes curling round the ribs of the wretched, ill-fed, galloping

horses, and natives darting into their houses on each side to save themselves from death, as the furious procession, in clouds of dust, rushed by. The cause of this sudden madness is found in the fact that the two best-known orders of these Mohammedan monks (one calls them monks for want of a better name; they have some resemblance to monks, and some to Freemasons) go through their rites once a week only, and upon the same afternoon; by making this desperate haste it is possible to see both services; and as travellers, for the most part, make but a short stay in Cairo, they find themselves taking part, *nolens volens*, in this frantic progress, led by their ambitious dragomans, who appear to enjoy it. The service of the Dancing Dervishes takes place in their mosque, which is near the square of Sultan Hassan. Here they have a small circular hall; round this arena, and elevated slightly above it, is an aisle where spectators are allowed to stand; over the aisle is the gallery. This January brought a crowd of visitors who filled the aisle completely. Presently a dervish made the circuit of the empty

OUTER ENTRANCE OF THE CITADEL, CAIRO.

After a photograph by Sebah, Cairo.

GARDEN HOUSE AT CHOUBRA, SHOWING PART OF THE LAKE NEAR CAIRO.
After a photograph by Sebah, Cairo.

arena, warning, by a solemn gesture, those who had seated or half seated themselves upon the balustrade that the attitude was not allowed. As soon as he had passed, some of the warned took their places again. Naturally, these were spectators of the gentler sex. I am even afraid that they were pilgrims from the land where the gentler sex is accustomed from its earliest years to a profound deference. Two of these pretty pilgrims transgressed in this way four times, and at last the dervish came and stood before them. They remained seated, returning his gaze with amiable tranquillity. What he thought I do not know— this lean Egyptian in his old brown cloak and conical hat. I fancied, however, that it had something to do with the great advantages of the Mohammedan system regarding the seclusion of women. He did not conquer.

At length began the music. The band of the dervishes is placed in one of the galleries; we could see the performers squatting on their rugs, the instruments being flutes or long pipes, and small drums like tambourines without the rattles. Egyptian music has a marked time, but no melody: no matter how good an ear one has, it is impossible to catch and re-sing its notes, even though one hears them daily. Pierre Loti writes: "The strains of the little flutes of Africa charm me more than the most perfect orchestral harmonies of other lands." If by this he means that the flutes recall to his memory the magic scenes of Oriental life, that is one thing; but if he means that he really loves the sounds for themselves, I am afraid we must conclude that this prince of verbal expression has not an ear for music (which is only fair; a man cannot have everything). The band of the dervishes sends forth a high wail, accompanied by a rumble. Neither, however, is distressingly loud. Meanwhile the dervishes have entered, and, muffled in their cloaks, are standing, a silent band, round the edge of the arena; their sheykh —a very old man, much bent, but with a noble countenance—takes his place upon the sacred rug, and receives with dignity their obeisances. All remain motionless for a while. Then the sheykh rises, heads the procession, and, with a very slow step, they all move round the arena, bowing toward the sacred carpet as they pass it. This opening ceremony concluded, the sheykh again takes his seat, and the dervishes, divesting themselves of their cloaks, step one by one into the open space, where, after a prayer, each begins whirling slowly, with closed eyes. They are all attired in long full white skirts, whose edges have weights attached to them; as the speed of the music increases, their whirl becomes more rapid, but it remains always even; though their eyes are closed, they never touch each other.

From the description alone, it is difficult to imagine that this rite (for such it is) is solemn. But, looked at with the actual eyes, it seemed to me an impressive ceremony; the absorbed appearance of the participants, their unconsciousness of all outward things, the earnestness of the aspiration visible on their faces — all these were striking. The zikr, as this species of religious effort is named, is an attempt to reach a state of ecstasy (hallucination, we should call it), during which the human being, having forgotten the existence of its body, becomes for the moment spirit only, and can then mingle with the spirit world. The Dancing Dervishes endeavor to bring on this trance by the physical dizziness which is produced by whirling; the Howling Dervishes try to effect the same by swinging their heads rapidly up and down, and from side to side, with a constant shout of "Allah!" "Allah!" The latter soon reach a state of temporary frenzy. For this reason the dancers are

THE ROAD TO CHOUBRA.
After a photograph by Sebah, Cairo.

more interesting; their ecstasy, being silent, seems more earnest. The religion of the Hindoos has a similar idea in another form, namely, that the highest happiness is a mingling with God, and an utter unconsciousness of one's humanity. Christian hermits, in retiring from the world, have sought, as far as possible, the same mental condition: but for a lifetime, not, like the dervishes, for an hour. These enthusiasts marry, if they please; many of them are artisans, tradesmen, and farm laborers, and go only at certain times to the monasteries to take part in the zikrs. There are many different orders, and several other kinds of zikr besides the two commonly seen by travellers.

Travellers see also the Mohammedan prayers. These prayers, with alms-giving, fasting during the month Ramadan, and the pilgrimage to Mecca, are the most important religious duties of all Muslims. The excellent new hotel, the Continental, where we had our quarters, a hotel whose quiet and comfort are a blessing to Cairo, overlooked a house which was undergoing alteration; every afternoon at a certain hour a plasterer came from his work within, and, standing in a corner under our windows, divested himself of his soiled outer gown; then, going to a wall faucet, he turned on the water, and rapidly but carefully washed his face, his hands and arms, his feet, and his legs as far as his knees, according to Mohammed's rule; this done, he took down from a tree a clean board which he kept there for the purpose, and placing it upon the ground, he kneeled down upon it, with his face toward Mecca, and went through his worship, many times touching the ground with his forehead in token of self-humiliation. His devotions occupied five or six minutes. As soon as they were over, the board was quickly replaced in the tree, the soiled gown put on again, and the man hurried back to his work with an alertness which showed that he was no idler. On the Nile, at the appointed hour, our pilot gave the wheel to a subordinate, spread out his prayer carpet on the deck, and said his prayers with as much indifference to the eyes watching him as though they did not exist. In the bazars the merchants pray in their shops; the public cook prays in the street beside his little furnace; on the shores of the river at sunset the kneeling figures outlined against the sky are one of the pictures which all travellers remember. The official pilgrimage to Mecca takes place each year, the departure and return of the pilgrim train being celebrated with great pomp; the most ardent desire of every Mohammedan is to make this sacred journey before he dies. When a returning Cairo pilgrim reaches home, it is a common custom to decorate his doorway with figures, painted in brilliant hues, representing his supposed adventures. The designs, which are very primitive in outline, usually show the train of camels, the escort of soldiers, wonderful wild beasts in fighting attitudes, nondescript birds and trees, and garlands of flowers. One comes upon these Mecca doorways very frequently in the old quarters. Sometimes the gay tints show that the journey was a recent one; often the faded outlines speak of the zeal of an ancestor.

While in the city of the Khedive, if one has a wish for the benediction of a far-stretching view, he must go to the Citadel. The prospect from this hill has been described many times. One sees all Cairo, with her minarets; the vivid green of the plain, with the Nile winding through it; the desert meeting the verdure and stretching back to the red hills; lastly, the pyramids, beginning with those of Gizeh, near at hand, and ending, far in the distance, with the hazy outlines of those of Abouseer and Sakkarah. The Citadel was built by Saladin in the twelfth century. Saladin's palace, which formed part of it, was demolished in 1824 to make room for the modern mosque, whose large dome and attenuated minarets are now the last objects which fade away when the traveller leaves Cairo behind him. This rich Mohammedan temple was the work of Mehemet Ali, the founder of the present dynasty. It is not beautiful, in spite of its alabaster, but Mehemet himself would probably admire it, could he return to earth (the mosque was not completed until after his death), as he had to the full that bad taste in architecture and art which, for unexplained reasons, so often accompanies a new birth of progress in an old country. Mehemet was born in Roumelia; he entered the Turkish army, and after attaining the rank of colonel he was sent to Egypt. Here he soon usurped all power, and had it not been for the intervention of Russia and France, and later of England and Austria, it is probable that he would have succeeded in freeing himself and the country whose leadership he had grasped from the domination of Turkey. Every one has heard something of the terrible massacre of the Memlooks by his order, in this Citadel, in 1811. The Memlooks were opposed to all progress, and Mehemet was bent upon progress. Freed from their power, this ferocious liberator built canals; he did his best to improve agriculture; he established a printing-office and founded schools; he sent three hundred boys to Europe to be educated as civil engineers, as machinists, as printers, as naval officers, and as physicians; his idea was that, upon their return, they could instruct others. When the first class came back, he filled his public schools by the simple method of force. The translators of the French text-books which had been selected for the use of the schools were taken from the ranks of the returned students. A text-book was given to each, and all were kept closely imprisoned in the Citadel a period of four months, until they had completed their task. Mehemet had a dream of an Arabian kingdom in Egypt which should in time rival the European nations without joining them. It is this dream which makes him interesting. He was the first modern. A Turk by birth, and remaining a Turk as regards his private life, he had great ideas. Undoubtedly he possessed genius of a high order.

As to his private life, one comes across a trace of it at Choubra. This was Mehemet's summer residence, and the place remains much as it was during his lifetime. The road to Choubra, which was until recently the favorite drive of the Cairenes, is now deserted. The palace stands on the banks of the Nile, three miles from town, and its gardens, which cover nine acres, are beautiful even in their present neglected condition; in the spring the fragrance from the mass of blossoms is intoxicatingly sweet. But the wonder of Choubra is a richly decorated garden-house, containing, in a marble basin, a lake which is large enough for skiffs. Here Mehemet often spent his

A MECCA DOOR.

evenings. Upon these occasions the whole place was brilliantly lighted, and the hareem disported itself in little boats on the fairy-like pool, and in strolling up and down the marble colonnades, unveiled (as Mehemet was the only man present), and in their richest attire. The marbles have grown dim, the fountains are choked, the colonnades are dusty, and the lake has a melancholy air. But even in its decay Choubra presents to the man of fancy— a few such men still exist—a picture of Oriental scenes which he has all his life imagined, perhaps, but whose actual traces he no more expected to see with his own eyes in 1890 than to behold the silken sails of Cleopatra furled among Cook's steamers on the Nile. Mehemet's last years were spent at Choubra, and here he died, in 1849, at the age of eighty-one. As he had forced from Turkey a firman assigning the throne to his own family, he was succeeded by one of his sons.

In 1863 (after the short reign of Ibrahim, five years of Abbas, and eight of Said), Ismail, Mehemet's grandson, ascended the throne. Ismail had received his education in Paris.

Much has been written about this man. The opening, in 1869, of the Suez Canal turned the eyes of the entire civilized world upon Egypt. The writers swooped down upon the ancient country in a flock, and the canal, the land, and its ruler were described again and again. The ruler was remarkable. Ismail was short (one speaks of him in the past tense, although he is not dead), with very broad shoulders; his hands were singularly thick; his ears also were thick, and oddly placed; his feet were small, and he always wore finically fine French shoes. There was nothing of the Arab in his face, and little of the Turk. One of his eyelids had a natural droop, and vexed diplomatists have left it upon record that he had the power of causing the other to droop also, thus making it possible for him to study the faces of his antagonists at his leisure, he, meanwhile, presenting to them in return a blind mask. The mask, however, was amiable; it was adorned almost constantly with a smile. The man must have had marked powers of fascination. At the present day, when some of the secrets of his reign are known—though by no means all—it is easy to paint him in the darkest colors; but during the time of his power his great schemes dazzled the world, and people liked him—it is impossible to doubt the testimony of so many pens. European and American visitors always left his presence pleased.

There are in Cairo black stories of cruelty connected with his name. These for the most part are unwritten; they are told in the native cafés and in the bazars. It does not appear that he loved cruelty for its own sake, as some of the Roman emperors loved it; but if any one rebelled against his power or his pleasure, that person was sacrificed without scruple. In some cases it took the form of a disappearance in the night, without a sound or a trace left behind. This is the sort of thing we associate with the old despotic ages. But 1869 is not a remote date, and at that time the present Emperor of Austria, the late Emperor Frederick (then Crown-Prince of Prussia), the Empress Eugénie, Prince Oscar of Sweden, Prince Louis of Hesse, the Princess of the Netherlands, the Duke and Duchess of Aosta, and other distinguished Europeans, were the guests of this enigmatic host, eating his sumptuous dinners and attending his magnificent balls. The festivities in connection with the opening of the canal are said to have cost Ismail twenty-one millions of dollars. The sum seems large; but it included the furnishing of palaces, lavish hospitality to an army of guests besides the sovereigns and their suites, and an opera to order, namely, Verdi's *Aïda*, which was given with great brilliancy in Cairo, in an opera-house erected for the occasion. Ismail, like Mehemet, had his splendid dream. He, too, wished to free Egypt from the power of Turkey; but, unlike his grandfather, he wished to take her bodily into the circle of the civilized nations, not as a rival, but as an ally and friend. An Egyptian kingdom, under his rule, was to extend from the Mediterranean to the equator; from the Red Sea westward beyond Darfur. His bold ambition ended in disaster. His railways, telegraphs, schools, harbors, and postal service, together with his personal extravagance, brought Egypt to the verge of bankruptcy. All Europe now had a vital interest in the Suez Canal, and the powers therefore united in a demand that the Sultan should stop the career of his audacious Egyptian Viceroy. The Viceroy might perhaps have resisted the Porte; he could not resist the united powers. In 1879 he was deposed, and his son Tufik appointed in his place. Ismail left Egypt. For several years he travelled, residing for a time in Naples; at present he is living in a villa near Constantinople. There is a rumor in Cairo that he is more of a prisoner there than he supposes. But this may be only one of the legends that are always attached to Turkish affairs. His dream has come true in one respect at least: Egypt has indeed joined the circle of the European nations, but not in the manner which Ismail intended; she is only a bondwoman — if the pun can be permitted.

The Gezireh road is to-day the favorite afternoon drive of the Cairenes. It is a broad avenue, raised above the plain, and overarched by trees throughout its course. At many points it commands an uninterrupted view of the pyramids. Two miles from town the Gezireh Palace rises on the right, surrounded by gardens, which, unlike those of Choubra, are carefully tended. It was built by Ismail. Of all these Cairo palaces it must be explained that they have none of the characteristics of castles or strongholds. They are merely lightly built residences, designed for a

THE KHEDIVE.
From a photograph by Sebah, Cairo.

climate which has ten months of summer. The central hall and grand staircase of Gezireh are superb; alabaster, onyx, and malachite adorn like jewels the beautiful marbles, which came from Carrara. The drawing-rooms and audience-chambers have a splendid spaciousness: the state apartments of many a royal palace in Europe sink into insignificance in this respect when compared with them. Much of the furniture is rich, but again (as in the old house of the Sheykh es Sadat) one finds it difficult to forgive the tawdry French carpets and curtains, when the bazars close at hand could have contributed fabrics of so much greater beauty. But Ismail's taste was French—that is, the lowest shade of French—as French is still the taste of modern Egypt among the upper classes. It remains to be seen

CHIEF WIFE OF EX-KHEDIVE ISMAIL, WITH HER PRIVATE BAND.

After a photograph by Schœfft, Cairo.

whether the English occupation will change this. During the festivities at the time of the opening of the canal, Ismail's royal guests were entertained at Gezireh. On the upper floor are the rooms which were occupied by the Empress Eugénie, the walls and ceilings covered with thick satin, tufted like the back of an arm-chair, its tint the shade of blue which is most becoming to a blond complexion—Ismail's compliment to his beautiful guest. During these days there were state dinners and balls at Gezireh, with banks of orchids, myriads of wax-lights, and orchestras playing strains from *La Belle Hélène* and *La Grande Duchesse.* During one of these balls the Emperor of Austria made a progress through the rooms with Ismail, band after band taking up the Austrian national anthem as the imperial guest entered. The vision of the stately, grave Franz Josef advancing through these glittering halls by the side of the waddling little hippopotamus of the Nile, to the martial notes of that fine hymn (which we have appropriated for our churches under another name, and without saying "By your leave"), is one of the sinister apparitions with which this rococo palace, a palace half splendid, half shabby, is haunted.

In the garden there is a kiosk whose proportions charm the eye. The guidebooks inform us that this ornamentation is of cast iron; that it is an imitation of the Alhambra; that it is "considered the finest modern Arabian building in the world"—all of which is against it. Nevertheless, viewed from any point across the gardens, its outlines are exquisite. Within there are more festal chambers, and a gilded dining-room, which was the scene of the suppers (they were often orgies) that were given by Ismail upon the occasion of his private masked balls. At some distance from the palace, behind a screen of trees, are the apartments reserved for the hareem. This smaller palace has no beauty, unless one includes its enchanting little garden; such attraction as it has comes from the light it sheds upon the daily life of Eastern women. Occidental travellers are always curious about the hareem. The word means simply the ladies, or women, of the family, and the term is made to include also the rooms which they occupy, as our word "school" might mean the building or the pupils within it. At Gezireh the hareem,

save that its appointments are more costly, is much like those caravansaries which abound at our inland summer resorts. There are long rows of small chambers opening from each side of narrow halls, with a few sitting-rooms, which were held in common. The carpets, curtains, and such articles of furniture as still remain are all flowery, glaring, and in the worst possible modern taste, save that they do not exhibit those horrible hues, surely the most hideous with which this world has been cursed—the so-called solferinos and magentas. Besides their private garden, the women and children of the hareem had for their entertainment a small menagerie, an aviary, and a confectionery establishment, where fresh bonbons were made for them every day, especially the sugared rose leaves so dear to the Oriental heart. The chief of Ismail's four wives had a passion for jewels. She possessed rubies and diamonds of unusual size, and so many precious stones of all kinds that her satin dresses were embroidered with them. She had her private band of female musicians, who played for her, when she wished for music, upon the violin, the flute, the zither, and the mandolin. The princesses of the royal house, Ismail's wives and his sisters-in-law, could not bring themselves to admire the Empress of the French. They were lost in wonder over what they called her "pinched stiffness." It is true that the uncorseted forms of Oriental beauties have nothing in common with the rigid back and martial elbows of modern attire. Dimples, polished limbs, dark long-lashed eyes, and an indolent step are the ideals of the hareem.

The legends of these jewelled sultanas, of the masked balls, of the long train of royal visitors, of the orchids, the orchestras, and the wax-lights, are followed at Gezireh by a tale of murder which is singularly ghastly. Ismail's Minister of Finance was his foster-brother Sadyk, with whom he had lived upon terms of closest intimacy all his life. The two were often together; frequently they drove out to Gezireh to spend the night. One afternoon in 1878 Ismail's carriage stopped at the doorway of the palace in Cairo occupied by his minister. Sadyk came out. "Get in," Ismail was heard to say. "We will go to Gezireh. There are business matters about which I must talk with you." The two men went away together.

Sadyk never came back. When the carriage reached Gezireh, Ismail gave orders that it should stop at the palace, instead of going on to the kiosk, where they generally alighted. He himself led the way within, crossing the reception-room to the small private salon which overlooks the Nile. Here he seated himself upon a sofa, drawing up his feet in the Oriental fashion, which was not his usual custom. Sadyk was about to follow his example, when he found himself seized suddenly from behind. The doors were now locked from the outside, leaving within only the two foster-brothers and the man who had seized Sadyk. This was a Nubian named Ishak, a creature celebrated for his strength. He now proceeded to murder Sadyk after a fashion of his own country, a process of breaking the bones of the chest and neck in a manner which leaves on the skin no sign. Sadyk fought for his life; he dragged the Nubian over the white velvet carpet, and finally bit off two of his fingers. But he was not a young man, and in the end he was conquered. During this struggle Ismail remained motionless on the sofa, with his feet drawn up and his arms folded. A steamer lay at anchor outside, and during the night Sadyk's body was placed on board; at dawn the boat started up the river. At the same hour Ismail drove back to Cairo, where, in the course of the morning, it was officially announced that the Minister of Finance, having been detected in colossal peculations, had been banished to the White Nile, and was already on his way thither. Sadyk's body rests somewhere at the bottom of the river. But Ismail's little drama of banishment and the steamer was set at naught when, after he had left Cairo, Ishak the Nubian returned, with his mutilated hand and his story. Such is the tale as it is told in the bazars. Ismail's motive in murdering a man he liked (he was incapable of true affection for any one) is found in the fact that he could place upon the shoulders of the missing minister the worst of the financial irregularities which were trying the patience of the European powers. It did him no good. He was deposed the next year.

During the spring of 1890, Gezireh awoke to new life for a time. A French company had purchased the place, with the intention of opening it as an Egyptian Monte Carlo. But Khedive Tufik, who has prohibited gambling throughout his domain, forbade the execution of this plan. So the tarnished silks remain where they were, and the faded gilded ceilings have not been renewed. When we made our last visit, during the heats of early summer, the blossoms were as beautiful as ever, and the ghosts were all there— we met them on the marble stairs—the European princes led by poor Eugénie; the sultanas with their jewels and their band; Ismail with his drooping eyelids; and Sadyk, followed by the Nubian.

The present Khedive (or Viceroy) is thirty-eight years of age. Well-proportioned, with fine dark eyes, he may be called a handsome man; but his face is made heavy by its expression of settled melancholy. It is said in Cairo that he has never been known to laugh. But this must apply to his public life only, for he is much attached to his family—to his wife and his four children; in this respect he lives strictly in the European manner, never having had but this one wife. He is a devoted father. Determined that the education of his sons should not be neglected as his own education was neglected by Ismail, he had for them, at an early age, an accomplished English tutor. Later he sent them to Geneva, Switzerland; they are now in Vienna. Tufik's chief interest, if one may judge by his acts, is in education. In this direction his strongest efforts have been made; he has improved the public schools of Egypt, and established new ones; he has given all the support possible to that greatest of modern innovations in a Mohammedan country, the education of women. With all this, he is a devout Mohammedan; he is not a fanatic; but he may be called, I think, a Mohammedan Puritan. He receives his many European and American visitors with courtesy. But they do not talk about him as they talked about Ismail; he excites no curiosity. This is partly owing to his position, his opinions and actions having naturally small importance while an English army is taking charge of his realm; but it is also owing, in a measure, to the character of the man himself. One often sees him driving. On Sunday afternoons his carriage in semi state leads the procession along the Gezireh Avenue. First appear the outriders, six mounted soldiers; four brilliantly dressed saises follow, rushing along with their wands high in the air; then comes the open carriage, with the dark-eyed, melancholy Khedive on the back seat, returning mechanically the many salutations offered by strangers and by his own people. Behind his carriage are four more of the flying runners; then the remainder of the mounted escort, two and two. At a little distance follows the brougham of the Vice-reine; according to Oriental etiquette, she never appears in public beside her husband. Her brougham is preceded and followed by saises, but there is no mounted escort. The Vice-reine is pretty, intelligent, and accomplished; in addition, she is brave. Several years ago, when the cholera was raging in Cairo, and the Khedive, almost alone among the upper classes, remained there in order to do what he could for the suffering people, his wife also refused to flee. She staid in the plague-stricken town until the pestilence had disappeared, exerting her influence to persuade the frightened women of the lower classes to follow her example regarding sanitary precautions. Tufik is accused of being always undecided; he was not undecided upon this occasion at least. It is probable that some of his moments of indecision have been caused by real hesitations. And this brings us to Arabi.

Arabi (he is probably indifferent to the musical sound of his name) was the leader of the military revolt which broke out in Egypt in 1881—a revolt with which all the world is familiar, because it was followed by the bombardment of Alexandria by the English fleet. Arabi had studied at El Azhar; he knew the Koran by heart. To the native population he seemed a wonderful orator; he excited their enthusiasm; he roused their courage; he almost made them patriotic. The story of Arabi is interesting; there were many intrigues mixed with the revolt, and a dramatic element throughout. But these slight impressions—the idle notes merely of one winter—are not the place for serious history. Nor is the page completed so that it can be described as a whole. Egypt at this moment is the scene of history in the actual process of making, if the term may be so used—making day by day and hour by hour. Arabi has been called the modern Masaniello. The watchword of his revolt was, "Egypt for the Egyptians"; and there is always something touching in this cry when the invaded country is weak, and the incoming power strong. But it may be answered that the Egyptians at present are incapable of governing themselves; that the country, if left to its own devices, would revert to anarchy in a month, and to famine, desolation, and barbarism in five years. Americans are not concerned with these questions of the Eastern world. But if a similar cry had been successfully raised about two hundred years ago on another coast —"America for the Americans"—would the Western continent have profited thereby? Doubtless the original Americans— those of the red skins—raised it as loudly as they could. But there was not much listening. The comparison is stretched, for the poor Egyptian fellah is at least not a savage; but there is a grain of resemblance large enough to call for reflection, when the question of the occupation and improvement of a half-civilized land elsewhere is under discussion. The English put down the revolt, and sent Arabi to Ceylon, a small Napoleon at St. Helena. The rebel colonel and his fellow-exiles are at present enjoying those spicy breezes which are associated in our minds with foreign missions and a whole congregation singing (and dragging them fearfully) the celebrated verses. Arabi has complained of the climate in spite of its perfumes, and it is said that he is to be transferred to some other point in the ocean; there are, indeed, many of them well adapted for the purpose. The English newspapers of to-day are dotted with the word shadowed, which signifies, apparently, that certain persons in Ireland are followed so closely by a policeman that the official might be the shadow. Possibly the melancholy Khedive is shadowed by the memory of the exile of Ceylon. For Tufik did not cast in his lot with Arabi. He turned toward the English. To use the word again, though with another signification, though ruler still, he has but a shadowy power.

Near the city gate named the Help of God, on the northeastern border of Cairo, is the old mosque El Hakim. Save its outer walls, which enclose, like the mosques of Touloon and Amer, a large open square, there is not much left of it; but within this square, housed in a temporary building, one finds the collection of Saracenic antiquities which is called the Arab Museum.

This museum is interesting, and it ought

to be beautiful. But somehow it is not. The barrack-like walls, sparsely ornamented with relics from the mosques, the straight aisles and glass show-cases, are not inspiring; the fragments of Arabian wood-carving seem to be lamenting their fate; and the only room which is not desolate is the one where old tiles lie in disorder upon the floor, much as they lie on the broken marble pavements of the ancient houses which, half ruined and buried in rubbish, still exist in the old quarters. Why one should be so inconsistent as to find no fault with Gizeh, where rows of antiquities torn from their proper places confront us, where show-cases abound, and yet at the same time make an outcry over this poor little morsel at El Hakim, remains a mystery. Possibly it is because the massive statues and the solid little gods of ancient Egypt do not require an appropriate background, as do the delicate fancies of Saracenic taste. However this may be, to some of us the Arab Museum looks as if a New England farmer's wife had tried her best to make things orderly within its borders, poor soul, in spite of the strangeness of the articles with which she was obliged to deal. It must, however, be added that the museum will not make this impression upon persons who are indifferent to the general aspect of an aisle, or of a series of walls—persons who care only for the articles which adorn them—the lovers of detail, in short. And it is well for all of us to join this class as soon as our feet have crossed the threshold. For we shall be repaid for it. The details are exquisite.

The Arab Museum has been established recently. Every one is grateful to the zeal which has rescued from further injury so many specimens of a vanishing art. One covets a little chest for the Koran which is made of sandal-wood. It is encrusted with arabesques carved in ivory, and has broad hasps and locks of embossed silver. There are many koursis, or small stool-like tables; one of these has panels of silver filigree, and fretted medallions bearing the name of the Sultan Mohammed ebn Kalaoon, thus showing that it once belonged to the mosque at the Citadel which was built by that Memlook ruler—the mosque whose minarets are ornamented with the picturesque bands of emerald-hued porcelain. The illuminated Korans are not here; they are kept in the Public Library in the Street of the Sycamores.

Perhaps the most beautiful of the museum's treasures are the old lamps of Arabian glass. In shape they are vases, as they were simply filled with perfumed oil which carried a floating wick; the colors are usually a pearly background, faintly tinged sometimes by the hue we call ashes of roses; upon this background are ornaments of blue, gold, and red; occasionally these ornaments are Arabic letters forming a name or text. These lamps were made in the thirteenth and fourteenth centuries; the glass, which has as marked characteristics of its own as Palissy ware, so that once seen it can never be confounded with any other, has a delicate beauty which is unrivalled.

Like the pyramids, Heliopolis belongs to Cairo. On the way thither, one first traverses the pleasant suburb of Abbasieh. How one traverses it depends upon his taste. The most enthusiastic pedestrian soon gives up walking in the city of the Khedive save in the broad streets of the new quarter. The English ride, one meets every day their gallant mounted bands; but these are generally residents and their visitors, and the horses are their own; for the traveller there are only the street carriages and the donkeys. The carriages are dubiously loose-jointed, and the horses (whose misery has already been described) have but two gaits—the walk of a dying creature and the gallop of despair; unless, therefore, one wishes to mount a dromedary, he must take a donkey. But the "must" is not a disparagement; the white and gray donkeys of Cairo—the best of them—are good-natured, gay-hearted, strong, and even handsome. They have a coquettish way of arching their necks and holding up their chins (if a donkey can be said to have a chin), which always reminded me of George Eliot's description of Gwendolen's manner of poising her head in *Daniel Deronda*. George Eliot goes on to warn other young ladies that it is useless to try to imitate this proud little air, unless one has a throat like Gwendolen's. And, in the same spirit, one must warn other donkeys that they must be born in Cairo to be beautiful. Upon several occasions I recognized vanity in my donkey; he knew perfectly when he was adorned with his holiday necklaces—one of imitation sequins, the other of turquoise-hued beads. I am sure that he would have felt much depressed if deprived of his charm against magic—

the morsel of parchment inscribed with Arabic characters which decorated his breast. His tail and his short mane were dyed fashionably with henna, but his legs had not been shaved in the pattern which represents filigree garters, and whenever a comrade who had this additional glory passed him, he became distinctly melancholy, and brooded about it for several minutes. There is nothing in the world so deprecating as the profile of one of these Cairo donkeys when he finds himself obliged, by the pressure of the crowd, to push against a European; his long nose and his polite eye as he passes are full of friendly apologies. The donkey-boy, in his skull-cap and single garment, runs behind his beast. These lads are very quick-witted. They have ready for their donkeys five or six names, and they seldom make a mistake in applying them according to the supposed nationality of their patrons of the moment, so that the Englishman learns that he has Annie Laurie; the Frenchman, Napoleon; the German, Bismarck; the Italian, Garibaldi; and the Americans, indiscriminately, Hail Columbia, Yankee Doodle, and General Grant.

In passing through the Abbasieh quarter, we always came, sooner or later, upon a wedding. The different stages of a native marriage require, indeed, so many days for their accomplishment that nuptial festivities are a permanent institution in Cairo, like the policemen and the water-carts, rather than an occasional event as in other places. One day, upon turning into a narrow street, we discovered that a long portion of it had been roofed over with red cloth; from the centre of this awning four large chandeliers were suspended by cords, and at each end of the improvised tent were hoops adorned with the little red Egyptian banners which look like fringed napkins. In the roadway, placed against the walls of the houses on each side, were rows of wooden settees; one of these seats was occupied by the band, which kept up a constant piping and droning, and upon the others were squatted the invited guests. Every now and then a man came from a gayly adorned door on the left, which was that of the bridegroom, bringing with him a tray covered with the tiny cups of coffee set in their filigree stands; he offered coffee to all. In the mean while, in the centre of the roadway between the settees,

an Egyptian in his long blue gown was dancing. The expression of responsibility on his face amounted to anxiety as he took his steps with great care, now lifting one bare foot as high as he could, and turning it sidewise, as if to show us the sole; now putting it down and hopping upon it, while he displayed to us in the same way the sole of the other. This formal dancing is done by the guests when no public performers are employed. Some one must dance to express the revelry of the occasion; those who are invited, therefore, undertake the duty one by one. When at last we went on our way we were obliged to ride directly through the reception, our donkeys brushing the band on one side and the guests on the other; the dancer on duty paused for a moment, wiping his face with the tail of his gown.

The road leading to Heliopolis has a charm which it shares with no other in the neighborhood of Cairo: at a certain point the desert—the real desert—comes rolling up to its very edge; one can look across the sand for miles. The desert is not a plain, the sand lies in ridges and hillocks; and this sand in many places is not so much like the sand of the seashore as it is like the dust of one of our country roads in August. The contrast between the bright green of the cultivated fields (the land which is reached by the inundation) and these silvery, arrested waves is striking, the line of their meeting being as sharply defined as that between sea and shore. I have called the color silvery, but that is only one of the tints which the sand assumes. An artist has jotted down the names of the colors used in an effort to copy the hues on an expanse of desert before him; beginning with the foreground, these were brown, dark red, violet, blue, gold, rose, crimson, pale green, orange, indigo blue, and sky blue. Colors supply the place of shadows; for there is no shade anywhere, all is wide open and light; and yet the expanse does not strike one in the least as bare. For myself, I can say that of all the marvels which one sees in Egypt, the desert produced the most profound impression; and I fancy that, as regards this feeling, I am but one of many. The cause of the attraction is a mystery. It cannot be found in the roving tendencies of our ancestor, since he was arboreal, and there are no trees in the strange tinted waste. The old legend says that Adam's first wife, Lilith, fled to Egypt, where she was permitted to live in the desert, and where she still exists.

> " It was Lilith, the wife of Adam;
> Not a drop of her blood was human."

Perhaps it is Lilith's magic that we feel.

Heliopolis, the City of the Sun, the On of the forty-first chapter of Genesis, is five miles from Cairo. Nothing of it is now left above-ground save an obelisk and a few ruined walls. The obelisk, which is the oldest yet discovered, bears the name of the king in whose reign it was erected; this gives us the date, 5000 years ago; that is, more than a millennium before the days of Moses. At Heliopolis was the Temple of the Sun, and the schools which Herodotus visited "because the teachers are considered the most accomplished men in Egypt." When Strabo came hither, four hundred years later, he saw the house which Plato had occupied; Moses here learned "all the wisdom of the Egyptians." Papyri describe Heliopolis as "full of obelisks." Two of these columns were carried to Alexandria 1937 years ago, and set up before the Temple of Cæsar. According to one authority, this temple was built by Cleopatra; in any case, the two obelisks acquired the name of Cleopatra's Needles, and though the temple itself in time disappeared, they remained where they had been placed—one erect, one prostrate—until, in recent years, one was given to London and the other to New York. One recites all this in a breath in order to bring up, if possible, the associations which rush confusedly through the mind as one stands beside this red granite column rising alone in the green fields at Heliopolis. No myth itself, it was erected in days which are to us mythical—days which are the jumping-off place of our human history; yet they were not savages who polished this granite, who sculptured this inscription; ages of civilization of a certain sort must have preceded them. Beginning with the Central Park, we force our minds backward in an endeavor to make these dates real. "Homer was a modern compared with the designers of this pillar," we say to ourselves. "The Mycenæ relics were *articles de Paris* of centuries and centuries later." But repeating the words (and even rolling the r's) are useless efforts; the imagination will not rise;

it is crushed into stupidity by such a vista of years. As reaction, perhaps as revenge, we flee to geology and Darwin; here, at least, one can take breath.

Near Heliopolis there is an ostrich yard. The giant birds are very amusing; they walk about with long steps, and stretch their necks. If allowed, they would tap us all on the head, I think, after the fashion of the ostriches in that vivid book, *The Story of an African Farm.*

Gerard de Nerval begins his volume on Egypt by announcing that the women of Cairo are so thickly veiled that the European (*i. e.*, the Frenchman?) becomes discouraged after a very few days, and, in consequence, goes up the Nile. This, at least, is one effort to explain why strangers spend so short a time in Cairo. The French, as a nation, are not travellers; they have small interest in any country beyond their own borders. A few of their writers have cherished a liking for the East; but it has been what we may call a home-liking. They give us the impression of having sincerely believed that they could, owing to their extreme intelligence, imagine for themselves (and reproduce for others) the entire Orient from one fez, one Turkish pipe, and a picture of the desert. Gautier, for instance, has described many Eastern landscapes which his eyes had never beheld. Pictures are, indeed, much to Frenchmen. The acme of this feeling is reached by one of the Goncourt brothers, who writes, in their recently published journal, that the true way to enjoy a summer in the country is to fill one's town-house during the summer months with beautiful paintings of green fields, wild forests, and purling brooks, and then stay at home, and look at the lovely pictured scenes in comfort. French volumes of travels in the East are written as much with exclamation points as with the letters of the alphabet. Lamartine and his disciples frequently paused "to drop a tear." Later Gallic voyagers divided all scenery into two classes; the cities "laugh," the plains are "amiable," or they "smile"; if they do not do this, immediately they are set down as "sad." One must be bold indeed to call Edmond About, the distinguished author of *Tolla,* ridiculous. The present writer, not being bold, is careful to abstain from it. But the last scene of his volume on Egypt (*Le Fellah,* published in 1883), describing the hero, with all his clothes rolled into a gigantic turban round his head, swimming after the yacht which bears away the heroine — a certain impossible Miss Grace—from the harbor of Port Said, must have caused, I think, some amused reflection in the minds of English and American readers. It is but just to add that among the younger French writers are several who have abandoned these methods. Gabriel Charmes's volume on Cairo contains an excellent account of the place. Pierre Loti and Maupassant have this year (1890) given to the world pages about northwestern Africa which are marvels of actuality as well as of unsurpassed description.

The French at present are greatly angered by the continuance of the English occupation of Egypt. Since Napoleon's day they have looked upon the Nile country as sure to be theirs some time. They built the Suez Canal when the English were opposed to the scheme. They remember when their influence was dominant. The French tradesmen, the French milliners and dressmakers in Cairo, still oppose a stubborn resistance to the English way of counting. They give the prices of their goods and render their accounts in Egyptian piasters, or in napoleons and francs; they refuse to comprehend shillings and pounds. And here, by-the-way, Americans would gladly join their side of the controversy. England alone, among the important countries of the world, has a currency which is not based upon the decimal system. The collected number of sixpences lost each year in England, by American travellers who mistake the half-crown piece for two shillings, would make a large sum. The bewilderment over English prices given in a coin which has no existence is like that felt by serious-minded persons who read *Alice in Wonderland* from a sense of duty. Talk of the English as having no imagination when the guinea exists!

France lost her opportunity in Egypt when her fleet sailed away from Alexandria Harbor in July, 1882. Her ships were asked to remain and take part in the bombardment; they refused and departed. The English, thus being left alone, quieted the country later by means of an army of occupation. An English army of occupation has been there ever since.

At present it is not a large army. The number of British soldiers in 1890 is given as three thousand; the remaining troops are Egyptians, with English regimental officers. During the winter months the short-waisted red coat of Tommy Atkins enlivens with its cheerful blaze the streets of Cairo at every turn. The East and the West may be said to be personified by the slender supple Arabs in their flowing draperies, and by these lusty youths of light complexion, with straight backs and stiff shoulders, who walk, armed with a rattan, in the centre of the pavement, wearing over one ear the cloth-covered saucer which passes for a head-covering. Tommy Atkins patronizes the donkeys with all his heart. One of the most frequently seen groups is a party of laughing scarlet-backed youths mounted on the smallest beasts they can find, and careering down the avenues at the donkey's swiftest speed, followed by the donkey-boys, delighted and panting. As the spring comes on, Atkins changes his scarlet for lighter garments, and dons the summer helmet. This species of hat is not confined to the sons of Mars; it is worn in warm weather by Europeans of all nationalities who are living or travelling in the East. It may be cool. Without doubt, æsthetically considered, it is the most unbecoming head-covering known to the civilized world. It has a peculiar power of causing its wearer to appear both ignoble and pulmonic; for, viewed in front, the most distinguished features, under its tin-pan-like visor, become plebeian; and, viewed behind, the strongest masculine throat looks wizened and consumptive.

The English have benefited Egypt. They have put an end to the open knavery in high places which flourished unchecked; they have taught honesty; they have so greatly improved the methods of irrigation that a bad Nile (*i.e.*, a deficient inundation) no longer means starvation; finally, they have taken hold of the mismanaged finances, disentangled them, set them in order, and given them at least a start in the right direction. The natives fret over some of their restrictions. And they say that the English have, first of all, taken care of their own interests. In addition, they greatly dislike seeing so many Englishmen holding office over them. But this last objection is simply the other side of the story. If the English are to help the country, they must be on the spot in order to do it; and it appears to be a fixed rule in all British colonies that the representatives of the government, whether high or low, shall be made, as regards material things, extremely comfortable. Egypt is not yet a British colony: she is a viceroyalty under the suzerainty of the Porte. But practically she is to-day governed by the English; and, to the American traveller at least (whatever the French may think), it appears probable that English authority will soon be as absolute in the Khedive's country as it is now in India.

In Cairo, in 1890, the English colony played lawn-tennis; it attended the races; when Stanley returned to civilization it welcomed him with enthusiasm; and when, later, Prince Eddie came, it attended a gala performance of *Aïda* at the opera-house—a resurrection from the time of Ismail ordered by Ismail's son for the entertainment of the heir-presumptive (one wonders whether Tufik himself found entertainment in it).

In the little English church, which stands amidst its roses and vines in the new quarter, is a wall tablet of red and white marble—the memorial of a great Englishman. It bears the following inscription: "In memory of Major-General Charles George Gordon, C.B. Born at Woolwich, Jan. 28, 1833. Killed at the defence of Khartoum, Jan. 26, 1885." Above is a sentence from Gordon's last letter: "I have done my best for the honor of our country."

St. George of Khartoum, as he has been called. If objection is made to the bestowal of this title, it might be answered that the saints of old lived before the age of the telegraph, the printer, the newspaper, and the reporter; possibly they too would not have seemed to us faultless if every one of their small decisions and all their trivial utterances had been subjected to the electric-light publicity of to-day. Perhaps Gordon was a fanatic, and his discernment was not accurate. But he was single-hearted, devoted to what he considered to be his duty, and brave to a striking degree. When we remember how he faced death through those weary days we cannot criticise him. The story of that rescuing army which came so near him and yet failed, and of his long hoping in vain, only to be shot down at the last, must always remain one of the most pathetic tales of history.

As the warm spring closes, every one selects something to carry homeward. Leaving aside those fortunate persons who can purchase the ancient carved woodwork of an entire house, or Turkish carpets by the dozen, the rest of us keep watch of the selections of our friends while we make our own. Among these we find the jackets embroidered in silver and gold; the inevitable fez; two or three blue tiles of the thirteenth century; a water jug, or kulleh; a fly brush with ivory handle; attar of roses and essence of sandal-wood; Assiout ware in vases and stoups; a narghileh; the gauze scarfs embroidered with Persian benedictions; a koursi inlaid with mother-of-pearl; Arabian inkstands—long cases of silver or brass, to be worn like a dagger in the belt; a keffiyeh, or delicate silken head-shawl with white knotted fringe; the Arabian finger-bowls; the little coffee-cups; images of Osiris from the tombs; a native bracelet and anklet; and finally a scarab or two, whose authenticity is always exciting, like an unsolved riddle. A picture of these mementos of Cairo would not be complete for some of us without two of those constant companions of so many long mornings — the dusty, shuffling, dragging, slipping, venerable, abominable mosque shoes.

"We who pursue
Our business with unslackening stride,
Traverse in troops, with care-fill'd breast,
The soft Mediterranean side,
The Nile, the East,
And see all sights from pole to pole,
And glance and nod and bustle by,
And never once possess our soul
Before we die."

So chanted Matthew Arnold of the English of to-day. And if we are to believe what is preached to us and hurled at us, it is a reproach even more applicable to Americans than to the English themselves. One American traveller, however, wishes to record modestly a disbelief in the universal truth of this idea. Many of us are, indeed, haunted by our business; many of us do glance and nod and bustle by; it is a class, and a large class. But these hurried people are not all; an equal number of us, who, being less in haste, may be less conspicuous perhaps, are the most admiring travellers in the world. American are the bands who journey to Stratford-upon-Avon, and go down upon their knees—almost—when they reach the sacred spot; American are the pilgrims who pay reverent visits to all the English cathedrals, one after the other, from Car-

THE INUNDATION NEAR CAIRO.

lisle to Exeter, from Durham to Canterbury. In the East, likewise, it is the transatlantic travellers who are so deeply impressed by the strangeness and beauty of the scenes about them that they forget to talk about their personal comforts (or rather the lack of them).

There is another matter upon which a word may be said, and this is the habit of judging the East from the stand-point of one's home customs, whether the home be American or English. It is, of course, easy to find faults in the social systems of the Oriental nations; they have laws and usages which are repugnant to all our feelings, which seem to us horrible. But it is well to remember that it is impossible to comprehend any nation not our own

A MOHAMMEDAN CEMETERY, CAIRO.

unless one has lived a long time among its people, and made one's self familiar with their traditions, their temperament, their history, and, above all, with the language which they speak. Anything less than this is observation from the outside alone, which is sure to be founded upon misapprehension. The French and the English are separated by merely the few miles of the channel, and they have, to a certain extent, a common language; for though the French do not often understand English, the English very generally understand something of French. Yet it is said that these two nations have never thoroughly comprehended each other either as nations or individuals; and it is even added that, owing to their differing temperaments, they will never reach a clear appreciation of each other's merits; demerits, of course, are easier. Our own country has a language which is, on the whole, nearer the English tongue perhaps than is the speech of France; yet have we not felt now and then that English travellers have misunderstood us? If this is the case among people who are all Occidentals together, how much more difficult must be a thorough comprehension by us of those ancient nations who were old before we were born?

The East is the land of mystery. If one cares for it at all, one loves it; there is no half-way. If one does not love it, one really (though perhaps not avowedly) hates it—hates it and all its ways. But for those who love it the charm is so strong that no surprise is felt in reading or hearing of Europeans who have left all to take up a wandering existence there for long years or for life—the spirit of Browning's "What's become of Waring?"

All of us cannot be Warings, however, and the time comes at last when we must take leave. The streets of Cairo have been for some time adorned with placards whose announcements begin, in large type, "Travellers returning to Europe." We are indeed far away when returning to Europe is a step towards home. We wait for the last festival—the Shem-en-Neseem, or Smelling of the Zephyr—the annual picnic day, when the people go into the country to gather flowers and breathe the soft air before the opening of the regular season for the Khamsin. Then comes the journey by railway to Alexandria. We wave a handkerchief (now fringed on all four sides by the colored threads of the laundresses) to the few friends still left behind. They respond; and so do all the Mustaphas, Achmets, and Ibrahims who have carried our parcels and trotted after our donkeys. Then we take a seat by the window to watch for the last time the flying Egyptian landscape—the green plain, the tawny Nile, the camels on the bank, the villages, and the palm-trees, and behind them the solemn line of the desert.

At sunset the steamer passes down the harbor, and pushing out to sea, turns westward. A faint crescent moon becomes visible over the Ras-et-Teen palace. It is the moon of Ramadan. Presently a cannon on the shore ushers in, with its distant sound, the great Mohammedan fast.

THE LAND OF THE MIDNIGHT SUN

THERE is no accounting for the tastes of travellers. Mr. Paul Du Chaillu was born in Africa, where he made wonderful journeys and discoveries that earn-

AN OLD NORSE CHIEF.

ed him world-wide honor; but although he proved himself superior to all the torments of equatorial travel, it was quite natural to suppose that yearly, after his return, he would, on the approach of winter, hurry shiveringly from New York to at least the shores of the Gulf of Mexico. What he really did, however, when seized anew by the fever of travel, was to cross the Atlantic and go as near to the north pole as the route by land would allow. For five years he remained within or near the arctic circle; and although thousands of his admirers declared that his imprudence would cost him his life, he returned in enviable health, having entirely escaped even the rheumatism that is supposed to claim for its own all travellers from milder climes. One important re-

sult of his trip is a large and extremely interesting book,* just published simultaneously in America, England, Germany, France, Sweden, and Denmark—an incident unparalleled in the history of book publication.

Like the author's other works, *The Land of the Midnight Sun* derives much of its charm from the novelty of the scenes and people described. Portions of Scandinavia have at times exerted mighty influences on the remainder of Europe, so it would seem that at least the southern parts of Sweden and Norway would have attracted the attention of many writers. To Mr. Du Chaillu, however, belongs the honor of having written the first comprehensive sketch of the country and its inhabitants. The Scandinavian peninsula now devotes its attention strictly to its own affairs. It is not on the road between the remainder of Europe and anywhere in particular; so, excepting a few English sportsmen and an occasional party whose first desire is to see the sun at midnight, their second longing being to get back to their comfortable homes as soon as possible, the foreigner is seldom seen in the land, so the natives are simply what their own surroundings have made them, and their dress, customs, and homes are in great part unlike those of any other country. Where else in the world is the buyer trusted to make out his own bills? Where else do parents go to bed at night before their daughters' lovers arrive? In what other part of Europe are there provinces where all the peasants bathe weekly, where there are jails that never are occupied, where the annual death rate is not one per cent., and where jurymen

* *The Land of the Midnight Sun.* Summer and Winter Journeys through Sweden, Norway, Lapland, and Northern Finland. By PAUL B. DU CHAILLU, author of *Explorations in Equatorial Africa, A Journey to Ashango-Land, Stories of the Gorilla Country,* etc. With Map and 233 Illustrations. In Two Volumes. New York: Harper and Brothers. London: John Murray.

are elected by the people, instead of being drawn hap-hazard from among such citizens as are not smart enough to shirk jury duty? Nearly every one of Mr. Du Chaillu's descriptions of the people compels the reader to believe that if the descendants of the Vikings are so honest, industrious, peaceable, and hearty, the dreaded incursions of alleged marauders did not do England any great harm after all.

The most striking quality of Scandinavian character seems to be hospitality. Throughout Norway, Sweden, and the far North the author was heartily received by every one, from the king in his palace to the Laplander in his tent. During five years of almost incessant travel, in the course of which every part of the peninsula was visited, Mr. Du Chaillu was coolly treated only once. The Swedes and Norwegians have the reputation of being reserved and cold, but this is true of them only when they meet strangers of the class best suggested by the word "tourist." To any one whose interest in them can not be measured by a stare or two and a few impertinent questions they are unsuspicious and communicative, as well as cordial to the verge of affection. Mr. Du Chaillu went among them freely, conversed with them in their language, wore garments like their own, and took part in their labors, sports, and ceremonies. The treatment he received in return causes him to speak most enthusiastically in praise of their sociability and kindness.

As in all other countries that retain primitive habits, hospitality in Scandinavia always implies eating and drinking. The poorest farmer or fisherman always

has something to offer the visitor, and lack of appetite is generally construed as a slight. The author mentions one occasion on which, to avoid hurting any one's feelings, he ate thirty times in two days, and drank thirty - four cups of coffee. Often strong cheese is offered just before a meal to provoke appetite, and in the cities a formal dinner is preceded by a *smörgås*, or lunch, at a table crowded with alleged appetizers. On a single *smörgås* table the author noted smoked reindeer meat, smoked salmon with poached eggs, raw salmon freshly salted, hard-boiled eggs, caviare, fried sausage. anchovy, smoked goose breast, cucumbers, raw salt herring, several kinds of cheese and as many of bread, and a salad made of pickled herring, boiled meat, potatoes, eggs, beets, and onions. There were also three kinds of spirits on the table, and

RUNIC STONE AT TJÄNGVIDE.

from these and the various dishes the guests helped themselves bountifully, and then did justice to an excellent dinner. An American who would attempt by such seldom complain of indigestion, and they certainly live longer than their Western neighbors.

There is delicious satire in the fact that

NORTH CAPE.

means to gain an appetite would be helpless before reaching the dinner table, and his dyspepsia would be one of the most wonderful cases on record; but the Swedes the Norseman of the present day, the descendant of the most famous robbers that overran Europe, is distinguished above all other Europeans for his honesty and sim-

plicity. Not once during his long residence in Scandinavia did the author lose
any of his property by theft, although he
often left his bag of money exposed in
sleigh or wagon. On two or three occasions he lost his watch or his money, but
invariably they were found, and brought
being careful to set aside those really
caught by his neighbor; once in a while,
too, the honest Lapp in the far North may
not make haste to report that a reindeer
or two have strayed into his herd; but
these offenses are winked at very much
after the manner of Americans toward

DRESSING THE BRIDE.

back to him without any assistance from
the authorities; and the bringer would
appear not only surprised but hurt if offered payment for what seemed a mere
neighborly service. Occasionally the
fisherman who finds other nets or lines
entangled with his own in the water
will remove all fish that he sees without
the saintly deacon who overreaches his
neighbor in a horse trade. Of common
thieves, however, there seem to be absolutely none outside of the cities. Simple
trust in the honor of every one seems to
be universal, and this feeling extends even
to the social relations. Conventional re-
straints are often set aside to an extent

THE SKJAEGGDAL, A WATER-FALL IN NORWAY.

that startles and horrifies the traveller, until he discovers that they are not maintained because they are not necessary.

The Scandinavian is earnest, industrious, and methodical in everything he does. He works, during the daylight season of the year, longer hours than any American would think of doing, and his industrial habits are as regular as those of the clock. He is equally thorough about his devotions; the church may be far from his farm, and the Sunday very stormy, but he attends service if he is not sick. Congregations of from three to five thousand persons are not unusual in the rural districts. He is just as much in earnest when at his diversions. An old farmer will fiddle all evening while his family—children and servants included— dance. He is very fond of visiting; and a wedding is sufficient excuse for a three days' jollification. Preparations for a wedding feast begin weeks beforehand, and are so extensive that M. Du Chaillu was utterly amazed at the quantity of solids and liquids that he saw stored against an approaching marriage feast. Invitations to weddings are sent out well in advance of the happy day, so that the guests may prepare for two or three days' absence from home; and the poorest person invited is never without a wedding garment. The happy couple eat, drink, and dance with everybody; and it seems never to have occurred to the people to inquire how they do it. There is a limit to the endurance of the native head and stomach, and this generally is found on the third day; then the guests, on bidding good-by to the bride, tender their wedding presents, which always consist of money, and are deposited, without being examined, in a box which the bride wears at her side. How many American girls will

THE WALLS OF WISBY.

wish—only to themselves—that a similar custom might prevail here can not easily be estimated, but all of them will understand why there are but few bachelors in the land of the midnight sun. Long as are the wedding festivities, those of Christmas far exceed them, for feasting and fun are industriously kept up from Christmas-eve to Twelfth-night, and quaint and charming are some of the attendant ceremonies.

The patriarchal mode of life seems to have been better preserved in Scandinavia than in any other part of Europe. Even in the cities, where the habits of good society are in no way inferior to those of similar circles in England and France, servants and other social inferiors are treated with thoughtfulness and consideration to a degree that is seldom approached even in our own land of boasted equality, and many large employers look to the general well-being of their workmen, caring for the sick, and pensioning the families

OLD DRINKING HORN.

of those who die in their employ. In the farming districts, where the people are fully as well educated as those of any rural district in the United States, the servants form part of the family circle at the table, around the hearth-stone, or in the pew at church; they share the best sleeping apartments of the family, wear just as good clothing as the master and mistress, and the maids, if they are as pretty, get as much attention from masculine visitors as the daughters of the house, too. One fine old farmer, Thord by name, who entertained the late king during that ruler's trip to Norway for coronation, sent the king word to bring no silver service with him, as there was enough on the estate for the whole royal party. While domestics can eat at the board at the head of which sits such a man, it is useless for American ladies to sigh for the "perfect Swedish servant" that they have heard so much about.

The author admires the scenery of Norway and Sweden as heartily as he does the people. There is a general impression that all Scandinavian landscapes are rugged and gloomy; some of them certainly appear to be sombre, though many of these are unspeakably grand; both countries, however, have regions as smiling and beautiful as any in England, and offer the traveller a variety that he can not find within similar area anywhere else in the world. The western coast of the Scandinavian peninsula is indented by numerous narrow, long bays called fiords, with water sometimes nearly a mile deep, while their sides are abrupt and mountainous. Farther inland there are wonderful water-falls in profusion: the author's volumes contain sketches of many of these, and the American trembles for the fame of some of the noted cataracts and cascades of his own country as he reads of rivers that tumble about a quarter of a mile at a single leap, and then repeat this gentle exercise once or twice. Enormous snowy mountains may be enjoyed in variety throughout the winter season, and reached without journeying half-way across a continent, as the American must generally do if he desires a first-class mountain view. The mountains of Northern Scandinavia make themselves particularly attractive by night, and so does everything else picturesque, for, as if to compensate the native for almost total

BORGUND CHURCH.

insisted on entertaining the author at a special table, but first he ate with his family and servants. Feeling sure that six meals per day instead of three would cause his host discomfort, Mr. Du Chaillu remonstrated with Thord, who replied that if he were to absent himself from his family table, the servants would think him proud. And yet this considerate old fellow was a descendant of King Harold the Fair-haired, and inhabited an estate that had been in his family a thousand years—an estate so rich that his father,

GOLDEN BOWL, BLEKINGE.—[ONE-HALF ITS SIZE.]

withdrawal of daylight during the winter season, nature gives him moonlight and starlight such as are seldom seen in lower latitudes. Where the scenery does not startle the beholder by its grandeur, it is quite likely to charm by its beauty, for the less hilly portions of the peninsula are fully covered by farms, the buildings of which are quaint and quite unlike anything to be seen elsewhere. The age attributed to some of these buildings seems impossible, for it is not assuring to national pride to know that some Swedish farmers lived in solid, comfortable, roomy houses when our English ancestors occupied mere hovels, but the evidence that some of these farm-houses date back five, seven, and even ten centuries seems conclusive. Equally old and interesting are many of the churches, and they are not, like most of those of a similar period in other lands, merely picturesque ruins, as will be seen by a picture or two which we borrow from the score or more that the author displays in his book. The interiors of some of these old churches indicate that Sweden had money enough to secure the best architects of the day, and to fully carry out their designs.

Indeed, for interesting antiquities Sweden may safely challenge comparison with any other nation in the north of Europe. Even had she only the remains of the old city of Wisby, she could outdo any of her neighbors in a competitive display of antiquities and of honorable historical record. In the days when London was merely the principal city of England, and centuries before Liverpool existed as a shipping port, Wisby was the centre of trade in Northern Europe, her business relations extending to Greece, Rome, India, and Persia. The present walls of the city, with towers sixty or seventy feet high, were built six centuries

ago, for even at that time the community was so rich as to require special protection. The merchants had their code of commercial laws, which still is held in high respect in business circles everywhere. The city was as full as London of rich guilds, and contained many large and beautiful churches, some of which remain to testify to the wealth and taste of their builders. Like all of the rich European cities, Wisby was one day captured, sacked, and almost destroyed. Perhaps it was at this time that the citizens buried the immense quantity of valuable portable property since discovered; or perhaps the Wisby savings-banks, like many of the present day, taught the people that the surest way of keeping their money was to take care of it themselves. But whatever the reason, the soil of Wisby has in late years proved particularly

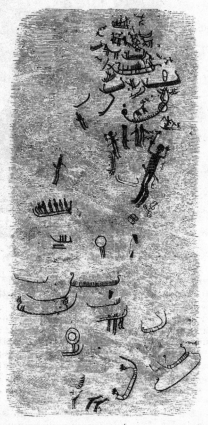

ROCK CUTTING NEAR BACKA.—[ONE SIXTY-SEVENTH ITS SIZE.]

INTERIOR OF RISINGE CHURCH, ÖSTERGÖTLAND.

auriferous: great quantities of European coins have been dug from the ground, many of those of Rome dating back to the first century of the Christian era, while of Asiatic coins more than ten thousand are known to have been found; and as men seldom tell about the finding of money, it is reasonable to suppose that the entire find has been enormous. Large quantities of valuable jewels, gold and silver vessels, etc., have been discovered, as well as the seals of some of the great guilds. Hundreds of buildings still remain as mute evidences of the substantial prosperity of the old merchants, and numerous ancient family tombs make interesting additions to the city's record.

But Wisby (which is on an island) is only one of the old Scandinavian cities; on the mainland were many others older and much larger, although perhaps not so rich, and their remains are equally interesting. How many of the valuables found in these cities really originated there is a somewhat delicate question to discuss, for the old Scandinavians, like all other powerful nations of the same period, had a habit of going in immense surprise parties to other countries, and bringing back whatever suited their fancy, dispensing entirely with the formality of asking the original owner's consent. Exquisite vases in gold, silver, and bronze have been found, and so have valuable ornaments in great profusion, while household utensils, armor, weapons, and even fairly preserved Viking ships are numerous enough to throw much light on Scandinavian life in the Middle Ages. As usual in old countries, the tombs yield valuable contributions to the general store of antiquities, besides being quite curious in themselves.

Most interesting, however, of all Norse remains are the rock tracings, which at what they are when he sees them, but there knowledge ends. Many students have labored over them as faithfully as others have done over our own darling obelisk, but the translations disagree as

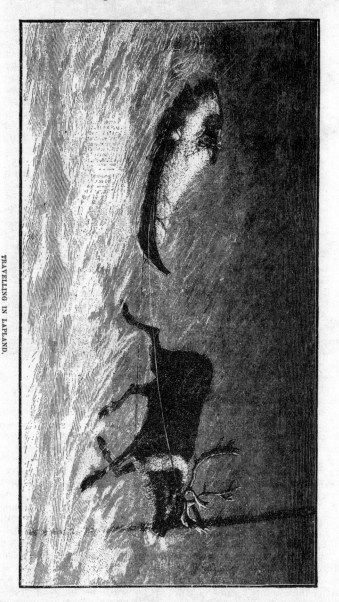

TRAVELING IN LAPLAND.

one stage of the country's development were the only substitutes for national and local records. Every one knows hopelessly as politicians. More legible in appearance, though sometimes just as puzzling in reality, are the rune stones,

REINDEER DIGGING IN THE SNOW.

by anything worth the name of night, a trip to the midnight sun costs much more than money, although the traveller will not admit that the cost is too great.

A sketch of the far North without some description of Lapland, its people and its reindeer, would be as disappointing as a performance of *Hamlet* without the melancholy Dane. Mr. Du Chaillu spent much time in Lapland, and

bearing inscriptions in characters that were designed to be mystical, and certainly succeeded in being mysterious. Among those that are decipherable are some inscriptions on memorial stones, which state that the late lamented departed this life in Greece, Rome, or the Saracen land—places to which the Norsemen have not generally been suspected of wandering.

Of course the author's first duty was to pay his respects to the midnight sun, which he saw from North Cape, the northernmost extremity of Scandinavia. As he approached the arctic circle he naturally expected to be delivered from the swarms of buzzing insects that sometimes make life miserable in lower latitudes; to his great surprise and disgust, however, the pests increased as he moved farther north. Mosquitoes were sometimes so numerous that it seemed a mystery how they could find enough air to breathe, and the author insists on being believed when he tells of a swarm so dense that it hid three men who were standing near by. In the middle of August these pests give way to a hard-biting gnat, which is nevertheless not wholly pitiless, for it remains out-of-doors, and does not bite at night. After these comes a sand-fly that lunches on poor humanity until cold weather suppresses him. As all of these tormentors attend to business throughout the whole summer day, which is not broken

declares the Lapps to be a much-misrepresented people. Instead of being dark of complexion, black-haired, stupid, heathenish, and murderous, as even some Swedes and Norwegians believe them to be, the author found them light of hair and color, agile, industrious, bright, hospitable, and as good Christians as any other people. They are not always as cleanly as some other races, for building material is scarce in Lapland, houses or tents are small, and washing-day preparations are sometimes impossible. Their morals are of a high order. Many of them are fairly educated, and nearly all of them are religious in both form and spirit. The author's religious beliefs were carefully investigated at length by men and women alike. Some of the Lapps go abroad and become rich; Mr. Du Chaillu refers to several of these who are in the United States, where one of them owns a brown-stone front; but most of them prefer to remain in their own land. In the words of the author: "Happy and contented with his lot in the world, endowed with a religious nature which a barren and lonely land contributes to intensify, the Lapp believes in God, in his Bible, in the Lord Jesus Christ as the Son of God, and in a future life. From that dreary waste his songs of praise and his prayers are uttered with a faith which ceases only with his breath, and he departs rejoicing that he is going to the 'better land.'"

The reindeer, which in one way or another manages to be almost the entire support of the Lapps who have herds, is a large, heavy animal with remarkable independence of character. He will not accept shelter under cover, no matter how inclement the weather may be. Neither will he eat any food that is offered him; he prefers to seek his own sustenance, which consists principally of a peculiar moss, and as this grows very slowly, requiring about seven years in which to reach maturity, the Lapp must shift his home from time to time to meet the necessities of his herd. In midwinter the moss may be covered by several feet of snow, but the deer digs a hole with his feet, and disappears from the surface, burrowing his way through the snow as he follows his nose from one tuft of moss to another. The flesh of the reindeer is quite palatable and nutritious, his skin makes very warm garments as well as durable harness, and cheese made of reindeer milk is very rich, although the quantity of milk yielded per day seems scarcely worth the taking, as it amounts to a mere teacupful.

Unlike the general traveller who writes books, Mr. Du Chaillu has interested himself in every intellectual, social, and industrial phase of the national life. To those who read his frequent allusions to the music and song heard everywhere it will no longer seem strange that Jenny Lind, Christine Nilsson, and Ole Bull should have come from Sweden instead of Italy, the supposed mother of singers. The dying art of vocal serenading seems to flourish vigorously in Sweden and Norway, and instrumental music is so common that the author reports pianos

AN OLD HOUSE IN SKANE—1558.

within the arctic circle, and towns farther south where these instruments are found in the ratio of one to every twenty-five people. Great attention is bestowed upon dress and the beautifying of homes, although taste is superior to the rage for display. Facilities for communication are good, cheap, and fully equal to the demand; the postal service is fully as good as our own, and a perfect telegraph system covers the peninsula, the operators being compelled to understand at least three languages. The common schools are as thorough in their methods as those of America, and considerably higher in grade, for the poorest child can obtain instruction in higher mathematics, the natural sciences, Latin, Greek, and modern languages. Excellent technical schools exist, and good universities crown the educational system.

Although in Norway and Sweden there are many mines and mills, most of the people gain their living either out of the soil or the sea. The farmer in either country is a marvel of industry and thrift; he would live upon what an American farmer wastes, and live more comfortably than our farming population do, as a rule. The amount of labor performed at the special dairy-farms, to which cattle are driven in summer, generally by girls, would horrify a Western maiden; but the Swedish and Norwegian girls thrive on it, enjoying rare good health, and consequent happiness. Still more exacting is the home care of cattle in winter, when much of the food must be specially prepared. On some soil that here would be condemned as good for nothing, fair crops are grown and harvested in the short summer, while in the southern provinces the yield is equal to that of model farms in America.

The maritime statistics of the two countries, and of Norway in particular, are simply staggering. Last year more than a thousand Norwegian vessels entered the port of New York, and seven times as many were busy elsewhere. More than sixty thousand sailors man these vessels, and yet Norwegian sailors are numerous in the merchant navy of almost every other country. About a hundred and twenty thousand Norwegians are engaged in the fisheries. The author minutely describes the great fishing stations of Norway, and here, as elsewhere, is struck by the attention paid by the government to all its resources. Every fishing station has a superintendent, appointed by the government, and the date of beginning the season's work, the time of starting out for the day, and even the places in which the fish are prepared for market, are determined by him; but the officer's duties seem to consist principally in preventing confusion or bad feeling. No liquor is sold at fishing stations, and yet the men, who are directly in the path of all the "American weather" that crosses the Atlantic, are a remarkably healthy and vigorous set of fellows; they wear good clothes, too, which is not done by fishermen in general. To their abstemiousness must be attributed the lack of strife; during a long visit to the fishing stations the author saw no fighting, and did not hear a single oath. No fishing is permitted on Sunday. Drunkenness and profanity are rare everywhere in Scandinavia; there seems to be absolutely no idle, non-producing, dangerous class, such as is the main-stay of vice in every other European country. At fairs and feasts there is a great deal of drinking, but the period is brief, and the fun never culminates in fighting.

So thoroughly has the author interested himself in Scandinavia that the reader can ask scarcely a question about the country that the book does not answer. The geology of the country, and the effect of the glaciers, many of which are still at work, are minutely set forth. The development of the people is traced from the stone age down to modern times, and even the dwellings, from the first departure from cave life, are described at length, the text being illustrated by many engravings of houses at different periods. Much valuable information is given about the fauna and flora, the climate, temperature, and rain-fall—the result being a general disabusing of popular impression. Unlike many books of travel, these volumes are illustrated solely from photographs and sketches made from the people and scenes described, so the pictures contribute directly to the reader's information. Mr. Du Chaillu can not claim to be the original discoverer of Scandinavia, but he certainly has the honor of being the first to make known to the world the country as it exists to-day.

CHARACTERISTIC PARISIAN CAFES

TYPES OF WAITERS AND WAITRESSES.

CHARACTERISTIC PARISIAN CAFÉS.

BY THEODORE CHILD.

IN Paris, public-houses where liquid refreshments are sold take many names,
of which "café" is the most general and
comprehensive. "Brasserie" is a café
where beer is made a specialty; "cabaret" is the old-fash-
ioned, but still used,
word meaning a place
where both drink and
food are sold. Then
there are the popular
names not recognized by the
standard dictionaries, such as
"caboulot," "boussingot," or
"bouchon," meaning a little
low café; "bouisbouis," meaning a low café with the attraction of music and singing;
and "mannezingue," "mastro-
quet," and "troquet," which
are equivalent to the "mar-
chand de vin"—the man who
sells liquor over a polished
zinc counter, and who varies
in worthiness from a respectable tradesman and prominent
elector down to the keeper of a "tapis
franc," or thieves' den. Such establishments of different kinds are to be found in
Paris by tens of thousands; furthermore,
the number of them is increasing, and, according to statisticians, alcoholism is increasing too, especially amongst the lower
classes. Far be it from me to distrust the

figures of the statisticians, or even to quote them, for statisticians, I have remarked, are willingly foreboders of evil, and their conclusions full of menace. My own experience during many years of peripatetic observation has been that it is a very rare thing to see a drunken man in the streets of Paris; and when, on two or three occasions within as many years, I have seen a man lying helpless on the sidewalk, I have always attributed the accident to the slipperiness of the pavement, or to the sleepiness of the man, or to his having thought that there was an earthquake.

The Frenchman does not get drunk; he becomes lively—or, as he says, *ému*—under the influence of liquor, and in such circumstances he is expansive, persuasive, and singularly eloquent. Frédérick Lemaître and Gambetta achieved their most brilliant successes, the one as an actor, the other as an orator, when they were exceedingly *ému*. In his younger days, I have heard, the Duc d'Aumale, passing at the head of his regiment the Clos Vougeot, halted his men, and made them salute the famous vineyard, as being one of the great nursing mothers of French wit. But, strange to say, the Parisian does not drink wine at a café: he drinks deleterious distilled liquors, such as vermouth, absinthe, various bitters supposed to have merits as "appetizers," or harmless syrups made from fruits or aromatic plants. On the other hand, he drinks but small quantities of these liquids, and that, too, so slowly that he is capable of sitting for two hours in a café before a single thimbleful of liqueur brandy, having thus paid for a pretext for lounging, talking, and reading the newspapers. In fact, the café and the newspaper came into vogue almost simultaneously about a century ago, when Louis XVI. was King. As the times became more interesting, the gazettes became more numerous, and the calm topics of art, the drama, and the scandals of the court gave way to hot discussions about the rights of man, in which the women also took part. At the Café Corazza the Jacobins gathered round Chabot and Collot d'Herbois, while the Royalists held their own as well as they could at the Café de Foy. Then, the summer of 1789 happening to be persistently rainy, and the gossips being more eager than ever for news, the politicians and their orators sought shelter in various other cafés, where they formed sympathetic groups, and so prepared the way for the clubs of the period of the Revolution. In those critical times, when the formidable subject of the rights of man was being argued and settled for all time, the politicians established clearly and by example that it was the right of the French citizen to read the gazettes, to talk loudly, and to enjoy all the other advantages of a café, during the space of at least six hours, on the condition of ordering one cup of coffee or a single thimbleful of brandy. And this right has been maintained by succeeding generations up to the present day. Thus we have one important point settled, namely, the Frenchman does not go to a café for the sake of drinking, nor does he drink at the café for the sake of drinking, much less because he is thirsty: he drinks simply because he wants to go to the café.

Why the Frenchman wants to go to a café is a complex question which can be answered only roughly and incompletely by noting the triple attraction which the café exercises. First of all, it satisfies the need of public life and life in public which the Latin nations in particular have felt since the Revolution of 1789; secondly, it takes the place of family life, which the conditions of modern existence have profoundly undermined; finally, it flatters a certain taste for degradation and lowness which is peculiar to male humanity, and which the wisest legislator will never be able to suppress. All men, it seems, feel the need of escaping occasionally from the gentle influence of their women-folk, and of enjoying masculine society and masculine talk; hence the café and hence the club, which is an outcome and modification of the café, and the most exclusively masculine of all the institutions of modern civilization. In itself the café is tiresome and full of ennui, like everything which is not natural, and the pleasure which it gives cannot be formulated.

Let us take a walk along the boulevard between five and seven o'clock, the "green hours," when the Parisians are wont to drink absinthe, read the evening papers, and gossip in the cafés. The boulevards extend for miles until they reach the Bastile Column, where they connect with other boulevards which surround the city. But the real boulevard —*the* boulevard—is a short stretch bounded at one end by the Madeleine and at the

CAFÉ TORTONI.

other by the Rue Montmartre, and the centre and quintessence of it is the Café Tortoni. The history of Tortoni is the history of the boulevard, and of that superior kind of Bohemian who bears the generic name of *boulevardier*. Under the First Empire the wits assembled there to comment upon the bulletins of the Grand Army, or to criticise the last tragedy of Luce de Lancival. In the little room at the back, Talleyrand was wont to sit, and through the window watch the gay movement of the Boulevard de Gand, which we now call the Boulevard des Italiens. Later, M. Thiers, aged thirty, elegant, ambitious, and determined to succeed, used to ride up to Tortoni's on a white horse, stay just long enough to eat an ice, and then quick to the saddle again, and *en route* for fortune. Throughout the Restoration and the Second Empire Tortoni was a centre of fashion, wit, and elegance, and the little café at the corner of the Rue Taitbout still remains, a monument, an institution, a tradition, the sanctum of the *chroniqueurs* of the Parisian newspapers of the *Figaro* type, the head-quarters of the wits, the gossips, and the scandal-mongers of the capital. At the Café Américain, novelists, poets, other *chroniqueurs*, literary men, and painters indulge regularly in "apéritifs," cigarettes, and piquant talk. At the Café Riche, the financiers and stock-brokers outnumber the literary men, who used to predominate in former days, when Offenbach, Clément Laurier, Wolff, About, and Saint-Victor were the habitués of a particular round table. On the other side of the boulevard, the Café du Helder is the rendezvous of military and naval officers, who on their brief visits to Paris are sure to find some friend there with whom to discuss the latest promotions and the newest reforms invented by their hierarchic chief the Minister of War, and in case of need they can appeal for information to the habitués, who are not all army men, but who have a particular affection for all that is military, and who sit at the little marble tables, drink absinthe, and are invariably decorated. One may be a retired captain with a rubicund nose, long shaggy mustaches, a goatee beard, and in his button-hole the rosette of the Legion of Honor, won perhaps by good service in Africa. With his hands in his pockets, he sits heavily on the red velvet divan, propping his gross body against the back,

and never removing his rather rakish hat from his denuded skull. Another may be a horse-dealer or an army contractor, whose sympathies and interests make him prefer to drink his green poison in a military café. A third, corpulent, apoplectic, faded, and sulky, smokes stolidly, with a cross expression on his countenance, his temper having been irremediably soured by long years of sedentary ennui in the bureaux of the War Department.

Then there is the Café de la Paix, the rendezvous of the gilded youth of Paris, and of the rich strangers, who sit at the little round tables placed on the sidewalk, and marvel at the animation and variety of the boulevard. At the Café de la Paix you can see any day and at almost any hour specimens of all the nationalities of the earth — Brazilians scintillating with diamonds, Englishmen conspicuous by their strange head-gear and light-colored clothes, Chinese clad in radiant silks, Arab sheiks who mar the majesty of their turban and burnoose by wearing yellow kid French gloves stitched with black. And in the midst of this cosmopolitan company the young French "dude" sucks the handle of his cane, cramped and angular in his tight-fitting garments, dull-eyed, stolid, and proud of the weary emptiness of his existence. At the Café de Madrid may be seen the members of the radical newspaper press, intermingled with business men and miscellaneous idlers, for the café is no longer the almost exclusively political rendezvous which it was in the later years of the Empire, when Ranc, Spuller, Gambetta, and Vallès were the chief orators in this sort of forum, where most of the prominent politicians and journalists of the present day took their first lessons in Republican arms. This was about 1886, when on the other side of the river the future chiefs of the Commune, Raoul, Rigault, Tridon, Dacosta, and Landowski, began to frequent the Café de la Renaissance on the Boulevard Saint-Michel. In 1871, when these gentlemen came into power at the Hôtel de Ville, they and their parasites, with their long boots, clanking spurs, and brilliant uniforms, transferred their custom to the Café de Madrid; but as they paid only when they pleased, and were pleased to pay never, the café soon closed through the ruin of the proprietor. The Café de Madrid is now a noisy and pestiferous cavern,

"WHO SIT AT THE LITTLE MARBLE TABLES, DRINK ABSINTHE, AND ARE INVARIABLY DECORATED."

where the voice of the talkers rises with difficulty above the clatter of the dominoes incessantly shaken up on the marble tables, and the rattling of dice on innumerable backgammon boards. Opposite, at the Café de Suède, the habitués are lyric and dramatic artists, and in the room on the first floor the diamond merchants meet to do business and to play dominoes. Next door, the Café des Variétés used to be the favorite resort of Rochefort, Murger, Barrière, and other vaudevillists and playwrights, and it was there, at the table where Théodore de Banville and Baudelaire presided, that Catulle Mendès founded the Parnassian school of poetry which has flourished since, and is now represented in the French Academy by Coppée and Sully Prudhomme. But gradually puffed up by the glory of his customers, the proprietor grew proud and insolent, and one day the literary men left in a body, and since then the Café des Variétés has remained nondescript and unrenowned. Further east, along the boulevard, the cafés become less and less elegant, and more and more crowded and noisy, while the German beer-houses, with their baskets of "pretzel," are more frequent as we approach the commercial quarters of the Boulevards de Sebastopol and Strasbourg, where there is much billiard-playing, domino-playing, and card-playing, and where the habitués sit round the tables in strident and vulgar groups, smoking, sipping absinthe, and talking all at once at the top of their voices, in an atmosphere thick with tobacco smoke, and heavy with the fumes of alcohol, boots, kitchen grease, and the natural exhalations of crowded humanity. As for the life of the Parisian café, it is much the same all over the city. In the morning a few homeless beings come there to take their coffee and milk; before lunch some customers arrive to take the morning *apéritif* and to read the papers; toward five o'clock the tables begin to fill, and until seven the crowd thickens; during the dinner hour there is a lull, and then toward nine o'clock the tables fill once more, and the activity continues until one or two o'clock in the morning, when the cafés are closed in accordance with the police regulations.

Such are the principal cafés of the boulevard *par excellence*, and it is at these cafés, and along the bitumen pavement between the Madeleine and Brébant's, that the *boulevardier* flourishes, exerting his powers of glittering more especially in the late afternoon at the absinthe hours. Then the trees between the endless lines of houses spread their bare branches or their sickly verdure in a perspective of luminous newspaper kiosques, green benches, and tall advertising columns crowned by a ring of gas jets, which light up the many-colored patchwork of play-bills announcing the amusements of the evening. The cabs and private carriages glide over the wooden pavement, dotting the scene with yellow and black patches; the monster omnibuses plough their way brutally through the surging current of wheels and hoofs; at intervals a refuge in the middle of the roadway is marked by a gas lamp surmounted by the blue dial of a pneumatic clock; the shops are all brilliantly lighted; the cafés fill rapidly, and the waiters hurry to and fro with strange cries: "Un Turin terrasse," "Boum!" "Absinthe anisette à l'as," and other cabalistic words, intelligible only to the initiated. At this hour of the day the aspect of the boulevard changes entirely; a curious tribe of men descends from all quarters to this central hunting-ground. Some come in search of wit; some in search of news; some in search of relations and influence; some to be seen, to prove that they are still living, and to make themselves and others believe that they occupy a place in Paris. Many again come simply to see and enjoy that unique spectacle of varied movement, life, and color, which the streets and boulevards of Paris alone can offer. And this is why it is difficult to define the *boulevardier*, for amongst those to whom this appellation is given you find men of all ages, all characters, all professions, and all reputations; the only bonds of union are certain daily habits, a special language, a love of gossip and scandal, a peculiar turn of wit, and a tendency to gyrate in the neighborhood of Tortoni's. The pure *boulevardier* is always indifferent and generally selfish, which is not strange when we reflect that he is an isolated unit struggling for life in the midst of the selfishness and indifference of Paris, where he daily shakes hands with a hundred of his fellows, and cherishes no illusions as to the incontestable insignificance of that ungraceful form of salutation. The typical *boulevardier* is a superior species of Bohemian, but generally a Bohemian with expensive tastes, whose existence is a perpetual problem which occupies himself and sometimes others; whereas the existence of the ordinary Bohemian is a matter to which he does not deign to give thought. The *boulevardier* is somewhat of a man of letters, somewhat of a lawyer, somewhat of a speculator, more or less an adventurer, and sometimes a gambler; in short, the multiplicity of his aptitudes and experience fits him for the most diverse positions; and

Deputies, and in official situations of all kinds. Amongst the *boulevardiers* whom one sees every night taking their absinthe or their bitter and gossiping on the sidewalk, there are twenty men of rare wit.

CAFÉ VACHETTE.

so, in Paris, we find *boulevardiers* everywhere—in the clubs, in the newspaper offices, in the directing boards of financial administrations, in the Chamber of

The others are more or less skilful workmen who paint, sing, write, or talk with a certain technical excellence, but who are wanting in originality, and who are mere parasites, living on the crumbs of wit, experience, and practical cynicism that the leaders let fall from their table.

Some observers pretend that the palmy days were those of the Second Empire, when the *boulevardier*, sleek, witty, elegant, and gallant, lived in the midst of the ambient luxury, heedless of politics and vulgar cares. After 1871 politics invaded all Paris; the habitués of Tortoni's had to choose an opinion; the first tendency of the *boulevardiers* was toward the Comte de Chambord and the white flag; then, veering with success, they turned toward Gambetta, thanks to whom many of the veterans now hold official positions. As for the young generation, say the critics, it includes few genuine *boulevardiers* of the old style; the boulevard is being gradually annexed by Montmartre, and in the bustle and promiscuity of triumphant democracy, the asphalt of the Boulevard des Italiens is losing its stamp of adventurous elegance and intelligent exclusiveness. It is always well to mistrust the praisers of the past, especially in France, where the prestige of the book and of the printed picture is so very strong. The boulevard such as Balzac and Gavarni have depicted probably never existed, any more than the Latin Quarter as Murger described it in his *Scènes de la Vie de Bohème*, and as Gavarni drew it in his beautiful lithographs. The creations of these great artists doubtless had a certain reflex action on a few of their contemporaries, just as nowadays Grévin's caricatures influence in a reflex manner the costume and bearing of certain frivolous French women. Or, to take another example, Alexandre Dumas's comedies are rarely studied from life, and yet such is the logical consistency of the persons whom his imagination creates, that you find women who have formed themselves after the impossible type of *L'Étrangère*, for instance. Thus, although at the time when it was written the heroine of this comedy was purely a fiction of the author's brain, it would be easy now to point to half a dozen women in Parisian society who have conformed themselves reflexly to this fictitious model, and thus rendered true that which was untrue a few years ago. The characters whom Murger placed in his famous novel were not students, but notorious and scandalous Bohemians. During the Second Empire Bohemianism was *à la mode;* the looseness of the Bohemian's habits, the brutality of his persiflage, the monstrousness of his paradoxes, the picturesqueness of his silhouette, represented a reaction against the affected respectability of a society whose hero was the Duc de Morny, and whose ideal was external correctness, *le chic* or *la tenue.* Democracy,

however, does not like these threadbare parasites, with their unkempt locks and greasy hats; in the Bohemian it sees and hates a useless member in a society where all work. The traveller must therefore be prepared to seek in vain for Bohemians of the Murger type in busy modern Paris.

In the Latin Quarter of the present day one rarely observes eccentricity of costume. On the contrary, the students affect rather the dress and bearing of the boulevard "dude," more especially the law students, who do not disdain to cross the Seine, go into society, and lose their money at the races. The real student is the medical student, for whom the eight or ten years which he passes in Paris are the heyday of his existence. After he has obtained his diploma, the medical student will have to leave the capital, settle down in some provincial town, and work up a practice; and so, while he is in Paris, he makes a point of having a happy time, but a happy time in his own fashion. The medical student is not a "dude"; he does not always wear a silk hat and varnished shoes, like the law student; he does not play cards and baccarat in the sporting cafés; nor does he cross the river and go into society, for he must be up early in the morning for the rounds in the hospitals. The medical students live very much together; they monopolize certain restaurants; they smoke and discuss at night in certain cafés, such as La Source, on the Boulevard St.-Michel; they are bound together by a sort of freemasonry, resulting from their special and almost secret studies, which are unknown to the uninitiated. On the other hand, the medical students love to make a noise, and to promenade in Indian file on little or no pretext. Occasionally a new policeman, who is unaccustomed to such manifestations of youthful exuberance, interferes, and then there is great agitation, which invariably ends by a procession to the Prefecture of Police of some hundred or two students, carrying Chinese lanterns, and crying: "Conspuez Gragnon! Conspuez Gragnon!" Gragnon being the name of the Prefect of Police, whom they invite the public thus to treat with contempt. Hearing the noise of tramping feet and seditious cries, the guard marches out of the court-yard of the Prefecture, and the students howl with laughter and return to their Latin Quarter, happy and contented with the success of their harmless escapade. The population of the Boulevard St.-Michel is accustomed to these noisy ways, but over the water such manners are not appreciated, and the jokes of the medical students have generally led to disturbances when they have ventured to practise them elsewhere than in their own Latin Quarter. Therefore the medical student will tell you that he does not care to cross the river, and that the grand boulevard has no charms for him. His boulevard is that named after St.-Michel, a fine modern thoroughfare, shaded with splendid trees, and lined with shops, restaurants, and innumerable cafés and brasseries, where the students take their "demi-tasse," their "bock," their vermouth, or their absinthe, and watch the characteristic movement of their " Boul' Mich'," as they call their favorite promenade. A characteristic corner is the Café Vachette, which is patronized by students of all categories — by the "swells," by the sporting and betting men, by the Bohemian student, by the southerner of the type of Alphonse Dau-

det, with long black hair, curly mustache, and forked beard, who wears a flat-brimmed hat tilted on the back of his head, and has a gay word to say to all the impertinent *étudiantes*, who are not all rigorously inscribed on the books of the University. Even the French school-boy goes to the café, and on Saturday especially you see the pupils of the state lycées, the *potaches* as they are called, airing themselves along the " Boul' Mich'," with their hands in their pockets, and their " semi-rigide" képi pulled well down over their ears, smoking gi-

NEOMEDIÆVAL CAFÉ.

gantic cigars, and looking as stolid and unintelligent as they can, for the ideal of the modern French school-boy of the silly class, as it is also of the modern French "dude," is to look stupid, or *abruti*, as the French term is.

In the Latin Quarter there are but few cafés of historical interest, and even those that have survived the transformation of the district do not retain even a vestige of their pristine glory. Thus the Café Procope, with its souvenirs of Diderot, d'Alembert, Jean Jacques Rousseau, Holbach, Voltaire, and Mirabeau, exists now with difficulty as a very cheap eating-house. The new Boulevard St.-Germain has swept away Andler's, in the Rue Haute-feuille, where the "realists" used to meet under the artistic chieftainship of Courbet and the literary guidance of Champfleury. From 1850 until 1860 Andler's, also called the "Brasserie des Réalistes," enjoyed great vogue in artistic Paris. It was there that the Parisians first learnt to drink beer; for forty years ago, it must be remembered, the Parisians went to the café to drink coffee: beer was then regarded as a strange drink, almost a gastronomic curiosity, which was always served with the accompaniment of cakes or nougat, while appetizing liqueurs, such as absinthe, vermouth, or bitters, were rarely seen, being looked upon as potions for the use of persons whose constitution had been debilitated by the African climate. In those days, too, the pipe was held in higher honor than the cigarette or the cigar, whereas now the use of the pipe has almost disappeared, in public at least; and in the hundreds of cafés and "brasseries" which now exist in the Latin Quarter the consumption of beer and of appetizing drinks far exceeds the consumption of coffee. Since the exhibition of 1867, when German, Swiss, English, Austrian, and Hungarian bar-maids were first seen in Paris, waitresses have taken the place of waiters in many of the beer saloons of the Latin Quarter, and that strange institution called the "brasserie à femmes" has gradually spread all over Paris, at the same time that it has become the custom to fit up the beer saloons in quaint, fantastic, and pseudo-historical styles, and to costume the waitresses as Opéra Comique nurses, with peaked caps and a doll in their pocket; as barristers, with long blond wigs, black gowns, white bands, and a bouquet of roses to mark the place of their easily won hearts; as almées; as Arlésiennes, and I know not what other disguises, which give to the humblest "caboulot" the suggestion of the coulisses of some ideal and inoffensive theatre, where there is never any acting of unreal comedies or tearful tragedies. The old-fashioned café, with its white walls picked out with simple gold beadings, its neat marble tables, its light chairs, its unpretentious looking-glasses, and its *comptoir*, where sits the waxen-faced lady book-keeper, is becoming more and more rare in modern Paris. The mediæval semi-German tavern is the fashion now, and in every street you find some paltry little establishment with stained-glass windows, heavy wooden tables, imitation tapestry on the walls, and imitation faience mugs, which are filled with Bavarian beer by waiters or waitresses more or less costumed.

The café being in itself a tiresome and unpleasing place, there is no objection to be made to costume or to any fantastic decoration which makes of the whole a spectacle amusing to the eye. In our modern civilization the development of the spirit of dilettanteism and of criticism has extended the museum beyond the public or private collection, and introduced what may be called the museum spirit into the smallest details of furnishing, and thus created the bibelot. And by the bibelot we mean that minute fragment of the work of art which puts something of the East, of the Renaissance, or of the Middle Ages on the corner of a drawing-room table or on the ledge of a dresser. It is this love of the bibelot which has transformed the decoration of our modern homes, and given them an archaic physiognomy so curious and amusing that, as a subtle analyst has said, our nineteenth century, by dint of collecting and verifying the styles of the past, will have forgotten to create a style of its own. This love of the bibelot, this research of the quaint, the dainty, and the bizarre, has naturally penetrated from the home to the café; and in the brasseries of the Latin Quarter, the son of the provincial bourgeois who has just arrived in the capital finds himself sitting in a beer saloon at a Renaissance table, drinking out of an imitation Venetian glass, and regretting that the view of the movement of the street is estopped by the painted mediæval windows. And so there

CABARET DU CHAT NOIR.

is no more curious excursion to be made in Paris than a rapid visit to the queer cafés and brasseries of the Latin Quarter. The personnel is a study in itself: the caissière who sits at the desk amidst sheaves of spoons, piles of saucers, and battalions of small carafons of cognac, and inscribes in a book every order that the waiters announce as they pass; the maître d'hôtel, corpulent and dignified, whose duty it is to superintend the general service of the café, and to inquire kindly after the health of habitués; the waiter who cries "Boum" in reply to orders, and carries five glasses of beer in one hand while he balances a heavy tray with the other; the "sommelier," or butler, who runs from table to table, laden with bottles, and distributes here and there strange liquids—Absinthe, Amer Picon, Chartreuse, Bitters, Groseille, Madère, Vermouth, Cassis, Guignolet, and a dozen other deleterious distillations; the "verseur," who carries a coffee-pot and a milk-pot, and fills the cups when the waiter bellows out "Versez 10!" thus indicating the number of the table; the waitresses in their innumerable fancy costumes. All these novel types, and all the amusing accessories of a Parisian café— the tables, the newspapers fixed on sticks, the water bottles, the glasses, the foaming bocks, the steaming plates of sauer-kraut— all help to form a curious vision of souvenirs in the brain of the observer, admirably prepared for dreaming by repeated stations in an atmosphere impregnated with the mixed perfumes of tobacco and onion soup, which are the dominant elements in the characteristic odor of a Parisian beer saloon of an evening.

Leaving the noisy brasseries of the Latin Quarter, we will recross the Seine, and direct our steps toward Montmartre, the Bohemia of modern Paris. On our way, however, we will pay a visit to the Café de la Régence, on the Place du Théâtre Français, the great rendezvous of the French chess-players. The present café is not the one where Bonaparte played, or even Alfred de Musset. The historic Café de la Régence was pulled down when the Place du Palais Royal was transformed, and the name and the habitués of the old café were transferred across the street to the present establishment, together with the table on which Napoleon used to play chess before he was Napoleon, or even First Consul. This café, thanks to its proximity, is naturally the resort of the actors of the Comédie Française; it has also its champion domino-player and its champion billiard-players; but its chief glory is chess, in which game the Régence has boasted a long line of champions, beginning a hundred and fifty years ago with Philidor, and continuing through Mouret, Deschapelles, Labourdonnaye, Saint-Arnaud, Kiezeritsky, Neumann, Harwitz, and Rosenthal, who has now abandoned the Régence, and left the chieftainship to Arnous de Rivière.

Now let us climb the Rue Pigalle or the Rue des Martyrs, and scale the heights of Montmartre. We have just been in the Pays Latin; we are now in the Pays de Bohème, a country inhabited by painters, sculptors, poets, budding novelists, struggling journalists, starving musicians, and even by well-to-do citizens, but essentially a country where all that is conventional is held in supreme abomination, so much so that Montmartre has come to be one of the most congenial camping-grounds in Paris for the modern personifications of those immortal prototypes of moral untidiness, Manon Lescaut and the Chevalier Des Grieux. But at Montmartre at the present day we do not find Bohemians of the Murger species any more than we have found them in the Latin Quarter. There was one generation and one only of grand Bohemians in modern France, and that was the generation of Théophile Gautier, Gérard de Nerval, and the leaders of the romantic movement of 1830—the Bohemians of the Impasse du Doyenné—a generation full of grand fantasy and singularly rich in talent, inasmuch as it produced artists of the rank of Delacroix, of Corot, and of Barye. The spirit of revolt against received ideas and somnolent institutions which animated these men in their youth was doubtless a necessity in the literary and artistic battle. The Bohemianism of Courbet and the realists under the Empire had little or no excuse, for the battle was already won. As for Bohemianism of the militant kind, it has nowadays absolutely no *raison d'être*, and carries with it inevitably an odor of vice and a stigma of impotence, even when it becomes pedantic and loses what talent it might have had in eccentric or tortuously ridiculous theories, such, for instance, as certain exaggerations of Impressionism in art, and certain manifestations of the recently

EDITORIAL BREAKFAST AT THE CHAT NOIR.

hatched literary sects of Symbolists and Decadents. The fact is that Bohemianism, which was originally a purely literary phenomenon and a purely literary conception, has become something else. The primitive province of Bohemia, a small and joyous country, has annexed two larger provinces, political and social Bohemia, which are far from sympathetic. The country of Bohemia is overgrown with thistles and poisonous plants; it is no longer a place for the gentle, the delicate, the dreamers, and the volunteers in the service of the Muses. Bohemian is a title which will soon be as unenviable as communist or anarchist.

Nevertheless, we need some term to express that hatred of ennui and that gay spirit of enormity and exuberant aspiration which characterize the artistic nature in its early developments; and if Murger had not perverted it there would be no objection to be made to Bohemianism, the more so as Saint-Simon and Madame de Sévigné both used it in the sense of exaggeration of the artistic sentiment. And it is only Bohemianism of this kind that we shall venture to glance at in our visit to Montmartre, for an examination of other kinds of Bohemianism and of the cafés where they glory in their depravation might lead us into unsavory details.

The two traditional artistic cafés of Montmartre are the Café de la Rochefoucauld and the Café de la Nouvelle Athènes. The latter used to be the rendezvous of Manet and the Impressionists, and at both these cafés you still see many known and unknown "celebrities," the unknown ones being, of course, in the majority, which is not astonishing when we reflect that in Paris there is not a single man, except the Secretary of the Academy, who knows by heart the names of the forty "immortals." Glory is a vain word. The devil and Sarah Bernhardt are perhaps the only two celebrities universally known. It is useless, therefore, to more than barely mention Babou, Duranty, and even Cazin and Zola, who were all in their day frequenters of the Nouvelle Athènes, and founders of schools of literature or painting or criticism. The men of that generation seem to have had a mania for enrolling themselves under some flag and chief. And this craze went so far, as I have heard the engraver Bracquemond relate, that one day Alphonse Legros, now a grave professor at London, calmly proposed, between two pots of beer, "Let us found a school, and I will be the chief."

Nowadays the glory of these two cafés is much diminished, and also the craze for founding schools, though it has not yet quite died out, and the most famous and curious café of Montmartre is at present the "Chat Noir," which is at once the prototype and beau ideal of the fantastic neomediæval tavern, a most amusing place, whose host, by dint of intelligent "cheek" and a keen prevision of the wants of the age, has become one of the celebrities of Paris. Formerly a painter and somewhat of a poet, he concluded one day, after due reflection, that drink was a greater necessity than art, and that he could better tempt the public to give him money in exchange for beer than in exchange for his pictures. But being an artist, he could not sell beer in ordinary and vulgar conditions; he must sell it in an artistic manner and in artistic surroundings. And so he hired a modest shop at Montmartre, and fitted it up with real old wood-work, old tapestry, old faience, and old arms; the fireplace was a vast open chimney, with the traditional chain and pot suspended therein; on the ceiling was fixed an immense "glory," bought at the Hôtel Drouot at a sale of old ecclesiastical accessories, and in the middle of the glory was placed a black cat's head; the windows were of stained glass and adorned with the emblematic cat; and the swinging zinc sign outside the door represented a black cat standing with mountainous back and tortuous tail on that astronomical abstraction, the crescent moon. In the room were rough wooden tables and a piano; gradually curious pictures by painters of talent covered the walls; the inn became a rendezvous for poets, painters, and actors; and in order to affirm its literary character, some of the habitués joined their host in founding a weekly newspaper, Le Chat Noir, which is now in the sixth year of its existence, and which has published prose, verse, and drawings of a whole host of young men of talent, who have since worked their way to reputation.

Now the "Chat Noir" has outgrown its modest cradle, and taken up its abode in the Rue de Laval, in a house whose façade is adorned with strange colored glass windows, with the old swinging zinc sign, and with a colossal cat enthroned in the rays of an immense golden sun. At the

A CAFÉ CONCERT.

door stands a messenger, or "chasseur," in radiant livery, and an ornamental janitor, who carries a halberd in sign of his office. Inside, the rooms on the first, second, and third floors are amusingly fitted up with queer bric-à-brac, stained-glass windows, tapestry, and pictures or frescoes by Willette—the painter of Pierrots—by Rivière, by Caran d'Ache, and by other odd geniuses, who have become known chiefly as illustrators and graphic satirists. But before being allowed to penetrate to the upper rooms you must show clean hands, *patte blanche*, or rather a hand stained with ink or with paint; for our host professes a violent hatred of *bourgeois* and philistines, and pretends to be at home and master in his inn, affable, bantering, *fantaisiste* in the highest degree, and making his *fantaisie* serve his interests and his industry of beer-selling. The moment the face of any one known in art or letters appears, our host prostrates himself before the "dear master" who honors the cabaret by his visit, and orders an "immortal" to offer "monseigneur" a cup of foaming ale; for the service is performed by waiters who are dressed literally in the costume of the members of the French Academy, in order, as the facetious host tells us, "to show the young what one may come to in literature by dint of industry and good conduct." Here we have the note of parody and persiflage; but in reality amongst the habitués of the "Chat Noir" I have seen many true men of letters, who scoff at the Academy only because they are not yet ready to knock at its doors. The Academy, as Voltaire said, is always the desired mistress of those who make songs and epigrams against her until they have won her favor. At the "Chat Noir" the epigram is a little heavy, and smells of advertising, and of that theatrical spirit of vanity and show which the French call "cabotinage." However, in reality nothing can be more academic than this café, where the hottest discussions are over a sonnet, and the most furious disagreements over the merits of a new comedy or the charms of a new picture.

But no one better than the "gentilhomme cabaretier," as he styles himself, can describe the merits of his inn. The "Cabaret du Chat Noir," he begins, "is a creation unique in the world. Situated in the centre of Montmartre, the modern capital of intellect, this inn is the rendezvous of the most celebrated poets, painters, and sculptors. It is an absolutely curious place, in the purest Louis XIII. style. You can see there the drinking-glasses which were used by Charlemagne, Villon, Rabelais, Cardinal Richelieu, the Duchesse de Chevreuse, Mme. de Rambouillet, Mlle. de Scudéry, Louis XIV., Mlle. de la Vallière, Voltaire, Diderot. Robespierre, Bonaparte, Mme. de Staël, Mme. Récamier...." Enough! enough! excellent "gentilhomme cabaretier"! The "Chat Noir," we will admit, is unique in the world; it is fitted up most artistically; it is even a marvel of the purest Louis XIII. style, if you will; but, above all, it is an amusing place, where Schopenhauer is held in execration; where people try to amuse themselves, and generally succeed; and where, when they do not succeed, they drink beer in order to deceive themselves into the belief that they are having a good time. From this item of the programme there is no escape, for during the evening, between every song, monologue, or witticism, at least every quarter of an hour, the "gentilhomme cabaretier" cries, with the voice of Stentor:

"Messeigneurs, c'est le moment où les gens bien élevés renouvellent les consommations!" (My lords, this is the moment when people who have been well brought up call for more drinks.)

One of these days some anecdotic historian of Paris will doubtless write a monograph on this fantastic "Chat Noir," on its newspaper, its habitués, and its literary evenings. The newspaper is a comic illustrated sheet, which is invariably put together by the joyous editorial staff around the breakfast-table, under the presidency of the worthy host and hostess; and as some of the smart junior members of the great daily press usually drop in for the sake of auld lang syne on the editorial morning, it generally happens that in this gastronomico-journalistic group the dog is the only serious member. As for the literary evenings of the "Chat Noir," they are of course private, and frequented only by the friends and invited guests of the members of the little cénacle; but amongst these friends and invited guests have figured all who have a name in art and letters in modern Paris—poets, journalists, painters, sculptors, men of fashion, actors, and actresses, and even some great ladies of high social rank, the last of course incognita. The taste of great ladies for seeing queer haunts is not new. Collé used to take duchesses to the Porcherons, and Mme. de Montarcy escaped occasionally from the court of Louis XIV., and in the guard-room, as Bouilhet tells us, "brûlait sa lèvre rose à la pipe des Suisses." But naturally in the quaintly decorated upper room of the "Chat Noir," with its marionette show, its revolutionary musicians, its droll monologuists, and its canopy of smoke floating in mid-air, you do not expect to find Parisian matrons and their daughters.

There remains only one type of café still to be noticed, namely, the café-concert, which is the French equivalent for the Anglo-Saxon music hall. The type might furnish the material for a long study, of interest from many points of view; for of late years the cafés-concerts have become the most popular form of amusement in Paris, and absorbed a large part of the public which used to support the theatres. And yet anything more inept and stupid than a French music hall it would be difficult to conceive. Why people go to them I cannot explain, unless it be because some mysterious destiny forces mankind in general to seek distraction perpetually, and the Frenchman in particular, to escape from the ennui of his own fireside. And so the cafés-concerts, which abound particularly in the commercial quarters of Paris, are always crowded; the shopkeepers of the neighborhood, their wives and their daughters, their cook-maids and their clerks, patronize them steadily night after night. In serried ranks they sit, packed literally so closely that they cannot move their legs six inches in any direction; in front of the seats is a narrow ledge on which is placed the "consommation" of each visitor—cherries preserved in eau-de-vie, coffee, beer, peppermint, or red currant syrup; with their hats on or off, the men smoke at their ease. As the evening advances the atmosphere of the hall becomes more and more hot and foul, the audience more and more swarming and more and more perspiring; the flaring gas jets become gradually obscured by the thick blue fog of smoke; while on the stage the lean and hoarse-voiced cantatrice, with awkward angular gestures, screams, over the bald heads of the musicians in the orchestra, the senseless refrain of some popular absurdity, or of some sentimental romance.

IN THE GARDEN OF CHINA

NO matter what one man writes of China, the next writer will contradict him. A description of anything Chinese in one standard work is little, if at all, like a description of the same thing in the next treatise upon that people. Marco Polo has been called a liar for centuries, and now it is his defamers who are accused of falsehood, while the truth stands between, holding out a friendly hand to each side. With that knowledge of my subject, I yet venture to describe what I saw and learned in China. And I smile as I think of the letters that will come declaring me unreliable, nonsensical, imaginative, and altogether wrong. They will come because China is a dozen and a half of different countries, of which we will persist in speaking as one nation. I shall try to be careful to tell of only what I saw and found in the Kiang-su and the Cheh-kiang provinces, but the men who have traded for twenty - five years in the north, those who have explored the west, and the missionaries who have worked lifetimes in the south will all find these things so different from those they have observed that they will forget and contradict me. When I began to read what has been published about China I took notes of the peculiar ceremonies attendant on betrothal and marriage. Upon reading a second book I corrected what the first one said, until nothing remained of my notes except the part that the go-betweens and the astrologers played. Then I read a third book, by an author who painstakingly described the ceremonies in detail, and as his account was still different, I threw my notes away. I reached China with eight varying accounts of the marriage custom fighting each other in my head. At once I set about getting my own version from a born Chinaman in Shanghai. That was plain sailing. He glibly described his own experience at the—I will not say court of Hymen, but the stock exchange of Chinese matrimony. Nearly all that I had read he proved to be wrong. "I know what you've been reading," said he; "you have told me some things they do in Sze-chuen province, some that are the custom in Chihli, where Peking is, and some things that are number one

proper in Hunan, but nowhere else." After I had written out what he told me I found that I was not fully informed upon some minor details. Becoming acquainted with a very intelligent dependent upon a mandarin, I went to him for more light upon the subject.

"Now," said I, "who tells you when the bride has arrived in her chair, so that you can go out and knock on the door of the chair with your fan and bid her come out?"

"My no go knock on door," said he; "no b'long Shanghai custom for man go knock woman's chair."

"Oh!" I gasped, seeing my own "special correspondence on the scene" begin to go the way of all the other literature.

"Tink um b'long Canton side go knockee chair. Shanghai custom b'long differlent. My waitee in my house, in my bedloom, topside. Bime-by woman have come. My flend he call out, 'Hiyah! woman have come; supposce you come down and see her.' Then—"

"Ah!" said I, "that is after she has been carried from her chair into your house, over the fire of charcoal on the door-sill?"

"No b'long cally into house. Woman get out chair, walkee in house. What piecee foolo man have talkee you? No b'long cally, b'long walkee. No savey foolo talk about makee fire in door-place."

"Well," said I, letting go all that I had read and heard and studied upon the subject, "but when she walks into your house, and your friend calls you to come down and see her, and you come down—"

"My no come down. My makee play pidgin. My cly out, 'You g'long; no wantchee gal';" here he paused, as if the effort he was making was too great, and said, "That makee long talkee; bime-by my tellee you."

"Well, but when you come down or she goes up—is it then that you stand on a tall chair, so that she must begin her married life by looking up to you, and must look up to you the rest of her days?"

"My no savey!" said my friend. "No gettee topside chair. Tink you talkee Canton custom. Some man speakee you have come Canton side. No got chair. Got big loom and plenty flend, and my makee bow to woman, and she makee bow, and then man and woman makee chin-chin joss-pidgin ["talk god-business," which is to say, religious worship] all alound the loom, and chin-chin to farder and mudder picture."

"Oh yes, I know," said I. "And is that when the bride tells your ancestors that she has come into your family, and is going to be a good, dutiful member of it?"

"No. Blide no can talkee. Shanghai custom blide no makee talkee for thlee days. More better you go look-see one piecee malliage."

"I think so too," said I, for at each stage of the investigation I knew less than before.

It was the same with everything. One day we discussed the funeral customs in a group of European residents in China. Mr. Weldon said that the queerest practice he had witnessed was that of concealing the mourners within four walls of white muslin carried by bearers, with the feet of the mourners showing as they walked inside the queer box. The other men were surprised. They had never seen that feature of the funeral service. Within a week I twice witnessed it. The reason that there could be a dispute upon such a point is that European Shanghai is peopled by Chinamen from many provinces. And the differing customs in the provinces account for all the confusion that is created by men who write of one province as if it were China. I should consider that book an authority upon China which could be written by an observant man who had spent a year each in her twenty-odd provinces and territories. As for what I write, it is to be a partial record of two months of incessant

A VILLAGE GIRL.

observation, travel, and study in two of the provinces within the Garden of China.

There are many Chinas, or many kinds of China, but the only one I expected to find was the one I did not see. It was an ideal I had been forming all along the years between my first geography and my latest purchased book—of a country peopled by men wearing broad-brimmed, cone-shaped hats, and carrying boxes of tea on each end of the bamboo poles they balanced on one shoulder. That sort of man I saw once or twice among the millions I met, but the whole combination I missed altogether. My China has its gentry, its merchants, its working-men, and its farmers—not to speak of beggars, actors, priests, conjurers, and sailors. We found its merchant class polite, patient, extremely shrewd, well-dressed, pattern shopkeepers. We found its gentlemen graceful, polished, generous, and amiable. But the peasantry constantly reminded us of the country folk of continental Europe outside of Russia. Theirs was the same simplicity of costume, intelligence, and manners. They lived in very much the same little villages of thatched cottages. Theirs was the same awkwardness, shyness, cunning in trade, the same distrust of strangers and of strange things. The sharpest fracture of the comparison was seen in the Chinese farms; for, where we were, every handful of earth was almost literally passed through the hands of its cultivators, every leaf was inspected, every inch was watered, manured, watched, and cared for as a retired Englishman looks after his back garden. The result was a fertility beyond compare, a glory of vegetation, a universality of cultivation that permitted no waste places. It was a system that always included the preparation of a second growth to be transplanted into the place of the main growth when the first reached its harvest. As compared with Japan, one feature of every view was strikingly in favor of the larger country. The dress and behavior of the Chinese will not offend Europeans. The women of central China are not merely most modest, they are as completely dressed as any women I have ever seen. They are covered from neck to heels in a costume composed of a jacket and trousers. As Mr. Weldon says: "Their complete freedom of movement

BOY OF THE LOWER CLASS.

is calculated to produce the most perfect nation, physically. It is God's providence that this menace to the safety of the world is offset by their innutritious food and their fondness for the crippling of women's feet." In Japan nakedness is what startles the new-comer on all sides. In China "the altogether" that Trilby posed for is a product that I saw only in the cases of less than half a dozen children. I am told that in the country one sees women half bared above the waist when the sun shines tropically, but I cannot prove that. I saw one farmer girl with only her padlike frontlet of cotton on above her trousers, but I cannot announce a national custom upon that slender basis. On the other hand, I saw the women at every sort of labor, squatted down upon the river's edge, climbing like boys, wrestling, frolicking, rowing boats with their feet, wading streams, yet never having occasion to regard that jealous modesty which is safeguarded in their dress and in their souls from infancy onward. I never—except in two instances among thousands—raised my eyes to have them meet those of a woman that she did not cast hers down, or turn and run in-doors as fast as her "golden lilies"—goat's feet, Weldon calls them—would carry her. Even in the night resorts of the gentlemen, where the bejewelled singsong girls ply their service of song and attendance during the formal dinners of men of means, I never saw the suggestion of improper behavior on the men's or the women's parts. To be sure, these

A WATER-SIDE REST-HOUSE.

women made bold to rub their hands softly against my hair (where I keep what I have, in the back) to see how our shorn hair feels. And they fingered my collar and cuffs, and gently touched my planklike shirt front, and giggled just as little children do under similar circumstances at home. So like little children were they that I could not bear to think them different in any respect—there in that garden where baby girls only fetched a dollar in the market, until the price rose recently, in Shanghai, because of the employment of girls in the silk-filature factories. Boys are different, of course. Just as I was leaving China an old man who wanted to adopt a son picked out a likely shaver of four years old and set his heart on having him. The fool of a mother did not see that the true price the old man offered was a comfortable home and the heirdom to his property. She only saw how much the old man wanted her boy. She would not sell him for less than eighty dollars. Therefore the prudent old fellow was obliged to stifle his budding affection and look for a cheaper child. He got a chubby little urchin for sixty dollars, which was his limit.

In spite of their modesty, the Chinese girls do flirt, and in proper European fashion. At a large mission college I was told that the perfect gravity of church service is ruffled at times by the manner in which the maidens steal glances at the young men out of the tails of their eyes on the only day and occasion when the sexes come together. And I was told, too, that it had been found necessary to forbid the girls to use a certain path which is part of the route to the boys' school, because the decorum of the girls, as well as their peace of mind, was seen to suffer by the meeting of the male procession and the girl paraders during exercise-time. Very strange indeed is that familiar accessory of European schooling in a land where men and women are strangers until they wed, where not even a brother may so much as touch his sister's hand, where courtship, even by letter, is practically unknown.

Are the women of China pretty? Most Europeans think not, though many admit that pretty ones are more numerous in central China than in Japan. The plump, round Chinese face lends itself to girlish beauty better than the long, narrow physiognomies of the Japanese. All agree that the most beautiful women in China are those of Soo-chow (which city the Chinese say is one of two that rank next to heaven), and in that neighborhood I saw the greatest and most frequent beauty. I certainly saw many very pretty women there, and a few in other places. But though their costume includes the famous divided skirt of common-sense and reformers' noising, theirs is not a dress that we can admire, or consider an effective setting for a woman's charms. Put feminine China, I say, into the graceful, picturesque drapery of feminine Japan, and clothe Japan's gentler moiety in China's trousers, and the chief magnet that Japan holds for the attraction of the globe-trotter would disappear.

"Maskee," said Ananias; "can do—bime-by."

"Maskee!" He spoke the motto of the Chinese, the password of all, their constant thought and refuge and consolation, and the curse of the empire.

He had forgotten to buy the four dollars' worth of five-cent pieces that would have saved us fifty per cent. in our pettier outlays upon priests and beggars, ferrymen, small traders, and the like. We must have had about a bushel, a peck, two quarts, and a pint of *cash*, the mud-and-brass currency of the realm, but that was for the crew and the cook and the boy. We wanted cleaner, more convenient money, and were vexed that the boy had forgotten to get it. "Maskee" was all he said—"never mind."

On that first night aboard the *Swallow* we turned into the cabin and ordered our beds made up as soon as we tired of the early night scenes around us. The noisy repartee of the crew, the occasional gasping steam-tugs, so unlooked-for in China, the long, shadowy trains of junks and smaller boats behind the panting launches, the yellow-specked villages by the waterside, and the dark flat country between them were the dim sights and loud sounds we soon tired of. Had we thought to see a second kickaway boat we might have staid up half the night for it, because that was one of the most weird, uncanny things we saw during all our stay in China. It came throbbing and drumming up to and beyond us, a great yellow box on a low broad hull. Huge beams of yellow lamp-light shot out of its many square windows upon the murky water beside it. Through the windows we saw the coolie passengers lying on bed shelves, and, next beyond them, the long-coated gentry in round, button-topped skull-caps, smoking and gambling and lounging about. And then came a fair third of the broad boat, open at the sides, half

A TYPICAL STONE BRIDGE.

lighted by a small smoky lamp, and filled with the ghostlike figures of many men, all walking, walking, walking, and yet standing in one place, as they clambered incessantly upon a tread-mill that worked a great naked stern paddle-wheel, toward which they walked, yet which they never reached. The trunks of the spectral men dripped with perspiration. The feeble rays of the lamp were caught upon their sweating sides and shoulders and reflected back. And when two or three turned their heads to look at our boat, the light leaped into their eyes and made them coals of fire. There were twelve or fifteen men on the tread-mill, though there might have been fifty, or none at all, but in their place a shapeless monster, all heads and legs and shadows, prisoned in a dark cell, and condemned to walk without rest to Soochow and back, and back again, forever. We saw the kickaway boats thrice every day while we voyaged (in the early gray, the high sunlight, and in black night), but Mr. Weldon did not sketch one. They made him shudder, he said, and they haunted him—they and their fiery yellow lights, their ceaseless plashing, their rising and falling chain-gangs, and their callous passengers gambling and smoking, as the Romans played, above the heads of the slaves bound to the galleys' oars. "Maskee," said the light-hearted passengers; "we must get to Soo-chow, and if the government will not permit steam passenger boats on that route we must go aboard the kickaway boats, and have ourselves kicked there by many relays of coolies, who get pay enough to buy rice, tobacco, and opium, and are glad of the chance."

"Maskee" was the last word we heard on that first night in true China. We felt the unpoetic square nose of the *Swallow* bump against the mud, and then tear through the sedge at the side of the creek. We ran on deck to see the place at which we were to lie up all night.

A STUCCO GARDEN WALL.

It proved to be the middle of a murky black night, edged at one side by the lamps and noisy activity of a little river town. To that town was wending a thin, steady stream of countrymen, beggars, and soldiers, who stumbled along the muddy towpath within an arm's-length of our cabin roof. We knew that our windows could not be fastened, and all the massacres, stonings of Christians, and atrocities of which we had read rushed back into our memories. We did not know then that there were pirates in those waters—but we knew enough. "Heavens!" said we, "can we not anchor out in the stream, or tie up far out in the country, or fasten the windows in some way?"

"No can rock the windows," said the boy.

"But any thief can slide a window

back and reach in and sweep out everything we've got."

"Maskee," said Ananias; "no can tief; too muchee fear."

"In the morning, very early," my notes say, "all life was astir. Though we are in a country where scarcely a house is to be seen, the towpath is lively with single travellers, and gangs of men tracking boats, women and children leading cows, tiny little girls tugging at great short-bodied, round-bellied, flat-horned buffaloes—and the water at the side of this procession fairly bustling with moving craft." But I must turn from my notes to speak of the impression on my mind, now that the days when the notes accumulated are all past and gone—the crowds of China! How continual, how incessant they were! I look back on China as if it were a vast imperial Wall Street or Charing Cross; for there is almost no spot along its highways, or time of any day, when the beholder does not rest his eyes upon crowds of people. The cities, towns, and villages are thronged; the highways are all alive; the fields are peopled—and if the eye rests upon a place deserted by men, it is almost certain to be crowded with the dead, still on the earth's surface, still breaking the line of the horizon as when they travelled their brief span.

Oh, but it was a beautiful country that confronted us on that first morning out. The land led forever away in great reaches of brilliant verdure, raised neck-high above the criss-crossed waterways. The tasselled, whispering rice stood knee-high and brilliant in uncountable fields, only broken by other multitudinous fields of cotton, dark green and brown, already plucked and wilting, but specked with white tatters of the garnered cotton-bolls. "It's all Holland magnified"—so they say who know Holland—the long low vistas of luxuriant green, the ever-lengthening, unbroken, flat view, the silvery water routes, and the great sails in every distance, seeming to glide over the land. To me the same scenes suggested Long Island at its best. To every one from America or England the comparisons would be as homelike and familiar. To be sure, there was every here and there the jar of something Chinese in the form of a pagoda rising polelike in the far distance, in the plenty of smooth-skinned buffaloes, in the quaint granite bridges, in the

swarming of people in loose and faded blue, and, now and then, in the little outside refuges or rest-houses along the only roads, the towpaths. And these resting-places were no more Chinese than the account that Ananias, our boy, gave of them.

"Velly good ting," said he. "Suppose one bakerman [beggar] got velly much lain or got velly much tired—too muchee walkee—can lest, can makee sleep nighttime. Plenty man can do."

No fling of the eye in any direction fails to compass many pump-sheds or irrigating stations. These are composed of a square roof of matting upon four short poles, and under it a horizontal cogged wheel that grinds a chain of buckets reaching down into the water. A blind-folded buffalo turns the great wheel by dragging its motor-bar around behind him—an ox of the African type, with a hide like a hippopotamus turned black, and with shapely flat black horns that curve back in line with his body. A man or a boy or a girl lounges on the earth near by to keep the solemn beast from forgetting his lot to labor. Over his eyes he wears a bandage of straw, or two old shoes, or the shells of a pair of tortoises, and yet at each creaking, gushing round of his wheel he steps over the chain of scoops with the precision of perfect sight, while the water pours into the field behind it in a solid liquid stream. Ofttimes the sheltering shed had a lush pumpkin-vine trained over its brown roof, and then the great green leaves and blazing yellow blossoms caused my artistic companion to wail for his oils.

In as full harmony with the sweet pure country are the numerous villages where the tillers of one-acre or three-acre rice and cotton farms huddle together, not merely as neighbors ruled by the usual ten heads of families, but very, very often as folk of one blood and family and surnames—for such are the villages of China. Beside the lesser canals and streams one sees these picturesque settlements—each a long line of low buildings overwhelmed to the vision by clouds of tree foliage. From a distance the thatched roofs peeping out of the greenery recall many hamlets that I have seen in Devonshire. But nearer at hand they look like villages made of matting, while nearer yet the houses are seen to be built of brick, wood, bamboo, or stone as well as matting—

which composes so many fences and compounds and sheds as to dominate the view.

Mr. Weldon and I often went into the villages, walking between the fields of shivering rice, but far oftener the villagers came to see us in our house-boat—men, women, babies, dogs, and all. Always some little side canal, the offshoot of a main waterway, was the only street between or before the village houses. There was always the towpath, but the best route was by a second path leading behind the houses. By following that we passed through the farms and yards. We saw the men and women thrashing the rice by beating a log with handfuls of it to scatter the kernels on the ground. We saw the farmers turning the soil over and breaking it up laboriously, or punching holes in the thick clay, dropping seeds in them, and then smearing the holes over with a rake. We went into the inner courts of the better houses, and noted how the men, and even the tiniest baby boys, thrust themselves forward to greet us, while the women and girls slunk behind or merely peeped through the doorways and open windows—the latter being Elizabethan contrivances, framed for little panes of oiled paper or the enamelled inner coating of sea-shells. White goats, wolfish dogs, common - sense chickens, humpbacked cows, and nose-led buffaloes made up the animal life that is so painfully missing in Japan and so abundant in China.

"Don't you have sheep?" I asked Ananias.

"Have got sheep," said he; "plenty—Shanghai side."

"I don't remember them."

"Sheep no tra-la," said he, meaning that they do not go roaming or tra-la-ing about like tourists. "No got sheep outside—all got in house so tief no can takee. Leave buffalo outside; so big no can tief."

Ananias never could look any one in the eye. It would not do to say that this was mainly because he was a liar and a cheat, or even because he felt above his position. He was a tall fellow, well built —like millions and millions of his countrymen, who are not a small-sized race, as we think, who only see the Cantonese. His costume of "long clothes," such as the gentlemen and commercial folk wear, became him as if he had the right to put

ORNAMENTAL COURT-YARD DOOR.

it on. He was grave and sad and sneaking and quick-fingered, and he could lie so easily and calmly that it is a wonder he was not a mandarin. He was the only Chinaman that I saw of that sort. Most of those who were in the employ of my friends inspired confidence, and were highly praised by all who knew them; in fact, all men depend upon their boys in

CORNER OF A TEA-GARDEN.

the treaty ports, as the bankers and merchants depend upon their Chinese compradores. But Ananias was a sad rascal. He did not work because he wanted to. He hated it. All he wanted was a salary of twenty-five cents a day for dodging work, for stealing, and for telling falsehoods. After Mr. Weldon stopped travelling and took a house as a studio, he used to discharge Ananias every night—and then take him back every morning, because that was less trouble than to hunt up a fresh parasite. It was during the trip on the *Swallow* that we studied Ananias and mastered his eccentricities.

What he liked best was buying things in Chinese, and next to that he liked to bring things to sell to us in pidgin-English. Either way he doubled the prices for us. Of plain work, such as running errands, he made a failure nine times in ten. If we sent him to ask any one to let us sketch him or her, or his or her belongings, Ananias went away lazily, and came back to say that the person "chop-chop lunned away."

"Go catchee one piecee woman," Weldon would say; "my wantchee make sketch."

"No can scotch," Ananias would say when he returned. "That woman he got velly much fear. Tink you make tlubble, makee bad joss. My go talkee—no can do—chop-chop lunned away."

"Look-see," Weldon would say, "my wantchee that man's coat, so can take home and put on man and makee sketch. You buy coat—savey?"

"No tink can do," Ananias would say. "He velly much fear; he chop-chop lunned away."

"Confound you!" Mr. Weldon would shout; "go and catch my that coat."

Ananias would drag himself away, and then would drag himself back again to report that the man imagined himself the butt of a practical joke. "He tinkee you makee play-pidgin," was the way he expressed it.

One day, when it began to look as though no one would sell us any "properties" or the right to make any portraits, we went off with one of the coolies of the crew—the boy being in a neighboring city shopping. To our surprise, we found that whenever Mr. Weldon expressed a longing for picturesque costumes—even some that were then on the persons of their owners—this coolie went straightway to the owners, and quickly returned with the coveted articles. It seems past belief, but one of the coolie's first feats was the following: There was a pretty girl of fourteen, the daughter of a miller whose beautiful mill and house lay up a picturesque little private canal. She wore a short black cotton jacket and a pair of trousers of a hue of faded blue that could not be had in a shop for money.

"Oh my! oh my!" said the artist. "I wish I had my paints with me to make a study of the blue of those trousers."

When the coolie went ashore to buy the clothes that hung on poles to dry in the miller's compound, he stopped to say a few words to the little girl, and, lo! out she came presently with the old blue garment in her hand and a new pair in their former place. The coolie bought a rare old pewter samsu-bottle for me, and a gentleman's walking-pipe for Mr. Weldon. It was obviously a gentleman's pipe, because it was four feet long, and never could be smoked unless the owner had a coolie to walk to the far end of it and light it. But the adventure with the girl in faded blue impressed us most. We told Ananias about it, before the crew, when we returned, and pledged ourselves to ship him home and put the coolie in his place if he did not prove as useful and as energetic. He lost so much "face" by that episode that from that time forward he did what we wanted, and squeezed us royally. I saw him pay twenty cents to one of Mr. Weldon's models one day, and when the man begged for more money, I heard Ananias say to Mr. Weldon:

"My tink he too muchee squeeze. My have pay him eighty cents. He wantchee catch one dollar."

"Give him the twenty cents," said the painter, "and drive him away."

"All light," said the boy, and gave the model another ten cents.

He sat down in the cabin with us on the second day out, which was an extraordinary piece of impudence, and on the next morning he began to serve breakfast with his pigtail coiled up. A Chinese house-servant should only show himself in his "long clothes" and with his queue down. It is said that they study to insult those whom they do not respect by thousands of little breaches of etiquette in speech, dress, and manners, but I only credit Ananias with a desire to show us how far he was above his place.

When he found that we knew our place, and his besides, he never failed in respect to us, outward at least.

He learned our wants and ways, and was, perhaps, worth all he cost. Certainly we got from him more than he dreamed that he was giving. I shall never see my gilt bronze idol, a goddess all crusted with jewels, without recalling his idea of a god.

"What kind of woman this b'long?" I asked.

"No b'long woman," said he. "B'long topside joss. He alle time sit in joss-house. Have got he stomach velly full. Alle time makee laugh. He say: 'Ha! ha! what ting? You wantchee chow? My got stomach velly full good chow. My velly happy—you go 'long.'"

If the reader understands that "he" is "she," that "my" means "I," that "chow" is "food," and that "what ting?" means "what's the matter?" this study of a god's character will be intelligible.

The Chinese fancy that three spirits inhabit their bodies—compose their souls, perhaps. One spirit goes topside with them when they makee die, one stays in their grave, and one inhabits the tablet that is kept at home to be reverenced. On one day we sent Ananias to a fisherman's cottage to ask the man's wife to pose for a sketch. He came back crestfallen.

"No can do," said he; "woman too muchee fear—too muchee chin-chin joss pidgin" (religious business). "He tink you wantchee catch he face. Bime-by you go 'way, you takee scotch [sketch]. makee chin-chin, and he makee die. Man got house he chin-chin woman. 'Lun in house,' he say, 'you big foolo. No wantchee have European catchee face —makee die.'"

The essence of that unexpected curio, which we added to our collection, was that both the man and woman were superstitious. They imagined that a European could take away one spirit from the body in making a counterfeit presentment of it on paper. Then the artist could go home and wish the woman dead, when she would straightway die.

But our sights, adventures, and experiences must form another chapter, this being merely on account of the manner in which we travelled and were attended.

On one Sunday we tied up near a pretty green-bowered village; but we found no Sunday there, for that glad day is not in all China. That was pitiful. All over the fields, in the pelting rain, the women were at work—as one sees them in Europe. These had rolled up those strips of cloth that serve them as skirts, loin-high, out of the wet of the fields. Their square trousers legs were furled also, yet were in such evidence that but for their back hair and rounded outlines they would look as much like men as their husbands, all of whom, by-the-way, appear, as most Orientals do, decidedly like women. One thing about the coolie dress we never could grow accustomed to. That is the national habit of cutting their trousers out with a jig-saw. When one sees a pair hanging on a pole to dry, the inside line of the legs and middle forms a perfect crescent. On the women they fit well enough, but every pair that a man puts on has the seat hanging like a bag even with the knees. The coolie women have legs inside their trousers, as we see when a wet day comes. That does not surprise the reader as it surprised us, for we had been told by the ladies at the foreign missions that the women walked on "broomsticks"—on mere soft and pudgy undeveloped understandings. They were right as to the better class of small-footed women, it seems, who have to be carried, because they cannot walk and thus develop muscle. But the coolie women showed all the graceful outlines of proper physical development. They showed them as much as their loose jackets and looser drawers will permit display in a land where men and women marvel how our women can be so shameless as to model their dresses upon stays that reveal those outlines which modesty would rather be murdered than disclose.

We stopped near an irrigation shed at this village, and sent Ananias to the nearest house to ask the farmer to bring out his buffalo and hitch him to the wheel while the scene was being added to Mr. Weldon's collection. Across the rice-fields, sighing and shuddering in the fresh breeze, came men and maidens, women and boys, to stand behind the artist and watch him, wondering, agog, and curious. "And," as the old ditty has it, "the buffalo walked around."

The black hair of the wives was coiled behind, and held in place by a narrow bar of either gilt metal or imitation jadestone, that pierced the loop in the heart of the coil. The ends of the bar shone prettily against the jet coil, and the younger women increased the same effect by adding a gilt stick-pin or two at the sides of the coil. The young girls, especially the little ones, wore the coil at one side of the head, and decked it with a white bud, a green leaf, or a tiny row of blossoms. The boys wore pigtails, and the urchins had their hair shaved so as to leave tufts or tails here and there. The baby boys wore ridiculous red worsted crowns, or gorgeous open topped caps of red cloth and tinsel, to emphasize their importance as boys and the pride of their parents in possessing them. For the rest, all, young, old, male, and feminine, wore a cotton jacket, broad trousers, and plaited-straw shoes. The women, of course, carried a frontlet of white cotton under their jackets—if hearing is believing.

"How much?" Weldon asks when his sketch is made.

After a great deal of talk twenty cents is agreed upon and paid. And does that end the bargain? Not in China—never. The man who has been paid announces that the buffalo bull belongs to such and such a woman, to whom he hands the money. And now he ought to have five cents for his trouble. The painter pays manfully, and then announces that he will give twenty-five cents to any woman or girl who will stand for her picture. Two old women move off when this is repeated in Chinese. Then a young girl takes the hand of a companion, and pulls her until both take to their heels and scamper. Presently only the men and boys remain, laughing at the flight of the women.

"Chinese custom," says Ananias. "Countly peeper [people] talkee money alle time; but talkee picture, alle makee lun away chop chop."

At one of these villages a man passes us on the tow path, carrying a string of straw shoes that the peasants wear. Mr. Weldon tried to buy a pair, but, though his foot is small in America, it is bigger than any shoes that he could buy. The man said that he would set his boys to work and fit us out by night with monster shoes. He did so, and we paid him three cents, Mexican, for each pair—that is, a cent and a half. Afterwards we learned that we had been swindled into paying many times too much for them.

Such are the wages of labor in China. They are almost as amazing as the profits of our neighbors at home who deal in Oriental merchandise. The very last thing I coveted in China was a porcelain inkstand, whose form was a pair of white dragons holding up a white apple. In a rather dear shop, frequented by Europeans, it was offered at thirty-seven cents. The first Chinese object I saw on my return to New York was the mate to that inkstand—a modern product, and not a curio. It was one of a million Oriental things in a great and popular store, and it was labelled "twelve dollars"!

But all this time we have confined our attention to the land, to the path beside the water. That is like trying to describe a street by telling only of the sidewalks. Beside us on the water was tenfold more that was strange, for the true highway was the water, and the most picturesque life, outside the towns, was the boat life. After looking upon it for an hour, Mr. Weldon declared that it had spoiled Japan for him, for him who has established himself in what the Chinese call the country of the *wo jen*—the black dwarfs.

A military drawbridge is before us, stuck all over with flags. And flags are on both banks of the river, while near at hand is a square stone-walled soldier camp, with its little house-tops showing above its six-foot play-at-war walls. Many broad, low, open boats, crowded with coolie recruits, are hurrying to the seaboard for enlistment, uniforms, and war. Always there is one man in a red-bordered coat standing in the stern—the recruiting officer, presumably. A mandarin's chop-boat heaves along. It is a hull with a great varnished house upon it, and with that cut up into rooms. The mandarin has ordered his coolies out upon the bank to "track" or tow him along. The dried-up old official, in his tall stiff cap and huge round goggles, stares at us as if we had dropped from the skies. We too are tracking. We have turned down our hinged mast, and put up a short jury-mast. From that we have sent a stout line ashore, and each coolie of the crew has hitched himself to the line. Each one carries a bamboo yoke, and a loop of rope from it to the long line. He presses against the yoke, while the loop tautens behind him, over one shoulder and under the other arm. There is a great "bobbery" every time we pass a boat going the other way or a boat warped to the bank, and yet each is passed cleverly in a systematic way.

The activity on the water is marvellous. The craft are as numerous and as varied as the water will hold or the mind can fancy. The most impressive are the junks, with preposterous sails that hide everything behind them from earth to sky. These junks ride low in front, and are built up behind like the *Pinta*, *Niña*, and *Santa Maria*. They have great goggle-eyes painted and carved on their bows, and turned to look down at the water. Every European in China loves to tell a stranger why nearly all the boats, of every shape and size, are thus ornamented. It is because, "if no hab eye, how can see? If no can see, how can savey? If no can savey, how can walk?" Then there are large cargo-boats shaped like long barrels or large cigars. Their rounding tops are made of bent mats that can be piled on top of one another in one place to make a little cabin, or can be pulled out, end to end, to cover all the cargo. There are other long narrow boats, laden high with garden truck, with potatoes or pease or beans or rice straw, and looking like so many Flatbush farm wagons afloat. There are little sampans, from which men and women fish with nets. And there are innumerable other small boats, wherein men, women, and children are working those tools, like oyster-tongs, with which they tear up the weeds that grow beneath the water. These they spread on the farms, and thus raise all central China higher and higher above the water of the creeks and canals, which is where the ocean water once was, though the land now rises from four to six feet above it. The express boats are very interesting. They are slender long row-boats roofed over with mats, for one or two passengers, and carrying in the stern a muscular Chinaman, who propels a big-bladed oar with his feet. With a small oar in one hand to steer with, with the other hand holding a parasol or fan, the while he may be puffing at his pipe, he toils calmly on, all night or all day, seated on the point of his spine, and describing endless circles with his muscular legs and his dexterous feet.

Thousands of the vessels, even the smallest, are the only homes of the people in them. In them men take wives; in them children are born and reared; in them death pursues his rounds. In them we saw whole families at work making baskets, making lanterns, busy at many sorts of labor. The family cat or dog, or the melancholy chicken perched on an outrigger and watching the family duck at his ablutions, tail up in the water, with a string tied to his leg to keep him at home—these were some of the assurances we had that certain of the craft were floating homes. Often, on the cargo-boats, the dwelling-place was beneath a great square mat in the stern. There the man slept, the woman cooked the rice and fish, and the tiniest children worked the yoolo to send the boat ahead. Baskets hanging behind served as closets and clothes-chests. On the chop-boats, which are floating homes of the best grade, we saw pots of pretty flowers, and kitchens and cooks, and gentle ladies and solemn-looking mustachioed old grandees, as well as nurses and children. Finer yet were the flower-boats, with their cargoes of those painted women who are not allowed to pollute the cities, and therefore float outside in little palaces, all gilt and glass and carved wood. Very ornate and often beautiful were these bulky square boats, masses of fine carving and loud with red and gold. The slave women, in their beautiful silks and jewel-crusted hair, peeped out at us from chalk-white faces, or we glanced in at the windows and heard and saw them practising to please with high-keyed lute and shriller voice.

Most of all were we interested in the cormorant fishing-boats. These are the size of a Whitehall row-boat, and are all open within, to permit the fisherman to walk from bird to bird between bow and stern. Often he is alone; often he carries a boy or a wife to work the yoolo. The birds sit at the sides of the boat, on projecting sticks over the water. They perch in pairs, and there may be ten of them or two dozen. They are the size and look very like the fish-hawks of the Atlantic coast; but they are dirty birds, with ragged wings, plucked to keep them from flying. In color they are a metallic black, with mottled or creamy or even white bosoms. They have long, narrow, curved bills of the flesh-tearing character. Their perches are wrapped with straw, to give the birds a good foothold. When fishing is to be done their master tightens the noose that each wears round its neck, and putting a stick before each one, lifts it down to the water. When they have caught fish enough, or, more likely, have become so soaked that they must be taken aboard to dry, he rows among them and lifts them back on their perches. Their skill lies in their greed, and their greed has doomed them to servile labor.

perches. They yawn and flap their wings to dry themselves, and he prepares for them a fairly good dinner of rice and small fish, or whatever is cheapest, stopping now and then to scold or to beat one with a cane if one is quarrelsome. The man that Mr. Weldon painted sat for his portrait in the rain, protected by a hat of

PASSING THROUGH A FISH-SNARE.

They are caught on the sea-coast when young, and are trained by their purchasers until they become worth ten dollars, Mexican, apiece. Their training consists in starving them all day and in throttling them so that they cannot swallow what they catch. When they are in the water they not only dive for fish, but are said to swim swiftly under the water after their prey. When a fish is caught, the bird rises to the surface and gasps and chokes to get the fish down. The other birds rush at him to wrest his prey from him. The fisherman hurries to the spot, beats the other greedy birds away, and lifting the successful cormorant into the boat, takes his fish from him, loosens his throttling-string, and pokes some food into his ravenous beak as a reward of merit. At last the birds are all returned to their

thatched straw and a great cape of the same material—the water-proof of the common folk in both China and Japan. He was the second who sat for the artist. The first one made a bargain and tried hard to keep it, but as he sat in his boat alone on the water, with the "foreign devil" of Franklin Square looking at him and putting him down on paper, all the ages-old superstition that was in him began to tug at his heartstrings, and he surrendered to it and fled. If Mr. Weldon had offered to use a camera, which is made to work by being packed full of the eyes of dead Chinese babies—as they think over there—he would not have sat at all. But Mr. Weldon used a pencil, and since pencils are only milder inventions of foreign deviltry, who can guess what that ignorant fisherman thought of it?

THE WEST AND EAST ENDS OF LONDON

T has seemed so difficult to write of the social side of the London season that I have put off, from month to month, saying anything of it directly until now, that the last of these articles has been reached, it is necessary to touch upon it here, or to leave it out of consideration altogether. To do the latter would be like writing of the Horse Show and omitting everything but the horses, and doing the former puts the writer in the unpleasant light of criticising those who have been civil to him. It may be possible, and I hope it may prove so, to avoid speaking of the social side of the London season in anything but glittering generalities. Of course the most obvious difference between the season in London and the season in New York is due to the difference in the season of the year. We cannot give garden parties in December or February, nor, were the American fashionables given to that form of amusement, attend race meetings in January. So the out-of-door life of a London season—the lawn parties in town, the water parties on the Thames, the church parade, and the gatherings in the Row in the morning and on the lawn opposite Stanhope Gate before dinner, the week at Ascot, and the closing of the season at Goodwood—is of a kind with which there is nothing similar to compare in New York. The elements of fashionable life which are most alike in both cities are the dinners and dances and the opera. Dinners, I imagine, are pretty much alike all the world over, and the dances in London, at the first glance, are like as smart dances in New York, as far as the young people and the music and the palms and the supper and such things go. There is, however, a very marked difference in the solemnity of the young men and in the shyness and sedateness of the young girls. There are certain interests to offset this, which are lacking with us, one of which is the number of married women you see whose faces are already familiar to you on both sides of the Atlantic through their photographs in shop windows, and who keep you wondering where you have come across them and their tiaras before, and another is the greater number of servants, whose livery and powdered hair add color to the halls, and who, when they pass on the word that "Lady Somebody's carriage blocks the way," are much more picturesque than Johnson in his ulster and high hat calling out " 23 East Twenty-second Street." There is a more brilliant showing of precious stones in London, and the older men in the sashes and stars of the different orders of the empire add something of color and distinction which we do not have at home. Otherwise the scene is much the same. It is only when you leave the ballroom and go out on to the lawn or into the surrounding rooms that you come across an anomaly which is most disturbing. The American girl who seeks corners and the tops of stairways, or who, when the weather permits, wanders away from the care of her chaperon and the lighted rooms into the garden around the house, if the house has a garden, is sure to suffer the penalty of being talked about. Young married women may do that sort of thing with us, but a young girl must remain in evidence, she must be where her partners can reach her, and where whoever is looking after her can whisper to her to hold herself straight, or that she is dancing her hair down. If she wants to talk to a man alone, as she sometimes does, and her mother approves of the man, she can see him at her own home over a cup of tea any afternoon after five. But she cannot do this if she is an English girl in London. So when the English girl goes to a dance at a private house she takes advantage of the long waits between each dance, which are made very long on purpose, and rushes off, not only into rooms leading from the ballroom, but up stairs to the third and fourth story, or out into the garden, where she sits behind statues and

"YOU ARE CONSTANTLY INTRUDING."

bushes, and so, when you wander out for a peaceful smoke, you are constantly intruding upon a gleaming shirt front and the glimmer of a white skirt hidden away in a surrounding canopy of green. It is most embarrassing. I have been brought up to believe that English girls were the most overridden and over-chaperoned young women in the world, and I still think they are, except in this one particular license allowed to them at dances. It struck me as most contradictory and somewhat absurd. Why, if a young girl may not see a young man alone at her own house, should she be allowed to wander all over some other person's house with him, and penetrate with him into the third floor back, or move on considerately to the fourth floor if she finds the third is already occupied? It seems to me it is in so much better taste to do as we do and let the girl see the man under her own roof.

The most novel feature of the dance in London, which does not obtain so frequently with us, is the sudden changing of night into day, at the early hour of two in the morning. Daylight obtrudes so late in New York that it is generally the signal for going home; but it comes so early in the game in London that one often sees the cotillon begun in a clear sunlight, which does not mar, but rather heightens, the beauty of the soft English complexions and the fair arms and shoulders of the young girls, even while it turns the noblest son and heir of the oldest house present into something distressingly like a waiter.

This is one of the prettiest sights in London. A room full of young girls, the older women having discreetly fled before the dawn, romping through a figure in the smartest of *décolleté* gowns, and in the most brilliant sunlight, with the birds chirping violently outside, and the fairy-lamps in the gardens smoking gloomily, and the Blue Hungarian Band yawning over their fiddles. It is all very well for the women, but, as one of the men said, " I always go home early now; one hates having people one knows take one for a butler and ask after their carriage." There is a decorum about an English dance which, I should think, will always tend to keep the hostess in doubt as to whether or no her guests have enjoyed themselves

as keenly as they signify they have done when they murmur their adieus. And I do not mean by this that there is any indecorum at a dance in America, but there is less consciousness of self, and more evident enjoyment of those things which are meant to be enjoyed, and no such terribly trying exhibitions of shyness. Shyness, so it struck me, is the most remarkable of all English characteristics. It is not a pretty trait. It is a thing which is happily almost unknown to us. The Englishman will agree to this with a smile because he thinks we are too bold, and because he believes that shyness is a form of modesty. It is nothing of the sort. It is simply a sign of self-consciousness, and, in consequence, of bad breeding; it is the acme of self-consciousness, and carries with it its own punishment. People with us are either reserved or over-confident,

" PEOPLE ONE KNOWS TAKE ONE FOR A BUTLER."

or simple and sincere, or bold and self-assertive; but they are not shy. And what is most aggravating is that the English make shyness something of a virtue, and think that it covers a multitude of sins. If a man is rude or a woman brusque, his or her friends will say, "You mustn't mind him, he's so shy," or, "She doesn't mean anything; that's just her manner; she's so shy." The English are constantly laughing mockingly at their French neighbor on account of his manner, and yet his exaggerated politeness is much less trying to one's nerves than the average Englishman's lack of the small-change of conversation and his ever-present self-consciousness, which render him a torment to himself and a trial to the people he meets.

There are different kinds of shyness, and different causes for it. To be quite fair, it is only right to say that in many cases the Englishman's shyness is due to his desire not to appear egotistical, or to talk of himself, or of what he does, or happens to have done. His horror of the appearance of boasting is so great that he often errs in the other direction, and is silent or abrupt in order that he may not be drawn into speaking of himself, or of appearing to give importance to his own actions. Modesty is, I think, the most charming of all English characteristics, only it is rather in some instances overdone. In our country a man likes you to refer to the influence he wields; he likes you to say, "A man in your position," or, "Any one with your influence," or, "Placed as you are, you could if you would." It is the breath of his nostrils to many a man. But an Englishman detests any reference to the fact that he is a Member of Parliament as if it were something over which he ought to be pleased; he wears his honors awkwardly; more frequently leaves them at home. He does not wear his war medals with civilian dress. He is quite honest in his disregard of title if he has one, though, being mortal, he thinks as much of it if he lacks it as the chance American does. But he does not say, "Come down to *my* house and ride *my* horses and look at *my* pictures." If he takes you over his place, he is apt to speak of his ancestor's tomb as a "jolly old piece of work," just as though it were a sundial or a chimney-piece, and he is much more likely to show you the family skeleton than the family plate and pictures. I was in a boy's room at Oxford last summer, and saw a picture of one of the peers of England there, a man who has held the highest offices in the diplomatic service. "Why do you have such a large picture of Lord —— here?" I asked. "Do you admire him as much as that?"

"He's my father," he said. "Of course," he went on, anxiously, "he doesn't dress in all those things unless he has to. Here is a better portrait of him."

And he showed me one of his father in knickerbockers. It struck me as a very happy instance of English reserve about those things of which the average American youth would have been apt to speak. I had known him a couple of weeks, but on account of his bearing the family name I did not connect him with his father. The "things" to which he referred were the grand crosses of the orders of the Bath, and of the Star of India, and of the Indian Empire. An American boy would have pointed out their significance to you; but the English boy, fearing I would think he and his father thought overmuch of them, proffered the picture of his father in a tweed suit instead. I have heard Americans in London tell very long stories of our civil war, and of their very large share in bringing it to a conclusion, and as no one had asked them to talk about it, or knew anything about it, it used to hurt my feelings, especially as I remember having tried to drag anecdotes of the Soudan and India out of the several English officers present, and without success. So, on the whole, one must remember this form of shyness too. But the shyness which comes from stupid fear is unpardonable.

As an American youth said last summer, "It is rather disappointing to come over here prepared to bow down and worship, and to find you have to put a duchess at her ease." I asked an Englishman once whether or not people shook hands when they were presented in England. I told him we did not do so at home, but that English people seemed to have no fixed rule about it, and I wanted to know what was expected of one. "Well, you know," he said, with the most charming naïveté, "it isn't a matter of rule exactly; one is generally so embarrassed when being introduced that one really doesn't know whether one is shaking hands or not." And he quite

"ONE OFTEN SEES THE COTILLON BEGUN IN A CLEAR SUNLIGHT."

expected me to agree. If the English themselves were the only ones to suffer from their own lack of ease, and of the little graces which oil the social wheels, it would not so much matter; one would only regret that they were not having a better time. But they make others suffer, especially the stranger within their gates. Mr. Robert Louis Stevenson, in his essay on "The Foreigner at Home," tells of the trials of the Scotchman when he first visits England. He says: "A Scotchman is vain, interested in himself and others, eager for sympathy, setting forth his thoughts and experience in the best light. The egotism of the Englishman is self-contained. He does not seek to proselytize. He takes no interest in Scotland or the Scotch, and, what is the unkindest cut of all, he does not care to justify his indifference."

If the Scotchman, who certainly seems reserved enough in our eyes, is chilled by the Englishman's manner, it is evident how much more the American must suffer before he learns that there is something better to come, and that the Englishman's manner is his own misfortune and not his intentional fault. The English say to this, when you know them well enough to complain, that we are too "sensitive," and that we are too quick to take offence. It never occurs to him that it may be that he is too brusque. If you say, on mounting a coach, "I am afraid I am one too many, I fear I am crowding you all," you can count upon their all answering, with perfect cheerfulness, "Yes, you are, but we didn't know you were coming, and there is no help for it," and it never occurs to them that that is not perhaps the best way of putting it. After a bit you find out that they do not mean to be rude, or you learn to be rude yourself, and then you get on famously. I have had Americans come into my rooms in London with tears of indignation in their eyes, and tell of the way they had been, as they supposed, snubbed and insulted and neglected. "Why," they would ask, "did they invite me to their house if they meant to treat me like that? I didn't ask them to. I didn't force myself on them. I only wanted a word now and then, just to make me feel I was a human being. If they had only asked me, 'When are you going away?' it would have been something; but to leave me standing around in corners, and

to go through whole dinners without as much as a word, without introducing me to any one or recognizing my existence— Why did they ask me if they only meant to insult me when they got me there? Is that English hospitality?" And the next day I would meet the people with whom he had been staying, and they would say, "We have had such a nice compatriot of yours with us, such a well-informed young man; I hope he will stop with us for the shooting." As far as they knew they had done all that civility required, all they would have given their neighbors, or have expected from their own people. But they did not know that we are not used to being walked over rough-shod, that we affect interest even if we do not feel it, and that we tell social fibs if it is going to make some one else feel more comfortable. It is as if the American had boxed with gloves all his life, and then met a man who struck with his bare fists; and it naturally hurts. And the most pathetic part of the whole thing is that they do not know how much better than their own breeding of the American really is. It is like the line in the *International Episode*, where the American woman points out to her friend that their English visitors not only dress badly, but so badly that they will not appreciate how well dressed the Americans are. I have seen a whole roomful of Englishmen sit still when a woman came into her own drawing-room, and then look compassionately at the Americans present because they stood up. They probably thought we were following out the rules of some book on etiquette, and could not know that we were simply more comfortable standing when a woman was standing than we would have been sitting down. And it will not do to say in reply to this that these Englishmen of whom I speak were not of the better sort, and that I should not judge by the middle class. I am not writing of the middle classes. "It was the best butter," as the March hare says.

I have had Americans tell me, and most interesting Americans they were, of dinners in London where they had sat, after the women left the room, in absolute isolation, when the men near them turned their backs on them, and talked of things interesting only to themselves, and left the stranger to the mercies of the butler. Imagine anything like that with us!

Imagine our neglecting a guest to that extent—and an Englishman too! We might not like him, and would find him probably a trifle obtuse, but we would not let him see it, and we would at least throw him a word now and again, and ask him if he meant to shoot big game, or merely to write a book about us. It might not be that we intended to read his book, or cared whether he shot moose or himself, but as long as he was our guest we would try to make him feel that we did not consider our responsibility was at an end when we gave him his bread-and-butter. But the average Englishman and English woman does not feel this responsibility. I remember a dinner given in New York last winter to a prominent Englishman who was visiting this country, and there happened to be a number of very clever men at the table who were good after-dinner talkers, and not after-dinner story-tellers, which is a vastly different thing. The Englishman's contribution to the evening's entertainment was a succession of stories which he had heard on this side, and which he told very badly. The Americans were quite able to judge of this, as they had told the stories themselves many different times. But they all listened with the most serious or amused interest, and greeted each story with the proper amount of laughter, and by saying, "How very good," and "Quite delightful!" Then they all reached under the table and kicked the shins of the unhappy host who had subjected them to this trial. In England it would not have been the host nor his English friends who would have been the one to suffer. I went with a man who had never been in London before to a garden party last summer, and warned him on the way that he would not be introduced to any one, and that after he had met his hostess he would probably be left rooted to a block of stone on the terrace, and would be as little considered as a marble statue. He smiled scornfully at this, but half an hour after our arrival I passed him for the third time as he stood gazing dreamily out across the park just where I had left him. And as I passed he dropped the point of his stick to the ground, and drew it carefully around the lines of the slab of marble upon which he was standing, and then continued to smile significantly out across the lawn. I do not think they treat us in this way because we are Americans, but because we are strangers,

and London is a very busy place, and a very big place, and those who go about there have their time more than taken up already, and have but little to spare for the chance visitor. It is the same with their own people. The governor's lady of some little island or military station in the colonies, who has virtually boarded and lodged and danced and wined the

"NOTHING TO SHOW FOR IT BUT CLUBS AND THEATRES."

distinguished English family who visited the station in their yacht the winter before, thinks, poor thing, when she reaches London that she will receive favors in return, and sends her card expectingly, as she has been urged not to forget to do, and she is invited to luncheon. And after luncheon her hostess says: "Goodby. We are going to Lady Somebody's musical. Shall we see you there? No? Then we shall meet again, I hope." But unless they meet at a street crossing, it is unlikely.

It is the same with those young English subalterns who come back from India and Egypt tanned and handsome and keen for the pleasures of the town, and who have been singing, "When will we see

London again?" and who find their three
months' furlough slipping by with nothing
to show for it but clubs and theatres, and
who go back abusing the country and the
town that have failed to mark their return
or to take note of their presence. I know
one woman in London who expends her
energies in asking cards for things for
young lieutenants back on leave, who appoints herself their hostess, whose pleasure
is in giving these others pleasure, and who
makes them think the place they call
home has not forgotten them, and so,
when they have gone back to the barracks
or the jungle, they have more to thank
her for than they know, and many pleasant things to remember. I rather like
her missionary work better than that of
Dr. Bernado's. There are a great many
Americans who will tell you that we, as
Americans, are very popular in London;
that the English think us clever and
amusing on account of our "quaint
American humor," and our curious enthusiasm over their traditions and their
history and its monuments. It may be
that I am entirely mistaken, but I do not
think we are popular at all. I think we
are just the contrary. As for our American humor, they do not understand what
is best of it, and they laugh, if they laugh
at all, not with us, but at us. Those
Americans who are willing to be a success through being considered buffoons,
are perfectly welcome to become so, but it
does not strike me as an edifying social
triumph. The Americans who are very
much liked in London, whether men or
women, are not the Americans of whose
doings we hear at home; they are not
likely to furnish the papers with the material for cablegrams, and do not take the
fact that they have been found agreeable
by agreeable people as something of so
surprising a nature that they should talk
about it when they return to their own
country. As a matter of fact, I think the
English care less for Americans than they
do for any other foreigners. They think
us pushing, given to overmuch bragging,
and too self-assertive. They judge us a
good deal by the Americans they meet at
Homburg, who give large tips to the
head waiter to secure the tables near that
of a certain royal personage at luncheon-
time, and those whom they chance to meet
in a railway carriage, and who spend the
time in telling them, uninvited, how vastly inferior are their travelling accommodations to those of the Chicago limited
express, with its "barber shop, bath-room,
type-writer, and vestibule-cars, sir, all in
one." I used to get so weary of the virtues of this American institution that I
vowed I would walk the ties when I returned home sooner than enter its rub-
ber portals again. You can see what
they think of our bragging by the anecdotes they tell you, which are supposed
to be characteristic of Americans, and
the point of which, when there is a point,
invariably turns on some absurdly prodigious or boasting lie which one American
tells another. They also judge us a great
deal, and not unnaturally, by what we
say of each other, and one cannot blame
them for thinking that those of us whom
they meet in town during the season must
be a very bad lot.

It is almost as impossible to hear one
American speak well of another American in London as to hear the cock crow
at dinner-time. "Oh, she's over here,
is she," they say, smiling mysteriously.
"No, I don't know her. She's not exactly—well, I really shouldn't say anything about her; she is not a person I
would be likely to meet at home." I
used to get so tired of hearing one American abuse another because he happened
to know a duchess and the other one did
not, because she was asked to a country
house to which the other wanted to go,
that I made it a rule to swear that every
man they asked me about was considered
in America as one of the noblest of God's
handiworks, and I am afraid now that I
may have vouched for some very disreputable specimens. They were not worse,
however, than those Englishmen who
come to us each winter vouched for by
equerries of the Queen and several earls
each, and who go later to the Island in
our cast-off shoes and with some of our
friends' money. If the English judged us
by the chance American, and we judged
them by the average English adventurer,
we would go to war again for some reason or other at once. And yet that is
almost what we do. We judge by the
men who make themselves conspicuous,
who force themselves on our notice,
whether they do it by bragging offensively in a railway carriage, or by borrowing
money, or failing to pay their club dues.
We forget that the gentleman, whether
he comes from New York or London or
Athens, is not conspicuous, but passes by

SATURDAY NIGHT IN THE EAST END.

unheard, like the angels we entertain unawares, and that where a gentleman is
concerned there can be no international
differences. There can only be one sort
of a gentleman; there can be all varieties
of cads. An Englishman used to argue
last summer that he was quite fair in
judging the Americans as a people by
the average American, and not by those
he is pleased to like and respect. He said
they were not "representative" Americans, and that we could not urge that
our best exponents of what Americans
should and could be should represent us,
which was of course quite absurd. If the
English were entering a yacht for an international race they would enter their
best yacht, not the third or fourth rate
yachts. No women are more intelligent
and womanly and sweet than the best of
the American women, and no men that I
have met more courteous and clever than
the best American men, and it is by these
we should be judged, not by the American who scratches his name over cathedrals when the verger isn't looking, or the
young women who race through the halls
of the Victoria Hotel.

All of this of which I have been speaking refers to the Englishman's manner,
his outside, his crust, his bark, and bears
in no way upon his spirit of hospitality
which it disguises, but which is, nevertheless, much his best point, and in which
he far outshines his American cousin. If
you question this, consider what he gives,
and how generously he gives it, in comparison with what we give him. Of course
hospitality is not to be judged or gauged
by its expense, or how much one makes
by it. The mere asking a man to sit
down may breathe with truer hospitality
than inviting him to consider all that is
yours his, as the Spaniards do. What
do we for the visiting Englishman who
comes properly introduced, and with a
wife who happens to be his own? We
ask him to dinner, and put him up at
the clubs, and get invitations to whatever is going on, sometimes to give him
pleasure, and sometimes to show him how
socially important we may happen to be.
In doing any of these things we run no
great risk, we are not placed in a position
from which we cannot at any moment
withdraw. He does much more than this
for the visiting American. For some time,
it is true, he holds you at arm's-length, as
I have just described; he looks you over

and considers you, and is brusque or
silent with you; and then, one fine day,
when you have despaired of ever getting
the small-change of every-day politeness
from him, he, figuratively speaking, stuffs
your hands with bank-notes, and says,
"That's all I have at present; spend it as
you like, and call on me for more when
it is gone." He takes you to his house
and makes you feel it is your home. He
gives you his servants, his house, his
grounds, his horses, his gun, and his
keepers, and the society of his wife and
daughters, and passes you on eventually
to his cousins and his sisters and brothers. This is a show of confidence which
makes a dinner and a theatre party, or a
fortnight's privileges at a club, seem rather small.

It is true he does not meet you at the
door with his family grouped about him
as though they were going to be photographed, and with the dogs barking a
welcome; he lets you come as you would
come to your own house, as naturally
and with as little ostentation. But you
are given to understand when you get
there that as long as you turn up at dinner at the right hour, you are to do as
you please. You get up when you like,
and go to bed when you like; you can
fish for pike in the lake in front of the
house, or pick strawberries, or play tennis
with his sons and daughters, or read in
his library, or take the guide-book and
wander over the house and find out which
is the Rubens, and trace the family likeness on down to the present day by means
of Sir Joshua and Romney to Herkomer
and Watts, and Mendelssohn in a silver frame on the centre table. He has
much more to give than have we, and he
gives it entirely and without reserve; he
only asks that you enjoy yourself after
your own fashion, and allow him to go
on in his own house in his own way.
When a man has as much as this to give,
you cannot blame him if he does not
cheapen it for himself and for others by
throwing it open to whoever comes in his
way. The club with the longest waiting
list is generally the best club.

All of this is rather far away from the
London season of which I began to write,
but it is the manners and characteristics
of people which make society, even fashionable society, and not Gunter or Sherry.
You may forget whether it was the regimental band of the First or Second Life-

guards, but you do not forget that the
hostess was gracious or rude.

The East End of London is entirely too
awful, and too intricate a neighborhood
to be dismissed in a chapter. It is the
back yard of the greatest city in the world,
into which all the unpleasant and un-
sightly things are thrown and hidden
away from sight, to be dragged out occasionally and shaken before the eyes of
the West End as a warning or a menace.
Sometimes, or all the time, missionaries
from the universities and restless spirits
of the West End go into it, and learn
more or less about it, and help here, and
mend there, but they are as impotent as
the man who builds a breakwater in front
of his cottage at Seabright and thinks he
has subdued the Atlantic Ocean. They
protect themselves against certain things
—*ennui* and selfishness and hard-hearted-
ness—but they must see in the end that
they gain more than they can give; for
where they save one soul from the burning, two are born, still to be saved, who
will breed in their turn more souls to be
saved.

There is more earnest effort in the East
End of London than there is, I think, in
the east side of New York. I do not mean
that it is more honest, but that there is
more of it. This is only natural, as the
need is greater, and the bitter cry of out-
cast London more apparent and continual
than is the cry that comes from the slums
of New York. I have heard several gentlemen who ought to know say that the east
side of the American city is quite as appalling as is the Whitechapel of London, but
I do not find it so. You cannot judge by
appearances altogether; dirt and poverty,
after a certain point is reached, have no
degrees, and one alley looks as dark as
another, and one court-yard as dirty; but
you must judge by the degradation of the
people, their morals, and their valuation
of life, and by their lack of ambition.
If one judged by this the American
slums would be better in comparison, although when I say "American" that is
hardly fair either, as the lowest depths of
degradation in New York are touched by
the Italians and the Russian Jews, as it is
by the latter in London, and by the English too.

This must necessarily be a series of
obiter dicta, as I cannot quote the incidents or repeat the stories which go to

prove what I say, and if I did attempt
to prove it, somebody who works in the
slums would come down with a fine array
of statistics and show how wrong I was.
So it would be better to take the East End
of London from the outside entirely. The
best time to see the East End is on Sunday morning in Petticoat Lane, and on
Saturday night in the streets which run
off the Commercial Road or Whitechapel
Road, or in such alleys as Ship's Alley,
off the Ratcliff Highway. On Sunday
morning Petticoat Lane is divided into
three thoroughfares made by two rows of
handcarts, drays, and temporary booths
ranged along each gutter. The people
pass up and down these three lanes in a
long continuous stream, which stops and
congests at certain points of interest and
then breaks on again. Everything that
is sold, and most things that are generally
given or thrown away, are for sale on
this street on Sunday morning. It is
quite useless to enumerate them, "everything" is comprehensive enough; the fact
that they sell for nothing is the main
feature of interest. It is the most excellent lesson in the value of money that
the world gives. You learn not only
the value of a penny, but the value of a
farthing. A silver sixpence shines like
a diamond with the rare possibilities it
presents, and a five-pound note will
buy half a mile of merchandise. All of
the dealers call their wares at one and
the same time, and abuse the rival dealers by way of relaxation. The rival dealer does not mind this, but regards it as
a form of advertisement, and answers in
kind, and the crowd listens with delighted
interest. "Go on," one of the men will
cry from the back of his cart—"go on
an' buy his rotten clothes. O' course he
sells 'em cheap. 'Cos why! 'Cos he
never pays his pore workin' people their
waiges. He's a blooming sweater, 'e is:
'e never gives nothink to his workers but
promises and kicks; that's all 'Ammerstein gives. Yes, you do; you *know* you
do. And what 'appens, why, 'is clothes
is all infected with cholera, and falls to
pieces in the sun and shrinks up in the
rain. They ain't fit for nothink but to
bury folks in, 'cos if yer moves in 'em
they falls ter pieces and leaves you naked.
I don't call no names, but this I *will* say,
'Ammerstein is a —— —— —— —— thief,
'e is, and a—— —— —— liar, and 'is clothes
is —— —— moth-eaten cholera blankets,

robbed from 'ospitals and made over."
Then "'Ammerstein," on the next cart,
who has listened to this with his thumbs
in the sleeves of his waistcoat, smiles
cheerfully and says: "You musd egscuse
that jail-birt on the nexd cart. He vas
a clerk of mine, but he stole oud of der
till, und I discharged him, and he feels
bat aboud id."

Saturday night is naturally the best
time in which to visit the East End, for
the reason that the men and the women
have been paid off, and are out buying
the next week's rations and visiting from
public - house to public - house, and are
noisy and merry, or sullen and bent on
fighting, as the case may be. The streets
are filled with carts lit with flaring oil-
lamps, and the public - houses, open on
every side, are ablaze with gas and glittering with mirrors and burnished pewter, and the sausage and fish shops, with
these edibles frying in the open front
windows, send out broad rays of smoky
light and the odor of burning fat. It
is like a great out-of-door kitchen, full
of wonderful colors and flaring lights
and inky shadows, with glimpses of stout,
florid, respectable working-men's wives,
with market basket on arm, jostled by
trembling hags of the river-front, and
starving wild - eyed young men with
enough evil purpose in their faces to do
many murders, and with not enough
power in their poor ill-fed and unkempt
twisted bodies to strangle a child.

There are no such faces to be seen anywhere else in the world, no such despair
nor misery nor ignorance. They are
brutal, sullen, and gladless. A number
of these men together make you feel an
uneasiness concerning your safety which
is not the fear of a fellow-man, such as
you might confess to if you met any
men alone in a dark place, but such as
you feel in the presence of an animal, an
uneasiness which comes from ignorance
as to what it may possibly do next, and as
to how it will go about doing it. One
night an inspector of police woke fifty of
these men in McCarthy's lodging-house
on Dorset Street, off the Commercial
Road, to exhibit them, and I felt as though
I had walked into a cage with the keeper. They lay on strips of canvas naked
to the waist, for it was a warm, close
night, and as the ray from the policeman's lantern slid from cot to cot, it
showed the sunken chests and ribs of

some half-starved wrecks of the wharves,
or the broad torso of a "docker," or a
sailor's hairy breast marked with tattooing, and the throats of two men scarred
with long dull red lines where some one
had drawn a knife, and some of them
tossed and woke cursing and muttering,
and then rested on their elbows, cowering
before the officers and blinking at the
light, or sat erect and glared at them defiantly, and hailed them with drunken
bravado.

"The beds seem comfortable," I said to
McCarthy, by way of being civil.

"Oh, yes, sir," he answered, "com-
for'ble enough, only it ain't proper, after
paying twopence for your bed, to 'ave
a policeman a-waking you up with a
lamp in your face. It 'urts the 'ouse,
that's wot it does." He added, gloomily,
"It droives away trade." The most interesting group of these men I ever
saw gathered together in one place was
at Harwood's Music Hall. This is a
place to which every stranger in London
should go. It is a long low building
near Spitalfields Market, and there are
two performances a night, one at seven
and another at nine. The price of admittance is fourpence. The seats are long
deal benches without arms, and the place
is always crowded with men. I have
never seen a woman there. The men
bring their bottles of bitter ale with them
and a fried sole wrapped in paper, and as
the performance goes on they munch at
the sole in one hand and drink out of the
bottle in the other. When a gentleman
in the middle of a bench wants more room
he shoves the man next him, and he in
turn shoves the next, and he the next,
with the result that the man on the end
is precipitated violently into the aisle, to
the delight of those around him. He
takes this apparently as a matter of course,
and without embarrassment or show of
anger pounds the man who has taken his
end seat in the face and ribs until he
gets it again, at which this gentleman
pounds the man who had shoved him,
and so it goes on like a row of falling
bricks throughout the length of the bench.
Sometimes you will see as many as
three or four of these impromptu battles
running from bench to bench in the most
orderly and good - natured manner possible. Harwood's has a tremendous sense
of humor, only the witticisms of its cli-
entèle are not translatable. The first

RIVAL DEALERS IN PETTICOAT LANE.

time I went there we were ushered into
the solitary private box, and as our party
came in, owing to our evening dress, or
to the fact that we looked down, I suppose, too curiously on the mass of evil,
upturned faces, one of the boys sprang
to his feet and cried: "Gentlemen, owin'
to the unexpected presence of the Prince
of Wailes, the audience will please rise
and sing 'God save the Queen,'" which
the audience did with much ironical solemnity.

The orchestra at Harwood's, which consists of five pieces, is not very good.
One night the stage-manager came before
the curtain and stated that owing to the
non-arrival of the sisters Barrow, who
were to do the next turn, there would be
a wait of ten minutes; "this, however,"
he added, "will be made up to you by
the gentlemen of the orchestra, who have
kindly consented to play a few selections."
Instantly one of the audience jumped to
his feet, and waving his hands implor-
ingly, cried, in a voice of the keenest fear
and entreaty: "Good Gawd, governor, it
'ain't *our* fault the ladies 'aven't come.
Don't turn the orchestra on *us*. We'll
be good."

The East End of London sprang into

prominence of late on account of the murders which were committed there. These murders are not yet far enough off in the past to have become matters of history, or near enough to be of "news interest." It is not my intention to speak

suers as effectively as though they were running in a maze. This fact explains, perhaps, the escape of the Whitechapel murderer, and serves to excuse in some degree the London police for having failed to find him.

"'OWIN' TO THE UNEXPECTED PRESENCE OF THE PRINCE OF WAILES."

of them now or here, but twenty years or so from now the story of these crimes must be written, for they are undoubtedly the most remarkable criminal event of the century. But the elements which made them possible exist to-day in the nature of the neighborhood and in the condition of the women of the district. In a minute's time one can walk from the grandly lit High Street, Whitechapel, which is like our Sixth Avenue filled with pedestrians from the Bowery, into a net-work of narrow passageways and blind alleys and covered courts as intricate and dirty as the great net-work of sewers which stretches beneath them. A criminal can turn into one of these courts and find half a dozen openings leading into other courts and into dark alleys, in which he can lose himself and his pur-

The East End of London is either to be taken seriously by those who study it, and whose aim and hope are to reclaim it as a great and terrible problem, or from the outside by those who with a morbid interest go to walk through it and to pass by on the other side. The life of the Whitechapel coster as shown by Albert Chevalier and *The Children of the Ghetto* is a widely different thing, yet both are true and both untrue as showing only one side. I confess to having in no way touched upon the East End of London deeply. I know and have seen just enough of it to know how little one can judge of it from the outside, and I feel I should make some apology for having touched on it at all to those men and women who are working there, and giving up their lives to its redemption.

THE LORDS OF THE SAHARA

OF the Tawareks — or Touaregs, as the French spell the name, — the inhabitants of the open Sahara, and, in spite of European treaties and French spheres of influence, the real rulers of the country, very little is known. Most of the information that we have concerning them was gathered from some members of this race who were captured during a desert raid and confined for some time in a fort at Algiers. They are, however, known to be an educated race, as a rule, nearly white in color, who, since they inhabit practically the whole of the Sahara, possess a territory more than half the size of the United States.

Ethnographically speaking, they belong to what is known as the Caucasic race —the race that originated in that part of Africa that lies to the north of the Sudan, when the Sahara was a highly productive country, dotted with swamps and intersected by huge rivers, in which crocodiles, hippopotami, elephants, and other tropical creatures abounded. This race, according to scientists, were our own immediate ancestors, and the Mediterranean branch of it to which the Tawareks belong are closely related to the Iberians, Corsicans, Italians, and Greeks. Owing perhaps to the fact that as the northern part of Africa gradually dried up it afforded insufficient sustenance for its inhabitants, these European branches of the race in the dim ages of the past left their country in several successive migrations and settled in the more fertile lands lying to the north of the Mediterranean, where under happier circumstances they rapidly increased and became highly civilized races.

The Tawareks, however, remained in the ancestral home of their family, which during the course of ages has so changed that at the present time it forms one of the most desolate wastes on the face of the earth. The result has been that while the Tawareks still retain the physical characteristics and intellectual qualities of the race from which they

A GUARDIAN OF THE CARAVAN

tongue—Tamahak—and a considerable percentage of them in Arabic in addition; some of them can speak a Sudanese language, and as a race they seem to have a considerable linguistic capacity.

The barren character of the Sahara compels them to lead the life of restless nomads, pasturing their herds and flocks on the desert scrub, and condemned to perpetually flit from place to place in search of the scanty supply of water and pasture upon which the flocks to which they mainly look for a livelihood subsist. Being as a race miserably poor, they supplement the scanty living which their beasts afford by preying upon their neighbors or acting as guides and guardians to those caravans that traverse the country of the tribe to which they belong.

The rich caravans— consisting sometimes of thousands of laden camels — which cross the Sahara offer, when passing through the country of a rival tribe, an irresistible bait to these lawless nomads, and it is seldom that one succeeds in traversing this desert without having at least one serious encounter with these redoubtable robbers. The Arab camel-drivers— who, though capable of the most reckless bravery at times, are by nature a very cautious

have sprung, their method of life, owing to the nature of the country which they inhabit, is entirely different from that of their more civilized cousins. They are educated to the extent that they almost all can write and read in their own race—go in fear of their lives of these dreaded marauders, and no power on earth will induce them to venture into the Tawarek country until they have come to terms with the chiefs of those tribes through which their road lies and paid the blackmail demanded by them in return for a safe-conduct and protection while in their territory.

Their fears are by no means ill founded, for graves of the victims of these raids and even whole cemeteries, with mounds of earth or mud pillars instead of gravestones, marking the places where caravans have been cut up, are frequently to be seen by the side of the Sarahan trade routes. Owing, however, to the recent French occupation of the northern part of the Sahara, the roads leading into Algeria have become, comparatively speaking, safe.

All the Tawarek men conceal their faces with a cotton mask, which is usually black in color. This mask is never removed even in the family circle. Whatever may be the origin of this curious custom, it certainly is one that has its advantages in a climate like that of the Sahara; for not only by covering the mouth and nostrils does it prevent evaporation and

so enable the Tawareks to travel for long periods without drinking, but it shields the mouth and eyes from the flying sand during the violent storms which are so common in this region, and protects to some extent the eyes from the contrast in temperature between the day and the night, which is such a fruitful source of ophthalmic diseases.

On account of this peculiarity and of their marauding propensities the Tawareks have been nicknamed by the French "the masked pirates of the Sahara." But, like every one else, the Tawareks are a compound of good and bad. They are seen at their worst in their relations with their neighbors, for in their domestic circle they are almost model family men, and their good qualities are nowhere more apparent than in their treatment of their womenkind, which in many respects recalls the romantic and chivalrous customs of the feudal ages in Europe.

The young Tawarek gallant, mounted on his swiftest camel, armed with sword,

ARAB FALCONERS

THE WOMEN MAKE AMULETS FOR THE WARRIORS

dagger, and lance, roams the Sahara like a knight errant of old, protecting and guiding the caravans under the charge of his tribe, redressing and avenging the wrongs done to his slaves and serfs, or, in order to bring glory to his ladye-love, whose *gage d'amour* he wears, and to find the necessary dowry to settle upon her, engaging in adventurous forays upon his neighbors' herds and the caravans under the protection of the neighboring tribes.

From time to time, when an opportunity occurs, he sends a letter to his adored, giving, in a somewhat vainglorious tone, an account of himself and his exploits. These letters are written in the old characters of the Berber alphabet, which at the present day is in use among the Tawareks alone. They are sometimes il-lustrated with rough but spirited drawings of the incidents referred to. Occasionally they are written in a cipher, of which the writer and the recipient alone possess the key, and not unfrequent-ly they take the form of a short poem addressed by the absent Tawarek to his *inamorata*.

When a Tawarek woman wishes to obtain some intelligence of her absent lover, if no other means are available for doing so, she arrays herself in her best dress, dons the whole of her jewelry, and be-takes herself at nightfall to the nearest Tawarek grave, where, lying at full length upon it, she summons a spirit known as the Idebni to appear before her. If he answers to her call, he takes the form of a huge Tawarek, and seating

Half-tone plate engraved by C. E. Hart

"HIS STEED WAS A HUGE WHITE CAMEL"

himself beside the grave, enters into conversation with her. Should she succeed in winning his approbation, he gives her the information that she requires. Should she, however, be so unfortunate as to fail in so doing or to offend him in the slightest degree, the spirit immediately strangles her and carries her bodily off into the gloomy recesses of the unseen world which he inhabits. That at least is what is supposed to happen when a Tawarek woman does not return after invoking the Idebni; but as the missing damsel is sometimes afterwards discovered as the wife of a Tawarek belonging to some distant camp, it may be assumed that these mysterious ceremonies are sometimes intended merely to afford an opportunity for a faithless maiden to escape from her paternal custody to elope, in the absence of her betrothed, with some more favored swain. In any case, when a woman disappears in this way, it is not considered etiquette to refer to her again in the presence of her relations.

The Tawarek warriors return at intervals to the family circle from their forays in order to lay at the feet of their beloved the spoil that they have collected. On these occasions the women of the camp come out to meet them, chanting to the accompaniment of a guitar songs of victory and extempory odes in praise of their exploits and valor. If the raid has been unusually successful, the whole community gives itself up for several days to festivities, in which huge feasts, sham fights, and performances after the nature of "Punch and Judy" shows, with clay puppets dressed in rags, take a prominent part.

During two visits to Algeria I had heard much of these curious Tawareks and of their romantic predatory method of life, and what I had learned had so aroused my curiosity that when, on a subsequent visit to that country, I was told that a camp of these people had been seen near one of the oases in the northern part of the Sahara, I could not resist the temptation to go in search of them to see for myself what manner of men they were. Owing, however, to their frequent migrations, I found them extremely hard to come up with. Like the mirage, they seemed to perpetually retreat from before me, and though I continually heard rumors that they were in my neighborhood, it was only after a protracted hunt that I found their camp.

The wayfarers to be met with in the desert show an endless variety. A day seldom passes without encountering at least one or two groups of human beings. Nomads watering their herds at the wells; Arab shepherds changing their pasture; whole tribes migrating northward to their quarters for the summer months; native hunters and falconers; squat, bandy-legged merchants from the Mzab oases with their strings of camels or mules; and caravans of lithe, wiry Arabs bringing dates into the market-towns—are frequently to be met with upon these roads. Nor are the oases less interesting and varied. Each little Saharan city has, as a rule, a character peculiar to itself, and is totally different in the nature of its buildings from its neighbor some two or three days' march distant. Often, too, the races inhabiting adjacent oases are entirely distinct from each other, and speak, if not different languages, at all events distinctive dialects. The markets in these towns are always full of quaint and picturesque scenes and figures, and afford an artist or photographer endless opportunities of exercising his art.

In spite of the bad character which the Tawareks bear, my own dealings with them, so far as they went, were, with one exception, of an entirely amicable nature. The exception was in the case of a grizzled, scarred, and battered veteran of a hundred desert fights, who, if his history could only have been discovered, would probably have proved to have been as hoary an old sinner as ever lifted a herd of camels or swooped down like a hawk in the windy dusk before the dawn upon a defenceless caravan. We met him riding, accompanied by a servant mounted upon a mule, into one of the desert towns. His steed was a huge white camel some eight feet at the hump. The Tawarek himself, like nearly all the men of his race, was extremely tall. He had apparently injured his leg, for he sat his beast in a curious sidelong manner, which, however, did not seem to interfere in any way with the firmness of his seat. In addition to his crippled leg, he had lost the little finger of his left hand, and even the mask which only partly covered his

"MARKETS FULL OF PICTURESQUE SCENES AND FIGURES"

features could not conceal that his nose had been smashed across his face. He had clearly been very much " in the wars."

In spite of the fact that he was badly armed and that our party outnumbered his in the proportion of two to one, he treated us with all the overbearing insolence for which his race is notorious. He rode past us at first without returning our salutation—this in itself is an unpardonable offence in the desert. When addressed by one of my men, he commenced heaping the most insulting epithets upon him. My Arab, who was not blessed with too serene a temper, retaliated in the same manner, and if I had not interfered, the incident would have ended in that insolent Tawarek receiving a shot in the back from my infuriated Arab as he rode past us.

The distrust that the Tawareks inspire in others is an entirely reciprocal emotion. They are as suspicious and as shy as wild beasts in their dealings with their fellow men. I employed a young Tawarek for a few hours as a guide. One of the Arabs belonging to my caravan happened to be a member of a tribe with which his was at blood-feud, and it was very amusing to see the way in which my hulking guide sidled away and furtively handled the hilt of his dagger whenever his enemy approached him. The latter, feeling that he had the whole of my party on his side, abused the position shamefully, and chaffed that sulky Tawarek in such a merciless and insulting manner that he ground his teeth audibly in his impotent fury.

In the middle of the day, when we halted for a meal, the young Tawarek absolutely refused to eat some dates that I offered him until I had partaken of some of them myself as a guarantee that they were not poisoned, and he had watched for about a quarter of an hour to assure himself that I did not suffer from any ill effects in consequence. When at length I prevailed upon him to accept a few, he squatted down upon the ground at a little distance from us, opened several of the dates and examined them minutely, smelling and licking them all over before he became quite satisfied that they were innocuous. Then he made up for lost time by bolting nearly three pounds of them in about five minutes.

It was very curious to watch him eating. Like all the Tawarek men, he considered it immodest to show his face, so he passed the food up under his mask in such a way as to show not even his chin.

Before dismissing him, I bought the whole of his arms, with the exception of his dagger, for which he asked an enormous price, wishing to retain it, as he did not like to go about unarmed. The possession which he most prized was a large stone bangle which he wore upon his arm above the right elbow. This had been given him by his *fiancée,* and she had inscribed her name upon it. He would not part with that, he said, for " all the camels in the Sahara."

A French soldier, whom I met passing with despatches between two of the small military posts in the Sahara, told me that he had orders not to allow any member of this race to approach him, but to fire a shot over his head if he came within a thousand metres, and to shoot the pariah dead if he did not immediately take the hint and sheer off. This soldier was what is vulgarly known as a " *sans souci*"—that is to say, he was a member of one of the condemned corps who together with the " foreign legion "—the Turcos, Spahis, and other native troops—form the bulk of the garrisons of the French forts in the Sahara. As these condemned corps consist of those soldiers who have been convicted of serious crimes during the term of their military service, in point of depravity they are quite a match for any Tawarek, and, with the exception of the almost equally disreputable " foreign legion," are the only troops for whom the Tawareks and other warlike desert tribes have any real respect. My *sans souci* was a typical specimen of his class, and informed me with a leer that even at a thousand metres it was difficult to miss these huge Tawareks, and consequently the first shot often took effect. In accounting to the authorities on his return for his missing cartridge it was, he said, merely necessary for him to show that he had killed a Tawarek with it, and no further questions were likely to be asked. The weapons of the deceased were the French soldier's by right, and he could sell them as curios to the officers, who were always glad of an opportunity to purchase them.

AN ELEPHANT DRIVE IN SIAM

IT is no easy matter in these days to find a country or place unmarred by the mere sight-seeing globe-trotter; yet if such places do exist, Siam has a right to be included in the number. The generally entertained idea about that country, as expressed by the untravelled Briton, is "a swampy, uncivilized land, inhabited by savages, smells, and diseases"; also (and this, in his opinion, is against it) it is not in the general round of tours. My friendship with H. R. H. the Crown Prince of Siam at Oxford had, however, given me something of the truth, and when (on hearing of my projected trip to the East) he most kindly offered me letters of introduction to members of his family, should I feel inclined to go there, I readily accepted, and made arrangements accordingly.

On May 7, C. K. Hoghton (my companion on many travels) and I boarded a small German steamer at Singapore, and after a warm and uneventful passage arrived at the mouth of the Menam, and waited for high water to cross the bar. Then, slowly feeling the way, we steamed up the glorious tropical river to the muddy wharf at Bangkok. Of our reception in the Siamese capital, the friends we made, and our many doings I will not speak; it is sufficient to know that the time leading up to the subject of this story was amply filled. Our chief host was Prince Charoon, a cousin of the Crown Prince, and one of the most charming of men; he had spent thirteen of his twenty-seven years in England, and is, moreover, a B.A. of Trinity College, Cambridge. From him and his brother, Prince Sithiporn, we first heard of the hunt.

The Siamese army possesses the finest elephant corps in the world, and to keep its ranks up to the requisite number it is necessary every few years to have a "drive" in order to capture a few promising youngsters from amongst the wild herds. Such an expedient appeared necessary at this time, and as H. I. H. Prince Boris of Russia was shortly to arrive, the hunt was so arranged as to fit in excellently with our stay. We were naturally desirous of seeing what a hunt of these great beasts was like, and were promised excitement such as we had never before experienced,—nor, I think it will be admitted, were we disappointed. The country chosen for the operations is to the north of the ancient capital Ayuthia, where the dense jungle almost completely shuts in the town. For our convenience during the "hunt week" the Prime Minister, H. R. H. Prince Damrong, very kindly placed his palace at Bang-pa-In at our disposal, and, that we might do the journey to Ayuthia by river, a fine launch was also provided for us.

All arrangements being completed, we impatiently awaited Prince Boris, who at last arrived, and we were told that the hunt would take place two days later, and that, the evening before, the festivities would begin with a "Lakon," or special theatrical display, in Phya Taywate's Royal Opera House. We received invitations, and witnessed the Siamese rendering of *Beauty and the Beast*. The play was remarkable in that all the actors and actresses were members of the royal family; the programmes and words were printed on books of the purest white silk,—a memento I often look at as recalling a truly novel experience. Halfway through the play we were summoned to the door by an officer, who said our host, Charoon, desired to speak to us. We went to him (for we had wondered at his non-appearance), and he told us the sad news that his uncle, H. R. H. Phya Maha Yotha, had that evening fallen dead from heart trouble whilst making an after-dinner speech, and that

THE ROYAL BOX, LOOKING ACROSS A CORNER OF THE PANIET

he and his brother could not, therefore, come with us to Bang-pa-In on the morrow, but that he had wired to the majordomo to meet us and escort us to the palace.

Next morning we rose at 5.30, and caught the 7.40 train out — only by chance, though, for on the drive to the station the off-side rein gave at the buckle, and the little ponies pitched our gharry into a deep sewer, from falling into which we barely escaped. All's well that ends so, however, and at nine we drew into Bang-pa-In, and found a number of liveried servants awaiting us, with red baize laid to the station door. With us were Captain Hartnell of the Western Division of Police, and Lawson, who controls Bangkok—excellent fellows and good sportsmen. Behind the station a stream led to the palace, and at the bottom of the steps a richly fitted gondola, with four gorgeously apparelled oarsmen, waited to convey us to our destination. After proceeding half a mile up the picturesque backwater which ran between the grounds of Prince Damrong's and the imperial palaces, we reached the river, and there found our

launch awaiting us, with some dozen men in attendance. After transshipping, and leaving our baggage on the palace steps to be arranged for us during the day, we veered round and headed up-stream towards Ayuthia, which is situated fourteen miles distant.

The Siamese elephant-hunt is not a short entertainment like tiger-shooting or shark-catching; for, in the first place, it requires three months' preparation, during which time the small, wandering herds of wild elephants, numbering anything from three or four to fifty in the herd, have to be collected and driven together from the outlying districts, and on the last day gathered into one vast mass. The number collected for this hunt constituted an absolute record, there being, we are told, close upon five hundred of the great brutes — a total never before approached.

The "hunt" itself extends over three days: on the first the elephants are merely driven into the corral, or kraal, or "paniet," as it is variously called; on the second, likely-looking calves are captured inside the paniet; and on the third the whole herd, with the exception of the captives, is driven out, and the hunt devolves into a series of rushes by the infuriated brutes amongst the spectators.

The paniet consists of an enormous square enclosed by a wall built of solid stone, about twenty feet high and perhaps thirty thick. At one end is the royal box, and on another side double steps lead to the seats that surround the top of the wall. It is placed in a convenient position between two branches of the river, the two openings for the use of the elephants facing the water on each side. To guide the great beasts into the narrow neck of the entrance there is a line of posts, each made of a single tree, about twelve to fifteen feet in height and two feet apart; similar posts form the inner square of the paniet, and a large space is left for the spectators on the ground between the wall and these posts. In the very centre of the paniet is a pagodalike erection for the use of the King's head elephant-man, who takes up his position inside and points out to the mahouts of the tame elephants those beasts he desires to have captured. The

photographs accompanying this article, taken by Hoghton and myself, will, with the above explanations, give a fair idea of the paniet and its surroundings.

On arriving at Ayuthia we found our launch to be too deep to go up the klong (creek) abutting on the paniet ground, so we steamed through the main river, and landed on the side from which the elephants were to approach, to see if the herd was in sight. As we ascended the sloping bank we came upon a large open plain, perhaps a mile in breadth, shut in at the back by dense jungle. Hillocks and clumps of trees were dotted over it, and Hartnell pointed to a cloud of dust rising steadily behind one of these, about four hundred yards away.

"Here they come," he said, and a moment later the first elephant, a gigantic tusker, mounted the crest of the hill, and stood clearly outlined against the blue sky; he was not long alone, though, for within half a minute the main herd, squealing and snorting, rushed into view, upon which one of our party hinted that it was time to "trek." This

CHARGING FURIOUSLY TOWARDS THE SPECTATORS

THE HERD IN THE PANIET

we did with some speed—to a sampan (native boat), the boatman of which (a Chinaman) was in mortal terror lest he should be caught by the oncoming elephants. A slight breeze brought the noise of the brutes closer, and also something of their odor. We arrived at our positions in the paniet (above the entrance, on the first day) in good time, and shortly afterwards four Siamese flags fluttered out from the top of a quartet of high trees—the signal for the "drive-in" to commence. Then, slowly moving toward us, we espied the herd coming up the river bank. There were 470 in all, and of these about 150 were young ones of ages between a few months and five years; these were hidden under the great flanks of their mothers, and consequently the herd did not appear as numerous as it really was. The air smelt of the huge beasts, the whole place resounded with their trumpeting, bellowings, and hoarse buglelike cries—in all keys, from the low, deep grunt of the aged tusker to the high treble of the newly born calf.

They were not long in reaching the mouth of the paniet; but once there,

they hesitated, until a large tame male with a single glistening tusk, the hero of many battles no doubt, came forward at his mahout's bidding and led the way. As the tame elephant entered the narrow gate—made so that only one animal could pass through at a time—the leading wild ones rushed forward, followed closely by the whole herd, and in a moment a veritable bedlam was let loose as the huge beasts jammed into the funnel-shaped passage; and then ensued a scene that beggars description. Of course there was no stopping them, and they were left to fight it out as best they could. The stout teak posts creaked and groaned under the great pressure; and once, as a loud crack rang out, the multitude of natives who had gathered to watch the fun scattered in all directions, and soon every tree possessed of sufficient solidity was as thick with human fruit as it could well be packed. It was only a false alarm, however—one of the many that occurred during these exciting three days.

The way in which the cow elephants protected their calves was truly remarkable; they kept the little things under their bodies while in the herd, and on arriving at the entrance of the paniet, placed themselves across it, bearing the whole weight of the charging mass until the youngsters had got through in safety. Two or three got killed and trodden in the mud, however, in spite of the care bestowed on them. The mahouts of the tame elephants were all the time pressing the herd on from behind, and, goaded to fury by repeated spear-thrusts, a wild male occasionally backed a few yards and, with lowered head and curled-up trunk, the piglike tail stuck out stiffly behind, would charge the struggling mass with all his might, shrieking defiance in his rage. The poor recipients of the charge would then turn round and give battle— and such battles, too; bull-fights are mere child's play in comparison. Blood ran freely, and the thunder of the impact as two great heads came together, with the various cries and shrill calls, made fitting music to the extraordinary scene.

Once inside the paniet, the herd quieted down, and to enliven matters a young female was let loose amongst the crowd. After one or two futile charges, it made the turn of the wall and crossed the klong, rushed across the island to which our launch was moored, and stumbled into the main river between it and another boat—belonging to a friend of ours, Trotter by name—from which waved the Siamese imperial flag, a white elephant on a scarlet background. This emblem attracted the attention of the escaping brute; she seized it with her trunk, and holding it defiantly aloft, swam the river, and ambled triumphantly away into the jungle. The men in the launch were of course almost mad with fear, and were pleased to see the brute's tail disappear in the distance. This ended the first day's work—the least interesting of the three,—and we went down-stream to Bang-pa-In for dinner, finding, on arrival, a note from Charoon, saying that he and his brother were coming up the following day. After a game of billiards we turned in, and rose for breakfast at 8.30; at 9.30 we fetched our hosts from the station, and proceeded at once up to Ayuthia. On arrival we found the mahouts were already inside the paniet, noosing the elephants for taming. The method of procedure is simple: a large slip-noose is made in a stout rope, this being fastened to the end of a fifteen-foot bamboo; the mahout then follows the animal he desires to capture, until at last he manages to slip the noose under one of his hind feet; this done, at a touch his intelligent steed forces his way to the nearest post, where men are always waiting to fasten the end of the captive's rope. This operation took up the morning, and then came the driving out of the whole herd to bathe—and sadly they needed it. It required some encouragement to persuade the great beasts to again trust themselves in a narrow passage—they still remembered the squeezing at the entrance. At last one huge fellow, more courageous than the rest, darted through, and at his best speed made for the river.

In the stockade the mahouts on the tame elephants were having a lively time. One large cow, maddened possibly at the loss of its calf, became infuriated, and repeatedly charged the tame ones. These used their tusks savagely to meet the onslaughts; yet one was brought to its knees by the weight of its opponent, and for a moment it seemed that the mahouts (there are two to each elephant) must inevitably be swept off by the slashing blows aimed at them by the great trunk. Another of the tame ones shirked meeting the beast, and in self-defence the mahouts had to protect themselves with their lances till the poor brute was all over blood. Once the blood spurted several inches from its trunk. The stand in the centre was full of men with spears, and this animal attacked them also in the most savage manner. It was reported that one of the men was killed, but this happily proved incorrect. It was a relief to all when the maddened elephant was finally got out of the kraal. Several of the captured herd, however, though they would not face the tusks, charged savagely at the tame elephants when their backs were turned.

After the serious business came the comic interlude. The last of the herd left there was a tiny baby, born the day before in the paniet, and small enough to get between the fence-posts into the outside passage, where it caused no end of fun. Finally a man seized the end of its trunk and led it off, squealing like a pig.

SECURING THE CAPTURED CALVES

Many times the elephants, coming in twos and threes, made rushes into the crowd of spectators, numbers of whom had hair-breadth escapes. Somehow tragedy seemed to be in the air, and we expected fearful things to happen. The Siamese are very fond of running up to an elephant as it comes out of the narrow way and making it rush at them; having got the ponderous animal at full speed, its tormentors suddenly dodge, and, carried on by its weight, the elephant lumbers by. The game of course requires a great deal of nerve, and had been going on for some time, when we heard a general yell of horror, and saw two great male elephants chasing a rather heavy middle-aged man; they were close on him, and in his fear he dared not dodge. Suddenly he stumbled, and by the merest fluke the two animals lurched past him. Just ahead of them was a white-haired old man hiding behind a tree; and catching sight of him, the leading elephant, lowering its head, snapped the obstruction like a reed. With a yell of agonized fear the old fellow turned and bolted directly towards a large crowd of several hundreds of people standing on the edge of the river, just where there happened to be a

perpendicular drop of about fifteen feet; there was absolutely no escape, and the shrieks of horror which arose as the savage brutes approached sent a cold shiver down my spine. I can never forget that scene. A number of the crowd dropped over the precipitous edge and sought refuge below, but all to no purpose. In a moment the great animals were amongst them, kicking right and left, and we saw the old man, the unfortunate author of it all, hurled into the air like a feather, to fall to the ground a bloody, inanimate mass, broken in every part of his body. The yells of the spectators were fearful. But worse was still to come. Carried forward by the impetus of the rush, both the elephants, squealing with fear and rage, shot headlong over the edge; an ear-piercing shriek, the dying note of an anguished soul, rent the air—and two minutes later we learned the dreadful truth. A hapless man, sheltered, as he thought, by the bank, had been crushed to pulp by one of the falling brutes.

It was the most ghastly scene I have ever witnessed, one to which some unknown power drew the eyes—it was impossible to look away. In one short minute two human lives had been crushed out as by the snuffing of a candle. Of the elephants, one was drowned; the other joined the herd unharmed. This incident had scarcely closed—and it had taken away the taste for elephant-hunts from most of the Europeans there—when an equally exciting happening took place. An elephant, a young tuskless male, chanced to come out by himself, and seeing none of his kind to follow (for the elephant is very short-sighted), appeared quite at a loss as to the way he should turn. He stood for a few moments, all four legs well apart, his ears stretched out, and his trunk " feeling " the air with undulating movement, trumpeting shrilly the while. Suddenly, as though struck by an idea, he turned to the left and made off round the paniet wall, keeping close under it.

Now it chanced that Follet and Trotter (of the police) were walking from the klong landing - stage to the steps when the elephant burst round the corner, and perceiving that he must inevitably reach the steps before they could, they sought safety in flight. Turning, they, with a Chinaman who chanced to be near, fled before the charging animal, which had now scented them. Follet—wise man that he was—did not stop until he had placed the row of posts, forming the V-shaped entrance to the kraal, between himself and the enemy. Trotter and the Chinaman stopped at the turn of the corner, imagining that the elephant would certainly continue his headlong rush. To their horror, the great beast whipped round at right angles and at once gave chase. They went like the wind, with death in its most awful form to urge them on. When only thirty yards from the posts the elephant, squealing and trumpeting with pleasure at his success, came up to them; and they, seeing the huge trunk waving above their heads, branched off with a final spurt. Trotter —the fates were with him that day— happened to be in khaki, the Chinaman in spotless white. The elephant gave the matter no thought, but took the lighter figure; in a few seconds pursuer and pursued were level, and then, thud! the ponderous foot shot out sideways and flung the poor Celestial, with one last despairing shriek, against the posts. These

shook with the impact, and when the hapless creature was picked up after the departure of the elephant he was quite dead, with nearly every bone in his body broken by the force of the blow. When Trotter came up to us, three minutes later, with full details of his marvellous escape, he was shaking with terror, and his lips were colorless.

After allowing the elephants three or four hours to bathe, the tame ones (of which thirty were employed) commenced driving the herd back into the corral for the night. During the operation a score or more of those newly captured managed to break away; they spread into the town, and on the island over which we had to pass to reach our launch.

The third and last day of the hunt dawned, and with our hosts we went up in our launch, and had not long to wait before the mahouts started driving the herd out into the open. One elephant, a heavy tuskless male, could not be forced out, and no efforts of the tame beasts would induce him to leave. He charged these on sight with unusual ferocity, and at last the mahouts were obliged to leave him in possession. Seeing no living foe, the huge animal butted violently at the posts and made frantic endeavors to get at the natives beyond them. At other times he would turn round and back with all his weight into the fence, at the same time letting out a double kick—and then look round for the effect.

Then he rushed for the entrance, and seizing one of the four great trees placed as a gate, flung it above his head as though it were but a straw. It was a wonderful object-lesson of the strength these brutes possess. At last, by order of the officer in charge of the ceremonies, the single-tusk tame elephant went in to give battle. With a furious trumpet of uncontrollable rage the mad beast rushed at its enemy, and so great was the onslaught that the tame one turned away and would not face the charge. With a sullen thud the ponderous head of the attacker took the single - tusker in the ribs, and over he went like a ninepin, the fore legs kicking in an unavailing effort to right himself. For a moment it was feared that the mahouts were crushed to death, but it seemed that they had both been shot far away and close to the posts

TAME ELEPHANTS SECURING A SMALL WILD TUSKER

by the shock of the blow. Another tame tusker was sent in—and indeed except for this intervention the prostrate elephant would have been battered to death by his savage foe. The new enemy distracted him, and this time he met a foe worthy of his metal. Lowering his head, the tame elephant took the charge on his forehead, and with a jerk threw his opponent to the ground. The fight was over; having met his match, it took but little persuasion to send the defeated animal out to the remainder of the herd.

Meanwhile the elephants outside had been amusing the people in another way, and we were just in time to see a most amusing sight — an elephant walking

through houses for the mere fun of it. All the buildings near the river are raised on posts, and it was really laughable to watch the beast calmly charging everything within sight, the lightly built houses falling before him like packs of cards. Having cleared away the houses (they were empty, and would be replaced by the government), he went along the fences, ripping them away bar by bar. Then some foolish man attracted him, and he turned his attentions to the people who were enjoying his antics; but to avoid a repetition of the tragedy of the previous day, a bullet was put through his head.

We witnessed another incident worth relating. The mahouts had "legged" a

A TUSKLESS MALE CHARGING THE PANIET POSTS

little two-year-old and tied him firmly to a stump, just before driving the herd into their native jungle. As these disappeared behind the trees, the poor little beast set up a piteous squealing, and amidst cries of astonishment from the spectators two full-grown elephants, the parents evidently, broke post-haste back to their offspring, and took up positions on each side of the youngster, facing different ways, and trumpeting defiance. Then the father, seeming for the first time to notice the rope, curled his trunk around it and did his best to pull it away, the cow meanwhile pushing her calf to add to the strain; seeing this to be ineffectual, they tried running off a few yards and calling out to it to follow. Then they appeared to give up hope, and ambled slowly after the rest of the herd; but a few minutes later the little one was released and literally flew after its parents, pursued by an immense crowd, yelling with delight.

POPULAR LIFE IN
AUSTRO-HUNGARIAN CAPITALS

IN THE STADTPARK, VIENNA.

DO you envy the man who, on arriving in a large city, registers, classifies, and records in his head all the impressions he has received; investigates carefully the museums, the water supply, the markets, the canals, and the sewers, and becomes a peripatetic "annual report" of the kind which municipal governments issue?

In the eyes of such profound students the frivolous pleasure-seeker will find little favor. The latter may be endowed with but slight profundity, but he keeps his eyes open and his nose in the air while he saunters through the streets, delighting in all that is picturesque, as a connoisseur enjoys the flavor of fine wine. He views the public monuments only *en passant* as something to look at. In the show-windows of the publishers he takes special note of the books with piquant titles and striking illustrations. He cannot resist the attraction of a green garden, or a jolly company, or a good restaurant. He likes to drift with the human current, and life in the midst of the people is to him a source of inexhaustible pleasure.'

The writer of these lines willingly—and, if you like, penitently—confesses that he belongs to this class of harmless loafers, who are in danger of being accounted mere unliterary curiosity-hunters, because they only put down that which they have seen and heard, and don't care a button for legends or anything which already has been beautifully described by others. To unite into a mosaic the frivolous, genial, and jovial phases of popular life is the object of the present article, and the author has no higher ambition than to draw by his harmless levity a smile of satisfaction from his reader.

Few are the travellers who do not recall with pleasure their sojourn in Vienna

TYPE OF VIENNOISE.

—provided they did not get mixed up in the social and political quarrels which, for the moment, are threatening to injure the ancient reputation of the Viennese for genial good-nature, but surrendered themselves without reserve to the delightful impressions of the city and its characteristic folk-life. The Viennese folk-life is easily understood. The chief factors are —or were at least formerly—a mixture of naïve careless gayety, an impetuous, sanguine temperament, love of song, fun, and laughter, and appreciation of a good bumper. Those who boast of belonging to the upper classes have, to be sure, donned the stiff uniform of European social etiquette, but in moments of overflowing vitality the Viennese characteristics will yet victoriously assert themselves. Of the very highest class I am not now speaking, for its members constitute a separate and distinct caste, with habits and customs of their own, which the Viennese snob (for this variety is also extant) finds enviable and worthy of imitation.

It is amazing what a number of experiences a man can get through within a single day in Vienna. The native rises early, because he does not go to bed late. If he be a bachelor, his first visit is to a restaurant. Only a few Viennese cafés are permitted (as they are in Paris) to take possession of the sidewalk with chairs and tables. Whoever is desirous to drink his coffee in the open air will find a friendly reception in the City Park (Stadtpark), in the vicinity of the small "Kurhaus," in the shadow of trees and with fragrant flowers round about him; and he will, moreover, find a pleasant pastime in watching the groups at the neighboring tables.

The Stadtpark is a small, well-tended garden, in whose arbors devotees of the *dolce far niente*, old pensioners (and young ones too, for that matter), enthusiasts reading a love romance, or on the lookout for one, idle away their time, listening to the song of the birds and the sirens. For it is a fact that Cupid also gets up early in the morning in Vienna, and at quite an unseasonable hour one may catch glimpses of loving couples under the leafy crowns which shade statues of artists, or a sculptured fountain, with the perpetual plash of water.

Those who are fond of museums may take an inventory of the Ambrose collection in the Belvedere, and admire the Theseus who, in the midst of the charming Volksgarten, slays the Minotaur for the edification of the peaceful newspaper-reading citizen. We prefer first to take a drive in a fiacre through the Ringstrasse, with its splendid display of monumental buildings, and then to make a little excursion into the country. The Viennese cabmen have the reputation of being the best whips in the world. In speed and skilful driving they are, indeed, not easily excelled. Their cabs are light and kept in good repair; their horses are racers of a very respectable sort. The driver cultivates a certain elegance, in accordance with his station. He does not, as in many other cities, wear a uniform, but mostly a jacket, tight-fitting trousers, a shirt with

AT KAHLENBERG.

tall starched collar, and on his head either a small felt hat with a feather in it, or a straight-brimmed, excessively shiny cylinder, known in popular parlance as a *Stösser*.

Scarcely any city in the world has so charming an environment as the Austrian capital. Its seal and its sentinel is the ancient wooded Kahlenberg, with its villas and monasteries. From the city to the Kahlenberg is a short drive in a fiacre. It is also possible to go by boat. An inclined railway runs to the top of the mountain, from which one may enjoy a delightful view of the wide-spreading city, girdled by the Danube. An incomparable adornment is the extensive Wiener Wald (Vienna Forest). Wherever one turns he is likely to strike a picturesque corner where jolly pleasure-seekers rejoice in God's creation. Around the primitive tables, in the neighborhood of which industrious hens are frequently seen scraping up a scanty living, sit gay Viennese men and women drinking the native wine, mixed with soda-water (known in local parlance as a *Gespritzter*), and munching the national "rolls." The demands for modern improvements are, to be sure, beginning to assert themselves here and there, in the erection of pretentious hotels in Swiss style; but, for all that, the little cozy inns are not yet extinct, with their verandas and projecting

OVER THE NEW WINE.

balconies, wreathed in vines and ivy, beneath which it is so pleasant to sit, and, oblivious of the world and its problems, gaze out upon the trees nodding in the wind, and whispering their ineffably home-like melody. The connoisseur of good Austrian wine will find a hospitable welcome under the arbors of the famous monastery Klosterneuburg. Probably he will be tempted to tarry there longer than is good for him, for he will not easily find an environment more conducive to conviviality than the prospect from the summit of the cloister, especially when the sun is beginning to sink beneath the distant horizon, and the ghostly shades of night spread over the wide landscape.

The hour for dining is between three and four o'clock, and does not conform to the custom in other cities. In some hotels an attempt has been made to domesticate the *table d'hôte*, but the prejudice of the Viennese in this particular is not to be overcome. His independence in the choice of his viands, and his predilections in reference to the composition of his prandial circle, amount to obstinacy.

He clings to his fixed, habitual table companions as he clings to his religion. There are hotels and taverns where for a long series of years the same people have dined daily at the same tables. Each has his own glass, his own pipe, and his tastes and habits are known and respected both by landlord and waiters. These "fixed guests" (*Stammgäste*) get always the best portions; they are most attentively waited upon, and constitute a kind of hereditary bibulous aristocracy. It is almost impossible for a stranger to be admitted to any of the so-called *Stammtische* without the permission of the company. The fixed or habitual guests are mostly married citizens of Vienna who like to spend their evenings at a tavern. As slender and modest youths these freemasons of the eating and drinking fraternity first took their seats at these tables; but with the lapse of years they have grown stout and gray and highly respectable; and there they now sit, listening to all sorts of anecdotes, even the hoariest, and relating the same kind. The *Stammtische* are a less frequent institution in the larger hostelries, conducted according to the pattern of the great and fashionable restaurants on the Continent; but they yet flourish in the small smoky taverns which the Viennese call *Beisel*. This is, to be sure, a derogatory term, but is used in its present significance as a pet name. The *Beisels* are mostly situated in out-of-the-way streets, hidden away in hallways and upper stories, where in the period of police persecution (now long since forgotten) the citizen could withdraw from the too curious scrutiny of the vigilant guardians of order.

The excellent Viennese beer halls are, in a certain sense, in spite of all their simplicity, the *salons* of the *bourgeoisie*. No one will object to their cheapness. In these places, barring a certain number which have furnished a gathering-

fingers of his despotic chief, and who in the evening, when weariness prematurely closes his eyes, is more frequently aroused from his sweet slumber by a well-applied box on the ear than by the beneficent fee of a customer. He, too, wears, like his superiors, the swallow-tail, whose cleanness, to be sure, is not always beyond question. Only in the last months of his apprenticeship does the youngster betray an aspiration toward elegance; for he is then soon to enter upon the second stage of his development as a dish carrier, and his art, which will then demand a low-cut waistcoat and neatly parted hair, is a very advanced one. The Viennese waiter who has been promoted to this point, when he is competent to receive orders from the bill of fare, knows how to build up with mathematical exactness a

VIENNESE WAITERS.

place for stupid political malcontents, one is apt to meet some of the most prominent and cultivated people of Vienna, and one is often surprised to hear conversation concerning literature, art, and science. Here one has furthermore a chance to observe a notable phenomenon, viz., the Viennese waiter in all the stages of his development. First, the small and clever beer apprentice, who carries a bouquet of large and small glasses in his red, toil-worn hands, and dodges about among the little tables with express-train velocity, whose hair-fashion is often disarranged by the energetic intrusion of the

perfect tower of dishes, in the distribution of which from table to table he evinces the most extraordinary dexterity and skill.

The third stage of development is represented by the head waiter (*Zahlkellner*), who cultivates a certain ease of manner and *embonpoint;* who will condescend to wait only upon the most distinguished *habitués;* who, moreover, receives the money and the larger tips, while the dish-carriers and beer apprentices must content themselves with more modest fees. The generalissimo of the beer restaurant is the superintendent or business manager.

VIENNESE FIACRE.

He has divested himself of that badge of servitude, the swallow-tail, and he is also above accepting fees.

Besides the tower of St. Stephen's Church, with its pinnacle looming against the sky, the Prater is the pride of the genuine Viennese. To be sure, the ancient simplicity which formerly manifested itself in respect for unspoiled and unimproved nature, only here and there interrupted by some picturesque barracks, is now no longer to be found in the Prater. The demands of a great city have also penetrated into this pleasure-ground, and have there found modern expression in paved roads, railway bridges, and ships with mechanical contrivances in the way of engines, etc. Besides, the World Exhibition of 1873 subjected the democratic part of the natural garden—the so-called Wurstel - Prater — to a transformation which the old local patriots have never ceased to lament. To this day lies in the Prater, like a gigantic turtle, the rotunda of the exposition building.

The Prater ought not to be compared to the Hyde Park of London or the showy Bois de Boulogne. The Prater is some-thing apart by itself, in spite of the aristocratic tone which has been imparted to it by the Constantine Hill, which was laid out in imitation of the Paris Cascade, surrounded by a lake and adorned with a restaurant. For what constitutes the chief charm of the Prater is its ancient groups of trees, which yet remain unmolested, and a certain primitive grandeur in the *tout ensemble* which rebels against all attempts at transformation. A part of the great park, which is traversed by a wide avenue of chestnut-trees, is known as the Nobel-Prater. Here private equipages and nimble fiacres are continually parading. The plain citizen, sitting before the three coffee-houses (so called because hardly any coffee, but almost exclusively beer and wine are drunk there), contemplates with delight the display of luxury in the carriages, while the magnificent Austrian military music is ringing in his ears.

Of the popularity of this military music one may form an idea any day when, about noon, a military band marches up toward the Imperial Palace, in order to play at the relief of the sentries. Whoever has sound

CAFÉ CONCERT IN THE PRATER.

legs marches bravely along with the band. There is the Vienna loafer, with his hair parted on his temples, his hands in his trousers pockets, his patched felt hat perched on the side of his head, a long Virginia cigar in his mouth, and a bright necktie with flying ends. There, too, are the witty, impudent apprentice, the plain citizen, who happens just to be going the same way, and the slender gazelle of a laundry girl, with a yoke on her back, and her hands gracefully resting on her hips. Here we meet also the numerous train of the unemployed, who run along as if electrified by the spirited tunes of the horn-blowers, the stirring noise of the triangles, the drum-beat, the clash of the cymbals. But let us return to our Prater.

Whoever does not care to sit idle and let the sun shine into his face will take a seat at one of the tables in the coffee-houses and sip the good light Vienna beer, while listening to operatic arias and Vienna waltzes. From this coign of vantage he may in spring, and particularly on the 1st of May, behold, passing in review before him, everything that Vienna has to show of rank, distinction, wealth, beauty, and also of false glit-ter and sham. Here he may also observe the affectionate reverence of the Viennese for the Emperor and the Empress. The latter they hold to be the noblest of women, and they express their admiration for her distinguished bearing by the most enthusiastic homage. The archdukes, each with his special court, are also like-ly to pass here. The members of the

PROMENADE IN THE PRATER.

Austrian imperial house wear almost always uniforms, even though they may, like Archduke Rainer, devote themselves in an enlightened manner to art and scientific study.

From this same post of observation the Viennese has also a chance to philosophize concerning the aristocracy, who have now become useless, and therefore unjustly enjoy their privileges, but who, nevertheless, yet form a world by themselves, and consume a certain annual revenue, whether it be their own or borrowed from somebody else. Their principal occupation consists in getting up horseraces, gambling, and riding. They are most elegant in their attire, and display a kind of physical chivalrousness, which impels the snob and the *parvenu* to make themselves ridiculous by caricatured imitations, and awake in them a certain respect—shall I say?—or, at least, an unconfessed consciousness of the distance which separates them from the aristocrat —or "gavalier," as they style him.

Furthermore, we find in this Vanity Fair the rich banker who has been knighted, and who strives to attract attention by luxury and excessive display. We shall encounter wealthy manufacturers too, and merchants with heavy watch chains and broad rings, and at their sides their usually well-fed and buxom wives. Actors with smooth-shaven faces pass also in review, and over-dressed actresses, who assume the most absurd attitudes in their carriages, betraying a high-nosed consciousness of being known to all the world. Lastly, the ephemeral beauties of Vienna seize this opportunity to show themselves.

In fine, the Nobel-Prater, in spite of its Viennese character, bears the stamp peculiar to the gathering-place of the *classes dirigeantes* in all large cities. Characteristic of Vienna in a far higher degree is the Wurstel-Prater, the gathering-place of those whom Richard Wagner would call the less cultured, and unhappily also the less prosperous classes. We will pass by the buxom servant-maids who here, upon the green grass under the old trees, receive the court of military Don Juans (from the corporal down), while the children with noisy laughter play their innocent games. Such scenes are to be found in all cities. Neither will we linger in the company of the flea trainers, bearded women, red-nosed prophets, faded somnambulists, female ser-

pent-charmers, and lion-tamers in threadbare velvet, women with fish tails, ladies with hairy necks and a mustache which would not ill become a drum-major—all these belong to the international brotherhood of roving jugglers who are distributed over the entire earth. Nor are we inclined to place the theatre in the Wurstel-Prater in the first rank of Viennese "specialties," although plays are there performed which deal in a language perfectly well adapted to the mode of thought of the lower strata of the Viennese population.

What particularly deserves consideration as a distinctly Viennese feature is, for instance, the swings in which girls with glowing cheeks and a wild grace of motion shout and scream merrily, while stalwart fellows in shirt sleeves, urged on by their encouraging cries, hurl them high into the air. The spirited, fleet-footed dance

SHOWS IN THE WURSTEL-PRATER.

on the green, under the open sky, deserves to be seen, for here all types, in all sorts of costumes (only none that are elegant), form a picturesque *tout ensemble*. So also it is entertaining to hear the ladies' bands in the restaurants play Viennese tunes. It is advisable, however, in order to gain an insight into the harmless and genial manifestations of the Viennese popular character, to take a seat under the leafy roof of the chestnuts in certain

A FEMALE ORCHESTRA.

parts of the park, and participate in the lively drama which is there being enacted. To be sure, one must, in order to comprehend the pleasure of an old Viennese in these scenes, try to share sympathetically his old Viennese sentiment. A stranger is not unlikely to find fault with the large-flowered and not always immaculate table-cloths, the not altogether stainless napkins, the plain and often bent forks and spoons, ascribing all their shortcomings to a defective sense of comfort. He will conclude, perhaps, that a little sausage and cheese from a dealer in

" delicatessen," or a breaded veal-cutlet (Wiener Schnitzel) procured from the waiter, or a couple of small sausages with vinegar (of the kind which in Vienna are called Frankfurters, and in Frankfurt Wieners), constitute too frugal a meal according to his notion. He may insinuate, too, that the dishes presented excel more by the generous abundance of their quantity than by the fineness of art displayed in their preparation. Granted. But just in this simplicity there is an inexpressible charm to the native, who has brought with him as spice a generous dose of health, good cheer, pleasure in living, and, above all, a good appetite, and has the faculty to laugh heartily at a stupid witticism. He bravely admires the jugglers on the stage in their faded tights, and he is particularly well disposed toward the musicians who perform the Viennese yodel, or melodious Viennese ballads in soft and soothing strains. If the old Viennese, to boot, has consumed his fair share of excellent beer, then he is filled with a blissful sense of oblivion of all the world, which finds vent in the saying, "Sell my coat; I am in heaven."

"Get up, doctor. It's time." With this call we are aroused from our dreams, for in Vienna every man who wields a pen is styled doctor, even though he really be one. Accordingly the doctor dresses himself rapidly, locks his trunk, distributes fees right and left, mounts a fiacre, and at full speed he is driven to the Danube Canal, where a slender ship awaits him, already overloaded with people and luggage. Don't worry about that. The voyage to Pesth is not to be made upon this tiny craft. Her destiny is only to convey us to the large Danube, where a spacious steamer, with a well-furnished saloon, offers us a friendly reception. One feels, at being transferred from the small to the large steamer, like a man who exchanges a tight-fitting dress-

VIEW OF BUDA.

coat for an easy lounging coat, or a pair of tight boots for a pair of soft slippers. One is not likely to wait long before finding pleasant company, if one is content with simple conversation about things which, to be sure, are not vitally interesting, but yet interesting enough to kill time with. Some of the passengers begin at once to play cards, and do not stop until they are summoned to a meal. We had the opportunity to make the voyage to Buda-Pesth in the company of a troop of Viennese actors, with their manager, famous both in Germany and Austria.

The affected posing of these people, aching to attract attention, was extremely amusing. With a certain instinctive skill they selected the places which could best serve as a setting for their unnatural attitudes, while the old manager walked up and down upon the deck with his lieutenant. If he had been the captain he could not have looked about him with a more anxious air of responsibility, as if we were sailing upon the stormy ocean, and not upon the beautiful blue Danube, which, by-the-way, is always green. It flows calmly through the midst of flat country, and occasionally through a wooded landscape, from which, now and then, a ruin upon a hill-top or a straw-thatched village emerges. After a sail of about two hours, the ancient royal city of Pressburg,

with its picturesque castle, glides into view, like a beautiful transformation scene in a theatre. Later the fortress of Komorn attracts some attention. Then the ship ploughs its way onward between meadows, fruitful fields, and irregular banks, on which, occasionally, some straw-thatched cottages are scattered. Then come, perhaps, a little church (before which a flock of geese and a couple of jolly little pigs), some playful children in primitive toilet, a peasant in wide linen trousers with a broad hat on his head, or a peasant woman with picturesque head-dress and a figure in the style of Rubens. Then one has to kill time smoking, chatting, sleeping, as the German poet Nicholas Lenau (who was of Hungarian descent) has remarked in one of his poems. But when evening comes the monotony of the landscape vanishes, to be replaced by charming and, in part, romantic scenery. From a hill in the distance rises upon its many pillars the dome of the Gran cathedral, which, as the steamer presses forward, constantly presents itself to the people on board in new shapes, until, like a scene in a fairy tale, it vanishes behind a cloudy veil. Parallel with the river runs the railway, upon which trains are constantly hurrying by. Nor should Wischegrad be forgotten, which in solemn majesty mirrors itself in the current. With the

change in the landscape the character of
the passengers, who are becoming more
and more numerous, also changes. Large,
well-fed Hungarian figures, in braided
coats and top-boots, with yellow complexions and dark mustaches, predominate.
A band of gypsies come on board, and in
order not to make the trip at their own
expense, but rather to profit by it, they
begin to fiddle to us one piece after the
other, with a truly stirring *verve*. When
the water in the Danube is high, the
steamer arrives in Buda-Pesth by daylight, otherwise the journey is prolonged
until the artificial light has begun its im-

Attila.   Now the ship has come to a full
stop.   On the pier stand, sure enough,
the committee of reception.   The porters
yell in wild confusion; the band of gypsies strike up the national hymn with its
rousing rhythm.   Yes, we are in Buda-
Pesth.   *Eljen! Eljen!*

Like all large cities, Buda-Pesth has
beautiful hotels, on which we need waste
no words.   When we arrive in a strange
town we do not go in search of those
things which it has in common with other
municipalities, but we look for those
things which are distinct and peculiar.
We will then take advantage of the beau-

GYPSY MUSICIANS.

potent competition with the starry sky,
and the landscape melts away in shadowy
outlines.   We arrived in the evening.

With increasing garishness the rows of
gas lamps dazzled our eyes, and with every moment the noise of the city became
more audible.   The steam-whistle sounded.   Great commotion among the passengers, who stood laden down with travelling bags, boxes, and packages.   Now
we are passing under an enormous suspension-bridge, and land in the heart of
the town.   Our troop of actors crowd
about their manager, who, knowing that
an ovation is in store for him, strikes an
attitude worthy, at the very least, of an

tiful evening not to visit the National
Theatre, where the Hungarian language
is used (which, unhappily, we don't understand), or the New Opera, which
strives to compete with the opera-houses
of other cities, but to enter a Hungarian
restaurant in the court-yard of a house,
where some dusty oleanders form a sort of
garden, covered with an awning.   Peculiar, wondrously appetizing odors of the
kitchen greet our nostrils, for we are here
on the classical soil of the Hungarian
"gulyas," which the Viennese pronounce
"gollasch," and the Hungarians "gu-
jaasch."

What is, then, a "gulyas"?   Meat

roasted in a peppery onion sauce. But what a stupid definition that is! It is like saying that an opera by Mozart is a combination of sounds. One thing, however, is beyond dispute—if there is a Hungarian heaven, "gulyas" is sure to be eaten there. "Gulyas," then, is a concoction of onions, pork, meats of all sorts, and paprika (red Hungarian pepper). But who can praise in fitting language its savoriness? Who can describe with adequate eloquence the blood-and-marrow-penetrating strength of the paprika, this boasted national product? Who can praise sufficiently the pungent pepper with which the "gulyas" is seasoned in such abundant measure that the stranger who eats it feels something dissolve inside of him? Stars dance before his eyes, and the perspiration breaks out upon his brow. But this excessive pungency is tempered and enriched by the potatoes cooked into a mealy liquid and the little dumplings known as "nokerln." In "gulyas," as in music, there are infinite variations possible, but the key-note is always the paprika. With the "gulyas," one or more bottles of fiery Hungarian wine are drunk. Ho, ho! Hungarian brother! *Eljen!*

As an accompaniment to "gulyas" and paprika belongs gypsy music. One of the many bands, whose chief is a local celebrity, installs itself in a corner of the room. In foreign countries one sees gypsies of questionable origin. Often they are Bohemians, or even Germans (in Hungary they are called *Schwooh*), who in meretricious huzzar costumes exhibit themselves to their guests. But in Buda-Pesth such playing at gypsies would not be practicable. Here the brown, brawny fellows, with their shrewd, deep, dark eyes, and their mustaches, show themselves in all their native picturesqueness. Their clothes present a mixture of peculiarly Hungarian and European costumes; on their heads they wear small round hats with turned-up brims. The men play without notes, and it is asserted that the

TYPE OF HONGROISE.

majority of them do not know one note from another, but play by ear, if not to say by instinct. The leader of the band plays the first violin, turning constantly with nervous alertness to the right and to the left, and the others simply accompany his melody with all sorts of variations. An important rôle belongs in every gypsy band to the cymbal-player, who with two little hammers beats a kind of big zither. According as the leader with nervous, almost convulsive motions belabors his fiddle, the others file away after him, until they work themselves up, just as he does, into a musical delirium. Long-drawn, plaintive, melancholy, sighing tunes alternate with sudden, unbridled bursts of joy. Like the clever psychologist that he is, the leader of the gypsies instantly picks out some quiet patrician in the audience, to whom he addresses the music. Boldly he places himself in front of him, sticks his

A HUNGARIAN MAGNATE.

a time that the gypsies, when they have earned money enough, have vanished one by one just as the company had been seized with a desire to dance. To guard against this contingency each one of the band had to pull off one boot and keep the other, playing with one foot bare. The confiscated boots were flung into the cellar, and only surrendered when the dance and jollification were at an end. This ingenious procedure does not express, perhaps, a high degree of mutual confidence; but practical and effective it is, which is, after all, the main consideration.

He whose sleep is not disturbed by fantastic dreams and reminiscences of the previous night is apt to wake up in the morning in a good humor for exploring a town of fascinating beauty and romantic charm. From whatever side one contemplates the twin city, divided but not separated by the broad current of the Danube, it affords a most delightful spectacle. If one looks from Pesth toward Ofen a view is presented of the royal castle, situated upon a hill, surrounded by a girdle of houses, shaded by green trees. It is flanked on one side by that mighty sentinel the high-crested Blocksberg, and upon the other by the Schwabenberg, the villa region in Anwinkel, where a refreshing spring leaps out of a black sow's head sculptured in the rock.

If, however, you take the inclined railway as far as the plateau, not far from the royal castle, then you will from this elevated station see Pesth spread out like a fan, with its quays and its new streets, which during the last twenty years have given evidence of a marvellous progress. For we have known the old Pesth, with its narrow and crooked streets, which from an architectural point of view were anything but imposing. Where formerly mostly small, squatty houses jostled each other, expands now the Pesth Boulevard, the Radial or Andrassy Street, with the Grand Opera at one end, and with long rows of houses and villas, built in all kinds of styles, extending all the way to the City Forest (*Stadtwäldchen*). The latter is a gem of a public garden, which, however, were worthy of less modest dimensions. Where formerly stood dancing-halls surrounded by board fences are now seen lofty apartment-houses; street cars rush by, and none of the modern improvements applicable in large cities are

fiddle almost into his face, and performs first tearful tunes, which make the listener gaze with a serious intentness into space; then the gypsy accelerates the tempo until he reaches the delirium, which kindles such an intoxicating ecstasy in the patrician that, with a half-smothered "Jai!" he grabs his head. When the playing is at an end he says not a word, but pulls from his big leather purse a bank-note of considerable value, and spitting on the back of it, pastes it on the gypsy's forehead. Not so quiet is the scene when the whole company have been wrought into ecstasy; then some one present is apt to tear a bill of a high denomination in two, give one half to the gypsy and stick the other half into his pocket, surrendering it only when the gypsies have given the company their fill of music. Frequently a struggle for existence arises between the musicians and the carousers. It has happened many

wanting here. A wise government, conducted during the last fourteen years almost entirely by the iron hand of Herr von Tisza, does everything possible to heighten the splendor of the capital. The city now even permits itself the luxury of raising statues to its great men, as, for instance, to the organizer Szechenyi, to whom Buda-Pesth, among other things, owes its connection by the great suspension-bridge. There is also a statue of the parliament buildings, and churches (one of which had no sooner been completed than it tumbled down, and has not since been re-erected) which vividly impress the image of Pesth upon our memory, but it is its fairest and most imposing adornment—the broad, majestic Danube, upon whose bosom the large, heavily laden ships and passenger steamers of all sizes are the jewels. During our promenade along the quay, in the company of some

DANCING THE CZARDAS.

eminent statesman Deak, which, however, from an artistic point of view, has been subjected to severe criticism, because the great legislator appears altogether too enormous in the big chair in which he is seated. The contrary is true of the slender statue of the noble poet Petöfi, who looks as if he wanted to run away from his pedestal.

It is not, however, the statues, museums, highly ornamental Hungarians and fascinating ladies, we cast a glance upon the animated Danube, with the picturesque Ofen in the background. We feel the caress of the soft breeze and the Southern sunshine, which induce a wanton sense of well-being, light-heartedness, and delight in living, of which we have never been so conscious in any other city.

MARGARET ISLAND, BUDA-PESTH.

archs and persons who have given up ambition and the struggle for wealth do not prefer Buda-Pesth as a residence to the larger and noisier cities. For surely Buda-Pesth is a hospitable place. At all events, among the good old Hungarian race hospitality is a chivalrous virtue, which scarcely anywhere else is practised with the same heartiness and vigor; though here, as elsewhere, a part of the younger generation appears to be degenerate.

Buda-Pesth has also a sufficiency of intellectual life. We need only mention the fact that a man of genius and a thoroughly modern spirit like Moritz Yokai has his residence here. The city has, moreover, its universities, academies, and conservatories, and lies by no means beyond the currents of the world's intellectual intercourse. The latter, to be sure, are perceptible only in slight ripples, and the wearisome clamor and quarrelling of the philosophical and literary cliques find so far only a feeble echo in the Hungarian capital. The eminent works of the world's celebrities are offered for sale; people read French novels, even the spiciest and most exaggerated, written by authors who regard themselves as great classics, because they find among their contemporaries, perhaps, none greater than themselves. One is, accordingly, not in danger of intellectual starvation in Buda-Pesth. But, on the other hand, material existence could not easily be richer, more lavish, and fuller of enjoyment.

Buda-Pesth boasts an advantage over nearly all other large cities in the possession of wonderful medicinal springs. In

Old Homer makes the people of Phæakia say:

"Daily our joy is the feast and the dance and the zither,
Frequent change of attire, the quickening bath, and sweet slumber."

Homer might have said the same of the Hungarians. But to account for these qualities by a study of their ethnic psychology would lead us too far. As mere idle observers we shall have to fall back upon our personal experience in asserting that people in Hungary take no end of comfort in mere material existence; and we have often wondered why exiled mon-

Ofen, not far from the castle, we catch sight of the very comfortably arranged bathing establishment, where for very little money we may have a bath in water welling forth warm from the bowels of the earth.

Ladies and gentlemen, a fig for the so-called civilization! It forces all the world into its own uniform, and robs the nations of their peculiarities. With sincere regret we see in Buda-Pesth cylinder hats, dress-coats, and the long trousers, hiding the shape of the leg and destructive of all poetry, taking the place of the chivalrous Hungarian costume. What is the reason that the Magyars now appear only on great holidays (as on St. Stephen's day) in their shining *czismen* (cavalry boots), tight-fitting, richly braided breeches, flying fur-trimmed dolmans, and round *kalpaks* (hats), in which a plume gallantly points toward the sky? Why do we not see them more frequently in this costume on horseback? For they are capital horsemen, and seem with their steeds to form one single creature. Why do they no more carry their curved swords at their sides? If a Maria Theresa were to come to Hungary to-day she would, perhaps, find the same chivalrous spirit, but hidden away under claw-hammer coats and white neckties, as in the *blasé* audience of a first night at the opera. It would be a pity to lose the magnificent figure of the portly, broad-shouldered, well-fed Hungarian, whose round skull is covered with thick dark hair, whose half-shrewd, half-challenging eyes, shaded by bushy brows, express so much self-confidence, who wears above his necktie a narrow strip of beard, which frames his yellowish face, but whose chief mark of distinction is a defiant mustache, both of whose ends (by means of a kind of indestructible beard wax) have been made stiff and pointed, so that they stand out like two bayonets. For such a Hungarian, as he proudly strides along, flourishing his silver-headed cane, is, in truth, a lord of creation. By his genius for governing he asserts his supremacy over all other races resident in Hungary. Almost every Hungarian is an excellent orator, and as such no less fond of striking images and similes quietly presented than of that grand, kindling eloquence for which the Hungarian language is peculiarly well adapted, when the audience feel their flesh creep, clinch their fists, and burst into frenzied shouts

of *Eljen!* Are we never more to see those bold election agents ride on their smart horses around the carriage of the recently elected member of Parliament, who stands up bareheaded, bowing in all directions? Are we henceforth to admire the Hungarian costume, with the richly colored, braided *burnus*, reaching almost to the earth, only on the persons of pompous janitors? Why can you not keep your picturesque attire, which constitutes the charm of your city? Do not lose yourselves in the general European indistinctness. We could more easily put up with the loss of the proud Magyar who promptly knocked down every one who ventured ever so slightly to step on his toes, but who with sweet quiescence finds it perfectly natural to have his fellow-men, of the lower classes, sentenced to twenty-five lashes, administered by a functionary in national costume with a waxed mustache. These five-and-twenty lashes have played no inconsiderable rôle in the popular education in Hungary.

No man is without his foibles, and it will therefore surprise no one to learn that the Hungarian also has some. A worthless minority of agitators, who through gambling and carousing have been reduced to poverty, and through violence hope to get on the top again, have even a good many. In the Hungarian women we purposely overlook any that may exist, for, without palaver, the Hungarian women are among the most beautiful in the world. They are not languishing, diaphanous creatures, composed of cobwebs and the odor of musk, with a sickly pallor or a hectic flush in their cheeks. No; erect and straight as a candle, hearty and vigorous to the core, the rare pictures of good health and abounding vitality. They are gifted with small feet, full arms, plump hands with tapering fingers, and wear long braids. The sun has spread a reddish-golden tint or a darker tone over the complexion. The Hungarian woman is not a beauty of classical contour, nor does she perhaps frequently present a riddle to the psychologist, and ethereal poets will scarcely find a theme in her for hypersentimental reveries. She is rather the vigorous embodiment of primeval womanhood.

As her exterior, so her whole character is enchantingly fresh and positive. She likes to eat well, is fond of a drop of wine, takes naturally to swimming, dancing, gymnastics, and has not the least objection to being admired. Although not specially inclined to sentimental effusiveness, in one sense of the term, she may, in moments of love and passion, give a profoundly stirring expression to her emotions; she may clothe her sentiment in words of enrapturing *naïveté*, drawn from the depths of the national temperament, if it does not find utterance in the all-expressive "jai," whispered in the acme of ecstasy, accompanied by an ineffably blissful glance. This is true of the so-called girls of the people no less than of women of the higher classes, for grace and beauty know no difference between high and low, and often bestow upon a poor, barefooted, short-skirted peasant girl (with her face framed in a kerchief tied under the chin) the same enchanting form, the same graceful walk, the same magically attractive glance, as upon her more favored sister.

Perhaps it would now be in order to visit the casino of nobles, and listen there to political conversations, so as to become competent to estimate at its worth the important social and national mission of the nobility. Perhaps, too, we ought to pay our respects to all the national celebrities. We might also have paid a visit to the Parliament, and heard ancient revolutionists accuse the Prime Minister of all sorts of crimes, which accusations the Prime Minister receives with a quiet chuckle. We preferred, however, to saunter on the quay, and with delighted eyes to observe the sun-bathed fruits and melons in the market-place. The picturesque, many-colored confusion of buxom peasant girls, heaps of fruit, fragrant canteleups, bargaining and gesticulating customers, formed a sensuous symphony of colors, voices, and perfumes which was extremely effective. Our next preference was to take a stroll through Königsgasse, and let the turmoil of carriages, carts, peddlers, barefooted servant-girls, children, beggars, loafers, street dirt, small merchandise, and open omnibuses driving to the Stadtwäldchen defile before us. These omnibuses were probably once upon a time fresh as to color, and their leather upholstering uncracked. It was a perfect salad of men, horses, and conveyances—of persons and things—which crowded upon our view. Particularly we observed with pleasure the Hungarian peasant, with his tall shiny top-boots, his wide canvas

breeches, short cloth jacket, round hat, and, of course, an enormous mustache. He is not to be confounded with the Slowak, whose whole toilet consists of a coarse canvas shirt, and whose small eyes and upturned nose form an easily recognizable contrast to the features of the Hungarian type. We take an interest, too, in the gypsy, the expression of whose face alternates between a sly appreciation of his own advantage and well-acted humility. We watch the porters, often nude to the girdle, whose language is richly spiced with curses. Especially pleased we were at the sight of the beautiful peasant girl, with her short bunchy skirt, the embroidered bodice, the silk kerchief about her head, and a coy good-nature in her face. No end of services were offered us by the many peddlers and hucksters and other street characters in shabby, threadbare, and ragged clothes. And as we happen to be in a mood for confession, then let us just as well add that we are so hardened as not even to repent having fallen into "the Blue Cat." Yes, not to mince matters, into "the Blue Cat!" "The Blue Cat" is a low-ceiled, smoky place in the Königsgasse, where one drinks beer, and, leaning back in his seat with a cigar between his lips, gazes at a stage where, in a German jargon (which, by our soul, we did not always understand), songs were sung by ballad-singers, and where Hungarian girls in bold rhythms performed Hungarian folk-songs, which, unhappily, we were unable to translate into our language, but which, judging by the rapture, the hullabaloo, the enthusiastic *Eljen* and applause with which they were greeted by the audience, must have been extremely moving. Youthful representatives of the so-called aristocracy often come in a state of blissful intoxication to "the Blue Cat" for the purpose of making scandal. In a corner of the room sit a couple, full of an ardent desire to tell each other something which nobody else need know anything about, touching the perennial theme of love in its introductory stage.

In another place we witnessed a genuine Hungarian "czardas," which is danced in the highest as in the lowest circles, with the same passion and with the same inventiveness in the sequence and accumulation of *nuances* of exciting motion. For a "czardas" two young people are required—a young man and a girl of robust physique—and a gypsy band. If the youth and the maiden are in love with each other, the "czardas" will be the more passionate, attractive, and fascinating. If they are not in love with each other, but dance only for the sake of dancing, it makes little difference, for the "czardas" is itself volcanic passion expressed in hops, leaps, and gestures. The gypsies play at first with measured rhythm. The dancers, who ought to wear the Hungarian costume, stand *vis-à-vis*, with their arms akimbo, and make short *chassez* motions with their legs, while gazing steadily into each other's eyes. So far one might call the dance a slightly peppered minuet. But soon the storm breaks loose. The gypsies change their rhythm. All the instruments give a sudden wail, as if quivering in the intervals between electric shocks; the action of the limbs becomes more rapid, with bolder *chassez* movements. The youth raises now one, now the other hand to his head, dances toward the girl, who roguishly tries to escape him, but again approaches him and again slips away, until, after a great deal of such playful teasing, she permits him to put his arm about her waist and to swing her about in a ring. Nothing can be more charming than this *allegro* which intervenes between the *andante* of the beginning and the bacchantic fury which is to follow. The music of the gypsies begins to rage, and infuses a wild glow into the excited blood of the dancers. Now the legs fairly twinkle as they fly to the right and to the left; the feet touch the floor, now with the heel and now with the toe, the cheeks burn, and the eyes are wide open. With the enraptured cry "Jai!" the youth grabs his head like a drunken man, while the girl, like a sylph, skips before him. The music fairly lashes them; the excited spectators burst into tremendous shouts of "Eljen!" until the dancers seize each other by the shoulders and spin about in a wild whirl.

And now to thee, thou small paradise, fair Margareten Insel, last in order of sequence, but not last in our affection! From the great quay in the middle of the city commodious steamers carry merry pleasure-seekers to the large green island in the Danube, adorned with old trees, shrubbery, and groves. Even if the Margareten Insel were only as nature made it —grass-grown, wooded, and cooled by soft breezes, having, moreover, an abundance of retired spots, where one might pleasant-ly kill the time in sweet reveries, or with a dear friend discuss the affairs of the heart, while the waves of the Danube murmured mysteriously at our feet—it would still be a delightful bit of earth, which fancy might without effort populate with figures in the style of Watteau. But, at the instigation of the Archduke Joseph, ingenious man has transformed the island into a river-girt sanatorium, in which a large bathing establishment and a *Kursaal* have been erected; and moreover a tramway has been laid, which runs the entire length of the island, and hospitable pavilions have been built, which afford pleasant shelter to promenaders. On the Margareten Insel one sees the beautiful women of Pesth walking about, refreshed by a recent bath, in bright costumes, laughing and merry, listening to the music. All day long the steamers carry passengers to and from the city. In a happy mood the stranger contemplates this ever-changing picture.

With the coming of evening the visit to the Margareten Insel culminates. The restaurants on the island are crowded with people. Under the ancient trees, whose branches gently creak and groan in the evening breeze, and whose crowns nod with mysterious confidence, heads of families, with their ever-hungry progeny, take their places at the small tables, which are lighted with torches. A romanticist may take offence at this desecration of the poetry of the place through prosaic nourishment; but the people of Pesth are not troubled with that kind of sentimentality. The waiters bring very respectable portions of highly seasoned food—chicken swimming in peppered cream sauce, veal in a sauce of cream and paprika (*Pörkelt*), and finally the classical "gulyas"—all to accompaniment of gypsy music.

Many a one will, perhaps, come to the conclusion that we have indulged in too much enthusiasm in our description of Buda-Pesth. Quite possible. The unfavorable sides of this city may have impressed others more than they did us. To be sure, much that is worthy of censure has not escaped our attention. But then it was not our intention to set up as a critic; nor do these cursory sketches make any pretense of including the entire life of the city. Wherever anything struck our fancy we simply put our photographing apparatus in order, in the hope of obtaining a fairly felicitous picture.

WILD MOUNTAIN TRIBES OF BORNEO

UTUS SIBAU is the last
Dutch outpost on the
Kapuas River, and Fort
Kapit guards the conflu-
ence of the Balleh and
the Rejang rivers in
Sarawak. Between these
two fortresses lies an unbroken and, for
the most part, uninhabited forest,—uninhabited because the people of the Rejang
River Valley have been at war with the
tribes living in the Kapuas Valley longer
than their oldest inhabitant can remember, making this wide area the theatre for
many an unrecorded duel and bloody battle scene, perpetuating tribal feuds and
racial hatreds, and rendering waste the
mountains and valleys in which the Balleh and Kapuas rivers find their sources.
Well-armed natives venture into the deserted mountains in search of gutta-
percha; a few families of a nomadic
tribe conceal their miserable huts in the
dense forests; and at long intervals a
band of Kyans cross the water-shed on
their visits to and from the widely separated settlements. But no Taman builds
his long-house or clears his rice-field; no

Malay tethers his floating cabin to the
banks of the streams; and no Chinaman,
that pioneer of Eastern commerce, dares
erect his bazar so far from military support. The wild-boar and the sambur-deer
feed undisturbed on the banks of the
streams, the rhinoceros treads his pathway along the *tohen's* crest, monkeys
swing athwart the leafy highway, the
hornbills trumpet across the misty valleys, and the argus-pheasant struts amid
the ferns; but, to all human knowledge,
no foot of white man had ever passed
that way.

The government bungalow, a small
bazar, and a few scattering Malay houses
form the settlement of Putus Sibau,
where the controlleur and a dozen Javanese soldiers maintain the feeble authority of the Netherlands over the vast territory around. There we remained several
weeks, visited daily by the members of
various tribes inhabiting the upper Kapuas, learning the legends of mountains
and streams, listening to unchronicled
history, and to the recitals of duels and
assassinations, of deeds of valor and of
treachery, the gossip of the upper waters.

At length, wearied of watching through countless days the level stretches of jungle that reached out to the foot of Gunong Telong, and debarred from further progress up the Kapuas by a taboo which a recent murder had placed there, we decided to cross this unknown forest on our way to the sea on the north side of the island. The controlleur lent his aid and counsel, advising us to secure the services of Tegang, a young Kyan chief, who would bring a number of his men to act as boatmen, porters, and guides, and if necessary as warriors.

ed before us. He wore the customary loin-cloth; heavy metal rings elongated the lobes of his ears; a fillet of cloth confined his long black hair; and here and there on his arms and chest were the tattoo marks of the Kyan tribe.

Tegang readily consented to accompany us to Fort Kapit, provided he could find a sufficient number of men who dared follow us across the border, and also provided the omens should be propitious. All the natives of Borneo are more or less superstitious, and consult various omens before all undertakings, whether it be the most ordinary duty, or, as in this instance, an unusual and dangerous expedition. From the cradle to the grave they live in fear of the unknown, and of the mighty horde of spirits that infest every animate and inanimate object which enters into the weal or woe of their daily life. Birds are the especial messengers of the spirits, and, if approached in an orthodox manner, give notice by good or bad omens to these trusting jungle folk, who are thereby braced for an honest endeavor, or else are afforded an excuse to abandon an expedition of doubtful issue or propriety.

Tegang returned to his home to repair the canoe, collect his men, and consult the birds, leaving us ample time to buy rice, dried fish, salt, and tobacco for the men, and to pack everything in small sacks of matting to facilitate portage, and also to arrange our own provisions and outfit for a journey which might require from three to six weeks to accomplish. Conflicting rumors came down the river to us from the Kyan settlement: one time, that the birds had given good omens, then again that the expedition must be abandoned, or that a sufficient party could not be obtained. At the end of the second week Tegang himself

TEGANG, THE YOUNG KYAN CHIEF

He was short of stature, thick-set, and strong, with a good-humored expression on his broad face; eyes ever twinkling with merriment, a forehead betokening intelligence, a flat nose, but a mouth which marred all; for his teeth were stained with betel-nut, and when he opened his mouth a cavern of blackness yawn-

came down to tell us that the "hisit" had given good augury, that the "nihoblah," the white-headed hawk, had also been propitious, but that unfortunately just as they began their search for the "telajan" a woman had died in a neighboring house, and further search had to be given up. Twenty-three men were collected together, however, the boats were in readiness, and, if we were willing to allow them to stop on the way and follow their own customs in the event of accident or signs of danger, they would be ready to accompany us. Tegang assured us, moreover, that the Kyans would not have undertaken such an expedition alone, and that they trusted to the white men's gods also to bring us a safe journey.

One morning we saw them coming down the river, their boats lashed together, drifting with the current. Their war-bonnets and plumes, the gala garments of the women who came to see the start, and the sunlight flashing on their ornaments and weapons made a very gay appearance. Even now we feared that some unexpected event had again befallen them, and that this unusual inactivity was intended to impress us with their sorrow at the disappointment in store for us.

A skilful steersman brought them to the bank below the fort, and in an instant all was bustle and excitement, arranging the bags of provisions in the five canoes, rushing to the bazar to buy an all but forgotten cooking-pot, repairing a boat, or building the palm-leaf shade over the central part of the canoe, where sit the drones who toil not. Then, with last messages, promises, and farewells, we began the ascent of the river on our long journey across the mountains. The controlleur waved his cap for the orderly to apply the fuse, and the rusty little cannon roared a farewell salute, sending the news of our departure to the Kautus down-river, to the Tamans up-stream, and far away to the Mendalam River, where the wives and mothers of our men sat in the Kyan long-house. As the echoes came back across the level jungle, they bore the message from them all: "Salaamat jalan."

Half an hour after leaving the fort the canoes drew up to the bank of the stream, and one of the older men kindled a fire of twigs, using for this purpose his flint and steel, for the sacred fire may not be lighted by the modern match. As the

smoke column rose straight up in the still atmosphere it carried a message to the small bird of omen which had first given them the propitious signs, and once again

THE CANOES WERE DRAWN UP TO THE BANK

that day they halted to build a fire to insure the luck the white-headed hawk had promised. Had they failed thus to notify by the smoke that the good omens had been seen, no luck would have followed them beyond the first catch of fish, and evil spirits would have come trooping after them, bringing sickness and disaster. Pandora's box does not contain one-half the ills which beset the Kyans' path unless they keep a vigilant eye for the warnings of the birds. There still remained one more bird, the telejan, the last of the three which they deem it necessary to consult before a journey. Many days passed without seeing its glossy plumage or hearing its liquid note. But late one afternoon Ung Juan heard its distant call deep in the forest on our right hand. They said the omen was propitious, called a halt upon a gravelly bank, kindled the smoke signal, and went on. But they did not disregard other warnings whenever the birds crossed our path. Once a busy little brown bird flew across the stream from left to right in advance of our boats, uttering its sharp cry, hi-sit, hi-sit, and the older men let loose such a flood of language that any one could tell it was a warning of evil. Again, as we were leaving a camp, we heard a bird call near at hand. Each man dropped his burden where he stood, tore a piece from his loin-cloth, and hung it upon the remaining poles of the hut's framework. We waited half an hour before resuming our journey. The evil spirit, seeing so many pieces of clothing hanging about the hut, would naturally conclude that this was a permanent camp, and would go away, leaving us to pursue our journey unmolested. These are but a few of the many similar incidents on the journey. When we crossed the *tohen,* when we first drank of the waters of the river in the new country, when we saw signs of the enemy, or even when we had bad dreams, an appropriate and impressive ceremony followed.

When the lengthening shadows warned the men that night was near, the canoes were drawn up to the bank, preferably upon a pebbly beach, called a *karungan.* While some of the men were securing the canoes by means of the rattan painters, others were searching the jungle for dry branches to be used as firewood, and the remainder built the rude shelter under which the men usually slept. A few poles lashed together by thongs of rattan or of creepers constituted the framework, while palm-leaf mats, called *kajangs,* or, failing these, leaves, would be employed as thatch, and the resulting structure would suffice to protect them from the heavy dews or the frequent night storms. Long before a shelter was finished, a dozen small fires would be kindled. Over each would hang a small rice-pot, and a native would squat beside each tiny blaze to feed the fire and watch for his pot to boil.

When the meal was finished, the men were wont to smoke their cheroots and talk over the events of the day. Then some would repair to the hut or to the canoes, spread out their mats, hang their mosquito-curtains, and fall asleep. Others, if the night was clear, would stretch themselves out on the *karungan* wheresoever drowsiness overtook them, with neither mat nor curtains for protection. Often when sleepless I have left my mat to stroll down by the river-side, passing here and there the prostrate forms, where, wrapped in the sleeping-cloth, once white, the tired native slept oblivious of toil and danger. Here one had improvised a pallet by placing the paddle blades side by side, there another pillowed his head upon a shield, while one and all slept within easy reach of his spear and the long-bladed knife, or *mallat.* The dogs would follow me. A light sleeper would raise himself on one elbow and pass the word, "*Ada baik Tuan?*" The river sang lullaby, the stars kept vigil, and the men slept like tired children at the end of a long summer day.

When the gray dawn begins to fade before the rosy flush of day, and the birds try their first notes before they break into the jubilant chorus of their morning song, the men go silently down to the stream and plunge into the water;

THE RUDE SHELTER UNDER WHICH THE MEN SLEPT

THE MEN SQUAT AROUND THEIR FOOD

soon afterward the smoke rises from the cooking-fires, the meal of rice and fish is spread out upon the leaf platters, and the men squat around as they hastily swallow their food. The hut is then torn down, the boats are repacked, and long before the sun has grown hot they are under way again, with lusty paddle-stroke or strong pull and haul.

There were many interesting characters among our men, and we soon learned the names and peculiarities of each. We knew the strong man, the councillor, the one who steered best, the patient worker, and also the pessimist. We knew those who were freemen and those who were slaves. The work of the slaves was never over, and we pitied them heartily. There was Tegang, our chieftain, and Tama Imang, his grand vizier; Ung Juan, experienced, cool, steady, and true; the wise man he, who knew the omens and lighted the sacred fires; Ngoh, who always sat in the prow, and Paran the Iban, who held the steering-paddle; Nigi the Bukitan, a lesser chieftain, who had brought his own seven men; Laioh the Bukit, who bore on his back a long scar that an Iban had left there when he failed to take the Bukit's head. And there were many more whose individuality was not so pronounced, or who played minor parts.

These men were savages, all of them, and at times given to cannibal rites, desperately superstitious, blood-thirsty head-hunters on occasion, skilled only in the most primitive needs of life, barely emerged from the iron age, deadliest of enemies, transmitting their feuds through generations. But, like many uncivilized peoples they were not without some excellent qualities. They had sworn friendship to us; our dangers were their dangers, and our foes were their own. To us they were for the most part honest and truthful, courteous and kind, and under a strong leader would not only have tried to lessen all the difficulties and unpleasant features of the journey, but would have remained true to us even in the last extremity. But Tegang was young, and, moreover, jealous and vain, easily flattered and influenced by Tama Imang, and fearful of the growing popularity of Nigi, the courteous, pleasant young Bukitan chief.

For the first few days all worked in apparent harmony. When Tegang gave his commands, they were promptly executed, and all joined in the councils, and stood share and share alike in the divisions of food, or toil, or danger. But the jealous rivalry, the smouldering feuds, and the secret hatreds which breed so easily among savage peoples soon became manifest. There were small groups that sat apart conversing in low tones; the orders of the chief were tardily executed, or completely ignored. Tegang, advised by the wily Ung Juan, gradually drew away from the general camp, attended only by his slaves; Nigi drew his men

A KYAN WARRIOR

were sadly demoralized, and we began to think that an open quarrel among our own men was much more to be feared than an encounter with the Ibans from across the watershed. But a common danger unites even foes, and more than once we saw them temporarily forget their disputes and work together for mutual protection until the danger had passed, when they returned to their individual hatreds or grievances as though no interruption had occurred.

We were punting slowly and laboriously up against the current when all at once a tiny chip was seen floating on the stream, and the first boat abruptly halted, and the word of warning was sent back to the others. There was a hurried consultation, followed by a prompt rush for weapons and war-coats, and before we were fairly aware of the cause of the excitement, every one of our followers stood armed for battle. Each man had donned his war-bonnet, decorated with the feathers of the hornbill and argus-pheasant, a padded coat, or one of rawhide, a spear, a shield, and his long-bladed knife. Their excitement was contagious, and we too felt it. Hastily buckling on our revolvers and filling the chambers of our rifles, we joined them in their council of war. This chip, fresh and white, was unmistakable evidence that somewhere, higher up stream, some one, friend or foe, had that day felled a tree, and, since in this land of feuds it was most probably an

about him in a closer band, and the two factions grew further and further apart. Then the river, swollen by rain, changed from a crystal stream to a muddy torrent, and held us in camp for days. This enforced idleness increased the opportunities for quarrels and conspiracies. By the end of the first ten days our followers enemy, we made our plans for an encounter. Nigi and Laioh, armed with the blow-pipe and *mallat*, crept through the brush by the side of the stream, while Tegang, Ung Juan, Tama Imang, Itani, Harrison, and I went forward in the smallest and fastest canoe, and the others followed more slowly with the laden boats.

HEWING OUT A CANOE

The stillness of death seemed to have settled over the jungle, the rushing waters alone broke the silence, and the desire of combat alone possessed us. With pulses throbbing, eyes sharpened, ears alert, and muscles tense, we sent the boat quickly onward against the current, keeping abreast with the two scouts on the bank. Now and then another chip or freshly cut twig floated past; or Nigi and Laioh would stoop over a sandy beach to examine footprints, and turning to us would hold up two fingers, at the same time pointing up stream. Two men had recently passed that way.

The warning boom of a big brass gong reverberated through the forest, and we thought that the Ibans must have heard us, and were calling their comrades for the defense of the camp; but we rushed on, and a moment later broke through the jungle into a clearing about a small hut. Nigi was beating the gong, Laioh stood near him, and at that instant an Iban chief with one of his men, each with his spear poised in readiness to throw, sprang into the clearing from the opposite side. There was a pause as we surveyed each other, rifle and spear in readiness, a pause scarcely long enough for each to catch his breath, before the chief, seeing that he was outnumbered, said to his son,

"They are going to kill us;" and in token of submission their spears slid through their hands, striking point downward into the soft earth at their feet.

Then Nigi, holding up his hand, replied, "Have no fear; we are honest people." And to assure them that he spoke the truth we left our weapons outside as we entered the hut.

The Iban chief handed around tobacco and banana-leaf wrappers, the long cheroots were quickly rolled and the curling smoke arose, which signs the bond of peace and friendship throughout the world. Then, from time to time, another Iban would break into the clearing, with startled gaze and pallid skin, but seeing us all so peacefully occupied, he would in turn plant his spear in the ground, and join the circle of newly formed friends. The young men looked at one another in silence, while the elders explained the unexpected meeting.

They were seven men after gutta from the Rejang River, who had been out in the hills for several months. "Had we any tobacco or salt to spare?" they asked. We had, and in turn asked for information concerning the best trails, the chance of finding boats cachéd beyond the mountains, and the likelihood of meeting with other members of the tribe, either hostile

THE CAMP AT NANGAH

or friendly. They told us there were hundreds of Ibans seeking gutta in the mountains, and our men shook their heads in doubt as to the chances of peace at our next meeting. They told us, however, how to find a boat they had concealed at the base of the water-shed beyond, and asked for one of our canoes in exchange. To this we added a gift of rice and salt, heard their good wishes for a safe journey, and left them to recover from the shock of our sudden appearance.

Beyond the Taman houses a bend in the river disclosed a wooden javelin and a stone suspended over midstream by means of a long creeper which hung from the overarching trees. This well-known *sign* gave notice to a possible hostile party descending the stream that their coming was known, and that the Tamans were prepared to resist them.

At the evening of the second day's march after leaving our boats we had gained the summit of Bukit-Aseh, which separates Sarawak from the Dutch possessions, a narrow water-shed, from which the water flows on the one hand into the China Sea, and on the other into the Sea of Java. Through a narrow rift in the

forest on either side we could see mountains gradually falling away to hills, but in the deep blue valleys we knew that there were tiny brooks which were destined to become rivers that would bear canoes on their swift current. At this height the mists hung low, the air was chilly, and the wind at times suggested the early autumn days at home.

Along the *tohen* we saw the broad pathway made by the rhinoceros as he travelled to and fro on the mountains, and Larong, the slave, was afraid to sleep that night lest a rhinoceros, in his nocturnal wanderings, should crash through our huts. The old men had told Larong tales of such incidents in the past; and a few hours after abandoning this camp a man returning for some forgotten utensil found that a rhinoceros, enraged at finding his path blockaded, had totally destroyed our huts.

It was long after dark before the camp on the *tohen* was completed; and here, on the border of their own country, the *Negri Kapuas*, our Kyans had to propitiate the mountain spirits before they dared to descend into the new country, the *Negri Rejang*. For this purpose they had brought eggs all the way from their home, which, with some uncooked rice, they placed in a dish, this dish the chief passed round, and each of us had to lay his hands upon the eggs and to pass his fingers through the rice, while all looked on with solemn faces. Four small sticks had been thrust into the ground by the side of the narrow pathway, and into the forked top of each an egg was placed. The flickering lamps threw a feeble light over the small circle of men, who, with upturned faces, peered silently into the inky blackness beyond, as though to see the mountain spirits floating by on the ribbons of mist that blew across the crest of the mountain. Then Tegang threw the rice by handfuls into the air, and uttered the invocation: "Spirit of the *tohen,* these offerings of rice and eggs we make to show that your children never forget you; in return we beg that you will give us your protection in the new land we are about to enter. Let no evil spirits pursue us, no sickness befall us, no one poison or kill us; grant us good omens, and a safe return to the home of our fathers."

The northern slope of the water-shed is very steep; we hung to boughs and creepers to avoid plunging headlong as we rapidly descended to a small brook which they called "a child of a river," —*anak sungei.* We followed this stream down, down, until often the waters reached above our waists as we plunged through the pools; then they called it a river, the *Tevulohpi.* Where a small tributary enters this river on the south side there is a large tree, whose spreading branches bear a great burden of small stones, placed there by the passing travellers. Some of the stones had been lodged there long enough to become embedded in the tree, while others had fallen to the ground, forming a mound at its base. If the Kyans are asked why each person must halt and add his contribution, they will tell us they know no reason, only that any one who fails to conform to the customs of his ancestors will certainly meet with misfortune. So we paid a tribute to Kyan superstition, and placed our pebbly offerings on the overburdened altar.

The *Bukit,* returning one afternoon from an unsuccessful day's hunt far away in the mountains, rushed excitedly into camp with the announcement that he had encountered an Iban on the mountain-side who had told him there were thousands of his people collecting gutta-

A TYPICAL IBAN CHIEF

percha along the streams below us. Laioh had not quarrelled with the Iban; he had not even staid to question further, but had hurried back to warn his comrades; and the excitement which followed in our camp was ample proof that he had acted wisely. Every trace of fatigue, of laziness, or of quarrelling vanished instantly, and the question on every tongue was, "What shall we do?"

Some counselled that we return to

A KYAN LONG-HOUSE

Negri Kapuas the way we had come; others, discrediting the Iban's assurance that they were gutta collectors, advised that part of the men return to warn their families that a hostile invasion was imminent; while a few, among whom we were numbered, stoutly maintained that the wisest course was to pursue our way toward Kapit. They consulted omens of various kinds, but the warnings were either uncertain, or else yielded them scant comfort. They formed hurried plans for advance or for retreat, and as quickly abandoned them; and night came on leaving us still in doubt as to their intentions. We wondered if they would leave us there in the heart of the island, our journey but half completed, or whether they would have the courage to advance, believing, as most of them did, that the Ibans were on a head-hunting expedition under the guise of peaceful pursuits. The next day we renewed our arguments and entreaties, and late in the afternoon we finally prevailed upon them to start.

There were many wild adventures to be undergone before our long journey was ended. Finally, however, we reached the fort at Kapit, which stands on a high bank of the Rejang River, half an hour below the mouth of the Balleh. A well-built wooden stockade houses a dozen native soldiers and

a single government official, who keep guard over the trading bazar and the fertile valley below. Kyans and Kenyahs from the hills, Malays and Ibans from the lowlands, hear and answer the challenge "Who goes there?" which the sentinel shouts at every passing boat.

Year after year Minggu has sat at his desk, listening to lawsuits and collecting taxes, while the advent of the trading-steamer or the visit of the *Resident* from Sibu breaks the monotony of his lonely life. Day after day the barefooted sentry paces to and fro in the lookout, groups of natives come and go bringing jungle produce to exchange for the stamped paper which makes them "children of the Rajah." The harvest follows the monsoon, and the feasting follows the harvest, but the unexpected rarely happens to Minggu.

When the sentinel ran in to tell him that "two white men have just arrived from the upper waters," he would not believe it. "No white men have passed up stream; how could they be returning?" But for once he was mistaken. Twenty-three days after leaving Putus Sibau we

THE SACRIFICE

entered the gates of Fort Kapit, and the well-known voice of Minggu welcomed us back once more to the outskirts of civilization.

IN FOLKESTONE OUT OF SEASON

HOW long the pretty town, or summer city, of Folkestone, on the southeastern shore of Kent, has been a favorite English watering-place I am not ready to say. Very likely the ancient Britons did not resort to it much; but there are the remains of Roman fortifications on the downs behind the town, known as Cæsar's Camp, and though Cæsar is now said not to have been aware of camping there, other Roman soldiers must have been there, who could have come down to the sea for a dip as often as they could "get liberty." It is also imaginable that an occasional Saxon or Dane, after a hard day's marauding along the coast, may have wished to wash up in the waters of the Channel; but he could hardly have inaugurated the sort of season which for five or six weeks of the later summer finds the Folkestone beaches thronged with visitors, and the surf full of them. We ourselves formed no part of the season, having come for the air in the later spring, when the air is said to be tonic enough without the water. It is my belief that at no time of the year can you come amiss to Folkestone; but still it is better for me to own at the outset that you will not find it very gay there if you come at the end of April.

Our sitting-room windows did not look out upon the sea, as we had planned. The front of our house was not upon the Leas, as the esplanaded cliffs at Folkestone are called, and you could not see the coast of France from it as you could from the house-fronts of the Leas in certain states of the atmosphere. But that sight always means rain, and in Folkestone there is rain enough without seeing the coast of France; and so it was not altogether a disadvantage to be one corner back from the Leas on a street enfilading them from the north. After the tea and bread and butter which they always have so good in England, and which instantly appeared, as if the kettle had been boiling for us from the beginning of time, we ran out to the Leas, and said we would never go away from Folkestone. How, indeed, could we think of doing such a thing, with that lawny level of interasphalted green stretching eastward into the town that climbed picturesquely up to meet it, and westward to the sunset, and dropped southward by a swift declivity softened in its abruptness by flowery and leafy shrubs?

If this were not enough inducement to an eternal stay, there was the provisionally peaceable Channel wrinkled in a friendly smile at the depth below us, and shaded from delicate green to delicate purple away from the long, brown beach on which it amused itself by gently breaking in a snowy surf. In the middle distance were every manner of smaller or larger sail, and in the offing little stubbed steamers smoking along, and here and there an ocean liner making from an American for a German port; or if it

UNDER THE LEAS

was not an ocean liner it ought to have been.

Certainly there could be no question of the business-and-pleasure-shipping drawn up on the beach, on the best terms with the ranks of bathing-machines patiently waiting the August bathers with the same serene faith in them as the half-fledged trees showed, that end-of-April evening, in the coming of the summer which seemed so doubtful to the human spectator. For the prevailing blandness of the atmosphere had keen little points and edges of cold in it; and vagarious gusts caught and tossed the smoke from the chimney-pots of the pretty town along the sea-level below the Leas, giving way here to the wooded walks, and gaining there upon them. Inspired by the presence of a steel pier half as long as that of Atlantic City, with the same sort of pavilion for entertainments at the end, we tried to fancy that the spring was farther advanced at home, but we could only make sure that it would be summer sooner and fiercer with us. In the mean time, as it was too late for the military band which plays every fine afternoon in a stand on the Leas, the birds were singing in the gardens that border them; very sweetly and richly, and not obli-

ging you at any point to get up and take your hat off by striking into "God save the King." I am not sure what kind of birds they were; but I called them to myself all robins of our sort, for upon the whole they sounded like them. Some golden-billed blackbirds I made certain of, and very likely there were larks and thrushes among them,—and nightingales, for anything I knew. They all shouted for joy of the pleasant evening, and of the garden trees in which they hid, and which were oftener pleasant, no doubt, than the evening. The gardens where the trees stood spread between handsome mansard-roofed houses of gray stucco of the same type as those which front flush upon the Leas, and which prevail in all the newer parts of Folkestone; their style dates them as of the sixties and seventies of the last century, since when not many houses seem to have been built on the Leas at Folkestone.

There are entertainments of an inoffensive vaudeville sort in the pavilion on the pier at Folkestone, and yet milder attractions in the hall of the Leas Pavilion, which for some abstruse reason is sunk ten or twelve feet below the surrounding level. The evening I spent there, the tea was yet milder than the other attractions: than the fair vocalist; than the prestidigitator who made a dozen different kinds of hats out of a square piece of cloth, and personated their historical wearers in them; than the cinematograph; than the lady orchestra which so mainly played pieces "By Desire" that the programme was almost composed of them. A diversion in the direction of ice-cream was not lavishly fortunate: the ice-cream was a sort of sweetened and extract-flavored snow which was hardly colder than the air outside.

It seemed, in fact, somewhat relaxed by those atmospheric influences which in England are of such frequent and swift vicissitude. At Folkestone we were early warned against the air of the sea-level, which we would find extremely relaxing, whereas that of the Leas, fifty feet above, was extremely bracing. We were not always able to note the difference, but at times we found the air even on the Leas extremely relaxing when the wind was in a certain quarter.

The sun is, of course, the mild English sun, which seems nowise akin to our flaming American star, but is quite probably the centre of the same solar system. The birds are in the wilding shrubs and trees which clothe the front of the cliffs, and in the gardened spaces on the relaxing levels, spreading below to the sands of the sea; and they are in the gardens of the placid, handsome houses which stand detached behind their hedges of thorn or laurel. This is the houses' habit through the whole town, which is superficially vast, and everywhere agreeably and often prettily built. It is overbuilt, in fact; well toward seven hundred houses lie empty, and half of those which are occupied are devoted to lodgings and boarding-houses, while the hotels, large and little, abound. There are no manufactures, and except in the season and the preparatory season, there is no work. Folkestone has become very gay, but is no longer the resort of the consumptive or the aristocratic, or even the æsthetic. These turn to other air and other conditions, where they may sleep out-of-doors, or wander informally about the fields or over the sands.

But the birds say nothing of all this,

especially in the first days of your arrival, when it is only a question whether you shall buy the most beautiful house on the Leas, or whether you shall buy the whole town. Afterwards, when the birds are a little franker, your heart is gone to Folkestone, and you do not mind whether you have made a good investment or not. By this time, though the Earl of Radnor still owns the earth, you own the sky and sea, for which you pay him no ground rent. Of your sky perhaps the less said the better, but of your sea you could not brag too loudly. Sometimes the sun looks askance at it from the curtains of clouds which he likes to keep drawn, especially out of season, and sometimes the rainy Hyades vex its dimness, but at all times its tender and lovely coloring seems its own, and not a hue lent it from the smiling or frowning welkin. I am speaking of its amiable moods; it has a muddiness all its own, also, when the Hyades have vexed it too long. But on a reasonably pleasant day, I do not know a much more agreeable thing than to sit on a bench under the edge of the Leas, and tacitly direct the movements of the fishermen whose sails light up the water wherever it is not darkened by the smokes of those steamers I have spoken of. About noon the fishermen begin to make inshore, toward the piers which form the harbor, and then if you will leave your bench, and walk down the long sloping road from the Leas into the quaint old seafaring quarter of the town, you can see the fishermen auctioning off their several catches.

Their craft, as they round the end of the breakwater, and come dropping into the wharves, are not as graceful as they looked at sea. In fact, the American eye, trained to the trimmer lines of our shipping in every kind, sees them lumpish and loggish, with bows that can scarcely know themselves from sterns, and with stumpy masts and shapeless sails. But the fishermen themselves are very fine: fair or dark men, but mostly fair, of stalwart build, with sou'westers sloping over powerful shoulders, and the red of their English complexions showing rank through their professional tan. With the toe of his huge thigh-boot one of them tenderly touches the edge of the wharf, as the boat-load of fish swims up to it, and then steps ashore to hold it fast, while the others empty a squirming and flopping heap on the stones. The heaps are gathered into baskets, and carried to the simple sheds of the market, where the beheading and disembowelling of fish is forever going on, and then being dumped down on the stones again, they are cried off by one of the crew that caught them. I say cried because I suppose that is the technical phrase, but it is too violent. The voice of the auctioneer is slow and low, and his manner diffident and embarrassed; he practises none of the arts of his secondary trade; he does nothing, by joke or boast, to work up the inaudible bidders to flights of speculative fancy; after a pause, which seems no silenter than the rest of the transaction, he ceases to repeat the bids, and his fish, in the measure of a bushel or so, have gone for a matter of three shillings. The day of my visit, a few tourists, mostly women, of course, formed the uninterested audience.

The affair was so far from having the interest promised that I turned from it toward the neighboring streets of humble old-fashioned houses, and wondered in which of them it could have been that forty-three years ago a very homesick, very young American going out to be a Consul in Italy, stopped one particularly black night and had a rasher of bacon. It could not be specifically found, but there were plenty of other quaint, antiquated houses, of which one had one's choice, clinging to the edge of the sea, and the foot of the steep which swells away toward Dover into misty heights of very agreeable grandeur. In the narrow street that climbs into the upper and newer town, there are old curiosity-shops of a fatal fascination for such as love old silver, which is indeed so abundant in the old curiosity-shops of England everywhere as to leave the impression that all the silver presently in use is fire-new. There are other fascinating shops of a more practical sort in that street, which has a cart-track so narrow that scarcely the boldest Bath-chair could venture it. When it opens at top into the new wide streets you find yourself in the midst of a shopping region of which Folkestone is justly proud, and which is said to suggest, "to the finer female sense," both London and Paris. Perhaps it only suggests a difference from both; but at any rate it is very bright and pleasant, especially when

THE PIER WITH ITS PAVILION

Half-tone plate engraved by G. M. Lewis

THE FISH-MARKET AT FOLKESTONE

it is not raining; and there are not only French and English modistes but Italian confectioners; one sees Italian names almost as commonly as in New York, and they seem rather fond of Folkestone, where they mistake the air for that of the Riviera. This street of shops (which abounds in circulating libraries) soon ceases into a street of the self-respectful dwellings of the local type, and from the midst of these rises the bulk of the Pleasure Gardens Theatre, to which I addicted myself,

in my constant love of the drama, without even the small reciprocation which I experience from it at home. In the season, the Pleasure Gardens adjacent are given up to many sorts of gayety, but during our stay there was no merriment madder than the wild hilarity of a croquet tournament; this, I will own, I had not the heart to go and pay sixpence to see.

The note of Folkestone is distinctly formality. I do not say the highest fashion, for I have been told that this is "The tender grace of a day that is dead" for Folkestone. The highest fashion in England, if not in America, seeks the simplest expression in certain moments; it likes to go to little seashore places where it can be informal, when it likes, in dress and amusement; where it can get close to its neglected mother nature, and lie in her lap and smoke its cigarette in her indulgent face. So at least I have heard; I vouch for nothing. Sometimes I have seen the Leas fairly well dotted with promenaders toward evening; sometimes, in a brief interval of sunshine, the lawns pretty fairly spotted with people listening in chairs to the military band. On other days—and my experience is that out of eighteen days at Folkestone fourteen are too bad for the band to play in the pavilion—there is a modest string band in the Shelter. This is a sort of cavern hollowed under the edge of the Leas, where there are chairs within, and without under the veranda eaves, at tuppence each, and where the visitors all sit reading novels, and trying to shut out the music from their consciousness. I think it is because they dread so much coming to "God Save the King," when they will have to get up and stand uncovered. It is not because they hate to uncover to the King, but because they know that then they will have to go away, and there is nothing else for them to do.

Once they could go twice a day to see the Channel boats come in, and the passengers, sodden from seasickness, come limply lagging ashore. But now they are deprived of this sight by the ill-behavior of the railroad in timing the boats so that they arrive in the middle of lunch and after dark. It is held to have been distinctly a blow to the prosperity of Folkestone, where people now have more leisure than they know what to do with, even when they spend all the time in dressing and undressing which the height of the season exacts of them. Of course, there is always the bathing, when the water is warm enough. The bathing-machine is not so attractive to the spectator as the bath-house with the bather tripping or hobbling down to the sea across the yellow sands; but it serves equally to pass the time and occupy the mind, and for the American onlooker it would have the charm of novelty, when the clumsy structure was driven into the water.

I have said yellow sands in obedience to Shakespeare, but I note again that the beach at Folkestone is reddish brown. Its sands are coarse, and do not pack smoothly like those of our beaches; at Dover, where they were used in the mortar for building the castle, they are to blame for the damp coming through the walls and obliging the authorities to paint the old armor to keep it from rusting. But I fancy the sea sand does not enter into the composition of the stucco on the Folkestone houses, one of which we found so pleasantly habitable. Most of the houses on and near the Leas are larger than the wont of American houses, and the arrangement much more agreeable and sensible than that of our average houses; the hallway opens from a handsome vestibule, and the stairs ascend from the rear of the hall, and turn squarely, as they mount half-way up. But let not the intending exile suppose that their rents are low; with the rates and taxes, which the tenant always pays in England, the rents are fully up to those in towns of corresponding size with us. Provisions are even higher than in our subordinate cities, especially to the westward, and I doubt if people live as cheaply in Folkestone as, say, in Springfield, Massachusetts, or in Buffalo.

For the same money, though, they can live more handsomely, for domestic service in England is cheap and abundant and well-ordered. Yet on the other hand they cannot live so comfortably, nor, taking the prevalence of rheumatism into account, so wholesomely. There are no furnaces in these very personable houses; steam heat is undreamt of, and the grates which are in every room and are not of ignoble size, scarce suffice to keep the mercury above the early sixties of the thermometer's degrees. If you would have warm hands and feet you must go out-of-doors and walk them warm. It is not a bad plan, and if you can happen on a little sunshine out-of-doors, it is far better than to sit cowering over the grate, which has enough to do in keeping itself warm.

One could easily exaggerate the sum of sunshine at Folkestone, and yet I do not feel that I have got quite enough of it into my picture. It was not much

THE SHELTER UNDER THE LEAS

obscured by fog during our stay; but there were clouds that came and went, but came more than they went. One night there was absolute fog, which blew in from the sea in drifts showing almost like snow in the electric lamps; and at momently intervals the siren horn at the pier lowed like some unhappy cow, crazed for her wandering calf, and far, far out from the blind deep, the Boulogne boat bellowed its plaintive response. But there was, at other times, sunshine quite as absolute. Our last Sunday at Folkestone was one of such sunshine, and all the morning long the sky was blue, blue as I had fancied it could be blue only in America or in Italy. Besides this there remains the sense of much absolute sunshine from our first Sunday morning, when we walked along under the Leas toward Sandgate as far as to the Elizabethan castle on the shore. We found it doubly shut because it was Sunday and because it was not yet Whit-Monday, until which feast of the church it would not be opened. It is only after serious trouble with the almanac that the essentially dissenting American discovers the date of these church feasts which are confidently given in public announcements in England, as clearly fixing this or that day of the month; but we were sure we should not be there after Whit-Monday, and we made what we could of the outside of the castle, and did not suffer our exclusion to embitter us. Nothing could have embittered us that Sunday morning as we strolled along that pleasant way, with the sea on one side and the seaside cottages on the other, and occasionally pressing between us and the beach. Their presence so close to the water spoke well for the mildness of the winter, and for the winds of all seasons. On any New England coast they would have frozen up and blown away; but here they stood safe among their laurels, with their little vegetable-gardens beside them; and the birds, which sang among their budding trees, probably never left off singing the year round, except in some extraordinary stress of weather, or when occupied in plucking up the sprouting pease by the roots and eating the seed-pease. To prevent their ravage, and to restrict them to their business of singing, the rows of young pease were netted with a somewhat coarser mesh than that used in New Jersey to exclude the mosquitoes, but whether it was effectual or not, I do not know.

A SUNNY AFTERNOON

The sun shone impartially upon the birds and upon us, so that an overcoat became oppressive, and the climb back to the Leas by the steep hillside paths impossible. If it had not been for the elders reading newspapers, and the lovers reading each other's thoughts on all the benches, it might have been managed; but as it was we climbed down after climbing halfway up, and retraced our steps towards Sandgate, where we took a fly for the drive back to Folkestone. Our fly driver (it is not the slang it sounds) said there would be time within the hour we bargained for to go round through the camp at Shorncliffe, and we providentially arrived on the parade-ground while the band was still playing to a crowd of the masses who love military music everywhere, and especially hang tranced upon it in England. If I had some particularly vivid pots of paint instead of the cold black and white of ink and paper, I might give some notion in color of the way the red-coated soldiery flamed out of the intense green of the plain, and how the strong purples and greens and yellows and blues of the women's dresses gave the effect of some gaudy garden all round them. American women say that English women of all classes wear, and can wear, colors in this soft atmosphere that would shriek aloud in our clear, pitiless air. When the band ceased playing, and the deity had been musically invoked once more to save the King, and each soldier had paired off and strolled away with the maid who had been simple-heartedly waiting for him, it was as gigantic tulips and hollyhocks walking.

The camp at Shorncliffe is for ten thousand soldiers, I believe, of all arms, who are housed in a town of brick and wooden cottages, with streets and lanes of its own; and many of the officers have their quarters there as well as the men. Once these officers' families lived in Folkestone, and something of the decay of its prosperity is laid to their removal, which was caused by its increasing expensiveness. Probably none of them dwell in the tents which our drive brought us in sight of, beyond the barrack-town pitched in the middle of a green, green field, and lying like heaps of snow on the rank verdure. The old church of Cheriton, with a cloud of immemorial associations with Briton, and Roman, and Saxon, and Dane, and Norman, rose gray in the background of the picture, and beyond the potential goriness of the tented field was a sheep-pasture, full of the white innocence of the young lambs, which, after probably bounding as to the tabor's sound from the martial bands, were stretched beside their dams in motionless exhaustion from their play.

It was all very strange, that sunshiny Sunday morning, for the soldiers who lounged near the gate of their camp looked not less kind than the types of harmlessness beyond the hedge, and these emblems of their inherited faith could hardly have been less conscious of the monstrous grotesqueness of their trade of murder than the poor soldiers themselves. It is all a weary and disheartening puzzle, which the world seems as far as ever from guessing out. It may be that the best way is to give it up, but one thinks of it helplessly in the beauty of this gentle, smiling England, whose history has been written in blood from the earliest records of the heathen time to the latest Christian yesterday. Her battle-fields have merely been transferred beyond seas, but are still English battle-fields.

What strikes the American constantly in England is the homogeneousness of the people. We have the foreigner so much with us that we miss him when we come to England. When I take my walks in Central Park I am likely to hear any other tongue oftener than English, to hear Yiddish, or Russian, or Polish, or Norwegian, or French, or Italian, or Spanish; but when I take my walks on the Leas at Folkestone, scarcely more than an hour from the polyglot continent of Europe, I hear all but nothing but English. Twice, indeed, I heard a few French people speaking together; once I heard a German Jew telling a story of a dog, which he found so funny that he almost burst with laughter; and once again, in the lower town, there came to me from the open door of an eating-house the sound of Italian. But nearly everywhere else was English, and the signs of *Ici on parle Français* were almost as infrequent in the shops. As we very well know, if we know English history even so little as I do, it used to be very different. Many of those tongues in their earlier modifications used to be heard in and about Folkestone, if not simultane-

ously, then successively. The Normans came speaking their French of Stratford-atte-Bowe, the Danes their Scandinavian, the Saxons their Low German, and the Italians their vernacular Latin, the supposed sister tongue and not mother tongue of their modern parlance. If it was not the Latin which Cæsar wrote, it was the Latin which Cæsar heard in his camp on the downs back of Folkestone, if that was really his camp and not some later Roman general's. The words, though not the accents, of all these foreigners are still heard in the British speech there; the only words which are almost silent in it are those of the first British, who have given their name to the empire of the English; and that seems very strange, and perhaps a little sad. But it cannot be helped; we ourselves have kept very few Algonquian vocables; we ourselves speak the language of the Roman, the Saxon, the Dane, the Norman, in the mixture imported from England in the seventeenth century and adapted to our needs by the newspapers in the nineteenth. We may get back to a likeness of the Latin which the hills back of Folkestone reechoed two thousand years ago, if the Italians keep coming in at the present rate, but it is not probable; and I thought it advisable, for the sake of a realizing sense of Italian authority in our civilization, to pay a visit to Cæsar's camp, one afternoon of the few when the sun shone. This took us up a road so long and steep that it seemed only a due humanity to get out and join our fly driver in sparing his panting and perspiring horse; and the walk gave us a better chance of enjoying the entrancing prospects opening seaward from every break in the downs. Valleys green with soft grass and gray with pasturing sheep dipped in soft slopes to the Folkestone levels; and against the horizon shimmered the Channel, flecked with sail of every type, and stained with the smoke of steamers, including the Folkestone boat full of passengers not, let us hope, so seasick as usual.

Part of our errand was to see the Holy Well at which the Canterbury pilgrims used to turn aside and drink, and to feel that we were going a little way with them. But we were so lost in pity for our horse and joy in the landscape that we forgot to demand the well and its associations from our driver till we had remounted to our places, and turned aside on the way to Cæsar's camp. Then he could only point with his whip to a hollow we had passed unconscious, and say the Holy Well was there.

"But where, where," we cried, "is the pilgrim road to Canterbury?"

Then he faced about and pointed in another direction to a long, white highway, curving out of sight, and there it was, just as Chaucer saw it full of pilgrims five hundred years ago, or as Blake and Stothard saw it four hundred years after Chaucer. I myself always preferred Stothard's vision of those pious folk to Blake's; but that is a matter of taste. Both visions of them were like, and they both now did their best to re-people the empty white highway for us. I do not say they altogether failed; these things are mostly subjective, and it is hard to tell, especially if you want others to believe your report. But we were only subordinately concerned with the Canterbury pilgrims; we were mainly in a high Roman mood, and Cæsar's camp was our goal.

The antiquity of England is always stunning, and it is with the breath always pretty well knocked out of your body that you constantly come upon evidences of the Roman occupation, especially in the old, old churches which abound far beyond the fondest fancy of the home-keeping American mind. You can only stand before those built-in Roman brick, on those bricked-up Roman arches, and gasp out below the verger's hearing: "Four hundred years! They held Britain four hundred years! Four times as long as we have lived since we broke with her!"

But observe, gentle and trusting reader, that the Roman remains are of the latest years of the Roman domination, and very long after they had converted and enslaved the stubbornest of the Britons, while at Cæsar's camp, if it was his, we stood before the ghosts of the earliest invaders, of those legionaries who were there before Christ was in the world, and who have left no trace of their presence except this fortress-grave. Very like a grave it was, with huge, long barrows of heavily sodded earth made in scooping out the bed of the moat, and building upon some imaginable inner structure of stone or brickwork. They fronted the landward side of a down which seawardly was of too sharp an ascent to need their defence. Rising one above another, they formed good resting-places for the transatlantic tourists whom the Roman engineers could hardly have had in mind, and a good playground for some children who were there with their mothers and nurses. A kindly-looking young Englishman had stretched himself out on one of them, and as we approached from below was in the act of lighting his pipe. It was all, after those two thousand years, very peaceable, and there were so many larks singing in the meadow that it seemed as if there must be one of them in every tuft of grass. The place was profusely starred over with the small English daisies, which they are not obliged to take up in pots, for the winter here, and which seized the occasion to pass themselves off on me for white clover, till I found them out by their having no odor.

The effect was what forts and fields of fight always come to if you give them time enough; though few of the most famous can offer the traveller such a view of Folkestone and the sea as Cæsar's camp. We drove round into the town by a different road from that we came out by, and on the way I noted that there was a small brickmaking industry in the suburb, which could perhaps account both for the prosperity of Folkestone and for the overbuilding. Sadly we saw the great numbers of houses that were to be let or sold, everywhere, and the well-wisher of the sympathetic town must fall back for comfort as to its future on the prevalence of what has been waiting to call itself the instructional industry. Schools for youth of both sexes abound, and one everywhere sees at the proper hours discreetly guarded processions of fresh-looking young English-looking girls, carrying their complexions out into the health-giving air of the Leas. As long as one could see them in their wholesome pink-cheeked blue-eyed innocence, one could hardly miss the fashion whose absence was a condition of one's being in Folkestone out of season.

WITH THE AFGHAN BOUNDARY COMMISSION

LASGIRD.

THE present condition of Central Asia, as well as of the countries around it, can scarcely be understood without giving some account of the Turkoman raids. For a long period of time this raiding system has gone on, but, owing to the out-of-the-way position of the region, the people of the West knew little or nothing of what was taking place. It is only lately that a few daring travellers have ventured, at great risk to themselves, into the Dasht-i-Turkoman, as the great plain of Central Asia is called, and revealed to us a slight knowledge of its present condition. Having gone with the Afghan Frontier Commission through Persia to the banks of the Heri-Rud and the Murghab, I thus passed over one of the favorite raiding grounds, and had the opportunity of seeing the results which it produced, and of realizing to a certain extent the appalling character of the system. The raiding of the Turkomans was essentially a slave-dealing system, founded on the assumption of a right of property in human flesh and blood. Men, women, and children were carried off to Khiva and Bokhara, thus placing the impassable desert between them and

their homes, so that escape was all but impossible—this security producing a corresponding value in the slave markets of these places.

These predatory excursions were known as "chapows" by the Persians, and as "alamans" by the Turkomans. The number of men engaged in one of them depended much on the character of the leader: if he had a previous reputation for success in such expeditions, large numbers would flock to him when a new raid was projected; at times as many as five or six thousand men would engage in one of these expeditions. Horses were put under a peculiar diet and training to fit them for the necessary endurance, for it must be understood that the Turkoman's horse formed the essential part of the raider, where long rides and sudden surprises were the main tactics of the game. As the Thugs of India converted their system of murder into a kind of worship, so the Ishans, or Mohammedan mollahs, gave a religious sanction to the foray by blessing it before starting. At first the "alaman" would move slowly across the desert; but as soon as the Persian frontier was passed, it made long and stealthy marches by unfrequented routes, avoiding all large towns, till the selected district was reached. Small parties were then detached; these in the dusk of the early dawn crept under the cover of hollows or rising ground toward villages, on which they came down with a lightning sweep, so as to catch the men or women at work in the fields, or by the surprise to seize the cattle before they could be driven in. Men, women, and children, as well as horses, cattle, and sheep, were all fish to the Turkomans' net, and whatever was taken they carried off to the main body of the alaman, who guarded the plunder while the detachments carried on the work. If a village could be taken, then every living thing in it became spoil; whatever the robber's horse could carry, or whatever could be forced to move on its own legs, was borne away. Young girls—if they were pretty—and children were looked upon as the most valuable prizes, as they could be sold to the highest advantage in the bazars of Khiva or Bokhara;

If not too much overburdened with spoil, the plundering would go on during the return march. When a successful expedition had been made, and each returned rich from robbery and crime, there was great rejoicing in the auls, or collections of kibitkas, which form the villages of Turkestan; the Ishans again came forth and uttered prayers of thanks to Allah for all the good things which had come to them.

Sir Peter Lumsden and the portion of the Afghan Boundary Commission which started from London had to pass through Persia, and we had not marched far from Tehran when indications of this raiding system began to appear. The capital of Persia is about 600 miles due west from the frontier on the Heri-Rud, and the raiders were in the habit of carrying their expeditions up to less than 100 miles of the seat of government. To realize this state of things we have to picture to ourselves the Highlanders regularly coming to Derby, as they did in 1745, or even nearer to London, and plun-

TOWER OF REFUGE.

it was also considered a lucky stroke when any one of wealth or rank was caught, a heavy ransom being expected for his release. We were told of one raid in which 130,000 sheep, goats, and other animals had been swept away; this large number has much the appearance of an exaggeration, but supposing we subtract a large discount from the figures—say twenty-five or even fifty per cent.—the sum will yet present a calamitous loss to the people who were despoiled. When the operations on the ground selected were completed, the alaman began its retreat, generally taking another route from that by which it came.

dering the whole region as they came and went, to give us an idea of the condition of Persia up to the present day, for it is only a couple of years since the raiding ceased. The Turkomans were not without daring, but this state of things must be looked upon not so much as an illustration of their character, but rather as showing the imbecility of the Persian government, which either permitted such things to take place or connived at them through its subordinates on the frontier. The people had to do the best they could to protect themselves. Villages, through insufficiency of numbers, could not oppose large bands of well-

GREAT HIGHWAY OF CENTRAL ASIA.

armed marauders; but strong walls could be constructed as a means of defense. Mud is the building material in Persia, and in a dry climate it fulfills every necessary requirement; we found the village walls were made of this, and often of great thickness, so that a breach could not be easily made. Through this there was only one small entrance, so low that a Turkoman on horseback could not pass through, which, had it been large, he might possibly have done when in chase of those flying for refuge, and the village might have been taken through this means. The door in many instances was of stone, so that it could not be destroyed by fire. The raiders never thought of laying siege in any way to a place. They made a sudden dash; if it failed, they went off to try the same process on the next village; hence all that the villagers required was refuge and safety from these momentary assaults.

We found a remarkable instance of a village with the necessary defensive conditions on our route; it is called Lasgird, and it is within 100 miles, to the eastward, of Tehran, thus illustrating how near to the capital protection was essential. In plan the outer wall was a circle, this being an exceptional feature; its antiquity may be presumed, as the marking out of the circular form is ascribed to *Las* or *Last*, a son of Noah—a character not generally known to Biblical students—*gird* having a meaning something like ring or girdle, being that which goes round or incloses. This circular wall may be about 20 or 30 feet thick, and it rises in a solid form to perhaps 30 or 40 feet; on this the houses are built in two irregular tiers all round. Perched at this height, the people were out of all danger, while the only entrance was closed by a massive granite door 45 by 37 inches, and about 7 inches thick, working on pivots, like the old stone doors found still existing in the Hauran. The central part of the inclosure was filled up with a honey-combed mass of houses which were used for the storage of grain, and for receiving the horses, cattle, sheep, etc. The means of communication round this strange structure was by a balcony formed of projecting trees, rudely trimmed, covered or interlaced with branches, and then laid over with mud, and without any external protecting railing. On this dangerous and rickety support we saw women, children, sheep, and goats moving about; the goats may have been quite at home, but what percentage of children tumbled down every year we did not learn: such accidents seemed to us—strangers—as something inevitable under the conditions. When a raid took place, all that could manage to get inside were safe; there was no intermediate position; it was necessary to be either in or out; to be inside was salvation, on the outside was destruction. Where there were hills or rising ground near the villages, towers were constructed, and men kept constant watch. When the cloud of dust was seen in the distance—a sure indication of horsemen in a dry climate—muskets were fired to give warning, beasts were driven into the village, and every one sought the protection of walls. In many cases the fields were too distant for those working in them to have time to run to the village, so towers of refuge had to be erected; these could either be entered by a ladder, which was drawn up afterward, or by a narrow opening, through which it would have been certain destruction for the pursuer to attempt to follow. The mills for grinding corn had to be placed wherever a stream of water could be found, and I noticed that there was a tower of refuge attached to each of them, and it was so placed that the miller could run up into it without having to go outside.

Such were the conditions under which agriculture had to be carried on. Commerce had also to struggle against the same difficulties. If the raiders got information of a rich caravan of merchandise or of pilgrims passing between Tehran and Meshed, they lay in wait for it at some convenient spot, where its capture became almost a certainty. To insure safety, caravans always went in large numbers, and an escort went with them, but merchants, mule-drivers, pilgrims, and escort were all impressed with such terror of the Turkomans that their powers of defense might be compared to that of sheep when the hungry wolves make an attack. A piece of artillery was often sent, which, like artillery in battle, might have carried a moral power along with it, but practically nothing could have been more useless. Its moral effect on those belonging to the caravan was that they looked upon it as something in the light of a talisman, which had the virtue of counteracting all the powers of evil; if the cry of an "ala-

man" was raised, the mob of pilgrims and merchants at once crowded round the gun as a place of security, and supposing the gunners had retained the necessary courage to have fired it—a most doubtful supposition under the circumstances—the effort would have been an impossibility.

At regular stations on the road, caravansaries exist for the accommodation of travellers; these are large structures, generally built of brick, and with a strong door which could be secured, and the Turkomans defied. These places could receive camels, horses, and all beasts of burden, as well as men and women; they are what might be called the "hotels" of the East, and in the season when the pilgrims visit "Meshed the Holy" those on this route become crowded with a varied mass of humanity, which presents a fine field of study to all who are interested in Eastern habits and customs. The journey from Tehran to Meshed occupies the most part of a month, and in the days of Turkoman alamans it was a time passed in constant terror and alarm; but the desire among Sheah Mohammedans to visit the tomb of the Imam Reza is so great that thousands of men, women, and children yearly risked all the difficulties and dangers of the route. It will be easily understood that commercial operations could not flourish under such opposing influences; the wonder is that any trade could have existed under such an order of things. Caravans with merchandise never ceased to pass; but business under such circumstances must have been of a very limited kind. We had on our way a tangible evidence of the amount of mercantile activity which goes on; this was the postman between Tehran and Meshed: he passed only once a week between these two places, and he could carry all the correspondence, not only of these two important cities, but also of the region between, which is over 500 miles—about the distance from London to Aberdeen—in the saddle-bags of the horse he rode, and he never seemed to be overburdened by his load.

The road we travelled on eastward from Tehran is an ancient one, and in addition to the interest it presented to us in connection with the raiding system, it had historical associations which belong to a far past date. From the earliest times it must have been the great highway of Central Asia. The Dasht-i-Kuvir, or Great

PENJDEH.

Salt Desert, comes close up to it on the south, and the Elburz range is on the northern side. The road passes along close to the base of the hills, thus avoiding them; and as the desert on the other side is impassable, this road is almost the only line of communication between east and west through Persia. By this route Alexander pushed his conquests to Bactria and India; in the opposite direction the hordes of Genghiz-Khan brought death and devastation westward. Timour-Lung must have trodden over the same ground. At a later date the cruel Nadir Shah marched his army on this line when he invaded India and slaughtered the inhabitants of Delhi. The road led to "far Cathay," and Marco Polo must have made its acquaintance in his travels. It was from the earliest times the route of commerce as well as of conquest, and caravans bearing the productions of India, China, and the far East have for many long ages toiled along this dusty way.

Meshed is only about 100 miles from what used to be the Turkoman frontier. It was rather a surprise to find it such a large and important city in such near proximity to the home of the terrible raiders, but, as already explained, these scourges never attacked large towns; hence Meshed enjoyed a condition of safety. It is the capital of Khorassan; the Governor-General of that province resides there, and he has always a body of troops at his disposal. The great importance of

Meshed results from the tomb of the Imam Reza being within its walls. Thousands of Sheah pilgrims come every year to worship at this shrine. The rich spend money, and the poor are fed at the expense of the saint, who, although dead nearly a thousand years ago, is enormously wealthy. He possesses villages and lands in every part of Persia, the revenue from which amounts to a large sum every year.

Mirza Abdul Wahab Khan, the Governor-General of Khorassan, received the Afghan Frontier Commission with much ceremony on its arrival at Meshed. The istikhbal, or procession of welcome, met Sir Peter Lumsden a mile or so outside of the city, bringing carriages with it, in which the members of the Commission were driven to a camp of magnificent tents pitched in a garden. Here the chief cook of the Governor-General had a splendid breakfast in readiness, in which Persian pillaus and other dishes peculiar to the country appeared in such profusion that, although we all had appetites in good condition from the early morning march, our powers were not sufficient for the occasion, and dishes had to be removed untouched.

In the plain around Meshed there are villages with people living in them, but our first march eastward brought us to a region where they had long ceased to exist. Here and there ruined walls and mounds told that a population had lived upon the ground. This had been so long

PUL-I-KHISTI AND AK TAPA.

ago that the soil had returned to the condition of a jungle, and it was only by discovering the old irrigation channels—and time had left only the faintest traces of them in many parts—that we felt certain of former cultivation. Between Tehran and Meshed we had seen the thick walls of defense around each village, and the towers of refuge in the fields, all telling of danger and of the precarious conditions of life; men told us of the raids, and many who had been made prisoners and carried off recounted their experiences to us. To the eastward of Meshed, as we neared the once dreaded Turkoman country, the change was marked: we found that human beings had long ceased to live here, and the powers of destruction had been so great that a desert only was left. All the way to Sarakhs, and from that south along the Heri-Rud to Kuhsan, which is close to Herat, not a single village is to be seen. Herat is two-hundred miles from Sarakhs, and nearly the whole of that space is a desert. Scarcely a soul is met with over this large extent of ground. Once or twice we passed shepherds with their flocks, but it is only within the last year or so that they have ventured where the danger was once so great.

Our way eastward to Sarakhs was along the Keshef-Rud, a stream which flows into the Heri-Rud at Pul-i-Khatun. At Ak Durbund there is a wretched mud fort, in which we found about half a dozen scarecrows, which in Persia are supposed to be soldiers. Here the valley of the Keshef-Rud had become narrow, and there were towers on the hills, with walls between them, which had been intended to prevent the raiders from passing—a purpose in which success had not been attained.

After passing Ak Durbund we left the Keshef-Rud, and struck northeast on the direct line to Sarakhs; this soon brought us to high ground, from which we looked down on the Heri-Rud, and where I got the first glimpse of the great plain of Central Asia. Having for some weeks before been passing through the desolation caused by the inhuman forays of the Turkomans, every day bringing us to some further illustration of their doings or tale of their cruelties, here at last we could gaze down on the source from which they came. It recalled the ascent of Vesuvius after having seen the remains of Pompeii and Herculaneum. I was looking on the crater from which torrents of human lava had poured out, carrying ruin and death on their way. On a line eastward were the low undulations where the northern slopes of the Paropamisan range sank into the flat level of the great Dasht-i-Turkoman, the line of which extended away to the north as straight against the sky as the horizon of the sea. This straight line recalled the theory that the plain of Central Asia had been at some far remote period the basin of an inland ocean, when this, with the Caspian and the Euxine, was probably but one sheet of water. As we gazed upon the scene it was peaceful enough; not a living soul was to be seen, for a desert had been produced. While standing on this spot and thinking of what the past had been, and knowing the changes which had lately occurred, I began to realize the fact that the present time is a turning-point in relation to this portion of the earth's surface. A great and important chapter in the history of the human species had been closed; a new order of things was about to begin. This part of Asia had become a den of thieves and murderers; it had become all but separated from the rest of the world; civilization had been shut out; its people had grown to be a nation of Ishmaelites, their hand against every man, and every man's hand against them. Law and order were now to appear; safety for men and property would be the rule in the future; commerce, with

view as the ultimate aim of her extension into Central Asia, but for the accomplishment of this she deserves the gratitude of the whole civilized world. The occupation of Bokhara and Khiva extinguished the two great markets for the sale of slaves; after Geok Tepé was taken, and Merv was held by the Russians, the alamans became an impossibility. While the raiding system went on, all the countries round were demoralized, so that any development or progress was out of the question; but now they will have a chance of a settled condition, and their prosperity is certain. The only influence in that quarter that can be seen at present as likely to disturb the future is in the probable schemes of Russia in relation to Afghanistan and India, and perhaps the annexation of territory in Persia.

Sir Peter Lumsden arrived at Sarakhs on the 8th of November. He thus duly appeared at the place of meeting where the Russian Commission ought also to have been, according to the arrangement. We made a halt there of a couple of days. Our camp was at New Sarakhs, which is on the Persian frontier, the Heri-Rud being the boundary line. At the time of our visit the bed of the river was dry. It is a peculiarity of many of the streams hereabouts that in places the water sinks below the surface during the dry season, and comes up again beyond. The Heri-

OLD SARAKHS.

all its train of what is new and progressive, would soon take the place of war and man-stealing; and better conditions would result, not only for those who had suffered, but also for those who had been the cause of the suffering.

The honor of suppressing this raiding system and all its manifold evils is due to Russia. She may have other objects in

Rud disappears about ten miles above Sarakhs, and when it re-appears, further on to the north, it is called the Tejend. In the spring, when the snow on the Koh-i-Baba begins to melt, the supply of water makes a continuous stream. Old Sarakhs is about a mile or so from the east bank of the river. New Sarakhs was constructed only a few years back by the

Persians. The work well illustrates the character of all things military among that people. Instead of making a place capable of resisting the modern means of attack, this fortress, which is within three-quarters of a mile from the boundary line, is formed of high mud walls—a primitive style of fortification which has existed in this part of the world from the earliest times, and the original type of which may be seen in the Assyrian sculptures. Old Sarakhs had been occupied by the Russians only about four or five months before our arrival, and the troops were in a small camp formed of kibitkas. General Komaroff, who is the head authority in the trans-Caspian province, had come on a visit, so I rode over to ask permission to make sketches of the old place. The general received me most graciously, and

which the Turkomans of to-day live. The only building left is an old tomb, called Ugle Baba, said to be the tomb of Abel. On the west of New Sarakhs there is a similar tomb, which tradition declares to be that of Cain. These are no doubt connected with another tradition that Adam had his garden at Sarakhs, and came up every morning from Serendib, or Ceylon, to work in it. As the Mohammedans have legendary stories about Adam with Ceylon and Adam's Peak there, this should, I think, be ascribed to them, but General Komaroff told me that there were a number of traditions associating Noah with Merv, and he believes in some early Jewish connection as the source from which these legends originated. These, with the Jewish origin of the Afghans, and a number of similar inquiries, must be left to the future investigations of archæologists.

On leaving Sarakhs we moved south along the western bank of the Heri - Rud, which brought us to Pul-i-Khatun: *pul* in Persian means "bridge," and *khatun* is "lady." It is supposed that the bridge at this place is as old as the period of Timour, and that it was built by one of the ladies of his family; it is constructed of brick, with six arches, and although much decayed, it would be still serviceable if

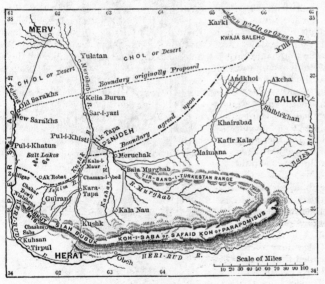

THE NEW RUSSIAN-AFGHAN FRONTIER.

sent a couple of Akhal Teké horsemen as my attendants. Colonel Alikhanoff was with the general. He most kindly invited me to pay him a visit at Merv, of which he is the Governor—an invitation which I greatly regret it was out of my power to accept at the moment, our stay being so short. All that remains of Old Sarakhs is a large mound, square in form, and covered with bricks. Scattered around it are portions of mud walls, and a number of rude huts made of reeds, in

the central arch were not broken. About thirty miles further south we could see the entrance to the Zulfigar Pass on the eastern side of the river; it is a grand gorge among bleak, rocky hills. Zulfigar was the name of Ali's sword; it means "the two-edged," and was given to him by Mohammed. The weapon seems to have been as wonderful as the "Excalibur" of Arthur, for the pass was produced by a stroke from it. Ali, who has been all but deified by the Sheahs, never could have been in his lifetime further east than the Euphrates Valley; still faith has created legends about him which extend as far as Ali Musjid in the Khyber. From Sarakhs to Herat is about 200 miles, and nearly the whole distance is now a desert; it is known as "the District of the 350 Ruined Villages." As far as Kuhsan, which is about sixty miles from Herat, we found no habitation, and with the exception of a shepherd here and there—for they now venture over the ground with their flocks—we scarcely saw a human being on our way. This desert condition has resulted from the raiding; the most of the ground might be as fertile as the Herat Valley is celebrated for being, and no doubt but it was so before the villages were destroyed and the people exterminated.

At Kuhsan we met the Indian camp and that portion of the Commission which had come with it. They had, under the charge of Colonel Ridgeway, made a remarkable march north through the deserts of Beluchistan and Seistan. With it was the Survey Department, which has done a large amount of good work, and given us accurate maps, which we had not before. It was now nearing the end of November, and winter-quarters for the camp had to be thought of. It was arranged that the main body of the camp should move eastward to the Murghab, while Sir Peter Lumsden, with a light camp, struck away in a northeast direction to visit Penjdeh. This took us across the district of Badghis, once a province of the old kingdom of Ariana, to the Kushk, the principal tributary of the Murghab. We descended that stream to Ak Tapa and Pul-i-Khisti, or "the bridge of bricks." It was here that the fight took place afterward between the Afghans and the Russians at the end of March; it is now generally spoken of as Penjdeh, but the old remains of that place are in reality about six miles to the south, on the Murghab. *Ak Tapa* means the "white mound," from a large heaped-up mass of earth which is there; these mounds are a peculiarity of the sites of old cities in this part of the world, and there is some difficulty in determining their original purpose. There is no doubt but they are old, and it has been suggested that they were the "high

SARIK TURKOMAN WOMAN.

places" on which the Guebres placed their fire altars. One theory is that they were tombs. The most probable explanation is that they were heaped up to form strong places of defense, and were the citadels of a primitive period. Scattered round these mounds are lower heaps and ridges marking the remains of the town. The building material in this part of the world was, as it is to-day, principally mud, or sun-dried brick, which is the same; and earth heaps are all that is now to be seen of the remains of cities. There are no ancient temples which tell their tales of the past, such as those which are to be seen in Greece, Egypt, or India. The structures were of dust, and into dust they have returned. Ak Tapa was the largest of the mounds which we saw, and the ground round it is filled with fragments of pottery, showing that a town had existed at some far back date. If the Tapa was a defensive work, its great size would show that the strategic importance of the place had been no new discovery on the part of the Russians; it derives this importance from the command it gives of the upper portion of the Murghab Valley as well as the Kushk, the line of the latter leading straight south upon Herat, and forming part of the direct road to that place from Merv. From the absence of water, no force of any size could move south except upon the Heri-Rud or the Murghab and the Kushk. When Russia chooses to attack Herat, she will now be able to utilize both lines, and march two armies upon that place.

We found the Sarik Turkomans in occupation of the Murghab Valley from near Ak Tapa all the way south to Meruchak, a distance of nearly thirty miles. They were living, not in houses, but in kibitkas, which are a kind of hut formed of wicker-work and pelts; these are movable, and are peculiar to the people of Turkestan, who are all more or less nomadic. The kibitka does not require a central pole like a tent, which allows of the fire-place being in the middle of the structure, and the smoke escapes by a hole in the top, the light being admitted by the same aperture. No tables or chairs are used; all sit on carpets in the Oriental fashion, and the making of these carpets is one of the occupations of the women. These articles, although produced by the most primitive means, are of the most beautiful kind. The only thing to be regretted about them in the present day is that bright colors of a fugitive kind have found their way into Central Asia from Europe, which have had a tendency to destroy the artistic harmony of design, and at the same time to deprive them of the old value they possessed from the permanency of their dyes. The raiding having been now entirely suppressed, the Sariks, who had been as much given to that as their neighbors, have taken to agriculture, and we found them busy with the plough, while groups were clearing out the old

irrigation channels, and bringing more ground under cultivation. We found a village or two of them in the Kushk Valley, in which they were extending their operations. I find that writers and speakers at home suppose that the region is a desert. This is only so far true at the present day from the land having been, from causes explained in this article, out of cultivation for many years. It is important to understand that the country need not necessarily be a desert; in former times it was not so; on the contrary, it was rich and fruitful, with a large population. About the middle of the third century B.C., Antiochus Theodorus, the grandson of Seleucus, was called "the Governor of the Thousand Cities of Bactria." It could not have been a desert at that period; Bactria itself, the modern Balkh, now a mass of shapeless mounds, was known as "the Mother of Cities." Merv was called "The Queen of the World." The Bundahis mentions a district which must have been in this part of the world, and states that "in the days of Yim a myriad towns and cities were erected on its pleasant and prosperous territory." The vast quantities of mounds, extending all the way from the Caspian to the base of the Hindu-Kush, attest to the truth of these historical declarations.

There could not have been in the past a more "pleasant and prosperous territory" than what the banks of the Murghab must have presented. The Bundahis speaks of the "Marv River" as "a glorious river in the East"; its water at the present day is clear and bright, of a delicate grayish-blue tint. It is a much longer stream than the Heri-Rud. Merv is wholly indebted to it for its fertility, and the river was known as the Mawr-i-ab, or water of Mawr or Merv. In this we have a much more probable etymology of its name than that usually given, which is explained as being from *murgh*, a "fowl," and *ab*, "water," this being evidently a modern Persian derivation. The valley south of Ak Tapa is what in Scotland would be called a "strath"; that is, the river flows through a flat ground between hills. In many places this level soil is three or four miles wide, and by means of canals the whole space can be cultivated. At Penjdeh—the word meaning "five villages" (this is modern Persian, the ancient name being lost)— the remains extend for miles, and are only known to the natives as "Kona Pendie," or old Penjdeh. Captain De Lassoe, one of the officers attached to the English Commission, discovered an extensive and very remarkable group of caves at this place, which were, in all probability, at one time a Buddhist vihara, or monastery. There were a large number of such establishments in Balkh, of which we have descriptions, in the seventh century; and there is every reason to suppose that they existed as far west as Persia. Meruchak is the next place which must have had an importance in the past. It is on the eastern bank of the river, and about twenty-two miles south of the present Penjdeh. The mounds here are very numerous, and the crumbling mud walls belonging to a later town of considerable extent are still in existence, showing that it must have had a large population at no far distant period. The piers of a well-built brick bridge are still standing, and close to them is a ford, by which we crossed the river—an operation which, from the depth of the river, was not without some danger. About eleven miles farther south is a place now known as Karaoul Khaneh, or the "guard-house." Here, again, the old name is lost, and we have nothing left to identify the mounds of an old town which exist at it. From Meruchak to about a mile or so south of Karaoul Khaneh there are no inhabitants; owing to this, the pheasants have increased in great numbers, and our party had splendid shooting, which, it was declared, the best preserves in England could not have exceeded. Another march brought us to Bala Murghab, where we took up our winter-quarters. We arrived there on the 12th of December, and remained till the 15th of February, a little over two months. It was not till the 2d of January that the severe winter came on. There was snow occasionally, but it did not lie long on the ground. The piercing cold blast which sweeps along over Turkestan when the thermometer is far below zero is called "the cimeter of Central Asia"—a name suggestive of a cutting wind.

The camp was moved to a place called Gulran, which was nearer to the Heri-Rud, and not so distant from Meshed and Herat, from which places supplies were drawn. As it appeared that everything connected with the boundary was uncertain, and the coming of the Russian Commissioners seemed as far off as ever, I determined to return home; so toward the end of February I recrossed the Heri-Rud, and came back by way of Meshed and Shahrud to Astrabad. At Bunder Gez, the port of Astrabad on the Caspian, there is a line of steamers, which brought me to Baku, and there I was again on the route by which our party travelled on the outward journey in September. The Caspian and the Black seas are connected by the railway from Batoum to Baku; from Batoum steamers run to Odessa. By this line of communication I returned to Europe, after an absence of about eight months.

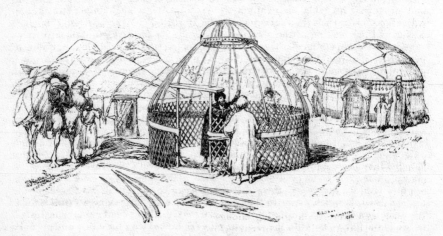

A KIBITKA.

THE LOTUS LAND OF THE PACIFIC

THE fierce noonday sun blazed upon the roofs of the straggling line of houses that fringes the beach and forms the township of Apia. In the harbor a couple of small trading-schooners lay idly at anchor. Farther out to sea the tiny canoe of a solitary fisherman, restlessly rising and falling just inside the line of breakers that marks the edge of the outer reef, was the only sign of life and motion visible through the hot, palpitating air. I sat on the veranda of the hotel, gazing idly seaward, thinking of the ten days

THE MAIL STEAMER.

yet to be endured ere the mail-steamer should call and take me back to civilization and cooler weather, and wondering how I should kill the time.

"Why don't you go on a *malanga*?"* said the owner of one of the trading-schooners, who had dropped in to refresh himself with a tepid brandy and soda. "Go and see something of the natives and native life. You'll enjoy the trip, and you'll find the people very different from the Samoans you see round about Apia."

The mere idea of any change from the deadly dulness of the town inspired me with energy, and having made a few inquiries, I engaged a young half-caste as interpreter and guide, and a boat and crew of three Samoans. The rest of the day was spent in fitting out with the necessary provisions and a goodly store of "trade," tobacco, cloth, etc., to be given as presents at the various stopping-places, and soon all was ready for an early start on the morrow.

Early next morning, a light favorable breeze springing up, we pushed off from the pier, and were soon gliding along through the calm shallows between reef

* Pleasure trip.

and shore, under an almost cloudless sky. High and dry upon the edge of the inner reef of the harbor lies the skeleton of the German war-ship *Adler*, the *Little Murderer*, as the natives with justice called her, cast there in the disastrous hurricane of 1889. We passed close under her stern, and saw myriads of brilliantly colored fishes darting in and out among the shallow pools on the ledge of rock upon which she lies, her gaunt frame-work, from which all the valuable metal and timbers have long ago been stripped, standing out against the sunny sky, a grim memento of man's impotence and the power of the angry sea.

Our way lay due west along the coast of the island of Upolu for about sixteen miles, and then across to Apolima, which is about four miles from the extreme western end of the island. It would be hard indeed to imagine a more pleasant journey than ours that day, travelling lazily along midway between the coast and the line of reef, past a succession of beautiful stretches of scenery, with here and there little villages nestling in among the waving palms and glorious tropical foliage that fringe the silvery sand. Groups of natives sat chatting and smoking among the trees or bathing in the crystal pools that mark the spot where some tiny stream empties itself into the sea. Behind lay the dark green mountain range of Upolu, rising some two thousand feet, and forming a beautiful background to the brighter coloring of the coast-line. On the other hand was the open sea, the great sullen-looking rollers breaking into a dazzling line of white along the reef, and subsiding into the calm clear lagoon through which we were sailing. Looking down into the water, one could see alternately patches of golden sand and miniature forests of

THE SKELETON OF THE "LITTLE MURDERER."

the wondrous submarine growths peculiar to these coral reefs—dark waving patches of rich green sea-weed, or masses of coral, fantastic in outline and of every shade of color, in and out of which brilliant-hued fish, blue, purple, golden—some with all the tints of the rainbow—dart here and there like the variegated denizens of some tropical forest.

Sometimes, as we rounded one of the countless points that jut out from the shore, we would come upon a merry party of laughing girls, knee-deep in the water, filling their baskets with dainty edible mussels and other kinds of shell-fish. From these damsels we never failed to get a smiling greeting, and after many interchanges of compliments, through the medium of Tialli, the half-caste boy (who proved to be a most accomplished orator, with an inexhaustible flow of flowery language), and when the girls had partaken, not without -many giggling protestations, of a mild brew of claret and water, we would pass on our way, they kissing their hands and calling after us "To-fa"* till we were out of hearing.

About three o'clock in the afternoon I landed, and having sent the boat on, took Tialli with me and sauntered along the road which skirts the beach and forms the main highway round the island. At intervals of every half-mile or so we passed through little villages, each with its neat white church and open thatched houses, where the women sat making mats or weaving garlands of flowers, and the men lay about smoking and talking, languidly brushing away the flies, and only looking up to give us a kindly greeting or an invitation to step in and rest and drink the friendly kava. As I was anxious to reach Apolima before night, these invitations had to be declined, with a promise, in most cases, that we would stop if possible on our return.

The spot from which we were to cross is an outlying trading-station belonging to a German firm with an utterly unpronounceable name. Here the gentleman in charge insisted on my halting for refreshment, and in his charming little cottage presently produced cool foaming lager-beer in genuine old stone tankards, the sight of which brought back to me memories of the "Drei Raben" at Dres-

*Good-by.

GATHERING MUSSELS.

den, the "Hofbrau Haus" at Munich, and many a pleasant "Gasthaus" by the banks of the Rhine. As we smoked and chatted and drank our lager, we were waited on by two pretty nut-brown maidens, each clad in a single flowing garment of softest muslin, while a chubby brown urchin stood behind each chair, with fan and flapper, to drive away the flies that lazily buzzed about the room.

The time sped so pleasantly that I had almost forgotten the four-mile row yet before us and the difficult passages between the reefs, which would be more safely made at daylight. But Tialli arrived to say that it was time to start, and that he had induced an old chief, a noted pilot, to make the passage with us. So bidding my kind host good-by, I went down to the boat, where our pilot, Lekéli, a handsome white-haired old gentleman, was already at the tiller.

By this time a heavy bank of clouds had begun to form away to the east; there was a choppy ripple on the now leaden-colored sea, and every indication of an approaching storm. Ere we had gone a mile, down came the rain in bucketfuls, drenching us to the skin, while the choppy ripple swelled into ugly white-capped rollers that rendered it difficult to find the passages and avoid the sunken rocks. Our ancient mariner evidently knew his business well, and we dodged about in and out of the breakers, making slow but steady progress, till, ere we were within a mile of our destination, darkness was upon us.

Before long, from the sound of waves breaking upon the shore, and from the indistinct outline of a black wall of rock dimly looming out of the darkness, I knew that we were skirting close to the side of the island. Suddenly there appeared to be a break in the huge mass of rock, a number of twinkling lights appeared, towards which, with a shout of warning to the rowers, Lekéli brought the boat's head sharp round. In a moment we appeared to sink deep down into the trough of an immense wave, while right behind us in the murky gloom a wall of water seemed about to fall upon and overwhelm us. Half a dozen quick strokes with the oars; for an instant the boat remained stationary ; the mass of water from behind came hissing and gurgling round us; we were lifted, poised high in air; then, at a yell from our helmsman, another half-dozen quick oarstrokes, and we were in smooth water within a few yards of the shore.

Soon dusky figures came hurrying down to the beach, and by the time we had grounded our boat the whole village had turned out to welcome us. After much chattering, and an explanation by Tialli, I was presented to the chief of the village, who promptly despatched men and girls to prepare the guest-house for our reception.

The Samoan house consists of one large oval-shaped apartment, from twenty-five to thirty-five feet long by twenty broad, formed by a thatched roof resembling an immense beehive, which is supported by two or three large posts in the centre, and a number of short posts placed round the side about four or five feet apart. In the spaces between these outer posts are cunningly contrived shutters made of plaited palm leaves, which are let down only in bad weather, the house ordinarily being open on all sides. The floor, which is raised five or six inches, is paved with smooth round pebbles, upon which are laid long strips of coarse cocoanut matting. Over these are placed here and there a finer species of mat, woven out of the fibre of the pandanus leaf; and both paving and matting, and, in fact, everything in the interior, is kept scrupulously clean. In many of the houses a number of cords stretched across from the rafters support mosquito-nets, which are rolled up in the daytime, and at night let down, so as to form a series of tents.

Under one of these I promptly retired to put on some dry clothing, while our hosts prepared a meal.

After the meal we sat and smoked, and a few visitors dropped in to welcome the stranger. I learned from the chief that times had sadly changed on the once happy island of Apolima. In 1888, during the late war, the island was shelled by that same *Adler* whose skeleton we passed on leaving Apia, many houses were burnt, and the larger number of their bread-fruit and banana trees, the main source of their food-supply, destroyed. This act of barbarity had forced the greater number of the inhabitants gradually to migrate to the larger islands, there being indeed barely sufficient food for the few who were left behind. Consequently, said my host, they had but sorry entertainment to offer me, and he sadly recalled the days when the little island was a very paradise, where want and care were unknown, and the coming of the stranger was the occasion for feasting and enjoyment. They made up, however, for the lack of material offerings by their courtesy and cheerful kindness, the girls in particular being full of fun, and evidently delighted with this break in the monotony of their lives.

By-and-by the visitors, one by one, retired to their houses, and at about ten o'clock, the rain by this time having ceased, and the moon coming out in all her splendor, the girls suggested a bath. So off we started, singing, laughing, and chattering like children just released from school, till down by the beach we came to a miniature fresh-water lagoon. Each girl as she reached the water's edge untwisted the *lava lava*, or linen waistcloth, that formed her only garment, and as it fell to her feet, dived into the pool. Having improvised a bathing-suit with a towel, I followed, and there in the moonlight we splashed about and dived and swam, the girls with their lithe, graceful figures, and dripping, gleaming locks, looking like a band of dusky waternymphs from some old pagan paradise. After the bath the girls ran races, and I was initiated into the mysteries of a game that was the Samoan equivalent of the old English kiss-in-the-ring. All went merrily, till the shouting and laughter brought an angry old gentleman on the scene, who informed us that it was quite time that all decent people, Samoan or otherwise, were asleep. Not altogether sorry to take the hint, I retired under my mosquito-nets, while the girls stretched themselves out on the mats around the house, and soon we were all asleep.

At daybreak next morning I was up and off to bathe in the surf, and then for the first time realized the danger of our landing of the night before. The little island is a horseshoe-shaped volcanic hill, about a mile in circumference, which rises sheer from the water, part of the precipitous wall of rock having in some bygone age been broken down by the molten lava rushing to the sea. This break in the rock, the open portion of the horseshoe, forms a tiny harbor, guarded by a black, ugly-looking reef, in which, as the tide was now running out, I could see a long narrow passage, through which we had come the night before; and truly it was a wondrous feat of skill to bring us safely through in the darkness, for the opening is in places only a few yards wide, and even in daytime and with a favorable tide there is danger in entering it with a large boat. Sometimes when a heavy sea is running the passage is closed for weeks, and the natives, thus cut off from the sea and from communication with the other islands, suffer great privation, as they depend largely upon the outside fishing for their food-supply.

The inner portion of the horseshoe, the crater of the volcano, is a gently sloping plateau, divided by a little stream, on either side of which are the fifteen or twenty houses that form the village. Here and there are cultivated patches of taro and the kava-plant, and a few bread-fruit and banana trees, while the steep sloping sides of the crater are covered with dense tropical undergrowth. The little plateau is aptly described by its name, *Apolima*, which means "the hollow of the hand."

After a dip in the surf, a light breakfast, and a stroll round the summit of the volcano, I decided to make for Manono, where I was sure of a great reception,

having a recommendation to the chief from a trader in Apia who is deservedly popular with the natives all through the group. So, having said good-by to our kind friends and distributed a good store of biscuits, tinned meats, tobacco, and cloth, with a few little knickknacks for the girls, we made a start. All the villagers came to the beach to see us off, and two sturdy fellows volunteered to help us

"'VAVÉ!' SCREAMS LEKÉLI."

over the barrier and through the passage. They waded out to the bar, one taking the bow and one the stern, and then, the men being ready at the oars, we put her head to the breakers and waited for the word. Suddenly an immense wave comes in, lapping and curling round the boat, and just covering the huge rock we have to cross. "Vavé!"* screams Lekéli, and with a shout our friends push us off, the keel grates heavily over the reef, and we plunge down into the seething, boiling caldron, and are in the narrow channel. The boys bend to the oars and we shoot ahead. In comes another tremendous roller, that buffets us back almost to the rocks; we are stationary an instant; and then, as the waves rush swirling out through the channel, away go the oars; we shoot ahead, and are clear of the reef and safe on the open sea. I had wanted to give our two kind helpers some tobacco, but in the excitement had neglected to do so, so I now held up a large foot-long twist of the peculiar black leaf that the Samoan dearly

* Quick!

loves. In an instant one of the men, a big, powerful fellow, jumped off into the breakers, which would assuredly have dashed any ordinary swimmer in pieces on the rocks, and diving through the waves as he met them, soon reached the boat, grabbed the tobacco, and with a quick "Fafetai lava,"* swam back with his prize, smiling and happy. A shout of "To-fa," a farewell wave from the watchers on the beach, then a few oar-strokes, and the wall of rock shuts them and the village from our sight; and before us lies beautiful Manono, the garden island of Samoa, and the nearest approach to the ideal lotus land to be found even in these Southern seas, where all nature is at its loveliest.

Manono is about three miles in circumference, is surrounded by the usual barrier-reef of coral, and fringed with a ribbon-like strip of white sand, from which the ground slopes up in gentle undulations to a tiny hill in the centre. Bananas, palms, cocoanut and breadfruit trees grow in profusion, while the flaming hibiscus and the trailing passion-flower give brilliant touches of color here and there, and the magnolia, lemon, wild orange, and a hundred aromatic shrubs and flowers steep the drowsy languorous air with perfume. Down among the ferns and mosses tiny springs bubble up from the cool depths and trickle to the sea, while here and there beneath the palms are shady bathing-pools hollowed out among the smooth round stones, with clean sandy bottoms and fairylike vine-trellised grottos that tempt one to plunge in and seek shelter from the heat of the tropical noonday.

We landed at a village on the eastern side of the island, and I was presented to the chief, Fakatta, a tall and handsome man of about forty, who received me with a stately courtesy and dignified bearing

* Many thanks.

"THE MERRIEST, SAUCIEST LITTLE MAID."

that in these degenerate days is seldom met with save in these happy islands. A large house was dedicated to my use, snowy mats were spread, messengers were sent about to announce the arrival of a visitor, and I was welcomed with an invitation to drink kava. On reaching the house I was presented to the chief's daughter, Faké, the "Taupo," or "Maid of the Village," of Manono, and her three attendant maidens, and was told that these damsels would take charge of me and see to my comfort and amusement during our stay.

The "Taupo" is always a young and good-looking girl, generally the daughter or adopted daughter of the chief. She is chosen as "Maid of the Village," and maintained by contributions levied from all the inhabitants, who supply her with food, clothing (the latter not a heavy or expensive item), and a large, well-built house, in which she is expected to dispense hospitality to all important visitors. Three or four attendants are always with her, whose duty it is not only to serve her, but to keep a watchful eye upon her and see that she never strays from the path of propriety, she being destined eventually to wed some great chief. On the ceremony taking place, the village to which the bridegroom belongs must make an offering of valuable mats, large quantities of food, and various kinds of property to the village of which she is the Maid; so that, apart from any considerations of abstract morality, she is looked upon as a valuable asset, and is guarded accordingly. Should she, however, yield to the fascinations of some handsome young *manaia*,* her hair is cropped short, she is stripped of her simple finery, and degraded to the post of attendant on the more prudent virgin who may be chosen as her successor. On the other hand, the young "blood" plumes himself

* Dandy.

on his conquest, and the more adventures of the kind he can boast of, the more highly he is considered. Thus, though the less culpable of the two, the woman has to make all the sacrifice and bear all the punishment; so that in this matter at least the savage is quite in touch with the humane sentiments of civilization.

Faké was a tall slight girl, with long wavy black hair, clear-cut features, and a pleasant though somewhat sedate expression. Sassa, one of her attendant maids, was plump and pleasing, the very picture of health and happiness; Epinessa, who was rather short and sturdy, with an air of bustling activity unusual in a Polynesian, was evidently the working partner of the firm; while

A SAMOAN STREAM.

prettiest of them all was laughing, bright-eyed Maua, the merriest, sauciest, and most mischievous little sixteen-year-old maid that ever poet sang or dreamed of. They soon had my things stowed away and everything in order, when a message came bidding us to the chief's house for the ceremony of the kava-drinking.

Here were assembled Falatta himself and a number of old men and chiefs, prominent among whom were the "talking-man," or public orator of the village, and an extraordinary-looking individual named Peisano, the chief's jester. They were all seated in a semicircle round the floor, cross-legged in that peculiar attitude only possible to the supple-jointed Polynesian. In the centre sat the two girls who were to prepare the kava. Having first carefully rinsed their mouths and washed their hands with water brought to them by an attendant, they proceeded

solemnly to chew pieces of the kava-root cut up and handed to them by one of the men. When the mass had been thoroughly masticated it was placed in a large four-legged wooden bowl, which stood between the girls. Water was poured upon it from the cocoanut shells always kept hanging in the cool shade of the thatch, and they proceeded to knead and squeeze it till all the juice was extracted. They then strained and skimmed it with long wisps of delicate pandanus fibre, till at last the bowl was filled with a liquor that in appearance was not unlike *café au lait*.

All being ready, one of the girls clapped her hands twice, while the other dipped a polished cocoanut - shell cup into the bowl and filled it to the brim. The "talking-man" now stood up and called "Ooatenah," which was the nearest approach a Samoan could make to the pronunciation of my name. The Maid of the Village took the cup, and advancing slowly, with bended head, to where I sat, bowed to the ground and handed it to me. Having first turned aside, and, in correct Samoan fashion, spilled a little on the threshold as a libation, I looked towards the chief, said, "Manuia,"* to which they all replied, "Manuia lava,"† drained the bowl, and handed it back to the Maid. The talking-man now called the name of Falatta, the cup was handed to the chief, and the same routine gone through; and so on until each man, in his turn, according to his rank or seniority, had been served. The whole ceremony, from the commence-

* Good health to you.
† Very good health to you.

ment of the preparation of the kava to the drinking of the last cupful, was conducted with the utmost solemnity, as the Samoan looks upon it almost as a religious function, the libation being always poured out as a propitiatory offering to the household gods. The method of preparation is apt, at first, to rather shock a European, but one soon grows accustomed to it, many white men becoming very fond of the liquor, which has a peculiar bitter flavor, and is extremely refreshing. A red-pepper pod is sometimes crushed and mixed with the kava to give it an extra "bite," and is, indeed, a great improvement. When taken in great quantities it is said to be intoxicating, but in all my travels through the islands the only drunkenness I have seen has been among the whites—the Samoan, though invariably a great eater, being in other respects extremely temperate.

The kava-bowl having been removed, the girls made us each a *sului*, or cigarette. A few tiny shreds of tobacco are first carefully dried with a piece of live charcoal, then rolled in a strip of dry banana leaf, lighted, and handed to each in turn. While we enjoyed our smoke, Tialii went round with the whiskey-flask and gave each a "wee drappie." The *kava papalagi** was pronounced a great success, and one stout old gentleman in the corner cast his eyes to heaven and rubbed his stomach with an air of such supreme beatitude that I felt bound to invite him to "wet the other eye," which he promptly did, in spite of much good-natured chaff from the others, who seemed to look upon this as rather a breach of etiquette.

In the mean time a feast had been prepared, and we now adjourned to the guest-house. Down the centre of the floor were laid long strips of green banana leaf, and on these were piled all sorts of edibles, conspicuous among which a couple of small roast pigs held the place of honor. Fowls, fish, bread-fruit, taro, yams, and bananas were mingled with the contributions from our store in the shape of biscuits, tinned meats, salmon, sardines, and jam, for which last the Polynesian has the true child's love. We all took our places on the mats, and the chief proceeded to chop the pigs into enormous portions, which were distributed among the guests. A wooden trough of clean

* White man's kava.

water was passed round, in which each one rinsed his hands, and then proceeded to fall to, though not until it was seen that the stranger had been served with the noblest portion; for the Samoan, though he dearly loves the pleasures of the table, is the personification of true hospitality. A clean, freshly cut breadfruit leaf served each man as a plate, fingers took the place of knives and forks, and soon the pile of good things began to disappear in wondrous fashion. Outside the house sleek, well-fed dogs prowled, on the lookout for the bone or scrap of meat which was thrown to them from time to time, and in a corner a group of children feasted on the portion that had been set aside for them. And surely nowhere out of fairyland are there such children as these happy, laughing, crowing little savages, with their chubby round bodies, smooth shining skins, and heads close shaven, save for the fantastic tufts of hair left growing, sometimes on the top and sometimes on the side of the skull. The girls sat round me, heaping my plate with the choicest morsels, one offering in her dainty fingers a piece of snow-white fish, another a slice of the soft and delicious inner pulp of the bread-fruit, while the laughing Maua held a freshly gathered cocoanut full of the cool milky liquor, that, tempered with a thimbleful of gin or brandy, makes a delightful drink. All sorts of strange delicacies were produced from various little bags made of breadfruit leaves, drawn together at the four corners and tied with pieces of fibre. There was raw "beche-de-mer" cut in pieces, and a delicious mixture called *pālo sāmi*, made of the young green tops of the taro-plant cooked in salt water and flavored with the soft creamlike kernel of the cocoanut, and many other artfully concocted dishes, fit to tickle the jaded palate of the most fastidious epicure. At length the feast came to an end, hands were again dipped into the trough of water, and after a smoke and chat the guests dispersed to their several houses for the siesta which invariably follows the Polynesian meal.

The hospitable Faké, ever thoughtful of my comfort, was anxious that I should experience what she called the "lomi lomi." A pile of soft mats was laid, and on it was placed one of their curious pillows, formed of a piece of bamboo about three feet long, which is raised about six

inches from the mat by a short pair of
legs placed at each end. I stretched myself out, one of the girls seating herself at
my head and one on either side of me.
The former deftly ran her fingers through
my hair and over my face and neck,

themselves on one side, and proceeded to
beat a sort of wooden drum, at the sound
of which the guests began to assemble.
Neither the chief nor the old men showed
themselves, as the *siva* is looked upon
with great disfavor by the missionaries,

KAVA-DRINKING.

and the elders doubt-
less thought it would
not be decorous of
them to be present,
though they gave me
to understand that
they had no objection
to the dance taking

while the others rubbed, kneaded, and
punched my back, chest, arms, and legs
with a skill and lightness of touch that
no professional "masseur" could imitate.
By-and-by I began to feel as if charged
with electricity, and glowed and tingled
from head to foot, till gradually a delicious drowsy feeling stole over me and I
dropped off to sleep.

The girls having announced that they
would give a *siva** that night, after a
short interval of rest, spent the remainder
of the afternoon weaving wreaths of flowers and dressing their hair. When night
came the guest-house was lighted with
two or three lamps placed upon the floor,
and a screen was arranged at the far end,
behind which the girls retired to make
their preparations. Four musicians seated

* Dance.

place. The house was soon filled with the
young men and girls, who sat chatting,
laughing, and smoking, and facing a clear
place left in the centre for the performers.

The musicians beat a sharp tattoo on
the drums, and, at a great round of applause and clapping of hands, the four
girls appear from behind the screen and
take their places in the open space. Their
handsome brown bodies glisten with cocoanut oil, their hair is decorated with
shells and white and scarlet flowers, and
each is clad in a very short *lava lava* of
about the size of a large pocket-handker-
chief. Over this is a fringed and tasselled girdle made of pandanus fibre and
dyed in brilliant colors, and each wears
round the neck and falling over the
breasts a wreath of strongly scented
flowers.

THE SIVA.

The lamps are now placed upon the edge of the mats, and the girls seat themselves in a line facing them. One begins singing in a shrill high-pitched voice, and the others in turn take up the strain, the four voices blending in a weird sort of harmony, to which the beating of the drums and the deep bass voices of the musicians make an effective accompaniment. As the girls sing, their bodies sway from side to side, the arms wave gracefully in perfect time, while the music, which commences slowly, gradually quickens, until arms, bodies, and voices are going at lightning speed; then they gradually slow down again, and the song dies away in a soft, tender whisper.

After more applause, and loud shouts of "Lelei! lelei!"* the girls stand up, the music starts again, and they begin to dance the real Samoan *siva*, the *anathema maranatha* of the missionary, and the chief delight of the pleasure-loving islander. The brown bodies, glistening in the fitful light, sway from the hips in dreamy languorous motion, while the arms are waved from side to side, quivering, rising, and falling like the rippling of water when the breeze kisses its surface; the air is heavy with the sensuous odor of the wreaths and the scented oil with which their bodies are anointed; the limpid brown eyes gleam with strange light, and are veiled again by the drooping lids. Again the music quickens, and is intermingled with quaint barbaric discords; the drums give forth a louder, harsher note, and the voluptuous swaying motion gives place to quick leaps high in the air, wild gestures, and tempestuous tossing of the limbs; the wreaths and girdles whirl and twist, the eyes that were so soft and dreamy now gleam and sparkle like burning coals; louder still sounds the shouting and the drums, quicker speeds the dance, till at length with one wild cry it ceases, and the girls sink on the mats, panting and quivering with excitement and exhaustion.

After an interval of rest, the four musicians come forward and perform a war-dance, while the girls take their places at the drums. The men wear loin-cloths, and are tattooed from the waist to the knee. They go through all sorts of dramatic gestures with imaginary spear and club, and give a realistic representation

* Good! good!

of savage warfare, the music gradually working them up to a state of frenzy, till they too desist from sheer exhaustion.

At this stage there were loud cries of "Peisano! Peisano!" and the jester came forward and took his place upon the mat. He was a long, lean, three-cornered-looking creature, with a small conical-shaped head, little twinkling reddish eyes, an enormous mouth, and extraordinarily elastic features, which he could twist and contort into every conceivable variety of expression. He produced from the folds of his loin-cloth a small mouth-organ, fitted it into the capacious chasm that seemed to stretch almost from ear to ear, and by blowing hard, and at the same time keeping up a vigorous lateral movement of the lower jaw, succeeded in producing a series of hideous sounds, not unlike an exaggerated form of the effect obtained by the small boy with a piece of tissue-paper and a comb. He kept time to this discord by waving his arms, snapping his fingers, slapping his chest and thighs, and jumping, writhing, and twisting in strange serpentlike contortions. These antics were received by the audience with yells of laughter and huge delight, they evidently regarding him as an artist of no ordinary ability. Finally he was greeted with a burst of applause, which he acknowledged with a stately bow, and then looking towards me, said, "Now Peisano go dead!"

From the enthusiasm aroused by this announcement I concluded that he was about to give us the gem of his *répertoire;* and certainly the performance which followed was, in its way, the most marvellous piece of acting I have ever seen. The musicians softly beat the drums and broke into a lugubrious chant, repeating over and over again, with every variety of mournful expression, a few words in their language, which were translated to me as: "Poor Peisano's going to die! Oh, poor Peisano!" Meanwhile Peisano himself stood bolt-upright on the mat, his arms hanging rigidly at his sides, his stomach drawn in and his ribs protruding, till, in the uncertain, fitful light, he seemed but a mass of skin and bone. The red eyes grew dull and fishlike, the cheeks were sunken in, and save for an occasional shiver from head to foot, a short gasp, and a motion with the mouth exactly like that of a fish

when taken from the water, he seemed lifeless. First one eyelid dropped, and then the other, the gasping grew almost imperceptible, till at last the head bent forward, the jaw dropped horribly upon the chest, and he was to all appearances a corpse. The dirgelike music had now died away to an awful whisper of "Poor Peisano's dead! Oh, poor Peisano!" Suddenly the corpse lifts an eyelid, gives a short gasp, and begins to show gradually increasing signs of returning animation, working up by degrees to a wild dance, in which arms and legs swing loosely here and there as though jerked by invisible wires, while the song has changed to a joyful shout of "Peisano's come to life!"

After this there was more singing and dancing, and the fun was kept up till far into the small hours. At last I was glad to turn into my mosquito-nets, but only to dream of a wild carnival, in which fierce warriors and laughing brown-eyed maidens were jostled by hideous skeletons with grinning, sightless skulls, to the music of a ghostly drummer playing with a pair of cross-bones on a coffin lid.

Next morning I was wakened by the sound of singing, and looking out from my tent, found the whole household on their knees. They were facing the east, where the first flush of dawn appeared behind Upolu, and all in unison were chanting a strange morning hymn. After the hymn one of the old men began a long, rambling prayer, during which Peisano looked over at me, winked, and proceeded for my amusement to put his mobile features through some of their lightning changes. Little Maua, happening to look up, at once burst into a fit of giggling, whereupon the old gentleman, checking for the moment his flood of eloquence, solemnly gave her a sounding whack over the head that sent her howling from the room. While this little passage of arms was taking place, the villain Peisano had cast his eyes heavenwards and assumed a seraphic and intensely devotional expression.

The days passed away, the happy hours speeding all too quickly. We swam in the surf, fished on the reef, sailed round the island in canoes, strolled among the perfume-laden trees, or lounged through the heat of the day in the cool shade of the houses, till the time came for me to return to Apia to catch the mail-steamer.

SPANISH VISTAS

THE LOST CITY.

I.

IT was of Spain's past and present that we were speaking, and "What," I asked, "have we given her in return for her discovery of our New World?"

"The sleeping-car and the street tramway," answered Velazquez, with justifiable pride.

He was right, for we had seen the first on the railroad, and the second skimming the streets of Madrid.

Still, the reward did not appear great, measured by the much that Spain's ventures in the Western hemisphere had cost her, and by the comparative desolation of her present. The devoted labors of Irving and Prescott, which Spaniards warmly appreciate, are more in the nature of an adequate return.

"It strikes me also," I ventured to add, "that we are rendering a service in kind. She discovered us, and now we are discovering her."

If one reflects how some of the once great and powerful places of the Peninsula, such as Toledo and Cordova, have sunk out of sight and perished to the modern world, this fancy applies with some truth to every sympathetic explorer of them. It had been all very well to imagine ourselves conversant with the country when we were in Madrid, and even an occasional slip in the language did not disturb that supposition. When I accidentally asked the chamber-maid to swallow a cup of chocolate instead of "bringing" it, owing to an unnecessary resemblance of two distinct words, and when my comrade, in attending to details of the laundry, was led by an imperfect dictionary to describe one article of wear as a *pintura de noche*, or "night scene," our confidence suffered only a momentary shock. But, after all, it was not until we reached Toledo that we really passed into a kind of forgotten existence, and knew what it was to be far beyond reach of any familiar word.

With the first plunge southward from the capital the reign of ruin begins—ruin

ENTRANCE TO TOLEDO.

and flies. The heat becomes intense; the air itself seems to be cooked through and through; the flies rejoice with a malicious joy, and the dry sandy hills, bearing nothing but tufts of blackened weeds, resemble large mounds of pepper and salt. Here and there in the valley is the skeleton of a stone or brick farm-house withering away, and perhaps near by a small round defensive hut, recalling times of disorder. Between the hills, however, are fields still prolific in rye, though wholly destitute of trees. Verdure re-asserts itself wherever there is the smallest water-course; and a curve of the river Tagus is sure to infold fruit orchards and melon vines, while the parched soil briefly revives and puts forth delightful shade trees. But although the river-fed lands around Toledo are rich in vegetation, the ancient city itself, with the Tagus slung around its base like a loop, rises on a sterile rock, and amid hills of bronze. So much are the brown and sun-imbued houses and the old fortified walls in keeping with the massy natural foundation that all seem reared together, the huge form of the Alcazar, or castle—where the Spanish national military academy is housed—towering like a second cliff in one corner of the round, irregularly clustered city. Our omnibus scaled the height by a road perfectly adapted for conducting to some dragon-stronghold of misty fable, and landed us in the Zocodover, the sole

open space of any magnitude in that tangle of thread-like streetlets, along which the houses range themselves with a semblance of order purely superficial. Most of Toledo is traversable only for men and donkeys. These latter carry immense double baskets across their backs, in which are transported provisions, bricks, coal, fowls, water, bread, crockery—everything, in short, down to the dirt occasionally scraped from the thoroughfares. I saw one peasant, rather advanced in years, helping himself up the steep rise of a street on the hill-side by means of a stout cane in one hand and the tail of his heavy-laden donkey grasped in the other. To make room for these useful beasts and their broad panniers, some of the houses are hollowed out at the corners, in one case the side wall being actually grooved a foot deep for a number of yards along an anxious turning. Otherwise the panniers would touch both sides of the way, and cause a blockade as obstinate as the animal itself.

Coming from the outer world into so strange a labyrinth, where there is no echo of rolling wheels, no rumble of traffic or manufacture, you find yourself in a city which may be said to be without a voice. Through a hush like this, history and tradition speak all the more powerfully. Toledo has been a favorite with the novelists. The Zocodover was the haunt of that typical rogue Lazarillo de Tormes; and Cervantes, oddly as it happens, connects the scene of *La ilustre Fregonde* with a shattered castle across the river, which by a coincidence has had its original name of San Servando corrupted into San Cervantes.

Never shall I forget our walk around the city walls that first afternoon in Toledo. A broad thoroughfare skirts the disused defenses on the south and west, running at first along the sheer descent to the river, and a beetling height against which houses, shops, and churches are crammed confusedly. I noticed one smithy with a wide dark mouth revealing the naked rock on which walls and roof abutted, and other houses into the faces of which had been wrought large granite projections of the hill. After this the way led through a gate of peculiar strength and shapeliness, carrying up arches of granite and red brick to a considerable height —a stout relic of the proud Moorish dominion so long maintained here; and then when we had rambled about a church of Santiago lower down, passing through some streets irregular as foot-paths, where over a neglected door stood a unique announcement of the owner's name—"I am Don Sanchez. 1792"—we came to the Visagra, the country gate. This menacing, double-towered portal is mediæval; so that a few steps had carried us from Mohammedan Alimaymon to the Emperor Charles V. Just outside of it again is the Alameda, the modern garden promenade, where the beauty and idleness of Toledo congregate on Sunday eves to the soft compulsion of strains from the military academical band. Thin runnels of water murmur along through the hedges and embowered trees, explaining by their presence how this refreshing pleasure-ground was conjured into being; for on the slope, a few feet below the green hedges, you still see the sun-parched soil just as it once spread over the whole area. The contrast suggests Eden blossoming on a crater-side.

At the open-air soirées of the Alameda may be seen excellent examples of Spanish beauty. The national type of woman appears here in good preservation, and not too much hampered by foreign airs. Doubtless one finds it too in Burgos and Madrid, and in fact everywhere; and the grace of the women in other places is rather fonder of setting itself off by a fan used for parasol purposes in the street than in Toledo. But on the *paseo* and *alameda* all Spanish ladies carry fans, and it is something marvellous to see how they manage them. Not for a moment is the subtle instrument at rest: it flutters, wavers idly, is opened and shut in the space of a second, falls to the side, and again rises to take its part in the conversation almost like a third person — all without effort, with merely a turn of the supple fingers or wrist, and contributing an added charm to the bearer. The type of face which beams with more or less similarity above every fan in Spain is difficult to describe, and at first difficult even to apprehend. One has heard so much about its beauty that

THE NARROW WAY.

in the beginning it seems to fall short; but gradually its spell seizes on the mind, becoming stronger and stronger. The tint varies from tawny rose or olive to white: ladies of higher caste, from their night life and rare exposure to the sun, acquire a deathly pallor, which is unfortunately too often imitated with powder. Chestnut or lighter hair is seen a good deal in the south and east, but deep black is the prevalent hue. And the eyes!—it is impossible to more than suggest the luminous, dreamy medium in which they swim, so large, dark, and vivid. But above all, there is combined with a certain child-like frankness a freedom and force, a quick mobility in the lines of the face, equalled only in American women. To these ele-

SINGING GIRL.

ments you must add a strong arching eyebrow and a pervading richness and fire of nature in the features, which it would be hard to parallel at all, especially when the whole is framed in the seductive folds of the black mantilla, like a drifting night cloud enhancing the sparkle of a star.

As we continued along the Camin de Marchan we looked down on one side over the fertile plain. The pale tones of the ripe harvest and dense green of trees contrasted with the rich brown and gray of the city, and dashes of red clay here and there. In a long field rose detached fragments of masonry, showing at different points the vast ground plan of the Roman Circus Maximus, with a burst of bright ochre sand in the midst of the stubble, while on the left hand we had an old Arab gate pierced with slits for arrows, and on the crest above that a nunnery; St. Sunday the Royal, followed by a line of palaces and convents half ruined in the Napoleonic campaign of 1812. Out in the plain was the roof of the sword factory, where "Toledo blades" are still forged and tempered for the Spanish army; although in the finer details of damascening and de-

sign nothing is produced beyond a small stock of show weapons and tiny ornamental trinkets for sale to tourists. Nor was this all; for a little further on, at the edge of the river, close to the Bridge of St. Martin and the Gate of Twelve Stones, the broken remains of an old Gothic palace sprawled the steep, lying open to heaven, and vacant as the dull eye-socket in some unsepulchred skull. Our stroll of a mile had carried us back to the second century before Christ, the path being strewn with relics of the Roman conquest, the Visigothic inroad, the Moorish ascendency, and the returning tide of Christian power. But the Jews, seeking refuge after the fall of Jerusalem, preceded all these, making a still deeper substratum in the marvellous chronicles of Toledo; and some of their later synagogues, exquisitely wrought in the Moorish manner, still stand in the Jewish quarter for the wonderment of pilgrim connoisseurs.

It was from a terrace of this old Gothic palace near the bridge that, according to legend, Don Roderick, the last of the Goths in Spain, saw Florinda, daughter of one Count Julian, bathing in the yellow Tagus under a four-arched tower, which still invades the flood, and goes by the name of the Bath of Florinda. From his passion for her, and their mutual error, the popular tale, with vigorous disregard of chronology, deduces the fall of Spain before the Berber armies; and as most old stories here receive an ecclesiastical tinge, this one relates how Florinda's sinful ghost continued to haunt the spot where we now stood until laid by a good friar with cross and benediction. The sharp fall of the bank looked at first glance to consist of ordinary earth and stones, but on closer scrutiny turned out to contain quantities of brick bits from the old forts and towers which one generation after another had built on the heights, and which had slowly mouldered into nullity. Even so the firm lines of history have fallen away and crumbled into romance, which sifts through the crannies of the whole withered old city. As a lady of my acquaintance graphically said, it seems as if ashes had been thrown over this ancient capital, covering it with a film of oblivion. The rocks, towers, churches, ruins, are just so much corporeal mythology—object lessons in fable. A little girl, becomingly neckerchiefed, wandered by us while we leaned dreaming above the river, and she was singing one of the wild little songs of the country, full of melancholy melody:

> "Fair Malaga, adios!
> Ah, land where I was born,
> Thou hadst mother-love for all,
> But for me step-mother's scorn!"

All unconscious of the monuments around in front of St. John of the Kings. a venerable church, formerly connected with a Franciscan monastery which the French burned. On the outer wall high up hangs a stern fringe of chains, placed there as votive tokens by released Christian captives in 1492; and there they have remained since America was discovered.

CLOISTER OF ST. JOHN OF THE KINGS.

her, she stopped when she saw that we had turned and were listening. Then we resumed our way, passing, I may literally say, as if in a trance up into the town again, where we presently found ourselves

To this church is attached a most beautiful cloister, calm with the solitude of nearly four hundred years. Around three sides the rich clustered columns, each with its figures of holy men supported un-

slants upon the pavement, falling between the leaves of aspiring vines that twine upward from the garden in the middle. There the rose-laurel blooms, and a rude fountain perpetually gurgles, hidden in thick greenery; and on the fourth side the wall is dismantled as the French bombardment left it. Seventy years have passed, and though the sculptured blocks for restoration have been got together, the vines grow over them, and no work has been done. We mounted the bell tower part way, with the custodian, and gained a gallery looking into the chapel, strangely adorned with regal shields and huge eagles in stone. On our way, under one part of the tower roof, we found a hen calmly strutting with her brood. "It was meant for celibacy," said the custodian,

der pointed canopies, mark the delicate Gothic arches, through which the sunlight

SPANISH SOLDIERS PLAYING DOMINOES.

"but times change, and you see that family life has established itself here after all."

I don't know whether there is anything particularly sacred about the hens of this district, but after seeing this one in the church tower I began to think there might be, especially as on the way home we discovered another imprisoned fowl disconsolately looking down at us from the topmost window of a venerable patrician residence.

II.

Its antiquities are not the queerest thing about Toledo. The sights of the day, the isolated existence of the inhabitants, are things peculiar. The very sports of the children reflect the prevailing influences. A favorite diversion with them is to parade in some dark hallway with slow step and droning chants, in imitation of church festivals; and in the street we found boys playing at *toros*. Some took off their coats to wave

WOMAN WITH BUNDLE.

as mantles before the bull, who hid around the corner until the proper time for his entry. The bull in this game, I noticed, had a nice sense of fair play, and would stop to argue points with his antagonists—something I should have been glad to see in the real arena. Once the old rock town accommodated two hundred thousand residents. Its contingent has now shrunk to twenty, yet it swarms with citizens, cadets, loafers, and beggars. Its tortuous wynds are full of wine-shops, vegetables, and children, all mixed up together. Superb old palaces, nevertheless, open off from them, frequently with spacious courts inside, shaded by trellised vines, and with pillars at the entrance topped by heavy stone balls, or doors studded with nails and moulded in rectangular patterns like inlay-work. One day we wandered through a sculptured gateway and entered a paved opening with a carved wood gallery running around the walls above. Orange-trees in tubs stood about, and a brewery was established in these palatial quarters. We ordered a bottle, but it was a long time in coming, and I noticed that the brewer stood

A NARROW STREET.

THE SERENADERS.

regarding us anxiously.   At last he drew
nearer, and asked, "Do you come from
Madrid?"
   "Yes."

"Ah, then," said he, in a disheartened
tone, "you won't like our beer."
   We encouraged him, however, and at
last he disappeared, sending us the beverage

diplomatically by another hand. He was too faint-spirited to witness the trial himself. Though called "The Delicious," the thin, sweet, gaseous liquid was certainly detestable; but in deference to the brewer's delicate conscientiousness we drank as much as possible, and then left with his wife some money and a weakly complimentary remark about the beer, which evidently came just in time to convince her that we were, after all, discriminating judges.

The people generally were very simple and good-natured, and in particular a young commercial traveller from Barcelona whom we met exerted himself to entertain us. The chief street was lined with awnings reaching to the curb-stone in front of the shops, and every public doorway was screened by a striped curtain. Pushing aside one of these, our new acquaintance introduced us to what seemed a dingy bar, but by a series of turnings opened out into a spacious concealed café —that of the Two Brothers—where we frequently repaired with him, to sip chiccory and cognac or play dominoes. On these occasions he kept the tally in pencil on the marble table, marking the side of himself and a friend with their initials, and heading ours "The Strangers." All travellers in Spain are described by natives as "Strangers" or "French," and the reputation for a pure Parisian accent which we acquired under these circumstances, though brief, was glorious. To the Two Brothers resorted many soldiers, shopkeepers, and well-to-do housewives during fixed hours of the afternoon and evening, but at other times it was as forsaken as Don Roderick's palace. Another place of amusement was the Grand Summer Theatre, lodged within the ragged walls of a large building which had been half torn down. Here we sat under the stars, luxuriating in the most expensive seats (at eight cents per head), surrounded by a full audience of exceedingly good aspect, including some Toledan ladies of great beauty, and listened to a *zarzuela*, or popular comic opera, in which the prompter took an almost too energetic part. The ticket collector came in among the chairs to take up everybody's coupons, with very much the air of being one of the family; for while performing his stern duty he smoked a short brier pipe, giving to the act an indescribable dignity which threw the whole business of the tickets into a proper sub-

ordination. In returning to our inn about midnight, we were attracted by the free cool sound of a guitar duet issuing from a dark street that rambled off somewhere like a worm track in old wood, and, pursuing the sound, we discovered by the aid of a match lighted for a cigarette two men standing in the obscure alley, and serenading a couple of ladies in a balcony, who positively laughed with pride at the attention. The men, it proved, had been hired by some admirer, and so our friend engaged them to perform for us at the hotel the following night.

The skill these thrummers of the guitar display is delicious, especially in the treble part, which is executed on a smaller species of the instrument, called a *mandura*. Our treble-player was blind in one eye,

A PLENTIFUL SUPPLY OF PLATES.

and with the carelessness of genius allowed his mouth to stay open, but managed always to keep a cigarette miraculously hanging in it; while his comrade, with a disconsolate expression, disdained to look at the strings on which his proud Castilian fingers were condemned to play a mere accompaniment. For two or three hours they rippled out those peculiar native airs which go so well with the muffled vibrations and mournful Oriental monotony of the guitar; but the bagman varied the concert by executing operatic pieces on a hair-comb covered with thin paper— a contrivance in which he took unfeigned delight. Some remonstrance against this uproar being made by other inmates of the hotel, our host silenced the complainants by cordially inviting them in. One

A PATIO IN TOLEDO.

large black-bearded guest, the exact reproduction of a stately ancient Roman, accepted the hospitality, and listened to that ridiculous piping of the comb with profound gravity and unmoved muscles, expressing neither approval nor dissatisfaction. But the white-aproned waiter, who, though unasked, hung spell-bound on the threshold, was, beyond question, deeply impressed. The relations of servants with employers are on a very democratic footing in Spain. We had an admirable butler at Madrid who used to join in the conversation at table whenever it interested him, and was always answered with good grace by the conversationists, who admitted him to their intellectual repast at the same moment that he was proffering them physical nutriment. These Toledan servitors of the Fonda de Lindo were still more informal. They used to take naps regularly twice a day in the hall, and could not get through serving dinner without an occasional cigarette between the courses. To save labor, they would place a pile of plates in front of each person, enough to hold the entire list of viands. That last phrase is a euphuism, however, for the meal each day consisted of the same meat served in three separate relays without vegetables, followed by fowl, an allowance of beans, and dessert. Even this they were not particular to give us on the hour. Famished beyond endurance one evening at eight o'clock, we went down stairs and found that not the first movement toward dinner had been made. The *mozos* (waiters) were smoking and gossiping in the street, and rather frowned upon our low-born desire for food, but we finally persuaded them to yield to it. After we had bought some tomatoes and made a salad at dinner, the management was put on its mettle, and improved slightly. Fish in this country is always brought on somewhere in the middle of dinner, like the German pudding, and our landlord astonished us by following the three courses of stewed veal with sardines fried in oil, and ambuscaded in a mass of boiled green peppers. After that we were contented.

The hotel guest, however, is on the whole regarded as a necessary evil, a nuisance tolerated only because some few of the finest race in the world can make money out of him. The landlord lived with his family on the ground-floor, and furnished little domestic tableaux as we passed in and out; but he never paid any attention to us, and even looked rather hurt at the intrusion of so many strangers into his hostelry.

THE TOILET—OPEN-AIR SOIRÉE ON THE ALAMEDA.

Nor did the high-born sewing-women who sat on the public stairs, and left only a narrow space for other people to ascend or descend by, consider it necessary to stir in the least for our convenience. The fonda had more of the old tavern or posada style about it than most hotels patronized by foreigners. The entrance door led immediately into a double court, where two or three yellow equipages stood, and from which the kitchen, store-rooms, and stable all branched off in some clandestine way. Above, at the eaves, these courts were covered with canvas awnings wrinkled in regular folds on iron rods—sheltering covers which remained drawn from the first flood of the morning sun until after five in the afternoon. Early and late I used to look down into the inner court, observing the men and women of the household as they dressed fish and silently wrung the necks of chickens, or sat talking a running stream of nothingness by the hour, for love of their own glib but uncouth voices. People of this province intone rather than talk: their sentences are set to distinct drawling tunes such as I never before encountered in ordinary speech, and their thick lisping of all sibilants, combined with the usual contralto of their voices, gives the language a sonorous burr, for which one soon acquires a liking. Sunday is the great hair-combing day in Toledo, if I may judge from the manner in which women carried on that soothing operation in their doorways and *patios*:

" Stone walls do not a prison make,
Nor iron bars a cage."

A TOLEDO PRIEST.

and in this inner court below my window one of the servants, sitting on a stone slab, enjoyed the double profit of sewing and of letting a companion manipulate her yard-long locks of jet, while others sat near fanning themselves and chattering. Another time a little girl, dark as an Indian, came there in the morning to wash a kerchief at the stone tank always brimming with dirty water; after which she executed, unsuspicious of my gaze, a singularly weird *pas seul*, a sort of shadow dance, on the pavement, and then vanished.

All the houses are roofed with heavy curved tiles, which fit together so as to let the air circulate under their hollow grooves, and a species of many-seeded grass sprouts out of these baked earth coverings, out of the ledges of old towers and belfries, and from the crevices of the great cathedral itself, like the downy hair on an old woman's cheek.

The view along almost any one of the ancient streets, which are always tilted by the hilly site, is wonderfully quaint in its irregularities. Every window is heavily grated with iron, from the top to the bottom story, even the openings high up in the cathedral spire being similarly guarded, until the whole place looks like a metropolis of prisons. In the stout doors, too, there are small openings or peep-holes, such as we had seen still in actual use at Madrid, the relics of an epoch when even to open to an unknown visitor might be dangerous. White, white, white the sunshine, and the walls of pink or yellow-brown, of pale green and blue, are sown with deep shadows and broken by big archways, often surmounted by rich knightly escutcheons. Balconies with tiled floors turning their colors down toward the sidewalk stud the fronts, and long curtains stream over them like cloaks fluttering in the breeze. At one point a peak-roofed tower rises above the rest of its house with sides open to the air and cool shadow within, where perhaps a woman sits and works behind a row of bright flowering plants.

Doves inhabited the fonda roof unmolested by the spiritless cats that, flat as paper, slept in the undulations of the tiles; for the Toledan cats and dogs are the most wretched of their kind. They get even less to eat than their human neighbors, which is saying a great deal. And beyond the territory of the doves my view extended to a slender bell spire at the end of the cathedral, poised in the bright air like a flower-stalk, with one bell seen through an interstice as if it were a blossom. At another point the main spire rose out of what might be called a rich thicket of Gothic work. Its tall thin shaft is encircled near the point with sharp radiating spikes of iron, doubtless intended to recall the crown of thorns, and in this sign of the Passion held forever aloft, three hundred feet above the ground, there is a penetrating pathos, a solemn beauty.

III.

The cathedral of Toledo, long the seat of the Spanish primate, stands in the first rank of cathedrals, and is invested with a ponderous gloom that has something almost savage about it. For six centuries art, ecclesiasticism, and royal power lavished their resources upon it, and its dusky chapels are loaded with precious gems and metals, tawdry though the style of their ornamentation often is. The huge pillars that divide its five naves rise with a peculiar inward curve, which gives them an elastic look of growth. They are the giant roots from which the rest has spread. Under the golden gratings and jasper steps of the high altar Cardinal Mendoza lies buried, with a number of the older Kings of Spain, in a grewsome sunless vault; but at the back of the altar there is contrived with theatrical effect a burst of white light from a window in the arched ceiling, around the pale radiance of which are assembled painted figures, gradually giving place to others in veritable relief, all sprawling, flying, falling down the wall inclosing the altar, as if one were suddenly permitted to see a swarm of saints and angels careering in a beam of real supernatural illumination. A private covered gallery leads above the street from the archbishop's palace into one side of the mighty edifice; and this, with the rambling, varied aspect of the exterior, in portions resembling a fortress, with a stone sentry-box on the roof, recalls the days of prelates who put themselves at the head of armies.

TOLEDO SERVITORS AT THE FOUNTAIN.

leading in war as in everything else. A spacious adjoining cloister, full of climbing ivy and figs, Spanish cypress, the smooth-trunked laurel-tree, and many other growths, all bathed in opulent sunshine, marks the site of an old Jewish market,

preserved in one of the chapels. A former inscription said to believers, "Use yourselves to kiss it for your much consolation," and their obedient lips have in time greatly worn down the stone. Later on, the church was used as a mosque by

A GROUP OF MENDICANTS.

which Archbishop Tenorio in 1389 incited a mob to burn in order that he might have room for this sacred garden. But the voices of children now ring out from the upper rooms of the cloister building, where the widows and orphans of cathedral servants are given free homes. Through this "cloister of the great church" it was that Cervantes says he hurried with the MS. of Cid Hamete Benengeli, containing Don Quixote's history, after he had bought it for half a real—just two cents and a half.

A temple of the barbaric and the barbarous, the cathedral dates from the thirteenth century; but it was preceded by one which was built to the Virgin in her lifetime, tradition says; and she came down from heaven to visit her shrine. The identical slab on which she alighted is still

the infidel conquerors, and when they were driven out it was pulled down to be replaced by the present huge and solemn structure. But by a compromise with the subjugated Moors, a Muzarabic mass (a seeming mixture of Mohammedan ritual with Christian worship) was ordained to be said in a particular chapel; and there it is recited still, every morning in the year. I attended this weird, half-Eastern ceremony, which was conducted with an extraordinary, incessant babble of rapid prayer from the priests in the stalls, precisely like the inarticulate hum one imagines in a mosque. On the floor below and in front of the altar steps was placed a richly draped chest, perhaps meant to represent the tomb of Mohammed in the Caaba, and around it stood lighted candles.

During the long and involved mass one of the younger priests, in appearance almost an imbecile, had the prayer he was to read pointed out for him by an altar-boy with what looked like a long knife-blade used for the purpose. Soon after an incense-bearing acolyte nudged him energetically to let him know that his turn had now come. This was the only evidence I could discover of any progress in knowledge or goodness resulting from the Muzarabic mass.

At one time Toledo had, besides the cathedral, a hundred and ten churches. Traces of many of them are still seen in small arches rising from the midst of house-tops, with a bell swung in the opening; but the most have fallen into disuse, and the greatest era of the hierarchy has passed. The great priests have also passed, and those who now dwell here offer to the most unprejudiced eye a dreary succession of bloated bodies and brutish faces. Sermons are never read in the gorgeous cathedral pulpits, and the Church, as even an ardent Catholic assured me, seems, at least locally, dead. The priests and the prosperous shop-keepers are almost the only beings in Toledo who look portly: the rest are thin, brown, wiry, and tall, with fine creases in their hard faces that appear to have been drilled there by the sand-blast process.

The women, however, even in the humbler class, preserve a fine, fresh animal health, which makes you wonder how they ever grow old, until you see some tottering creature who is little more than a mass of sinews and wrinkles held together by a skirt and a neckerchief—the *pañuelo* universal with her sex. At noon and evening the serving-women came out to the fountains, distributed here and there under groups of miniature locust-trees, to fetch water for their houses. They carried huge earthen jars, or *cantaros*, which they would lug off easily under one arm, in attitudes of inimitable grace.

If religious sway over temporal things has declined, Toledo still impresses one as little more than a big church founded on the rock, with room made for the money-changers' benches, and an unimaginable jumble of palaces once thronged with powerful courtiers and abundant in wealth, but at this day chiefly inhabited by persons of humble quality. Nightly there glows in the second story of a building on the Zocodover, where *autos-da-fe* used

to be held, a large arched shrine of the Virgin hung with mellow lamps, so that not even with departing daylight shall religious duty be put aside by the commonplace crowd shuffling through the plaza beneath. Everywhere in angles and turnings and archways one comes upon images and pictures fixed to the wall under a pointed roof made with two short boards, to draw a passing genuflection or incidental *ave* from any one who may be going by on an errand of business or—as more often occurs—laziness. Feast-days, too, are still ardently observed. With all this, somehow, the fact connects itself that the

A PROFESSIONAL BEGGAR.

populace are instinctive, free-born, insatiable beggars. The magnificently chased doorways of the cathedral festered with revolting specimens of human disease and degeneration, appealing for alms. Other more prosperous mendicants were regularly on hand for business every day at the "old stand" in some particular thoroughfare. I remember one especially whose whole capital was invested in a superior article of nervous complaint, which enabled him to balance himself between the wall and a crutch, and there oscillate spasmodically by the hour. In this he was entirely beyond competition, and cast into the shade those merely routine professionals who took the common line of bad eyes or uninterestingly motionless deformities. It used to depress them when he came on to the ground. Bright little children, even, in perfect health, would desist from their amusements and assail us, struck with the happy thought that they might possibly wheedle the "strangers" into some untimely generosity. There was one pretty girl of about ten years, who laughed outright at the thought of her own impudence, but stopped none the less for half an hour on her way to market (carrying a basket on her arm) in order to pester poor Velazquez while he was sketching, and begged him for money, first to get bread, and then shoes, and then anything she could think of.

A hand opened to receive money would be a highly suitable device for the municipal coat of arms.

My friend's irrepressible pencil, by-the-way, made him the centre of a crowd wherever he went. Grave business men came out of their shops to see what he was drawing; loungers made long and ingenious détours in order to obtain a good view of his labors; ragamuffins elbowed him, undismayed by energetic remarks in several languages; until finally he was moved to get up and display the contents of his pockets, inviting them even to read some letters he had with him. To this gentle satire they would sometimes yield. We fell a prey, however, to one silent youth of whom we once unguardedly asked a question. After that he considered himself permanently engaged to pilot us about. He would linger for hours near the fonda dinnerless, and, what was even more terrible, sleepless, so that he might fasten upon us the moment we should emerge. If he discovered our destination,

he would stride off mutely in advance, to impress on us the fact that we were under obligation to him; and when we found the place we wanted, he waited patiently until we had rewarded him with a half-cent. If we gratified him by asking him the way, he responded by silently stretching forth his arm and one long forefinger with a lordly gesture, still striding on; and he had a very superior Castilian sneering smile, which he put on when he looked around to see if we were following. He gradually became for us a sort of symbolic shadow of the town's vanished greatness; and from his mysterious way of coming into sight and haunting us in the most unexpected places, we gave him the name of "Ghost." Nevertheless, we baffled him at last. In the Street of the Christ of Light there is a small but exceedingly curious mosque, now converted into a church, so ancient in origin that some of the capitals in it are thought to show Visigothic work, so that it must have been a Christian church even before the Moorish invasion. Close by this we chanced upon a charming old *patio*, or court-yard, entered through a wooden gate, and by dexterously gliding in here and shutting the gate we exorcised "Ghost" for some time.

The broad red tiles of this *patio* contrasted well with its whitewashed arcade pillars, on which were embossed the royal arms of Castile; and the jutting roof of the house was supported on elaborate beams of old Spanish cedar cracked with age. It was sadly neglected. Flowers bloomed in the centre, but a pile of lumber littered one side; and the house was occupied by an old woman who was washing in the arcade, her tub being the half of a big terra-cotta jar laid on its side. She spread her linen out on the hot pavement to dry, and a sprightly neighbor coming in with a basket of clothes and a "Health to thee!" was invited to dry *her* wash on a low tile roof adjoining.

"Solitude" served at once as her name and to describe her surroundings. We made friends with her, the more easily because she was much interested in the sketch momently growing under my companion's touch.

"And *you* don't draw?" she inquired of me.

I answered apologetically, "No."

Having seen me glancing over a book, she added, as if to console me, and with emphasis, "But you can read!" To her

AN OLD PATIO.

mind that was a sister art and an equal one.

She went on to tell how her granddaughter had spent ten years in school, and at the end of that time was able to read. "But now she is forgetting it all.

She goes out and plays too much with the *muchachas*" (young girls).

This amiable grandmother also took us in to see her domicile, which proved to be a part of the old city wall, and had a fine view from its iron-barred window. She

51*

"MEN AND BOYS SLUMBER OUT-OF-DOORS EVEN IN THE HOT SUN."

declared vaguely that "a count" had formerly lived there; but it had more probably been the gate-captain's house, for close by was one of the fortified ports of the inner defenses. A store-room, in fact, which she kept full of pigeons and incredibly miscellaneous old iron, stood directly over the arched entrance, and there we saw the heavy beam and windlass which in by-gone ages had hoisted or let fall the spiked portcullis.

The majority of people in the hill city who can command a daily income of ten cents will do no work. Numbers of the inhabitants are always standing or leaning around drowsily, like animals who have been hired to personate men, and are getting tired of the job. Every act approaching labor must be done with long-drawn leisure. Men and boys slumber out-of-doors even in the hot sun, like dogs; after sitting meditatively against a wall for a while, one of them will tumble over on his nose—as if he were a statue undermined by time—and remain in motionless repose wherever he happens to strike. Business with the trading class itself is an incident, and resting is the essence of the mundane career.

Nevertheless, the place has fits of activity. When the mid-day siesta is over, there is a sudden show of doing something. Men begin to trot about with a springy, cat-like motion, acquired from always walking up and down hill, which, taken with their short loose blouses, dark skins, and roomy canvas slippers, gives them an astonishing likeness to Chinamen. The slip and scramble of mule hoofs and donkey hoofs are heard on the steep pavements, and two or three loud-voiced, lusty men, with bare arms, carrying a capacious tin can and a dipper, go roaring through the torrid streets, "Hor cha-ta!" Then the cathedral begins wildly pounding its bells, all out of tune, for vespers. The energy which has broken loose for a couple of hours is discovered to be a mistake, and another interval of relaxation sets in, lasting through the night, and until the glare of fiery daybreak, greeted by the shrill whistling of midst of the most sublime emotion aroused by the associations or grim beauty of Toledo, you are sure to be stopped short by some intolerable odor.

The primate city was endowed with enough of color and quaintness almost to

STREET SCENE WITH GOATS, TOLEDO.

the remorseless pet quail, sets the insect-like stir going again for a short time in the forenoon. Because of such apathy, and of a more than the usual Latin disregard for public decency, the streets and houses are allowed to become pestilential, and drainage is unknown. Enervating luxury of that sort did well enough for the Romans and Moors, but is literally below the level of Castilian ideas. In the compensate for this. We never tired of the graceful women walking the streets vestured in garments of barbaric tint and endlessly varied ornamentation, nor of the men in short breeches split at the bottom, who seemed to have splashed pots of vari-colored paint at hap-hazard over their clothes, and insisted upon balancing on their heads broad-brimmed, pointed hats like a combination of sieve and inverted funnel. There was a spark of excitement, again, in the random entry of a "guard of the country," mounted on his emblazoned donkey saddle, with a small arsenal in his waist sash, and a couple of guns slung behind on the beast's flanks, ready for marauders. Even now in remembrance the blots on Toledo fade, and I see its walls and towers throned grandly amid those hills that were mingled of white powder and fire at noontide, but near evening cooled themselves down to olive and russet citron, with burning rosy shadows resting in the depressions.

One of the first spectacles that presented itself to us will remain also one of the latest recollections. Between San Juan de los Reyes and the palace of Roderick we met unexpectedly a crowd of boys and girls, followed by a few men, all carrying lighted candles that glowed spectrally, for the sun was still half an hour high in the west. A stout priest, with white hair and a vinous complexion, had just gone down the street, and this motley group was following the same direction. Somewhat in advance walked a boy with a small black and white coffin held in place on his head by his upraised arms, as if it were a toy; and in the midst of the candle-bearers moved a light bier, like a basket-cradle, carried by girls, and containing the small waxen form of a dead child three or four years old, on whose impassive, colorless face the orange glow of approaching sunset fell, producing an effect natural yet incongruous. A scampering dog accompanied the mourners, if one may call them such, for they gave no token of being more impressed, more touched by emotion, than he. The cradle-bier swayed from side to side as if with a futile rockaby motion, until the bearers noticed how carelessly they were conveying it down the paved slope; and the members of the procession talked to each other with a singular indifference, or looked at anything which caught their random attention. As the little rabble disappeared through the Puerta del Cambron, with their long candles dimly flaming, and the solemn childish face in their midst, followed by the poor unconscious dog, it seemed to me that I beheld in allegory the departure from Toledo of that spirit of youth whose absence leaves it so old and worn.

A STRANGE FUNERAL.

A LITTLE JOURNEY IN JAVA

"TAKING it as a whole, and surveying it from every point of view, Java is probably the very finest and most interesting tropical island in the world."

It was a beautiful day in the late autumn when we read the above statement of Alfred Wallace, the celebrated English naturalist, who visited the Malay Archipelago over thirty years ago, and published an interesting volume of his experiences. Since then very little has been written or told of this gem of the Southern seas. Therefore it was with something of the feelings of an explorer that we resolved on deviating from the beaten track of tourist travel, and investigating for ourselves the charms of the island paradise.

This decision was reached only after long and earnest discussion on the shaded balcony of the Hong-Kong Hotel. A week later we were standing on the deck of the *Rosetta*, in Singapore Harbor.

"The Java steamer sails at nine," said the hotel runner, "and the wharf is some two or three miles distant."

It was then half past eight, and our baggage was still in the hold.

"I am very sorry," said our informant, "but our hotel has every comfort, and there is another steamer next week."

The outlook was gloomy; but we had gone too far to lose even the slightest chance. Hurrying on shore amid crowds of shouting and gesticulating coolies, whose naked bodies, smeared with oil, glistened in the sunlight, we made our way through a throng of eager gharri-wallers (cab-drivers), and placed our belongings on the nearest vehicle, a square box on four wheels, with a roof raised several inches above the body to allow a free circulation of air, and surrounded with slats in lieu of glass. With a last injunction to make haste, we settled back and drew a long breath, the first since leaving the steamer.

The day was warm and the reflection from the macadamized road was almost blinding. In the dazzling light everything seemed strange and unreal. Long lines of carts passed on either side, drawn by cream-colored or gray bullocks with mild eyes and gentle faces and huge flabby humps. Their drivers, stately Hindus in breech-cloth and snowy turban, or slender Malays with coppery skin and snaky eyes, gazed at us with Eastern indifference. What were we to minds busy with the Nirvana of forgetfulness? The loud shriek of a steam-whistle roused us from our meditation, and a modern dummy dashed by drawing after it a long train of open cars. As the road curved along the water-front we came now and then on clusters of rude huts thatched with palm leaves and supported on slender poles that raised them some three or four feet above the water that ebbed and flowed beneath. These were the homes of fishermen, and, with the ever-ready boat fastened beneath the entrance, had the merit at least of nearness to the field of labor.

Our sturdy little horses, hardly larger than ponies, breaking into a wild gallop, whirled us at last through a narrow gateway, and threading their way between piles of machinery and merchandise, stopped at the edge of the wharf, panting with exertion. It was considerably past the supposed hour of sailing; but the steamer was still there, and no one showed the slightest hurry or excitement. In answer to our eager questions the captain replied that the advertised hour of departure was twelve o'clock, but it would probably be an hour or two later before he could get off.

Everything was in confusion on the little *Cheribon*. Native passengers were constantly arriving in large numbers, and porters carrying heavy burdens were passing to and fro. Under the double awning of the quarter-deck an Indian juggler was displaying his skill. Squatting upon the deck, and with only the crudest appliances, he performed the old trick of the three cups and balls with marvellous dexterity. Under his nimble fingers the little spheres passed hither and thither as if enchanted, leaving the spectators completely bewildered. Then came the two pillars and the cut string, an old friend of every school-boy, but here revised and improved. Two carefully polished sticks, about half an inch in diameter and seven or eight inches in length, were shown pressed tightly together. Through the upper ends passed a stout string, which the conjurer drew back and forth to prove it was continuous. Inserting a

MOLENVLIET STREET, BATAVIA.

sharp knife between the sticks, he separated the upper ends, holding the lower firmly together. The string moved freely, as before, apparently passing down through the centre of the sticks and across at the joined ends, as in our form of the trick. But now, wonder of wonders, he separated the lower ends, and holding them some two or three inches apart, pulled first one string and then the other, the other moving in strict accord as though still connected.

The "Dutch Mail Steamer *Cheribon*" had an imposing title; but it was really a comical little side-wheeled craft of only four hundred and eighteen tons, making on an average ten miles an hour. One curious thing in the arrangement of the sleeping accommodations attracted our attention — the entire absence of upper sheets. Repeated calls and long-continued discussion at last softened the flinty heart of our "boy," and the desired article was produced. No one needs a blanket in this part of the world; but sheets are a luxury to which the extravagant Americans are still somewhat addicted.

Leaving Singapore late in the afternoon we did not reach our first landing-place, Riouw, until after six, when the short tropical twilight was over, and the darkness was so dense we could only see a dim outline of the shore. A large proa, heaped high with freight, had been waiting for us since early morning. Creeping slowly forward, propelled by clumsy oars in the shape of long poles with pieces of flat board fastened at the ends, it finally reached our side, and one of the Malays, climbing with the agility of a monkey, fastened a rope to the railing. The field of labor was illuminated by a single candle, and the sailors worked in Oriental fashion—as deliberately as if time were of no value whatever.

The life on the steamer was a curious and interesting study. Travelling in the saloon with us were a Dutchman and his wife and child. With the frank disregard of the conventionalities of life, which one soon learns in the tropics, they reduced their clothing to the lowest permissible limit. The wife appeared in skirt and waist, with bare feet thrust into heelless slippers, the child sported about in guileless freedom in a pair of sleeping drawers, and the husband lounged on deck in calico trousers and a white jacket.

PRIVATE HOUSE, BATAVIA.

On the forward deck were gathered a motley concourse of Chinese, Javanese, Malays, and half-breeds. Some of the half-breed girls, as white as ourselves, were remarkably pretty. The costumes were varied and picturesque. One little fellow, of some four or five summers, with limbs the color of rich chocolate, was tastefully attired in a chest-protector. This dress certainly has the advantage of economy and compactness. Most of the men wore calico trousers of brilliant and variegated patterns. Their close-fitting jackets are usually pink or green or some other strongly contrasting color. Each little family group selected its place on deck at starting, and camped there during the rest of the trip. Their provisions consisted chiefly of bananas and pineapples, with a moderate supply of rice. They are most inveterate gamblers, never missing an opportunity of indulging in their favorite pastime.

The Java Sea, which is nearly a thousand miles in length, is very shallow, and is sprinkled over with low-lying coral reefs, that are covered for the most part with a dense growth of palm-trees. Half-forgotten tales of Malay pirates thronged upon our minds, and we almost expected to see a long rakish craft dart out from the shadow of the palm groves and seize our defenseless bark. And, if these imaginary fears had proved real, the bold corsairs would have had a rich reward, for we were carrying $48,000 in specie to pay the wages of the tin-miners on the island of Banca. We saw several piratical-looking crafts with dark, blood-red sails and low, snakelike hulls; but they all proved to be harmless traders.

On the evening of the third day, five hundred miles from Singapore, we sighted the lights of Tandjong Priok, the port of Batavia. Early next morning we had passed the customs inspection, and, after a short ride on a narrow-gauge railroad, found ourselves in the streets of one of the prettiest cities we have ever visited. Batavia the beautiful, known throughout the East as the "gridiron," on account of the heat of its climate, and considered to be one of the most unhealthy towns in the world, is wonderfully attractive. The streets are wide and well kept, and are shaded by the most luxuriant tropical growth. The stores and private residences stand back from the road in the midst of ample grounds or compounds, beautifully adorned with flowers and foliage. This, of course, is in the Dutch quarter. The native town is more sordid; but in this favored land everything is picturesque.

The canals that form the centre of the principal streets in true Dutch fashion, in which the natives perform their morning ablutions as well as cleanse the family linen, have a very sluggish current; and this, in connection with the fact that the city is surrounded by marshes, is a sufficient explanation of its unhealthfulness. The general experience of the world holds true here. There is no Eden without its serpent.

The Hotel Nederlanden, a large, rambling, one-storied structure, with a spacious central court, is the last place in which one would expect to meet the decrees of fashion, and yet at the table d'hôte the ladies were dressed in a style that would have done credit to any European capital. These same ladies had appeared earlier in the day in a decidedly unconventional attire, and this rendered our surprise all the greater. They have learned to adapt themselves to the climate by keeping their heavier garments for the cool of evening. Even when making ceremonious calls in their carriages many adhere to the native costume — a white jacket and a calico sarong or skirt. The toes of their bare feet are thrust into gayly embroidered slippers that flap up and down as they walk. Girls of fifteen or sixteen appear on the veranda in the morning, and, indeed, until long past noon, in a sort of union costume such as young children sometimes wear with us when sleeping.

Notwithstanding these preparations for warm weather the heat is not excessive. During our stay the thermometer only once reached 88°, and even then it was easy to find a refreshing breeze. It must also be remembered that this was in the height of summer. The 22d of December is theoretically the turning-point of their warm season; but as a matter of fact the temperature is nearly the same all the year round. Lying about 450 miles south of the equator, Java enjoys a never-ending summer. This uniformity, to be sure, is somewhat enervating to the system; but for those having the requisite means and time there is a remedy within easy access in the districts remote from the sea. It would seem as if the climate of the interior of Java were as near perfection as it is possible to discover. At Bandong and Garoet, situated four thousand feet above the sea, we slept under blankets every night.

The island is very mountainous, over thirty-eight volcanic peaks dotting its surface, some of which rise to the height of ten or twelve thousand feet. There have been many terrific eruptions, destroying thousands of lives; but at present none of the volcanoes are in active operation.

In the mountainous regions the scenery is a never-ending source of delight, and the luxuriant vegetation gives softness

FARM HOUSE NEAR BUITENZORG.

and beauty to the lofty volcanic peaks. The volcano of Tangkoebanprahoe, near Bandong, is upward of eight thousand feet in height, and yet it is clothed to the very summit with dense and varied foliage. We saw ferns growing by the roadside that were fifteen or twenty feet in height. These gigantic plants are really trees with the same habit of growth as the smallest and most delicate ferns of our own clime. Interspersed among them were large forest trees in infinite variety, and huge parasitic vines that clung to trees hardly stouter than themselves. Here and there were wild flowers and flowering shrubs and long coarse grass with thick wiry leaves. The various palm and fruit trees had ceased at a lower altitude. The cinchona plantations flourished high on the mountain slopes. In fact, these trees seem to do best on high lands. Their red and green leaves and delicate white blossoms make a beautiful contrast to the deeper greens about them.

The cultivation of cinchona, or quinine, has become a large and profitable industry in Java since the partial failure of the coffee crop. A few years ago the trees producing the coffee for which the island has long been famous were badly injured by some mysterious disease, and their place is now being gradually taken by the Liberia coffee, which has a much larger and coarser berry.

The path to the summit of the volcano, made wide enough in the first place for a wagon road, had been so badly gullied by the heavy rains that it was hardly practicable for horses. In some places, where the way was particularly steep and the ruts alarmingly deep, the writer, who is somewhat of a novice in horsemanship, refused to trust his precious frame to anything less reliable than his own trusty legs. An ordinary mountain road was bad enough; but when it came to ascending a dry watercourse whose surface was covered with rough stones varying from six inches to a foot in diameter, he positively drew the line. In addition, the Javanese horses, which are usually small, like the people, are not apt to induce confidence. They are overworked and are frequently weak in the knees. The different portions of the harness have an unpleasant habit also of parting company at the most inconvenient time.

Near the summit we met two native hunters armed with slender blow-pipes, some four or five feet in length, and tiny darts of bamboo. These means of offence or defence were probably ample during the hours of daylight, but at night they would hardly suffice. Then the savage tiger grows bolder, and creeps forth in search of his favorite meal. Many villages on the west side of the island have been abandoned by their inhabitants on account of the nightly incursions of the tigers. The houses of a Javanese village offer but scanty protection against the assaults of the weather, and certainly none against the attacks of wild beasts. The thin walls, made of strips of bamboo pleated into mats, give way at a touch, and the doors, equally light in their construction, are easily forced.

As we advanced further inland the scenery became more and more attractive. The deep, sequestered valleys, with their wonderful growth of palms, bananas, coffee-trees, tea-plants, pineapples, and myriads of strange and interesting shrubs, are like visions of fairyland. Indeed, our daily experience seemed like a dream. The small, childlike people, with their quiet, deferential manner and scanty clothing, certainly belonged to a different realm from this commonplace world of ours. Java is the only country it has been our fortune to visit where the people sank down in the dust of the road-side as we passed. Men carrying heavy burdens on their shoulders turned on hearing the sound of wheels, and seeing who was coming, immediately squatted down in the most deferential manner. Sitting on your heels is the proper position to assume in this country in the presence of a superior.

Three hours by rail from Bandong is the little mountain village of Garoet. It is delightfully primitive and picturesque, and the rank growth of the tropic zone surrounds it in a fond embrace. Flowers bloom and palms wave on every side. In the neighboring fields a large crop of rice is raised, and the people look contented and prosperous. The average pay of a Javanese day-laborer is $2.40 a month, and out of this he pays ten cents to the government. Think of supporting a wife and family on less than eight cents a day! To be sure, the wife and older children assist in the work; but even then existence would be simply impossible were it not for the bounty of nature in a country where food is almost as cheap as air, and clothing is a luxury easily dispensed with.

DANCING GIRL

NATIONAL COSTUME

KADESH WOMAN

COCOA GATHERER

JAVANESE MUSICIANS.

JAVANESE TYPES.

In the country districts men and women alike usually wear only one article of clothing, a sort of petticoat, fastened tight around the waist by the men and just above the breast by the women. Some of the women adopt the style of the men as giving greater coolness and freedom. In the neighborhood of the towns they generally add an upper garment made somewhat in the style of a close-fitting nightgown, and either fastened in front or not, according to the taste of the wearer. The children in many cases omit even the chest-protector worn by our young fellow-traveller on the steamer. These little brown cherubs, with rounded bodies and well-formed limbs, look like bronze statues as they stand in the bright sunshine gazing curiously at the passing strangers.

About ten miles from Garoet is a small lake called Bagendit. The road, smooth and in good order, runs between rice-fields rising on either side in well-kept terraces. Men and women, standing up to their knees in mud, were turning up the rich black soil and preparing for the new crop. Gray or flesh-colored buffaloes, with hides like pig-skins, wallowed in the muddy water, looking up with languid, indifferent gaze as we rattled past. Sturdy brown children sported gayly among their four-footed companions in all the freedom and innocence of nature's own garb. We felt that we were nearer the great warm heart of Mother Earth than ever before.

As we neared the lake the villagers turned out in force to receive us. Ten or twelve hastened away to prepare the boats, while the remainder squatted down in silent respect. It was like the villages one reads of in the works of African explorers. The low, one-storied huts of light bamboo poles, enclosed with palm mats and thatched with leaves, seemed hardly

GARDEN OF THE GOVERNOR GENERAL, BUITENZORG.

BANYAN-TREES IN THE PARK, BUITENZORG.

capable of affording protection against the fierce rays of the sun. We made our way through the single street, followed at a respectful distance by a throng of curious but timid natives. At the water's edge we found the advance-guard busily engaged in constructing a most peculiar craft. Four long narrow canoes, each hollowed from the trunk of a large tree, were arranged side by side. On these was placed a sort of summer-house of light bamboo poles, roofed and floored with bamboo matting. In this floating house, which was about eight feet square, chairs were placed for our accommodation. Sitting at our ease we were paddled slowly out into the lake, our rowers squatting upon the bow and stern of each dugout, and propelling their cumbrous vessel with small spoon-shaped oars not unlike a child's sand-shovel. We forced our way through large fields of lily-pads, each leaf being two feet or more in diameter. The flowers, as large as a quart measure, were a beautiful pink and deliciously fragrant. The seeds, as we proved by actual experiment, make excellent eating, and are much prized by the natives.

The prevailing faith of the Javanese is Mohammedanism; but it does not seem to weigh very heavily upon them. In fact, not once during our sojourn did we witness the scene, so familiar in other Moslem countries, of a merchant praying at his shop door. The religion of Mohammed was introduced about the year 1478, replacing the old Brahminical faith, which had flourished from a period of unknown antiquity, and whose power is attested by the extensive remains of cities and temples that are scattered throughout the interior of the island. Under the Moslem rule the island steadily deteriorated, and it was not until it came into the possession of the Dutch that this downward movement was checked. Since that period, nearly three hundred years ago, its progress in wealth and population has been wonderfully rapid.

At the beginning of the present century there were about 3,500,000 inhabitants; in 1850 they had increased to 9,500,000; in 1865 the census showed 14,168,416, a remarkable increase; and in 1891 the population had reached 23,000,000. We should remember in this connection that the island of Java is only 600 miles long and from 60 to 120 wide.

YORK

> "York, York, for my monie,
> Of all the cities that ever I see,
> For merry pastime and companie,
> Except the city of London."

FIRST impressions are neither of antiquity nor of "merrie companie." Engine sheds, fitting shops, greasy mechanics in corduroy and fustian, shrieking locomotives, and a bedlam of nerve-shattering discords are furiously eloquent of a "pastime" that is not of bubbling gladness or riotous glee. Railroad corporations have taken the places of Percys and Nevilles; and if they don't own manors by the dozen, do own the principal lines of communication between the great manufacturing and commercial centres. The Northeastern owns or controls all the railways passing through the place, and employs several thousands of the inhabitants in constructing and repairing engines, trucks, and carriages. Without the walls all is of the nineteenth century; within them, minster towers, castled keeps, Norman spire, and Saxon turret warn us to expect an architectural medley of all the ages.

The railway station of York is said to be the largest in the United Kingdom. In precise terms, its measurement is said to be 800 by 234 feet. The Grand Central Depot of New York, though vastly superior in architectural effect, must yield to it in respect of size.

Opposite the parlor of the railway company's hotel are the grounds and museum of the Yorkshire Philosophical Society, the picturesque ruins of St. Mary's Abbey, and the famous Roman multangular tower. Beyond, the glorious Minster looms up in Gothic vastness and grayest gloom, and on the right appear the crenellated bar walls of the city. Past and present are incongruously blended. The present retains whatever is interesting and instructive of the past, but, whenever convenience requires, does not hesitate to convert Roman cemeteries into hurrying caravansaries, or dismal reminders of the 1832 cholera into festive flower gardens. This is just what it has done here. Bustling station and crowded hotel occupy the site of an old necropolis, in which, judging from the number of stone, lead, and wooden coffins that were dug up, not less than six thousand persons were sepultured.

With map of York—white walls, Clifford's Tower, colossal cathedral—imprinted on memory, and fortified by fresh relay of England's roast beef, we are now strong enough to begin circumambulation of said walls, or as much of them as will permit the pedestrian feat. Museum, etc., etc., can wait until after this walk around the Brigantine Jerusalem.

The plan of modern York and ancient Eburacum as drawn in Wellbeloved's invaluable work is not complete, such streets only being laid down as are connected with the discoveries of the Roman city and its suburbs. Our erudite local guide scoffs at the myth that Brutus,

STREET SCENE.

the size and splendor of ancient Eburacum, we cannot resist the conclusion that they can be understood only in the light of contemporary ideas. Remains of villas, palaces, and tessellated pavements, of urns, tablets, arms, and ornaments, prove that it was a civic and military station of much importance. The course of its enclosing rectangular wall, about 1950 (or, as some say, 1410), by 1650 feet, has been distinctly traced. A rampart or mound of earth lay outside the wall on the river side, and a moat or fosse outside that. A multangular tower like the one remaining stood at each corner of the defences, which embraced an area of about fifty acres.

great-grandson of the pious Æneas, erected the primeval city and gave his name to it. Nor does he think that Geoffrey of Monmouth is much nearer the truth when he says that Ebrauc, great-great-grandson of the aforesaid Brutus, and contemporary of David, the Israelitish king, built it on his return from a victorious invasion of Gaul, and called it *Caer-Ebrauc*—the city of Ebrauc. How it finally became York is a question as utterly mysterious as the name of William Patterson's occult assailant. In "Domesday-book" it is written *Euerwic.* Worsae maintains that the Britons named it *Eabkroic*, the Romans, *Eboracum* or *Eburacum*, the Anglo-Saxons, *Eoforwic*, and the Danes, *Jorvik.* It is now unmistakably "York." Constantine the Great was proclaimed emperor here somewhere about A.D. 306. He is reported to have permitted Christianity to be first preached in the city on the very spot where the Minster now stands.

Listening to or reading old accounts of

The circumference of the present fortifications is 4840 yards, enclosing 263 acres —more than four times the size of the Roman town.

With a cursory glance at the red-tile-capped tower on the river's brink, whence a chain formerly spanned the stream to a similar erection on the opposite shore, we pass on. Tanner Row, on our left, is the locality where formerly dwelt the odorous guild whose trade was prosecuted in Tanner's Moat, at the base of the walls. Micklegate Bar, at the head of a principal street, is a square tower surmounting a single arch. An embattled turret sustaining the stone figure of a warder adorns each corner. The memory of English rule in France appears in the arms of both countries sculptured upon shields on the external front. Side arches accommodate foot-passengers. The dreams of even lymphatic sleepers, occupying the rheumatic rooms of this dingy tower, may once in a while be disturbed by visions of the traitors or patriots whose heads grinned in ghastly mockery from spikes on the summit.

Here on the right is the famous nunnery, or St. Mary's Convent, of the Institute of the Blessed Virgin, founded in the reign of the second Charles, for the education of young ladies. Members of many noble families have been and are identified with it.

Descending from Baile Hill to the

VIEW FROM THE WALLS NEAR THE RAILWAY STATION.

highway, our antiquary remarks that here, in the thirteenth century, was the gate or postern of Hyngbrig, so called because the city moat at this point was crossed by a drawbridge. He also points to the rudiments of the graceful circular bastion, in which the wall once ended, on the riverbank. Crossing the Ouse by Skeldergate Bridge, which has recently supplanted the old penny ferry, we see some remains of the old city walls running up to the Castle. If, as an ingenious scientist declares, all scenes are successively photographed on flat surfaces in proximity to them, then these melancholy palimpsest structures have hidden impressions of some singular spectacles. Hard by was kept the cucking or ducking stool, in which derelict dames who had used false measures, brewed bad beer—a vice that Anglo-Saxons could never tolerate—or acquired the reputation of fliters, or common scolds, were tied and lowered thrice under the waters of the river. More to the taste of the multitude would be the pictures of pageants exhibited, preachers and audiences assembled in the grass field known as St. George's Close, at the festival of the patron saint in honor of whom the Hospital or Guild-house was raised. Loss of the life, color, and costumes of such sights is deeply deplored by the *dilettante* modern artist, who finds little of compensation in those of the sturdy lads who here exhibit so much of grace, strength, and purpose in their national

games of cricket and foot-ball. Yet the latter have had infinitely more to do with the training of the recent English for the leading part assumed in the world's affairs.

The crumbling tower of the Cliffords within the clean-cut walls of the Castle shows the way over the Foss by Castle Mills Bridge to the dolorous square keep of Fishergate postern, where we again ascend the walls, catch glimpses of the new War-office and the beautiful campanile of a Wesleyan Methodist church, and contemplate at leisure the busy traffic of the Cattle Market. The shepherds' dogs seem to be gifted with more than human resources. Flocks of sheep meet in one enclosure, but are kept apart by little lanes just wide enough to admit the passage of the canine guardians. Woe to the wrongheaded bleater that crosses the narrow path! The collie runs over the backs of the strangers, seizes the stray by the neck, and in a twinkling whisks him back into the company of his own brethren.

But here is Walmgate, most unique of all the four original bars, and the only one with barbican complete that remains in England. Its square tower and turreted angles soar not so high as those of Micklegate. The rusty iron portcullis threatens to drop on the pate of the cautious observer, the battered folding-doors trampishly lean against the walls, and the whole structure—to the policeman's Elizabethan mansion of timber and plaster on the top

THE PAVEMENT.

—wears a soured, discouraged aspect, as if sullenly resenting the battery inflicted by the last siege. Not less disheartened are the mean low streets and courts that house or hovel a poor, hard population within the walls. Somehow or other squalid poverty and gray antiquity evince special affinity. Here antiquity is grayest. The wall rests on irregular arches of rude stone-work, supposed to be the labor of Roman hands, and ends at the Red Tower—presumably piled up by the same rough artisans. Thence, for the space of 3500 feet over the marshy ground denominated the Foss Islands, and along the river, heavy iron chains are said to have been strung to the next tower at Layerthorpe Bridge.

Jewbury—the mediæval quarter of the D'Israelis and Rothschilds—county hospital, city gas-works, and St. Cuthbert's Church follow in quick succession. The last, older than the Norman conquest, is so sooty, rickety, and indubitably aged that it ought to be replaced by a new one, if not in honor of the forgotten St. Cuthbert, most certainly in that of the talents and fame of the rector, Rev. J. B. Fausset, whose popular *Commentary on the Scriptures* and other works have made his name a household word wherever the English language is spoken.

Monk Bar, loftiest of the quartet, is said to be the most perfect of feudal sort in the kingdom. From the angles of its boldly corbelled and embattled turrets grotesquely massive figures forever insanely hurl heavy rocks at imaginary foes. It is called Monk Bar in honor of the venal general who arrogated to himself, and indeed received, the credit due to Lord Fairfax, of valorous memory, for securing the peaceful restoration of the worthless Charles Stuart.

From Monk to Bootham Bar, a distance of 1950 feet, battlement and rampart have been skilfully restored, and a flagged promenade laid on the top of the latter, from which charming and advantageous views are obtained of the north and east aspects of the Minster. From Bootham Bar to the multangular tower, and thence to the Lendal bastion, the walls, although severed by the street of St. Leonards, and as yet unrestored, are in a hopeful state of preservation.

What St. Peter's is to Rome, that is the Church of St. Peter to York. Towering high above the city and country, like the cathedral of Cologne, it is a stirring ecclesiastical poem in stone. Guide-books record its dimensions, the length of its choir, and the height of its central tower. The Rev. Canon James Raine, joint author of *The Lives of the Archbishops of York* and other valuable antiquarian and ecclesiastical works, kindly volunteers to guide. There is something very congruous in this pleasant proffer. He is also rector of the Church of All Saints, Pavement, a building of the old perpendicular style, with clere-story and aisles, and a curious octagonal lantern, filled with perforated work, gracefully sitting upon a square tower. This church lantern, in the long ago, is said to have contained a beacon-fire that guided belated travellers through the forest of Galtres.

York Minster is in the form of a cross. Some enthusiastic critics maintain that it is the finest specimen of Gothic cathedral architecture extant. Professor Willis states that it is "an aggregate of various styles, having Early English transepts, a decorated nave, of which the body has geometrical tracery, and the west end flowing tracery. The choir is in two portions, of which the most easterly is of very early Perpendicular, and the western of later Perpendicular. The central tower and the western towers are all Perpendicular, and subsequent to the choir. In the crypt are remains of earlier buildings "— all of which has professional interest for church architects. Laymen are equally certain that dignity and massive grandeur are special features of this glorious structure. Like Niagara, it grows upon them the longer it is contemplated. The view across the great transept is one of the finest architectural effects of Gothic build-

ing. Lovers of stained glass here go wild with enthusiasm. From the thirteenth through all following centuries it abounds. The "Five Sisters" silently but loudly call for admiration. This noble window in the north transept is filled by five smaller lancet windows, and owes its name to the legend that just so many sisters from the same mother designed the pattern of the kaleidoscopic glass. This window, with the arcade of trefoil arches forming the base, constitutes "the most noble early English composition in the kingdom."

MICKLEGATE BAR.

EAST END, FROM MONK BAR.

Of course the curious must climb to the top of the central tower, the largest in England, even if aching limbs afterward remind him that he has seen the vale of York. Did not the infallible Chevalier Bunsen declare that to be "the most beautiful and most romantic vale in the world, the vale of Normandy excepted"? After that, if resolve hold out, as ours did, he must no less necessarily descend into the crypt, which contains the only remains of the first building of Archbishops Thomas and Roger, if not of the earliest "herring-bone" church built by King Edwin. Here that celebrated Northumbrian monarch received Christian baptism at the hands of the missionary Paulinus.

From the Minster we proceed to the Mansion-house and Guildhall. Furred scarlet and velvet robes of aldermen, scarlet cloak and massive gold chain of "my Lord Mayor," sword of state presented by Emperor Sigismund, richly adorned mace, corporation plate, portraits of defunct dignitaries—all quickly pass under notice. But what most invites minute criticism is the cap of maintenance, given by King Richard II. when

he made William de Selby the first Lord Mayor of York, to be worn by the mayoral sword-bearer in all presences on all state occasions. "I wear it at the banquets of my Lord Mayor; also when he goes to the banquets of the Lord Mayor of London, and to other banquets," says the sword-bearer, and adds: "I have appeared eight times before his Royal Highness the Prince of Wales. We're old friends now, and give each other a faint nod when we meet." Whether Olympus shakes on such occasions is not known.

The State-room, in which the "at homes" of the Lady Mayoress and the civic banquets are held, is quite as noteworthy for the gallery in which the band plays while the guests dine, and into which "my Lady Mayoress" and ladies go to listen to the postprandial eloquence of the dined and wined, as it is for artistic effects. The Mayoralty is an office that some of the elected have escaped only by the payment of a handsome composition. It is decidedly refreshing to find a city where the chief magistracy seeks an incumbent, and cannot hold him when he is found. Yet in his own jurisdiction the Lord Mayor takes social precedence of all persons except the sovereign and heir-apparent.

history, the $14,000 bell looted in Burmah, and the Magistrates' Room, in which

The Guildhall, gray and ghostly with the Great Council of the North held its

THE MINSTER, FROM THE MARKET-PLACE.

the memory of many centuries, with its fine oak carvings and stained-glass windows, in which are spirited artistic illustrations of prominent events in English

sessions, is the subject of many stereotyped and not invariably accurate chronological comments. But what are a few hundred years, one way or other, to a

THE FIDDLER OF YORK, CARVED ON THE TOP OF A PINNACLE.

man with a hat six hundred years old?

Dinner at the ancient hostelry of the Black Swan, in Coney Street, revives memories of Chaucer's "Canterbury Tales." Bits of deep rich color of the "merrie" past greet the eye in the oak panellings and stained glass, while the generous fare imparts *couleur de rose* to what is waiting for a visit in the museum and grounds of the Yorkshire Philosophical Society. Happy is the visitor whose cicerone is vivacious, and withal exaggerative as ours. He will hear jubilant tones telling of wonderful improvements since the stupid dawn of the century beheld common dumping-grounds and apple orchards where lawn and gardens now are; when the Hospitium was a cow-stable, the cloisters of St. Mary's Abbey a wine-vault (not for the first time), and the ruins of the monastery a prolific quarry, or covered by dwellings of abject look.

The Roman multangular tower, with its regular courses of small ashlar stones, and five-inch large Roman tiles inserted between, and solidly united thereto by cement as hard as the stone, has witnessed many such improvements and correspondent declensions. How the sick ever recovered in the ambulatory, or covered cloisters, of the secular St. Leonard's Hospital in close contiguity to the Ouse, may have been plain to the Saxon Athelstane who built it, but is puzzling to modern believers in the therapeutic virtues of sunlight, fresh air, and warm couches. These solid stone beds needed all the strains of Gregorian music from the adjoining chapel to make them at all tolerable.

Etchers and painters gloat over the singular beauty of the Benedictine St. Mary's, or what remains of it. Coeval with the conquest, it was one of the richest and strongest monkeries in the realm. Its fortifications speak the militant character of its spiritual occupants, who, if not belied, rather enjoyed a free fight with the worldly citizens.

Now, the Guest Hall of the monastery is the Hospitium, which provides permanent lodgings for a certain and sundry collection of antiquities, including the inevitable Egyptian remains, glass and Samian ware, Mithraic tablet, headless Æon, Roman tessellated pavements, altars, coffins, cinerary urns, and ornaments of bone, bronze, gold, silver, and jet. Deep-

BARBICAN, WALMGATE BAR.

ly touching is the sight of two fine pins of polished jet, passing through the stiff coil of coarse reddish-black hair of a young Roman lady or British princess—probably the latter—whose remains were discovered in a lead coffin contained in a sar-

bars and waist-belts of Dick Turpin and Nevison the highwaymen; and also the antiquities from Ireland, in which country England has a similar interest to that of St. Paul in the "thorn in the flesh." The small bronze tablet, on which is a

DOORWAY OF THE SCHOOL FOR THE BLIND.

cophagus of stone. Style has not changed much in seventeen centuries—in hair-dressing, we mean. Lime or gypsum in a liquid state, poured over the body when deposited in the coffin, preserved its form intact, and now enables antiquaries to reproduce that form—even the texture of garments, shape of nails, rings, and coins, ornamentation of sandals, etc., etc.—by means of plaster casts.

The rich collection of British birds and fossils is very interesting. So are the leg-

Greek inscription in punctured uncial letters—

"To The Gods Of The Governor's Prætorium"—

explains John xviii., 28. No strict Jew would enter a prætorium thus manifestly dedicated to heathen deities, and containing an altar for their worship.

The complete presentation in these buildings and grounds of all that was characteristic of the past reveals the making of the nation, and by what instru-

THE BLACK SWAN.

leading female vocalist—of singular purity, pitch, precision, and compass—somehow or other sound like voices of the receding past. An unconscious undertone, lamenting irrecoverable loss, and breathing unutterable yearning for completeness of life, enters into the melody. It plaintively appeals to what is tenderest and most Christ-like in the audience, and meets fullest response from the most highly gifted natures.

ments and through what throes it became what it now is. It reflects no less credit on the "well-beloved" Yorkshiremen whose spirit and energy effected the task.

One of the checkered, ivy-grown bits of old York as it was under the Tudors and Stuarts is the King's Manor-house, which is in part the building where the wealthy abbots of St. Mary's dispensed princely hospitality. Little of the abbatial palace remains except the wide and heavy staircase. Here successive monarchs were received, and here Charles II. held Parliament. Now, after instructive vicissitudes, it is a school for the blind; and, as such, the county memorial of the immortal philanthropist William Wilberforce. Sixty blind children here receive education and instruction in useful handicrafts. Quadrangular of form, and of architecture in which the Jacobean predominates, it is warningly suggestive of coughs, colds, and rheumatisms, which, strange to say, are not there in unusual number. Royal and noble coats of arms, which task all the pedantry of heralds to explain, adorn the principal entrances and some of the rooms.

The Thursday concert of the inmates is in progress as we enter. The performance of the blind organist, and the tones of the

The United States are graciously represented here by raised and dissected maps, books in the Boston raised and in the New York point type, and writing guides, presented by the American Printing House for the Blind at Louisville, Kentucky; wool-work articles and books presented by Mr. Anagnos, superintendent of the Perkins Institution and Massachusetts School for the Blind; and by a pathetic lace collar worked by the deaf, dumb, and blind Laura Bridgman. All these lent added interest to the jubilee of the institution in 1883.

One of the many historic rooms—now used as a dormitory for blind boys—that display the taste and magnificence of the builders contains a curiously grotesque Tudor fireplace, still intact. This was Lord Huntingdon's room, and "is probably the place in which Strafford held his Court of Star-chamber."

Our next walk, by way of contrast, should be in and around the Castle. The walls enclose about four acres, on which

ST. WILLIAM'S COLLEGE.

THE MINSTER TOWERS, FROM PETER GATE.

stand the prisons and assize courts of the North and East Ridings. "Nothing remarkable about these," is the silent remark, as the fair-haired daughter of the warder explains their several uses; and with glibness, tempered by awe, touches the identical spot where Jack Ketch has publicly "turned off" so many doomed to the halter. Executions are now private, and the city is spared the demoralization of judicial killings.

Enough of this! Clifford's Tower is more attractive. The books say it is the citadel or keep of the Norman castle built on mound of Saxon fortress by William the Conqueror to overawe the hard-fighting rebels of the north. Over the grooved gateway is a small chapel, also the royal arms and those of the Cliffords. Once upon a time George Fox, bellicose founder of the Society of Friends, was a constrained inmate. His hands are said to have planted the flourishing walnut-tree in the interior. The dry well possesses an interest more ghastly than the well of Hougomont. Victor Hugo's lurid pen is needed to describe the massacre of the Jews at this fatal spot. William of

AT THE SIGN OF THE SHIP.

Newburgh states that they appeared in York with the luxury and pomp of kings —*cultu fastuque pœne regio procedentes* —and had the reputation of cruel and pitiless creditors. Crusaders, impoverished by their exactions, in March, A.D. 1190, began the work of revenge. Five hundred Jews fled from the bloody weapons of the slayers to the castle. The absent castellan, enraged by refusal to admit him on his return, and also the sheriff, declared their act to be the "treason of air, where matters of highest moment in church and state were debated by baron, bishop, and commoner. Crowds now assemble there at the hustings for the nomination of representatives to the imperial Parliament in London. Saturdays are market-days, and bring hither the sturdy yeomanry and their buxom spouses, bearing the products of fat and fruitful farms. Color is in the eye, the cheek, and the hands of the venders, in the green of the fruit, and the gold of butter and cheese.

ST. MARY'S ABBEY.

Jewish dogs." Siege followed. For several days the assault raged. Capture was inevitable. "Let us, like men, choose death; and death not at the hands of a laughing enemy, but in the most honorable and painless shape—a free surrender of life to Him that gave it," advised an aged rabbi. Hiding all indestructible wealth, the desperate Hebrews then set fire to the castle, and threw all that could be consumed into the flames. Husbands and brothers killed the women and children, and next turned fatal daggers upon themselves.

About a mile away, on the Fulford Road, are the barracks of the Dragoon Guards, part of the "Heavies" who fought at Balaklava. York is one of the principal military centres of the kingdom.

The bits of old York to which we are introduced are as full of history, life, and color as minster or castle. Parliament Street preserves in its name the memory of at least twenty parliaments, summoned by kings from Henry II. to Charles I., and held for the most part in the open

All else is sombre—black in the dress, and gray in the streets and skies. At the annual Martinmas statutes, or hirings, servants still receive the "God's penny," which binds bargains with masters. St. William's College is of curious architecture. Founded in 1460 for the residence of cathedral "parsons and chantry priests," it is now the dwelling of poor families.

Another queer portion of the city bears the very euphonious title of "Mucky Peg Lane," possibly in memory of some slatternly matron who loved gossip better than work. In that and other sections are houses of remote antiquity. Constructed of timber and plaster, each of the upper stories overhangs the one immediately below; and so companionable are the uppermost that cronies may almost shake hands across the street. Not only this, and the additional house-room secured by such special construction, but the women could take a part in any scrimmage raging below by pouring hot water or melted lead on the combatants, or crack some unfriendly Abimelech's crown by hurling down huge fragments of stone.

One of the ripest, mouldiest bits of mediæval York is the Merchants' Hall, in Fossgate. The excellent, conservative guild-governor who points out its mani-

mission of the guild-governor, is sometimes let for religious assemblies. The connection of gain with godliness is further acknowledged by the York Penny Bank in the corner. But the most "feeling" illustration of their affinity is the

OLD HOUSES, FOSSGATE.

fold uses and beauties can hardly be expected to regard it with any eyes save those of affectionate pride. Over the entrance are the sculptured arms of the corporation, and the laudable prayer that is still their motto: "*Dieu nous donne bonne adventure.*" Paintings depicting the city as it was in the "good old times," and portraits of former worshipful masters, garnish the interior. As if in penitence for unsound ethics or doubtful commercial habits, one part of the hall is used for a Sunday-school; and the whole, by per-

underground chapel, entered by a large trap-door. This is the one entrance to the queerest place of worship in this queer old capital. The one service a year, when members of the company are expected to attend in guild dress, is justly deemed sufficient. The assistance of All Saints' choir is needed to cheer the impatient congregation into endurance of privilege in that damp, fusty, unwholesome sanctuary.

Trinity Hospital, one of nineteen Eborite eleemosynary establishments (three for lepers) endowed for the relief of poor men and women, is under the management and Hall of the Merchants' Company. Only one man was an inmate, and that of the women's ward. Flooded in the cold months, and vocal o' nights with feline melodies, both departments have been mercifully closed by the governors.

Despite all the care so lovingly lavished upon the crumbling erections of hoary eld, they totter to a final fall. Candor compels the admission that some of the churches are more conducive to other moral conditions than the sweetness and light of cheerful Christianity, even though, like Holy Trinity, Goodramgate, they possess "three old bells— a piscina"—and "the only example in York of a hagioscope, or oblique opening in the walls, to enable persons outside to see the elevation of the Host." Norman porches, like that of St. Margaret's, Walmgate, whose sculptured arches show the signs of the zodiac, the thirteen months of the Anglo-Saxon calendar, and figures emblematic of the months, may help to prolong existence, but not to prevent ultimate relegation to the domain of the worn-out and unused.

Lovers of deep rich color, violent contrast, and humanitarian iridescence find flavorous gratification in St. Anthony's Hospital, Peaseholme Green—another odd bit of the by-gone. Its four centuries are checkered by changes as countless as the temptations of the patron saint. House of religion, charity, festivity, business, workhouse, poorhouse, playhouse, school of archery, prison, arsenal, hospital, and lastly a house of Christian education, it has had experiences enough to satisfy the hero of a dime novel. Wandering through its wards and chatting with its conductors, we leave it with the profound persuasion that seventy healthy boys in "blue coats faced with yellow, sad-colored waistcoats and breeches, gray stockings, bands, and round bonnets," can do much to try the patience of the meekest saint on the calendar.

All the hitherto partial attempts at scholastic instruction are slowly converging toward the perfection of a system of national education worthy of the fame and adapted to the need of the British

THE SHAMBLES.

people. Some relics of the past will be preserved with religious solicitude. The eight hundred acres, more or less, in six different "strays" without the walls, belonging to the four ancient wards, and on which freemen have exclusive right to depasture their cattle, will be jealously guarded as property, lungs to the city, and resorts for recreation. This survival of beneficent communism interests us. It conserves the sense of solidarity in the citizens; it strengthens the democratic spirit of the sturdy toilers.

York, with 60,000 inhabitants, is a "great city." Always permeated by the literary and scientific spirit, it cherishes the memory, together with that of other native or adopted sons, of Daniel Defoe, the inimitable creator of *Robinson Crusoe*; of Lister and Wintringham, the celebrated physicians; Lambert and Etty, the painters; Giles, Price, and Peckitt, the glass painters; Goodricke, the astronomer; Guye Fauxe, the *bête noire* of English Protestantism; Matthew Poole, the author of *Synopsis Criticorum*; Wellbeloved and Davies, the antiquarians; and, above all, of Lindley Murray, the grammarian.

THE SLAVE MARKET AT MARRAKÉSH

IN the bazars of the brass-workers and dealers in cotton goods, in the bazar of the saddlers and the bazar of the leather-sellers, in all the places where the retail trade of Marrakésh is carried on, the auctions of the afternoon are drawing to a close. The delals have carried the goods to and fro in the narrow path between two lines of True Believers, obtaining the best prices possible on behalf of the merchants who sit grave and dignified in their boxlike shops. No merchant worries customers; he leaves the auctioneers to sell for him on commission, while he sits at ease, beyond the reach of elation or disappointment, in the knowledge that the success or failure of the day's market is decreed by Allah the One. Many articles have changed hands, but there is a greater attraction for men with money outside the limited area of the bazars, and I think the traffic here passes before its time.

The hour of the sunset prayer is approaching, and the wealthier members of the native community, leaving many attractive bargains unpursued, and heedless of the delals' frenzied cries, are setting out for the Sok es Abd — wool-market in the morning and afternoon, slave-market in the two hours that precede the setting of the sun and the closing of the city gates.

We follow them through a very labyrinth of narrow, unpaved streets, roofed here and there with frayed and tattered palm-leaves that offer some protection, albeit a scanty one, against the blazing sun. At one of the corners, where the beggars congregate and call for alms in the name of Mulai Abd el Kader el Jilani, I catch a glimpse of the great Kutubieh Tower, and the pigeons circling round its golden dome, and then the maze of streets, shutting out the view, claims me again. The road is by way of shops with every kind of native goods, and stalls of fruit and vegetables whose scent is as refreshing as the sound of running water. And at a turning in the crowded thoroughfare, where all the southern tribesmen are assembled and heavily laden camels compel the pedestrians to walk warily, we see the gate of the slave-market.

A crowd of penniless idlers, to whom admittance is denied, clamors on this side of the heavy door, while the city "rats" fight for the privilege of holding the mules of wealthy citizens, who are arriving in large numbers in response to the report that the household of a great wazeer, recently disgraced, will be offered for sale. Portly Moors from the city, wearing the blue cloth jellabias and selhams that bespeak wealth; country Moors, who boast less costly garments, but ride mules of easy pace and heavy price; one or two high officials of the Dar Maghzen — all classes

SLAVE-AUCTIONEERS

of the wealthy, to be brief, are arriving rapidly, for the market will open in a quarter of an hour, and bidding will be brisk.

We pass the portals unchallenged, and the market stands revealed — an open place of bare, dry ground, hemmed round with tapia walls, dust-colored, crumbling, ruinous. Something like an arcade stretches across the centre of the ground from one side to the other of the market, roofless now and broken down, just as the outer wall itself, or the sheds like cattle-pens that are built all round it, but an imposing structure enough in days of old. Behind the outer walls the town rises on every side; I see mules and donkeys feeding—apparently on the ramparts, really in a fondak overlooking the market. The minaret of a mosque is at the side of the mules' feeding-ground; there is the great white tomb of a saint behind the wall, with swaying palm-trees round it. Doubtless the saint's tomb gives the Sok es Abd a sanctity that no procedure within the walls can remove.

On the ground by the side of the human cattle-pens the wealthy patrons of the market seat themselves at their ease, arrange their robes in leisurely fashion, and start to chat as though the place were a smoking-room of a club. Water-carriers (lean, half-naked men from the Sus) sprinkle the thirsty ground, that the tramp of slaves and auctioneers may not raise too much dust. As they go about their work with the apathy and indifference born of long experience, I have a curious reminder of the Spanish bull-ring, to which the slave-market bears some remote resemblance; the gathering of spectators, the watering of the ground, the sense of excitement, all strengthen the impression. There are no bulls in the torils, but there are slaves in the pens, and it may be that the bulls have the better time, since their period of suffering is brief.

Within their sheds the slaves are shrinking, huddled together. They will not face the light until the market opens. I catch a glimpse of bright coloring now and again as some woman or child moves in the dim recesses of the retreat, but there is no suggestion of the number or quality of the victims.

Two storks sail leisurely from their nest on the saint's tomb; a little company of white ospreys passes over the burning market-place with such a wild, free flight that the contrast between the birds and the human beings forces itself painfully upon me. Now, however, there is no time for these thoughts; the crowd at the entrance parts to the right and left to admit twelve grave men wearing white turbans and jellabias. They are the delals, or auctioneers, and the sale is about to begin.

Slowly and impressively the delals advance in a line to the centre of the slave-market, almost up to the arcade where the wealthy buyers sit expectant. Then the head auctioneer lifts up his voice and — oh, hideous mockery of it all!—he prays. With downcast eyes and outspread hands he prays fervently. He recites the glory of Allah the One, who made the heaven above and the earth beneath, the sea and all that is therein; his brethren and the buyers say amen. He thanks Allah for His mercy to men in sending Mohammed the Prophet, who gave the world the true belief, and he curses Shaitan, who wages war against Allah and His children. Then he calls upon Sidi bel Abbas, patron saint of Marrakésh, friend of buyers and sellers, imploring the saint to bless the market and all who buy and sell therein, granting them plenty and length of days. And to these prayers, uttered with an intensity of emotion quite Mohammedan, the listeners say amen. Only to Unbelievers like myself, to men who have never known, or knowing, have rejected, Islam, is there aught infamous in the approaching business, and Unbelievers may pass unnoticed. In life the True Believer despises them; in death they go to the unquenchable fire. So says the "perspicuous Book." Throughout this strange ceremony of prayer I seem to see the bull-ring again, and in place of the delals the cuadrilla of the matadors coming out to salute, before the alguazils open the gates of the toril and the fight for life and death begins. The dramatic intensity of either scene connects this slave-market in Marrakésh with the plaza de toros in the shadow of the Giralda Tower of Sevilla. Strange to remember now and here that the man who built the Kutubieh Tower for this thou-

ROUND THE CIRCLE OF BUYERS THE AUCTIONEER LED THE SLAVES

sand-year-old city of Yusuf ben Tachfin gave the Giralda to Sevilla.

Prayers are over, the last amen is said, the delals separate, each one going to the pens he presides over and calling upon their tenants to come forth. These selling-men move with a dignity that is quite Eastern, and speak in tones that are calm and impressive; they lack the frenzied energy of their brethren who traffic in the bazars.

Obedient to the summons, the slaves face the light; the sheds are emptied, and there are a few noisy moments bewildering to the novice, in which the auctioneers place their goods in line, rearrange dresses, give children to the charge of adults, sort out men and women according to their age and value, and prepare for the promenade. The slaves will march round and round the circle of the buyers, led by the auctioneers, who will proclaim the latest bid offered, and hand over any one of his charges to an intending purchaser, that he may make his examination before raising the price.

In the procession now gathering for the first parade five, if not six, of the seven ages are represented. There are old men and old women who cannot walk upright, however the delal may urge; others of middle age, with years of active service before them; young men full of vigor and youth, fit for the fields; young women—moving, for once unveiled, yet unrebuked, before the faces of men— and children of every age—from babies, who will be sold with their mothers, to girls and boys on the threshold of manhood and womanhood. All are dressed in bright colors and displayed to the best advantage, that the hearts of bidders may be moved and their purses opened widely.

"It will be a fine sale," says my neighbor, a handsome, dignified Moor from one of the Atlas villages, who had chosen his place before I had reached the market. "There must be well-nigh forty slaves, and this is good, now that the court is at Fez. It is because Our Master—Allah send him yet more victories!—has been pleased to 'visit' Sidi Abdeslam and send him to the prisons of Mequinez. All the wealth he has extorted has been taken away from him by Our Lord; he will see

no more light. Twenty or more of the women here are from his house."

Now each delal has his people sorted out, and the procession begins. Followed by his bargains, he marches round and round the market, and I understand why the dust was laid before the procession commenced. Some of the slaves are absolutely free from emotion of any sort; they move round as stolidly as the blindfolded horses that work the water-wheels in gardens beyond the town. Others feel their position.

I think that the most sensitive must come from the household of the unfortunate Sidi Abdeslam, who was reputed to be a good master. Forced from the home where perhaps they were born, or at least lived a long time, these poor human chattels do not know what master will take them now, and whether they will be well or badly used. If the master be kind, well and good; if not—well, let it be put as briefly and concisely as possible: he can gratify any passion at their expense, even to the extent of torturing them to death, and the law (!) will not step in. Small wonder if they shrink or if the black visage seems to take some tint of ashen gray when a buyer whose face is an open defiance to all the Ten Commandments calls upon the delal to halt, and picking one out as though she had been one of a flock of sheep, examines teeth and muscles, and questions her and the delal very closely about past history and present health. I can understand now the delight sailors take in overhauling a slave-dhow and meting out rough justice to the blackguards in charge.

"Ah, Tsamanni," says my gossip from the Atlas to the big delal who led the prayers and is in special charge of the children for sale, "I will speak to this one"; and Tsamanni pushes a tiny little girl into his arms. The child kisses the speaker's hand. Not unkindly the Moor makes his critical survey, and Tsamanni enlarges upon her merits.

"She does not come from the town at all," he says, glibly, "but from Timbuctoo. It is more difficult than ever to get children thence. The accursed French people have taken the town, and the slave-market droops. But this one is desirable; she understands needle-

MOTHER AND SON SOLD INTO SLAVERY

work, she will be a companion for your house, and thirty - five dollars is the last price bid."

"One more dollar, Tsamanni. She is not ill-favored, but she is not well fattened. Nevertheless, say one dollar more," says the Moor.

"Praise be to Allah, who made the world," says the delal, piously, doubtless thinking of his commission, and hurries round the ring, saying that the price of the child is now thirty-six dollars, and calling upon the buyers to go higher.

I learn that the delal's commission is two and a half per cent. on the purchase-price, and there is a government tax of five per cent. Slaves are sold under a warranty, and are returned if they have not been properly described by the auctioneer. Bids must not be advanced by less than a Moorish dollar—that is, about three shillings—at a time, and when a sale is concluded a deposit is paid at once, and the balance on or after the following day. Thin slaves will not fetch as much as fat ones, for corpulence by the Moor is regarded as the outward and visible sign of health and prosperity.

"I have a little boy," says the Moor from the Atlas; "he is my only child, and must have a playfellow, so I am here to buy him one. In these days it is not easy to get what one wants. Everywhere the French. The caravans come no longer from Tuat—because of the French. From Timbuctoo it is the same thing. Surely Allah will burn these people in a fire of no ordinary heat, a furnace that shall never go out. Ah, listen to the prices!" The little girl's market value has gone to forty - four dollars — say, seven pounds ten shillings in English money at the current rate of exchange; it has risen two dollars at a time, and Tsamanni is doing good business. One girl, aged fourteen, has been sold for no less than ninety dollars, after spirited bidding by two country caids; another, ten years older, has gone for seventy-six.

"There is no moderation in all this," says the Atlas Moor, angrily; "but prices will rise until our lord the Sultan ceases to listen to the Christians and purges the land. Because of their Bashadors we can no longer have the markets at the towns on the coast; if we do have one, it must be held secretly, or a slave must be carried in the darkness from house to house. This is shameful for an unconquered people."

I am only faintly conscious of my companion's talk and action as he bids for child after child, never going beyond forty dollars. Interest centres in the diminishing crowd of slaves, who still follow the delals round the market in monotonous procession.

The attractive women and strong men have been sold, and have realized good prices; the old people are in little or no demand; but the auctioneers will persist until closing-time. Up and down tramp the unhappy creatures nobody wants, burdens to themselves and their owners, the useless or nearly useless men and women whose life has been slavery as long as they can remember. Scarred and bent by taskmasters and tasks, they make a pathetic picture, and it is impossible to avoid the knowledge that they feel the shame and humiliation of their position. Even the water-carrier from the Sus country, who has been jingling his bright bowls together since the market opened, is moved to compassion; for while two old women are standing behind their delal, who talks to a client about their reserve price, I see him give them a free draught from his goatskin

water-barrel, and this kind action seems to do something to freshen the tainted air, just as the mint and the roses of the gardeners freshen the heated bazars in the heart of the city. Surely this journey round and round the market is the saddest of their lives, worse than the pilgrimage across the deserts of the Wad Noon, the Erg, or the Draa in the days when they were carried captive from their homes, packed in panniers upon camels, travelling by night, and half starved; for then at least they were valued. Now they are little more than the broken-down mules and donkeys left to starve by the roadside.

It is fair to say that auctioneers and buyers treat the slaves in a manner that is not actively unkind. They handle them just as though they were animals with a market value that ill treatment will diminish. The unsold adults and little children seem painfully tired; some of the latter can hardly keep pace with the auctioneer, until he takes them by the hand and leads them along with him. The procedure never varies. As a client beckons and points out a slave, the one selected is pushed forward for inspection, the history is briefly told, and if the bidding is raised, the auctioneer, thanking Allah, who sends good prices, hurries on his way to find one who will bid a little more. On approaching an intending purchaser the slave seizes and kisses his hand, releases it, and then stands still, generally indifferent to the rest of the proceedings.

"It is well for the slaves," says the Atlas Moor, still rather angrily, for the fifth and last child has gone up beyond his limit. "In the Mellah or the Medina you can get labor for nothing, now the Sultan is in Fez. There is hunger in many a house; it is hard for a freeman to find food, but slaves are well fed. In times of famine and war, freemen die, slaves are in comfort. Why, then, do the Christians seek to free the slaves, and put barriers against the market, until at last the prices are foolish? Clearly it was written that my Mohammed, my first-born, my only one, shall have no playmate this day. No, Tsamanni; I will bid no more. Have I such store of dollars that I can buy a child for its weight in silver?"

AUCTIONEERS PRAYING FOR A SUCCESSFUL SALE

The crowd is thinning now. Less than ten slaves remain to be sold; and I do not like to think how many times they must have tramped round the market, neglected and despised. Men and women —bold, brazen, merry, indifferent—have passed to their several masters. All the

Half-tone plate engraved by Frank E. Pettit

A Slave Girl and her Master

Once again the storks from the saint's tomb pass circling over the market, as though to tell the story of the joy of freedom. It is the time of their evening flight. The sun is setting rapidly and the sale is nearly at an end.

"Twenty - one dollars — twenty - one," cries the delal at whose heels the one young and pretty woman who has not found a buyer limps painfully. She is from the western Sudan, and her big eyes have the terror-stricken look that reminds me of a hare that was run down by the hounds a few yards from me on the marshes near my country home last winter.

"Why is the price so low?" I ask.

"She is sick," says the Moor, coolly; "she cannot work; perhaps she will not live. Who will give more in such a case? She is of Caid Abdeslam's household, though he bought her a few weeks before his fall, and she must be sold; but the delal can give no warranty, for nobody knows her sickness. She is one of the slaves who are bought from the dealers for rock-salt."

Happily the woman seems too dull or too ill to feel her own position. She moves as though in a dream — a dream undisturbed, for the buyers have almost ceased to regard her. Finally she is sold for twenty-three dollars to a very old, infirm man, who, whatever her state of health, can hardly

children have gone; the remaining slaves, weighed down by the shame and degradation of their position, with shuffling gait, downcast eyes, and melancholy looks, are in pitiful contrast to their bright clothes — the garments in which they are dressed for the sale because their own rags might prejudice purchasers.

be farther removed from the grave. Surely if her disease is quick it must be accounted merciful. Granting that the buyer's face is a true index to character, death would be a better master than the decrepid purchaser.

"No slaves, no slaves," says the Atlas Moor, impatiently, "and in the town they are slow to raise them." I want an explanation of this strange complaint.

"What do you mean when you say they are slow to raise them?" I ask.

"In Marrakésh, now," he explains, "dealers buy the healthiest slaves they can find, and raise as many children as is possible. Then, so soon as the children are old enough to sell, they are sold, and when the mothers grow old and have no more children they too are sold; but they do not fetch much then."

The infamy underlying this statement takes all words from me; but my informant sees nothing startling in the case, and continues, gravely:

"From six years old they are sold to be companions, and from twelve they go to the harems. Prices are good—too high, indeed; fifty-four dollars I must have paid this afternoon to purchase one, and when Mulai Mohammed reigned the price would have been twenty, perhaps less; and for that one would have bought fat slaves. Where there is one caravan now, there were ten of old times."

Only four slaves now, and they must go back to their masters, to be sent to the market on another day, for the sun is below the horizon, the market almost empty, and the guards will be gathering at the city gates. Two delals make a last despairing promenade, while their companions are busy recording their prices and other details in connection with the afternoon's business; and the purchased slaves, the auctioneer's gaudy clothing changed for their own, are being taken to their masters' houses. We who live within the city walls must hasten now, for the time of their closing is near, and he who stays outside runs more risk than need be set down here.

It has been a great day. Many rich men have attended personally or by their agents to compete for the best-favored women of the household of the fallen caid, and the prices in one or two cases ran into three figures, English money, so brisk was the bidding.

Outside the market-place one country Moor of the middle class is in charge of four young boy slaves, and is telling a friend what he paid for them. I learn that their price averaged eleven pounds apiece in English currency—two hundred and eighty dollars in Moorish money,— that they were all bred in Marrakésh by a dealer who keeps a large establishment of slaves as one in England might keep a stud-farm, and sells the children as they grow up. The purchaser of the quartet is going to take them to the north; he will pass the coming night in a fondak, and leave as soon after daybreak as the gates are opened. Some ten days' travel on foot will bring them to a certain city where his merchandise should fetch four hundred dollars. The lads do not seem to be upset by the sale of their future; and the dealer himself seems to be as near an approach to a commercial traveller as I have seen in Morocco. To him the whole transaction is on a par with selling eggs or fruit, and while he does not resent my interest, he does not pretend to understand it.

From the minaret that overlooks the mosque, the muezzin calls for the evening prayer. From the Kutubieh Tower and the minaret of Sidi bel Abbas, as well as from all the lesser mosques, the cry is repeated. Lepers pass out of the city on their way to the Hara, where they will be shut in for the night. Beggars shuffle off to their dens. Storks, standing on the flat housetops, look gravely down at the unchanging city. Doubtless the delals and all who sent their slaves to market to be sold this afternoon will join the muezzins in the declaration of faith with grateful hearts, and Sidi bel Abbas, patron saint of red Marrakésh, will not go unthanked.

NEW ZEALAND

I RECENTLY made the circuit of the self-governing colonies of Great Britain. Beginning with those in Africa, where still, as of old, something new is always being found, I went on to Tasmania, New Zealand, and the Australias, and from there by Hong-Kong—the new Liverpool of the East—to Vancouver, and across Canada to Atlantic tide-water. Each colony and group of colonies visited had about it something noteworthy, but none presented so many points of interest in small compass as New Zealand. It has the raw material out of which can be made something fairer and better than the mother country. Business enterprises are not laid out on the continental lines already traceable in Sydney and Melbourne. The two islands are scarcely as large as Great Britain and Ireland. But they have an existence of their own. They stand on their own feet, or "hang by their own head." They are no part of Australia, geographically or geologically, in their fauna or flora. They have no immediate intention of becoming one politically with their big neighbor, but hope to occupy as important a relation to it as Britain did and does to Europe, and they are satisfied that their connection with the Empire gives them the necessary conditions for free development.

Through what perversity was this land of mountain and flood, of forest and fiords, of glittering glaciers and bright sunshine, of geysers and pools of exquisitely tinted water fit for naiads to bathe in, called after foggy, swampy Zealand? Probably only the perversity of ignorance. Though Abel Janssen Tasman discovered it in 1642, he did not land, the wild natives frightening him off from their shores. But the Dutch cartographers saw that it adjoined New Holland. The thousand miles of wild waters intervening amounted to no more under the Southern Cross than the distance between old Holland and old Zealand. On a small map the distance is a trifle, and the incongruity is no greater than the names of Rome, Syracuse, Utica, and Ithaca—plundered from a classical dictionary—sown broadcast over northern New York.

Americans have little idea of the actual and prospective importance of New Zealand. They touch at Auckland on their way to Sydney, and, if they can spare two or three weeks, run out to where the pink and white terraces were. Having thus done full justice to the country, they take the next steamer for Australia. Mr. Froude wrote authoritatively concerning it on the strength of having seen that much, and why should an American, who has half a continent of his own, be more particular? New Zealand is not a world like the United States. But neither is it one locality, not even in the sense in which the great colonies of New South Wales and Victoria are local. There you find the whole life of the country in the capital of each, whereas New Zealand has at least four distinct centres, each the capital of a province, and each certain to remain an important centre of business and of characteristic life. The man who has not visited the four does not know New Zealand. Yet the population of the four put together is not as great relatively to that of the colony as the population of Melbourne is to that of Victoria. The mass of the people are to be found in the country or in small towns and villages.

It was the variety of New Zealand that struck me most. So far as scenery is con-

AUCKLAND HARBOR AND MOUNT RANGITOTO.

cerned, we get an approach to it only by combining Switzerland, southern France, Norway, and the Yellowstone Park—I might throw in the Tyrol and North Italy —into one not very big country. As Switzerland is the point to which tens of thousands of tired men and women converge every summer, so shall it be before long with New Zealand. What a godsend the sight of it must be to people who have lived on the waterless plains of Australia, who have beheld with straining eyes every blade of grass burnt down to the roots, and their vast flocks withering away along the line of march from one dried-up water-hole to another! Instead of low-lying shores, the noble line of the Southern Alps, snowy ranges, and lofty peaks curtained with glaciers, rising into the clear air from eight to twelve thousand feet. Instead of a "bush" without trees, or melancholy eucalypts, girdled, ghostly, stretching out skeleton branches, dense green forests! What a play-ground for the squatter!

A brief itinerary will show how great is the variety of scenery. Take a steamer from Melbourne for the sounds at the southwestern extremity of the South Island. There are thirteen of them along a hundred and twenty miles of coast, the

nearest being Milford, Bligh, and George sounds. Beyond the long wash of Australasian seas and noisy breakers on an iron shore, you pass into still and serene channels two or three hundred fathoms deep, precipitous mountains a mile high rising sheer from the water's edge, clothed with richest forest, tier above tier, to the line of snow or glacier. At every turn new beauties are revealed; water-falls, embowered in trees, leaping out from the sides of mountains, or concealing the faces of cliffs with spray-like bridal veils. From the sounds the steamer runs through the Foveaux Strait, separating Stewart from the South Island, and lands you at the Bluff. Stewart Island is sometimes counted as a third in the New Zealand group, and then the South is called the Middle Island—an enumeration that reminds one of the parish minister of the Cumbraes, who regularly prayed for "the muckle and the lesser Cumbraes, and the adjacent islands of Great Britain and Ireland." From the Bluff you run up by rail to Invercargill, a singularly clean, pretty town, as Scotch as it can be, with all its streets named after Scottish rivers, and from there find your way to the lake and mountain region. Lake Wakatipu is sixty miles long, and, being well provided with steamers, makes the best base for expeditions. Tourists who are in a hurry stop at Queenstown, or strike off to visit the gold fields that brought the town into existence. But to see Wakatipu it is necessary to go on to Glenorchy or Kinloch, on the upper branch of the lake. The water has all the charm of coloring reflected from surrounding heights that characterizes Como, Lugano, and Maggiore, and the mountains are as interesting as those of the Tyrol. The glaciers on Mounts Aspiring and Earnslaw, formidable as they look, are only the feeble representatives of the old Anakim that scooped out these beautiful lakes as deep as the sounds on the opposite coast, not many miles away. After a short holiday in this district, cross the Southland plains to Dunedin, and thence to Timaru, to follow the trail that Mr. Green, with Emil Boss and Ulric Kaufmann, made to the summit, or rather the *arête*, of Mount Cook, the great Aorangi or sky-piercer of the Maori. Better not attack this monarch of the mountain world of the southern hemisphere without Swiss guides, though it is easy enough to travel to the highest ridge of the Downs, and see him towering over parallel ranges of grand

Alpine heights. There is no great risk in going even so far as the southern ridge, to get the view described with the glow of anticipated triumph by the surefooted Irish clergyman, his only conqueror: "Ranges upon ranges of peaks in all directions and of every form, from the ice-capped dome to the splintered aiguille, standing up out of the purple haze." Only a member of the Alpine Club can fully sympathize with the reflection that follows: "And then to think that not one had yet been climbed! Here was work not for a short holiday ramble merely, not to be accomplished even in a lifetime, but work for a whole company of climbers, which would occupy them for half a century of summers, and still there would remain many a new route to be tried." We must hurry away from Aorangi, and leave on one side the marvellously beautiful west coast road, running from Christchurch over a high pass of the Southern Alps to Hokitika, and omit, too, the rich Alpine valleys of the provinces of Nelson and Marlborough, if we are to see anything of the North Island. At Lyttelton (the port of Christchurch), where we get on board the steamer for Wellington, great graceful-looking ocean

MILFORD SOUND.

steamers, equal to Atlantic liners, show how important the trade of New Zealand is. Each of them carries as one item of its cargo 30,000 carcasses of frozen sheep to feed hungry London. Embarking at night, we see the lofty Kaikoura Range in the morning, and soon after get the swell from Cook Strait, and before noon run into the landlocked harbor of the capital. It is a far cry of four hundred miles from it to Auckland. If we go by the railway that skirts the northwesterly coast as far as the Manawatu River, we there

MAP OF NEW ZEALAND.

take coach and drive through a gorge, that cleaves the mountains down to the roots, right into the interior of the island. This Manawatu gorge, terrible or magnificent, according to the weather, is the pass of Killiecrankie on a large scale. If we go by the Masterton line over the Rimutacca Range, grades are encountered worse than on the Canadian Pacific Railway down the Kicking-horse and over the Selkirks. These are overcome not by the powerful engines of the C.P.R.,

but by a third rail elevated between the two ordinary rails, and a special engine with extra wheels fixed horizontally to grip the elevated rail on each side. This works us slowly up and down the mountain range. At points on the line barriers are erected to save the train from being hurled into the abyss by the storms that sweep down gorges denuded of their forests. It does blow, be it remarked, both in the North and South islands. All the way to Auckland we get what is generally considered the characteristic scenery of New Zealand: open and park-like plains alternating with the richest forest, active volcanoes, like smoking Tongariro, and extinct snow-clad Ruapehu, the sacred Lake Taupo, and the full-fed Waikato flowing from it, striking water-falls, hot springs, baths blessed with healing virtue, fumaroles, geysers, sinter terraces that recall the glory of Rotomahana, so recently destroyed (1886)—in a word, two hundred miles of wonder-land, whose varied beauty it is impossible to overrate, and parts of which have been described by hundreds of tourists. Not the least remarkable feature—seen to good advantage when travelling by coach—is the forest. Even the scrub, which consists usually of the ti-tree or manuka-bush, shows the luxuriance of vegetation. The ti-tree is very like an enormous heather, only that its flowers are white. But it is the forest itself that attests the richness of the soil. In some places huge trees shoot straight up like masts, and at the top spread out umbrellas of branches, which, intertwining with others, form a complete roof overhead. Most beautiful are the cabbage-tree, the nikau-palm, the rata, whose glorious red flowers blaze out in January, and the graceful fern-tree. So dense is the underbrush that progress through the forest is almost impossible, as the soldiers found to their cost in the wars with the Maori. Supple-jacks, or trailing and creeping plants, lianes and parasites, bind the bush together, and fasten themselves to every intruder. A thorny creeper, popularly known as the lawyer, is perhaps the worst of the species. The under side of the leaf is covered with prickles, which

tear clothes and flesh on the slightest provocation. Among the tussock-grass on the plains, the needle-pointed green bayonets of the Spaniards and a sturdy bramble called the wild-Irishman are just as much dreaded by horse and man. The commercial value of the New Zealand forest is very great. The Kauri pine gives the best wood in the world,

The Remarkable from Ben Lomond.

QUEENSTOWN AND LAKE WAKATIPU.

large, durable, easily worked, and without knots. The Totara ranks next to the Kauri in utility. Black, red, and white pines, the broad-leaf, iron-wood, and mapou, are everywhere. In the settlements blue-gums imported from Australia, with other useful and ornamental trees of every description, are being extensively planted.

This run from the southwest coast through the two islands, made in one or two summer months, between December and March, will show any one that no other country of the size of New Zealand enjoys so great a variety of extraordinary natural beauty. But it is a total misconception of the country to fancy that this is its chief claim to the love of its people and the consideration of its neighbors. It has claims infinitely more substantial. Men cannot live upon scenery, nor even, like the wild pigs of New Zealand, upon the parsnip-like roots of Spaniards. Emigrants have gone there for the last half-century because they were told that they could make a living by farming or keeping sheep, by cottage husbandry, coal or gold mining, or other forms of labor. They have not been disappointed. The resources of the colony are as varied as its scenery, and partly for the same reason. It extends for twelve hundred miles from the cold south bordering on antarctic seas to the warm north, and thus has every kind of pleasant climate, through all the ranges of temperate and sub-tropical. When the native of another country sees its unequalled capabilities for tillage and pasturage, his instinctive patriotism makes him almost thankful that it is not any bigger, like the French marshal, whose comment on the British infantry, "the best in the world, sire, but luckily few in number," is so often repeated in England.

If New Zealand were as large as Australia it would supply the English market, and Canada and the United States could hardly be expected to be grateful. Its average yield of wheat is twenty-six bushels to the acre. It is better adapted for raising the best kinds of wool and mutton than even New South Wales, which truthfully boasts of having more sheep per capita than any other country under the sun; but then its runs and paddocks are not so vast, or so capable of indefinite expansion. The amount of business done by its handful of people—

less than two-thirds of a million—is astonishing. For the last few years the exports averaged sixty dollars per head, and for the year ending June 30, 1889, they had increased about eight millions over the previous year. The imports are nearly as large. No wonder that its ports are crowded with shipping! The great bulk of its business is done with the mother country and with the Australian colonies, though it sends almost its entire production of some articles to America, such as Kauri gum, an amber-like fossil resin, which is used as a base, instead of gum-mastic, for fine varnishes. Kauri-gum-digging is one of the industries peculiar to New Zealand. In former ages vast forests of the Kauri pine must have been burnt in the north part of the North Island, and the resin melted down into the ground and became deposited in lumps. These lumps vary in size from a thimble to an anchor, and can be dug up by any one able to handle a spade. Gum land is considered worthless for any other purpose, but as it yields to the value of nearly two millions a year for export, and the supply seems inexhaustible, it has an unquestioned worth of its own. As no apprenticeship is needed to make a gum-digger, and no capital but a shovel, the unemployed take to it when they have nothing better to do; waifs and strays also, because of the element of uncertainty in it that appeals to the gambling instinct. The regular army of labor looks down on the work, and classes the workers with the "sundowners," or "swaggers," who roam over the country in search of employment, terribly afraid lest they may find it. To run as little risk as possible, they take care not to appear at farmsteading or station till a little before sundown, sauntering then into the yard, swag or red blanket rolled into a pack on their back, requesting, in humble or insolent tones as may be, food and a night's lodging. The request is always granted, as the farmer or squatter has no wish to quarrel with men whose friends may drop accidentally a lighted match near his ricks on a dark night. They may be told to chop a little wood or do some chores in the morning, in exchange for their supper; but as a rule they feel that this implies a reflection on the hospitality of their entertainers, and before the household is astir, they have folded their swag and silently stolen

MOUNT COOK.

GLACIER, MOUNT COOK.

away. It is only fair to add that I have heard of this class of the population not at first hand. The "swagger" has probably a different story to tell from the squatter. So, doubtless, has the Kauri-gum-digger; but neither had I the good fortune to fall in with any member of that interesting profession. It is difficult to understand why in a country like New Zealand there should be so many tramps, but it is unnecessary to enter on social questions at present.

The great industry of the land is sheep-grazing, for the sake of the wool, and latterly for the sake of the mutton as well. When Captain Cook visited it in the year 1769 and the years succeeding, the only mammal worth mentioning was a rat that contributed to the food of the natives on feast-days. It has been killed off by our brown rat, a fate that is considered by the Maoris to prophesy their own, according to the saying: "As the English grass kills the Maori grass, and the English rat kills the Maori rat, so must the Maori himself be swept from the fern home of his fathers by the Pakeha." He deserves, and I anticipate for him, a better fate. There is no race antipathy between him and the "Pakeha," and the number of half-breeds is steadily increasing. What better fortune could be desired than absorption into a common New Zealand stock, the most vigorous in the Southern seas? The great sailor to whom I have referred, who may be called the discoverer as well as the first colonizer of the country, equally great as a navigator, an observer, and a man, introduced on the islands pigs, poultry, and potatoes. These have thriven amazingly. Indeed, every animal and vegetable, almost every bird, insect, and fish, that has been introduced since has thriven, some well and others too well, sheep taking the lead, and rabbits closely following. The value of the wool exported is now about twenty millions annually. Up to 1881 the sheep-masters did not know what on earth to do with their mutton, but the discovery was then made that it could be sent in a frozen state to Britain. Great was the alarm among the classes, from dukes to butchers, who controlled the British meat market. Strong prejudices were stirred up against frozen meat, and as at first some of the mutton was discolored, there was ground for prejudice. But the New-Zealanders got hold of the scientific truth that intense cold can be produced in a chamber with walls impervious to heat through the simple process of compressing air by steam-power and then letting it into the chamber, where it expands to its natural bulk. They gradually perfected their machinery and plant, established freezing-works near the ports of shipment, and sent the frozen carcasses, nicely encased in clean bags, to the freezing-chamber of the steamer. There they keep hard as marble and perfectly sweet for months, and, for aught I know to the contrary, could be kept for years. I sailed from Plymouth in the *Aorangi*, and from Cape Town in the *Ionic*, both of them magnificent steamers, belonging to different lines, and on board both the mutton brought to the table had made the voyage round the Horn, and then been in the Thames for weeks, yet better mutton I never ate. New Zealand now sends a million carcasses annually to the London market. It not only spares easily, and to the actual advantage of the flocks, that number annually from its total of seventeen millions of sheep, but believes that every year the number can be increased. Firms in Britain are establishing houses in all the great cities, where the carcasses can be stored and kept frozen till needed. Competition has brought down the cost of freight from three to two pence, and now, I believe, to one penny, or two cents, a pound. Great is the boon that has been conferred on two communities on opposite sides of the globe—meat-producers

and meat-eaters—by practical application of the familiar scientific truth at the basis of the trade. The gains from this one industry would pay for all the physical laboratories in the Empire, just as Germany makes more from the discovery of aniline dyes than it spends on its universities.

The sheep-masters, or squatters, are the aristocracy of New Zealand. But notwithstanding the success of the frozen-meat trade, they are not always happy. To hear members of the class in the clubs at Dunedin, Christchurch, or Wellington discussing their losses and crosses and the best ways of meeting their enemies, convinces us that life, even to the owners of runs in bright New Zealand, is a stern conflict, and that no business is exempt from hazards. There are no all-destroying droughts, as in Australia, but there are snow-storms, imprisoning the flock far back among the hills. The snow-storm of 1867, followed by pitiless rain, driven by a furious freezing southwester, killed half a million sheep, and the marvel was that any out of the flocks overtaken by it survived. Wild pigs descended from Captain Cook's domestic animals, great boars cased in hides and gristle that would turn a musket ball, were frozen stiff, while, hard by, thin-skinned creatures with only a few months' growth of merino wool on their backs stood the stress of the storm without injury. Such a calamity, however, as that of 1867 is not what vexes the squatter most. That comes direct from the Almighty, he thinks, and why should a living man complain? He frets more over the loss of a few score annually from the rascally kea, or the lessening of the carrying capacity of his run by the innocent rabbit. All the resources of civilization have to be invoked to meet these dread enemies, especially the latter of the two. The kea, or mountain-parrot, a greenish-brown bird, formerly as harmless as others of his class, has developed a carnivorous habit as fastidious as that of epicures. It used to feed on the berries that grew luxuriantly on the hills, but it has changed that simple diet since the multiplication of sheep; perhaps fires, too, made that natural food scarce. It now takes a terrible revenge on its unconscious enemy. Fastening itself on the back of a poor sheep, perhaps stuck in a snow-drift, and savagely tearing away wool, skin, and

HOT SPRINGS, WHAKAREWAREWA.

SHEEP ATTACKED BY KEAS.

flesh, it plunges its powerful beak into the kidney fat, which it devours, and then, leaving one victim to die in agony, goes off in search of another. Though it is as difficult to feel individual affection for sheep where they are slaughtered by millions as it would be to care for hogs in Chicago, the most unsentimental shepherd cannot refrain from pitying one of his own flock that he finds in such a condition, and from invoking maledictions on the whole race of keas. How they found out that kidney fat was such a delicacy can only be conjectured—perhaps in the same indirect manner in which Charles Lamb's Chinaman discovered that young roast pig was good: a kea saw a sheep devouring his regular supply of food, and defending his property with what beak and claws he had, his tongue came in contact accidentally with kidney fat. From that moment the satisfaction of appetite and the gratification of vendetta were united.

But compared to the rabbit, the kea is an enemy scarce worth mentioning. Numbers overwhelm. A single locust or a single rat can do little, but a cloud of locusts is terrible to the farmers of the Northwest, and a swarm of rats devoured Bishop Hatto. What vexes the run-holders of New Zealand and Australia most is that members of their own class introduced the plague — hares for coursing, rabbits for pets, food, or auld lang-syne. Great was the joy when the first shipment arrived safely in Invercargill. At a dinner that night Bunny's health was enthusiastically drank, and soon afterward special legislation was passed to protect him. A few pairs were turned out to make a warren, and all went well. Every one was satisfied.

"How do you like tiger-hunting?" was the question put to a returned Anglo-Indian.

"No sport better, so long as it stays that way," was the answer; "but when the tiger hunts you, it is a different matter altogether."

The legislator needs protection now, and not Bunny, as in the old Joe Miller concerning catching a Tartar:

"Why don't you let him go?" "Because he has caught me."

The run-holder has been caught. His sheep are being eaten out of their rich pastures, and he feels as helpless as he would against invasions of mice, mosquitoes, or microbes. Graphically did a member of the Dunedin Club describe to me the resistless advance of the timid creatures as beheld by him in the gray of a sharp morning, when the first snowfall drove them from the mountains to the lower slopes, where he had hoped to feed his fat sheep through the winter. Birnam Wood coming to Dunsinane was nothing to it. For miles and miles the hills and downs below the snow-line were living gray. The multitudinous gray mass was moving on, burrowing, nibbling, as it advanced. Poor man! He may have been

MAORI CARVING.

humbugging me; but if so, he did it well. His cheek actually lost a portion of its deep ruddy hue as he recalled the scene and began to compute in pounds sterling what the rabbit had cost his beloved New Zealand.

All sorts of remedies, from cats, weasels, stoats, and iguanas, to snakes, gunpowder, phosphorus, and cholera microbes, have been tried, and not wholly in vain. Bounties for rabbit-destruction at so much per thousand have called into existence professional trappers; but these are now found to contribute to the perpetuation of the pest. No profession, it would seem, can be

MAORI WHARRÉ.

unitedly and honestly willing to abrogate or annihilate that on which it lives. The "rabbiters" therefore take care to keep up the supply, by now and then waging war on the stoats and cats, professedly, of course, when taxed with the fact, in the interest of the housewife, whose yard and hen-roosts have suffered

MAORI DOORWAY, THAMES.

more from one stoat than from all rabbitdom, and whose anger is so kindled against such bloodthirsty brutes that she actually pities poor Bunny. I journeyed over the Rimutaccas with a squatter— like all the rest of his class whom I met, a singularly intelligent, well-educated man—and learned from him that he had found out nature's own remedy for the plague. In proof of his assertion, he said that he had cleared his own and his neighbors' runs. He had applied for the $125,000 prize that New South Wales had

offered, and considered that he was much better entitled to it than Pasteur, whose microbe remedy might in the end be worse than the disease. Nature's checks and counterchecks could always be depended on. In this case the remedy was the tapeworm of the dog, fox, wolf, cat, or other enemies of the rabbit. When, in spite of one or all of these, the rabbit multiplied excessively, his natural enemies, from feeding on him exclusively, got the tapeworm illness, and infected with it the grass. In that way the rabbits next got the disease, and it swept them out of existence. My squatter acquaintance made his discovery accidentally. Observing that his dogs, who had lived on rabbits, were becoming mangy, he physicked them, and a few weeks after he declared that the rabbits, which had previously held their own against trapping. shooting, poisoning, and suffocating in their warrens, had disappeared, with the exception of one or two of the hardiest, who proved their fitness to survive anything.

It ought to be mentioned here that in some districts even rabbits are turned to good account. They are shot or trapped by the thousand for food. The meat is tinned, and a profitable demand is rising in England for canned rabbit. The skins sell for the lining of coats and for felt hats.

New Zealand has all the elements of a great mining and manufacturing as well as of an agricultural and pastoral country. In mines, gold and coal take the first place, and are likely to hold it for some time. The story of the discovery of gold, and the influence it has had on settlement, is too interesting to be summarized. Coalmining is growing more rapidly than any other industry except the frozen-meat business; and instead of being localized in one grim "Black Country," the deposits— in all stages of lignite, brown, and bitumi-

WELLINGTON.

nous—are distributed over both islands, and the miners live like human beings.

Among the peculiar productions of New Zealand is the well-known flax *Phormium tenax*. This is a gigantic lily, with leaves nine or ten feet long, growing on hill-sides and in every swamp, and now finding a deserved place in gardens and pleasure-grounds. It was as useful to the Maori as the palm to the Arab, the cocoanut-tree to the Hindoo, or shaganappi to the Northwest half-breed or Hudson Bay trader. A sweet drink was extracted from its flowers, and an edible gum from the roots of the leaves. It was used for building and thatching their huts or wharrés, for nets, thread, ropes, sails, sandals, mats, baskets, bags, cables, clothing, and every conceivable textile purpose. So wonderfully fine and strong is the fibre that no one need be at a loss for thread or stout rope in any part of New Zealand. He has only to cut a leaf from a flax plant, and slit it into broad or narrow ribbons. There is an increasing demand for the fibre in commerce, especially when a partial failure of Manila hemp or Mexican sisal is threatened. Besides all that have been mentioned, New Zealand has other strings to its bow. The production of cereals and root crops, of butter and cheese, of sub-tropical fruits and flowers—in a word, of everything raised in temperate climates or in the favored lands along the shores of the Mediterranean—is steadily increasing. And better than richness and variety of soil is climate. There is no cli-

mate better suited to the Anglo-Saxon race, and no colony has been settled so exclusively from the British Islands and from the best classes of British people. I saw fewer alterations from the original stock than in Australia, the southern coast from Gippsland to Adelaide excepted, and any changes in physique were not for the worse. The climate, too, is far more pleasant than that of Britain, simply because there is far more sunshine. One is tempted to ask, for what other spot on earth has the Almighty done so much?

Yet, strange to say, these Fortunate Islands went a-begging from Captain Cook's time down to 1840, and the South Island was within an ace of being picked up by France. In that case it would have been probably used as a home for *récidivistes*, for in default of it New Caledonia was selected and is still used for that purpose. Captain Stanley, of the *Spitfire*, arrived three days before the vessels of the French Company, and had hoisted the union-jack. The Frenchman laughed good-naturedly, landed his emigrants, and sailed away for New Caledonia. Before long United Australia will politely ask France to consume her own smoke, or, at any rate, not to puff it offensively into a quiet neighbor's face. The way in which

New Zealand became British in spite of the Colonial Office is an illustration of how the Empire has grown. Fifty years ago Great Britain thought herself "the wearied Titan." Statesmen fancied that the occupation of fresh fields by her over-crowded children at home meant an additional load to be carried, instead of a lessening of burdens or the opening of new safety-valves. Filled with the paternal idea, they did not understand that such a people carried with them the principle

TAWHAIO, MAORI KING.

in 1839. Edward Gibbon Wakefield and Lord Durham formed a company, and sent out twelve hundred settlers, who founded Wellington. The statesmen had been laboriously seeking to build up a card castle called a Native State; this step was manifestly of the nature of treason; but as it could not be undone, it forced the creation of New Zealand into a separate colony. In 1840, by the treaty of Waitangi, the chiefs of the North Island ceded the sovereignty to the Queen, and that of the South Island was assumed on the ground of discovery. The Maoris and the settlers soon quarrelled, and wars followed from 1843 to 1869. These could have only one ending, notwithstanding the pluck of the Maoris, backed by their dense bush and supple-jacks. The flat meree of greenstone or whale blade-bone and tomahawk were no match for the bayonet, nor muskets bought from whalers for rockets and shells. The wars are over, and have left no bad blood behind. The Maoris form an integral portion of the community, with recognized place and rights. It is not considered at all improper for a white man to marry a Maori girl, especially if she is heiress to a tract of good land. They are a middle-sized, stuggy race, and though some say that they are dying out, better authorities maintain that they are holding and will continue to hold their own. They have representatives in both Houses of Parliament, and any of these, if unable to speak English, is allowed an interpreter, who stands up beside him and translates his speech sentence by sentence. This double-barrelled membership looks odd, but it works well. I heard Taipua, one of the four in the House of Representatives, make a speech after this manner on a proposed native lands bill. As a parliamentary utterance it was a miracle of condensation, perhaps because he had time to think over what he was going to say next, while the interpreter explained in English what he had said. "You have

and power of self-government. The last of that race of statesmen—let us hope—was Lord Derby, who snubbed Sir Thomas McIlwraith, of Queensland, for annexing New Guinea, with the result that the great island which overlooks the northern shores of Australia is now partitioned among different European powers. Individual Englishmen, however, have a way of acting for themselves, regardless of the Colonial Office, and fortunately there were men of that stamp in England

SUPREME COURT AND VICTORIA BRIDGE,
CHRISTCHURCH.

CATHEDRAL. CHRISTCHURCH.

passed twenty acts about our lands in as many years, and they have all been bad. This is the worst. You propose to tax our land. Had you not better leave the matter to ourselves? Or, as there are now a number of our leading men in Wellington to give evidence on a disputed will case involving land titles, I advise you to take counsel with them. They can give you light, if light is what you want. At any rate, keep lawyers away from us." Thus spake Taipua, and, amid the cheers and laughter of the House, took his seat, leaving the ministry in no doubt as to the side on which he intended to vote.

Some of the Maoris still keep up the old hideous practice of tattooing, the men puncturing the whole face to increase their importance, and the women their lips, chins, and eyelids to increase their personal attractions. A friend of mine told a married woman in Japan that he wondered at her disfiguring herself by blackening her teeth. "What do you mean?" was the indignant answer. "Any dog has white teeth." Probably the Maori damsel thinks along the same line, but after looking at her slaty-blue lips I thought her mistaken.

All New Zealand was in the blues in 1888. The cause was the public-works policy on which the government embarked in 1870, which landed the country in a quagmire of debt, threatening its credit for a time. It had given work at extravagant wages to every one as long as the borrowing went on, and there had to be a pause. There can be no doubt that the pace was too rapid, but the notion of the Cassandras, male and female, that the debt is simply a huge horse-leech draining away their life-blood

PRINCESS STREET, DUNEDIN.

for the benefit of the English bondholders, seems to me a delusion. Heavy as the burden is, amounting to somewhere about two hundred millions, it is a bagatelle compared to the resources of the country. The value of one product, the gold that has been entered for export, is larger, and there is still gold on government land, probably more than enough, to pay the whole debt; besides, there is money's worth to show for the money borrowed. For instance, the colony owns all the railways and the telegraph lines, and could sell these any day for what they cost, and so reduce the public indebtedness by nearly a half. Roads, harbors, piers, light-houses, and other public improvements the colony constructed in too great a hurry, and with all the waste incidental to democratic government, but not one of them would it be willing to do without.

Colonization proceeded from so many centres, distinct in climate, soil, popula-
tion, and history, and still unconnected by rail, except in the cases of Dunedin and Christchurch, that it was extremely difficult to carry out a comprehensive policy. Very naturally, too, each of the four principal cities continues to look upon itself as the real present, or, at any rate, the assured future, capital of New Zealand. Each points to its increasing commerce and special industries, and declares that the climate is the best in the world. Auckland, the old capital, bears itself with the dignity of a discrowned monarch, calmly convinced that the king must have his own again. There is room, certainly, for an immense surrounding population, alike in the great peninsula stretching from it far to the North Cape, and south to the King country, and its position as the port of call for steamers from America gives it special commercial importance But the people of Wellington calmly point to the map, and show you that their central position and command of Cook Strait settle the question. Their chief drawback is the limited area available for business or residence on account of abrupt hill-sides; but hills can be cut away, and there is a great deal of room at the

two wings of the city. Additional ground was formed by the earthquake of 1848, which raised the town site from three to six feet, and turned a swamp, reserved for a dock, into a capital field for recreation. No wonder that earthquakes, though dreaded elsewhere, are rather regarded with pride by Wellingtonians as one of the features of their city!

I think Wellington is likely to hold its own, especially as possession is nine points of the law. Its position, its excellent and well-defended harbor, and the two railways extending from it into the heart of the island are in its favor as the national capital and a distributing centre, although its growth was slow at first, owing to the steep hills crowding down to the water's edge, and the mountain ranges that cut it off from the back country.

To the Church of England was assigned the settlement of the province of Canterbury, and to the Free Church of Scotland the settlement of Otago. Hence Christchurch, the capital of the one, is essentially English in type, and Dunedin, the capital of the other, essentially Scottish. Port Lyttelton was intended as the capital of Canterbury, but the high, rugged, volcanic rocks enclosing the harbor left no room for a city, and the settlers began to stream across the ridge to the great plains beyond. There they found Scotchmen who had rented or bought large sections of choice land from the natives, and conquered the first difficulties that beset pioneers. Some of the Anglicans were disgusted that there should be intrusive Presbyterian Scots where they had resolved to plant a copy of England, with church and schools modelled on a type that is rather out of date even in the Old World. It was almost enough to warrant the declaration that when the north pole is discovered a Scotchman will be found sitting astride of it. However, all has turned out for the best. "The City of the Plains" is Anglican in tone, and all its streets are named after the sees of the Anglican Church; but education is public, unsectarian, and, it may be added, costly to the revenue, as in the rest of New Zealand. All kinds of churches, from a Free-thought temple to a Salvation Army barrack, have a fair field. The toilsome journeys to and from the harbor over the lofty volcanic spur still linger in the memories of the oldest inhabitants; but in

1861 the infant colony girded itself up to the work of boring a tunnel through the eight thousand feet of rock, and succeeded grandly. The pioneers came in 1850, and already the city has the equipment of a European capital—magnificent public buildings, college, museum, high schools, normal schools, cathedral, botanic gardens, park, hansoms, club with gorgeous red-waistcoated waiters, and fifty thousand people, all satisfied that the capital must come to Christchurch. Dunedin, they say, is too cold, Auckland too far north, and Wellington too windy, and so exposed to seismic disturbances that the public buildings have to be of wood. Their cathedral is on a splendid model. The nave only is sufficiently completed for worship, but it makes a serviceable church. The font at the entrance is the gift of the late Dean Stanley, in memory of his brother, who was so lucky as to anticipate the French. Christchurch is the real monument both of him and of the pioneers who came after him, "Alteram ut Angliam matre non indignam condant," as the parchment under the cathedral's foundation-stone reads.

The public gardens and Hagley Park are wonderful for size and possibilities. A pretty little stream—the Avon—meanders through them; not Shakespeare's Avon, but so named by the Scottish settlers after a stream that flows into the Clyde in their native Lanarkshire. The museum is simply astonishing. It owes its unique excellence to one great man, Sir Julius von Haast. The moa room alone, with its peerless collection of moa skeletons, the great wingless bird of prehistoric New Zealand, is well worth a long visit. The living representative of the moa, the kiwi, is a humble-looking bird, apparently as much related to its mighty ancestor as a wingless partridge to an ostrich or emu. The *Dinornis maximus* stands nearly thirteen feet high, and in life must have towered over its hunters like a giraffe.

When Dunedin is reached, its handsome buildings of Port Chalmers and Oamaru stone, the curbed and asphalted pavements and well-paved streets, make the traveller think that he has at last come to the capital. His impressions are strengthened as he sees ivy-clad Presbyterian churches like cathedrals, and extensive suburbs, not visible even from the surrounding hill-tops. The city climbs up and round steep green acclivities, and thus in great part is hidden away in nooks and glens. One might well be content to live in Dunedin. Its people are sure that there is no place like it, and they have good reason for their pride. Few communities are more hospitable or self-reliant. Indeed, their vigor seems hardly tempered with Scottish caution when you find them unsatisfied with Port Chalmers, eight miles off, as a harbor, and spending fabulous sums dredging out the connecting shallow arm of the sea, with the determination that the ocean liners shall come right up to the Dunedin wharves.

The threatened cold of Dunedin was not of the kind to frighten a Canadian. As I sat at dinner in the home-like club on the first day of my arrival, and looked out through the windows, it was difficult to realize that it was midwinter. The lawn was green as the Oxford quads in May. Beds of flowers gave color to the grounds—snowdrops, pansies, wallflowers, violets, stocks, chrysanthemums. Roses were about over, and camellias budding. Different species of veronica, fuchsias, laurestines, and the British and native holly with bright red berries backed the lawn. Beyond the shrubs towered graceful evergreens, the broadleaf, mapou, the cabbage-tree, bluegums, the macrocarpa, the *Pinus insignis*, and native pines. A cold rain fell steadily, much more unpleasant than a snow-storm, but there was no arrest of vegetation.

Next day a railway ride to Mossgiel and a drive through the valley of the Taieri showed the advantages for mixed farming that Otago possesses. No ice or snow; no dead leaves, for there are no deciduous trees except a few imported oaks and elms; no need of hay. The grass in the fields was green, and the cattle and sheep were pasturing. The gorse hedges were rich with golden blossoms, except where they were kept sternly clipped. The cozy-looking manses were surrounded with shrubbery, and covered with ivy or trailing vines. The people are a different race from the weedy Cornstalks of New South Wales or the Banana Boys of Queensland. For ruddy faces and strong frames one may back Barracoutas, even though taken from the factory of Mossgiel, against any part of the world. I saw a Dunedin crowd of ten or twelve thousand on my second visit. They had

gathered on the wharves to see the *Rotamahana* start for Melbourne, as it was a Sunday afternoon. Such a crowd of well-fed, well-clad, sturdy, red-cheeked men and women, business depression notwithstanding, surely no other city of the size could produce. Not one looked sick or even seedy. "Ah!" said one of the Dunedin pioneers, whom I was congratulating on the abounding evidences of order, comfort, and thrift that I had witnessed throughout the province, "few of them think now what it cost to lay the foundations." Thereupon he sketched vivid pictures of the difficulties and privations of the emigrants of 1848, and told with subdued enthusiasm how they triumphed over all, sustained by the native vigor of the race and faith in the God of their fathers. The immigrant to a new country has a hard time of it. He is smarting from the sundering of old ties, and new ones have not yet formed. In New Zealand the very seasons were turned upside down. But these men have their reward. They see their children growing up with a love for the land equal to that which brings tears to their own eyes as they think of the old home. Gradually their patriotic fervor becomes transferred to New Zealand, till to their astonishment they find themselves vehemently telling new-comers how much better it is than the old country.

"O fortunati nimium!" I am tempted to exclaim as I think of these old-timers. For nowhere is there a fairer land. Nowhere is labor more sweet, or recreation more shared in by all classes. Every township has its park, race-course, and play-ground; the cities have these and everything else that can be imagined. Picnics are universal. The long summers and bracing winters make open-air amusements delightful. Sports are taken up eagerly, from coursing matches over rough ground and pig-stalking, to cricket, foot-ball, and volunteering. From the beginning generous provision was made for schools and colleges, the people—in the South Island especially—having the spirit of the men who colonized New England. No one with eyes in his head can fail to see that the New-Zealander of to-day is laying the foundations of a mighty state, though he may not be able to believe that one of his descendants is likely to sit on a broken arch of London Bridge and sketch the ruins of St. Paul's.

CAMPAIGNING WITH THE COSSACKS

MIDWINTER.

as in its shape. The lash is made of rawhide closely braided into a flexible piece about as large as a lead-pencil, smooth and round, and almost as hard as iron. On one end of this is a flap of thick rawhide perhaps two inches in length, and on the other a similar bit which serves as a sort of hinge by which the lash is attached to the handle. This attachment is made by small thongs of rawhide, which are bound around with the skill of a sailor, and then are carried in a twist like the thread of a screw along the handle, both to ornament it and to add to its strength. There are as many qualities of nagajkas as there are of any other manufactured article, but the best varieties are rarely, if ever, to be bought in the shops. My own whip was of unusually fine workmanship, with a handle of some foreign cane like malacca joint, and a silver ferrule, which I have before described. To the practised Cossack eye it was evident at a glance that the whip was of home manufacture, and could have come into my possession only by theft or gift. To the uninitiated it represented only so much money value. The nagajka is such an indispensable part of the Cossack equipment that it is highly prized in active campaign, where there is little opportunity of replacing a lost one. But they often last for years, and when, as is frequently the case, they are the handiwork of some sweetheart or dear relative, they are preserved with great care, and never parted with for money. Naturally enough, I clung to my nagajka with the loyalty of a Cossack, both because it was a souvenir of the major and because it had served

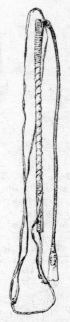

THE NAGAJKA.

THE little nagajka which had often served as a passport to the acquaintanceship of Cossacks all through the early summer campaign proved no less efficacious as a talisman when the fortunes of the field obliged me to leave the major, and to watch the more serious operations of the main army in Bulgaria. It was by no means such a prominent object in my outfit that it would have attracted the eye of the casual observer. Like all the Cossack whips, it had a small straight handle about eighteen inches long, with a lash a few inches longer attached to one end. The peculiarity of the nagajka consists quite as much in its construction

me a good turn in more ways than one. I steadily refused all offers to part with it, and guarded it jealously lest it should be stolen.

Weeks rolled by with great rapidity, and a dreary rainy season set in. About the middle of autumn we made a reconnoissance in the direction of Rasgrad, to endeavor to discover the strength of the enemy there. Three regiments of Cossacks made up the force, and we marched all day and part of the night be-

were riding a little ahead of the column could see the characteristic conical Turkish tents assembled in a little valley a short distance beyond. At the same instant our scouts engaged the enemy's pickets, and the column halted. The camp in sight was evidently only a large outpost, and the general immediately gave orders for one regiment to form and charge through the camp. We could see the men of the designated regiment uncover and cross themselves, and in a moment

CIRCASSIAN COSSACK AND PRISONER.

fore we came in the vicinity of the enemy. On the morning of the second day it was reported that a considerable detachment of Turkish irregulars was encamped a short distance in front of us. We had been moving during the night with as little noise as possible, and had bivouacked in the rain without building a fire, in order to give no notice of our approach to the enemy's pickets. It was only just daybreak when the orders to march were given, and the column proceeded cautiously with a few scouts in advance. In a half-hour or so we who

the head of the detachment was rapidly moving past us. Among the officers rode the major, my old friend of the Dobrudscha, who, unknown to me, had been promoted to a lieutenant-coloneley, and transferred to another regiment. As he dashed past he made a gesture of recognition and waved his hand for me to follow. I believe it was more the horse's fault than my own, for certainly I never had a deliberate intention of riding in a charge if I could help it, but before I knew it I was at the major's side. Off we went at a trot, changing our formation to regimental front. Then, in an irregular line, much broken by the inequalities of the ground, we swept down the slope at a gallop. There was some firing, and a few Cossacks fell, but I doubt if anybody heard a shot. The thunder of the hoofs, the shaking of the grain-bags, the rattling of the cooking utensils, and the resounding whacks of the nagajkas filled the air with a multitude of noises which drowned all other sounds. The exhilaration of the moment was supreme. Horses as well as men felt its unique stimulus, and we rushed through that camp, sweeping it away as the sudden cloud-burst in the Rockies tears out the bed of the arroya. It was one of those rare moments of life when all sense of individuality is

AN AUTUMN BIVOUAC.

merged in that utterly overwhelming feeling of exaltation, in that intoxication of magnetism, which often possesses large masses of men moved by some grand and simultaneous impulse. It was, perhaps, after all, a very trivial affair from a military point of view, but the sensation I experienced was by no means insignificant or easily forgotten.

Part of the Turkish force took to flight in time and escaped; those who remained to defend their camp were sabred, spitted like fowl on the lances, or captured and led back to the main column at the end of a lariat. The *finale* of this little incident was fully as impressive as the charge itself, although in quite another way. After we made camp that night the men of the regiment which had engaged the enemy were drawn up in line with uncovered heads and sang a religious hymn in chorus. How different now were those faces which a few hours before had been distorted with the cruel expressions of hatred of the infidel, or glorified by the excitement of the charge or with the consciousness of victory! Uniforms apart, the men looked like a rank of devout, peaceful farmers, bronzed by the sun in the fields, and begrimed with the dust of agriculture. The hymn rolled forth in quaint, sad cadences tuned to a minor key, like most of the native melodies. Along the ranks a gap purposely left here and there showed where a comrade had stood the day before. Although I could not catch the words they sang, the significance of the hymn could not be mistaken. Many rough hands brushed tearful eyes before the last mournful note died away, and the regiment then dispersed about the camp with a quiet step, as if the least noise were an insult to the memory of the dead.

The approach of cold weather fully developed all the resources of the Cossack as a campaigner. During the summer months there had been little necessity of shelter, and, except during rainy weather, no tents or other coverings were used. The common Russian soldiers were slow to learn to dig ditches around their tents, or to provide themselves with comfortable shelters of any kind. But the Cossacks, with the *sang-froid* of experienced veterans, made the best of everything, and surrounded themselves with all the comforts the circumstances allowed. In the construction of winter-quarters they displayed much the same ingenuity and fertility of resource which distinguished our volunteers in the civil war, except, perhaps, the devices were more primitive, and indicated a different if not a lower order of civilization. They are very skilful in thatching and in weaving together slender poles so as to make a rude basket-work serving as a foundation upon which to plaster clay or mud for the walls of a house. Most of the Bulgarian houses are so constructed, and the materials for Cossack huts were found readily enough. Conical thatched wigwams, built of a few sticks and hay or straw, sprang up like mushrooms in every camp. Accustomed to the use of the axe and spade, there was no contrivance of wood and earth and stone which they did not try their hand at. Grotesque but serviceable fireplaces; dining-tables with seats on four sides, all excavated out of the earth under the hut or tent; warm and cozy retreats in the side of a hill, or burrowed out of level ground, like rabbit holes — everywhere were found these ingenious constructions of the Cossacks, who seemed to be always building and always deserting their habitations.

Notwithstanding the strict discipline of the Russian army, it was quite impossible to keep the Cossacks within bounds as regarded appropriation of the Bulgarian live-stock. They could not be made to distinguish between the rights of property belonging to the enemy and the rights of property belonging to the Bulgarian allies. The poor Bulgarians suffered greatly in consequence. Incidents similar to the following were constantly occurring. The advance guard I was with halted one night after dark in a little deserted village among the foot-hills of the Balkans. As we were in the heart of the enemy's country, and some distance in advance of the main army, every precaution was taken against surprise, and we turned in, finding what shelter we could from the November storm in the half-ruined houses and stables. About midnight the rain ceased and the moon came out. Suddenly the quiet of the camp was interrupted by the sound of a rifle-shot close at hand, followed quickly by two others. The village was alive with men in an instant. Cossacks mounted and skurried off in every direction; the two companies of infantry fell in, and marched away in the direction of the firing. Teams were

BURIAL OF COMRADE.

hitched up, baggage thrown in the carts, and everything hastily prepared for retreat. The infantry disappeared, and the last tardy Cossack hurried off. The few of us who were left in camp anxiously awaited the attack. Revolvers were looked to, saddle girths tightened, and the countless little details of preparation were made which indicate uneasiness and nervous anxiety. Minutes dragged on slowly, but no further shots were heard. The excitement in the camp was still painfully intense, although visibly decreasing as the silence continued. After the lapse of half an hour everybody came back again, covered with mud and out of humor. A young Cossack, with two dead sheep he had shot, was brought in by the guard as the cause of the whole disturbance. I was present the next morning when the commanding officer interrogated the disturber of our night's rest. The culprit was a young recruit fresh from home, who had stolen out of camp, when the moon came out, to forage for his breakfast. In the excitement of chasing the sheep, which he could not catch, he thoughtlessly fired upon them.

"But," thundered the officer, "you knew, you scoundrel, that there are strict orders against killing sheep unless they are paid for. The orders were read to your sotnia only last night!"

"Yes, your excellency," sobbed the youth, who foresaw only a small chance of escape from the lash; "but—but—but I thought they were wild sheep!" He was turned over to the gendarmes to be flogged.

Among the numerous superstitions of the Cossacks there is none stronger than the belief that they will enter heaven in a better state of moral purity if they are personally clean at the time they are killed. Consequently before an expected battle they perform their toilets with scrupulous care, dress themselves in clean garments, and put on the best they have. This superstition is not confined to the Cossacks alone, but is widely prevalent in all branches of the Russian army. Skobeleff, in common with many other officers, professed a similar faith, and did not fail to dress himself for a battle as he would for a soirée. The Cossack sotnias, being often composed of men who belong to the same community at home, have a harmony of interest among the members which extends further than the ordinary matters of discipline. Their sick and wounded are generally more sedulously cared for than in other corps, and even in the excitement of active service they appear to have a reverence for their dead uncommon with soldiers who are accustomed to the daily spectacle of a comrade's death. Many a touching little

burial-service have I witnessed among the Cossacks, but none more moving than one which I accidentally saw in the beginning of winter. We had been making a rapid forward movement, and had captured a pass in the Balkans. In the late afternoon, after the engagement was over, I was making my way by a short-cut across the hills to a point where I expected to find the head-quarters, when I came upon a singular scene. Near the top of a bare knoll, strongly relieved against the sunset sky, three riderless horses came out in sharp silhouette. A little to the right of them, and on the very summit of the knoll, two Cossacks were stooping over, busy with something, I could not see what. The landscape, desolate, sombre, and brown in the near foreground, deepened to intense purple in the middle distance, and beyond and on either side of the knoll, which was the dominant object in the scene, the jagged mountain-tops sharply cut the wintry sky. The glory of a rich sunset mystified the details of the masses, while it seemed to sharpen their contours and heighten their contrasts. It was one of those evenings when there steals into the mind a sense of the solemnity of the hour almost amounting to religious fervor, and when one contemplates the departure of the daylight with an inexplicable feeling of sadness, and a scarcely formed but still vivid realization of the fathomless mystery of the near future.

As I approached the group the two men rose to their feet, and, without looking in my direction, uncovered their heads and stood motionless. Between them a long low mound disturbed the rounded outline of the hill, and a rude cross made of an unhewn tree trunk added its unexpected silhouette to the shapes of the men, seen as irregular masses against the deep crimson of the western sky. I involuntarily paused, and waited cap in hand until their silent prayer was finished, and they had slowly turned away toward the three horses; then, skirting the knoll crowned by the mound and cross, kept on my way. All that friendly hands could do to honor the victim of the day's fight had been religiously done by his two comrades. In the midst of the turmoil of war he had been given a decent, dignified, Christian burial. And what more impressive funeral could there be than the one I saw in the twilight of the glorious Balkan sunset? The place, the hour, the simple

FIFTY LASHES.

ceremony, the symbol of Christian faith, and proof of comrades' love—it was the poetry of a soldier's burial.

During the winter campaign part of the army was obliged to subsist on quarter rations of bread alone, and for many days suffered the deprivation of various articles of food which, if not actual necessities, are at least important elements of diet. Sugar grew scarce, and at last the remaining grains of dust which was once tea were shaken out of the corners of pockets and boiled. But the failure of both sugar and tea, two commodities dear to every Russian heart, was a trifling misfortune compared with the lack of common salt. Russians are proverbially improvident, and most of the men had neglected to lay in any store for the future, even after the total failure of the rations had been threatened. Gunpowder proved to be an unpalatable substitute as a seasoning article, and those who were fortunate enough to possess a small fragment of the crude rock-salt served to the army carefully concealed it, and only indulged in the taste of it on the sly. The Cossacks with their unflagging energy scoured the country for the needed supplies. Honey was found in considerable quantities, but only a little salt was obtainable by theft, capture, or purchase. About this time the Bulgarians continually complained at head-quarters that they were plundered by the Cossacks, and the strictest orders were issued against this practice. In the height of the salt famine a squad of Cossacks, eight in number, were prowling about a Bulgarian village, ostensibly on the watch for the enemy, but really in search of salt. They observed a peasant woman with a lump of the precious stuff

A CUP OF TEA.

as large as a quart measure, and following her to her house, first tried to persuade her to part with it, and then undertook to compel her by threats to sell it to them. They were engaged in this unjustifiable mode of bargaining when they were surprised by a patrol of gendarmes, were arrested, and led to camp. The case was speedily brought before the commander, and they were condemned to fifty lashes apiece. I happened to be quartered with the captain of gendarmes at the time, and heard all about the case from him. It certainly seemed a severe punishment for such a misdemeanor, but the officers were determined to stop such lawlessness, and refused to take into consideration the arguments of the culprits that no actual violence was used.

We were discussing the case in the quarters one afternoon when an orderly entered and announced to the captain that the Cossacks were there to receive their punishment. We went out upon the porch of the house, and saw drawn up in single file eight sturdy, honest-looking fellows, standing without their overcoats under the guard of a number of gigantic gendarmes. A heavy fall of snow was on the ground, and the mercury was almost down to zero. There was a strange expression on their weather-beaten faces as they stood shivering in the cold in the attitude of "attention," with their freezing fingers stiffly extended along the seam of the trousers. Not one of them had ever been flogged before, and in their eyes was the frightened, nervous look of new offenders, not the sullen glance of the experienced victim of the lash. I could not determine from their bearing whether they fully realized that they were to be submitted to the indignity of the most cruel and degrading punishment in the list. One or two of them were of the ordinary type, but the majority were young men of particularly good appearance, quite above the average, and with the unmistakable tone of the better class of Cossacks. I was led to notice the third in the line because of his handsome type of face and fine figure, and also because he appeared to be superior to the rest either in blood or in education. He was a blond of medium height, and could scarcely have been out of his teens, for a straggling soft beard, full cheeks, and unwrinkled skin marked the period of youth or early manhood. I watched him under the gaze of the captain, and saw a painful flush of anger, shame, and wounded pride color his face for an instant. No other visible sign of emotion did he show, but stood stoically with the rest in unwavering line.

The captain walked along the file, said a few words which I could not hear, came up the steps again, and turning to me, said, "Lend me your nagajka."

I went in and returned with it, venturing to protest as I handed it to him, "For

DANCE.

Heaven's sake let it be used as tenderly as possible, for it is a cruel weapon to punish human flesh with."

Without replying, he gave it to the sergeant of the gendarmes, who in turn passed it to one of the men.

At a word from the sergeant four gendarmes advanced in front of the file of Cossacks, and took their position in the form of a rectangle, facing inward. They were all very powerfully built men, having been selected, like all the gendarmes, not less for their physical strength and immense size than for their military record. The sergeant now read a name from a list he held in his hand, and the first Cossack stepped out of the file and stood between the gendarmes. At a second command he partially stripped and lay down in the untrodden snow, face downward. The three stalwart gendarmes immediately seized a limb apiece and held the culprit out flat, like a victim of the Inquisition strapped to the rack. The man who had my nagajka now advanced and raised it in the air, prepared to strike the exposed part of the prostrate Cossack.

"Ras!" shouted the sergeant.

Whack! went the cruel lash with a sound that made my flesh creep.

"Dva! Tri! Chetiri!" slowly counted the sergeant; and at each blow the Cossack seemed to shrink into half his natural size. Not a groan nor a sound escaped his lips until the fifty lashes were half spent, and then he moaned pitifully during the rest of his punishment. When the last blow fell, the gendarmes sprang to their feet, the Cossack scrambled up, his face distorted with suffering, arranged his uniform with trembling hands, and without stopping to shake the snow from his hair, hobbled off, under guard, out of sight among the horses. The seven comrades of the Cossack, enforced spectators of the brutal scene, were now very pale, and their hands nervously clutched their trousers while they still preserved the rigid attitude of "attention." A fresh hand took the nagajka, and the second name was called. A short, broad-shouldered fellow with a small head and a square face stepped briskly out, threw aside his cap with a careless flirt of the hand, jauntily removed his coat, as if preparing for a pleasant exercise, and lay down with a marked air of bravado. His courage did not hold out long, however, for at the very first blow he writhed and groaned and prayed and shouted, and after the third or fourth stroke wrenched one hand free and tried ineffectually to protect himself from the lash. But the gendarme quickly held the arm in place again, and the count was made with aggravating deliberation and precision. When the whole fifty had been put on he was led away shrieking and sobbing and dancing like a whipped school-boy, forgetful of cap and coat, snow and cold, and insensible, indeed, to everything but the pain of his punishment.

The third name was now called, and the young fellow whose appearance I have described took his place in the snow, now partly packed by the struggles of the first victims. There was no show of emotion on his face except a quivering lip, and he gave no indications of bravado or of fear. He bore the first dozen lashes without a sign except an involuntary quivering of the flesh. Suddenly, about the fifteenth blow, he seemed possessed with the strength of a maniac. Flinging aside the muscular gendarmes as if they were no stronger than children, and ignominiously tumbling one of them in the snow, he sprang to his feet, the picture of rage and indignation. He made no attempt to escape, but shrieked: "You have no right to whip me! You have no right to whip me! I am the son of an officer! I am the son of an officer!"

But this astonishing spurt of mad strength did not avail him, for the imperturbable gendarmes seized him again, and stolidly forced him to the ground, when the remaining blows were counted.

The foolish fear of becoming the butt for the laughter of the officers kept me a spectator of the whole of this disgusting and degrading performance. After the last blow had sounded, I could restrain my indignation no longer, and turning to the captain, asked—having in mind, of course, the moral effect of the flogging— "What will become of these men?"

"Oh," said he, indifferently, "they'll be sent on picket duty now for two weeks without being relieved."

"Captain," I continued, "if I were one of them, the moment I got my rifle again I would shoot you through the heart."

"Oh, nonsense!" he replied. "You are an American; these men are Russians. I don't like this business any better than you do. I'm used to it, that's all. Come in, let's have some tea, and forget all about it."

The amusements of the Cossacks in camp are not numerous. They are fond of gambling, as all Russians are; and games of chance as simple and as uninteresting as those indulged in by the Chinese and by the American Indians will keep them absorbed for hours together. Dancing is their favorite pastime, day and evening. The company either squats on the ground like Indians, or else forms a circle, standing in close ranks around an open space a dozen feet across. Some leader of song strikes up an inspiriting tune, and all begin to keep time with the

CIRCASSIAN COSSACKS.

measure, clapping their hands in the same way that the Southern negroes "pat juba." The song may rise to the dignity of a full chorus, or descend to the level of a medley of whistles, shouts, and uncouth noises. It usually takes some little time to work the company up into the proper state of excitement, but when the fever pitch is reached, two young men spring into the ring as actively as cats, and begin to dance like marionettes. The step can only be described as something between the Hungarian czardas and a negro breakdown. They patter with their feet with as rapid a succession of knocks as a skilful clog-dancer. They throw their heavily booted legs about with the agility if not the entire grace of a *maître de ballet*. They caper, they jump, and they whirl one another with giddy rapidity. Faster and faster goes the music, shorter and shorter are the measures forced by the hurried clapping of a hundred hands. At last, long after they have far surpassed the expectation of the uninitiated spectator, these marvels of endurance spring breathless out of the ring, and a fresh couple occupy their place almost before they have vacated it. Judging from the faces of the spectators, the dancers would be supposed to be performing solely for the entertainment of their comrades, for everybody is interested, exhilarated, and absorbed. If any argument may be drawn from the fact that the soloists are even more eager to follow one another than the company is to have them, there must be an intoxication in the motion which is at once irresistible and satisfying.

Another amusement, and one which is frequently enjoyed when there is a jollification of any kind, is tossing in the air. A crowd of sturdy young fellows seize the one selected for this honor, and throw him up bodily as high as they can, catching him as he falls, and repeating the operation as many times as their strength will allow. Speaking from experience of this game, I must say the honor should be very great to make up for the unpleasant sensation of the ceremony. Face or back upward, heels or head foremost, it makes little difference to the tossers which way the victim rises, provided he flies high. The catching is, too, a no more careful operation. Clothes are torn, pockets emptied, and the toilet sadly disarranged,

CIRCASSIAN SKIRMISHERS.

but the damage is inflicted with such a show of good-will and jollity that it is rarely objected to. The highest in rank may not be exempt from the honor of this horse-play. I have seen a general tossed for several minutes on the occasion of a festival in honor of his birthday, and I know from his own lips that he prized very highly this proof of his popularity. This game is but one of many examples of the peculiar democratic relations which exist between all classes in the Russian army. It is generally lost sight of in the pomp and display of authority and discipline, but it still remains a strong element in military life. This democratic forgetfulness of rank on some occasions, and almost servile obedience to the superior authority on others, is a strong characteristic of various Asiatic tribes with whom the Russians come in contact. I cannot imagine anything less likely to happen in the other European armies than tossing an officer of high rank like a rollicking school-boy.

Vodki is commonly introduced as an element of exhilaration at all festivities, and the fiery liquor rapidly increases the boisterous riot of the occasion. The Cossacks are often sad drunkards, and the vice is one for which they are most justly blamed. They brew a harmless sort of barley beer like all the Russians, but prefer to indulge in the doubtful delights of intoxication from vodki. This liquor is a high-proof spirit distilled from barley, is colorless, but makes up for the lack of tint by other less innocent qualities. It is served to the army in regular rations, increased according to circumstances. The officers drink it neat, although it is often above proof, but it is dealt out to the men in a slightly diluted form. The Cossacks being in a measure independent of rations, and continually bartering their forage and plunder both publicly for the common purse and privately for their own profit, are consequently exposed to more temptations than the infantry men. The custom of taking a dram before each meal with a bite of some appetizing delicacy is a prevalent one all over Russia and northern Europe, and is not neglected in the army. As long as there is a drop in the canteen it is passed around among the Cossacks as a second ceremony before each meal, the prayer, of course, being the first.

In winter the necessity of protection from cold metamorphosed the Cossacks, in external aspect at least, into a cross between a moujik and a Bulgarian. Bundled up in great-coats made of goat-skins or of sheep-skins, wearing clumsy mittens on the hands, wisps of hay around the feet, and the characteristic bashlik or pointed hood on the head, they gained in startling picturesqueness what they lost in style and jauntiness. A troop of cavalry thus attired was indeed a wonderful affair. Insignia of rank were often entirely obliterated by this costume, and ridiculous mistakes were often made.

The Kuban and Terek Cossacks, with whom I chanced to be thrown at frequent intervals during the winter, proved to be quite as interesting to study as their cousins of the Don and the Ural, although much less numerous. Next to the Mexican *Rurales*, they are the most picturesque cavalry I have ever seen. They wear at all seasons of the year a high cylindrical hat of Astrakhan wool, usually black, and sometimes ridiculously thick and long. This has a top of cloth or velvet. The coat is similar in general pattern to the Russian Cossack coat, but the skirts are usually longer and fuller, and the sleeves broad at the bottom. The outside coat has no collar, but is cut low in front to disclose a red undercoat hooked high in the neck. Full trousers and boots complete the ordinary dress. In the place of the gray Russian overcoat they carry a bourka, or circular cloak, made of peculiar fabric, which is somewhat like thick, coarse felt, with a long nap like goat's hair on one side of it. This bourka is water-proof and wind-proof, and ample enough, when worn on horseback, to cover the rider entirely and part of the horse as well. It serves, of course, as a bed by night as well as a cloak by day. It is, by-the-way, an interesting fact that among the articles of dress found in the peat-bogs of Denmark there are caps and cloaks of the same textile and approximate in shape to those worn by the Circassians to-day. The Circassian arms are quite as characteristic as their dress. A Berdan carbine is slung across the back in a case of shaggy goat-skin, or of felt like that of which the bourka is made. The sabre is a guardless one, like those carried by the Russian Cossacks, and is hung from the shoulder by a narrow strap. From the waist belt dangles in front a long, leaf-shaped, pointed dagger,

STRANGE BOOTY.

and behind, a quaint flintlock pistol altered to the percussion system, and with a
large round knob on the butt. One of the
most curious portions of the Circassian
dress is the row of cylindrical cases which
fit into cloth pockets on the breast of the
coat, ten on either side. In the days of
muzzle-loading guns these held a cartridge
apiece, and a tiny flask of priming powder hung around the neck. The cases
are still preserved as a portion of the
regulation dress, chiefly as an ornament,
partly to hold charges for the pistol,
which still remains of the antique pattern, but largely for the more prosaic
purpose of holding salt, tea, and various

trifles. These cases are sometimes made of silver, but are usually of wood and ivory, with little stoppers ornamented with tufts of red wool. The saddle and bridle are similar to those in use among all Cossacks. The uniform gives great scope to the love of glitter and ornament, and it is a favorite dress in the Russian army.

General Skobeleff, the father of the young Russian hero, was very proud of his silver-mounted equipments and richly decorated uniform. The son, whose position obliged him to confine his inherited love of display to the selection of pure white saddle-horses, had on his staff a number of Circassian Cossacks of distinguished bravery, one of them bearing the great red and yellow battle flag which always waved where the white horse was seen. The harness straps and sword-belt are often studded with silver, and the saddle loaded down with the same material beautifully worked. The cartridge cases and the stirrups are sometimes of the same precious metal, and cost enormous sums. As for the arms, they are marvels of workmanship, the Circassians having the strong Oriental pride in this regard, frequently going in rags, but always wearing an arsenal of expensive weapons. The dagger sheath and handle, the sword scabbard and hilt, are frequently covered with masses of intricately chased silver of native workmanship. The uniforms for the most part are quite plain, without buttons or braid, but occasionally is seen a man with silver braid all over his coat and around the top of his cap.

At all times, but particularly in winter, when the bourkas and the bashliks were worn, the Circassian Cossacks presented a decidedly savage and warlike appearance. They were very active in harassing the Turks, and were always raiding over the country in advance of the Russian army. In these expeditions they frequently captured military supply trains belonging to the enemy, but oftener they brought destruction to caravans of innocent fugitives or refugees who had left their homes at the advance of the Russians. Sometimes these caravans were turned back peacefully into the Russian lines, but on other occasions the fanatical resistance of the refugees brought upon themselves speedy destruction. All sorts of promiscuous plunder were brought into camp, and the Circassian quarters looked more like robbers' dens than soldiers' shelters. Copper uten-sils of the strange and picturesque shapes common in Turkey became a drug in the market, and the wily Bulgarian camp-followers reaped a rich harvest. Books which nobody could read, rugs which nobody could carry, farming implements, carpenters' tools, even American air-tight stoves—every conceivable article of household use found favor in the eyes of these plunderers.

One cold afternoon at the end of December a young Circassian Cossack came to camp head-quarters with an article of booty which attracted more attention than any other object before exhibited as a relic of the war. He was dressed in a worn and shabby uniform, and rode an underfed, carelessly groomed, and overworked animal. There was a merry, kindly expression on his face, and but for his uniform he would never have been suspected of belonging to the race whose name is widely synonymous with ferocity and cruelty. He had gathered up the long mane of his horse in such a way that it made a primitive sort of hammock. The fingers of his left hand were twisted in the knotted horse-hair, and in this ingenious bed lay, or rather reclined, half seated, a little girl-baby perhaps a year and a half old. She was dressed in the peculiar antiquated costume made of figured calico which the poorer Turkish women use for their own and for their children's dresses. She was apparently happy enough in her strange cradle, delighted with the motion of the horse, and diverted by the multitude of strange sights and sounds. She sat there and rolled her great brown eyes unconcernedly and fearlessly about, contentedly sucking a crust of black bread. In reply to our questions the Cossack reported that he had been with his sotnia that morning in pursuit of a Turkish wagon train. They were unable to capture the train, but had gathered up a great quantity of booty thrown away by the fugitives to lighten their loads. On the side of the road he noticed a bundle of ragged counterpanes, and dismounted to examine it. To his surprise he discovered that a child's cries proceeded from the bundle, and unrolling it, he disclosed the baby lying quite warm and comfortable, just as it had rolled off one of the wagons. He said he couldn't leave the creature there to die, and couldn't take care of it himself, so he rigged a cradle out of his horse's mane, and came directly to head-quarters. I took the child to hold it while the Cossack dismounted. When she saw a strange face bent over her she cried with a strength of lung which proved that her hardships had not yet undermined her physical health, and refused to be comforted by any one but her adopted Cossack nurse. Arrangements were easily made to have her carried over the mountains to the nearest Red Cross station, there to be given in charge of the women nurses, and the next morning we saw the waif depart on the shoulders of a stalwart Bulgarian.

The last excursion I made with my friend the major was noteworthy for only one incident. We spent the night in a large Bulgarian village, and had our quarters at some distance from that part of the town through which the great highway ran. The morning was so cold and the quarters so comfortable that we delayed some time after the detachment had gone on, a couple of men only remaining with us. When at last we mounted and set off, we rode through the village, and reached the highway at some distance from the irregular line of houses bordering it. Just as we came out upon this main street, the head of a great train of Turkish refugees which had been turned back homeward by the advance guard entered the village on their peaceful journey toward the farms in the Danube Valley which they had deserted the previous summer. A wretched set they were indeed. The lean and feeble oxen could scarcely draw the creaking carts laden with women, children, and what remain-

ed of the household goods. The men, exhausted by privation and by long marches, trudged painfully along, urging the beasts forward by voice and by blows. Near the head of the train an old woman, a shapeless mass of ragged quilts and dirty wraps, rode a miserable donkey. Quite a crowd of Bulgarians, both men and women, assembled as this sad caravan entered the village. Not perceiving our approach from the other direction, this band of poltroons attacked the defenceless refugees, pulled the old woman shrieking from the donkey, tumbled the terrified occupants of half a dozen wagons out upon the ground, and proceeded to make away with the animals and the household goods. The major rode up, closely followed by the two Cossacks, and ordered them to desist. At the sight of Russians and Cossacks the Bulgarians dropped their booty and took to their heels in all directions. In common with other human beings, Cossacks take an exaggerated dislike to seeing others do what they are forbidden themselves, and our two men began to lay about them on all sides with their nagajkas. The major and I immediately followed suit, and chased the rascals all over the village, thrashing them without mercy. For once I took pleasure in the pain inflicted by the nagajka. Leaving the Cossacks to escort the train to a safe distance from the village, we rode on, congratulating ourselves on our morning's work, and followed by the blessings of the refugees.

F. D. Millet

A NEW SWITZERLAND

IF the "Play-ground of Europe" is over-crowded, there is still plenty of room in the adjoining province of the Dauphiné. It has long been known to Alpinistes, and not a few of the famous English climbers who have conquered peaks the world over, in the interests of art, science, and sport, have first tried their skill and endurance on its redoubtable aiguilles, succeeding in some instances, after long having believed them to be impregnable.*

The writer feels a certain degree of hesitation, and even reluctance, in approaching this subject. The written page which might attract the attention of the summer tourist, and cause him to turn his steps hitherward, might also bring down on the writer's head the execrations of Alpine enthusiasts, who are now seeking less accessible and crowded centres than Zermatt. The hotel-keepers only would profit by it, while to the guides it would be of doubtful value. Many a knight of the piollet, in the lack of any braver service, now earns a daily pittance by prodding pack-mules up the Riffel Alp, or superintending the baggage of the ladies. But there is little danger that the improvement of this region will come about too rapidly, although it needs must follow in course of time. One may now make the entire circuit of it without meeting a single American tourist, but in every hotel and public conveyance there is an Englishman or two—usually clad in some rusty semi-ecclesiastical garb—with their patient wives, always a British kodak, and

a bundle of rugs. The two-storied American trunk, brass-bound and glittering, with its trays full of "chiffons" and ruffles, has not yet made its appearance here. In fact, this is almost the only picturesque bit of Europe which has not been consecrated by royalty, and it has not yet become the mode, like the Engadine. Neither has any provision been made for the entertainment of tourists on rainy days, which during this season at least have been only too frequent. There is not a café chantant in the whole country; there are no "little horses," nor brass bands, nor Tyrolean singers; there are no Alpine horns or Swiss wood-carvings. Neither the heroine of the pearl necklaces nor the Belle Otero has yet attracted her train of followers to these remote solitudes. If there are no Americans, there are but few Parisiennes, and at the table d'hôte their high-pitched voices are seldom heard. Most of the guests seem to have come from Lyons, Marseilles, Grenoble, and other provincial centres. The few who might approach the standard qualified by the term "chic," and that not from the French point of view, are the English members of the Alpine Club. In a talk with the gérant of the Hospice du Lautaret, who is the autocrat of that region, and who knows how to provide his guests with every substantial comfort, I commented on the absence of our countrymen. The gérant, who seemed somewhat afraid that they might descend upon him suddenly and before he was prepared, had rather exalted notions as to their requirements. "In a few years he hoped to be ready for them, but could not yet offer the luxuries to which they were accustomed in the Engadine, where they had private salons and dining-rooms, and expected to spend at least forty francs a day."

* On the authority of a recent climber's manual, one of the most noted of the fraternity once passed the Aiguilles d'Arves, with some of the best guides in Europe, and having taken a look at the most difficult one of the three, went away convinced that it was practically impossible. It has since been found easy of accomplishment, except for one difficult passage.

In a few years, doubtless, the tourist will have no occasion to marvel at low prices. Of absolutely untrodden summits the Alpinist in quest of sensational adventures will find few, if any, and those among the minor peaks, which are often the most difficult. The guides are full of reminiscences of mad Britons who seemed to come with the sole object of breaking their necks, probably with sufficient reason, and have made straight for the steepest passes, such as the Col du Diable, which has as yet resisted their best efforts, and is in every way worthy of its name.

II.

If there is one sound more than another characteristic of the summer tourist centre, it is the unceasing tinkle of mule-bells, accompanied by the cracking of whips. In the Place de Grenette, at Grenoble, stand the various wagons, diligences, "char-à-bancs," and other nondescript vehicles which start at fixed hours for the monastery of the Grande Chartreuse and local points of interest. This is also the starting-point for the different omnibuses and little tram-cars which rattle through the narrow streets quite independently of rails. Here are the busiest cafés, shaded by awnings, with rows of orange-trees standing in square green boxes along the curb-stone; and here, as everywhere in Grenoble, the street vistas are closed in by rocky or wooded heights crowned by fortifications. Nature obligingly accommodates herself in this region, as at Briançon, to the chief object of man, which seems to be the rearing of Gibraltars and Bastilles one above another. The natural fortresses of rock, which are already partially hewn and shaped for purposes of defence, require but a touch here and there, a few lines of wall in places, to make them impregnable. But none of these elevated positions

THE PLACE DE GRENETTE, GRENOBLE.

can be visited without a written order from the commandant, the military authorities supposing, naturally enough from their stand-point, that the stranger can have no other object than that of surreptitiously making plans or photographs of their fortifications. From the other side of the river, near the foot of the Bastille, which rises abruptly from the broad quais, there is a fine retrospective view of the mountain chain behind, beginning with the three Pics de Belledonne, and this may be enjoyed without exciting suspicion. This is the snow-capped background seen in panoramic views of the city. On fête nights and on Sunday evenings military bands play in the Place de Grenette and in the public garden, entered by an archway at the end of the Place. The garden is a charming little spot which fronts on the quai opposite the heights of the Bastille; it is crowded with fine old trees; it has a sunken flower-garden, and a broad elevated terrace, bordered by a low stone balustrade, such as Rico loves to paint in Venice. The city improves as one lingers in it, and is attractive even in showery, unsettled weather, when the mists hang about the heights on every side, investing them with a mystery and grandeur which are somewhat lessened under a clear sky. Every day one may discover some new charm in its environs.

Grenoble, which is within easy reach of every point of interest, is the natural tourist centre of this region. It is the seat of two or three organizations instituted with the object of developing the resources of the country in the matter of hotels, routes, and ways of communication. There is, first of all, the "Société des Touristes du Dauphiné." Here are the opening lines of a pamphlet explaining its object and end: "The Society of

Tourists of the Dauphiné was founded in 1875. Its chief object is, first, the study of the Alps of the Dauphiné from a scientific point of view as well as from that of the excursionist; afterwards the execution, as far as its scope allows, of such improvements as it may judge best calculated to facilitate excursions and to attract tourists, both French and foreign, to the Dauphiné."

Although its financial resources are limited, it has already accomplished a great deal; in fact, were it not for the labors of this organization, one would still have to rough it quite as much in the Dauphiné as in the Caucasus. It has built the "Chalet Hotel" at La Berarde, and placed an excellent manager (M. Tairraz) in charge of it; the charges, according to a fixed tariff established by the society, are moderate, considering the remoteness of La Berarde from the nearest supply centre. It has also constructed many of the refuges or club-huts, and it has organized and equipped as efficient a body of guides and porters as can be found anywhere, with a well-regulated schedule of charges.

Another society, also of great practical utility, is the "Syndicat d'Initiative," which concerns itself more especially with railways and other means of transport, the improvement of hotels, advertisements, etc. It has established offices everywhere to furnish gratuitous information to tourists, and to supply hotel coupons. And there is yet another, the "Syndicat Général des Alpes Françaises," which works on similar lines.

III.

The route to Briançon passes through Vizille, whence a steam tramway runs along the side of the highway, winding through rugged glens and the narrow streets of mountain villages to Bourg-d'Oysans. This town lies on the side of an elliptically shaped valley completely surrounded by cliffs and mountains of bold and varied outlines, which shut out all but occasional glimpses of the higher summits. In regard to hotels, as the inhabitants do not yet expect any great influx of tourists, the primitive inns of the town are still amply sufficient to accommodate all comers. There are, however, a "Grand Hotel"* and a smaller one of

* Recently constructed by the Syndicat d'Initiative.

the same character, opposite the station, where one may find the table d'hôte and the traditional menu which the traveller may now enjoy from Dieppe to Constantinople—and also the orthodox waiter. Both these hotels are said to be well kept and moderate in price, like all the hotels of this province. One would have every right to protest if he found them dear. The writer chose to alight at an ancient "auberge" in the town, which he found on the list of the "Touring Club of France." A book might be written about the inns of the Dauphiné. Mr. Whymper,* who was among the very first of the Alpine pioneers in this region, was emphatic in his condemnation of these inns and the unclean ways of the villagers. They have, most of them (the inns), improved since that day. It would be unwise to recommend the cuisine of these hostelries to the American tourist. I remember with poignant regret having once commended a remote "fonda" in Spain, where we were treated with fraternal affection by the landlady and her brother, the head waiter. We lost caste and fell forever in the estimation of the friends who went there on our recommendation, and who suffered alike from the Spanish

* *Scrambles among the Alps in the Years* 1860–1869. By Ed. Whymper.

ENTRANCE OF THE PALAIS DE JUSTICE, GRENOBLE.

cookery and the well-intentioned but persistent kindness of the landlady. Since then I dare to speak well, and that in barely tolerant fashion, of but two hotels on the Continent, the "Grand" and the "Schweitzerhof," which exist everywhere, and which are always unobjectionable. At this auberge of Bourg-d'Oysans the patron was sitting on a bench outside the door, under his swinging sign, smoking a pipe of German dimensions, while his wife, in the local costume of rusty black, sat on the door-step shelling pease. The house was entered through the kitchen, where several sturdy handmaidens were bustling about the range preparing dinner. A door at one end led up two steep flights of stairs to the bedrooms. The bedrooms of the Dauphiné are full of little surprises, where the element of the unexpected plays a prominent part. You must either pass through several others to reach your own, or the occupants of the others must needs use yours as a passage. Mine lay between two others which were unoccupied, and it was sufficiently furnished, as well as clean. It had also an electric bell within

A SUBURB OF BRIANÇON.

easy reach, and the dining-room was electrically lighted. This auberge has probably changed little in other respects since the days of Rabelais, and it must have been a good one then. But the quantity and quality of its viands seem better adapted to the solid stomachs of that era than to the capricious requirements of the modern Babylonians. Dinner was served in a sort of waiting-room opening out of the kitchen. There was no table d'hôte, and one missed the long rows of tourists watching each other across the pots of artificial flowers. The patron and his family, with an occasional cousin, occupied one table, and each guest —there were never more than two— had a table to himself, as well as a separate dinner. There was always a whole tureen of very substantial soup, and a large trout, which might appear at the beginning or at the end of the repast, as it happened. Now these trout, which were often of the pink variety known as "saumonée," were not at all "according to Hoyle." They were sometimes too large for one man; they were too fresh, having just been taken out of the water, and not having had time to acquire that flavor by which we recognize them at the usual table d'hôte, and one could see them taken sizzling off the kitchen fire and placed still smoking on the table. There was often a large platter of macaroni "au gratin," made after some local fashion, and also very hot. A whole filet or gigot d'agneau seasoned with sage followed, wine and desserts, melons and grapes à discrétion. If the undiscriminating and brutal appetite which is usually the penalty of a long day on the hills did not suffice to enable one to clear the table, there were the patient but persistent dogs, five of the fox-hound type, of all ages, from puppyhood to maturity, and two shaggier-coated but very sociable brutes of the collie persuasion. They had all been substantially fed out of great smoking porringers by the kitchen range, but they wanted more, and frequently deserted the patron's table to take up their station under mine, or to stand, one on each side, with their paws on my knees.

One liver-colored puppy with pendent
ears usually stood on the opposite side of
the table, with fore paws crossed on the
edge, watching every movement with pathetic and supplicating eyes. These im-
portunities were frequently interrupted
by a sudden raid on the part of the patron, who would dislodge his canine followers with stick or napkin. I returned
to that inn when I passed through the
town on the way to La Grave, in order
to have another trout. It was the last,
for at all the other properly conducted
hotels it is considered good form to ignore the local trout, and serve the guests
with the fish to which they are accustomed, more or less fatigued by their journey
from Dieppe, or with canned salmon. It
was at Bourg-d'Oysans that I first became
acquainted with the bread of the Dauphiné. That exquisite phrase of Howells's,
"the stony bread of Italy," would be
hardly appropriate to it. It may be questioned whether nickelled steel would make
a better cuirass for armored ships. To
be attacked with safety, it should be firmly
fixed in a vise, and divided with some
keen weapon of the nature of an adze.
When the unfortunate novice tries to
slice it with a table-knife, it usually
glances and buries itself in his flesh.

IV.

There are many pleasant excursions
which one may make from Bourg-
d'Oysans, returning the same day. There
is a path which mounts steeply near a
cascade across the valley to the upper
terraces of the cliffs: here a crooked
mule-path, paved in places, winds upwards, shaded by great trees, to the village of Huez; a further ascent leads to a
group of chalets, seen against the sky, on
the edge of a green and treeless plateau.
From this point smooth green meadows,
where the haymakers are at work, roll
upwards towards a range of steep rocky
ledges, beyond which rises the chain of
La Herpie and other summits patched
with snow. High up in a hollow beyond
the first rocky ridge lies the little "Lac
Blanc," reflecting in its green depths the
white expanse of a small glacier which
slopes down to its very margin. It is at
Bourg-d'Oysans that one is first impressed
with the Southern atmosphere and the
magnificent coloring of this country, so
like that of the Italian lake district.

From Grenoble, by steam tramway and

train to Bourg-d'Oysans, by a service of
wagons or char-à-bancs passing through
La Grave to Briançon, and thence by
train *viâ* Gap, one may make the entire

THE INN AT BOURG-D'OYSANS.

circuit of the principal mountain groups
in two or three days, returning to the
original starting-point. But to reach La
Berarde, which is in the very centre of
the horseshoe group formed by the chief
summits, one must make a détour from
Bourg-d'Oysans, whence a daily conveyance starts every morning for Bourg-
d'Aru, some two hours distant. From
this point the rest of the day's journey up
the valley may be made on foot or on
muleback, passing St.-Christophe perched
steeply on the side of the valley and em-
bosomed in foliage. The ancient mule-
track, roughly paved, winds upwards to
the village, where there are two inns of
the old order. Here one begins to catch
glimpses of the higher mountains and
glaciers at the end of the valley, or rising
above the rocky heights on either hand.
St.-Christophe is also a well-known centre
for mountaineers, but less advantageous
than La Berarde, being placed much
lower down. The carriage-road is now
being continued from Bourg-d'Aru to this
point. The valley becomes more stony
and desolate as one mounts upwards.
The group of low stone huts with tall

chimneys, with dark and mossy thatched roofs, which is all there is at La Berarde, walled in by barren rocky cliffs, has much the character of a Highland village in Scotland. The Chalet Hotel, built and equipped by the "Société des Touristes du Dauphiné," is the most conspicuous object in the landscape. It is under

LA BERARDE.

excellent management, and, like many of the most desirable spots on the globe, has been annexed by Great Britain.

By the little group of people sitting at iron tables in front of the house, and having afternoon tea and jam—a spectacle seldom seen at places not frequented by our English cousins—as well as by the general neatness of the service and the air of Sabbath-day stillness and propriety which reigned, it was easy to guess that England had taken possession. This state of things was brought forcibly home to the writer when he found that all the single bedrooms were occupied, and the only thing obtainable was a bed in a "dortoir," or many-bedded room. In spite of the regret shown by the hospitable manager, he removed his chattels to the ancient auberge close by, which was kept by "La Mère Angélique," one of the privileged characters of the locality, while he made the Chalet Hotel his headquarters.

The only available bedroom in this auberge was a little cell walled with pine boards, and with one small grated window; according to Mother Angélique this room had been occupied for many seasons by Mr. Coolidge, the famous conqueror of virgin summits. On the pine boards of

the partition wall four members of the French Alpine Club had pencilled "Notre admiration pour Sir Coolidge. Juillet, 1885."

La Mère Angélique spoke most intelligible French, for the good reason that, like most natives of the valley, who use patois among themselves, she kept her best French for the passing stranger. She was much interested in stray articles of toilet from the world below, but shook her head doubtfully over a hair mitten, which she considered much too thin and flimsy for the cold of the mountains. She had never seen a bicycle, and seemed unacquainted with the use of cold water. There were two Swiss climbers at the hotel. One of them had brought his young wife, and the three together had been "doing peaks" without guides. The other guests belonged to the British contingent. On contemplating this group of pioneers, one could not help being impressed with the uniformity of their attire; wherever you meet the English Alpinist or aspirant, he invariably wears a peculiar low-crowned felt hat, with a wide brim, which gives him a semi-clerical appearance, but never by any chance a hat of the Tyrolean shape, now so much in vogue, although the Prince of Wales has given it his official sanction. He may perchance don that article of head-gear in the streets of Paris or Vienna, but would not care to be "found dead with it" in any Alpine fastness. If a regiment of them could be gathered together from their various haunts, it would be found that they were uniformly equipped enough to pass muster as a military organization; and it would not be easy to find a more fearless or a hardier body of men. The nations which border on the Alps may boast of their rival battalions of Alpine chasseurs, but a regiment of these primly attired civilians could easily leave them "out of sight" when it came to scaling cliffs, and still have a reserve fund of energy for the enemy on the other side.

The little room at the auberge was

reached by a series of rude stone steps, a
kind of side alley between two thatched
roofs, which usually dripped for an hour
or so after a shower. The steps were
muddy and strongly scented by cattle and
goats, but the little chamber, which opened
into a hay-loft, was fairly clean and well
kept. When it rained at La Berarde
there was even less to distract the visit-
or's mind than in most of the Swiss
mountain resorts, and his situation strongly resembled that of the traveller who is
weather-bound in some isolated Moorish
town. He might use his broad window
ledge as a work-table, or gaze through the
diminutive iron-barred squares at the po-
tato-field in bloom, at the stone chalets
with tall chimneys from which the smoke
drifted downward in the slanting rain, at
the green, stone-bestrewn bank threaded
with zigzag paths which rises across the
torrent to the rocky buttresses of
"La Grande Aiguille" opposite.
He had better do this: it is safer
than to turn tail on a wet day and
flee down the valley; for he is liable to be pelted by falling stones
from the cliffs, loosened by the
rain at various points in the road
down to Bourg-d'Oysans. But
when the clouds rolled away the
sky became at once of the deepest
violet, and the sunlight had that
intensity, the local color of things
that peculiar vibration and life,
rendered more vivid by the opposition of sharp black shadows,
which are characteristic of the
Italian summer. For here we are
well to the southward of Turin.

V.

As the Matterhorn is to Zermatt, so is the "Meije" to La Berarde and La Grave. There may
be other European peaks known
to experienced Alpinists which
present greater difficulties, but the
Meije bids fair to rival the Matterhorn as a slayer of men. It
remained unconquered for three
years longer, and Whymper, in his
Scrambles among the Alps, refers
to it as being almost the only untrodden summit left. Its architecture is of the most fantastic imaginable, although it has not the
simple and impressive outline of
the Matterhorn, so isolated, so ap-

palling and yet fascinating to the novice,
and which rises more than sixteen hundred feet higher than the Meije. But
mere height has little or nothing to do
with the inaccessibility of mountain summits. Let one figure to himself a Gothic
cathedral of strange, elaborate, flamboy-
ant design. Far above its mighty foundations, approached by miles of moraines
and steep glacier, from a point only
reached after a stiff scramble up a couloir equal in difficulty to many well-
known Swiss peaks, rises the smooth
brown wall of the edifice, supporting a
steeply pitched, ice-covered roof, known
as the "Glacier Carré." High above this
glacier rise the towers and spires, slender
ice-coated finials, obelisks of ruddy stone
which flame orange in the cloudless morning or at sunset; and there are not lacking gargoyles of grotesque form or mam-

GLACIER DE LA PILOTTE BY MOONLIGHT (AT LA
BERARDE).

moth proportions to complete the resemblance. Only the great "Pic Occidental" of the Meije seems to rise with a mighty sweep of vertical lines, straight from the lower glacier, and may be likened to the main tower of the cathedral. At other times it suggests a fortress which Nature has done her best to defend against the assaults of men. Like the moats of such a fortress, yawning "bergschrunds" protect certain sides of it, and above them rises the steep glacis of ice to the foot of the walls, here absolutely perpendicular, there overhanging, and in other places sloping inward like the towers of a Persian gateway. It was long before a safe way of scaling this stronghold was discovered, and even now the proper day and hour must be chosen.

VI.

Four English climbers had been waiting for some weeks to make the ascent, and during two perfect days, when the Meije was accessible for the first and only time during the entire season, they set out, two at a time. The two more experienced members of the Alpine Club left the Refuge du Châtelleret first, and as they descended, late on the following day, they met two Frenchmen, members of a society at Grenoble, who were working their way slowly, and without guides, along the Glacier Carré.

The Englishmen had first passed them early in the morning at a point lower down, called the "Promontory." During the night after their return to La Bérarde the weather suddenly changed, and a cold rain began to fall on the following day. As this usually means snow on the higher altitudes, they naturally began to feel some anxiety in regard to the Frenchmen, from whom no news had been heard. The two Frenchmen, it should have been stated, had come from La Grave, on the opposite side of the Meije, accompanied by their wives and two porters. They had all passed the night in the cabane, but the French Alpinists, without mentioning their destination, had set out alone, soon after midnight, while the ladies returned to La Grave, with the two porters, by way of the Col known as the Brèche de la Meije. The Englishmen, aside from the anxiety dictated by common humanity, felt a sense of responsibility as members of the C. A., and with three guides, a supply of

provisions and restoratives, they set out on their quest, but without feeling at that moment any marked degree of apprehension. We saw them start off quietly and prosaically enough in the rain, with umbrellas, one with a water-proof, the other with a golf cape, quite as if they were contemplating a game of golf in the intervals of the showers. But all knew that should they find no trace of the missing men at the refuge, neither peril of wind nor snow nor wreathing vapor would prevent them from attempting a second ascent under the most trying and hazardous conditions imaginable, so long as guides could be induced to go with them. But their endurance was not put to that severe test. Early in the evening one of the party came down with the news that the bodies of the two men had been found. The guides had pressed on up the glacier and had first discovered one of them lying at the foot of the grand couloir; the other, still fast to the rope, which had caught on the rocks, hung in the opening of the crevasse formed by the shrinking of the ice at the foot of the cliff.

A larger party was organized at once to bring them down, and by noon on the following day they reached the refuge of Le Châtelleret with the two victims of the Meije. As they descended, picking their way along the crest of the moraine, carrying the two bodies corded to poles and wrapped up like mummies in rough canvas, the rain still fell, but from time to time, through rifts in the dense curtain of vapor, the crags of the Meije appeared for an instant apparently supernatural in height, and the Glacier Carré shone out like a fragment of white cloud, and again disappeared. There can be but little doubt that they reached the summit, since two figures were seen there from La Grave late in the day, so late that they must have been obliged to pass the night on the mountain, somewhere above the Pyramide Duhamel, in all probability. They were both tried mountaineers, and one of them was already familiar with the ground; had it not been for the tempest which took place at night, they would without doubt have reached the bottom in safety. But benumbed with cold, and blinded by the snow, which obliterated every trace left the day before, they could have been in no condition to make the descent of the couloir when the rocks were glassy with frozen sleet, and it was

VICTIMS OF THE MEIJE.

here, beyond a doubt, that the fatal slip was made. They were laid in the little chapel at La Berarde, with flowers about them, and a few lighted candles. Messengers had been sent to summon the mayor of St.-Christophe and two gendarmes, in order that the legal formalities might be accomplished. The official examination of the English Alpinistes and the guides, who had given such proof of their courage and devotion, took place in the little sitting-room of the chalet, where the broken rope and other relics were produced. The honest pomposity of the officers of the law, their lack of familiarity with English, and the way in which they contrived to mix themselves up and everybody else, lent a touch of serio-tragic humor, a slight flavor of opera-bouffe, which somewhat relieved the general depression. But the saddest event of the tragedy was the arrival, at dusk, of the two young wives, and the moment when they were led out to the chapel by the English ladies of the colony.

VII.

A few days afterward, when the weather had again become brilliant, the gérant proposed that we take Christophe Turc, the well-known guide, with a sturdy young porter, and ascend the Meije to look for traces of the two men.

We reached the cabane of Le Châtelleret before sundown, although the narrow Vallée des Étançons lay in shadow for the greater part of the afternoon, and while the gérant busied himself in concocting a savory mess for dinner, I made for a sheltered spot among the rocks, well bundled up to guard against the gathering chill, and proceeded to note down the changing effect of sunset on the Meije, half hidden by the evening mists. They descended at times quite to the lower edge of the Glacier des Étançons, shrouding the peak completely, and there seemed to be little chance of accomplishing anything more; and then for an instant the mists rapidly dissolved, the highest pyramid shone out like a tongue of flame against the purple above, and the whole range appeared in sharp relief, and again they curled and writhed slowly upwards like a column of smoke, and through it, as through a veil, the sharp arêtes of flaming orange, illuminated by the setting sun and the rich coloring of the whole mass, could be dimly seen.

The refuge of Le Châtelleret is like most of its class in Switzerland; a sloping bed of straw, provided with blankets, a stove, and cooking utensils are the only furniture. As the guides had no hope of reaching the summit in its present state we did not leave the refuge until 5 A.M. The ascent of the moraines is exceptionally long and irksome, but the glacier being only slightly crevassed at this point is soon gotten over, and we clambered up the rocks on the right of the couloir by which we were to ascend. At this point it is customary to halt and partake of a second breakfast, for guides are creatures of habit. Just above this breathing-place occurs a curious bit of rock-scrambling, where a poor gymnast has a chance to display his lack of grace. Having wriggled up this crevice as best we could, we came to the jagged rock arête by which the "Grand Couloir" is reached, well above the spot where it opens on the glacier, and where the bodies were found. Here one may look up through the gloom of this deep and narrow cleft, as through a telescope, to the crags and turrets above, now glowing red in the light of sunrise, and which seem almost directly overhead. It did not look an easy road, but it is the only available one known at present, and it certainly was not yet in good condition in spite of the burning sun of the last few days.

The couloir or chimney, lying in shadow for the greater part of the day, was still choked with snow, and for some distance we worked carefully along the ledges above it, here turning a sharp corner and groping for some projection on the hidden side which might offer either hand- or foothold—one is contented with little at such times—there lowering ourselves by finger-tips till we could drop with safety to the next ledge or projection below. Owing to the icy sheathing which glazed many of the rocks, but one man could move at a time, while the others were securely placed. To my way of thinking, the most unpleasant part of that couloir was the long snow slope—soft, granulated, and treacherous in some places; frozen hard in others. This long ice ladder was about as steep as it could well be without being vertical, and the nearest rocks on either side did not offer inviting handhold, since, owing to their stratification, they presented a series of smooth and slender points leaning down-

THE MEIJE AT SUNSET, SEEN FROM LA GRAVE.

wards, and mostly varnished with thin black ice. There was also the constant preoccupation in order to avoid dislodging a stone or piece of ice which might knock the man below out of his steps. In this fashion we moved slowly upward, making slight détours in order to peer down the walls of the ravine, but without finding trace of the lost men. At one point, a thousand feet, more or less, above the glacier, a steep bed of snow adhered to the rocks, and from the way in which it was ploughed and furrowed in every direction, quite to the glassy ice-clad edge of its lower lip, one might imagine that a desperate struggle for foothold had taken place. But upon closer inspection it appeared to have been cut and broken up by falling stones from above. In some similar spot the accident must have occurred; for two men, however skilful, might easily lose their traces in descending, particularly in bad weather; and even now a slight deviation of a foot or two on either side might have ensured a rather sudden descent to the glacier.

At the Pyramide Duhamel, so named by the gentleman who could get no further (at that time), which was our case to-day, we sat down, or rather anchored ourselves by such portions of our anatomies as would fit into the crevices, and emptied a bottle of champagne provided by the kindness of our host. It did not taste badly, drunk from leather cups at this altitude. Either the boring rays of the sun or the champagne, or both, had a soporific effect on the gérant, and pulling his hat over his eyes, he stretched himself out on the very edge of the declivity and fell asleep —after the guides had given a double turn of his rope around a projecting rock. Over our heads rose the vertical wall which has to be scaled in order to reach the Glacier Carré, that sloping, square, white patch which one sees from afar, invisible from this point, and only to be divined by the fringe of icicles along the upper edge of the wall. Above this, again, rose the battlements, towers, and pinnacles of the three summits, crowning all by a few feet, the main peak resembling

THE BRÈCHE DE LA MEIJE, FROM THE FRONT OF THE HOTEL AT LA GRAVE.

in one's memory like the fragment of a bad dream. This was a crevice in a ledge of overhanging rocks barely wide enough to turn in, and which could only be descended by twisting face in and face out alternately. Half-way down occurs a smooth bit of rock sloping outwards in such a way as to conceal the next man below; the points of support for the right hand and foot are readily found, but the others are not at once evident, and had it not been for the man below, I should have been obliged to rely altogether on the rope. This was humiliating, for the couloir is considered the easiest part of the whole business, and when one descends from the summit of the Pic Occidental and reaches the top of this couloir, it is with a sense of relief. For the "Thorough Expert," mentioned so often in Baedeker, there is no particular difficulty about this ascent when the conditions are favorable; but it certainly adds to the interest to adopt at times the point of view of the man who looks at the picturesque side of things and tries to realize their dramatic possibilities. His enjoyment will be somewhat marred, however, by the conviction that he is powerless to express by any form of art the impressions which rapidly succeed each other.

somewhat in outline the Rothhorn from the Hörnli. Below us, connected with the slope on which we lay by a thin, wedgelike cornice, rose a slender spire sprinkled with snow; a crow soared across the abyss and perched on its apex. High up on our right a red obelisk leaned over toward the white slopes of the Brèche de la Meije, almost too dazzling to look at.

As we descended, the views of Christophe, and his assertion that all the rest of the mountain was in an utterly unsafe condition, were well borne out, for a series of avalanches poured down the wall from the Glacier Carré, looking at that distance quite like cataracts of water. Getting down was a slower process than getting up, and I rejoiced in having had the foresight to leave my piollet below. That of the leader was of course necessary in hewing a way, but it seems much easier for the novice to imitate the clinging cat, and to have four points of support to depend on. Just above the spot where we had left our provisions we again reached the point which somehow lingers

VIII.

Most of the refuges and club-huts of the Dauphiné are situated too low down, and much lower than those of Switzerland. Thus the ascent of the rugged and inhospitable little peaks of this region necessitates more time and effort than many of the higher Swiss mountains. The refuge of Le Carrelet, built against a rock beyond La Berarde, in the valley of the Veneon, is no exception to this rule. Here we passed the night comfortably enough, preparatory to attempting the Pic Coolidge. This is a rocky pyramid of respectable height, commanding a fine view of "Les Écrins," the highest summit of them all. We were desirous of ascertaining the state of the

mountain, as hitherto it had been inaccessible during nearly the whole season.
The night was warm and close. When
we left the cabane at dawn the moon
still shone through the clouds; but as
we reached higher ground the entire horizon behind us became black and menacing, while the successive mountain
ranges appeared of that deep and sullen
violet so ominous in this region; balloon-
shaped puffs of gray vapor rose upwards
towards the zenith, and a few drops
of rain fell. We still had hopes that
the storm, which we saw was inevitable, might take some other direction;
but as we mounted the glacier towards the Col du Temple, furious gusts
of wind followed us, and once on
the ridge we were exposed to the
full force of the gale, which nearly
swept us off our feet, while the snow
cut our faces like volleys of fine shot.
The Pic Coolidge was now out of the
question, but we clambered up the
rocks on its lee side, hoping to get
out of the wind; our position there becoming untenable by reason of cold,
we hurried down the Glacier Noir,
where we found shelter under a huge
rock, partly surrounded by a rough
stone wall; the enclosure was filled
with snow, but the wind, which whistled and shrieked around us, was a
degree less piercing than on the Pic.
Looking across through the driving
snow at the frowning black walls of
the Pelvoux, I remembered the device
on the wine-merchant's shop opposite
the Cimetière Montmartre: "Ici on
est mieux qu'en face." Although we
were somewhat better off
than if we had been on
the cliffs of Pelvoux, we
were fast becoming stiff
and generally uncomfort-
able. The only thing left
for us to do was to face
the blast again, and make
a rush homewards over
the summit of the Col.
Within an hour we were
picking our way down
the moraine, genially
thawing at the anticipa-
tion of the skinful of hot
wine which we should
drink at the refuge.
From there down to La
Bérarde we had to face a

deluge of rain, but were none the worse
for the wetting.

IX.

At La Grave we are again on the diligence road which climbs upward from
Bourg-d'Oysans to the Col du Lautaret,
and then descends to Briançon, where the
railway from Grenoble terminates. The
long drive upwards through the wintry
rain, and the arrival stiff and benumbed

THE GRAND COULOIR OF THE MEIJE.

ÉMIL PIC CROSSING A SNOW BRIDGE ON LA
GRANDE RUINE.

As this is the northern side, it presents a very different aspect from that seen from Le Châtelleret. In the hotel hangs a fragment of broken rope, a relic of Dr. Zsigmondy, who was lost in traversing the arête from the Pic Central to the main summit. Three hours beyond La Grave is the Chalet de l'Alpe, at the height of six thousand nine hundred and seventy feet, built and equipped by the "society," and placed in the charge of a gérant. Although much more primitive in its arrangements than that at La Berarde, it is quite luxurious when compared with the ordinary refuge. I had been fortunate enough to fall in with Émil Pic, one of the pioneer guides of this region, and still in his prime. One of the finest glacier passes in the range has been christened after him. Although he felt confident that in a few days, if the snow continued to melt, we might be able to do the Pic Central, I had seen too much of Dauphiné weather to place any reliance on its stability. While we waited there came one glorious day, but only one, which, after much discussion, we devoted to the ascent of "La Grande Ruine," that being the only peak worthy of respect which was then accessible. Seen from the other side it appears to be a bare, rocky spur of the Meije group, but on this side it proved to be quite buried in snow. When we reached the Chalet de l'Alpe, just before dusk, for our progress had been agreeably retarded by frequent clusters of huckleberry bushes, it was so cold that even the guides hung about the stove. Josef, the son of Émil, a brawny young giant of twenty (there are six more of them), accompanied us as porter. Émil Pic is to all intents and purposes a young man still; his complexion is of the richest mahogany, and his blue-black hair and beard are without a streak of gray, although he owns to fifty summers. The light of the full moon was so brilliant when we started at two A.M. that we could dispense with lanterns as we stepped gingerly over the bowlders of the long moraines. Out of the thirteen hours which this expedition occupied from the refuge and back, nearly half were spent on toiling over endless heaps of angular fragments.

The steep, ragged arête just below the summit, which is usually bare at this sea-

at the hospitable Hôtel de la Meije, were enough to make one forget his Italian imaginings, inspired by the sunshine and heat of the previous day. But the view from the hotel windows on the cloudless morning which followed was a lavish compensation for such mere passing discomforts. One may travel far without finding a more noble and impressive mountain landscape, a wilder and more savage chaos of deeply furrowed towers and pinnacles of rock surmounted by cliffs and cataracts of ice, than that which rises so grandly from the deep green valley of the Romanche. On the terrace across the road, in front of the hotel, which overlooks the windings of the valley, are two gay little pavilions, with scarlet and yellow awnings, café tables, a comfortable array of lounging-chairs, and a telescope pointing upwards at a steep angle and focussed on the Meije, now dazzling with newly fallen snow.

son, protruded only a few inches above the level of the snow. It was here that the only incident occurred in what is usually an easy climb. Josef, who had relieved his father in "tracking," had kicked and cut steps a metre or so to the right of this rocky backbone, and having perched securely above us, we followed in turn. Half-way up, the snow began to slide down over the foundation of ice beneath; Émil, taking in the situation at a glance, crept swiftly up the rocks on all fours until he reached Josef, and I was then able to follow by hanging on the rope, for there was but one step left, the others having made themselves the nucleus of a miniature avalanche.*

No finer point of view could have been chosen, for the whole mass of the Meije rose almost within gunshot. Behind us towered the Écrins, with its formidable arêtes buried deep in fresh snow—the Pelvoux—and just across the glacier which we had toiled up stood the "Roche Méane," with four slender pinnacles, two of which have not yet been ascended, according to Stephane Juge. Mont Blanc, toned by a mellow haze, and Monte Viso, were the highest points in sight. As we looked down from the summit into the Vallée des Étançons, I remarked to Émil that if they would build a refuge higher up, the ascent of the Meije need not take longer than that of the Matterhorn. He replied, with the tone of a priest who is speaking of unseen powers, "Il faut respecter La Meije."

Our descent from the summit to the lower edge of the glacier, which had taken us four hours to mount, was accomplished in one, owing to the long glissades, and the tremendous gambols of the younger Pic, who towed us after him, in spite of his father's protestations.

X.

It was almost an Asiatic landscape which lay before us when we arrived in front of the hospice on the Col du Lautaret. We were on the side of a green cup-shaped hollow like the crater of an extinct volcano. The barren angular ridges

on the east, sparsely streaked with snow, burned crimson in the sunset, while the heights on the other side were unmistakably Alpine in character, and the freshly fallen snow descended almost to our level. What might be termed the minor ranges of the Dauphiné, which are even more interesting and bizarre in character, pictorially speaking, than the principal group, first appear here, and follow the route to Grenoble by way of Briançon and Gap. They rise in castellated, turreted forms, seamed with deep vertical fis-

GUIDES UNROPING IN LA GRANDE RUINE.

sures, which add to their apparent height, while their sky-lines are deeply notched and indented, or rise in splintered crags, or take the form of fortresses like the "Mont Aiguille," which seems to have been shaped by rule and compass, so square, so massive are its outlines. High up in these rocky gorges, barren of all vegetation, one might fancy one's self in Arabia, while beyond Gap the lower slopes often have the pale dotted character of Provence, which is close at hand. As one passes through the villages by diligence or post-wagon, the men are all playing at bowls, the local pastime. After the quiet of the higher solitudes, Briançon is a giddy little world in itself.

---

* For once Baedeker is inexact. He says of "La Grande Ruine"—"Fairly easy, especially when there is plenty of snow." The admirable little work, *Guide Bleu Illustré*, by Stephane Juge, says: "Difficult of access. The difficulty increases in direct ratio with the quantity of snow."

The approach to Briançon by the winding road from the Col du Lautaret is strikingly picturesque : every rock is crowned with a fortress. The most interesting feature of the town is the Grande Rue, which begins at the fortress gate and climbs a hill of amazing steepness, so steep that it would be unsafe to venture on it in winter without an ice-axe and a rope. Through this narrow street, between tall houses decidedly Italian in character, for Briançon is but eleven kilometres from the frontier, runs a stone channel, down which courses a stream of water, carrying old boots, paper boxes, and tin cans.

This is the headquarters of the Chasseurs Alpins, one of the most efficient and active bodies of men in the French army. Their uniform of dark blue with knickerbockers, and "berets," worn carelessly over one ear, gives them a rather brigandish appearance.

From Briançon to Gap and onward, the train to Grenoble passes through gorges of ochre and sienna tinted rocks, as blinding in the light of noon as those of Andalusia. The engineering of this line is remarkable, and the landscape has a dramatic quality, if one may so call it, abounding in abrupt transitions.

So long as the stranger keeps to the beaten route, with occasional excursions into the centre of the mountain district, he will find all that is needful. The Alpinist, who is usually less exacting than the tourist, will fare quite as well as in the Tyrol. Everywhere the innkeepers, or gérants in the service of the "Société des Touristes," who generally have an intimate personal acquaintance with the mountains, and second only to that of the guides, are ready to supply him with information, and often to accompany him on important expeditions. If he has time to penetrate into the lesser ranges on foot, which border on Provence or on the Italian frontier, or by post-wagon, he must, from all accounts, be prepared to do without even comfortable inns. In fact, this is a smaller intensified edition of Switzerland, with more than its extremes of temperature, under a Southern sun, and offering within its limited area a greater variety of contrasts.

BRIANÇON.

DOMESTIC AND COURT CUSTOMS OF PERSIA

A PERSIAN mounts his horse on the right side; he writes from right to left. These may seem unimportant, trifling characteristics, but they are cited as forcible illustrations of the radical and permanent difference between the nations of the East and the West. The difference in the external customs and institutions is more apparent, perhaps, but is less important and profound than the divergences existing in the thought or the intellectual cast of these two great divisions of the human race.

The Persians resemble Europeans, or rather the Latin people, more than do other Asiatics, and yet, from the great gulf existing between Persian and Frenchman, one who has never been in the East may form some conception of the vast and seemingly irreconcilable space that separates the Asiatic in general from the European type.

Oriental life must possess charms for the student of human nature for ages; that of Persia is of especial interest, because, while apparently cast in fixed moulds of immemorial usage, it is more plastic and mobile than that of other Eastern countries. The Persian is of a vivacious, mercurial disposition, and has none of that aversion to change, as such, which is so marked a characteristic of the Chinese or the Indian. The climate suggests certain customs which, being suited to the circumstances, require only slow modification, and the rigidity of the theocratic code retards social movements. Were it not for these the Persians would be inclined by nature to be less distant in the rear of this progressive age. As it is, we find in Persia a somewhat complex civilization, and a diversity of races which by their individual traits give variety to the study of life in that ancient country. Three points are especially prominent when one comes to an analysis of Persian life: one is the fact that it is essentially an out-of-door life; another point is the seeming publicity of life there, the absence of reserve; and thirdly, in direct contrast with this characteristic is the profound seclusion and mystery of the domestic life of Persia. The former two characteristics of Persian society are the direct result of the climate, and necessarily partake of the simplicity which attends primitive life in all lands; but the reason for the character of the domestic institutions is more obscure; it can not be attributed wholly to the teachings of the Koran, for it has been a marked feature of Oriental life in all ages, the English sentiment that a man is lord in his own castle seeming to be a concise statement of the Persian ideas on the question of home life.

The physical conditions underlying the customs of Persia are as simple as the habits to which they have given rise—a country twice the size of France, representing, except in the Caspian provinces, a vast plateau 4000 to 6000 feet above the sea, skirted by tremendous snow-clad ranges, and including vast tracts of waste lands strewn with sand and salt. These spaces, where the onager and the gazelle wander at will, and the vulture poises in the cloudless heavens above, are broken at intervals by water-courses, giving sustenance to tufts of luxuriant verdure, which are as distinctly marked on the red waste lands as a dark shadow of a cloud on a summer day.

Here is a climate where rain never falls from April until December, where the temperature is uniform for the entire season, and the transition from one season to another as gradual as the approach of old age. For the greater part of the year the heat of mid-day obliges one to travel by the light of the moon, and to remain in the cool until the sun nears the west. For thousands of years these physical conditions have existed, and have maintained the character and customs of the Persians without change. The Persian who, smoking his kaliân at Teheran to-day, meditates "treasons, stratagems, and spoils," is in no essential sense different from his "burned fathers," whom Xenophon describes, no less unscrupulous, no less acute and wily and intellectual, no less addicted to the discussion of mystic philosophy and poetry, no less devoted to corrupt thoughts, and no less inspired by a wonderful feeling for the beautiful.

A third of the population of Persia is still composed of nomads, and all travel and freightage are still, as of old, conducted by means of horses, asses, camels, and mules, even though it be the choice wares and inventions of Europe, which they carry from the frontier over lofty rocky passes to the royal saloons of Teheran. It is at early morning, after a long toilsome night over the mountains and plains, that these caravans enter the gates of Teheran, with the tinkle of donkey bells or the sonorous, monotonous clang of the larger bell which announces the stately march of the otherwise noiseless train of camels. Here and there among the confused throng of beasts of burden and vociferous drivers surging into the capital, one sees some man of rank coming from Meschêd or Ispahân. He is of dignified mien and dark but handsome features, and is superbly mounted. A train of mounted attendants clear the way for his approach, and perhaps his wives are also with him in tachtravans, or litters, borne by mules, or in kajevêhs, which are covered boxes slung on each side of a mule. Attaching ourselves to this imposing train, and borrowing some of its splendor, we enter the Gate of Meschêd, so called because one coming from that celebrated shrine of the Sheah faith, and from the now famous frontier of Afghanistan in dispute between England and Russia, must enter Teheran at this point. It is a lofty arched structure, resembling a Roman triumphal arch in size and plan. It is crowned with four pinnacles, and the entire surface is decorated with elegant geometric designs composed of glazed bricks of several indestructible colors.

Having fairly entered the city, one is surprised to find a bustling, thriving place of 180,000 people, rapidly spreading out in all directions, and destined soon to outgrow the limits now prescribed by the extensive earth-works and fosse laid out in modern style of fortification by the late General Büler, who captured Herat under Mohammed Shah. The nucleus or centre of the city is composed of the Ark, or the vast inclosure which embraces the palace now occupied by the Shah and the Foreign and War offices, with the arsenal and barracks. Adjoining the Ark are the extensive covered bazars, the finest in the East after those of Constantinople, less magnificent, perhaps, in the external display of goods, but more solidly and elegantly constructed. From the centre the city radiates in all directions, occupying the space of a European city of thrice the population, owing to the numerous and extensive gardens it includes, and the large ground-plan of the dwellings. It is now divided into the so-called Old and New parts, the latter being laid out with considerable regularity, with broad streets lined with trees, parks, and esplanades. Avenues of trees by the street sides are not, however, a feature of Teheran borrowed, as one might hastily suppose, from European usage. The finest avenues of Ispahân and Shiraz were thus beautified in the palmy days of Shah Abbas and the good Kerim Khân, the Zend.

Open water-courses, distributing water to all parts of the city, are on either side of these avenues of Teheran, and daily the dust is laid by sakkâhs, or water-carriers, who also supply the tea-shops and families of the better class with drinking water from sources presumed to be uncontaminated by the impurities defiling the ordinary connaughts, or channels. Water is the most precious article in Persia. Agriculture is entirely dependent upon irrigation, while the depth to which wells must be carried, and the absence of either rain or dew for ten months, require the expenditure of enormous labor and treasure to bring water from the mountains, or to divert the few existing streams into the public service.

We entered Teheran in the morning, and following the direction taken by the caravan, we came to one of the numerous caravansaries, which serve at once as inns for the lodging of strangers, and depots for the deposit of goods until distributed. On the country roads they are generally small, and the animals and loads rest outside in the open, generally free from molestation, for the country is at present in good order, and far more safe from brigandage than the disturbed adjoining territories of Turkey. Men of wealth or position travelling in Persia usually send in advance and hire a house during their stay in a place, or they are entertained by friends. The vaunted hospitality of olden times, still in full vogue in Oriental countries, is no indication of superior amiability or breeding; it is the result of circumstances—a system of mutual accommodation under unavoidable conditions, in which the host dispenses a courtesy which he knows he may need in turn. But the men of the middle and lower classes generally resort to the caravansaries, where they take a room, cook their own meals, and sleep on a rug they carry with them. In Teheran it is usual for a traveller to resort to an inn where he may find fellow-townsmen. Availing myself of this fact in several instances when I was obliged to cause the arrest of fugitive criminals, I was able to trace and secure them through information obtained from those sojourning there.

After unloading his goods, the travelling merchant finds it next in order to take a bath, which is one of the institu-

practice. They resemble the Turkish baths, but in those of Persia the cold plunge bath in an immense tank is a most important feature. The water in these tanks becomes foul from frequent use and insufficient care to change it, and diseases

WEIGHING MERCHANDISE IN A CARAVANSARY, TEHERAN.

tions of Persia. Public baths abound at Teheran, and every one visits them at least once a week; many do it daily. The wealthy have private baths attached to their houses, which are sometimes elegant and luxurious. Christians are never permitted to enter the public baths of Persia—a point in which the Persians are far more fanatical than the Turks. But I am able to judge, from several private baths I have entered, what are the arrangements and

are undoubtedly thus communicated. Notwithstanding this fact, these public baths are in the main useful and indispensable institutions in such a climate.

After completing his bath, the Persian traveller goes to the bazars, to transact the business which brought him to Teheran. This net-work of covered streets is cool even when the heat is unbearable elsewhere. Where two streets meet, the roof forms a Saracenic dome, groined or

WATER-CARRIER.

elegantly decorated with the beautiful honey-comb work called Saracenic, although in reality Persian in its origin. Each trade or fabric has certain streets allotted, the dealers in carpets and embroideries in one street, the shoe-makers in another, the workers in brass in another, the cotton beaters and weavers in still another street, and so on. In each avenue, however, are found confectionery or bakers' shops or eating shops, where one gets kebabs, ragouts, and the various native dishes of rice, classified under the general heads of chillô and pillô. All the shops are open to the street like booths, the buyer standing outside, liable to be jostled or run over by the ever-shifting, bustling, confused throng of pedestrians, and riders, porters, horses, and loaded mules.

Of course business is not confined to the bazars or covered market. Grocers, hucksters, butchers, carpenters, or blacksmiths are found in every quarter. It is curious to see, with all this thriving activity and apparently complex artificiality of a busy capital, a prevailing simpli-

city which carries one back to primitive times or nomadic usages. Everything is open to the public. The carpenter finds his shop too small for the window-sash he is framing; the good fellow takes it out to the shady side of the street, and shapes it on the pavement, regardless of passers-by. The carpenters of Teheran are a curiously independent set, who require so little to live on that they spend half the time in sleeping and smoking; this habit is encouraged by the fact that custom allows them to have an advance on what they are to receive for a job, ostensibly to buy the materials; but, if lazy, they spend it in smoking, and then have to resort to make-shifts to get their wood and nails. They are clever fellows, however, and do very good work when in the mood; but they labor under great disadvantages, for, having no wood like our soft pine, with a smooth, tenacious, but easily worked fibre, they must make even the simplest objects out of the chenar, the poplar, the hard pine, and the walnut, and this, too, with tools far inferior to ours. The saw, the Persian carpenter draws toward him in cutting; instead of a hatchet, he uses an adze, at the imminent risk of splitting himself asunder; in order to saw a bit of plank, he squats on the ground and holds the wood between his toes. In one respect the Persian has, I think, a means for drilling holes superior to our common gimlet. It is practically a drill, which is worked by a bow and cord, the latter twisted around the handle of the drill. The hole is made with much less effort than with the ordinary gimlet, especially in hard wood.

The out-of-door-ness of Teheran life is again seen in the publicity of the schools, which are open to the street exactly like the shops. The old master, with goggles on his nose, glances alternately at the passers-by in the street and on the pupils seated on their heels in rows before him, and reciting their lesson in chorus. The barber performs his functions in the same public manner, barber and barbered alike being indifferent to the common gaze; but, in fact, the sight is so ordinary, no one notices it. As it is the custom and law for Persians to shave the head, it is evident that the barber is a person of some consequence there, and he adds to it by pulling teeth, leeching, and venesection, the latter a very important pursuit in Persia, for even well persons are in the habit of being bled once or twice a month as a preventive to disease, while the slightest colic or neuralgic pain sends them in haste to the barber, who at the same time gives them in return advice *ad libitum* and the latest scandal of the neighborhood as a panacea to the soul of the patient. It is the custom, also, to bleed horses once a month in Persia. As the Persian horses are in every way admirable, and possess great endurance, and as the Persians have in all ages been noted for their knowledge and management of horses, it would seem that this custom is at least not injurious, and possibly in such a climate has decided advantages.

The baker is another absurd character of Teheran, who has the faculty of pursuing his vocation in violation of all Occidental notions about professional secrets. Whatever the baker of Teheran does is done "free and above-board," and if the customer is cheated, he has only himself to blame. He kneads and rolls his bread before the public, flattens the loaves into long thin sheets on his bare arms, and after the bread is baked, lays it on a ledge in the street wall by his shop to dry, or flings it over his shoulder like so many sides of leather, and peddles it. This bread, which, when baked, is only the tenth part of an inch thick, is very palatable when just from the oven, and even foreigners come to prefer it to any other, for it is sweet and easily digested.

But the growing heat of mid-day suggests that the hour for lunch and repose has arrived. The noonday meal is light, composed of fruit, grapes, figs, or melons, with salads and bread. After it perhaps follows a cup of tea and a kaliân, and then a nap, in which high and low participate. In the middle of the day, during the warm season, the whole city, the very streets and walls, seem asleep, gradually waking again as the sun begins to approach the west. After his siesta, the Teheranee says his prayers, or is supposed to say them: in spite of, or perhaps as a result of, their intense external fanaticism, the modern Persians are but little addicted to praying; their religion is rather like a shibboleth, a *mot d'ordre* to swear by, than a code of guidance to shape life and

EXTERIOR OF COUNTRY CARAVANSARY.

COTTON BEATER.

character. But the Persians are not singular in this respect at the present day. After another smoke, the Persian gentleman sallies forth toward the cool of the evening with a rosary in his hand, attended by a servant or companion.

It is the hour of peace; a rosy light bathes the house-tops, but the stately avenues leading north and south are in shadow, and cooled by the water thrown by the sakkâhs. The tender evening light also rests on the snowy crests of the vast ridge of the Shim Irân, or Light of Persia, which soars to a height of 13,000 feet across the northern side of the plain, but nine miles away. The evening glow, before it fades into twilight, lingers last on the snowy cone of Demavend, 21,000 feet high, ever present in every view, like the presiding genius that protects the capital of Persia.

With slow and dignified steps the Persian gentlemen stroll through these inviting avenues, engaged in genial converse. Their long robes, their massive beards, their lofty caps or voluminous turbans, give them a lofty stateliness as they wend along, undisturbed by the numerous horses or carriages, or the hideously unkempt and filthy dervishes who claim alms on account of their sanctified rags.

At this hour the tea-houses are in full blast. The reader may be surprised to learn that the national beverage of Persia is not coffee, but tea. One would naturally suppose that a country so near Araby the Blest and the aromatic groves of Mocha would, like the Turks, prefer coffee. Of course a great deal of coffee, prepared in the Turkish way, is consumed by the Persians, but the fact remains that they are essentially a tea-drinking race, drinking it in vast quantities, flavored with lemon or tourchee, which is the prepared juice of the lime, and sweetened almost to a syrup. The habit is probably the result of the commercial intercourse which at an early period existed between Persia and China, and which, as is now well known, gave an impulse to the arts of Persia, of which evidences appear at various stages of her æsthetic history. At Teheran the tea-houses take the place of the coffee-houses of Constantinople. One meets them at every turn, of every rank, but all alike resorts for rest, leisure, and entertainment. There one may see public dancers, who by law are now invariably men, although women of questionable repute contrive to evade the laws sometimes and exhibit in the harems. The male dancers are brought up to this vocation from boyhood, and invariably wear long hair in imitation of women, and shave their faces smooth.

What interests an intelligent European more at these tea-houses than the dances are the recitations from the poets. The songs of Hafiz may be heard there, and entire cantos from the great epic of Ferdoonsee, repeated with loud, sonorous modulation, heard sometimes at quite a distance at the more inspiring passages, and listened to with enthusiastic rapture. Here, too, one may hear the *Arabian Nights* tales given without any attempt at expurgation, exactly as in a recent translation. The reader will recollect that the characters in the *Arabian Nights* are constantly and at every opportunity quoting long and appropriate passages from the poets. This may to the European appear to be an affectation or a freak of poetic license on the part of the author of these tales. On the contrary, he was simply giving us another of those traits of Oriental character the record of which has given to those inimitable narratives immortality as the finest picture ever given of the life of the East, which, after thousands of years, is only just beginning to feel the transforming influence of Western civilization.

As one continues his ramble through Teheran at this hour, he sees a crowd amused by baboons dancing to the beat of tambourines—animals which, if they do not get all the happiness they deserve, at least well fulfill their mission in ministering to the pleasure of myriads by their absurd antics and grimaces. Or we see a chained lioness put through her paces, or, fatigued by the part she has been forced to play in life, and unable to escape from it by suicide, is sleeping heavily on the pavement. But one of the most common spectacles of Teheran in the late afternoon—a sight which always draws a crowd—is a match of trained wrestlers, or athletes exercising with clubs, at both of which the Persians are very expert, although they make no great figure in jugglery.

The afternoon is also the time when the gentlemen of Teheran exchange calls. A gentleman in Persia never calls on a lady; he does not even dare to inquire after her health, or even mention her to her husband. Notwithstanding this, the exchange of visits is a most formidable affair at Teheran, affording an opportunity for the full display of the elaborate etiquette for which Persia has always been celebrated. I make no apology for describing with some minuteness the details of such a visit, as doubtless no such social ceremony is elsewhere in vogue to such a degree at the present day. All the ceremonies attending such an affair are shaded

A BUTCHER.

off to the finest point, and are expected to form part of the education of every Persian, or, in fact, to be a second nature to him.

Before making the visit, a servant is sent, generally the previous day, to announce it. The rank of the servant who is sent is suited to the rank of the gentleman who is to receive the call. If a person of very high rank is to call on one of similar position, it is considered eminently proper to announce and accept the visit in an autograph note. If the caller is of the higher rank, he simply states that he proposes to call at such an hour; if of equal or lower rank, he asks permission to call. The call must be made on horseback or in a carriage, and the number of mounted attendants depends upon the rank of the person visited. Xenophon in his Anabasis states it as a custom peculiar to the Persians that they always went abroad accompanied by many retainers. The usage exists to this day, and is still carried to such a degree that it has a material effect on the resources of the country, so large is the number of servants who are consumers but not producers. The Prime Minister has in his employ two thousand men, of whom many, as well as their fathers, have been in his family all their lives. He rarely goes out with less than sixty to one hundred attendants. There are many gentlemen at Teheran whose households include one hundred domestics. Most of them are assigned some special duty, but often a number are merely retained to assist in the display of the *ménage*, fed by, and receiving the protection of, their lord, and picking up pishkesh, or presents, as they can.

On approaching the house, the visitor, if of high rank, is met by mounted heralds, who immediately return at full speed to announce the approach of the guest. If of very high rank, the host will try sometimes to see the effect on his guest by coming into the reception-room after the arrival of the guest. Supposing that he has not tried such a manœuvre, a courteous skirmish occurs when the guest enters the door; each seeks to outdo the other in politeness, while each is exceedingly careful not to accept or allow a position to which he is not entitled by rank. The corner of the room the most remote from the entrance is the place of honor; the guest, if he outranks the host, while strenuously declining to take that seat, will be

very careful that his host does not occupy it instead, and quite as careful not to accept it if of inferior rank, although urged, for to do so under such circumstances would be to affront the host, and invite an affront in return. I should state here that the host advances outside of the door of the reception-room to receive one of superior rank; meets him at the door if of equal rank, and leads him by the hand to his seat; goes half-way the length of the apartment to meet one of slightly inferior rank, but does not condescend to advance a step for a guest far below in social or official position. When the host and guest are of equal rank, chairs or cushions are arranged in equal position opposite the refreshment table, and so on through all the various social grades. Other things being equal, the left hand, and not the right, is the place of honor.

The serving of refreshments is another important question, regulated by undeviating custom. The nazir, or head steward of the household, enters in his stocking feet, ushering in a number of servants equal to the number to be served. If host and guest are of equal rank, the cup is presented to each exactly at the same moment; but if one outranks the other, he is first served. When there is present a member of the royal family, or one of the cabinet or council of the Shah, or a foreign minister, the servants must always retire backward to the door. The number and character of the refreshments depend on the rank, the hour, and the season. In the morning tea is served once. In the afternoon, the guest being of equal or higher rank, he is first served with tea in dainty glasses. This is followed by the kaliân, or water-pipe, which differs from the Turkish nargileh by having a short straight stem. In it is smoked the tobacco called tumbakee, a species grown only in Persia. That of Shiraz is very delicate in flavor, and the best. The tumbakee must first be soaked in water and squeezed like a sponge, or it will cause vertigo. A live coal made from the root of the vine is placed on the tobacco, and the smoke is drawn through water with a gentle inhaling, depositing the oil in its passage through the water. When several persons of equal rank are being served, it is the proper thing to bring an equal number of lighted pipes; but if one present outranks all the others, only one pipe is brought in, which is handed to him. Before smoking, he makes a feint of offering it in turn to all present, but woe be to him who incautiously accepts it before he of higher rank has first smoked, for he will be made to feel the withering scorn of which a Persian gentleman is capable. I knew of such an instance. The pipe was offered by the host in this perfuncto-

After the first kaliân, tea is served again, followed by a second pipe. After a proper interval, whose length is regulated by the acceptability of the visit, coffee is served in tiny cups, followed in turn by the pipe. This is the signal that the limit of the entertainment has been reached, and the guest in honeyed words ex-

ITINERANT BEGGAR.

ry manner to one of lower rank, and it was accepted; but when he of lower rank had smoked and returned it to the other, the host ordered the servant to take out the pipe, wash it thoroughly, and prepare it afresh. The Mestofi - Mamolêk, the highest man in Persia after the king, has not smoked for forty years. He took a solemn resolution against tobacco, because, when a young man, the kaliân was on one occasion given in his presence to a man whom he considered of lower rank before it was offered to him. He dashed aside the pipe, and swore never to smoke again, in order to avoid the possibility of being again subjected to such an affront.

presses his acknowledgments for the courtesy of the host, and requests permission to depart. When the Persian new year begins, with the spring equinox, the season is indicated by the substitution of a cool sherbet for the first cup of tea, and sometimes of an ice in the place of the coffee; but after the September equinoctial the tea and coffee are resumed. These may seem trivial matters, but in Persia they have great weight; and not only is the taste of the host indicated by the quality and style of the refreshments, but the *savoir-faire* and the rank of the guest are weighed by his bearing on such an occasion. It is of no slight importance that

NIGHT PROCESSION WITH LANTERN.

a European in Persia should understand these laws of etiquette; otherwise he is liable not only to have his breeding as a gentleman misunderstood, but to be assigned purposely such an inferior rank that he loses influence, while by strongly asserting his claim to all the privileges which he has the right to expect and demand, suitable to his rank, he receives the respect which is his due, but which no Persian will give except when he sees him firm on these points.

Thus far we have been considering life at Teheran as it appears in public to a man. From this aspect it appears to be an open-air, a public existence. But there is another phase to life in Persia of which even he who lives years in that country knows little and sees less—a state of mystery, a system hidden in the midst of a city busy and apparently open to the widest publicity. I refer to the domestic life of Persia, and the existence of

woman in that land of romance and song. Without woman, how can there be romance and song? and where are the women of Teheran? and how is the poet who would sing their praises to see and appreciate the charms that quicken the chords of his lyre? Pope has said, and been applauded for ages for saying, that "the proper study of mankind is man." I venture to assert that the great sage and satirist stated only half a truth, and showed that he but dimly perceived the complex character of woman, or he would have said, instead, "The proper study of mankind is woman." But at Teheran one sees but rarely the face of a woman, unless she be a Nestorian, an Armenian, or a Guebre, or Fireworshipper, who all go but slightly disguised, or if he be a Mussulman, in which case he may have all the concubines he pleases. It is a little singular that there are still about twenty-five thousand Guebres left in Persia; persecuted from the

time of the Mohammedan conquest, a few
faithful ones still cling to the cult of Cy-
rus and Darius.   Unlike the Mohammedan Persians, they have intermarried with
no other race, and thus present to-day the
original Persian race.

secular law called the Urf, based on oral
traditions and practice, and employed in
unimportant cases; but the Shahr is always the final authority.   The laws relating to marriage and the relations of
the sexes are a marvel of minuteness, and

STROLLING MUSICIANS.

The laws of Persia are theocratic. They
are founded on the Koran, and a system
has been deduced which, like the common
law, consists of the opinions of priests of
especial sanctity and wisdom. This code
is called the Shahr.   There is a lesser and

form the most extraordinary reading in
existence.   As it is simply impossible for
any one to remember and practice every
one of the regulations which govern the
great question of the sexes and domestic
life, a large portion of this burdensome

code is practically a dead letter; but enough yet remains in practice to produce an extraordinary system. Every Persian house is constructed upon a plan of secrecy; no windows are visible from the streets; but the interior is constructed around several courts, with lovely gardens, tanks, shrubbery, and even luxuriant groves of fruit and shade trees, of all of which one obtains not the slightest hint from the street. In the main dwelling the master of the house lives and transacts business during the day. But his business over, he retires for the night to his anderoon, which is the quarter of the residence devoted to the women. The anderoon is jealously guarded by the eunuch, and no man ever enters it but the proprietor. When he is there in the bosom of his family, he can not be disturbed; it is sufficient to say to any one who inquires for him, "He is in his anderoon." This is an asylum from outward cares which it would be well to import into the United States for those who seek effectual quiet and repose. To the

Persian it takes the place of a club—the more so as clubs, theatres, and other places for evening resort would not be permitted in Persia. The influence of the women would be sufficient to prevent the establishment of institutions which would result in a complete reversal of the present domestic system. Knowing nothing better, and able to compass their ends with

A SLEEPING LIONESS.

matters as they are, being accustomed to them, the women of Persia are satisfied to have the system continue. It would be a mistake hastily to conclude that this indicates a low order of intellect or an abject spirit. If uneducated according to our ideas, the Persian women, from all I can gather, are by no means stupid, and enjoy an influence and a controlling power in domestic and state affairs not inferior to that of women elsewhere, only it finds expression by different methods. It is not the semblance of power that is to be feared, but the unseen power behind the throne; and I can affirm emphatically that in no country do women have more influence than in Persia, where they are content to be the power behind the throne.

It is true, the laws of the country appear at first sight to discriminate against the women. Divorce, for example, is easy for the man but difficult for the woman who has a grievance. The husband may dismiss his wife by saying three times, "You are divorced."

Besides the usual form of marriage, which is presumably for life, there is the temporary marriage. During the period agreed upon, which must be specified in a written contract, neither party can be divorced from the other. It is not uncommon for ladies of social position to prefer this form, as, by making the term sufficiently long, they can insure themselves against divorce, and loss of the portion or jointure advanced by the husband.

Women of great talents are occasionally found in the anderoons, skilled in music, poetry, and painting, and in the diplomatic art. All of them show skill in embroidering, which has been carried in Persia to a degree never elsewhere surpassed. According to Persian law, a husband must divide his time equally among his wives; but if he has one he prefers, she can generally arrange with the others by presents to have part of the time to which they are entitled. Diplomacy, intrigue, and influence in Persia are dependent in a large measure on the force of character displayed by the women. If a man wishes to influence another in an affair of importance, he manages it by confiding the matter to one or all of his wives, who in turn visit the wives of the man to be influenced, or the wives of one who has influence over him, and by urging and presents seek to attain the object. Most of the important transactions of Persia are conducted in this manner. The greatest difficulties I had to encounter in Persia were against the intrigues of women who were deputed to bespeak in this manner the opposition of the high officers of the government, or of the Shah himself; while, on the other hand, it was by availing myself of this usage that I was able repeatedly to win the advantage in certain difficult affairs.

The profound disguise worn by the women of Teheran in the street, supposed by foreigners to be a serious inconvenience, is, under existing conditions, an enormous advantage, and the women themselves would be the last to advocate a change, so long as polygamy exists. No argument

is required to show what a power for intrigue exists in such a costume. In her mantle or veil, completely covering her from head to foot, a woman can go wherever she pleases without the slightest possibility of detecting her identity, and not even her husband would dare to raise her veil: to do so would render him liable to instant death. On the other hand, if a woman wishes to disclose her charms to any one, she generally contrives to find a chance to withdraw her veil for an instant. The rest is arranged by third parties, who are always on hand. The women of Teheran can thus go anywhere with little risk of detection; only the wives of the Shah and of his sons are debarred from the privilege, never going abroad without numerous attendants. The former are always accompanied by the royal guards, who, at a certain distance before and behind the royal ladies, keep the

A GUEBRE.

way clear. When these ladies propose to leave the palace, the event is announced by heralds in all the streets by which they are to pass; the shops are closed, and every one is expected to take himself out of the way. Until recently it was impossible, for this reason, to construct windows overlooking the principal avenues, and any unlucky person found in the passage of the royal cortége was put to death on

for color and embroidery, but otherwise there is no difference in the home dress worn by the Persian ladies of Teheran from the palace to the meanest hovel.

The simplicity of this dress is, again, in strong contrast with the very elaborate and costly costume worn by gentlemen of the court. There is a tendency to adopt a modification of the European dress, resembling a military uniform. But on state occa-

GUEBRE WOMEN.

the spot. But the most that would now happen would probably be that he would be roughly handled, even if he turned his face to the wall.

There could hardly be a greater contrast than between the out-of-door and the indoor costume of the ladies of Teheran. What it is at home is shown by the picture on page 233, taken from a photograph. It was formerly more modest, but this fashion came in with the present century. Like the costume of short clothes worn by men in the last century in Europe, it requires a good figure to show it off to advantage. The moderate garments worn admit of considerable scope in the exercise of a taste

sions the magnificent and imposing robes of office are worn as of old, made of the richest stuffs of Cashmere and Kermân, worked with exquisite designs. At a royal audience the invariable kolâh, or black lamb-skin cap, is exchanged for a white turban, which is doffed on retiring from the royal presence, and given to a servant who has waited outside of the palace gate. As may be easily imagined from the account of visiting etiquette, the court ceremonials of Persia are of the most elaborate and punctilious character, although indicating at present an inclination to relax a little from a ceremonial that is burdensome in its details. It must be admitted that such

ARMENIAN WOMAN IN STREET COSTUME.

PERSIAN WOMAN, WITH VEIL RAISED, IN STREET COSTUME.

pomp is qualified to give majesty to a monarch, and to aid in the maintenance of power in a despotic government. It was the great court pageants and ceremonials of Byzantium which aided to prop up the decaying Roman Empire long after it had lost its vitality, presenting by its continued existence for centuries after it became moribund one of the most extraordinary phenomena in history.

Nusr-ed-Deen Shah, the reigning sovereign of Persia, is a man of good and progressive ideas, patriotically inclined, but often hampered by the character of his *entourage* and the menacing aspect of Russia, frowning upon any progress in Persia that would tend to add to the independence of an ancient monarchy that she hopes eventually to absorb without resistance—a problem that, in my opinion, is not likely to be as easy as she supposes. The Shah is a man fond of the chase, a bold and skillful marksman, of social disposition, and prefers, as far as possible, to drop the irksome ceremonies of state which surround him. On one occasion he said to an elegant and accomplished Persian gentleman whom he had honored by a visit to his superb country-seat, "If only I could for a while lay aside the embarrassments of my position, how I should enjoy a free conversation with a gentleman of your tastes and culture!"

He gives an audience to his ministers every morning about six, receives their reports, and gives his orders for the administration of affairs. In the afternoon, and sometimes in the evening, he engages in social converse with one or more of his favorite courtiers, or listens to the reading of foreign periodicals. On such occasions there is sometimes a freedom of expression allowed his courtiers which in former reigns would have cost them their heads. But Nusr-ed-Deen Shah is a man of noble and generous impulses.

The tendency to modify the strictness of the court etiquette at Teheran is shown by the manner of receiving foreign ministers. His Majesty receives them standing at the upper end of the audience chamber, which is the magnificent hall containing part of the crown jewels, when an audience is granted to the entire diplomatic corps on state occasions. When an audience is given to a single person for a special object, the king receives him in one of the smaller but scarcely less splendid apartments of

WINTER IN-DOOR COSTUME.

the palace. Nothing further is required of the minister except to leave his galoches, or outer shoes, at the gate of the palace. He is attended by the Zahiri Doulêh, or master of ceremonies, and when the massive embroidered portière is raised and discloses the Shah-in-Shah opposite him, resplendent in rubies and diamonds, he bows, and repeats this mark of respect when he has reached his Majesty, who stands as near to him as two gentlemen in ordinary conversation. The minister remains covered, as indicating the equality of the two powers, and waits for the Shah to begin the conversation, which becomes free and easy if his Majesty is in pleasant humor, or is favorably inclined to the minister and his country. The Shah speaks French, and sometimes condescends for a moment to dispense with the court interpreter and converse directly with the minister, although such condescension may be accepted as a mark of high favor. In former days the Shah would terminate the audience by saying, "You have leave to retire;" but the present king simply keeps silent or takes a step back, which is the signal for the minister to withdraw from the "blessed presence," taking care not to turn his back to the king until he reaches the door. This manœuvre is not an easy one when the entire diplomatic corps at Teheran is forced to retire down a hall over a hundred and fifty feet in length, and to be careful not to stumble over the chairs of beaten gold on either hand, and to avoid slipping on the highly polished pavement of variegated tiles.

But perhaps I can not better describe the intricate and time-honored ceremonies of the court of Persia than to give an account of the ceremonies of the No Rooz, or New-Year. The Persians, being now Mohammedans, pretend that the No Rooz comes at that time because it is the birthday of the Prophet. But in reality it is the time of the spring equinox, and the ancient Persians or Fire-worshippers made this the time for the opening of their new year. Traces of old religious customs of Persia still exist, such as looking over a row of burning heaps of brushwood the evening before No Rooz, and also the custom of hailing the new moon by covering the face with the hands, and then, as the hands are withdrawn and the moon appears, to stand several moments in that position and offer a prayer.

The celebration of the No Rooz continues for ten days; it is a period of rejoicing. All labor ceases; every one appears in a new suit of clothes, and visiting and feasting are universal. On the last day of No Rooz the entire city goes forth into the suburbs on a general picnic; the gardens of the wealthy are thrown open to the public, and for the only time in the year Persian gentlemen are accompanied by their wives in a promenade.

As the hour for the sun to cross the line approaches, the great officers of the realm gather in the grand hall of audience, around whose walls are clustered the crown jewels, the most costly and magnificent possessed by any court. The courtiers arrange themselves by prescribed rules, according to rank, on each side of the hall, the first in order being assigned places next to the celebrated peacock throne brought by Nadir Shah from Delhi, the lowest estimate of whose value has been placed by experts at fifteen millions of dollars. Between these two ranks of the distinguished men of Persia, who are glittering with innumerable gems, the Shah-in-Shah, or King of Kings, now passes with a slow and majestic step, and seats himself upon a silk carpet, embroidered with diamonds and pearls, at the foot of the peacock throne.

When his Majesty has taken his place, the chief of the Khajars approaches each courtier in turn, attended by servants bearing trays loaded with coins, of which a portion is now given to all in order, for good luck, that they may have money in their hands when the new year begins.

Numerous salvers containing the fruits of earth and water, or piled with silver and gold coins of Persia of different denominations, are also laid before the king, who now proceeds to burn incense on a

SUMMER IN-DOOR COSTUME.

small brazier until it is announced that the sun has crossed the line. A cannon proclaims the tidings over the capital, accompanied by the blare of trumpets. At the same instant the king takes up a magnificently bound Koran which is laid be-

COURTIER IN COURT COSTUME.

fore him, presses it to his forehead, lips, and bosom, and then turning to the mollahs, says, "Mombarêk bashêd!"—"May it be propitious to you!"

A mollah then arises, and in full, rich voice chants an invocation. This over, each personage present, according to rank, kneels before the Shah and receives from the royal hands a gift of coin, the amount depending upon the favor in which he stands with the king. This done, each retires from the hall until his Majesty remains alone. In the evening there are other imposing state ceremonies.

THE ARRAN ISLANDS

THE three islands known as the Arran Islands stretch like a natural breakwater across the entrance of Galway Bay. The largest, Inishmore, is nine miles long and one and a half broad. Inishman and Inishere, of which I shall speak hereafter, are respectively three, and two and a half miles long. A legend in the annals of Ireland states that Galway Bay was once a fresh-water lake known as Lough Lurgan, one of the three principal lakes of Ireland, and was converted into a bay by the Atlantic breaking over and uniting with its waters. Appearances go far to warrant such a belief, though I will not enter into the geological history of it, lest I should get beyond my depth, but will content myself with referring my readers to those geologists who have found in Ireland so inviting a field of research. Where verdure clothes these rugged rocks it is perpetual, and so rich that the finest cattle in the kingdom are grown here. There is no spot in Europe which for its size is richer in antiquities than this. More than one thousand years ago it earned the name of the Isle of the Saints, because holy men came hither in quest of that retirement and learned companionship which were deemed so conducive to sanctity. In a walk of nine miles one meets with the ruins of some fourteen churches, dating from about this period or earlier, along with the ruins of monasteries and hermitages, which show us how these men were content to live. There are, besides, round towers and fortresses which date earlier than any authentic historical record, and exhibit to the imagination these islands, now so desolate, filled with inhabitants active in war and peace. I believe they were in the time of the Druids favorite residences, and perhaps one of the latest strongholds of these people; at least the traveller and historian will find many reasons for such belief.

There are but two roads on the island, and being so little embarrassed in my choice, I took the first to the left, which leads to the once celebrated village of Killeany, and passed for a mile along the edge of the sea, the road being mostly upon a floor of rock. On either side were rude monumental structures, erected, as I learned, in the memory of those who lay buried in a cemetery some two miles off.

These solemn structures lining the road between the two villages of the island, the sea on one side, the stony hills on the other, seemed a novel and impressive way of recalling the dead to those who passed in their daily traffic. The inscriptions upon some of them were so late as the middle of the present century, and from the half-obliterated stones of others, mocking all record, I could not learn when or for whom they were erected.

As I proceeded I saw before me the lonely figure of a man, barefooted and meanly clad. His hands were crossed behind his back, and he held a farthing candle. I accosted him with a remark upon the beauty of the island. He turned his wolfish eyes upon me, and replied, with bitter scorn, "It is a very hard island."

"You are well acquainted with it, I presume?"

"None better. I was born here, and my forefathers before me. I have outlived every one of my family, and have been striving all my life to get away from here."

His tattered garb and wasted body were emblematic of the place, and befitting the progeny of this land of ruins.

Killeany, which I soon reached, is a large and well-built village. It was once of great note for the piety and learning of its founders. Hither came pious men from all parts of Europe to practice the austerities of a religious life; and the ruins which we see on every side tell us, too, that these men brought with them a taste refined by the arts. In those times Killeany was a village of wise men and sainted Tom Tiddlers, who retired to this solitude to prove that they were better than the world they had abandoned. Thus it acquired a renown which won it the name of the "Abode of the Saints." The inhabitants seem to have inherited nothing from the founders who made it so famous, except, perhaps, to imitate their rigid austerity of life, which, while it was chosen by the latter as a proof of piety, is enforced on these poor people by cruel poverty. I have not seen in any part of Ireland people more poorly clad and so pinched by hunger; even the children have wan, old faces, like hunchbacks. They possess no land, and depend entirely upon fishing. During the winter season the sea is so rough that it is impossible for them to venture out. Their principal food is fish dried upon the rocks. When one remembers that Christianity was introduced here by St. Endeus, or Eaney, so early as the sixth century, it seems impossible that they should have degenerated into such stupid barbarity.

The great church of St. Endeus was demolished by the soldiers of Cromwell to repair the fortified castle of Ardkyne, of which there is a ruin close to the sea. On the highest point of the eastern end of the island is the oratory of St. Benan, a unique specimen of the early Irish church. Near by, sunk in the rock, are the remains of the hermitage. This church, or oratory, is very small and unadorned—just such a structure as befitted the humbleness of the worshippers who lived in so inaccessible a region. It is useless to secure a guide in this country, for there is always some one living near the remarkable places who seems to consider that his duty is to offer his services, or rather, I should say, to accompany you, without any other preliminary than a careful scrutiny of your appearance, and a simple salutation. An old woman of the village, who appeared to have been able to buy some potatoes or other matter of generous diet, had trudged up the hill to the church. One charm of these dreary old places is the power of calling up vague reveries and pictures of the past, clothing realities with the illusions of the imagination. It needed but a slight exertion of the fancy to transform

THE ORATORY OF ST. BENAN.

my guide into St. Benan himself, taking his morning airing beside these gabled walls looking out over the sea. But my illusion, which bore so great an impress of reality, was dispelled by the whiffs of smoke from a modern clay pipe in the mouth of my portly guide.

Near by is a residence of the sixth century, which about two years ago was brought to light from a mass of earth and stones. It is built of small and undressed stones, without mortar, and is divided into numerous small compartments, barely large enough for a single person. There were little entryways not more than a foot in width, leading to the remoter rooms, destined, I presume, for the more meagre monks. There are probably twelve or fifteen rooms in this building; the floors and ceilings are all made of the same flinty and rugged stones. What was evidently the main entrance had somewhat an imposing appearance, being reached by four steps, at whose base there was built a little kennel, which, if it was not for a dog, was made by some monk more austere than the rest; he had, however, chosen a southern exposure for his penance.

As I gave a parting glance at the sea, I saw a bank of clouds melting into it in the distance. It looked like land, but in that

A DWELLING-HOUSE OF THE SIXTH CENTURY.

CHURCH OF THE FOUR COMELY SAINTS.

direction the nearest land was America. I remembered then that from these cliffs the famous Hy Brazil was said to have been seen. Arran is still believed by the peasantry to be the nearest land to the far-famed O'Brazil, or Hy Brazil, the blessed paradise of the pagan Irish. Mr. Hardiman derives the name Hy Brassil, or Brazil, from *bras*, fiction; *aoi*, island; and *ile*, great—*i. e.*, "the great fictitious island." The old bards and popular tradition describe it as a country of perpetual sunshine, abounding in rivers, forests, mountains, and lakes. Castles and palaces arise on every side, and as far as the eye can reach it is covered with groves, bowers, and silent glades; its fields are ever green, with sleek cattle grazing upon them; its groves filled with myriads of birds. It is only seen occasionally, owing to the long enchantment, which will, they say, now soon be dissolved. The inhabitants are ever young, taking no heed of time, and lead lives of perfect happiness. In many respects it resembles the Tirna-n'oge, the pagan Irish elysium.

On our way to the village I saw some odd-looking sheep nipping the grass from between the rocks. They had an absurd appearance of being in full dress, with bare necks and shoulders, which prompted me to ask the reason of such an unseemly out-door toilet. I learned that they were originally as well clad as others of their species; but in this region a

family rarely owns more than one animal, and they shear off as much wool at a time as they deem necessary for a pair of stockings; so the poor beasts are forced to go all day long in what would in civilized countries be called a strictly evening toilet. While our bare necks and shoulders, however, warm nobody, it is satisfactory to think that theirs are warming the lean legs of their owners.

Any one who has a fondness for shopping could, I think, be radically cured by a sojourn on these islands, as the nearest shops are at Galway, twenty-nine miles distant, and the only means of getting there is by a small yacht that goes once a week, weather permitting. One journey on board of it, along with pigs, fish, peasants, sundry oil cans, and musty boxes, with the prospect of tossing about for ten or twelve hours, will suffice for a long while. The luxuries of the table at the hotel are confined to mutton, boiled and fried, with the usual colossal platter of potatoes, varied only by bacon and cabbage. I saw a few chickens sheltering themselves under the walls, and observing me with an unfriendly eye, as if they saw in a stranger a Moloch who would reduce their number. Prompted probably by this idea, I asked for one for my dinner, but regretted having taken him from his companions, with whom he had lived so long; for he seemed to have been brought here by the early Christians, or, perhaps, had escaped at a remote date from some pagan sacrifice.

It was December, yet the sun was bright and the air soft and balmy, when I started for Dun Ængus, a fortress pronounced by Dr. Petrie to be the most magnificent barbaric monument now extant in Europe. The sun was so warm that I discarded my wrappings as the car jogged toward Kilmurrey. I am fond of loitering, and stopped to see the church of the Four Comely Saints, because the name attracted me. There was, however, so much mud on the road to this blessed chapel that I would have been disgusted with the Four Comely Saints ere I arrived at their sanctuary, had I not considered that the mud and slush might have been an accumulation of the eleven hundred years that lay between them and me. I can not tell how many stone walls I scaled, or through what grimy depths I waded, to reach the little ruin, which was covered with weeds and tangled vines. There is an east window and altar-place in excellent preservation, and, near by, a niche, the carving of the base of which was as fresh as if made yesterday; but all above was filled by the clustering ivy, which strove, I thought, to fill the cavity left vacant by the absent saint. Although the chapel is small, it is of beautiful proportion, and the four saints seem to have left their comeliness as a perpetual heirloom to these walls.

When I arrived at Kilmurrey, one of those storms which come from the Atlantic, and in an instant envelop these islands in a cloud of wind-driven mist, made me seek refuge in a cabin. It was a crowded, busy peasant's home, and as I sat by the fire—the warmest seat being given me with the invariable hospitality of these people—I found abundant material for observation and reflection. Whatever cleanliness was possible in a family of eight occupying one huge room along with two pigs was carefully maintained; at least, the mother and children were neatly and comfortably attired, the hearth well swept, and the pigs were confined to the limits assigned them. An old woman was carding wool, a little child rocking the cradle, and the mother spinning at a large wheel. The chickens, also driven in by the rain, one by one hopped up a ladder to their roosts among the rafters, from which they watched over their ruffled feathers the busy family and the blazing hearth with so much approval and satisfaction that I am sure, if chickens be susceptible to emotion, these were very tender ones indeed. A dog sneaked in, and seeing a stranger, went out into the rain again. The dogs, which are not numerous on the island, are of the most miserable and condemned aspect, and seem to feel their ignoble ancestry, as they invariably jumped over a wall or ran into some obscurity on the approach of a stranger. While drying my dripping garments, I saw for the first time, seated in a corner, as if to screen himself from observation, the figure of a young man clad in white flannel, the costume of the island. His face was thin and sad, and of the same color as the garments he wore, and he gazed at the fire with such a dejected and hopeless expression as led me to infer that he was the fated victim of some terrible disease—consumption, perhaps—and was feebly waiting through the long hours of the day and night the death he knew to be

so sure and near. I spoke to him, striving in my pity to appear unconscious of perceiving his misery. Without answering, he rose abruptly and left the cabin. The looks of concern and inquietude in the faces about me told me of some unusual sorrow, which the mother, leaving her spinning-wheel, explained to me in a low voice. She told me that the young man, her eldest son, poor Owney, as she called him, had until a month before been the most healthy and cheerful member of the family; ready and prompt at work, and the life of the household, when a letter came from America to a neighboring family inclosing money to pay the passage thither of their eldest daughter. It appeared that the young man had long entertained a secret passion for this girl, and when he heard that he probably would never see her again, he declared his love to her, and besought her to remain. So far from being unmindful of his affection, she avowed her willingness to marry him at once, if he would accompany her to America immediately afterward. This was impossible; his own family were unable to assist him, and the few people who possess money on the island would not lend it without security. The practical damsel saw on the other side of the Atlantic every prospect of improving her material condition, and doubted not that husbands were as plentiful there as elsewhere; while, if she remained, she knew the drudgery and hopeless slavery that were the lot of all around her would be hers also. Therefore she told her suitor if he could not accompany her she would not listen to his suit. When the young man found his upbraidings useless, he gave way to despair, and had not worked or spoken since his cruel sentence had been pronounced. Every day he grew thinner and more wan, and he did not partake of sufficient food to support life. All the solicitude and tenderness of his mother had not succeeded in arousing within him his former self, and with tears running down her cheeks she told me she thought he had lost his reason forever.

Some weeks previously the school-master had written for them to a priest, a distant relative of the family, who lived in Connemara; but they had received no reply, and she supposed he had neither help nor counsel to give. I pondered for a long while, as I sat by the fire, upon what often proves to be the unfortunate sin-

MY GUIDE AT FORT ÆNGUS.

were to start immediately afterward upon their long voyage. As I left, the damsel, whose month's delay to prepare her outfit had given such a fortunate respite to her lover, thrust her head in the door, and called upon Owney to be sure and wear the blue stockings she had knitted him to the chapel on the morrow; and then, with her little *retroussé* nose turned up to the sky, ran blushing away.

But to continue my narrative. When the mist had blown over, I left the cabin, and began a difficult ascent to Dun Ængus, which crowned the cliffs overlooking the sea on the opposite side of the island. My guide was a youth of about nine years, whose attire consisted of a red petticoat, and at least a shirt collar, which was ostentatiously displayed over his bodice, an Irish cap resembling the top of a mushroom, blue stockings, and sandals, called pampootees, made of untanned cowhide, universally worn by the inhabitants of these islands. Instead of the treacherous bogs, which my foot-padding in Ireland had familiarized me with, I had now rocks and stones of every dimension and ruggedness to contend with. I may here mention that in the Arran Isles there are no bogs, therefore no turf; and as trees are unknown, all fuel is brought, at considerable expense, from Connemara. My guide danced with such agility and recklessness from stone to stone that I was not only much concerned lest his thin legs should break beneath him, but was also a good deal out of breath and out of patience in my efforts to keep pace with him. In response to my repeated injunctions, however, he restrained himself so much as to run around me like a dog, instead of running ahead of me like a hare. Motion seemed to be a necessity of his existence, for I verily believe he did not remain a second in one spot. When I asked him a question as he bounded at my right, he answered me from the left, and it took some little circumspection to adapt my

cerity of men, and I could not refrain from deploring the no less frequent levity of my own sex. In passing through the village a week afterward I stopped to say good-day to these kind people, when I found the house a scene of bustle and confusion. My erewhile love-sick swain was, when I entered, making himself a pair of pampootees; and as he bade me good-day over a dangerously starched collar, his face glowed with health and energy. The now cheerful and happy mother informed me that since my last visit they had received a letter from the priest in Connemara, inclosing his blessing for her son, and the money to pay his passage to America. She had been very busy knitting him stockings, and making him a fine white flannel suit to be married in, and which thereafter he would not again wear till his arrival at New York, so that he would make a decent appearance in the New World, as became the relative of a priest. He was to be married to the object of his choice the next day, and they

conversation to the movements of this strange will-o'-the-wisp.

"Do you know how much gentlemen and ladies give me for showing them up to Dun Ængus? Two and three shillings," he continued, on my negative response. And then he eyed me with such a keen and mercenary expression that I was astonished to see it in so young a face. I expressed my surprise at the generosity of the ladies and gentlemen whom he had escorted; but this was not to his purpose, for he asked me point-blank how much I intended to give him.

" A shilling," I replied.

" Oh," he cried, "no lady or gentleman ever gives me a shilling, but always two or three."

My reader perceives that it is not always civilization which makes humanity sordid, as he will admit that this child of nine years displayed ere I bade him good-by a persistent rapacity worthy of the most accomplished Shylock. Until we arrived at the fort, he strove by every possible artifice and argument—so much beyond his years in skill that I would have believed him an elfish changeling had I been credulous in such matters—to convince me that two shillings was the lowest possible sum I could offer him consistent with my own gentility and his services.

The Dun, or fort, is built on the very edge of a precipice which stands three hundred feet above the sea. It is in horseshoe shape, the open side facing the sea. It consists of three inclosures, the innermost wall being the thickest; this inclosure measures one hundred and fifty feet from north to south. About the first century of the Christian era three brothers came from Scotland to Arran, Ængus, Conchovar, and Mil, and their names are still preserved in connection with buildings on the islands. The walls are eight or ten feet thick, built of comparatively small unhewn stones, without mortar, which manner of construction, we are told, affords less resistance to the wind, and is more durable, than the cemented edifices of later date. There is a doorway in perfect preservation, wherein the admirable ingenuity of the builders is shown; the immense thickness of the wall, and consequently great weight upon the lintel, is broken by several gradations, as it were, of supports, as shown in my sketch.

My youthful companion, who had been dancing about me with the utmost impatience during my researches, informed me, when we reached a certain point of the outer inclosure, that that was the consecrated place for paying him, and assured me that though he did not speak at all in his own interest, if I wished for good luck I would pay him then and there.

"It's many a shilling," he said, "you have given to people—mere robbers—while you've been travelling about; but all that'll be so much bad luck to you unless you pay me well now." With the respect which I always observe for the

DOORWAY, FORT ÆNGUS.

manners and customs of the country in which I travel, I immediately gave him a shilling, which he held between his thumb and finger, and with a look of indignant reprobation, his cold eye resting upon me as steadily as that of the Ancient Mariner on the wedding guest, he added, " Is that all you'll give me?"

I assured him that it was. " If you'll add twopence," he said, " good luck will be with you; but if you don't, you'll be misfortunate for all the days of your life."

I gave him the twopence, which I am sure the wedding guest would have willingly given the Ancient Mariner to have escaped his gimlet eye; and in some fear of this indefatigably mercenary child, I descended the cliffs as the shades of evening came on.

In the twilight I visited Teampull Mic Duach, a most interesting ruin, upon the grounds of a gentleman who rents the

DOORWAY OF TEAMPULL MIC DUACH.

work, but exercised a constructive ability not excelled in modern times. There is a window giving a curious example of a primitive kind of pointed arch. Two flat stones form the lintels, so nicely adjusted that, notwithstanding the extreme thickness of the walls, it is to-day as perfect as when constructed thirteen hundred years ago. The origin of the pointed arch has been claimed by many nations, but the best authorities declare that while it was introduced into England and the Continent in the time of the Crusades, probably from the East, it was used in Ireland long before there was any intercourse between the two countries; and Wilkinson says that though he does not claim that the pointed arch originated in Ireland, it existed there prior to the period when the pointed style was introduced through England to that country.

The doorway of this little church is, curiously enough, an almost perfect copy of an entrance to an Egyptian tomb, simple and grand.

At the northwestern extremity of the island are the ruins of the seven churches,

STONE WINDOW, TEAMPULL MIC DUACH.

larger portion of the island for grazing his cattle, while he resides elsewhere. His farmer, or overseer, takes a commendable pride in preserving the ruins on his master's domain. He told me, with swelling breast, that, although he had only lived on this island four years, and was not prejudiced in its favor, he did not believe there could be finer farming land. "Potatoes have been grown in the same ground for over one hundred years, and the cattle reared here, though never housed, and allowed no food save their pasture, take prizes in the English and Irish fairs." I thought the grazing must be rich, for even when in certain rocky wastes it grows in the fissures of the rocks, the land, if land it may be called, is carefully fenced off, and rented at so much per acre. Indeed, the whole island is fenced off in little plots, from a few yards to half an acre in extent, for no other reason, that I could perceive, than that they knew not what other disposition to make of the stones, although as many were left on the ground as would make a thousand such walls.

Teampull Mic Duach is certainly a beautiful little church. Antiquarians have decided that it was built in the sixth century, and the enormous undressed stones used in its construction, fitted with admirable exactitude, no cement being used, show that the builders of those times not only thought a great deal about their

lying in a hollow between a little village and the sea. There are portions of two which are in only a tolerable state of preservation; others have fallen, leaving an altar or some piece of carved stone that belonged to a window or doorway. An old man issued from a little hovel in the village, having evidently been informed of my arrival by some staring children who had retreated at my approach. He saluted me as he hobbled down from grave to grave, and asked me if I had ever been there before; if not, he might as well go with me, for he knew every inch of the place, having lived here nearly eighty years. Between his remarks he would stoop and pluck little wisps of grass, and brush some old tombstone with affectionate care, or break the brambles that crept over them.

Teampull Brecain, or the Church of St. Brecain, has a chancel of rude masonry, and a choir that is more modern—when I say modern in this case, I mean a date of four or five hundred years ago. In this, as nearly all the old churches of Ireland, the principal window is on the east, immediately over the altar. The floor is paved with graves, many of the slabs bearing recent dates, every nook and corner being filled with bones of the former occupants, which have been disturbed to give room to new-comers. The Old Mortality who acted as my guide slipped through the archway into the chancel, and pointing with his staff to a large stone in the corner, said, with an air of pride, that he had two sons — fine boys — under it. I asked if his name was upon it.

" No, your honor; but I know they are there, and there was nothing in it but this," pointing to a fragment of a skull that filled a gap made by a fallen stone.

We sauntered about among these relics for a long time, where at every turn something rare presented itself. The Aharla, or sacred inclosure, where only saints were buried, is still visible, with undeciphered inscriptions upon the slabs. A few rags fluttered on some bushes by what I thought was a

small cave; but the old man said it was a holy well, that it was dry just now, but when the day of the patron saint arrived it was always full—in the summertime. The greatest curiosity he reserved until the last. On an old tombstone was placed a rare and beautiful cross, broken evidently by force, for the stone shows no signs of decay, the fragments of which he told me had been found in various parts of these sacred grounds. Seating himself upon a grave, he related in the most solemn manner the history of the search for the pieces—how earnest had been his desire to bring together the remains, so that he could see the fulfillment of prophecy. When St. Brecain preached in this church a holy man visited him, and addressed the people; he meant only to say a few words to them, but as he stood by the altar a divine light descended upon him, and illuminated his face and breast. He was inspired to tell them that they would be

OLD MORTALITY—INTERIOR OF TEAMPULL BRECAIN.

DOORWAY OF TEAMPULL CHIARAIN.

persecuted and beaten, their churches and crosses destroyed, but their religion would outlive it all, and the crosses would be restored piece by piece. "And I have been allowed to see the truth of it," he added; "there is only one piece wanting to that cross, and it will be found in God's own time."

A Scotch mist had so much overcome its national prejudices as to visit Ireland the day I started for Teampull Chiarain, one of the many churches on this little island. Again I encountered a formidable array of stone fences. I reached the church, however—which stands in the midst of a potato field—after a great deal of difficulty. It is one of the best-preserved on the island, having a beautiful east window, and a striking doorway, which gives an instance of the simple construction and common application of the arch in the various ancient edifices of Ireland, formed in most buildings of two stones only, which appear to have been worked from one, and afterward split in the centre.

The next day I grew weary of the sheltered and inhabited side of the island, for the weather was so soft and balmy that one was invited to the open air. I sallied forth to where the cliffs present their rocky front as a barrier to the ocean, which in his wrath dashed against them with such mad fury that the surf rose in many places far above them, and the dark and awful green of the sea was thrown back from these terrible cliffs into the boiling caldron below as white as the driven snow. Here the Black Fort, as it is called, frowns over a fearful precipice. It resembles Dun Ængus in character, though it is much smaller, and in less perfect preservation.

I observed on the very verge of the cliff two figures manœuvring a large rope, as though they were fishing for sea-monsters. As I approached I saw that the end of the rope was attached to no monster, but to a man, who was delving into the crevices for some treasure, and the aerial anglers were moving the rope in accordance with signals made by a wave of his hand. When he arrived at the crevices in which the sea-birds made their homes, he seized dozens of them ere they could escape, and, loaded with his prey, he placed his feet against the perpendicular cliff, and while he was dragged by his friends above, walked up like a fly.

As I turned my steps homeward, the noise of the mighty waves as they broke against the cliffs filling my ears, I saw on the other side of the island the waters of the bay, quiet as a lake, reflecting the rosy blush of the sunset sky, and wondered that the waters of this great sea could here be so wild and there so calm.

BIRD-CATCHING.

A NIGHT'S RIDE WITH ARAB BANDITS

I SUSPECTED Muraiche, suspected him of an indefinite something, but the workings of his wily old Arab mind, its reasons and its purposes, were to me as mysterious as the great wastes of the Sahhra (Sahara) over which for days we had been crawling, and as elusive as the noxious sand-lizards which now and again scurried from beneath our horses' feet.

The long, hot caravan trail along which we had crawled during the day had led over the sun-scorched rocky wastes of the Djebel Nagahza (Nagahza Mountains), and at sundown emptied us into the little Arab town of Khoms. Here we parted with a small caravan forty camels strong bound for Misurata, with which we had travelled for the last three days. My two men, Mohammed and Ali, who were on foot, drove a large fast-walking pack-donkey; while Muraiche, like myself, rode an Arab stallion. His bent old figure, now ahead of me, now by my side, seemed lost in the folds of his barracan.

Some months previously, a viséed passport and other documents had landed me safely within the confines of the town of Tripoli, and later, after some difficulty, permission to travel into the desert had been granted by the Turkish Pasha who commanded the Turkish forces in that country. Many Arabs there were in the town who would gladly have risked the dangers of the desert as dragomen, but as my object was to obtain information of desert life, a man who could act also as interpreter was indispensable; and Muraiche proved to be the only available man. It is true that he had an unsavory record, and I was so warned by certain members of the little English colony there. But his broken English and lingua Franca were valuable assets; besides, forewarned was forearmed, so it came about that Muraiche picked the other men and became my dragoman.

Since sunrise, as we approached Khoms, a change had come over Muraiche; he no longer obeyed my orders with alacrity, and when several times it was necessary for me to repeat them sharply, he seemed to awaken with a start from deep meditation. This, at the time, I attributed to the fatigue of our journey and anticipated relaxation, for I had promised a rest at Khoms. Following the custom of the country, I reported to the Turkish governor on our arrival, and saw my men and animals comfortably fixed in a fonduk (caravansary), with orders to have everything in readiness to start at two the following afternoon, then spent the night at the house of Mr. Tate, the only Englishman in the place.

This night in mid-July and the following night, strangely different, stand out strongly in my memory—perhaps for the contrast with the dusty, monotonous travelling of other days, and the sleeping in dirty, crowded fonduks; or, perhaps, in contrast with each other. If you would know the pleasure of bathing, of sleeping between the snow-white sheets of a bed, travel day after day on the burning, scorching, yellow-red sand of the Sahhra; fill your eyes, nose and ears, your very soul, with its fine-powdered dust; tie your handkerchief, after the manner of the Touaregs, across your mouth to prevent evaporation, that your throat may not parch too much. Travel early and late to make the most of the cool of the morning and evening. Sleep lightly if you are a lone stranger, and do not mind the uncomfortable lump of your pistol-holsters under your arm: they are better in your hands than in the other fellow's. So when, sunburnt, saddle-sore, and tired with long riding and little sleep, you find, what I did, a bath of delicious cold water, brought from an old Roman well still used by the Arabs in Khoms, and a snow-white bed, give praise to Allah. Then let the barbaric noises of a wild Sudanese dance in the distance and the musical chant of the Muezzin melt away with your thoughts into the quiet of the African night.

Had it not been for a casual stroll through the Suk the next forenoon my men might now be recounting a different yarn over their smoking kief and coos-coos. I threaded my way among men, animals, shacks, scattered garden produce, grains and wares which covered the ground in interesting heaps, and as I pushed through a small crowd which had gathered about me, their curiosity and cupidity aroused by a gold filling in one of my teeth, I stopped for a moment. For there in the middle of an open space beside a Marabout (saint's tomb), Muraiche was engrossed in a low conversation with one of the irregular guards, an Arab in the Turkish employ. Disappearing unobserved to another part of the Suk, I should have thought no more of the matter, but for the fact that when later in the morning these two met in my presence, by the Governor's palace, they omitted the customary b'salaams and effusive greetings of Mohammedan acquaintances, and by no word or sign betrayed the least recognition.

Reminding Muraiche of my previous orders to have everything in readiness by two o'clock, I sauntered up to lunch at Mr. Tate's. The route to my next point of destination, the little town of Kussabat, was not only over a rough mountainous country, but it was considered by the Arabs dangerous on account of thieves. Being under the necessity of making the journey that day, I was anxious to arrive there by sundown. Consequently, when by half past two none of my outfit had put in an appearance, I despatched one of the house servants to learn the reason.

First by wily excuses, and then by open mutiny, my men delayed the departure until half past five, when by threats to appeal to the Turkish Pasha to have them thrown into prison and engage new men, we were finally ready to start.

"But a guard, Arbi (master)?" Twice Muraiche had asked the question, and twice I answered him that I had notified the Turkish officials of my intention to depart at two o'clock. Had they intended to send a guard they would have done so. However, being desirous of conforming to custom, I sent Muraiche to the Governor's palace with instructions to report our departure, but not to ask for a guard, as personally I shared in the common opinion that often the traveller is safer without one.

I watched Muraiche after he rounded a corner and disappeared at a gallop down the narrow street to the palace, from which, immediately reappearing, he set off to a different quarter of the town. Questioned on his return, he replied that an officer had sent him to notify a guard who was to go with us.

"You'll see your way all right, for the full moon ought to be up in about two hours, but ride last," were Tate's parting words. It was good advice and had often been given me before. To travellers in North Africa, particularly those among the French colonists of Tunis and Algeria, the saying, "Never allow an Arab to ride behind you," has become an adage, and this night in the Gharian I proved its worth.

We rode to the top of the steep trail, down which the slanting afternoon sunbeams shot by in golden shafts. Back and beyond us these sun shafts sped, until striking the white walls of Khoms they broke, spilling over them a flood of orange gold, diffusing her surrounding olive groves and date-palms with a golden green, and through the shimmering, sifting gold mist above it all sparkled a scintillating sea of blue.

Our course now lay almost due south to the region of the Djebel Gharian, the region I had hoped to enter and pass through by day.

Resting on the site of ancient Lebda of the Romans, my golden city of Khoms lay nearly an hour's ride behind us, and as yet no guard, to my entire satisfaction. This was short-lived, however, for soon a yell, such as I had never yet heard loosed from the throat of a human being, caused us suddenly to draw rein. Down the steep, rocky incline, where an ordinary horseman could but carefully pick his way, out on to the sandy plateau upon which we had just ridden, riding wild and giving his wiry little animal free rein, dashed a guard, and when abreast of us drew up short out of a full run, after the manner of Arab horsemen.

"B'salaam" to Muraiche, and a nod of the head to me, which I slightly reciprocated; yes, very slightly, for before me he was the one man out of all the Arabs I had ever seen that I would have chosen last for a companion that night. There in the glow of the late afternoon sunlight, the stock of his short carbine resting on his saddle, and the sweat making bright the high lights on his evil, brassy-bronze face, sat the worst cutthroat it was ever my fortune to look upon, — Muraiche's friend, he of the market-place.

Although I had learned not to judge men too much by appearances, I re-

MOHAMMED

solved to watch him. After a short conversation with Muraiche, during which the guard's peculiar eyes scanned me from the rowels of my spurs to the top of my sun-helmet, I knew that the main objects of his searching glance were in my holsters, covered by my jacket; meantime, however, I lost no detail of his weapon, a hammerless magazine rifle of modern make. Then he addressed me in Arabic, but not speaking the language, I turned to Muraiche.

"He tells us to start," the latter replied.

This sudden assumption of leadership came most unexpectedly, his seeming intention being to bring up the rear. Now Arabs are daring though ignorant; but like all Orientals, fully respect only one thing, and that is a just and strong hand, which they must feel in order to appreciate. Consequently my course was plain.

"Tell the guard to head the caravan, and that if he goes with me, he goes as one of my men." As we got under way, the guard rode slowly ahead, meanwhile taking sidelong glances at me, out of the corners of his villainous gray-green eyes, filled with all the hatred of the Moslem for the Christian. I realized that never in my life had the assets and liabilities of my *status quo* received such careful auditing.

When the great red lantern of the sun disk had sunk beneath the earth-line, from without the deep mysterious valleys crept the blue-violet mist films of twilight shadows, absorbing and leavening into their dark tones the brighter crimson afterglow, against which moved the dark shapes of horses and men. Suddenly they bunched themselves and the guard dismounted, then Mohammed and Ali went on with the pack-donkey.

"The guard's saddle-girth is broken," Muraiche informed me. "But we will fix it, and you can ride on very slowly."

"I will wait," I replied, my hand instinctively resting on one of my pistols. "But *you* ride on, Muraiche." The girth was soon "fixed," which consisted in a vain effort to hitch it up another hole.

Steeper and more rugged grew the trail, and we entered the range of the Gharian. As daylight dimmed, an uncomfortable darkness hung over the mountains for a short space; then the moon-glow appeared in the East, and soon the moon itself lifted its pale distorted shape above the horizon, and suffused everything with its pale blue-green light, so cool and satisfying to the eye and mind in contrast to the hot sun glare that during the day reflected through to the very brain.

But the dark shadow masses of boulders, parched shrub patches, and shaded slopes, what uncanny things might they not contain? And those gorges, too, which in the day reflected heat like an oven from their hot, red sides? Now they were cold, dank, and foreboding, and a shudder passed over me. For a moment a sense of weakness, of fear, of almost helplessness, took possession of me; then I reasoned with myself. I was

MURAICHE, THE WILY OLD DRAGOMAN

tired, unduly apprehensive, the conditions of heat and long days in the saddle had overtaxed my nerves. I fell to watching the agile bodies of my Arabs on foot, as, tiring of the pace, they dropped back, until just in front of me. Mohammed in particular; how the lights and shadows played over his great, powerful, animal-like form, how subtly his shoulder and calf muscles moved under the sleek, dark skin; how they fascinated me! Willingly through the long journey they had served me, save at Khoms. I started, my dreaming suddenly ended, and almost involuntarily my spurs caused my horse to start ahead. The two men had so imperceptibly lessened their pace that now they had dropped just back of me, one on either side of my horse, and in Mohammed's hand was a wicked-looking knobbed club, which usually he had kept stuck in one of the packs. I knew that each carried a long Arab knife, so I ordered Muraiche to tell the men to keep alongside the donkey.

Down the other side of the moonlit valley I saw a caravan coming towards us heading for Khoms. Taking a small note-book from my pocket, I wrote, "Should any accident occur to me, thoroughly investigate my men, including the guard," and signed it. Tearing the leaf from the book and folding it, I watched the great lumbering camels approach us, and dropped a little farther behind, intending to give it to the head man of the caravan for him to bear to

Drawn by Charles W. Furlong

A LOUNGING-PLACE IN KHOMS

the Pasha at Khoms. Then I decided that under the circumstances there was not sufficient evidence to thus prejudice the Turkish authorities against my men, so I chewed it up and spat it into a patch of sand-lilies.

From the distance came the faint report of a gun. Every one of my men heard it, I knew, but no comment was made, and we pushed deeper into the mountains. On our left, looking toward the moon, objects were indistinct in the half-tone and shadow, while seen from there we appeared in full moonlight. Now and again I sensed moving shadows from that direction, but it was some time before I was sure that they were living forms following us, perhaps hyenas, jackals, or some sly chetah.

As we made sharp turns at times in rounding the mountains, and their sides stood out in silhouette against the sky, I bent low on my horse's neck and watched intently. At one of these turns where the sky cut deep into the mountainside, leaving every irregularity in relief against it, I noticed that men were following us, parallel to our course and a little ahead of it. First, away up on the side, a fezzed head and the barrel of a long Arab flintlock bobbed against the sky for a second, as, dodging catlike among the rocks, their owner rounded the side. Then a second and a third appeared, and I knew we were followed by thieves. This was not comforting; but if we were attacked, the guard's rifle, Muraiche's old-fashioned five-shooter, and my two revolvers would be more than a match for them in point of armament.

One thing puzzled me, however, until later. The manner of these desert thieves being invariably to attack from the rear, I could not account for their seeming to forge ahead of us. Watching my men, I saw that they, too, were aware of the thieves; and Muraiche, who had been watching me closely when we occasionally rode abreast, remarked: "This is a bad country here; I think robbers are following us."

"Yes," I replied; "there *are* men off there,—I have seen three."

"Allah knows, everything is in the hand of Allah. 'There is neither might nor power save in Allah, the High,

the Mighty.'* La! Arbi, you must not ride behind, it is dangerous; you had better ride first."

"Then I will ride last, Muraiche, for I have the best weapons, and I can shoot better than any of you."

After a sharp turn we wound along a valley side. Just below us the dense foliage of an ancient olive grove shut out every gleam of light from its black interior, the gnarled old branches reaching out as though to drag into their depths any who might come within their grasp, and the same weird sensations of awe passed over me which I had felt as a boy when I pored over Doré's illustrations of the wandering Dante and Virgil in that wonderful, gruesome nether world.

My sensation was complete when, as though it was the most natural thing in the world for a small caravan to leave the trail, dangerous at its best, my guard led and the men proceeded to follow him toward the dark wood, which it was manifestly their purpose to enter.

"Muraiche," I called, "why are the men leaving the trail?" Perhaps he did not hear, for the ground was rough, and the stones rattled down the steep bank. "Muraiche," I called loudly and peremptorily, as I rode up to him, "tell the men to halt," at the same time drawing one of my pistols and resting it across my saddle. Then I repeated the question.

"The guard says it is shorter," Muraiche replied, still following the guard.

"Then let the guard take it if he chooses. Order the men on to the trail," and we scrambled our horses and donkey up the steep incline.

The guard turned in his saddle for a moment, made a low reply to Muraiche, then descended and disappeared in the darkness. Skirting the wood for half a mile, we passed beyond it, and my already well-aroused suspicions of intended treachery on the part of my men were confirmed, when in spite of the fact that the guard had by far the fastest-walking horse of our outfit and had taken a shorter route, there was no sign of him until we had passed a hundred yards beyond the grove and halted.

As he emerged I heard the faint click of his carbine as he pulled the bolt to a

* This saying is used by Moslems when anything alarming occurs.

THERE SAT MURAICHE'S FRIEND—HE OF THE MARKET-PLACE

full-cock, upon which, half turning my horse, I awaited him; as he neared us I saw that he had been running his horse, which was breathing hard and sweating. Then the truth flashed upon me: my men were in league with the thieves, who, by a preconcerted arrangement, had gone ahead and hidden in the grove,—there to set upon me in the darkness, relying on my confidence in the guard to follow his lead. Failing in their end, the guard had stopped to parley with them and then made up time. Had their place of ambush not been so evidently dangerous to enter, they might have been successful. Nor would it have been the first time a guard and outfit had returned without the Arbi, telling a good story of how they were attacked by thieves and escaped while he was killed.

Now here in front of me that picturesque, venomous-looking devil sat, his rifle full-cocked across the pommel of his saddle, my other men at a little distance to my right, and I a good mark with my white sun-helmet, but my revolver resting on my saddle covered the guard.

"Muraiche, tell the guard to uncock

My Revolver was pointing at the Breast of Mohammed

his rifle. It might go off by accident."
With a sullen look the guard obeyed.

"Now tell him to ride first to protect
the goods. Let the men with the pack-
donkey follow, then you behind them.
I'll ride last. If any thieves approach
within gun-shot, warn them away at once
or I shall fire. You understand?"

"Yes, Arbi," and we strung out in
single file. My purpose was to place the
guard who possessed the most effective
weapon where it was practically of no
use against me; for this gave me a screen
of the men and animals. The danger
from Mohammed and Ali depended entirely upon their ability to close in on
me, so while in that position there was
nothing to fear from them. As for Muraiche, he was under my direct surveil-
lance with the advantage all my way, as
I rode with drawn weapon.

But I knew the Arab well enough to
know that so long as he is not excited
or his fanaticism aroused he will not
risk his own skin while strategy will
serve his ends; and also knew that I had
no one to depend upon but myself, and
that my safety lay in maintaining as
far as possible a normal condition of
things. So I watched; watched my men

in front, and watched to the side and behind for signs of the thieves, of whom I
caught glimpses now and again. My
Arabs' conjunction with these men
thwarted, it was but natural that they
should communicate with each other to
further their plans, and in various ways
they sought to do this. While caravan
men, when marching through a safe district and many strong, often chant to
ease their dreary march or to pacify the
camels, in our circumstances the less attention we could draw to ourselves the
better. So when Mohammed started to
chant in a loud voice by way of giving
information, I ordered him to be quiet.

Again, as we rounded a sharp bend, Ali
made a break for the brush, but he
started a second too soon. I saw him,
and called his name sharply; he halted
and returned to the caravan.

When we passed within gun-shot of
objects which might conceal a foe I rode
abreast of Muraiche, using him to screen
myself, knowing well that they would
only attack from the side which from
their position placed us in the full moonlight. And in the narrow ravines,
though he growled, I often crowded him
close, affording little or no opportunity

to the Arabs to single me out for a shot without endangering Muraiche. So we travelled until a thong of one of Mohammed's sandals broke on the rocky ground, and he asked to be allowed to drop behind a little and fix it. Since we were entering a wide open stretch below a long slope of hill, I acceded; but as he fell behind some distance, I called to him to come, and when he approached us I turned my attention to the men ahead, feeling a sense of relief that we were in more open country.

The moon was slightly behind us, high in the heavens now, and cast our shadows diagonally to the right and ahead of us. I watched the shadows of my horse and myself squirm and undulate as they travelled over the ground. As I relaxed from the tension under which I had been for a moment gazing unthinkingly ahead, the movement of another shadow caught my eye, that of an upward-moving arm and knobbed club. There was no time to look first. Instinctively my right hand thrust my revolver under my rein-arm, and I turned my head sharply to find, what I had expected, that my revolver was pointing full at the breast of the big fellow Mohammed, who, stealing up quietly behind me with sandals removed, had intended to strike.

" Boor-r-ro!" (go on), I said. Lowering his club, without a sign of embarrassment, he took his place in line, the others apparently having been oblivious to the whole affair.

After he left me, and the excitement of the moment had passed, cold chills chased one another up and down my spine. From then on I saw no sign of thieves. For five hours I had ridden with my finger on the trigger of my pistol covering my men. For five hours I had sensations which I trust I shall not experience again.

About one o'clock in the morning, high up on the hilltop we sighted the white walls of Kussabat, and, after some hard climbing, we came into full view of the silver city—glistening in a bath of silver as Khoms had shone in a flood of gold.

A few words with the town guard, and the great doors of its main gate, the Bab El Kussabat, creaked and groaned as they swung open, and we entered the city, clattered up the steep, narrow streets, where, from the low housetops on either side, sleeping forms muffled in barracans awoke and peered over at us, and big white wolf-hounds craning their necks set pandemonium loose from one end of the town to the other, as they snarled and yelped in our very faces.

Soon we were in a small fonduk with doors heavily bolted. The other occupants were a selected stock of camels, goats, sheep, and fowls taken from the Arabs by the Turks in lieu of taxes; in fact, the fonduk had been converted into a sort of pound. On the roof were a dozen or so of Arabs and blacks asleep, and I preferred their company in the moonlight to that of my four men under the dark archways. To prevent scheming, I took with me Muraiche, the cause of all the trouble. Some of these blacks and Arabs raised up out of their sleep to see, probably for the first time, an apparition in khaki and a white helmet. Then we lay down, and, thanks to the previous night's rest, I managed to keep awake most of the night. When Muraiche rolled over in his sleep, or a neighboring black muttered in his savage dreams, I would start from my dozing.

True, I gave them no baksheesh at the journey's end. I might have had them thrown into the foul Turkish prison of the castle; but, after all, it was the life of these men of the desert,— they had only tried their little game and failed.

And the stakes? My revolvers and ammunition, the leather of my saddle and riding-leggings, and perhaps a gold filling in my teeth. They knew I had no money, for in the presence of Muraiche I had deposited it at Tripoli, and Muraiche himself carried only the necessary funds for the journey. But modern weapons are a prohibited import, save for the Turkish army, and are worth their weight in silver to the Arabs.

Why such a risk for such small stakes? Well, why will the desert thief risk his life for a barracan, or an Arab scavenger dig up the corpse of a plague victim for the miserable piece of sackcloth that girds his loins?

A QUEST IN THE HIMALAYAS

THERE came to our ears the rhythmic *shuff, shuff* of bare feet, as four brown-bodied, white-turbaned men passed our carriage, bearing on their shoulders a rope stretcher. So tiny was the white-swathed body thus swiftly borne to the burning ghat that there was scarcely a depression in the loosely woven fabric. In front of the sad little procession the incense-bearer swung his censer. A passing native ran forward, helped bear the wee body a few paces, and then went serenely on his way, having thus won for himself reprieve for some sin that lay heavy on his conscience.

It was all a perfectly commonplace, every-day occurrence in Calcutta; but to us, as we rattled along in the carriage to the Darjeeling train, it was typical of the Plains, where Death is so ever present among the natives that it seems to walk hand in hand with Life, and where the air is as laden with mysticism and fatalism as with the heavy incense of the East.

We were glad to be leaving the plains for the mountains. For months the great Himalayas had been drawing us with an irresistible power; almost like that magnetic force which they exert upon the waters of the Bay of Bengal, where geographers say one really sails up-hill from Ceylon to Calcutta.

In explanation of whither we were bound and with what purpose, I cannot do better than quote Mr. Ernest Thompson Seton: " You are taking the most wonderful trip in the world in search of the most beautiful of birds." Of this great expedition to monograph the pheasants of the world, I now found myself, unlike Æneas, a small part; but very happy and thankful to have so conducted myself on previous and less extended journeyings in quest of birds that, in spite of being a mere woman, it was now permitted to me to be that small part.

Thus I reflected while we awaited the departure of our train in the dark, close station, where big punkahs swung fitfully back and forth, reflecting the wandering attention of the unseen hands impelling them.

For the benefit of the Oriental temperament the engine whistled and puffed warningly for an hour before at last it started.

For four hours we flew across the flat dusty plains. Even in April and at five o'clock in the afternoon the heat was intense, and the clouds of dust so suffocating that we could scarcely breathe. I felt that at the end of the journey we should have to be excavated, like the ruins of a buried city.

Barren and dusty though the country was, yet signs of life—anticipation of a wetter, cooler season—were visible everywhere. Clods of dust were being turned by wooden ploughs dragged by zebus and buffaloes; a tiny patch of desert was made, even at this season, to yield something green by uncountable buckets of water dipped one by one from a deep well.

Here and there our train window gave us a momentary glimpse of a great tumultuous mass of vultures crowding about some dead thing. This was the season of plenty for them. Grim and monotonous was the whole tone of the country: vegetation, animals, human beings, all coated with dust, the air filled with it!

How welcome was the darkness of night and the cool current of the Ganges! We leaned over the railing of the river boat, which took us across to the sleeping train, marvelling at the strange faith by which these waters make life and death easier for their worshippers.

Early the next morning we changed cars at Siliguri, taking the little toy train up the mountains to Darjeeling.

The tropical jungle at the foot of the mountains was a distinct disappointment. We tried to imagine the unseen tigers with which it is said to teem; but not a bird or a beast was visible, and there was only an occasional blossom.

After we began the ascent, however, our disappointment in the tropical zone was forgotten in the beauty which on one side was unfolded thousands of feet below us, and on the other towered as high above our heads. We reached the clouds and looked down through them to the sunshine in the distant valleys and to the terraced tea estates covering the hillsides like forests of dwarf Japanese trees. Far, far below, the parched plains gleamed through the shimmering heat-waves that hung over them. Above us waterfalls dashed down through forests, dark, cool, and fragrant. At still higher levels were picturesque little settlements snuggling against the steep mountainsides.

Darjeeling itself not only illustrated for us Kipling's tales of the hills, but was of peculiar interest as being the refuge of the Delai Lama who had just fled from Tibet.

We were very anxious to see this Lama—the first for many years wise enough to refuse the golden draught sent by the Emperor of China to each Delai Lama when he reaches the age of eighteen, with the prophecy that it will give him "immortal life." Unfortunately for us, a missionary, more zealous than well-bred, had interrupted a solemn procession in honor of the first visit of the Delai Lama to his faithful subjects, to force a tract into the hand of the Lama, and women tourists had pushed their way into the house set apart for the Lama, whose religion forbids his meeting European women. So, to the shame of our race, the unfortunate Lama had withdrawn into a well-guarded retreat.

THE LITTLE TOY TRAIN UP THE MOUNTAINS TO DARJEELING

A very few days in Darjeeling sufficed to complete the preparations for our mountain trip; and the morning of April 9th found us in the courtyard of the hotel, surrounded by our possessions, the amount of which appalled us. They included a large photographic outfit, guns and ammunition, scientific instruments, provisions, cooking utensils, bedding, and the simplest possible camping - dress. Every want had to be provided for in Darjeeling, since the wilderness bungalows in which we were to live furnished only a roof over our heads. We had cut down our outfit until further reduction was impossible, and yet how formidable it was!

It seemed incredible that coolies could carry our heavy boxes on their backs over the many score miles of mountain trails before us. We did not then know

TANDOOK

our sturdy Tibetans; nor did we know that, as the Englishman in India goes into camp with a folding library, a collapsible drawing-room, and cases of his favorite beverages, our very practical outfit was modest indeed!

One of W.'s assistants was a taxidermist from the Indian Museum in Calcutta—Das, a native of Baluchistan. We had employed a Tibetan, with the singular name of Tandook, as our A. D. C.—otherwise chief cook and head of all the coolies; and we had left to him the engaging of the thirty-two luggage coolies and the sweeper. The sweeper, by the way, is a national institution in India. Without him any

travel off the beaten routes is impossible. His is the lowest caste in all the land, and since he can sink no farther, there is no work beneath him.

After this long digression let us return to the morning of our departure. The scene was one of wild confusion. "Your loads are all too light," cried Tandook, stormily, first in Hindustani and then in various hill tongues, as he rushed about with long, heavy strides, lifting one box after another and slamming it down in front of the coolie who was to carry it. On principle every one objected to his load and insisted that he had more than any one else. The women—for to our surprise six of our luggage coolies were sturdy Tibetan women—laughed and chattered and studied us with undisguised curiosity. The whole jolly horde was like a troupe of insubordinate children. In a miraculously short time, however, Tandook had brought order out of all this Babel.

Although our acquaintance with Tandook began in his sternest mood, no degree of severity could make him anything but an absurd figure to us—in the white dress reaching to his knees and tied at the waist with a red sash, and the long black queue, above which the most microscopic of hats was tilted over the forehead and kept in place by some mysterious unseen force. Fortunately for us, however, he was a formidable figure to his coolies, and they all trudged off very obediently with their loads on their backs, held in place by a strap passing around the forehead. These uncouth hill-people seemed to me like mountain crags to whom some elfish god had given life and human form.

Our first day's "march" was to the bungalow of Jorepokri, where we were to spend the night. Our way lay through the zone of oaks and maples—a dense jungle of moss-draped trees starred with white orchids and lilies, all in the lush growth of full-blown spring.

In the forest near the bungalow big soft eyes watched us intently—the eyes of sambur-deer, alert and anxious; black-backed kalij pheasants started up with whirring wings from under our very feet. Here later we studied this bird, ferreting out the secrets of its home and young.

The next day our destination was the solitary bungalow on the summit of Tonglu, 10,000 feet high.

The mossy jungle of Jorepokri became a thing of the past, and each hour in the saddle now brought us to new beauties. All the way from Darjeeling the wax-like flowers of the magnolia had shone like white lights in the dark woods; but when we reached an elevation of 9,000 feet we found ourselves in a forest of blossoms—*trees* of pink, cerise and crimson rhododendrons, with an under-growth of the pale pink fragrant paper-laurel, from which the Nepalese make a Japanese-like paper. Beneath all was spread a carpet of golden-hearted, white-petalled strawberry blossoms.

Stray bits of human life drifted along our trail. Strangest of all was a creature who suddenly appeared before us at one of the loneliest spots of all the lonely trail. The figure wore skirts and a stiff fringe of false hair, standing out like a black halo five inches around the head, and, holding up a gnarled old hand with one finger missing, begged *baksheesh*. As we had no money accessible and were anxious to reach Tonglu, we rode on, thinking him but a common beggar, with which species India is overrun. How were we to know, as I found later, that he was a lama from a solitary hill lamasery! Thus we lost our opportunity to "acquire merit."

The days at Darjeeling had shown us no hint of the lofty snow-clad mountains. Always they had remained hidden in mist, and in vain we had gazed at the snowy piles of clouds. It was as though the great mountains had held themselves not too cheaply. One must earn the right to see them in all their wonder. Now as we neared Tonglu, Kinchinjunga moment by moment grew clearer.

At Tonglu the vegetation showed but the first blush of earliest spring. Here we were later to seek and find the feathered Pan of the Himalayas, the splendid *Satyra tragopan*. Now after a night's rest we were again on the trail, with the bungalow on the top of San-dukphu as objective point.

Leaving Tonglu, we rode down fifteen hundred feet into full spring again, and then abruptly up never-ending zigzags, our horses' sides heaving in the thin air, to the cool clouds which overhung a little mountain tarn, or "pokri."

Here was the *city* of Kalapokri, consisting of two dilapidated huts just inside the Nepal boundary. To our casual glance they seemed forlorn and innocent enough, but we were to find to our sorrow that the *raison d'être* of the settlement was the Tibetan and Nepalese weakness for drink. Fortunately most of our luggage coolies had within them the fear of Tandook; but Tandook himself had, alas! no such restraining influence.

Quite ignorant of the temptation within those two ramshackle huts, we wandered about the valley of Kalapokri, while our horses munched their tiffin of bamboo leaves. Here the rhododendrons were at the height of their glory. The valley was massed on one side with the scarlet variety, and on the other with flowers of the warmest, loveliest shade of pink. Looking up at these forty-foot trees of blossom, I felt myself a small child in a big old-fashioned Virginia garden, with stately rows of huge box-bushes, and my grandmother's rose-garden looking as lofty to me then as these gorgeous rhododendrons did now.

Turning reluctantly from this vale of flowers, we saw Tandook and the sweeper both in sad plight. The alcoholic temptations of Kalapokri had been too much for them. In the sweeper it took the æsthetic form of incoherent raptures over flowers; but poor Tandook was literally tumbling down the mountain, his red

THE MORNING START FROM TONGLU

woollen dress half slipping off his shoulders, his queue falling across his face as he picked himself up and crammed his wee hat down on his head. Could this Tandook that we saw staggering and stumbling, scolding and whistling, be the same as the busy, capable Tandook of a few hours ago—packing, apportioning to each coolie his load, and finally cooking and serving a delicious breakfast! Later, on the trail, we passed his solitary figure, sitting on the ground with his back to the passing world, beating the earth with a stick in misery and remorse.

W. and I pushed on ahead of all the rest to the final steep and difficult ascent of Sandukphu.

Our horses had an uncomfortable preference for walking at the very edge of a trail overhanging some apparently bottomless precipice. In Tibet they were trained in their youth as pack-ponies, the loads on their backs forcing them to walk on the outer edge of the trails, to prevent a disastrous collision of the pack and the mountainside. Horses thus trained can never be broken of this habit, no matter how wide may be their trails.

At first I felt overpowered by the immensity of the world spread out before us. I think it was Herbert Spencer whose greatest horror was of being an infinitesimal atom floating in inconceivable, immeasurable space. I felt something like that now—so small a thing on my horse, slowly and laboriously climbing higher and higher. Wherever the eye rested there was immensity; in the deep, wide valleys, in the rugged range of lesser mountains, and finally in the silent, stupendous, snow-clad Himalayan peaks, clear and dazzling against the cloudless blue sky. Before us our trail lay like a white thread turning and twisting its way up a rough bold mountain.

It is not a peaceful picture that nature has moulded in these Himalayas. As soon as one rises from the valleys the panorama is rugged, stern, sublime.

As we went on we were reminded that

A VIEW FROM SANDUKPHU

Sandukphu means "mountain of the aconite," for we passed little flocks of sheep, all muzzled to prevent their eating the deadly plant.

There was little life along the trail, but when our horses stopped to draw big breaths at the end of some especially steep zigzag, we looked out over the valleys and saw great imperial eagles soaring below us.

At last we swung off our horses before the door of the bungalow, feeling as fresh as at the beginning of the day, but the crisp, high air had made us ferociously hungry.

When Tandook arrived, still the worse for Kalapokri, he announced in a chanting voice, "To-day you starve! You get no food!" and threatened to go on to another "grog-shop" some miles away. Discouraged in that, he set about preparing tiffin, simpering and giggling, with the little Tibetan hat, which was so expressive a part of him, over one ear. As time went on and no tiffin appeared, I went out to the kitchen to investigate. I had been in the habit every day of giving cheap cigarettes to the tired coolies, and I now discovered Tandook passing around imaginary ciga-

rettes with an elaborate bow to each coolie. Just inside the kitchen was the sweeper, dramatically acting out the rôle of Tandook intoxicated.

In the midst of this bedlam the pony-boys came to be paid off. It had always been Tandook's proud duty to pay all the men. Now W. appeared, telling Tandook that he was in no condition to be trusted with any responsible work, and delegating Das to manage it. At being thus humiliated before all the coolies, Tandook was frantic, bursting into the room where we were still hungrily waiting for tiffin, exclaiming: "To-morrow I go Darjeeling! I discharge myself! Thank you!"

"All right," said W.; "go now."

I quailed inwardly at hearing my majordomo so summarily dismissed. I could not forget what a treasure he was when sober, and drink was the well-known failing of his country. In Tibet Tandook had been "body-servant"—or, as the negroes in Virginia say, "waitman"—to the Tashi Lama, next in holiness to the Delai Lama himself. Surely what the Tashi Lama could overlook we, mere scientists, must forgive. However, I could not intercede for vice, particularly when my motives were so transparently selfish. So I held my peace and awaited developments.

We heard excited talk in Hindustani going on in his pantry, the word *Memsahib* predominating. Finally a somewhat subdued Tandook came in, throwing what he always called the "tablesheet" on the table. He served tiffin with decidedly uncertain movements, loudly clucking like a hen as he passed the dishes. It was a new domestic experience certainly; although after having seen "*Maestro*"—the cook on board our Venezuelan sloop—draw his huge knife on the captain of our little bark, I was quite prepared for the unexpected.

Later Das told me that in the wild flow of Hindustani Tandook had been saying that he wanted to die, he would kill himself, for "*Memsahib*" had seen him in this disgraceful condition, and what did she think of him! But "*Memsahib*" would neither look at him nor speak to him. The most cruel blow was that I quietly refused to discuss with him what he should have for dinner. He made a thousand unnecessary excuses to come into my room, making several attempts outside the door before he could sufficiently screw up his courage to enter. Although he had "discharged himself," all his talk was of future plans —should he send to the nearest village for fowls to-morrow, didn't we want him to engage horses for our return trip, etc.

In the middle of the afternoon we heard him in the next room, talking in a low tone to Das. After a while Das appeared, to say that he had been sent by Tandook "to ask his pardon of Mr. and Mrs. Beebe." W. saw him and said he must make his peace with me; but he said he *could* not, he was "too shameful" to see Memsahib. At last, however, Das—the bearer of the olive branch—tapped at my door, saying in a most virtuous and paternal tone: "Here is Tandook, Mrs. Beebe. I think he is really sorry for what he has done." Das was only eighteen, and thoroughly enjoyed acting as mediator and doing the heavy moral.

Tandook stood in the doorway, only his eyes visible above the ridiculous hat, with which he was covering the lower part of his face, both hands clasped tremblingly in front of the hat. He vowed, "I catch my ear never again to be so rude and bad"—catching one's ear evidently being Tibetan for crossing one's heart. In justice to Tandook I must add that he kept his word, although we often passed the alluring "grog-shops."

Tandook had always been faithful and willing, but now in his repentant mood he became my devoted slave, flying to answer every call. For obvious reasons,

MUZZLED NEPALESE SHEEP

as the dinner hour drew near I consented to tell him what to have; and I took advantage of his chastened mood to get enough water for a hot bath—a difficult achievement on these mountain-tops.

The Dâk Bungalow of India is a blessed institution for the weary Dâk, as the natives call the traveller. He finds these little shelters dotted over many of the out-of-the-way parts of the country, generally not more than one long day's march apart. They mean warmth when one has been chilled to the bone by biting winds, or shelter from the driving rain and hail storms, the latter so common in northern India that planters insure their crops against them, and so violent that both men and cattle are often killed by them. The bungalows usually consist of two bedrooms and a dining-room, with rough outside buildings providing a kitchen and sheds for horses and coolies.

After our life in the untrodden forests of South America, it was camping *de luxe*.

When we woke on the morning after our arrival at Sandukphu we rubbed our eyes as wonderingly as Rip Van Winkle after his twenty years' sleep. Had we slept ourselves into the next winter! Five inches of snow covered the ground. From the snow-capped peaks to our own door-step all the world was dazzling white. A great pile of nondescript blankets and rags on the floor of the enclosed porch told us that our coolies were still sleeping. The snow had drifted in over them; but when the big heap of humanity finally dissolved into units, each one shook off the snow with the merry good humor which we never saw daunted in these hill-people.

Wearing all the clothes we possessed, we hurried out into the frosty air. As we had not brought heavy gloves, we slipped our hands into stockings, which we found very satisfactory substitutes.

The beautiful snow-storm seemed to go to all our heads. Tandook bustled about getting breakfast and perpetrating such brilliant jokes as, "Very nice sugar on the ground. Put in box; send to Calcutta; get much money," laughing heartily at his own wit! The coolies, full of the joy of the hills, danced around in their thick moccasins and threw snowballs, while we photographed wildly, and our artist painted as fast as cold fingers would permit. Every moment was precious. At this season of the year we had not thought it possible that we should experience the wonder of a snow-storm in these middle Hima-

OUR TIBETANS AT PLAY

THE MORNING TOILETTE

layas, with the blossoming rhododendrons only a few feet below us on the sheltered side of the mountain. The great Himalayas had proved true to the translation of their name—an "abode of snows."

Here at Sandukphu, our many days of journeying over for the present, we unpacked our outfit and settled down to the serious work of studying the blood and the Impeyan pheasants. While we were making ourselves at home in *our* way, we found the Tibetans doing the same thing in their own quite different fashion.

Gathered together at the sunny end of the bungalow, the women spent the entire morning on their toilets. They combed and plaited one another's hair into long, thick black braids, to my surprise producing false hair from an old tin tobacco-box and judiciously working it in where it was needed.

I longed to tell the woman who wound her braid in coronet style about her head that her coiffure was the most recent thing in the great centres of fashion, but Paris, New York, or London would mean nothing to her. I remembered my Ceylon servant who asked me if America was in Japan, and contented myself with admiring her head-dress, at which she was delighted.

It was a very jolly little feminine party, and each unselfishly helped in the beautification of the others. In lieu of any much-advertised cold-cream the women had rubbed their faces with a strange, brown, greasy paste, for even the Mongolian skin was not proof against the burning, chafing winds of this high altitude. They all wore gold, silver, and turquoise charm-boxes suspended from necklaces of big coral beads, and huge turquoise earrings, so long that they touched their shoulders.

Meanwhile the men played at throwing pice. A pice is equal to a quarter of an anna, or about half a cent in American money. Each player, standing at a distance of fifteen feet, threw the pice at a small hole in the ground; the pice landing in the hole belonged to the thrower. The game was one of wild excitement, every one rushing to the hole to see if the pice was fairly in. Day after day they played this game, always with the same wild shouts and an enthusiasm which never wearied; although occasionally for variety they threw dice, with an old tin cup for dice-box. Thus the women prinked and the men gambled, and neither felt the lack of a more intellectual employment.

My housekeeping was a never-ending source of amusement to me. Tandook came every morning for the day's orders, saying "Verry-wellsir" to all my suggestions, running the words together as though the whole phrase was one, and rolling his r's as sonorously as a Spaniard. Certainly he had no idea of the masculinity implied, for he sometimes varied his response by saying, "Yes, Madame." One could write a volume on the eccentricities of a Tibetan's English. W. was always making Tandook say "sixteen meeleek," which is, being interpreted, "six tins of milk."

We were sometimes lucky enough to be able to buy a chicken from some passing Nepalese hillman. I have an aversion to making the personal acquaintance of my animal food before it is ready for the table, but *that* I could never make Tandook understand. He always sought me triumphantly with a squawking chicken under each arm. I *must* look at them, and even lift them to see how heavy they were and how good a bargain he had made! Day after day W. went tramping in search of pheasants, trips often too long and difficult for me. On such days I would go off to a certain sunny patch of rugged pines, where I knew I should always find redstarts, skylarks, and cole-tits twittering in defiance of the bleakest weather. The little cole-tits, in their dainty

MOUNT EVEREST FROM OUR HIGHEST POINT

plumage with crests erect, were very "smart" indeed, hopping about the rhododendrons, which were larger here than the stunted growth to be found higher up.

At this season the summit of Sandukphu was a ghost-world: the ferns of last year lay dried but perfect, while the tender young fronds were already beginning to dream of life and spring; stiff brown lily stalks still held their heads high, as if they had not forgotten their yellow and crimson glory of the past summer—grim reminders of the cycle of life.

The most charming days were those on which W. and I took the horses and our favorite coolies and went back along the trail for a day in the valleys. There we were again in the zone of sunshine, flowers, and butterflies. Little waterfalls murmured their way down between mossy rocks and solid banks of primroses, oxalis, and white and blue violets, while the wind played a tinkling accompaniment among the bamboos.

The coolies carried cameras, guns, and butterfly-nets. They made a gay holiday of it, deeply interested in all we did, standing very still while W. crept up with his camera to some bird or insect, or gathering flowers for me and watching as I placed these between sheets of blotting-paper.

Gayest of them all was "Satán," in whom we had early discovered a useful and a kindred spirit. With the silver paper, in which a roll of films had been packed, plastered over his front teeth and a huge pink rhododendron blossom behind each ear, he would skip about catching butterflies. He was always part of our expeditions, bursting with pride at his newly acquired knowledge of cameras and guns. On our travels we have always found an embryo naturalist, and Satán proved one of the best of them. It was Satán who invariably took unconsciously picturesque poses that simply *had* to be photographed, and who was always used in a picture to show the size of tree or rock, usurping my old place as measuring-rod. It was Satán, too, who, after I had bound up his badly cut finger, described me as "a good doctor, but *splendid* for baksheesh!"

We had now obtained photographs and paintings of the native land of our pheasants, but W. wanted more "ecological data," as a scientist would put it, particularly concerning the rare blood-pheasant. In the language of the uninitiated this pheasant seemed to be an exclusive creature who did not care to have his domestic affairs gossipped about in a big monograph.

In spite of the long tramps, this bird had so far succeeded in evading us. "Closed state or not," said W. one day, "we must try our luck in Nepal." We had frequently made little inroads along the border into this forbidden land. This time W.'s plan was to go straight into Nepal along a trail impassable for the ponies, and, alas! for me also; as W. wanted to make a forced march covering as much ground as possible. There was a wild rumor that pheasants had been seen at a certain shed, where some Nepalese shepherds were pasturing their yaks during the snowy months. Here—and as much farther as possible— W. proposed to go, "beating" the jungle all the way.

Had I been going along all would have been serene. As it was, I came dangerously near revealing a feminine unfitness for membership in this pheasant expedition to the Far East. I pictured to myself W. being marched off to Katmandu, the capital of Nepal, where he would probably have to go through endless red tape and certainly lose much time before he could return to the freedom of British soil. This sort of thing had been known to happen before and might very reasonably happen again. Being left alone at Sandukphu to wonder whether W. had fallen down a precipice, or merely been taken off by force to visit Katmandu, would not be cheerful; but I held my peace, hastily put a small lunch of biscuit and cheese into what Tandook calls a "whacket," and wished W. luck as he set forth.

With a volunteer force of ten Tibetans

THE BUNGALOW AT PHALLUT

I then went out to excavate the labyrinth of vole tunnels back of the bungalow. My coolies made wild work of it, pretending to see voles where there were none, throwing their caps over imaginary creatures with cries of excitement. They were tremendously interested in the little grass beds which the thrifty voles had made for themselves in the tunnels, and in the white grubs on which they said the voles feed.

Two of the women had come along, and after the work was over, the occasion became a very social one. To all appearances absorbed in my note-book and statistics on the subject of vole tunnels, I sat in the shelter of a great lichened rock and watched them. One of the women was quite graceful and a beauty—for a Tibetan. I am sure her world considered her so. I dubbed her the Coquette. Human nature is so pathetically and amusingly the same, whether in the rough Tibetan homespun or in broadcloth and chiffon. There was not a man among all our coolies who would not do anything to please the Coquette. Did the lady wish a cigarette, half a dozen men offered theirs at once, and on the trail her load was always the lightest. She was the spirit of every party. Many a more civilized hostess might well have envied her this genius for amusing her world.

W. returned late, having safely crossed the border just in time to escape the Ghoorkas, who must have had a busy day following his trail. He had made many interesting observations, but one bird—the blood-pheasant—still evaded us.

We therefore held a council of war, whose decision was to make a quick trip on to Phallut, travelling as light as possible. It was to be a last dash for the blood-pheasant. Only six luggage coolies were to go, and one of them could do what cooking was necessary, Tandook to his great chagrin being left behind in charge of things at Sandukphu.

The council issued its decree at ten o'clock at night, and by seven the next morning we were on our way, the wind cutting our faces, and the horses slipping and sliding unwillingly along the icy trail. The clouds about us were so dense that we could not see the trail a foot in front of our horses' heads. The mist and the cold brought with them an unreasoning and hopeless depression. There seemed to be no sunshine left in the world—and no blood-pheasants! The one consolation was that we were leaving no stone unturned.

When we had gone about four miles the coolies back of us cried, "Chilly-milly! chilly-milly!"—the blood-pheasant! Pausing only an instant to listen to its peculiar call, W. snatched his gun and was off down the valley. For more than an hour I waited, scarcely feeling the wind, now that there was hope. I experimented in the power of mind over pheasants; but, alas! in this case a dog would have been superior to mind, humiliating as that confession is, for W. returned empty-handed. In all our attempts to get a dog we were disappointed. However, W. had seen this most elusive among pheasants, and had learned its very characteristic call.

We remounted and went on. After a while the sun struggled out. We had descended to a height of about nine thousand feet. The snow peaks were out of sight and the face of nature was no longer rugged and vast. Our way led through fragrant pines, among whose branches floated pianissimo wind music.

As we left the pines and came out again upon the barren mountain, a wild dog ran along the trail ahead of us. A tiny white dot at the top of the mountain showed us the Phallut bungalow, toward which we urged our horses on and up, in a freezing wind, with a storm fast approaching.

We found the bungalow had been shut up for six months. We set up a cry for the *chaukidár,* the bungalow-keeper, who finally appeared, wheezing, puffing, and groaning, after the manner of chaukidárs, who are very like old bellows—useful only for making fires, and very rusty and unwilling.

While the chaukidár made the fires and opened the dusty, long-closed windows, we unpacked our bags and made all ready for the night. Soon there were fresh air and crackling fires in the musty little bungalow. A spread table promised food for the hungry, while beds drawn close to the fireplace and heaped with blankets prophesied warmth and rest.

We had reached the bungalow just in time. As the last coolie put down his load a terrific storm broke—beating sleet and hail, dazzling lightning, and peals of thunder which seemed to shake the very foundation of our mountain. Later the hail ceased to dance on our roof, softening into huge snowflakes which fell swiftly and silently.

The coolies became demoralized and began to complain that if we were snowed in their food would give out, nothing could be got at Phallut, and if covered with snow the trail back to Sandukphu would be impassable. We were so grateful to have escaped being caught in such a storm that we refused to think of to-morrow's troubles, although our own food-supply was equally scanty and had been planned to last only a day and a half.

After dinner we huddled over the fire and recalled tales we had heard of the wild dogs that hunt in packs and often kill tigers, horses, and men, always taking out a piece wherever they bite, like the schools of caribe fishes of South America.

At five o'clock the next morning we climbed to the top of the peak back of the bungalow. I cannot yet realize that the panorama spread out before us that morning was of this earth. From Everest—the world's highest mountain—to Kinchinjunga, said to deserve the second place in altitude honors, the wonderful Himalayan range stood out, as clear-cut as cameos, against a deep-blue sky. Under the spell of the newly risen sun the snows were pale pink, delicate blue, and lavender, or pure, dead, cold white. The tops of all the lower mountains were enveloped in mist; so that the great snow range seemed to rise straight from a pearl-gray sea of clouds. Like the lesser peaks, all that was petty in life was blotted out in this vision of the loftiest mountains of our planet. A little wedge driven through the stupendous majesty and silence of the snows marked Jelep La Pass, the most important trade route through the Himalayas from India into Central Asia. Through this gateway of the snows tobacco, indigo, iron, manufactured cotton, silk, and wool are poured into Tibet, which in turn sends into India hides, horses, ponies, musk, and the fluffy yak-tails used all over the East as "fly-flappers."

After our early breakfast I helped W. off for his final arduous tramp in pursuit of the blood-pheasant. This time he was to go into the state of Sikkim. I then eagerly loaded up my cameras for a blissful morning with the snows—to find that in the few minutes which I had spent in getting ready the clouds had blotted out everything, and I could not see clearly ten feet beyond the door-step.

I could not expect W. back for eight hours at the very earliest. Of the coolies only the cook knew a word of English, and his vocabulary of some dozen words was purely culinary—toast, cheese, fowl, etc. That was not enlivening, particularly as the larder was so painfully bare. It was decidedly wiser to fix one's mind on higher things. I had only my thoughts and my diary to occupy me; the former were anxious enough to send me many times to peer vainly out into the all-obscuring gray mist.

As the day wore on, the snow on the trail melted sufficiently for me to send the horses two miles down in the hope of giving the tired men a lift home. W. told me later that nothing could describe the joy of his heart when he saw the horse waiting to take him up the last stiff climb. It was almost nightfall when at last he came, looking aged and worn with the terrible hours of toiling knee-deep in snow up and down the mountains, repeatedly slipping back many of the painfully gained steps. At last the coolies with him had lost the way; and they had had to climb over several of the treeless snow mountains next to Phallut, instead of following the trail. Both the coolies had collapsed, and I had to become at once "Memsahib the doctor," doing for them all that lay in the power of hot food and my medicine-kit.

But the bird of our quest had at last been found, and W. had made many desired observations concerning its manner of life and the desolate haunts which it shares with the lammergeier, the skylark, and the snow - leopard; the drama of the pheasants, however, is W.'s story, not mine.

OUT OF NO-MAN'S LAND

THERE is a No-Man's Land that you may find anywhere from St. Petersburg to Tokio. It is the land of the big hotel—the hotel double-starred in the guide-book. Its essentials are space, elevators, electric lights, and baths—all very good things in their way, but things for which one may pay too high a price in more precious things than money.

Conformity is the ideal of No-Man's Land, and while the exigencies of the climate cause this outward expression to vary, yet every effort is made to do away with trying differences which may jar on the nerves of the fastidious traveller who takes this curious way of seeing the world. For instance, while the servants are perforce of different nationalities, this trying variation is overcome as much as possible by the training of the waiters. They seem to breed a polyglot tribe all through southern Europe to serve those who live in No-Man's Land, just as they breed tall and pompous grenadiers for *portiers*.

The general aspect of the inhabitants is curiously alike—as alike as the sequence of courses or the fashion of cooking. You may go at a bound from Paris to Rome, and yet eat the same dinner and sit down to it with the same crowd about you. In one place as in the other you will find well-dressed Americans, the same British matrons, the same scattering of titled people, and in one place as in the other the assembly will be heavily weighted with English-speaking people.

Like a rich and powerful family, these hotels have many poor relations. Some are enveloped with specious elegance and small comfort; others sternly respectable—all modelled as nearly as possible upon the lines of the most powerful and enduring; while still others, like old families who need not to put on any frills, have for so long had a standard of ex-

cellence that they keep on their own way tranquilly, without any concessions to fashion, secure of their patronage. There are two things about these hotels that one may be sure of — that they are all to be found in Baedeker, and that they are all appallingly and deadeningly alike. Through their dignified portals the wind of chance never blows; the atmosphere of the country in which they are is shut out as sternly as an Italian shuts out the night air.

But while the great hotels in No-Man's Land do things with a gesture, and although its fluctuating crowd has little to say about the country, still, viewed as a crowd, it is often more than amusing. It is in what one might call the well-connected hotel and pensions that middle-class dulness broods, and to these most of us are condemned.

In an excellent but depressing hostelry in Florence a company of Americans found ourselves. "Is this Italy?" we asked one another (the cooking and the company were overpoweringly virginal and English). We sat reflecting sadly how an ignorance of a language cuts one off from all but museums. We told one another mournful tales of our childhood, when we had walked through endless hotel corridors, our wistful eyes searching the eyes of other children to whom we never spoke; we didn't need to be told not to—the atmosphere of No-Man's Land did it as surely as if some great sign had been placed frieze-like along the wall—"No Talking Allowed Here." This is a sad way for friendly children to live. We confessed that good-tempered chambermaids, not yet broken into the rigorous service, had formed our only solace.

In childhood, too, we had all seen from railway carriages little red-roofed towns in which were comfortable smiling little hotels whose sun-bathed faces overlooked some sleepy piazza. We had wondered why we never stopped in places like these, and had wished very much indeed that sometimes one could get off the train before the place one had planned to stop the night before, and take one's chances along the road.

It was inflaming talk of this kind that led us into the real Italy, past the warning in all guide-books. You may find it under the heading " Hotels," as follows:

" The wise traveller will avoid the native hotels of the country. While there may occasionally be found one of excellence, for American and English travellers they are for the most part utterly impracticable, leaving much, if not all, to be desired in cleanliness, food, and lodging, as well as in service."

And it . is a warning that the traveller who is under the heel of the great god Comfort would do well to heed. If you are one who has gone through life leading by one hand a porcelain tub and by the other a radiator, such adventurings are not for you.

Our entrance into the real Italy might be described like a ride through a tunnel that brings you out on the other side of the mountain into a different climate and a different atmosphere, though in our case the tunnel was merely a ride under the stars in a *carrozza* after a time passed tediously on the railway—a ride up a hill to a town that can have no name, because of the personalities that I shall have to indulge in concerning my friends Amelia, Otillio, and Annunciata. Some busybody would be sure to go to them and tell them that I, a trusted friend, had delivered them and their ingenuous vanities to print, and this would be a poor recompense to pay to those who led us first really into Italy, and also helped us to learn their lovely language through their eager willingness to understand every broken word of ours.

It was Beppi, the *facchino,* who led us up the hill in the darkness, chatty and communicative. Instead of the clanging bell that greets one's arrival at the hotels throughout Europe as a signal for the *portier,* deferential of manner and ample of abdomen, to come forth with his military salute, Beppi entered the hotel and bawled informally:

" Amelia! Amelia! Le Signorine Inglese!"

And so we stepped over the threshold of what in our eyes seemed the Land of Romance, with Amelia, purple of cheek, curling of hair, ample, homely, wholesome, as guide.

Underfoot the floors of our rooms were covered with red tiles. The plastered and whitewashed walls were stencilled with a pretty blue pattern. Furniture there was little beyond a bed and an august wardrobe, which looked as though it had begun life with the ambition of becoming a mausoleum, but had been forced by circumstances into a humbler walk of life. The very bareness of the room was reassuring and grateful.

" Here," we said, " we are quit of those who live in No-Man's Land. The British matrons, the two gentle American spinsters who have haunted us under varying forms, will never find their way here. There is nothing to see here but Italy."

And we took to admiring the hotel garden—a mere little shelf of land tucked almost on top of the roofs of houses and overlooking other shelf-like gardens fifteen or twenty feet below. From its exterior one would not have suspected the Stella d'Italia of any garden at all, for it gave prosaically on a little narrow street on one side and on an apology for a square on the other. A humble little *trattoria* flanked it, where people sat and drank syrups or the wine of the country, on the sidewalk, and there were the symptoms of a cinematograph opposite; it had been or was to be, I don't know which, for in the small hill towns of Italy the cinematograph is apt to be like the " Free Lunch To-morrow" of the historic Bowery sign.

This garden itself was an eloquent and touching example of how Italy can make a great deal out of very little. Here was a little shelf of land, very little more than a long back yard, and, behold! by its artful divisions it had a wood at one end so dense that at a stone table set in the midst of the boskage one could have imagined oneself miles away in the very depths of a forest. Especially as evening drew on was this true, until Annunciata lighted an evil - smelling acetylene light, heated her irons on a tiny charcoal fire made in what seemed to be a square flower-pot, and thus performed her ironing *al fresco,* thereby, it seemed to me, making a fine example to our housewives, who perform the same task of ironing clothes in a hot kitchen and in the middle of the day.

There was a graceful path of complicated design through w h o s e intricacies one might really make a walk of several rods and pretend one was in a spacious garden, and on both sides this path was bordered by a small and very fragrant rose, while an opulent Dijon clambered masterfully up the side of the hotel. Here and there a marble table at which one might dine gleamed white against the trees, and in the remotest corner dense shrubbery made a little private dining-room; nor was there lacking a small fountain. Down below one could see the winding streets of the little village, other gardens, and, at a distance, terraces of lemons with their straw mattings to protect them from the too direct rays of the sun; and still farther a glimpse of the little beach, with fishing-boats drawn up upon it.

And as we looked out and reflected, with very much the feelings of children on their first escape from parental authority, Amelia entered, with a copper jug of hot water in her big purple fist.

"What will it please the Signore to eat?" she inquired. And with such an air of authority did she speak that we asked her if she were the *padrona.*

And at this she blushed and exclaimed quickly:

"Oh no! I am only the *cameriera.* Would it please the Signore to eat a duck?" she persisted.

We agreed to eat a duck.

"I will now go and kill it suddenly," remarked Amelia; as indeed she did, and very near our windows it was, for be-

neath the hotel terrace were arches where were poultry and wash-tubs; where the children made doll-houses, and where the numerous old women attached to the house sat and gossiped while they did everything from washing clothes to picking over old mattresses.

THE STELLA D'ITALIA GAVE PROSAICALLY ON A NARROW STREET

Presently we dined upon the recently slaughtered duck and irreproachable fried potatoes and a salad and fruits served on fresh leaves. We ate in the face of the sunset out-of-doors, with the air sweet with the scent of the roses, the wandering winds bringing us whiffs of lemon blooms from the neighboring terraces, and the dusk gathering over the white stretch of sea far below. In sweet contentment of spirit we listened to the prattle of Fede, the waiter, as he came and went. He told us everything that would make our stay more enjoyable, wishing to prove that the Stella d'Italia was a peerless place, I believe. He even mentioned that the composer Bizet had stayed there the season before; and when, in our ungallant Anglo-Saxon way, we mentioned the fact that we had ignorantly supposed him dead these many years, nothing daunted, he proved that this was not so by humming the *Toreador.*

And then, in the midst of our happi-

AMELIA

ness, he allowed the axe to fall upon our defenceless heads.

"The Signore are not the only English Signore here," he said. "There is another lady here—an English lady who paints; an English gentleman with his spouse departed yesterday." He ran away in quest of cheese.

Was it not possible in the uttermost parts of the earth to escape them, we wondered. What brought them to this little unknown town which had nothing to recommend it to the sightseer except a church—and what town in Italy hasn't a church and a pulpit and an altar-piece?

By the time Fede had returned, our pessimistic minds had formed a picture of the interloping English painter.

"Was she middle-aged?" we asked. "Had she long teeth?"

"Very long teeth," replied Fede, "very middle-aged." He smiled.

"What time does she have her meals?" we asked.

"She breakfasts very, very early and is off. She stays away all day to paint. She returns late. She goes down to such and such a town."

"And why does she not stay there?" we wanted to know.

"The air," replied Fede, without hesitation—"the air here is much finer. She comes back to sleep."

He changed the subject by announcing that Otillio, the padrone, had purchased a cageful of nightingales and a cageful of doves, both of which Annunciata was to cook for us.

"A brave cook, Annunciata!" prattled Fede. "Truly an accomplished woman! One time she was cook for long in an English family—*nobilissimi* they were. She only left because of the death of her padrone."

Indeed an accomplished woman was Annunciata, as Fede proclaimed her. She had, I suppose, the dirtiest kitchen that any woman was ever guilty of. We knew that its floor was covered with red tiling because the rest of the floors were; otherwise it might have been the beaten earth of the street. Scrubbings would have done it no good; the hoe and the rake and the hose of the fire department would have been the only things strong enough to have removed the grime of ages from that kitchen floor. The *batterie de cuisine* was of copper, but it did not shine.

In one corner of this kitchen an old and decrepit man and several elderly females sat and perpetually prepared vegetables or plucked the feathers from fowls and poultry of various kinds, for the Stella d'Italia had a fair business at luncheon-time, as people sometimes drove out from the large neighboring town for the sake of the view.

In one corner was a soapstone hearth as high as any ordinary kitchen range, and a hood built down upon it. Upon this were places for several tiny charcoal fires, and over a handful of inadequate-looking coals and dusky copper dishes Annunciata would turn forth as savory meals as it has ever been my lot to taste. She could roast to a nicety in a covered casserole, and I think, to do her justice, from the taste of the cookery, that the interior of these pots must sometime have been scoured.

At all hours one might find her, large and good-tempered, waving her dilapidated turkey-fan with a delicate hand toward the embers. When we descended the stairs at noon and Amelia or Fede cried out, "Annunciata! Le Signore Inglese!" she would boom out, "Prunto!" as resonant as a bell, and presently send forth, from the midst of the unspeakable disorder in which she cooked, succulent dishes.

We turned blind eyes upon the dirt of Annunciata's kitchen and concentrated our attention on the excellent food, and philosophized about the economy of fuel in Italy, whereby a whole hotel was supplied with meals at less cost for fuel than for a small family in this country, and went around our small town rejoicing, our only dark spot the haunting shadow of the long-toothed Englishwoman.

And if it hadn't been for the dog of the *paroco,* we might have gone away and really have missed the whole significance of our little hotel. It was our custom often to stray into the church of Santa Maria di Primavera near at hand, and more than once we had lured forth the dog of the parish priest, who had a fondness for eating his bones before the altar of Our Lady—to our Protestant eyes an unseemly act. And through this Scotch terrier, whom I have always suspected of having some Presbyterian leanings, we became acquainted with the parish priest, an ascetic, middle-aged man, possessed of some French.

"Brave people," he remarked to us, "with whom you stay. A good daughter is Amelia, and a fine cook the *padrona.*

Annunciata." (It was Otillio we had supposed to be *padrone.*) "Yes," went on the priest, "and well brought-up her children. When Annunciata took up this venture, a while back, her son Fede left the big hotel in which he was *cameriere,* to help his mother; and Otillio, though not a clever lad, is good enough for bookkeeper. It has been a great windfall for them to have you with them. You are the first English that they have had, and I hope you will recommend them to others. A fine thing for Annunciata to have all her rooms taken by one party, except the room for commercial travellers and that for the Signor Avvocato."

He called to his dog and went his way.

There never had been any English lady, you see. There was no house across the street; there was no Marjorie Daw. The lady of the long teeth, of the early

A HUMBLE TRATTORIA WHERE PEOPLE SAT AND DRANK SYRUPS

rising habits, had been a pure figment of the brain of Fede, touchingly invented to make us feel at home and that we were not strangers in a strange land; and to make their new hotel glorious they had all of them sunk their personalities—all but Otillio—who wore the dignity of padrone with all the youthful malaise in the world.

Now we understood why it was that it

was like digging for buried treasure to extract the weekly bill from them, and understood, too, conversations such as these that would occur:

We, looking the bill over sternly: "Otillio, you have neglected to place upon the bill the sandwiches and tea we had the other afternoon. How much are they?"

Otillio: "Signore, I do not know; I will ask ma—that is to say, I will ask Annunciata. I was in town that afternoon."

"The wash bill, did you not pay our wash bill last week when we were absent?"

Otillio, with deep discomfort, as though convicted of a fault: "Si, Signore."

We, sternly: "Find out how much it was and put it on the bill. And the extra wine that we had the other evening?"

Otillio, throwing forth his hands: "Signore, that I cannot count for you. If the Signore drink a little more or less, who can count that? We who buy wine at wholesale!"

"But it must cost something."

"Almost less than nothing," Otillio, hastily and with embarrassment: "That wine I buy from the *podere* of my uncle."

Thus inadequately did poor Otillio play the unfamiliar part of the grasping hotel-keeper. No doubt he got many scoldings from his "mamma"—otherwise Annunciata, the true and adequate proprietress.

But until our departure we never told them that we knew that Amelia was no ordinary *cameriera*. We let them go on playing their little parts for the glory of the Stella d'Italia of which they were so proud, and for us, their first *forestieri*, though it was true that at the last they became a little lax in calling Annunciata, and occasionally we would hear:

"Mamma! Le Signore!"

Partly because they were charming persons and partly because they opened the door of Italy to us, Otillio and his family, who deceived us so bravely for the glory of the Stella d'Italia, will always remain first to us, though the Minerva, in Capo di Sorrento, played it a close second.

There is no town of its size that I know of in the south of Italy where the No-Man's Land hotels flourish better amid a more successful *mise en scène*. They have every modern improvement—electric light and lifts and baths in connection with each room—well, almost every room—and marvellous views from each window; for you cannot escape views in that part of the country if you want to. The gardens are knowingly laid out, and full of roses; besides that, they dance the Tarantella every night that there are strangers enough to pay for it. Indeed, they do very well indeed, both scenically and every other way.

But there are some things they can't do for you that the little Minerva, out a couple of kilometres, can, though you may live there for five or six *lire* a day. Because if you live at the Minerva you can't help finding out how a big Italian farm is run. For a half-hour's walk out of the tourist-ridden town of Sorrento, the shops of whose main street proclaim it to be given up to the stranger, you may find yourself in the deep country. Your walk takes you winding around the edge of a mountain, up whose sides clamber terraces of olives, and down whose flanks slide lemon groves, and at each turn in the road you have a new picture. The sea below you is more like some clear jewel than water, and Vesuvius, as beautiful as Fujiyama ever was, dominates the whole. No wonder they love their country—the south Italians; no wonder they come back to it, and no wonder the nations of the earth—heavy Germans, and all the northern races—escape from their countries to look upon the pure beauty of this lovely land.

Capo di Sorrento is a tiny village, with its own church and its scattering of houses and a mysterious and ample Roman ruin of its own. The new Minerva until recently was not inaptly termed "Paradiso," for lovely enough its ornamentations were when we arrived. Perhaps too much wistaria clambered up the trellis, the roses clustered too richly, the view too magnificent, until the whole thing gave one the effect of being in a well-staged Belasco play instead of in a humble little pension-hotel, which was to Italy what the farmers' boarding-houses are to America.

At just what date the proprietor be-

THE KITCHEN—HOTEL MINERVA
Etched by B. J. O. Nordfeldt

came more hotel-keeper than he was farmer I cannot tell you. Tourists probably found him out one time in his *podere,* or perhaps it was his father or his grandfather, and boarded with him in his up hill, down dale house—the house under which are tucked away the cow-stables, the bake-oven, and the mill for the olive oil. Incidentally there is also a bath-tub, used only under great stress, such as in cases of severe illness; for, when we saw it, it was turned upside down and stored away among the rafters, with the dust of ages over it. The clothes

of the family were being washed in the substitutes for set-tubs opposite the bake-oven, where their wholesome brown bread was in the process of baking.

And the Minerva is still as much of a farm as it is hotel. They grow their own vegetables and their own fruit, and have their own cows, and make their own wine and their own oil; and more unusual yet, most of their own bread. The work is done as at the Stella d'Italia— by the sons and daughters of the family, only the old patriarch of a proprietor makes no pretenses for the sake of his

The Orange-tree Patio—Fonda Italia
Etched by B. J. O. Nordfeldt

hotel. And how many sons and daughters he had was a fact never fathomed; all we knew was that they were all handsome, red-cheeked, deep-bosomed, curly-headed, and that he fairly burst with pride over the beauty of his daughters, making a personal matter of it, as though it were through some special virtue of his that they were such a fine-looking race.

As business increased he bought the second pension-hotel, and there from his farm he feeds a horde of Northerners; for by some trick of the tourist business almost all of the people who go there come from the farthest corner of Europe. You may hear Russian talked and Finnish and the variations of Swedish and Norwegian, and German also, but hardly ever a word of English.

It is to be observed as one travels around in different places that the tourist only too often acts as though he were invisible; here he stops to gape at a market group; there you find him in a cathedral while high mass is in progress, making his way through the worshippers to survey some picture as though they were not there. So in the end the people of Italy have gotten to treat the mighty army of tourists as though in very truth they did not exist. It is different in Spain; you cannot visit that land without meeting Spanish people; they do not keep courteously out of your way as do the Italians. Even if you do not speak the language you will, whether you wish to or not, and whether you keep your eyes open or not, see more of Spanish people in a week's time than it is probable you will of Italians in a month. In Spain, even in the cities, every eye will follow you; you are an object of interest —not a flattering interest always, but from the small boy who follows you in mobs to the demurely observant eye of well-bred ladies on their way to mass they are never indifferent to you.

It was because of this interest we aroused that our hearts failed us for a moment—that and the guide-book warning of "No Thoroughfare" in front of the native *fondas*. I have seen Spanish guide-books, indeed, where the earnestness of the warnings reached the point of hysteria; so much so that it made any experimenting seem adventuresome enough. But as far as my experience goes I should rather have a jolly meal out-of-doors in the Fonda Italia in Algeciras than in any other hotel in that town. It depends on what you have come to Spain for, of course; if you have come to see a fine hotel, go by all means to the Reina Cristina; it is a most commendable and beautiful hotel. But if you have come to see Spain and feel adventur-

ously inclined, wander up the little ice-cream-colored side street, beyond the market on this side of the cathedral, and ask one of the dozen little boys that will be following you where the Fonda Italia is.

If it is the proper season of the year, you will eat in a charming patio where oranges grow to the second story, and there will be a good-tempered and talkative Spanish crowd eating around you; and if it is your first venture in Spain you will marvel over the length of the menu and the strange disposition of the courses; for if I remember rightly there were hors-d'œuvres, soup, fish, and that dish whose name I have never mastered and without which no Spanish dinner is complete—boiled dried peas of a huge size, with more or less fragments of boiled beef about it and shreds of greens, an excellent dish, though as I tell it sounding contrary to all known laws of cookery. Then the meat and some other fish, and finally dessert, nuts and raisins

THE "UP HILL, DOWN DALE" HOUSE

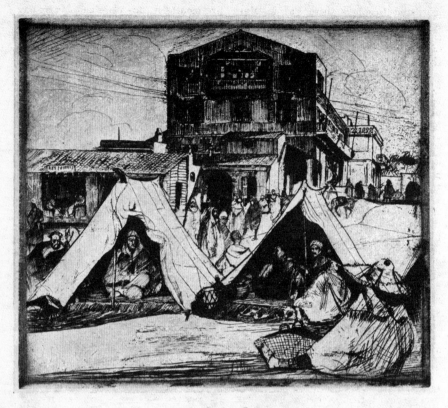

HOTEL CAVILLA—TANGIER

and oranges; and it seems to me that I have omitted mention of a fowl with salad in some portion of the menu where one would not expect such fowl and salad to appear.

Of the No-Man's Land in Spain I am in no position to speak; I never saw it, for right in the beginning of things we met Doña Amelia, a much-travelled business woman, who gave us addresses of tiny and inexpensive *fondas,* so that for the brief space of time we were in Spain we did not so much as see an English-speaking waiter, and were received as old friends by members of the family. Charming people gave us lessons in Spanish, reconstructed our Anglo-Saxon coiffures, and led us into the mysteries of the adjustment of the *mantilla,* until we felt that we were relatives returned from journeyings instead of board-paying strangers. It may be, for

all I know, that Spain has no true No-Man's Land; perhaps all Spain is off the beaten track.

It is not always sunshine, though, in the world outside of No-Man's Land; moments there are when one turns to the respectable if not heart-warming Baedeker for advice. There remain in our minds some vast tomb-like rooms in Frankfort-on-the-Main, in a hotel that acted as though its only visitors for a generation had been ghosts. The ordering of food was accompanied by dreary waits; panic followed on the heels of a request for the "Bath in the Hotel" advertised in four languages; and no wonder, for the family washing of the whole past month was at that moment soaking in the amorphous tank-like structure which the proprietors fondly looked upon as a bath-tub. And as a disreputable pendant of this respectable and moribund *Gasthaus* there was in Marseilles a whited sepulchre of a hotel of a snug enough and quiet exterior, but of dubious gayety o' nights. To offset these was the little Hôtel du Commerce in Saint-Raphael, whose windows looked forth on a populous beach on which were drawn up many boats; whose proprietor was the chef, and who brought to the preparing of meals that loving zeal so seldom found outside France.

The most rewarding of hotels is that hotel of paradoxes—Cavilla's, which is a Spanish hotel but which is not in Spain; Cavilla's, on whose roof live turkeys, and where the women sing the old coplas of Andalusia all the day long as they wash the clothes; on whose terraces dwell hoary turtles, and where you hear the perpetually disquieting beat of Moorish drums and the noise of the *gimbri* from the cafés underneath. For Cavilla's is a little island of Europe perpetually washed by the waves of Islam. It stands a big square place overlooking the Socco Grande in Tangier, and to get to it one must push one's way through the flocks and herds of the tribes. Before the very door the caravans of small camels lie down and the muffled women await the return of their lords, sitting with their backs against the hotel, looking at the Europeans with great and curious eyes. Outside, all is color and confusion; inside, all is quiet. You pass from one civilization to another, from Morocco to Spain, every time you cross the doorstep, and no matter how long you stay, the contrast never loses its sharpness.

They say that any one who knows the Sôk of Tangier and understands its currents, its drifts, and from which tribes the men come who wander through it, and who the holy men who beg there day by day (holy men who do not beg from Christians, in contradistinction to those who do), and who can understand the story-tellers, and knows how the snake-charmer lights straw by blowing on it after his tongue has been bitten by his snakes—it is said that any one who knows these things knows Morocco; but it is safe to say that the Europeans who do can be counted on one hand. There are not many Stricklands to be found in El Moghreb. But certain it is that you may

live months in this place and day by day the sights from your window will be new, and day by day the varying life of Tangier, full of color, will be unrolled before your eyes. Wedding processions with the bride cooped in a bright-painted wooden box will sway past at nightfall with torches and music, and the chanted dead march of the informal Moorish funerals break into the roar of the Sôk, while the skirling music of Sidi Mecfee, the patron saint of the Sôk, dominates every other sound.

After all, the little inns of a country are about the only point of contact that the average traveller has with the people of that country; for, indeed, what people eat and drink, and how they are contented to live out of their own homes, tells one a vast lot when you come down to it.

The moment you leave the land of big hotels and step into one of the little hostelries you find along the roadside you can make up the whole civilization of the country if you are clever, as a Buffon could reconstruct the whole animal from one bone. What more eloquent of the civilization of France, for instance, than the excellent omelet you may find waiting for you in almost any little hotel from Dieppe to the Midi? *"Der Mensch ist was er isst,"* and one could spend years in studying the customs and manners of France and Germany, and yet find it all in the contrast between that marvellous roast chicken, the art of which is lost the moment you put foot over the border, and the estimable salad of France with the beer and the ever-present productions of the pig in the small hostelries of the Fatherland. What more significant of at once the poverty and the richness of our own civilization in this country, where all the fruits of the earth—or at least the vegetables of it—are served in the country hotels in a series of chilly and forbidding birds' bath-tubs We are a nation who ask for a ruinous plenty and are content, in more things than food, to have this plenty cold, unappetizing, and ill-served. It is a far cry from the chain of fashionable institutions from Ponce up the coast to the little ordinary hotel of the small town. Could not a sagacious traveller plumb our heights and depths from these?

UNDER THE MINARETS

I.

IT was a small, not over-clean, and much-crumpled card, and it bore this inscription:

> Isaac Isaacs,
>
> *Dragoman and Interpreter,*
>
> Constantinople.

It was held very near my nose, and above the heads of a struggling, snarling pack of Turks, Armenians, Greeks, and Jews, all yelling at the tops of their voices, and all held at bay by a protecting rail in the station and two befezzed officers attached to the custom-house of his Serene Highness.

Beyond this seething mass of Orientals was seen an open door, and through this only the sunlight, a patch of green grass, and the glimpse of a minaret against the blue.

Yes; one thing more—the card.

The owner carried it aloft, like a flag of truce. He had escaped the tax-gathering section of the Sublime Porte by dodging under the guarded rail, and with fez to earth was now pressing its oblong proportions within an inch of my eyeglasses.

"Do you speak English?"

"Ev'ting: Yerman, Franche, Grek, Tearkish—all!"

"Take this sketch-trap, and get me a carriage."

The fez righted itself, and I looked into the face of a swarthy, dark-bearded mongrel, with a tobacco-colored complexion and a watery eye. He was gasping for breath and reeking with perspiration, the back of his hand serving as sponge.

I handed him my check—through baggage Orient Express, two days from Vienna—stepped into the half-parched garden, and drank in my first breath of Eastern air.

Within the garden—an oasis, barely kept alive by periodical sprinkling—lounged a few railroad officials hugging scant shadows, and one lone Turk dispensing cooling drinks beneath a huge umbrella.

Outside the garden's protecting fence wandered half the lost tribes of the earth, each one splitting the air with a combination of shouts, sounds, and cries that would have done justice to a travelling menagerie two hours late for breakfast. In and out this motley mob slouched the dogs—away out in the middle of the street, under the benches, in everybody's way and under everybody's feet: everywhere dogs, dogs, dogs!

Beyond this babel straggled a low building attached to the station. Above rose a ragged hill crowned by a shimmering wall of dazzling white, topped with rounded dome and slender minarets. Over all was the beautiful sky of the East, the joy and despair of every brush from the earliest times down to my own.

II.

Ever since the days of the Arabian Nights—my days—the days of Haroun al Raschid, of the big jars with the forty scalded thieves and the beautiful Fatima with the almond-shaped eyes, I have dreamed of the Orient and its palaces of marble. And so, when Baron de Hirsch had brought the home of the Caliphs within two days' journey of the domes of San Marco, I threw some extra canvases

But Isaac, the dragoman, is standing obsequiously with fez in hand, two little rivulets of well-earned sweat coursing down each cheek.

"Ze baggages ees complet, effendi."

Isaac crawled upon the box, the driver, a barelegged Turk with fez and stomach sash, drove his heel into the haunches of the near horse, once, no doubt, the pride of the desert, and we whirled away in a cloud of dust.

"I don't see my trunk, Isaac."

"Not presently, effendi. It now arrives immediatamente at the dogane. Trust me!"

CAÏQUE LANDING, GALATA BRIDGE.

into a trunk, tucked a passport into my inside pocket, shouldered my sketch-trap, and bought a second-class ticket for Constantinople.

I had only one object—to paint.

My comrades at Florian's—that most delightful of cafés on the Piazza—when they heard that I was about to exchange the cool canals of my beloved Venice for the dusty highways of the unspeakable Turk, condemned my departure as quixotic. The fleas would devour me; the beggars (all bandits) steal my last franc; and the government lock me up the very first moment I loosened my sketch-trap.

Five minutes more, and we alighted at the custom-house.

"This way, effendi."

For the benefit of those unfamiliar with the liquid language of the Orient, I will say that effendi means master, and that it is applied only to some distinguished person—one who has, or is expected to have, the sum of half a piastre about his person.

Isaac presented the check—a scrap of paper—to another befezzed official, and the next moment ushered me into a small room on the ground-floor, furnished with a divan, a tray with coffee and cigarettes,

PATIO OF THE PIGEON MOSQUE.

OVERLOOKING THE GOLDEN HORN FROM MOSQUE SULEIMAN.

and an overfed, cross-legged Turk. There was also a secretary, curled up somewhere in a corner, scratching away with a pen.

I salaamed to the Turk, opened my passport, sketch-book, and trap, and delivered up the key of my trunk.

The secretary undid his legs, stamped upon my official passport a monogram of authority looking more like the image of a fish-worm petrified in the last agonies of death than any written sign with which I was familiar, and clapped his hands in a perfectly natural Aladdin sort of way. A genie in the shape of a Nubian, immeasurably blacker than the darkest Africa, moved from behind a curtain, and in five minutes my trunk holding the extra canvases, with a great white cross of peace chalked across its face, was strapped to the carriage, and we on our way to the Royal.

As I said before, I had come to Constantinople to paint; to revel in color; to sit for hours following with reverent pencil the details of an architecture unrivalled on the globe; to watch the sun scale the hills of Scutari, and shatter its lances against the fairy minarets of Stamboul; to catch the swing and plash of the rowers rounding their caïques by the bridge of Galata; to wander through bazar, plaza, and market, dotting down splashes of robe, turban, and sash; to rest for hours in cool tiled mosques, with the silence of the infinite about me; to steep my soul in a splendor which in its very decay is sub-

lime; and to study a people whose rags are symphonies of color, and whose traditions and records the sweetest poems of modern times. If you are content with only this, come with me to the patio of the Mosque Bayazid—the Pigeon Mosque.

Isaac Isaacs, dragoman, stands at its door, with one hand over his heart, the other raised aloft, invoking the condemnation of the gods if he lies. In his earnestness he is pushing back his fez, disclosing an ugly old scar in his wrinkled, leathery forehead—a sabre cut, he tells me, in a burst of confidence, won in the last row with Russia. His black beard is shaking like a goat's, while his hands, with upturned palms and thumbs, touch his shoulders with the same old wavy motion common to his race. Standing now in the shadow of the archway, he insists that no unbeliever is ever permitted to make pictures in the patio, where flows the sacred fountain.

I had heard something like this before. The idlers at Florian's had all said so; an intelligent Greek merchant whom I met on the train had been sure of it; and even the clerk of the Royal shrugged his shoulders and thought I had better not.

All this time—Isaac still invoking new gods—I was gazing into the most beautiful patio along the Golden Horn, feasting my eyes on columns of verd-antique supporting arches light as rainbows, that shaded groups of priests brilliant in every color of the palette.

I crossed the threshold, dropped my trap behind a protecting column, and ran my eye around the Moorish square. The sun blazed down on glistening marbles; gnarled old cedars twisted themselves upward against the sky; flocks of pigeons whirled and swooped and fell in showers on cornice, roof, and dome; and tall minarets, like shafts of light, shot up into the blue. Scattered over the uneven pavement, patched with strips and squares of shadows, lounged groups of priests in bewildering robes of mauve, corn-yellow, white, and sea-green, while back beneath the arches bunches of natives listlessly pursued their several avocations.

It was a sight that brought the blood with a rush to my cheek. Here at last was the East, the land of my dreams! That swarthy Mussulman at his little square table mending seals; that fellow next him selling herbs, sprawled out on the marble floor, too lazy to crawl away, from the slant of the sunshine slipping through the ragged awning; and that young Turk in frayed and soiled embroidered jacket, holding up strings of beads to the priests passing in and out—had I not seen them over and over again?

And the old public scribe with the gray beard and white turban writing letters, the motionless veiled figures squatting around him, was he not Baba Mustapha, and the soft-eyed girl whispering into his ear none other than Morgiana, "fair as the meridian sun"?

Was I to devour all this with my eyes, and fill my soul with its beauty, and take nothing away? My mind was made up the moment I looked into the old scribe's face. Once get the confidence of this secret repository of half the love-making and intrigue in Stamboul, and I was safe.

"Isaac!"

"Yes, effendi."

"Do you know the scribe?"

Isaac advanced a step, scrutinized the old patriarch for a moment, and replied, "Effendi, pardonnez, he the one only man in Stamboul I not know."

This time, I noticed, he omitted the invocation to the gods.

"Then I'll present you."

I waited until the scribe looked up and caught my eye. Then I bowed my head reverently, and gave him the Turkish salute. It is a most respectful salutation. You stoop to the ground, pick up an imaginary handful of dust, press it to your heart, lips, and forehead in token of your

LIGHTER-BOATS IN THE BOSPORUS.

sincerity and esteem, and then scatter it to the four winds of heaven. Rapidly done, it looks like brushing off a fly.

The old scribe arose with the dignity of King Solomon—I am quite sure he looked like him—and offered me his own straw-thatched stool. I accepted it gravely, and opened my cigarette case. He unseated a client, dismissed his business for the day, and sat down beside me. Then, Isaac interpreting, I turned my sketch - book leaf by leaf, showing him bits of Venice, and, in the back of the book, some tall minarets of an old mosque caught on my way through Bulgaria.

It was curious to watch his face. He evidently had never seen their like before.

Before the book was closed, I had formally and with great ceremony asked and received permission to paint the most sacred patio, Isaac protesting all the time as he unbuckled my trap that the scribe was but a pauper, earning but a spoonful of copper coin in a day, with no more right to grant me a permit than the flea-bitten beggar at the gate. But then Isaac had not come to Constantinople to paint.

Half an hour later, when the arches were sketched in, and the pillars and roof-line complete, the shrill voice of the muezzin calling the faithful to prayer sounded above my head. I could see his little white dot of a turban bobbing away, high above me on the minaret, his blue robe waving in the soft air.

In an instant every occupation was abandoned, and priests, seal-maker, herb-doctor, and peddler crowded about the fountain, washed their faces and feet, and moved silently and reverently into the mosque. Soon the patio was deserted by all except Isaac, the pigeons, and the scribe—the kindly old scribe—who still remained glued to his seat, lost in wonder.

Another hour and the worshippers came straggling back, resuming their several avocations. Last of all came the priests, in groups of eight or ten, flashing masses of color as they stepped out of the cool arches into the blinding sunlight. They approached my easel with that easy rhythmic movement, so gracefully accentuated by their flowing robes, stopped short, and silently grouped themselves about me. I had now the creamy white of the minaret sharp against the blue, and the entrance of the mosque in clear relief.

For an instant there was a hurried consultation. Then a beardless young priest courteously but firmly expounded to Isaac some of the fundamental doctrines of the Mohammedan faith, one being, "Thou shalt not paint."

At this moment I felt a hand caress my shoulder, and raised my head.

It was the scribe's, who, with faded robe gathered about him, stood gazing into the face of the speaker. I held my breath, wondering whether, after all, I had left San Marco in vain. Isaac stood mute, a half-triumphant "I told you so" expression lighting up his face.

Then drawing himself to his full height, his long beard blending with his white robe, the old scribe waved Isaac aside, and answered in his stead. "I have given my word to the Frank. He is not a giaour, but a true Moslem, a holy man, who loves our temple. I have broken bread with him. He is my friend, bone of my bone, blood of my blood. You cannot drive him away."

After that, painting about Constantinople became quite easy. Perhaps the priests told it to their fellow-priests, who spread it abroad among the faithful in the mosques; perhaps the gossips around the patio took it up, or the good scribe whispered it into the veiled ear of his next fair client, and so gave it wings. How it happened, I know not; but from that day my white umbrella became a banner of peace, and my open sketch-book a passport to everybody's courtesy and everybody's good will.

III.

Let me remind those who may have forgotten it that there is really no such place as Constantinople. There is, of course, the old Turkish city of Stamboul, with all the great mosques.

Then there is the European city of Pera, rebuilt since the fire, up a hill, a long way up, with its modern tramway below, and the ancient tower of the Genoese crowning the top.

And last, across the Bosporus, is Scutari, only ten minutes by ferry - boat. Scutari-in-Asia, with mosques, archways, palaces, seraglios, fruit - markets, Arab horses, priests, eunuchs with bevies of houris out for an airing, gay awnings, silks in festoons from shop doors, streets crowded with carnival-like people wearing every color under the sun, Bedouins on

MOSQUE OF MOHAMMED ALI, SCUTARI.

horseback riding rapidly through narrow streets, tons and tons of grapes piled up in baskets, soldiers in fez and brown linen suits—everything that is foreign and un-European, and out of the common world. A bewildering, overwhelming, intoxicating sight to a man who has travelled half the world over to find the picturesque, and who suddenly comes upon all there is in the other half crammed into one compact mass half a mile square.

Isaac never quite understands why I go about absorbed in these things, and why I ignore the regulation sights—the mosque with the Persian tiles, three miles away and a carriage; the treasury at Seraglio Point, opened only by permit from the Grand Vizier (price £2); the dancing dervishes at Pera; the howling dervishes at Scutari; and the identical spot where Leander plunged in.

I finally compromised with Isaac on the dervishes. We had spent the morn-

had so humiliated him that he had suggested the dervishes to divert my attention. A dragoman of the opposition, a veritable son of Abraham, had betrayed him. He had bitten his thumb at him, not literally but figuratively, and this in very decent English—no, the reverse. He had charged him with fraud. He had said that his name was not Isaac Isaacs, but Yapouly—Dreco Yapouly; that he was not an honest Jew, but a dog of a Turk, who had stolen honest Isaac's name when he died. Yes, robbed him, ghoul, grave-digger, beast! He with a scar on his forehead, where he had been branded for theft! And here the opposition dragoman snatched Isaac's fez from his head, and ground it into the dirt with his heel.

After a gendarme had taken this very disagreeable dragoman away, Isaac confessed. So many Englishmen, Frenchmen, Americans, he said, had wanted Mr. Isaacs that he had concluded that it was

ing at Scutari, where I had been painting an old mosque. It was howling-dervish day—it comes but once a week, the howl beginning at 3 P.M. precisely—and to satisfy Isaac I had left the sunshine for an hour to watch their curious service.

I had, it is proper to state, wrung a confession that morning from Isaac which

cruel not to accommodate them. Of what use was a dead Jew? How infinitely better a live Turk! So one day, when hanging over the rail at the station, an Englishman had arrived holding the deceased Isaac's card in his hand, and since that time Yapouly had been Isaac Isaacs to the stranger and the wayfaring

MARKET DAY, VALEDÉ MOSQUE.

man. "See, effendi, here the Angleesh-man card."

It was the same the rascal had pressed into my own face!

Thus it was that Dreco Yapouly Isaacs—I will no longer lend myself to his villanous deception—preceded me up a steep hill paved with bowlders, entered the low door of the *tekkè* (house) of the dervishes, and motioned me to a seat in a small open court sheltered by an arbor covered with vines.

Five francs, and we passed the hanging curtain covering the entrance, and stepped inside a square, low-ceiled room hung with tambourines, cymbals, arms, and banners, and surrounded on three sides by an aisle.

The howlers—there were at least a dozen—were standing in a straight row on the floor, like a class at school, facing their master, an old, long-bearded priest squatting on a mat stretched before the low alcove altar.

As we entered, they were wagging their heads in unison, keeping time to a chant monotoned by the old priest. They were of all ages; fat and lean, smooth-shaven and bearded; some in rich garments, others in more sombre and cheaper stuffs.

One face cut itself into my memory—that of a handsome, clear-skinned young man, with deep, intense eyes that fairly flamed, and a sinewy, graceful body. On one of his delicate, lady-white hands was a large turquoise ring. Yapouly whispered to me that he was the son of the high priest, and would succeed his father when the old man died.

The chant continued, rising in volume and intensity, and a Nubian in white handed each man a black skull-cap. These they drew tightly over their perspiring heads.

The movement, which had begun with the slow rolling of their heads, now extended to their bodies. They writhed and twisted as if in agony, like a row of black-capped felons standing on an invisible gallows, swinging from unseen ropes.

Suddenly there darted out upon the mats a boy scarce ten years of age, spinning like a top in front of the priest, his skirts level with his hands.

The chant now broke into a wail, the audience joining in. The howls were deafening. The twelve were rocking their heads in a wild frenzy, groaning in long, subdued moans, ending in a peculiar "hough," like the sound of a dozen distant locomotives tugging up a steep grade.

"Allah, hou! Allah, hou! Allah, hou!" —the last word expelled with a jerk.

A dozen little children were now handed over the rail to the Nubian, who took them in his arms and laid them in a row, their faces flattened to the mats. The old priest advanced within a step of the first child, his lips moving in prayer.

Yapouly Isaac leaned over and whispered, "See! now he will bless them."

I raised myself on my feet to see the better. The old priest balanced himself for a moment, stepped firmly upon the first child, his bare feet sinking into its soft, yielding flesh, and then walked deliberately across the line of prostrate children. As he passed, each little tot raised its head, waited until the last child had

of athletes in from a foot-race. I looked for my young priest with the turquoise ring. He was sitting on a bench, rolling a cigarette, his face wreathed with smiles!

IV.

And yet the Mohammedan priest, despite his fanaticism, is really a most de-

PLAZA OF THE VALEDÉ MOSQUE.

been trampled; then sprang up, kissed the old priest's robe, and ran laughing from the room.

The dervishes were now in the last stages of exhausted frenzy. The once handsome young priest was ghastly, frothing at the mouth, only the white of his eyes visible, his voice thick, his breath almost gone. The others were drooping, with knees bent, hardly able to stand.

Suddenly the priest turned his back, prostrated himself before the altar, and prayed silently. The whirling child, who for half an hour had not stopped, sank to the floor. The line of dervishes grew still, one by one tottered along the floor, clutched at the hanging curtain, and passed into the sunlight.

I forced my way along the closely packed aisle, and rushed into the open air, impelled by a wild desire to render some assistance. The sight that met my eye staggered me. My breath stopped short. In the midst of the court stood the Nubian serving coffee, the howlers crowding about him, clamoring for cups, and panting for breath like a team

lightful companion. His tastes are refined, his garments spotless, his manners easy and graceful, and his whole bearing distinguished by a repose that is simply superb—the repose of unlimited idleness dignified by unquestioned religious authority.

I remember one in particular who spent a morning with me—a noble old patriarch, dressed in a delicate egg-shell-colored robe that floated about his feet as he walked, an under-garment of mauve, with waist sash of pale blue, and a snow-drift of silk on his head. For four broiling hours, with only such shade as a half-withered plane-tree could afford, did this majestic old fellow, with slippers tucked under him, sit and drink in every movement of my brush. When I had finished, he arose, saluted me after the manner of his race, and pointing first to the sketch, and then to the glistening mosque, said, in the softest of voices:

"Good dragoman, tell your master I have for him a very great respect. He has opened my eyes to many beautiful things. I am sure he is a most learned

MOSQUE OF THE SIX MINARETS.

man," and passed on with the dignity and composure of a Doge.

Everywhere else did I find this same spontaneous, generous courtesy and kindly good humor. Only once was I rebuffed. It was in the open plaza of the Valedé. I had been watching the shifting scene, following eagerly the little dabs of color hurrying over the heated pavement, when my eye fell upon a cobbler but a few yards off, pegging away at an upturned shoe. When my restless pencil had fastened his fez upon his head, and linked his body to his three-legged stool, a laugh broke out among the by-standers crowded about me, one jovial old Turk calling out to the unconscious model. In an instant he was on his feet, forcing his way through the throng behind me. Hardly had I matched this sketch with another— a long-robed Armenian who swung past— when I felt a hand tighten on my shoulder, and the next instant a wet leather sole was thrust forward and ground into my paper, spoiling both sketches.

It took five minutes of my most subtle Oriental diplomacy, sweetened with several cups of the choicest Turkish coffee, to convince this indignant shoemaker that I meant no offence. When I had succeeded, he was so profuse in his apologies that I had to smoke a chibouque with him, at his expense, to restore his equanimity.

And yet, under all the courtesy and good nature I found everywhere, I could not help noticing that a certain disquiet and nervous fear permeated all classes— priests and people alike. The government's extreme poverty and constant watchfulness are two things the inhabitant never forgets—one concerns his taxes, the other his liberty. This fear is so

MY SHOEMAKER.

FRUIT-STAND, SCUTARI.

great that many public topics worn thread-bare by most Europeans are never whispered by a Turk to his most intimate friend. Even my dear friend and confidential adviser, Mr. Yapouly, finds now and then a subject upon which he is silent. One day I asked him who had been suspected of murdering the predecessor of the present Sultan, and why it had been thought necessary to remove that luxurious son of the Prophet. To my surprise, he made no reply: we were in Pera at the time. When we reached the long cemetery, he stopped, looked carefully over the low wall, as if fearing the very graves, and then said, in his broken conglomerate, too shattered to reproduce here:

"Effendi, you must not ask such questions. Everybody is a spy: the man asleep on the sofa in the hotel, the waiter behind your chair, the barber who shaves you. Some night your bed will be empty. Nobody ever asks such questions in Constantinople."

Nor is this unrest confined to the people. I noticed the same anxious look on the Sultan's face the day of the *salemlik*—the day he drives publicly to the little mosque to pray, the mosque outside the palace gates. His face was like that of the acrobat riding bareback at the circus hoop—glad to be through.

But I am in Constantinople to paint, not to moralize, and these glimpses of the treacherous, deadly stream that flows beneath Turkish life are not to my liking. I want only the gay flowers above its banks and the soft summer air on my cheek, the tall grasses waving in the sunlight, and the glow and radiance of it all. So, if you please, we will go back to my mosque, and my delightful old priests, and the Greek who sells me grapes and weighs them in a pair of teetering scales, and my caïque with the pew cushion over the bottom, and the big caïkjis, with the chest of a Hercules and the legs of a satyr, who rows my Oriental gondola, and all the beautiful patches of color, fretted arch, and slender column that make life enchanting in this lotus-eating land; and even to Mr. Yapouly, Mr. Dreco Yapouly, who tells me he has reformed, and will never lie more, "so help him"—Mr. Dreco Isaacs Yapouly, who has lately ceased his unanswered appeals to the gods, and who has left off all his evil ways.

But then I remember that I cannot go back to my old life now, for the summer is ended. Last night there was a great storm of wind and a deluge of rain, the first for four months. All the gold-dust has been washed from the trees and the grasses. The plaza of the Valedé is scoured clean. The little waves around the Galata no longer lap their tongues indolently about the soggy, rotten floats, but snap angrily in the crisp wind. The doors of the mosques are closed, and outside, in the early morning, groups of natives are huddled over charcoal pans. The winter is creeping on apace, and I must be gone. Besides, they are waiting for me at Florian's on the Piazza in my beloved Venice; those scoffers with their cerise and Chianti and *grandi* of Munich beer. Waiting, not to mock, but to kotow, to bend the ear and genuflect, now that my portfolio is bursting, and to say, "Come, let us see your stuff!" and "How the devil did you get away with so much?"

So one morning I tell Isaac to pack my trap, and this time to slip it inside its leather travelling-case, and to get me a "hamal," a human burro—an Armenian, perhaps—who will toss my trunk, with the extra canvases now all filled, upon his back, and never break trot until he dumps it at the station two miles distant.

I instantly detect, in spite of our close intimacy, an expression of relief wrinkling over Mr. Yapouly's tobacco-colored countenance. He breathes out his regrets, but with a lightness of touch that shows his heart is not in them. He has been but a "hamal" himself, he thinks, lugging the trap about in the heat, and sitting for hours doing nothing—absolutely nothing. And I have bought so little in the bazars, and his commissions are so small. But then, as he reflects, is he not the dragoman of dragomans, and might not future wayfarers be my intimate friends and his special prey? So he becomes doubly solicitous as the time draws near. Would effendi allow him to place a few pounds of grapes in the compartment, the road to Philippopolis is so dusty and the water is so bad? Had not the umbrella better go above, and the rugs on the other seat?

Last of all, with a certain tenderness that he knows will appeal to me, where will effendi permit him to place the dear old trap, my companion over so many thousand miles of travel? At my feet? No; on the cushion beside me!

The guard blows his whistle; the carriage doors are locked. Yapouly—Dreco Yapouly, the reformed—leans outside. I move to the window for a parting word. After all, I may have misjudged him. He starts forward, and presses some cards into my hand.

"For your friends, effendi, when they want good dragoman."

I turn up their white faces.

They are clean and newly printed, and bear this inscription:

> *Isaac Isaacs,*
> ## *Dragoman and Interpreter,*
> *Constantinople.*

GREEK FISHING-BOATS.

THE NILE

AT this moment all eyes are turned eastward, and Egypt has become an object of actual and almost hourly interest. The papers bring us daily all the news that can be collected on the exciting development of events in that hitherto calm and dreamy land. It is not my intention to swell the volume of information which we already possess by any opinions or political prophecies of my own. I only wish to sketch for such of my readers as feel more than a passing interest in the land of Egypt some facts, traditions, and customs which may serve as background to the picture which the present unrolls before us. Owing to my lengthened stay on the shores of the Nile I have had ample opportunity of making observations and studies bearing upon the development of the Egyptian people. When I was a boy, and studying Greek, one of the first sentences I committed to memory was: "Egypt is the gift of the Nile," an opinion expressed by the father of history—Herodotus. Its meaning was at that time in no wise clear to me, and I had no reason then to suppose that fate would put me in the way of testing its truth.

Many a time during the years that I spent in Cairo have I stood on the immense Nile bridge, leading from the Oriental capital to the villages on the western shore of the river and toward the Pyramids, and have brooded over the mysteries of this wonderful and fascinating stream.

In winter and spring, when the waters sink deeper and deeper in their bed, and here and there a sand island appears, the river resembles a weary wanderer who is straining every nerve to reach the longed-for goal. In summer, when the tropical sun sears and scorches all exposed to its rays, it is quite the contrary; then is the time when Father Nile, in proud consciousness of his power and strength, tosses his brown and turbid waves, and hurries on, fierce and grumbling, under the arches of that imposing bridge, threatening to overthrow it, and all else, in his rapid onward course. There are other bridges spanning arms of the Nile further on, but this is the only yoke to which he deigns to bend his broad back while yet an undivided current sweeping onward to the sea.

It is through the Nile, as through an artery, that the body of Egypt draws life and nourishment; where its pulsations cease, death—the desert—begins. The soil is like a sponge, and during the time of the inundation absorbs such quantities of moisture that they suffice for the vegetation of the whole land until a year later, when new floods appear, awaking life, and calling forth an expression of renewed vitality in plants and animals. "First a desert, then a sweet water lake, then a blooming garden," are the words in which Amru, the Mohammedan conqueror of the land, characterizes in short and terse expression its three most salient phases.

At a time when geographical knowledge was in its infancy, Herodotus expressed an opinion, which modern science has confirmed, viz., that not only the Delta, but the whole lower valley of the Nile, had originally been a gulf, filled out gradually by the enormous masses of mud carried along and deposited by the tempestuous river. Nay, more, he even prophesied that, should the river ever change its course, and choose the Red Sea as point of exit, the same phenomenon would be repeated, and in twenty, or even ten, thousand years a new and fruitful continent would be formed where now all is water.

To give an approximate idea of the quantities deposited by the Nile during

THE CITADEL OF CAIRO.

the time of inundation, I will only mention that in a glass of water left standing for an hour, from one to two inches of sediment will be found.

In the immediate vicinity of Cairo are the ruins, scattered over a large space, of the City of the Sun—the "On" of the Bible (Genesis, chap. xli., vs. 45–50). It was the centre of Egyptian science, and has a peculiar interest for us in that Scripture tells us that the wife of Joseph was born here; and here, no doubt, Moses, as the adopted son of an Egyptian princess, became acquainted with the wisdom and learning of that time. One would hardly think it possible, on visiting the spot, that it has once been the scene of so much intellectual life and architectural splendor, for naught remains of the far-famed Egyptian university to speak of its past glory but heaps of débris, interspersed with orange groves surrounded by enormous hedges of cactus. The Nile, during the inundation, presses forward without let or hinderance, and covers with its flood the place where schools, temples, and palaces once stood. There is but one grand and characteristic memento of the past left standing—a huge obelisk, the oldest in all Egypt—a monolith of over one hundred feet in height, erected by the King Userteseu I. in the year 2803 B.C. Of all the family of obelisks which Greek wan-

derers once saw united here, and which now are scattered all over the world, this one alone is left in solitary grandeur, a fitting tombstone on the grave of the past. This obelisk, at whose base a Joseph and a Moses have wandered, stood before the great Temple of the Sun. But time and the Nile have been busy bedding it deeper and deeper, and full two meters of earth have accumulated at its foot in the more than 2000 years since the ruin of Heliopolis.

One of the peculiarities of the rivers of Africa—this land of mystery, typified by the Sphinx guarding its gates—is that they take the longest possible way to reach the sea. And the Nile is no exception to this rule. Its chief sources, situated the one in the mountains of Abyssinia, the other in the vast lakes of Central Africa, are comparatively near the eastern shore of the continent; and yet, in spite of this, and of the fact that the most southern of its sources takes its start south of the equator, the huge body of water turns northward, and after making a great circuit only reaches the sea at a latitude of thirty-two degrees north. The distance traversed by the Nile on its lower course, where on both sides there is desert, and no tributary whatever, is one of about 800 geographical miles.

The Nile and its inundations could not

be otherwise than a great mystery to the primitive inhabitants of Egypt, who were only acquainted with its lower range, and knew nothing of its sources or tributaries. Even at the time of the Romans, "caput Nile quærere" (seeking the source of the Nile) was a common saying, its meaning being, to try to discover something which was above and beyond the pale of human knowledge or discovery.

Notwithstanding this, there was in ancient times no lack of men who tried to solve the problem, and Herodotus gives us, with more detail than any other ancient writer, the different opinions on the subject which were then current. He stamps as merest legend the conviction entertained by some that the Nile was derived from the oceans surrounding the earth. Another version was that the cold northern winds, which in summer sweep uninterruptedly over the land, checked the flow of the river, and thus caused it to rise and overflow; but this he also stamps as untenable. On the other hand, he as positively rejects the theory held and defended by some few *savants* of the ancient time, especially Anaxagoras, and which we now know to be the true one, viz., that the melting of immense masses of snow accumulated on the mountains in Central Africa caused the Nile to rise. It is, above all, the Blue Nile which, during the rains in Abyssinia, and the time of thawing snow, contributes so largely to swelling the tide. Herodotus, who opposes this theory, says in relation to it: "How is it possible that snow in such quantities should exist in a region where the inhabitants are burned brown by the sun; and where the winds are scorching hot?" He had heard from Egyptian priests that the origin of the Nile was to be found in the deep ravines or chasms called Crophi and Mophi; but the rise and fall of its waters he explained as follows: "In winter, the sun on leaving us takes its course over the earth in more southerly direction. In consequence of this those regions become so intensely hot that the waters of the Nile—only just appearing on the surface of the earth—at once evaporate. When the sun returns to us in summer, and pours its burning rays over our land, those distant countries in Libya are comparatively cool, and the waters of the Nile can, quite unchecked, well up, accumulate, and flow down to us." Thus far

the speculation of the learned. Strongly contrasting with this is the popular tradition concerning the Nile, which, in consequence of its vast influence for good and evil, for plenty or for famine, attributed to

THE OBELISK AT HELIOPOLIS.

it divine power, and gave it a prominent place in the religious ideas and observances of that day—a tradition whose unimpaired transmission is mainly owing to the extreme tenacity with which the Oriental clings to all superstitions connected with his land and people.

The mythology of the ancient Egyp-

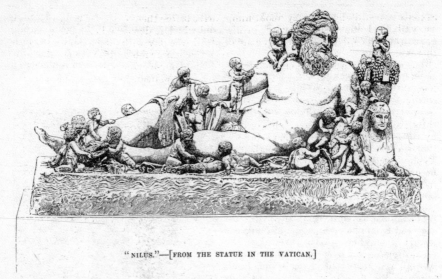

"NILUS."—[FROM THE STATUE IN THE VATICAN.]

tians, revealed to us in the many monuments on which it is recorded, impresses us at first sight as a chaos of color, letter, and design, and one into which the scholars of our time have brought but little order or system, comparatively speaking. It is a curious and interesting fact that this intricate maze of dogmas is reduced to simpler, clearer forms, the older the documents are in which we find its traces. In an extremely ancient sacred scroll, written on papyrus (known as papyrus Briss), we actually find only *one* God mentioned. To those who see in this only a proof of a long prehistoric development of the Egyptian people we will leave this theory, as well as the care of proving it, for as yet it has only been proposed.

It is quite natural that at a time when all manifestations of life, the human as well as the natural, were being deified, this river, representing moisture as a life-giving principle, the cause of all growth, should also be drawn within the magic circle of the deity, and be honored and worshipped as such. Was its appearance in the midst of desert and arid rocks not a miracle? What if not divine influence could be the cause of its yearly growth?

Most of us have no doubt seen pictorial reproductions of those peculiar Egyptian gods, invariably drawn in profile, and utterly without perspective. They are found in Egypt not only on the walls of temples and their gateways, monuments hewn out of the living rock, but also on the inner walls of tombs.

This most peculiar form of imagery has with wonderful tenacity preserved its rigid and inflexible character even at a time when Greek influence on art and religion was strong in Egypt, and when the Ptolemæi, who were desirous of uniting Greek art and beauty with Egyptian wisdom, sat upon the throne.

Among these portraits of their deities we find one—that of a man of greater height and fuller stature than the others—usually painted uniformly red or blue; on his head a wreath of lotus blossoms, in his hands aquatic plants and flowers. This is *the Nile*, the god *Harpi*. A beard gives proof of his manly prowess and strength, and a woman's breasts are symbolical of his nourishing, life-giving qualities.

The Greeks, who strove to clothe all mythological legends in gracious and winning forms, have chosen one far more pleasing than this crude Egyptian image. It is one of the finest specimens of classic sculpture, and such of my readers as have visited the Vatican in Rome will no doubt remember it—a male figure of athletic proportions, in a recumbent position, the left arm resting on a Sphinx. The head is crowned, here also, with aquatic blossoms; in his right hand are sheaves of wheat.

Sixteen graceful cherubs play about him, as symbolical of the sixteen yards of his growth and the universal prosperity caused thereby.

Isis and Osiris were brother and sister, as well as husband and wife—so says the legend—and reigned in prehistoric times in the land of Egypt: wise and gentle in their sway, maintaining peace throughout the land, and much beloved by their subjects. But they had a brother, full of envy and hatred, called Typhon, or Seth, who did not rest till he had murdered Osiris, cut up his body into many parts, and scattered them far and wide. With weeping and wailing Isis went in quest of the remains of her beloved; succeeded in finding all, save one, and gave them fitting burial. Her son, Horus, nurtured with thoughts of revenge, having reached maturity, failed not to seek and, when found, to slay in battle the enemy and murderer of his father. In the world of the immortals, however, Isis and Osiris were once more united, and continued, though invisible, to reign over their devoted subjects.

The manner in which Osiris is most frequently represented is that of King of Hades; the crown of Egypt on his head the scourge and crook in his hand, awaiting, as it were, the souls for judgment. He is monarch of the far west— the land of the dead; the King of Life, whom the souls of the departed must greet on their arrival in his realm with one hundred and twelve names and titles. According to Plutarch, the more intelligent of the priests interpreted this legend in various ways. One of the versions is that Osiris was the type of virtue, which, although often overcome by evil, is still in the end—and most surely in the hereafter—always victorious. But still another and most curious version is this: Osiris was the motive power in all fertilizing moisture, and they did not hesitate to call him plainly—the Nile.

Isis, the receptive, is the earth. Seth was, in their conception, the type of all aridity and dryness, all-scorching, wilting heat, transforming the fertility of the motherly earth (Isis) into a mourning widow; Seth is the wind that blows from the southwest, before whose withering breath all life and moisture disappear. Seth, yellow and reddish in color, comes from the Libyan desert, and resembles the hot sand that the fierce "chamsin" storms

drive before them in the early spring days, and which is dense and cloud-like, so that it fills the day with gloom, and causes the sun to appear moon-like through the haze.

The course which the Nile takes from the high plateaux of inner Africa to the

BASS-RELIEF OF QUEEN ISIS.
From the Cairo Museum.

lower lands of Egypt is one that leads over rocky terraces, and in that part of its journey, which is called "the Cataracts," it presses forward between opposing rocks and bowlders, causing picturesque waterfalls and rapids. Not till it reaches Assuan is there any calmness or method in the flow, but from this point on the river bears the stamp of a quiet and graceful stream. All "wild oats" are sown, and the Nile enters into the sedate demeanor of a good citizen. Its chief occupations are agriculture, but it disdains not to place its strength at the service of commerce and navigation.

Just before the last rapid, viz., the Pass of Silsileh, the rocky shores approach so

THE ROCK TEMPLES OF SILSILEH.

closely that the Nile, which in some parts of Egypt has a breadth of six thousand feet, in this place is crowded into a space of barely three hundred feet. At this spot were the quarries which furnished the building materials for the majestic temples, and here, too, the adoration of the "god of the Nile" was peculiarly fervent.

On the western rocky projection is a very curious rock temple, and quite near by, in the quarries, are two stone slabs (*stela*) containing the commandment issued by King Rameses II., and renewed by his son Merneptah, and Rameses III., to solemnize on this spot two feasts in honor of the Nile. These inscriptions contain accounts of these festivals, and also a hymn, which was, no doubt, sung on these occasions in adoration of the god Harpi. The moment selected for these festivities was, on the one hand, that at which the Nile in Egypt began to rise; on the other hand, when "the book of the Nile was laid aside," that is, when the feasts which annually accompanied the inundation came to a close.

I have repeatedly conjured up before my mind's eye the picture of that time, when on the heights of Silsileh the priests of the Nile-god, wrapped in gorgeous rai-

ment, with hands upraised, chanted the solemn anthem, while at their feet, in the deep ravine, the Nile rushed tempestuously on toward the thirsting Egyptian plains.

One of the grandest and most wonderful pages of Christian history is that which relates the triumphant march of the Cross through Egypt during the first centuries of our chronology.

The subject so often and justly selected by the Church for artistic representation, the infant Jesus forced to fly from his native land and his persecutors, and seeking shelter in Egypt, offers a parallel to the picture which history gives us of the infant Church, born into life in Bethlehem and on Golgotha, flying from the heights of Judæa and from the persecutions of the "chosen people" into the wastes and deserts of Egypt. The Egyptian religion, which had, till then, invariably conquered all those who had through power of sword swept over the land and possessed it, the Ethiopians, the nomad tribes of the East, the Persians, Greeks, and Romans, and had seen them, one and all, worshipping in its temples—this religion was forced to bow before the image of the Crucified, who, denuded of all outward power and glory, came into their midst. The ancient temples, which for thousands of years had been the nation's sanctuaries, were forsaken; on their ruins, in their vast courts and galleries, at their side, Christian churches sprang up.

And yet Egypt more than any other country showed great readiness in taking into its young Christian life alien elements, which, growing and developing,

edge of the sword, threw down the empty forms of doctrine, drove the no longer united brethren into open discord, and in its turn, in place of the Cross, erected the Crescent.

All that remains of this early Christian Church are the Copts of to-day. They resemble the petrified image of spiritual strife long past. Their Christian life now consists in, and is expressed by, a series of purely external and superficial

VIEW OF THE SECOND CATARACT.

could not fail to cause the early decay of Christianity within its gates. Side by side with the adoration of the one true God sprouts, like a luxuriant weed, the adoration of saints, and finds ample nourishment in the traditions of the people. In place of the Serapis priests, who fled from the world and its temptations, came numbers of Christian hermits, soon disciplined and united into orders, to inhabit the Egyptian deserts. A new race of priests, formed and regulated with great accuracy, in accordance with the model of a long-venerated hierarchy, sprang up among those who still called themselves "brethren." Strife of doctrine, whose subtle questions all too soon absorbed the Christian interest, was often fought out with the sword. But Divine punishment was near at hand: Islamism, with the

observances, lacking every element of warmth and vitality. And in their life, which bears but too plainly the stamp of long subjection, slavery of spirit has grown habitual. Their services, their small, humble churches and convents, built of clay, were to me always very touching, remembering what they once were, and what they had had to suffer.

It is curious to note how, in spite of such mighty spiritual revolutions, remains of the old heathen belief are to this day found in all classes of the Egyptian population. One finds customs, ideas, and convictions which, notwithstanding Christian and Moslem influence, date back for more than six thousand years. Especially the Nile is at this present day looked upon through the medium of ancient national traditions, and is the ob-

TOMBS OF THE SAINTS.
From a sketch by Sir Frederick Leighton, P.R.A.

ject of a custom which bears the marked traces of heathen ideas and practices.

Such of the "fellahs," or peasants, as have received some little culture know that the waters of the Nile come from the "land of dark men"—from the mountains of Abyssinia. In the year 1874, at the time of the war with Abyssinia, it happened that the Nile was slow to rise, and I have often heard, here and there in the villages, the opinion expressed that "no doubt the King of Dabeseh was revenging himself on the Egyptians by preventing the waters of the Nile from flowing down to them"; or that an ancient threat of Ethiopian kings, i. e., to lead off the Nile before its entrance into Egypt, through a canal into the Red Sea, was being carried out.

But the inhabitants of the more isolated inland villages have not even such lights as these, and should you chance to come across such a fellah crouching at the door of his mud hut, holding his kéf (siesta), and quietly content, with as little mental exertion as possible, smoking his waterpipe, and should you ask him as to his opinion of the Nile and its origin, you would in most cases find that instead of entering upon geographical questions and hypotheses, he would, with a grateful glance toward heaven, answer, simply, "Min Allah!" i. e., from God, or from heaven; and he would no doubt on his side turn questioner, and ask you, "Have you in your country also a Nile?" And great would be his astonishment and surprise on hearing that our vegetation, our crops, and our orchards are nourished by water which falls from the clouds. To him who hardly ever sees rain, and then only in a rare and passing shower, this seems a very precarious form of agriculture.

Nothing is more natural than that the Egyptian peasant, who has never been beyond his own village, and whose conceptions of the world, of men, and things are of the most limited, should, considering that the Nile gives him all he has and all he needs, look upon it as a direct gift of God.

Whether it be that his land is so favorably situated that the Nile flows over it at the time of inundation, or that the water reaches it through artificial irrigation by means of a water-wheel worked by the camel or the oxen of the peasant, or if he be very poor, owning neither camel nor oxen, and obliged to pull up the water in shallow buckets made of reeds, and with his own hand distribute it over his fields, this much is certain, that only in so far as the Nile has blessed his land will his corn or his cotton grow, and the harvest will be in exact proportion to the amount of moisture which the land has received.

And more than this, the Nile gives him so much besides. His hut is built of Nile mud, and thatched with reeds that

HEAD OF A PEASANT.

From a sketch by Sir Frederick Leighton, P.R.A.

grow in the canals; out of Nile clay is the beloved pipe, and also the water jar out of which he drinks (and he drinks incalculable quantities of water); and even for the "tarabooka," the peculiar kind of kettle-drum with which he accompanies all his monotonous songs and religious observances, does the Nile give him the clay. I have just said that the fellah is a great water-drinker, and I may add so are all foreigners in Egypt, for nowhere else that I know of is the water so clear and delicious. This is, no doubt, owing to the constant flowing over a bed of finest sand and loam. Filtered or cooled in a large urn of clay, it becomes perfectly cold, and is very refreshing.

I can well understand that the Bedouin of the desert, who for many months in the year has only briny springs wherewith to slake his thirst, and springs, too, that give but little, knows no greater luxury than to give his fleet camel the rein, and, having reached the green and fertile shores of the Nile, to deeply drink of its pure and limpid waters.

When the canals which furrow the land in every direction, and when the pools which the flood leaves behind it in every hollow and fall of ground, are dried up, when the cisterns grow empty and the women have far to go to fetch the water needed for their household, and are seen in picturesque groups carrying the large earthen jars on head or shoulders back to their humble huts, then is the time when men and animals thirst and yearn for the days when the glad tidings "the Nile is rising" shall meet the ear.

The night of the 17th of June (i. e., the 4th of the Copt or Christian-Egyptian month "Bauneh") is to this day known in popular parlance as "Leilet-en-Mekta" (i. e., the night of the drop). It is a time-honored creed, upheld even now, that during this night a wonderful, mysterious drop from heaven falls into the Nile. The ancient Egyptians believed that it was a tear which Isis wept, and the astrologers of the present time even pretend to calculate with great nicety the exact moment at which this drop is said to fall. Then, far away in the distance where the drop fell, the Nile begins to surge and swell, ever nearer and nearer, and soon the shores are too narrow to hold it.

Many of the inhabitants of Cairo and other towns on the river spend this night on the Nile shores or in adjacent houses or villas of their friends. The women make little rolls of dough, one for each member of the household, and place them on the "terrace," or flat roof, of the house. When the sun rises they go to inspect these rolls. Such as have burst open portend long life, health, and happiness to those whose names they bear; and such as show but small or no signs of development signify the contrary.

When the inundation approaches the capital—usually at the end of June or the beginning of July—the Nile criers (Muna-di-en-Nil) begin their work. These criers are men whose business it is to call out, or rather to recite, before the houses of those who wish it, how much the Nile has risen during the last twenty-four hours. The Oriental does everything, no matter what it is, gravely, slowly, with much dignity and verbosity, and is never chary of his time or breath. Even the form of his greeting in the street is a complicated ceremony of words and motions which usually takes some moments to perform. And in the same way this announcement of the river's rise, which seems to us such a simple matter, is a most serious affair.

The day before the crier begins his task he goes through the streets accompanied by a boy, whose part it is to act as chorus, and to sing the responses at the proper moment. The crier sings:

"God has looked graciously upon the fields."
Response: "Oh! day of glad tidings."
"To-morrow begins the announcement."
Response: "May it be followed by success."

Before the crier proceeds to give the information so much desired, he intones with the boy a lengthy, alternating chant, in which he praises God, implores blessings on the Prophet and all believers, and on the master of the house and all his children. Not until all this has been carefully gone through does he proceed to say, the Nile is risen so many inches.

This ceremony is carried on until the month of September, when the river has reached its culminating point, and the crier, as bringer of such good news, never fails to claim his "baksheesh," sometimes humbly, and sometimes, too, very imperiously.

The reports of these men, who in all Egyptian towns are the ambulant advertisers of the state of the Nile, are not always reliable. This is partly owing to the fact that, with true Oriental indifference, they do not take the trouble to acquire

HEAD OF AN OLD MAN.
From a sketch by Sir Frederick Leighton, P.R.A.

exact information at the only reliable sources, and also that the government intentionally spreads false reports in regard to the advance of the inundation. As the land tax can not be levied on certain large tracts of land until the rise of the Nile shall have reached at least sixteen Egyptian yards, it does not hesitate (a fact that has come within my own experience) to spread false reports; and although the imposition is patent to all, no one dares to raise his voice in remonstrance.

But my readers must not think that exact measurements in this important matter do not exist, or are not to be had. On the contrary, there are most carefully constructed Nile measurers in Cairo, near the First Cataract, and at Khartoom, at the junction of the Blue and the White Nile. The measurer at Cairo is a very remarkable building, erected (as we know with certainty) by the Caliph Motawakil I., A.D. 861, in place of a former measurer destroyed A.D. 716 by the river floods. A detail of peculiar interest, as far as the architecture is concerned, is that here, for the first time, is the Gothic arch employed.

This Nile measurer, called by the Arabs "Mekjas," is situated on the isle of Rhodda, quite near Cairo. It consists of a very deep and carefully constructed well, which is connected with the Nile by a subterranean canal, in consequence of which the height of the water in the well is always in exact accordance with that of the river. In the middle of this well we see an octagon pillar, on which a graduated scale gives us exact information as to the rise of the river. Steps lead down into the well, so that one can at any time reach the water's level and see for one's self. The height considered necessary for a favorable inundation is, in Cairo, eighteen Egyptian yards, or nine and a half meters, over and above the lowest water-mark. But the moment the flood rises above twenty-two yards, it becomes dangerous and devastating.

I wish that my readers might enjoy, what I have often enjoyed, the glorious view, which at the time of the inundation is peculiarly fascinating, from the summit of the mountains which bound the valley of the Nile on the eastern side. Let me try to lead you there, in fancy at least. It is an excursion which amply repays any one who undertakes it.

At other times of the year the valley of the Nile, seen from this height, resembles a green and blooming garden. Waving corn fields, deeply green clover meadows, high-grown Indian corn and beans, sugar-cane and cotton plantations, cover every inch of cultivated ground, interspersed with groups of palm-trees and groves of acacias, in the midst of which the villages nestle. Far away to westward the hills of the Libyan desert frame the picture, and the Pyramids of Ghizeh stand out in bold profile against the sky. If so be that the sun is setting behind them at the time that your eye is resting on this picture, you will enjoy a symphony of color such as once seen is never forgotten. The blue-green tints of the valley meet and blend with the warm browns and ochres of the desert, and through almost purple tints these again are united with and attuned to the deep blue of the sky.

The grand simplicity of subject, combined with the—I might say classic—harmony of lines and the marvellous blending of.colors, which go to make up the Egyptian landscape, can not but fascinate every artist; and all who have once seen and studied it are drawn irresistibly again and again to the deeper study of these problems of art. At the moment that I have selected for introducing this picture to my readers, the waters of the Nile, which at other times, hemmed in by the high shores, only resemble a silver ribbon winding in and out among the green fields, and glancing here and there as the sunlight falls upon it—these waters cover all, and the vast plain resembles an extensive lake. The villages, built on more elevated ground, and protected by high dikes, peep out of the vast expanse of water like islands in the sea. The palms, whose bluish-green feathery crowns are already burdened with heavy tassels of dates, red or brown or yellow, are more than halfway up their graceful stems in water. Numberless boats and small craft, with their picturesque lateen-sails, looking like sea-gulls on the wing, skim the water, speeding before the north wind, which at this season blows steadily and strongly, and sends them southward heavily laden with produce of the north, whence they return with cargoes of ivory, ostrich feathers, gum-arabic, and, alas! only too often, with slaves.

This is the time at which, in Cairo, a most curious and interesting fête is celebrated, one which has its origin in a heathen custom, namely, the so-called "break-

THE NILE ABOVE ASSOUAN.

ing through of the Nile," and takes place when the Nile has reached a certain height.

A canal traverses Cairo from east to west. This canal is closed, when the inundation begins, at the junction with the Nile, by a solid and well-made dike, and remains thus closed until the water-mark shall have reached a desired point. The rupture of this dike, which admits the water into the city, is accompanied by festivities in which all classes of the population share.

Already in the afternoon, and still more in the evening, of the day preceding the feast, numbers of dahabeeyahs—a kind of vessel found only on the Nile, and best described as a floating dwelling combin-ing great comfort with ship-like compactness and regard for space—are seen on the Nile approaching the spot where the canal and river meet, and there drop their anchors, while others continue tacking about. Some of these dahabeeyahs are the private property of residents of Cairo, who with their families spend this night on board; others are chartered for the occasion by a party who disperse, as best suits their taste, for the night, some retiring to the divans in the airy saloons, others preferring the deck, with its bright spectacle of illumination on all sides, for in the rigging of all these boats the colored lamps are twinkling and reflecting their light in the water.

One large boat among the many catches the eye in particular; it is that called "Akabeh," by the Arabs—painted in all the colors of the rainbow, its masts and rigging decked with countless lamps and flags. This boat leaves the harbor of Boolak, near Cairo, in the afternoon (and by paying a small sum one can obtain a passage), and sails on till it reaches the isle of Rhodda, quite near to which is the spot at which the festivities of that night are to take place. Here it is made fast by heavy cables, and prepares to remain till the morrow.

On the deck is an awning under which the passengers can wile away, with friendly cigarette and cooling sherbet, the intervening hours. In the imagination of the Egyptians of to-day, this boat represents the splendid vessel on which, in ancient times, the "Bride of the Nile" ("Aruseh"), a maiden, beautiful and of noble birth, was brought annually as a sacrifice to the god, and who, clothed in bridal array, was doomed to a watery grave.

The Arabs believe that Amru, the conqueror of Egypt, found this sacrifice still existing, and that only through Islamism has it been abolished. They say that during the year in which for the first time the sacrifice was wanting the Nile did not rise. On seeing this, Amru had, by the advice of the Caliph Omar, cast a letter into the river—a letter with the following words: "From Omar, the servant of the Lord and sovereign of the faithful, to the Nile of Egypt. If thou flowest of thyself, then cease to flow; but if it be God the Almighty who causes thee to flow, then we implore God the Almighty to let thee flow." And lo! in that same night the Nile rose sixteen yards.

We are more than justified in supposing that this is merely a pious legend—one in which the popular fondness for the wonderful and the tradition of a sacrifice to the Nile have united in glorifying Islam. We have, moreover, very reliable sources of historic information, through which we know that even in the heathen times in Egypt, when the Greeks first came into the land, the Egyptians no longer allowed human sacrifices. We know from a well-authenticated Greek author that the last sacrifice took place at Heliopolis, quite near Cairo, under King Amasis, and that the custom was abolished by him, and in its place a wax figure was annually offered to the Nile.

An Arab scribe states that in Christian times, instead of the yearly sacrifice of a maiden, it consisted in the finger of a mummy laid in a casket, and thus confided to the deep; but one finds it hard to credit such a tale, as it seems almost impossible to suppose that at the time when Christianity took root in Egypt it should have allowed human sacrifice, even in such harmless form, to exist.

Credulous tourists are apt to be told by their guides and dragomans that even to this day the fiction is upheld, and a "grandly attired doll is brought to the altar of sacrifice by the 'Akabeh,' and there, under various ceremonies, given to the river"; but such is not the case. What, however, does take place—and no doubt it points back to very ancient times, when the Egyptian people felt under obligation to give the Nile its best, its blooming, graceful womanhood—is as follows: Some few yards behind the dike already described in the canal through which the water reaches Cairo, the Arabs mould a kind of figure (somewhat resembling the "snow-man" of our school-boy days), and plant corn or clover on the top; this is a practical and prosaic, even if very grotesque, rendering of the old fable, and the Nile, on bursting the dike, has but few strides to make before it encircles this figure (which the Arabs call "el Aruseh," the bride of the Nile), and sweeps it away.

All Orientals, and the Egyptian is no exception to the rule, like to have their merry-makings at night. And they are right. The intense heat of the day is over; the sun, with its rays and its glare, no longer wearies eyes and nerves; the glorious star-lit sky—such a sky as only the far East can show—spreads its canopy over all; a soft, balmy breeze comes gently through the valley, and blows upstream, bringing the cool but never cold atmosphere of the Mediterranean, whose moisture and briny odors have been modified by the long journey it had to make before reaching the inland capital. This is the time, above all others, at which the river and its shores become the scene of animated life. At regular intervals the cannon boom, for without smell of powder, much shouting and screaming, and oft-repeated fire-works the proper holiday mood is wanting. Legions of small boats, like midges glancing over the water, move about in all directions as connecting links

ASSOUAN.

between the large, firmly anchored vessels.

From some one point the sound of the "tarabooka" is heard, and to its monotonous rhythmic accompaniment female singers warble their slow and melancholy ditties, ending generally in a chromatic scale. From another side the sound of castanets meets our ears—a sure sign that here the oft-mentioned and far-famed, though certainly not admirable, dancing-girls are in full performance. Along the shore hundreds of tents are erected, lighted, according to their rank and degree in the social scale, either by most primitive little oil lamps, or, progressing upward, most luxurious colored lanterns. In these booths refreshments of all kinds, but mostly coffee and sherbet, are to be had; and here one finds the sedate and well-to-do paterfamilias and the youthful though independent donkey driver side by side, smoking. The entertainment consists in listening to ballad singers, comic actors, reciters of Koran verses and romances; and all these artists manage to collect an ample public around them, and one which is very simple in tastes and most grateful and appreciative for whatever is offered it. Add to all this, constant, endless screaming and shouting, a maze of human forms ever rolling and unrolling itself, and my readers will be able to form some idea of what are the elements that go to compose every Arab festivity, and so also this "feast of the Nile."

Shortly after midnight the Arabs begin their work at the dike. To the accompaniment of a monotonous strain they dig away valiantly, so that at daybreak only a thin wall of earth remains as partition between them and the mighty flood beyond. At rise of sun the Khedive (viceroy), surrounded by the grandees of his realm, all in uniforms and gold-lace, arrives; he takes his stand in a tent prepared for him, and which commands the best possible view of all that goes on. A secretary takes a place at his side, and is prepared to take notes on this most important act, testifying that the Nile has reached the necessary height for bursting the dike, and for the land-tax on all the fellah to begin its work. This document is sent to Constantinople the moment the festivities are at an end.

A boat with a sharply built bow approaches, and steers straight at the dike, thus breaking through the thin wall of earth, and admitting the flood, which, tumbling and foaming, rushes through the opening, growing wider from minute to minute, and soon the rapid flow of the water has swept away even the last obstacle. Seated in a little boat, which dances on the top of the muddy waves, is the overseer of these earth-works, looking calmly victorious, as, floating onward with the current, he is carried back to the city. Many black and brown individuals hastily divest themselves of their, at best scanty, wardrobe, and jump into the water, swimming about and watching for the moment when the Khedive shall throw a

handful of coin into the river. Formerly these were of gold, then of silver, and
now, alas! are only given in copper. Hardly have the coins flashed in the sunlight
when the swimmers dive after them with
great adroitness, and happy the man who
returns with booty. By the rosy light of
the early morning the last batch of rockets and other fire-works is set off, salvos
of cannon and never-ending shouts and
hurrahs publish far and wide the good
news that the Nile has risen to its full
height.

My readers have kindly followed me on
an imaginary pilgrimage to the most ancient phases of human history, as well as
to the wholly modern times, tracing
through all the veneration, we may say
adoration, which one of the most remarkable nations of the world, in the past as in
the present, has offered to a stream. Not
only the scholars of our day, but every
cultivated person feels an interest in such
questions, and it is particularly Egypt
which has been selected as a frequent subject of study and attention. It is a fascinating problem to seek the source from
which the river of life proceeds, in whose
waters our thirst for knowledge is slaked.
Our civilization rests on the shoulders
of the classic nations, but these, in their
turn, have taken their first lessons of
philosophy, literature, and art from the
Orientals, and especially from the Egyptians.

More and more do our studies tend to
show that *there* was the root of the culture
which bloomed in the classic era. To-day
there are but few traces to be found of
this former grandeur; nothing but colossal ruins, and wastes covered with fragments, speak of the immense work of mind
and as great work of hand which once distinguished this epoch in history.

Any one who has lived in the midst of
Mohammedans, and has had occasion to
study Islamism in all its bearings, can
not, while admitting its power and importance, entertain any doubt of its destroying influence on all culture and
progress. Wheresoever in its triumphal
march it came upon an existing and well-
based civilization, it never failed, vam-
pire-like, to sap its vitality and to absorb its power, and as surely, also, to annihilate its existence in the end. It has
in no wise been able to further or develop
any good or beautiful institution found
blooming on its way. More than one of
our intelligent travellers and scholars,
men who are never disposed to advance
religious points of view in preference to
others, have yet expressed the conviction
that "the land of Egypt" can not rise again
until the Cross be planted where the Crescent now stands.

We Christians can but hope and pray
that, through the present mighty crisis
in the heart of Islam (and especially in
Egypt)—a faith whose political development is identical with its religious—a
day may dawn on which the Egypt that
is now so deeply fallen may "arise and
take a firmer and surer stand" in the
strength of a renewed Christian understanding and renewed Christian life; that
the Nile may become the thoroughfare on
which civilization, bearing onward the
glad tidings of a Saviour of all who have
strayed or are fallen, may bring light into
the inmost recesses of the "Dark Continent."

NEAR ASSOUAN.

IBEX-SHOOTING IN THE MOUNTAINS
OF BALTISTAN

FAR up in northern India, if you pass the first spurs of the Himalayas that rise gradually from the Punjaub, cross the great valley of Kashmir, and then again ascend and descend another mountain range that cuts off all behind it from the world below, you will come upon a country that for richness in all natural gifts, for healthfulness of climate, and for purity of atmosphere few parts of the world can rival, none certainly can surpass. You will find, if you are an artist or photographer, scenes of beauty and grandeur to inspire masterpieces; birds, flowers, rocks, if you are a scientist; tempting heights, if a mountaineer; native life, if you care to study; pleasing valleys, if you come to rest. But come as a lover of sport and you will have found the greatest resource the land can boast—a supply of game, both big and small, scattered over all the country from the lowest valleys to the topmost crags and snows. He is indeed fortunate who finds himself free to shake the burning dust of the plains from his feet and turn northward for a summer of shooting in the mountains of Baltistan.

The hot weather in Calcutta was at its height when April found us with our last preparations made for the trip northwards. I was glad that night, as we took the Punjaub express in Calcutta station, not to be numbered among those who had come down to see their friends off to the hills, who were themselves to stay behind, with two full months to look forward to before the welcome breaking of the rains would bring relief. Our short experience of that heat-parched city, its sleepless nights and furnace-breathed days, made doubly attractive the prospect of what awaited us and gave us no desire to prolong our stay.

There followed three interminable days of railway travel, fiery, sweltering days with the thermometer at 107 in our compartment and the breathless air enveloping us like a steaming blanket; two more days of dashing up into the mountains in that graceless vehicle the tonga, which for perfect discomfort is surpassed only by the Irish jaunting-cart, and then, one crisp, keen, glorious morning, which brought recollections of late October days at home, we awoke in the Dâk Bungalow at Baramulla, 7000 feet above the sea, to find the whole great valley of Kashmir spread out in all its freshness before us.

At our backs was the rugged mountain pass through which we had come in the night, before us a vast stretch of meadowland, brilliantly green, the blue Jhelum River winding in its midst, and around it, in a mighty panorama, the snowy summits of the Himalayas, with not even in the farthest distance a suspicion of haze to dull the clearness of the picture.

After a hot breakfast, prepared and served by the Chowkidar, we were off again, dashing down the long poplarlined road that leads to the capital of Kashmir.

It is a gay sight that greets the traveller as he rattles over the bridge into Srinagar—that delightful Venice of the north, with its canals, its bridges, its old rickety houses jutting out over the river, and behind them its great lawns and chenar groves. Merchants are paddling up and down in their "doongas," displaying or delivering their wares; barges and ponderous house-boats are making for the country; English residents are skimming by in their light "kishtis," their Kashmirian crews, in bright uniforms, moving together in perfect stroke. The sun seems to be always shining, the water sparkling, the natives laughing. Everything is bright, merry, and full of life.

On the evening of May 11, with everything finally in readiness for a start, we shoved off from the shore of the canal in Srinagar, and taking a glad leave of the crowd of merchants, coolies, and shikaris, clamoring up to the last moment for custom or employment, headed toward the Sind Valley, the road into Baltistan.

We were in two "doongas"—long, narrow boats with straw mattings at the sides to keep out the wind and rain—and a kitchen-boat for the supplies and servants. The next day about noon we reached our first halting-place, a village of a few little huts, called Gandarbal, and were obliged to spend the night, sending ahead a letter to the Tehsildar of the district to have forty coolies ready to take our outfit over the Zogi La Pass.

The route northwards is divided into stages or marches of from twelve to eighteen miles each, as a coolie, with his load, can travel only this distance in one day. Fresh coolies can generally be secured at the beginning of each stage, but in the approach and crossing of the Zogi La there are no villages large enough to supply them, which necessitates the employment of permanent ones for the five days' trip.

The coolies had arrived at dawn on the following day. Camp was broken, the luggage divided equally among them, and before the sun was well up we started on our first stage.

I may say that in point of size the personnel of our outfit, as I looked back and saw the cavalcade forming in single file behind us, fairly took my breath away. Kadera But and Salia Melik, our two venerable chief shikaris, headed on horseback what might have been called their respective companies; Sidka and Lussoo, the chota, or assistant shikaris, acted as their lieutenants; the seven or eight naukar, or servant coolies, who, unlike the relays of village coolies, were to serve as permanent camp servants, performed the duties of non-commissioned officers; while under their able guidance and the persuasion of several stout sticks our horde of forty-odd villagers composed the rank and file of this imposing if diminutive army. The two tiffin coolies, following close at our heels with their lunch-baskets, were certainly entitled to the regard usually accorded to color-bearers; and as for the commissariat, to leave nothing to be

THE REST-HOUSE AT NATAYUM

COOLIES CARRYING BAGGAGE

desired in this military showing, the cook and my old Cingalese servant Thomas ably represented that indispensable department.

The road led between rice-fields and was muddy from recent rains, but no such petty annoyance could prevent our enjoying the surrounding scene: ahead lay the entrance to the Sind Valley, flanked on one side by towering snow mountains, on the other by deodar-clad hills, and at their base were many little native huts with grass-grown roofs, while blue and white irises dotted the river bank in profusion. At noon we reached the village of Kangan, the end of the first march, but as the coolies did not arrive till afternoon, it was impossible to push on. A spot was chosen on the smooth lawn beside the village for the tents to be pitched when they should arrive, and after lunch, or "tiffin" (each sportsman has a tiffin coolie, who accompanies him with lunch, camera, dry socks, and such other things as may be needed on the march), we lay down on the porch of a native house, and rather wearied from our first walk, were quickly asleep.

In the morning our trail led up the valley, still following the course of the Sind River, now rocky and turbulent, and of a beautiful opalescent color from the snow and glacial streams which supplied it. The middle of the day was excessively hot—a great change from the frosty early morning air,—but we rested an hour for tiffin under a great chenar-tree beside a brook, and in the afternoon pushed on to Goond, the end of the stage. Here we took our last view of the valley of Kashmir, framed in a vista of blossoming apricot-trees, meadow-land, forest, and river.

Two more stages were to bring us into surroundings as desolate and wintry as the present landscape was warm and beautiful. Baltal, directly beneath the Zogi La Pass, was reached after a march of ten miles, the whole trail across snow, or mud where the snow was melting, and colored glasses were most necessary to protect the eyes from the glare. There was no village at Baltal—only a low windowless hovel, called a "rest-house."

We were up at 4.30 to attack the pass before the sun should soften the snow. After two hours of climbing—a long

A NATIVE-BUILT ROPE BRIDGE IN BALTISTAN

snow arête—apparently the top of the pass was reached, and from here on the going was level or slightly down-hill. It was well toward dark when the welcome village of Matayun appeared ahead in the distance.

A few straggling buildings, built of stones in the shape of hollow squares, with courtyards inside and flat roofs, composed the village of Matayun. None of these had windows, and the filth within, where several natives lived, was enough to disgust the most hardened. We had some food on the top of one of these buildings in the teeth of a bitterly cold wind which had sprung up toward the end of the march, and then repaired to the usual "rest-house," where a fire had been prepared.

The following day brought us down below the snow-line, the trail leaving the gorge in which we had been since Sonamarg, and broadening out into a wide, brown plain, with the few scattered huts of Dras at its feet, the Dras River flowing through it, and superb snow mountains all around. Since from here on we could secure fresh coolies at the be-

ginning of each stage, we paid off the thirty-seven who had taken our outfit over the Zogi La—eighty cents apiece, with eight cents as a present, or "baksheesh," for the full trip of five days. On figuring up our entire service expenses, I found that for the forty-eight men, two-thirds of whom would be dispensed with on reaching our new camp, my share amounted to $2 70 a day. Let one consider that a first-rate guide in the Maine woods at home is alone paid at the rate of three dollars a day.

The remainder of the journey to our first shooting-grounds was to be much less wearisome, since from now on the road led down into the valleys of Baltistan, bringing us among a new people and continually unfolding sights and scenes of the greatest interest.

The native Baltis are a wild-looking race; their heads are shaved on top and at the back, but at the sides their black hair is allowed to grow long and falls in unkempt locks; their dress is a single tunic of the roughest puttoo of the country—a coarse material which resembles sackcloth in texture. Their houses, in

STARTING ACROSS THE BRIDGE

the smaller villages, are often mere caves in the ground, with a hole leading straight down for entrance, or else low huts of stone, seldom higher than a man's height, with flat mud roofs, windowless, and with but a single opening in the roof for the smoke of their fires to pass through. Yet with all their rough exterior they are invariably respectful to the white man, and never pass without the customary raising of the hand and " Salam, sahib," to which the white man answers, " Salam "—that is, " Peace."

The villages, which come at intervals of a few miles down the valley, lie each beside a mountain stream; for, as the river‑basin narrows, the soil becomes dry and barren, and no vegetation can live without the necessary furrow irrigation. The wheat is cultivated in little terraces, banked by stone walls from the river to half-way up the mountainsides. Each village is an orchard of apricot and mulberry trees, which adds to the pleasant effect; and very refreshing it is, after tramping for hours through barren ravines and over hot, stony cliffs, to drop down into one of these villages, nearly

drown one's self in the icy stream, and then lie back at ease on a cool lawn, shaded by these fruit-trees, to watch the tents pitched and supper prepared.

At the end of our second stage from Dras, on turning suddenly into a narrow and wild ravine of the Dras River, we came upon a little cleared space on the very edge of a precipice, where a Balti polo game was in full swing. Some eight or ten natives, in their long puttoo coats, were tearing up and down the field on shaggy little ponies, with rude, short mallets, and chasing a rough-hewn ball. A small crowd of natives watched the game from a large rock, which formed a sort of grand stand, while a flute and drum supplied weird native music for the occasion; and as we took our seats on the rock the players, seeing their audience increased by two weary but appreciative sahibs, went at it with vim, and gave as fine an exhibition of polo as the primitive quality of field, sticks, and ball would allow—a strange scene to find in such a wilderness. The game finished, a native dance was performed for our further amusement, and we were then ceremoniously escorted by the Lumbardar, who was captain of one of the teams, to the serai, or rest-house, of the village, where the usual gifts of nuts

VIEW FROM THE MIDDLE OF THE BRIDGE

and dried apricots were brought us. The ripe apricot is too small to make a good fruit, but dried and pressed into balls of a dozen or so each, they form what is known as "kobani"—an indigestible but very delicious sweetmeat.

At the end of a long march of thirty-one miles the following day—four hours in the morning over a bad trail of difficult climbs and steep descents and seventeen miles in the afternoon to Tarkutti—we came upon our first "rope bridge" across the Indus. The ingenuity of the natives in making such a bridge with no material but twisted twigs, strong enough to hold the weight of any number of coolies with their loads

and long enough to be swung from cliff to cliff across this great river, is a source of wonder. Yet there it swings, with three strands of twisted twigs, one for each hand to grasp, one to guide the feet, sagging gracefully from the tops of the mighty cliffs that flank the river, occasionally swaying slightly in the wind, but firm and safe as a bridge of rock and iron. The sensation when one has felt one's way to its centre and stands looking down at the torrent swirling a hundred feet below is, to say the least, a strange one. I was glad enough to creep across unencumbered; to have had to lug the heavy loads our coolies carried would have been a handicap which I should as gracefully as possible have declined.

A twenty-six-mile march on the following day brought us to Parkutta—a village rather larger than the others through which we had passed,—and as we entered it an amusing scene greeted us. Under an enormous chenar-tree in the centre of the town and completely shut off from the outside world by the dense foliage of the fruit-trees, was a little round cleared space, where, apparently, all the villagers were gathered in a circle, five or six deep, and with shouting, clapping, and the usual discordant Balti music, were beating time for six men dancing in the centre. These, with waving riding-whips, singing and laughing, careered madly round in the space cleared for them. I soon discovered from the Rajah of the district, who lives here, that they were the victorious team of the afternoon's polo match, celebrating their victory; and not only had the men turned out to cheer them, but the housetops near by were crowded with women and children—all showing their enthusiasm in the most vociferous manner. Indeed, it was not unlike a college football triumph at home, and away out here in the heart of Asia it seemed strange and picturesque. As we dismounted, there was at once a respectful silence, and the Rajah, coming out of the circle and salaaming, led us under the tree, where a shawl and chair were at once brought. He then offered us cigarettes, which we felt out of courtesy bound to accept, though they were exceedingly vile, and ordered the festivities to proceed. After the main dance was finished, each of the players danced alone, retiring in turn as he finished and salaaming to us. The music was afforded by six tomtoms, three flutes, and a big horn, which as usual created the most painful discords imaginable, and the natives howled in unison. It then occurred to us that we were ravenously hungry, having had nothing to eat for eight hours; and as the luggage was still some distance back on the road, we intimated to his Highness the Rajah that anything eatable would be

most acceptable. Tea was at once brought in an enormous samovar—a kettle heated by coals in a chamber inside—and wheat cakes, which we gratefully received, and did not stand on much ceremony about falling to. The inner man having been temporarily satisfied, we repaired to our camp-ground, where the Rajah sat with us till the tents were pitched, smoking from a water-pipe held by a kneeling servant, and would not go even when we were most anxious to take our evening tub before dinner, though he looked at us in an appealing sort of way as if he too were quite ready to leave. Finally an interpreter came from the Rajah's house and whispered that his Highness had been awaiting our gracious permission to leave during the last half-hour. We gave it without delay, and are now wiser on points of Balti etiquette.

On the following morning the Rajah again appeared, no longer in his bright green riding-suit, English tan boots, and brilliant golf-stockings, but in white robes, and red slippers which turned up at the ends like the bow of a gondola. Having no extra knives, we were at a

A NATIVE DANCE

loss to know what sort of a present to give him, but at last tried ten shot-cartridges, which he received with the most evident delight, and we took leave at once.

As we proceeded down through the valleys we were, it seemed, moving gradually from winter to spring and from spring to full-blown summer—as mellow and fragrant a summer as ever made life doubly worth living. The wheat was higher in the fields, the apricot blossoms had given place to full-formed fruit, the birds were of the most brilliantly colored plumage and seemed to fill everything with their song. Every village was a little paradise in itself. And though the midday was as warm as could be without making our marches uncomfortable, the nights and early mornings were always crisp and delicious.

At last, after sixteen long days of marching, in which time we had accomplished two hundred and seventy-six miles, we found ourselves at the mouth of the valley of the Basha River, where our first shooting was to be found.

Ibex-stalking is not easy, for the habits of the animals are all conducive to their safety, and their senses of sight, smell, and hearing are very acute. Before sunrise they graze down to the slopes, but as the sun grows hot they ascend again to the snow, where they sleep in inaccessible positions during the day, always with one or more females posted as sentinels. Towards four in the afternoon they again graze downward till dark. The whole success of a stalk depends, of course, on getting behind a ridge to leeward of the herd, and having them graze to within range, or else on following them carefully from ridge to ridge as they move off. If they remain out in the flat ground, approach is absolutely impossible. The game-laws of Kashmir allow six to each gun.

It was a great pleasure to feel a gun in one's hands again: a two weeks' march to one's shooting-grounds whets one's keenness for the sport as nothing else can do. Kadera and Sidka, my shikari and chota shikari, were moving about camp before the first appearance of dawn; I awoke to the welcome sound of a crackling fire and dressed at once, my teeth chattering in the cold morning

air. A cup of steaming coffee, and we started single file for the head of the valley, where during the past few days several herds had been marked down. As we entered the upper section, the big mountain at its head was beginning to glow; the hillsides on the right were emerging from shadow, and gradually we could make out several dark spots about half-way up to the first ridge. They were the big herd of ibex which for two days past we had been watching eagerly from a distance, hoping vainly to see them move into a position where stalking would be possible. Now I saw at once that they were headed straight up toward the ridge which topped the first spur of the mountain; behind this there was a declivity; if they should disappear behind it, a successful stalk might be made, for the wind was towards us.

With the greatest caution we crept along the base of the mountain, crouched painfully, but not daring to let ourselves be seen for a second. A single glimpse of us would send the whole herd dashing off in a panic to their mountain retreats. When immediately below them, we halted, and without a whisper or motion waited and watched. They were maddeningly slow in their ascent to the ridge. This formidable mountainside which they were taking so deliberately and easily now would, I knew, have to be covered by us at top speed when once the last of the herd had disappeared, and the prospect made me doubly impatient to be off.

A full hour of shivering in the gully passed. Then the leader of the herd reached the top. He stood for a moment outlined against the sky, his great ridged horns curving gracefully over his back— I could see that they were over forty inches,—looked steadily over the ridge for several minutes to make sure that all was safe ahead, then turned to call his herd and disappeared. Without moving from my crouched position, I carefully removed all unnecessary clothing, shed my fur gloves, and slipped a cartridge into each barrel of the .450 cordite express. There might be no time for loading at the top. Kadera held the 30-40 Winchester, whose magazine was full, and started to follow my example of slipping a cartridge into the barrel, but

SEARCHING FOR GAME

I motioned him to stop. Put anything into the hands of an excited Kashmirian but a loaded gun. One by one the rest of the herd stood outlined on the ridge and dropped out of sight, but the stragglers were slow, and without the fur coat my joints were already stiffening with cold. I moved slightly to ease my position—there was a scurry above us, and the straggling cows dashed over the ridge. No time for regret! If I had spoiled the stalk, there would be ample opportunity for remorse afterwards; now my only object was to get up to the ridge in the least possible time, and we started.

In the first five minutes of dashing up a mountainside, no matter in how good condition is the hunter, his breath leaves him utterly, his throat seems pulled together as if by a strangling rope, and his chest feels like caving in. He tells himself that he cannot possibly do it, that he must slow up or choke, and the surer he is that he has taken his last step, the harder he goes at it. The second five minutes are easier; his muscles limber up, his throat loosens, his breath comes more regularly; in the third five minutes he has no desire to stop. But

this is just where a rest is necessary, for there is no use in coming on the game with the heart pounding like a trip-hammer. He must stop and imagine himself anywhere but about to reach, in the next minute, the point on which the whole success of his stalk depends. If he can do this, he will have almost immediate control of nerves and muscles.

I waited, then crept to the ridge and peered over. Two hundred and fifty yards away, filing slowly up a shale cleft in the mountain and totally unaware of our presence, were the whole herd, broadside on. With the telescope it was easy to pick out several fine heads, but they were shifting like a kaleidoscope, and at that distance we could hardly choose among them. It was fairly safe, though, to pick out any dark-colored buck. I rested the express carefully on the ridge, sighted, and fired. The buck I had aimed at stopped short, shot through the hind quarters; the second barrel sent him dashing off down the shale. The herd had split up and were dashing off in every direction, some tearing down the slope, starting small avalanches of shale and rocks in their flight, others making for the cliffs and scrambling up as only a goat can climb. Here was my second chance. I was sitting astride the ridge now. Kadera and Sidka had gone completely crazy with excitement; they were pounding me on the back and shouting: " Bara wallah, bara wallah, sahib! Maro!" (" Big one, big one, sahib! Shoot!") Needless to say their exhortations made shooting for the moment a physical impossibility, nor were they conducive to perfect coolness on my part. I seemed to see a regular kaleidoscope of " bara wallahs " in every direction. Then I managed to calm Kadera slightly, and taking the Winchester from him, held it on a buck who was trying to scale the apparently sheer face of a precipice to the left. He would have got up it, too, if I had waited a moment longer, but the first shot brought him tumbling, and he fell sheer twenty yards, quite dead. Another was still in sight far up the cliff, scrambling, slipping, leaping. I took the express and fired again, but it was a hard shot. The second barrel caught him amidships as he reached the level, and he made off, badly wounded.

The result of this first stalk was not all that could be desired, since of my three animals only one lay dead, and it was impossible to say how far the others might go before they dropped. Following a newly wounded ibex through the mountains is useless, for he will quickly distance the hunter and make for some inaccessible cliff before resting, but if allowed to go unwatched the chances are in favor of his soon lying down in a place whither he may later be tracked. But the first excitement of the hunt makes one keen for more.

The 1st of June dawned as all days in that wonderful country seemed to dawn, in a flood of sunlight, cloudless, and crisply cold. But before the great mountain at the valley's head had received the first tints of morning we were crouching behind a spur of the glacier and searching with the glasses the surrounding heights. It was but a few moments before a large herd was found far across on the steep mountainside which rose to the north, and though a full half-mile of serried glacier lay between, it seemed advisable to undertake the work and make our second stalk in country as yet undisturbed by firing.

The crossing was rather more than I had bargained for; again and again an impossible crevasse or an ice-covered slope that led to the edge of some ugly break in the glacier necessitated a retracing of our steps and a new start, and only at the end of two hours did we reach the farther side, weary and dripping.

A steep ascent of the mountainside followed, and once at the top, a sheltering tree afforded a few moments' rest, where we could observe the game unnoticed. The heads that appeared on that open mountain slope were larger than any we had yet run across. The larger bucks were all of the darkest brown, their horns curving magnificently over the backs and their beards hanging long and shaggy.

Before we had watched ten minutes the whole herd moved off behind a ridge, but as usual a solitary female was left posted, and the slightest movement from behind our tree would have spoiled it all.

The longed-for moment came after an impatient wait, the cow slowly moving behind the ridge, leaving a clear but hazardous slope for us to cross in order to get within range. It was surprising to me how we kept from slipping, but something on the plan of a hundred-yard dash and a rather studied nonchalance respecting the precipice just below brought us to the ridge without a stumble, and we dropped over.

The next five minutes made all the weary miles and days of travelling worth while many times over. My first impression was that we had somehow fallen in the very midst of a perfectly tame herd of the largest ibex on record, for the animals appeared so thunderstruck at seeing us quietly and suddenly drop in among them that for a moment they remained perfectly motionless. Then, of course, there was a scurry, and the sport began.

My first buck dropped before he had covered ten yards, and a careful shot from a knee rest brought down another that had gone but a short distance farther—two forty-inch heads. I was now allowed but one more by law and was unwilling to fire at any ordinary-sized head; several bucks were still in sight, but they

THE BIG IBEX; LENGTH OF HORNS FORTY-FOUR INCHES

were scattered and were tearing up the mountainside at a rapid pace.

Kadera had, however, stopped my hand after the first two successful shots and pointed to a ridge far above, from behind which in a moment dashed a magnificent animal, with horns very much larger than any I had yet noticed. As I found afterwards, he had been crouched behind a rock when we had first come upon the herd, and it was for this reason I had not aimed at him at once. Though still not too late, the mark was a small one. Some six shots ploughed up the sand about him; then he stumbled, but regained his feet and was immediately lost to sight behind a ridge.

The account of how that superb animal was tracked by his blood trail far into the mountains, how his horns were found to measure fully forty-four inches from base to tip, and how we returned at dusk across the glacier to camp, worn out by the hardest of stalks, but happy in the realization of complete success, would be, I fear, of less interest in the recounting than was the experience itself. To complete the satisfaction, a telegram was found awaiting me at camp from the secretary of the Game Association in Srinagar, stating that the Basha Nullah could rightly hold two guns, and that we were justified in having claimed our share of the valley.

NEAPOLITAN SKETCHES

NAPLES, FROM POSILIPPO.

LET the reader who does not know southern Italy or Naples picture to himself a city the leading characteristics of which are music, perfume, and color. In spite of all that has been said and written of the filth, squalor, and disgusting smells of Naples, and the too suggestive if not absolutely exact story of the English traveller who said that if the fleas could have been "quite unanimous" they would have dragged him out of bed, the fact still remains that this city is for beauty of situation and sensuous fascination one of the wonders of the world. Italy has majestic Rome, Florence, the centre of the glories of the Renaissance, and Venice, the Queen of the Adriatic, to be proud of; but for luxury, for brilliancy, for natural beauty and lazy enjoyment, Naples stands alone, and has stood alone from the time when the Cæsars set their seal upon it as a spot where all care might be laid aside, and existence become one protracted hour of soft delight.

Naples is a blaze of color. There seems to be a strife forever going on between nature and the inhabitants as to which shall produce the most gorgeous effects.

Nature is responsible for the brilliant blue of the bay, the splendor of the sky, the varied greens of the olive and the vine wherewith the hill-sides are clothed, and the bright tints of the flowers which spread themselves like a carpet in every public park and garden. Man is responsible for the red and yellow buildings and the general gorgeousness of coloring which characterizes nearly every object, from the fresco on a ceiling to the cap of a beggar. I am writing in a room where the gilding on the walls is positively dimmed by the orange-yellow of my bed-cover, and the roses on my table are put to shame by the brilliant crimson of furniture and hangings. By an effort I have shut out the sunshine, but no curtains will keep out the heavy breath of the orange grove beneath my window, or the sound of the bagpipe, lute, and mandolin that now at ten o'clock in the morning have begun the song that will not cease until after midnight.

It would seem that Naples has been long enough on the face of the earth to be old and worn and shabby. Her history extends back to a very remote age.

THE NATIONAL MUSEUM.

We read that somewhere about the year 1056 B.C. certain Æolians came from Chalcis in Eubœa and founded the colony of Kyme, or, in Latin, Cumæ, on a rocky eminence in the bay of Puteoli. The town of Puteoli, now called Pozzuoli, is to-day a suburb of Naples. It was the principal seat of the Jews in Italy. From Cumæ the colony Phaleron, or Parthenope, named, according to the elder Pliny, after the tomb of a siren of that name, seems to have emanated at a very early period, and to have been re-enforced at various times by emigrants from Greece. The latter founded the Neapolis, or new city, while Parthenope, the portion erected by the original colonists, was named Palæopolis, or old city, a distinction maintained until the conquest of Palæopolis by Rome in 326 B.C. Owing to the beauty of its situation, Naples soon became a favorite residence of the Roman magnates, but it continued to enjoy its municipal freedom and its Greek constitution. Its inhabitants spoke the Greek language, and were long distinguished by their attachment to the manners and customs of their ancestors. It was on this account, according to Tacitus, that Nero selected Naples as a place wherein to make his début on the stage, such a proceeding being less offensive to the prevailing sentiment among the people here than at Rome.

Wherever Rome went, she took her engineers with her. Naples, taken possession of by the Mistress of the World, felt at once the creative and adjusting impress of her touch. Public works were undertaken, roads were built, and to-day the visitor makes his way through the city and about the suburbs by way of thoroughfares built for the convenience of emperors. Among these undertakings the most remarkable are perhaps the tunnels that pierce their way through the great hill of Posilippo, which separates the town from what remains of Cumæ. One of these is called the Grotto of Posilippo, wrought—so mediæval legend tells us—by the magic arts of Virgil. Scholars insist that it was an outcome of the prolific age of Augustus; and Seneca and Petronius, writing in the time of Nero, speak of it as a narrow and gloomy pass. Alfonso I., about 1442, conceived the brilliant idea of enlarging it by lowering the level of the road, and a century later Don Pedro de Toledo caused it to be paved. Modern improvement has lighted it with gas, and to-day the long narrow passage, 757 yards in length, with a height varying from 87 feet at the entrance to 20 feet in the interior, and a breadth of between 20 and 30 feet, is the main thoroughfare between Naples and the small suburban towns lying toward the west. Just before the traveller enters the mouth of the gas-lit cavern he passes the tomb of Virgil. There is nothing but probability and local

in a line with the Grotto of Posilippo, illuminating the entire length of the gloomy cavern.

Naples owes little of her attraction to her buildings. Her National Museum was originally a cavalry barracks, erected by the Viceroy Duke of Ossuna in 1586. Subsequently it was ceded to the university, which was established there for a time, but in 1790 it was fitted up for the reception of the royal collection of pictures and antiquities. The museum contains treasures of antiquity from Herculaneum and Pompeii, together with rare objects from all parts of the world. The collection is unrivalled. Besides the various objects

STAIRCASE IN THE ROYAL PALACE.

tradition to prove that the ashes of the Latin poet once rested here. No trace remains of the hallowed urn, but there can be no doubt that Virgil once lived and wrote upon the hill of Posilippo. Beyond the tomb, at the entrance of the passage, stands a small chapel, and in the interior are others, where the faithful stop and say a prayer. There are certain days in March and November when the sun sets directly

taken from the two great buried cities, it includes the Farnese collection from Rome and Parma, those of the palaces of Portici and Capo di Monte, and also treasures resulting from the excavations at Rome and Stabiæ.

Naples abounds in royal palaces. There are five in the city and suburbs, which the traveller may visit at pleasure, provided they are not at the time occupied by any

THE VILLA NAZIONALE.

member of the royal family, simply by procuring a card from some one in Naples willing to vouch for his respectability and decent behavior within such hallowed precincts. Of these the grand Palazzo Reale is the largest, and most magnificent in its interior decorations and details, though on the outside it is a plain and monotonous building. It is situated in the midst of the city, in the Piazza del Plebiscito—so called from the popular vote which in 1860 united Naples with the rest of Italy. This palace, designed by the Roman architect Domenico Fontana, was begun in 1600 under the Viceroy Count de Lemol. It was burned in 1837, but some four years sufficed to complete the restorations. On visiting it we were first conducted by an obsequious guide up a side staircase to the Garden Terrace, which extends along the whole length of the palace, 185 feet, and affords a fine view of the harbor and arsenal immediately below. The magnificent grand staircase, constructed entirely of white marble, and adorned with reliefs and statues, dates from 1651. On the side toward the piazza are situated a small theatre and a superb dining-room. In the centre of the latter formerly stood a magnificent cradle, presented by the city of Naples to the present Queen Margherita in 1869. Beyond this apartment is the throne-room, furnished with crimson velvet embroidered with gold. The embroidery was made at the Neapolitan poor-house in 1818.

Adjoining the Palazzo Reale is the theatre of San Carlo, the native home of Italian opera.

Naples has a most beautiful public park. It was laid out just one hundred years ago, and has been enlarged and embellished and improved, until now it is one of the most attractive pleasure-grounds in the world. The Villa Nazionale, as it is called, or more frequently La Villa, was formerly a narrow strip of land close to the sea, but, like the Hollanders, the Neapolitans wanted more room for their flower beds and promenades, and they forced the waters back, planting long avenues of trees where the waves once danced and rippled. The grounds are all arranged in the profusely ornamented style characteristic of Italy, and imported trees and shrubs mingle their green with the splendid foliage natural to this favored clime. The most noticeable are the magnificent palms, which spread their fan-like branches more than a hundred feet above the heads of the passers-by. The statues which adorn the park are many in number, but they are chiefly imitations of ancient and modern works, and are sadly wanting in the merits of the originals. Formerly the celebrated group of the Farnese Bull stood in the Villa, but it was removed to the museum for preservation, and replaced by a large antique basin from Pæstum. Virgil and Tasso have here temples to their honor. During the early part of the day the Villa is

comparatively deserted, but
in the afternoon or even-
ing, when the daily con-
certs take place, the scene
is one of life and gayety
almost beyond description.
An Italian crowd is the
brightest and gayest to be
seen anywhere this side of
the gorgeous East; and the
Neapolitans bring their
worship of light, perfume,
and color to its utmost cul-
mination in their daily
promenade in the Villa.

In the centre of the Villa
stands a large white mar-
ble building, the celebrated
Aquarium of Naples. It
belongs to the Zoological
Station, and was established by the German natural-
ist Dr. Dohrn for the purpose of facilitating a thorough scientific investigation of the animal and
vegetable world of the
Mediterranean. The great-
er part of the expense was
borne by Dr. Dohrn him-
self, but the German gov-
ernment has repeatedly
contributed large subsidies.
Several prominent English
naturalists have also presented the institution with
important sums.

The inhabitants of Na-
ples number nearly half a
million souls. Yet in spite
of the generations of men
of different races—Greeks,
Goths, Byzantines, Nor-
mans, and modern peoples
—that have dwelt in this
beautiful region, Naples
has rarely attained even a
transient reputation in the
annals of politics, art, or
literature. All succumb to
the alluring influences of
the situation and the climate.

There are few people in
the world with whom it is
more difficult to arrive at
anything like familiar acquaintance than with the
higher class of Neapolitans.

EXTERIOR OF THE GROTTO OF POSILIPPO.

THE PUBLIC SCRIBE.

cat's-meat man, with his viands strung on a long pole, from which he detaches a piece and carves it with his knife for each of his four-footed clients, is a most extraordinary sight. The public scribe, protected from the rays of the sun by an umbrella, as he sits at a table inditing a love-letter, perhaps, for a Neapolitan damsel as beautiful as she is illiterate, is useful as well as picturesque. Another remarkable personage is the cigar scavenger, who at night goes about with his lantern hunting for old stumps, which he sells to manufacturers to be converted into the filling for fresh cigars. To these may be added the zampognari or bagpipers, and a host of other curious characters, ranging anywhere from a cardinal, attired in crimson and riding in a gilded coach, to a baby, bound up, after the manner of Neapolitan babies, in the straitest of swaddling-clothes, and looking more like a roll of linen just come from a draper's shop than a human being.

The advent of the zampognari in Naples always heralds the approach of one of the more important Church festivals. They come from their distant homes in the mountains of the Abruzzi to Naples and the surrounding towns to celebrate the Immaculate Conception and the ad-

They are exclusive to the last degree. Their pride seems to be in their birth, their lineage, the magnificence of their *entourage*, and the display they can make. The common people are at once the most careless, the most indolent, and the most indigent of the human race. Yet there is nothing that seems to be capable of depressing permanently the buoyancy of their spirits. Not all the political tempests that have swept over Naples, not the oppression of tyrants, or the terrible ills resulting from indolence, stupidity, and vice, have sufficed to take from its inhabitants the feeling that existence is a boon from the great Ruler of the universe for which they are deeply thankful, and which in their easy, unthinking, uncalculating manner they intensely enjoy.

The street scenes of Naples are a study in themselves, and would entertain a traveller for days even if he never entered a building. The curious garbs of the ecclesiastics, who seem to form a large proportion of the inhabitants, the grotesque appearance of the street venders, with their wares piled up above their heads, and hanging to all parts of their bodies, the brilliant dresses of the middle-class women, and the fantastic costumes of the beggars, who are picturesque in their very nakedness, give variety to the scene. The

ZAMPOGNARI PLAYING BEFORE A PUBLIC SHRINE.

vent of Christmas. Wearing pointed felt hats, wrapped in long brown cloaks, under which occasionally appears a goatskin jacket adorned with large metal buttons, their legs encased in tight-fitting breeches as far as the knee, and their feet of the city reclaimed from the sea. To the east of the long embankment and bridge which connect the shore with the rocky island whereon stands the Castel del' Ovo stretches what was once a long and narrow strip of dirty sand, but is now

ZAMPOGNARI IN THE STREET.

adorned with rags fastened by leather thongs about the ankle and calf, they are most picturesque objects. Thus attired, the zampognari go from house to house, singing and playing before the little gilded images of the Virgin and the Child, and stopping before the street shrines, where they repeat their monotonous song. On Christmas Eve, when there is a spirit of liberality abroad, the zampognaro usually receives a large number of coppers, and as much in the way of food and drink as his stomach can accommodate. When the festival is over they return to their mountain homes, there to pass their time as laborers or shepherds until the next occurs. The bagpipers of the Abruzzi frequently act as models, their picturesque costume adapting itself readily to artistic purposes.

A capital place to study some of the leading characteristics of Neapolitan life is along the broad and pleasant thoroughfare of Santa Lucia. This is another part a broad and handsome quay. Scenes of Neapolitan life may be witnessed here in perfection. The huts of the fishermen which once decorated the strand have given way to wharves and bridges, and handsome palaces form a background to the view from the water. But the people still claim a right to make this their lounging-place, the focus of the scene being a small promontory which is reached by a flight of steps, and where an elaborate fountain plays. Here, too, are the fish and oyster stalls, where passers-by may make a meal off the luxuries so expressively styled by the Neapolitans *frutti del mare*. The number of these aristocratic oystermen—for the majority traverse the city to sell their wares, carrying them in small baskets—is very limited, as the business and good-will can only be transmitted from father to son, or by extraordinary merit when the position is vacant. The stands are painted green, yellow, or black, and surmounted by sign-boards, on which

SANTA LUCIA AND CASTEL DEL' OVO.

the names of the owners are inscribed in large letters, and followed by such imposing words as "Ostricaro d'Europa," "Ostricaro fisico," etc.

The lower class Neapolitans live positively in the street. They occupy the thoroughfares with more than the determination shown by the upper classes in keeping out of them. In Naples it is not so much the quarter in which one lives—though certain parts of the town are always avoided by decent people—as the height at which one lives. The third and fourth stories of a building, for instance, will be occupied by families of considerable means, while in the rooms opening upon the street two or three poor families will be huddled. One room is, indeed, abundant space for the accommodation of a poor Neapolitan family, and sometimes they even take several boarders within its limits. This, so to speak, renders necessary the appropriation of a portion of the thoroughfare, and it is not at all unusual to see the single apartment filled up with beds, while the cooking stove, the dinner table, and the pots, pans, and dishes are accommodated in the street. The Neapolitan never hesitates to perform any part of his toilet in the street. He combs his hair or changes his clothing, the women nurse their infants, and adults and children hunt for uncomfortable insects on each other's heads and garments, with the utmost carelessness as to spectators.

These people are quite as fond of operatic and theatrical entertainments as are their superiors, and Naples abounds in theatres, concert halls, and shows of all kinds. The theatre San Carlino, the diminutive of San Carlo, and the home of the famous Pulcinello, to whom it was dedicated in 1770, is perhaps the most popular among these places. Pulcinello is a most amusing personage, and of most ancient lineage. He is usually attired in a loose jacket and exceedingly baggy linen trousers, with a pointed cap and a small black mask that conceals the upper part of his face. In character he is a vivacious sort of wag, cunning and foolish, cowardly and quarrelsome, good-humored and malicious, caustic, lazy, gluttonous, and thievish. The image of Pulcinello is said to have been found in Herculaneum, and near the Esquiline at Rome. He also appears on ancient Etruscan vases, and in the frescoes taken from Pompeii. His name changes frequently; it may be Aniello, Cinella, or Fiorillo; but his character remains the same. The performances at San Carlino generally turn upon domestic infelicities of some kind—conjugal quarrels, disputes in regard to property—

and the incidents are nearly always of a comic nature. Pulcinello is the life and soul of the whole, and generally succeeds in amusing a not overdifficult audience by his sharp speeches and ludicrous pranks.

The manner in which the people of Naples are supplied with food is most amazing to a stranger. The markets are peripatetic, and donkeys are the motive power.

tive carts, which, whatever their weight may be, are at least a dozen times his own bulk. In his leisure moments the donkey takes his master, and frequently two or three members of the family, for a ride upon his back.

A staple article of food in all Italian families, as is well known, is macaroni.

THE OYSTERMAN.

patetic, and donkeys are the motive power. Indeed, without the donkey, it seems as if the whole business of living in Naples would be brought to a stand-still. Articles of every description are conveyed from house to house by him. He is loaded with wine and water, for in Naples the drinking water is all procured from certain fountains, and sold by carriers; he carries bushels of vegetables piled in panniers, and spread upon shallow baskets, until nothing but his nose and tail are visible; and he draws loads piled on primi-

Having been convulsed with laughter one day by a sweet little American woman, who drew an immense endless attenuated pipe-stem into her mouth, and then announced, "It's peculiar, but very nice—where does it grow?" we organized a party to visit a macaroni factory. Our innocent little friend went with us, and has never eaten macaroni since. Nearly all the places where this commodity is produced are outside Naples, but a short drive brought us to a manufactory on the road toward Torre del Greco. We were received with *empressement*, not only by the proprietor, but by the whole staff of employés. The business of manufacturing macaroni is warm work, and the climate of Naples, save for three or four months in the year, excessively hot. As a general thing, there is a great indifference to the matter of clothing shown by the employés of such establishments; but on the appearance of a party of foreigners, two of whom were ladies, there was a grand scuffle for garments. The women were most successful, having had a foundation of under-clothing to begin upon. One boy secured a full suit. After this there were various toilets conspicuous by the absence of essential garments, while one poor fellow, oblivious of our presence to the last moment, could procure nothing but a towel. In this he arrayed himself, however, and tried to make up by extra

PULCINELLO IN A QUANDARY.

courtesy for what he lacked in the way of apparel. The process of manufacturing macaroni is very simple. The ground meal is mixed with water, kneaded or beaten by an immense wooden beam, and then transferred to the press. A perfo-

rated plate beneath, through which the dough is forced by means of a ponderous lever, produces the article. Upon this plate depends whether the macaroni has a diameter large or small, or whether it is flat like a ribbon. The sizes and varieties are many, and each is endowed with a different Italian name. When it issues from the press it is, of course, moist and limp. Large armfuls of it are seized by various attendants, and ranged upon long poles, suspended from the ceiling, to dry. It was this familiar handling of the dough and the macaroni, which is flung over the shoulder, wound round the arm, and patted and adjusted by the dirtiest of dirty hands, that deprived our little friend of any further appreciation of what she had taken to be a chaste product of Mother Nature.

Naples has a large foreign population, drawn hither by the fascination of the city and its beautiful suburbs. There is a considerable colony of Americans and English, and four or five Protestant places of worship. The largest and handsomest is Christ Church, situated in the Strada San Pasquali, where services are held on Sundays and saints' days, and the Holy Communion administered weekly by the English chaplain.

The city offers attractions as a permanent residence, if we except the few extremely warm summer months. The cost of living may be arranged very much as one pleases. There are the expensive hotels, arranged precisely on the plan of all other hotels throughout the world, with velvet carpets, heavy upholstery, a French cook, and a corps of waiters speaking any European language. For these luxuries one must pay, as one does in other large cities of Europe, anywhere from $3 to $5 per day, according to the length of stay. The Neapolitan *pension*, which is the refuge of a very large number of foreign residents, is usually kept by an English woman who has married an Italian, and found that he can not support a family without her assistance. At a *pension* one must pay from $1 to $2 per day. A very pleasant way of living in Naples is to take an apartment, the price of which varies according to the situation and number of rooms. A well-situated, comfortable apartment, with five furnished rooms, can be obtained for about $20 per month. Meals can then be procured either by going to or having them sent in from a trattoria,

MAKING MACARONI.

or restaurant. By going out, an excellent breakfast, and a dinner of four or five courses, with wine included, may be had at a cost of from eighty cents to a dollar per day. Housekeeping may be conducted at a moderate expense, meat and vegetables selling at low rates, and servants' wages ranging from two to eight dollars per month.

The business of living having been arranged, the person must be difficult to please who can not pass his time comfortably, and with no small degree of satisfaction to himself, in Naples. There is opportunity for occupation and amusement of every kind. Days may be passed in the museum, where the treasures of art are inexhaustible, and where there is a library open to the public which contains some 200,000 volumes and 4000 manuscripts. The number of excursions that may be made to different points of interest in the city and its environs is almost without limit. To the west, beyond Posilippo, lies ancient Pozzuoli; Baiæ, once famous as a watering-place, now silent and deserted; the baths of Nero, the chambers of which were heated by steam from a natural spring; the famous Lake Avernus, across

which, ancient story tells us, no bird could fly without meeting death; and last, but not least, the terrible river Styx. To the east are greater wonders. Here Vesuvius sends her clouds of smoke to heaven by day, and her glowing fires by night; Pompeii emerges from her twenty centuries of burial, and Herculaneum and other cities stand three deep upon the plain. Every foot of earth is classic ground, and replete with memories of the various races that have had their habitations here. When all other sources of entertainment have failed, hours may be passed in drifting about the shores of the bay, of which the poet Rogers writes:

"Not a grove,
Citron or pine or cedar, not a grot,
Sea-worn and mantled with the gadding vine
But breathes enchantment. Not a cliff but flings
On the clear wave some image of delight,
Some cabin roof glowing with crimson flowers,
Some ruined temple or fallen monument,
To muse on as the bark is gliding by."

Naples the beautiful has the same fascination to-day that she had when Cicero and Lucullus built their villas here, and when the potentates of Greece and Rome left their great capitals to pass their days in indolence and luxury upon her shores.

THE JAPANESE SPRING

BY ALFRED PARSONS.

WE had left Hong-Kong enveloped in its usual spring fog, and for five long weary days had steamed across the China Sea in regular monsoon weather, gray and wet and miserable, but during the fifth some rocky islands, outlying sentinels of the three thousand which compose the Mikado's realm, and occasional square-sailed, high-sterned boats, showed that we were near Japan, the Far East, the Land of Flowers and of the Rising Sun, the country which for years it had been my dream to see and paint, and by six o'clock in the evening, on the 9th of March, we were at anchor in Nagasaki Bay. The aspect of that port on a wet day was not inviting, nor were the little grimy girls, who in a chattering, laughing line carried their baskets of coal on board, so, difficult as it was to decline the hospitable invitations of the English residents, I decided to go on with the ship to Kobe. Early in the morning of the 11th we passed through the Strait of Shimonoseki —the sun shining brightly on the snowy hills and on the crowd of fishing-boats which had been sheltering there from the bad weather—and entered the Inland Sea. After so many days of monotonous gray ocean it was delightful to steam along in sight of land, and wind about among the islets and rocks, so near to many of them that we could see the little villages, the mists of white plum blossoms, the rows of beans and barley growing wherever a level patch could be made on the steep slopes, the people at work in their fields, and always in the distance the ranges of snow-covered mountains in Kiushiu and Shikoku, the islands which enclose this lovely sea on the south. I longed to land and begin work at once, with a nervous dread in my heart that I should find nothing so good elsewhere, and, indeed, though there is plenty of material to be found everywhere in Japan,

I saw nothing finer than these islands of the Inland Sea; to cruise about among them in a comfortable boat would be an ideal way to spend a summer, and would probably not be devoid of adventure, for our captain told me many tales of treacherous currents and sudden squalls and sunken reefs.

We reached Kobe next morning, and before I had been on shore more than an hour I had heard of a village six miles away which was celebrated for its plum orchards, and had started off to find it. Okamoto lies at the foot of the hills which rise behind Kobe on the north, and climbs a little way up them, and in front of the highest cottage, a modest tea-house with platforms arranged to accommodate the visitors who come in crowds to gaze at the blossoms, I unfolded my stool and easel, and in spite of a bitter wind and vicious little snow-storms made my first sketch in Japan. All round me and in the village below were the pink and white trees, then a band of rice-lands, pale green with young barley, and beyond them lay Osaka Bay, and the mountains of Yamato, which constantly changed in color as snow-storms passed over, or

IN THE INLAND SEA.

HILLS NEAR KOBE, FROM GAWA-YAMA.

gleams of sun lighted the shining water and the snow on the distant hills. It is an exciting thing to begin work in a new country, to compare the local color and the atmosphere with those you have tried before, and to find yourself half unconsciously using an entirely new set of pigments, and I was too absorbed to take any notice of the fact that my back was ach-

CHERRY BLOSSOMS IN THE RAIN.

ing, but after two hours, when I had finished my drawing, I found myself unable to rise from that sketching-stool, and for the next fortnight an attack of lumbago prevented my seeing anything more of the plum groves. The Buddhist pictures of their Inferno depict many ingenious tortures; I think they ought to add a man with lumbago doing six miles over a Japanese by-road in a jinricksha. When at last I got back to Okamoto there were still some blossoms, and the trees were tinged with the pink of withered petals, but the luxuriant freshness had gone.

On the 13th of April I said good-by to my friends and to the comforts of the Kobe Club, and started for Nara, stopping on my way at Osaka to have a look at the town and see the peach blossoms on Momo-Yama (peach mountain). The narrow streets leading up the hill were crowded with visitors, and among the orchards of dwarf trees temporary tea-sheds and resting-places had been erected for their comfort and refreshment. In spite of the many picturesque features in these fêtes the whole effect is at first disappointing: railings and stages of new raw deal, the untidy and unfinished look of rough bamboo structures, with corners of matting hanging loosely in places where they interfere with the perspective lines, the slovenly pathways, which are mud or dust according to the weather—all these things make unsatisfactory accessories for the figures and the flowers. After a time they obtrude themselves less on your notice, and you have learned to accept the fact that Japan is not a country of big masses and broad effects, but of interesting bits and amusing details. This is usually true of its landscape; the forms of mountains and trees are more quaint than grand, and the cultivated land has no broad stretches of pasture or corn, but is cut up into patches, mainly rice-fields, with various vegetables grown in little squares here and there. It was as yet too early in the year for any rice to be planted out. In the fertile valley through which the railway runs from Osaka to Nara some few fields were lying wet or fallow, others were being prepared by spade labor, and others again, not yet flooded, were covered with the bright green of young barley, or the strong light yellow of rape in flower.

Though I had read much about life in Japan, it was an embarrassing experience to be set down for the first time with my baggage in a Japanese room, and to try and adapt myself mentally to the possibilities of living under such conditions. In a bare hut or tent the problem is comparatively simple; there is always one way by which you must enter; but in a Japanese room there is too much liberty; three of the walls are opaque sliding screens, the fourth is a transparent, or rather translucent, one; you can come in or go out where you like; there is no table on which things must be put, no chair on which you must sit, no fireplace to stand with your back to—just a clean matted floor and perfect freedom of choice. Eu-

EARLY PLUM BLOSSOMS, OKAMOTO, NEAR KOBE.

ropean trunks look hopelessly ugly and unsympathetic in such surroundings, nor are matters much improved when the host, in deference to the habits of a foreigner, sends in a rough deal table, with a cloth of unhemmed cotton, intended to be white, and an uncompromising straight-backed deal chair. These hideous articles make a man feel ashamed, for though they are only a burlesque of our civilization, they are produced with an air of pride which shows that the owner is convinced they are the right thing, and one cannot but be humiliated by their ugliness and want of comfort. Yet if you want to read or write you have to keep them and make the best of them, for a long evening on the floor is only to be borne after a good many weeks of practice. Things begin to look brighter and pleasanter when the little waiting-maid

THE TORII OF KASUGA TEMPLE, NARA.

appears, bringing first some cushions and the hibachi, with its pile of glowing charcoal, and then the tea-tray and a few sweet cakes. This was more the sort of thing I had expected, and made me at once feel at home with my surroundings. It is the first attention shown you in every tea-house, no matter how humble; whether you go as an inmate, or whether you merely sit down for a few minutes' rest on a journey, the little teapot and the tiny cups are at once produced, and the hibachi is placed by your side, a pleasant and friendly welcome, which never failed to make its impression on me, however much the quality of the tea might vary. The Kiku-sui-ya (which means Chrysanthemum Waterhouse) is near the entrance to the great Kasuga Park at Nara; just outside it the road passes under a granite torii flanked with stone lanterns, and winds up to the temple through an avenue of cryptomerias, with rows of lanterns on each side, which get closer together as they near the temple buildings. There are booths here and there where pilgrims can rest and get a cup of tea, for pilgrimage in Japan is not made unnecessarily uncomfortable, and where the tame deer congregate to take the nuts and cakes which are sold for them to the passers-by. From early morning till nearly sundown this road is lively with groups of visitors. Nara is so near to Osaka that among them a sprinkling of men, mostly no doubt engaged in commerce, wore foreign dress, but the majority of the people were in their native clothes, and as I sat and painted by the road-side I could study the variations of Japanese costume—from that of the old peasant with his white or blue leggings, straw shoes, big hat, and robe tucked into his girdle, his head shaved down the middle, and the back hair turned up in a queue in the ancient mode, to that of the gay young musumé with her rich silk kimono, gorgeous scarlet petticoat, broad obi, and black-lacquered sandals on her pigeon-toed, white-socked feet. The cryptomerias are good, but the old wistarias are the glory of Kasuga Park. The great Fujiwara family formerly owned or were patrons of the temple, and though it is now imperial property, their crest the wistaria flower (*fuji no hana*) is still worn by the little girls who perform the sacred dance there, and all over the park the wistaria vines are allowed to grow as they choose, their great snaky stems writhing along the ground and twisting up to the tops of the highest trees. One very wet day, when painting out-of-doors was impossible, I went round to see the sights of Nara—Kobūkuji with its pagoda and fine old statues, the great bronze Buddha, a celebrated big bell, and beyond these the Buddhist temple Ni-gwatsu-dō, perched on a hill-side, the steps leading up to it lined with stone lanterns, little shrines, and booths for the sale of endless trifles. The platform surrounding this temple

is supported in front by a scaffolding of beams, at the back it abuts against the hill, and from the heavy projecting roof which covers it all hang hundreds of bronze lanterns, votive offerings. Each of these had been appropriated by a sparrow; trusting to the sanctity of the spot, they had piled in all the rubbish they could find to make their nests; odd ends of straw and cotton and paper

stuck out everywhere, showing that their stay in the East had not taught them tidy habits; but I am sorry to say that their confidence was misplaced, a temple festival came round before their eggs were hatched, and the whole of them with their embryo families were ruthlessly evicted.

The park at Nara is one of the few places in Japan where you can see real turf, and even there I was struck by the scarcity of ground flowers; there were plenty of scentless violets, some yellow and white dandelions, and in the damp ditches a little purple flower called jirobo by the country people, but there was nothing to compare with the masses of daisies, buttercups, and cowslips which make our English meadows so bright in the spring. Perhaps the mountain moorlands would have been as gay at that

CHERRY-TREE AND LANTERNS, NI-GWATSU-DŌ, NARA.

THE PAGODA OF KOBŪKUJI, NARA.

pointed herself my special attendant and protector at the Kiku-sui Hotel. One night at the theatre I saw a modern farce, with a policeman, an old-fashioned Japanese gentleman, a Chinaman, and an Englishman as the comic characters. They were ridiculous and amusing, but when all the earlier incidents of the piece were narrated with conscientious realism in the evidence before the magistrate the thing became monotonous, and struck me as faulty in dramatic construction. This was the only theatre I saw in Japan in which they had discarded the orchestra and chorus and other traditions of the old stage.

There is a modest little temple opposite Kobūkuji, which is visited by most of the pilgrims to Nara; in its court-yard is a pile of stones from which a stream of water flows, fed by the tears of the mother of Sankatchu, a sacrilegious man who killed some of the sacred deer, who was killed himself in consequence, and buried here by her. Day after day groups of visitors stand by the fountain, listening intently to the guide who tells them the pathetic story, and give their prayers and a few coppers to her memory. The family affections are strong in Japan, and the love between parents and children, and among the children themselves, is always pleasant to see. The little ones are

time as I found them later in the year; the fields are far too well cultivated for any weed to get a chance of flowering.

The earlier cherry-trees were in blossom by this time, and I lingered on, making studies of them, and learning Japanese words and ways from O Nao San, a young lady about twelve years old, who had ap-

SARU-HIKI-SAKA, NEAR YOSHINO—LATER CHERRIES.

CHERRY AND LATE PLUM, TEMA-CHO, NEAR NARA.

never slapped or shaken or pulled about roughly; you may wander through the streets for days without hearing a child cry, nor do they often quarrel in their play. But it is possible to go too far, even in filial piety. There was a murder trial while I was in the country, and by the evidence it appeared that the prisoner's mother was blind, that the doctor had prescribed the application of a warm human liver, and that he, as he could find no other way to get the remedy, had killed his wife in order to restore his mother's sight.

In most forms of Japanese art the technique which is admired by native connoisseurs, and the associations connected with the subject represented, can only be understood by those who have studied Japanese methods and traditions, but the old wooden statuary has more in common with Western art, and often reaches a high point of realism. In the religious figures certain traditions had to be followed, and in looking at these this fact has to be remembered; the exaggerated anatomy, unnaturally fierce expressions, and arbitrary number of limbs often disguise their true merits; but in the portrait figures of daimios, priests, and abbots the treatment is both simple and dignified. Mr. Takenouchi, a sculptor to whom I had letters, was making admirable copies of the principal sculptures at Kobūkuji, which were to be exhibited at Chicago, and afterwards added to the col-

A SPRING FLOWER—
JIRO-BO.

lection of the Fine Art Museum in Ueno Park, Tokyo. Among the old masters, Unkei, a sculptor of the twelfth century, is perhaps the most noteworthy; there is a mendicant ascetic by him in the Hall of the Thirty-three Thousand Kwannon at Kyoto, a lean old man, clad only in a few rags, resting on his staff and holding out his left hand for alms, which might rank with the work of Rodin.

On the 25th of April the cherry-trees were in full flower, and I left Nara for Yoshino, a village at the foot of Mount Omine, in Yamato, which has for centuries been noted for its cherry groves. Here the cult of the cherry blossom has its headquarters, and during the ten days or so which the blossoms last the little town is crowded with visitors. I was too late to see the place in its full glory; it stands at some height above the sea, and

I consequently imagined that the flowers would be later than those at Nara, but the cherry which grows there in such quantities is an early species, and three days of wind and rain had covered the ground with pink petals and left very few of them on the trees in the celebrated groves. Fortunately there were still some flowery trees to be found in gardens and sheltered corners, and at this time of year it would be impossible to settle down in a Japanese village without finding plenty of subjects to paint. The cherry in the Yoshino groves has a single flower, pale pink in color; this is followed by another kind with white blossoms, more like the European species. Both of these are wild, and from them the Japanese gardeners have raised many varieties, double and single flowered, some with the growth of the weeping-willow, and others with a spreading habit. The flowers vary in color from white to light crimson, and I noticed some young trees with large double blossoms which were pale yellow with a pink flush on the outer petals, like a delicate tea-rose. At the Tatsumi-ya, just by the remains of the huge bronze torii, which, until it was blown down by a hurricane, formed the entrance to the

A BUDDHIST TEMPLE AT YOSHINO—DOUBLE-FLOWERED CHERRY AND MAGNOLIA.

main street, I found a little suite of rooms built in the garden away from the rest of the house, and at once engaged them, in happy anticipation of quiet nights. These isolated rooms have some disadvantages, such as having to get to the bath and back on wet nights, but a very short acquaintance with life in a tea-house makes the traveller disregard such trifling inconveniences for the certainty of peaceful sleep. The Japanese wanderers usually finish their day's journey about five in the afternoon, and, after the preliminary cup of tea, discard their travel-stained clothes for the clean kimono which every well-regulated tea-house supplies to its guests, then bathe in water as near the boiling-point as possible, eat their dinner, sit talking and smoking till midnight, snore till five o'clock in the morning, and then begins the clatter of taking down shutters and the elaborate business of tooth-cleaning and tongue-scraping, with an accompaniment of complex noises suggesting sea-sickness in its worst stages, so it is not till they have departed at six or seven o'clock that a light sleeper gets much chance. In the daytime the tea-house is deserted, except by the proprietor, who sits in the front room and does his accounts, and by the little servant-girls, who, with their heads tied up in towels, kimono tucked into their obi, and sleeves fastened back, showing a good deal of round brown leg and arm, busily sweep and dust the rooms in preparation for the new set of visitors who will arrive in the evening. The thin sliding partitions would be little bar to sound even if they reached to the top of the room, and above them there is generally a foot or

so of open wood-work, which allows free ventilation and conversation between the different apartments. Privacy, as we understand it, is no part of the scheme of a Japanese tea-house. Real fresh air from outside is very difficult to get at night. During the hot weather I was always

MI KOMORI JIUJA, A SHINTO TEMPLE NEAR YOSHINO.

careful to examine the fastenings of the wooden shutters with which, after dark, every house is enclosed like a box, so that I could surreptitiously open a crack opposite my room, although by so doing I was disobeying the police regulations. These shutters do not keep out the noise of the watchman, who all night long wanders round and knocks two blocks of

CROSSING THE FERRY, MUDA ON THE GAWA.

ed constantly of a sentence which a friend had written in one of my books, "Take pains to encourage the beautiful, for the useful encourages itself." It is difficult for an outsider to determine how much of this is genuine enthusiasm and how much is custom or a traditional æstheticism; but it really matters little. That the popular idea of a holiday should be to wander about in the open air, visiting historic places, and gazing at the finest landscapes and the flowers in their seasons, indicates a high level of true civilization, and the custom, if it be only custom, proves the refinement of the people who originated and adhere to it.

wood together, just to let burglars know that he is on the lookout.

In these quarters I spent a week or so, painting all day when the weather would allow me, and in the evening struggling with the language and gambling for beans with the family and the servant-girls, who played *vingt-et-un* (*ni ju ichi*) with such keenness and discretion that I was generally made a bankrupt, with much laughter and clapping of hands, quite early in the game, and had to be set up again by general contribution.

Everything in Yoshino is redolent of the cherry; the pink and white cakes brought in with the tea are in the shape of its blossoms, and a conventional form of it is painted on every lantern and printed on every scrap of paper in the place. The shops sell preserved cherry flowers for making tea, and visitors to the tea-houses and temples are given maps of the district—or, rather, broad sheets roughly printed in colors, not exactly a map or a picture—on which every cherry grove is depicted in pink. And all this is simply enthusiasm for its beauty and its associations, for the trees bear no fruit worthy of the name. There is an old Japanese saying, "What the cherry blossom is among flowers, the warrior is among men." I was remind-

NOTES AT MUDA.

The village street of Yoshino winds up a spur of the hills, passing many temples and little hamlets, and gradually becomes a steep and stony mountain path, which ascends to Mount Omine. The great tracts of forest provide occupation for most of the people in this district; strings of men and women were constantly passing, carrying down heavy loads of wood and charcoal from the hills, and in front of many of the cottages match-wood was spread out on mats to dry. It was difficult to understand how it could ever get dry, for all the mists of Japan seemed to collect round these mountains and forests; the landscape was rarely free from them, and constantly looked like a Japanese drawing, all vague and white in the valleys, with ridges of hill and fringes of pine showing in sharp clear lines one behind the other.

It is a warm climate too, and everything grows luxuriantly. There are great clumps of bamboo, enormous azalea bushes, and thick undergrowths of palmetto. On the road-side banks, in this last week of April, there were ferns just unrolling, the fronds of maidenhair (*Adiantum pedatum*) all bright red, young shoots of lily and orchid and Solomon's-seal, and a lovely iris (*I. japonica*), with many lavender-colored flowers on a branching stalk, each outer petal marked with dark purple lines, and decorated with a little horn of brilliant orange. The gardens of tea-houses and temples were gay with azalea, camellia, magnolia, and cherry, and with the young leaves of maple and andromeda, as bright as any flowers. During a great part of the year these gardens have but few blooms—they are only an arrangement of greens and grays—but in the spring no amount of clipping and training can prevent the shrubs from blossoming. The cherry-trees and magnolias are let grow as they choose, but the others are trimmed into more or less formal shapes, considered suitable to the species, or helping the carefully studied arrangement of forms, which is the ideal of a Japanese gardener. There are no beds for flowers. In the little ponds the irises and lotus bloom, and in odd corners there may be clumps of lilies, chrysanthemums, or other plants, but these are mere accidents: the designer's aim is a composition of rocks, shrubs, stone lanterns, ponds, and bridges, which will look the same in its general features all the year round, and conform to established rules. One of my Japanese friends told me, as an instance of the complexity of the landscape-gardener's art, that if a certain shrub were used it would be necessary to place near it a stone from Tosa, the distant province where it commonly grows. The decorative garden is quite distinct from the flower garden, where the fine varieties of iris, pæony, and chrysanthemum, for which Japan is famous, are grown by professional florists, or by rich amateurs who can devote a special place to their culture.

On the 3d of May my host at the Tatsumi-ya brought me some pæony flowers arranged in an old bronze vase, which showed me it was time to move on to Hase, where there is a great display of them. So next morning I made an early start for a long jinricksha ride through the hills of Yamato.

THE STREET, HASE.

My baggage and painting materials could not be packed in less than two kuruma, two more were necessary for my boy and myself, and the four vehicles, with two men drawing each, made an imposing procession as we bumped down the steep village street. The whole staff of the Tatsumi-ya had turned out to say good-by; there was a row of little girls kneeling on the floor, their noses on the matting and their brown hands placed flat, palms downward, in front of their heads, and the landlord, after giving me the usual presents and a receipt for my "chadai" —the parting tip—insisted on accompanying me to the end of the town.

Our route for two or three miles, as far as the river Yoshino-gawa, was the same that I had climbed on my way up; but nine days had made a great difference in its aspect. Then many of the trees were still bare; now they were covered with spring leaves. After ferrying over to Muda we turned northwards, and a good road led us by low passes and through the grand forests at the foot of Mount Tonomine down to Tosa in the Yamato Valley. Jinricksha travelling is

ALFRED PARSONS.

WHITE WISTARIA, HASE-DERA.

IRIS JAPONICA.

very pleasant when the roads are good, the weather fine, and the men active; there is no noise of horses' hoofs to disturb the mind, the straw-sandalled feet of the coolies hardly make a sound, nor is your attention distracted from the landscape by having to drive; and the frequent short halts at wayside tea-houses give you a chance of airing your few phrases of Japanese and seeing the ways of the people. My lunch at Tosa was enlivened by two charming waitresses, who had evidently seen but few foreigners, and who were much interested in me and my belongings. My watch, match-box, cigarette-case, and other small articles had to be examined, talked over, and shown to the rest of the household, and I was plied with questions about my age, my family, and other personal matters, as Japanese etiquette prescribes.

This valley of Yamato is the earliest historic home of the present race; in it there are many tumuli which mark the burial-places of legendary emperors, including that of Jimmu Tenno, the first of all, and it is therefore considered sacred ground by the ancestor-loving Japanese. Every year crowds of pilgrims walk over the district, making their "Yamato-meguri," or tour of the holy places of Yamato, and thereout the innkeepers suck no small advantage. Hase was full of them, and every tea-house crammed; in the room next mine at least a dozen must have slept, and I thought myself lucky to get a place to myself. There were still some hours of daylight left after I had settled down, so I wandered up the street and climbed the long flight of steps to the great temple of Kwannon. On each side of the steps small beds were built up, and in these the pæonies grew, and their big flowers, ranging in color from white to dark purple, glowed in the afternoon light against a background of gray stone lanterns. The temple is built on a hill-side, like Ni-gwatsu-dō at Nara and many other Buddhist temples, and it consists of a wide veranda filled with incense-burners and votive pictures and bronze lanterns, and of an inner sanctuary. Across the entrance to this stands an altar, and over it an opening in the dark purple curtains allows a glimpse of the great gold figure of Kwannon, nearly thirty feet high, her face, with its expression of calm beneficence, only just distinguishable by the light of a few dim lamps in the gloom of the windowless shrine. Behind this main temple there are various other buildings, priests' houses and such like, and a little pond for the sacred tortoises.

The main street of Hase is cut up with rivulets; the middle one is used for all domestic purposes, and at all hours you may see the women, with skirts and sleeves tucked up, washing their clothes or their fish and vegetables, and ladling up water for baths and cooking with their long-handled wooden dippers. The side streams turn small water-wheels, which work wooden hammers for pounding and cleaning the rice — an important part of the day's work in every Japanese village. In the most primitive places it is done with a long-headed wooden mallet and the stump of a tree hollowed out for a mortar; in others big wooden hammers are fixed on a pivot, and are raised by stepping on the other end of the handle. A mountain brook, the parent of these little streams,

OLD WISTARIA IN KASUGA PARK, NARA.

tumbles along close behind the houses; its banks are overhung with bamboos, and the rocks at that season were covered with lavender iris. From Atago-Yama, a hill just across the river, the view is fine: below are the flat gray roofs of Hase, and the *cul-de-sac* in which it lies—bordered on either side with green hills, its windings indicated by the curves of road and shining river, its green surface spotted here and there with gray hamlets—gradually opens out into the wider Yamato Valley. Unebi - Yama, which marks the site of Jimmu Tenno's mausoleum, rises in the centre of the plain, and beyond it all is an enclosing barrier of cloudy mountains.

A morning's jinricksha ride took me back to my old quarters at Nara, and Kwannon must have rejoiced at my departure from Hase-dera, for while I was there most of the priests and all the acolytes sadly neglected her: they spent the day looking over my shoulder or gazing open-mouthed in my face.

A TALL WISTARIA, KASUGA PARK, NARA.

This was on the 9th of May, and I was glad to find that the wistaria in Kasuga Park was just in its glory. The masses of flowers turned the lower trees into big bouquets of pale mauve, and seemed to drip like fountains from the tall oaks and cryptomerias; and to add to the beauty, all the undergrowth of andromeda had put out its young leaves in many shades of color; as Chaucer says, "Some very red, and some a glad light green." One glade particularly attracted me: a tiny clear stream wound along through the brilliant grasses, and the trees which covered the steep banks on each side of this little meadow were completely overgrown with the vines, and

smothered with their blossoms. This too was a quiet spot, out of the track of tourists and pilgrims, and it was a blessed relief to work without a gazing crowd; the only passers were a few women and children collecting fire-wood or gathering the young fern shoots which were sprouting through the grass. These are cut just as they begin to unroll, and when they are boiled and flavored with soy, they are really quite good to eat, at least one thinks so in Japan.

The wistaria blossoms were almost gone when I decided that though there was still plenty to be done in Nara, it would be better to try some new sketching-ground, and having heard of a tea-house with a fine old garden at Hikone, on the

ANDROMEDA BUSHES IN KASUGA PARK, NARA.

shore of Lake Biwa, I determined to move on there for my next venture. I packed all my belongings, and made arrangements for the journey next morning, and then walked once more round the park and the temples, gazing regretfully at all the good things which still remained to be sketched, and climbed Mikasa-Yama, a steep grassy hill behind the park, which on fine days is dotted all over with picnic parties. From its summit there is a great view over the plains round Nara, with the Kizugawa, a good broad stream, winding through them. The grassy ridges and the few wind-beaten pines which grow on them made a fine foreground, and the little green gullies were spotted with low azalea bushes covered with flame-colored flowers. It was too good to leave, and I ought to have unpacked again and prolonged my stay for a few days; but laziness prevailed, the bore of repacking seemed intolerable, and to my lasting remorse it remained unpainted.

BADGE OF THE KIKU-SUI-YA.

PEEPS INTO BARBARY

A MOORISH VILLAGE.

COMPARATIVELY few, even of the ever-increasing number of visitors who year after year bring Morocco—the only remaining independent Barbary State—within the scope of their pilgrimage, are aware of the interest with which it teems for the scientist, the explorer, the historian, and students of human nature in general. A residence of nine years among the Moors, for the most part spent in gleaning information about them and their country, has enabled me to gain some insight into many things of which the mere passer-by never dreams, and I have come to look upon these people and their customs in a very different light from that of former years. Instead of "the poor rejected Moors who raised our childish fears," as Hood described them, they are a fine open race, capable of everything, but literally rotting in one of the finest countries in the world. The Moorish remains in Spain and the pages of history testify to the flourishing condition in which they once lived, but to-day their appearance is that of a nation asleep. Yet great strides towards reform have been made during the present century, and each successive decade sees more important progress than the last.

* For some years editor of the *Times of Morocco*.

One great cause which has ever worked disastrously in the history of Morocco, as of every country in which it has existed, is the lack of union among the constituent races of its population. The very name of Moor is a European invention, unknown in the land, where no more precise definition of its inhabitants can be given than that of "Westerns"—*Maghribeein*.* Our appellative is formed from the name we give to the country, itself a corruption of the native name for the southern capital, Marrákesh (Morocco city), through the Spanish version *Marruecos*. The genuine Moroccans are the Berbers, from whom the Arabs wrenched a great part of the country towards the close of the eighth century, introducing the blacks from Guinea in their raids across the Atlas. The remaining important body of the people are Jews of two classes—those settled in the country from prehistoric times, and those driven to it when expelled from Spain. With the exception of the Arabs and the blacks, none of these pull together, and in that case it is only because the latter are either subservient to the former or incorporated with them.

* Singular, Maghribi, from Maghreb, the Sunset (Land), the name by which Morocco is known to the Arabs.

First in importance, then, come the earliest known possessors of the land. These are not confined to Morocco, but still hold the rocky fastnesses which stretch away from the Atlantic opposite the Canaries to the borders of Egypt, from the sands of the Mediterranean to those of the Sahara, that vast extent of territory to which we have given their name, Barbary.

The character of the Berber is almost as great a contrast to that of the Arab as his language. Like mountaineers all the world over, his race has proved unconquerable, and it has defied for a thousand years the nation which has dominated the plains with ease. Phœnicians, Romans, Goths, and Vandals had already left their mark upon the country before the Arabs appeared, but none ever penetrated far inland. Had their many tribes been united, the followers of Islam would never have been masters of the country; but section after section was overcome, and adopted the religion of their conquerors, till it was professed from end to end of the land, and Arabic became the language of both creed and court. Beyond this and the introduction of a few Eastern customs, the masses of the people remain as unchanged as ever, and each successive Sultan of the various Fez and Morocco dynasties has in vain endeavored to subdue them entirely. Only a small proportion really amalgamated with the Muslim victors, and it is only to this mixed race which occupies the cities that the name of Moor is strictly applicable. Even at the present time the Sultan of Morocco undertakes annual expeditions against these Berber tribes, to maintain his nominal authority right in the heart of his kingdom, and to collect his tributes by force. As soon as his back is turned the governors he has imposed are slain or driven away, and the people do much as they like till another expedition comes their way.

"Powder has spoken on the hills of the Zemmoor." So runs the news from mouth to mouth, and it is thereby understood that one of the most powerful Berber tribes between Mequinez and the sea is in revolt once more. The proud, fierce clansmen are tired of quarrelling with one another, and wearied with the exactions and injustice of the imperial officials in their district. The heads of these worthies have been impaled above their dwellings; the whole country-side is up in arms. A period of comparative rest has allowed the tribe to recoup its energies: its corn-stores and its powder-flasks are full, and, forethought and discretion being cast aside, every male capable of shouldering a gun is eager for the fray. The Sultan and his army are away settling a similar account with a tribe on the other side of the empire, so for a time the spirits of the rebels rise as they give themselves to plunder. Those of their neighbors who have remained loyal to Shereefian* rule suffer continually from their forays, and the enriched insurgents, elated with success, openly dare their liege lord to attack them. But at last comes slow-fed vengeance.

The Sultan has passed a winter in the neighboring capital, and his warriors have recouped their strength at the expense of their purses. Now both they and their steeds fret and chafe to be away. The spring has come, and with it dreams of booty. On the appointed day a hundred thousand men camp round the imperial tent outside the walls. As the sun rises on the morrow they march away in a direction until then a secret in the Sultan's breast. It is to the homes of the rebel Zemmoor, whose boasts still ring in the air. At length their borders are invaded and their land laid waste on every side. Homes are burned; but they are empty. The arrival of so numerous a host has struck terror into the heart of the people, who have retired into their strongholds in the hills. As they are followed thither by the troops, a wild guerilla warfare is commenced. Every rock and every tree stump hides a shooter. Presently from across the valley rushes a line of mounted warriors, girded with flowing robes, brandishing above their heads their long quaint flintlocks, as their forefathers did their spears. They sweep onwards till they near the advancing foe. In a second each weapon is levelled at a signal from the leader, and, immediately it has been fired, their sturdy steeds are reined almost upon their haunches, wheeled about, and madly galloped out of range for a reload. At night the very mules are stolen from the Sultan's camp; his foraging parties are cut off, and his army becomes desperate from lack of provender, the rebels having de-

* The present dynasty is styled "Shereef," _i. e._, noble, as claiming descent from Mohammed.

stroyed all in their retreat. A pitched battle is seldom heard of. Meanwhile the fugitive undefended have been overtaken — women, children, and old men. Then begins a most heart-rending massacre; for, in spite of the orders of their imperial chief, the wild, fierce soldiery rush in and work their will. Such as are not fit for slaves are butchered, often after awful cruelties and insults. If peace is not yet sued for, the aid of the European officers* and cannon in the Sultan's service is called in. Strongholds are "removed" with dynamite, and a speedy termination is brought about by the submission of the rebels. The heads of the leaders are distributed among the chief towns of the empire, after having been pickled by the Jews, and are placed above the gates to warn all others, and dumbly tell of the prowess of "our lord." Many are loaded with chains and sent to rot in the dungeons of the capitals, while more than double the amount of tribute due is levied. A new governor and new

* These are "military missions" from France, Spain, and Italy, and two private English officers employed as drill-instructors.

assistants are appointed, and the army retires rich from a wasted country—"eaten up," as the native expression goes. Such are Moorish tax-gatherings.

I have already remarked how different the Berbers are from the Arabs, and I think this is shown in no way more than by their treatment of their women. Instead of that enforced seclusion and concealment of the features to which the followers of Islam elsewhere doom them, in these mountain homes they enjoy almost as perfect liberty as their sisters in Europe. I have been greatly struck with their intelligence and generally superior appearance to such Arab women as I have by chance been able to see. Once, when supping with the son of a powerful governor from above Fez, his mother, wife, and wife's sister sat composedly to eat with us, which could never have occurred in the dwelling of a Moor. No attempt at covering their faces was made, though male attendants were present at times, but the little daughter shrieked at the sight of a Nazarene. The grandmother, a fine buxom dame, could read and write—an astonishing accomplishment for a Moor-

A TANGIER MARKET.

ish woman—and she could converse better than many men who would in this country pass for educated.

The men are a hardy, sturdy race, wiry and lithe, inured to toil and cold; fonder far of the gun and sword than of the ploughshare, and steady riders of an equally wiry race of mountain ponies. Those who have always resided at home have a poor idea of Europeans, and will not allow them to enter their territories if they can help it. Only those who are in subjection to the Sultan permit them to do so freely. Their dwellings are of stone and mud, often of two floors, flat-topped, with rugged projecting eaves, the roofs being made of poles covered with the same material as the walls, stamped and smoothed. These houses are seldom whitewashed, and present a most ruinous appearance. Their ovens are domes about three feet or less in height outside; they are heated by a fire inside, then emptied, and the bread put in. Similar ovens are employed in camp to bake for the court. The Berber dress has either borrowed from or lent much to the Moor, but a few articles stamp them wherever worn. These are a large black hooded cloak of goat's-hair, impervious to rain, made of one piece, with no armholes. At the point of the cowl hangs a black tassel, and right across the back, about the level of the knees, runs an assegai-shaped patch of yellow, often with a centre of red. It has been opined that this remarkable feature represents the All-seeing Eye, so often used as a charm, but from the scanty information I could gather from the people themselves, I believe that they have lost sight of the original idea, though some have told me that variations in the pattern mark clan distinctions. I have ridden—when in the disguise of a native—for days together in one of these cloaks, during pelting rain, which never penetrated it. In more remote districts, seldom visited by Europeans, the garments are ruder far, entirely of undyed wool, and unsewn—mere blankets with slits cut in the centre for the head. There is, however, in every respect, a great difference between the various districts. The turban is little used by these people, skull-caps being preferred, while their red cloth gun-cases are commonly used turbanwise, and often a camel's-hair cord is deemed sufficient protection for the head.

Only on the plains are the Arabs to be found, but here their tents are scattered in every direction. From the Atlantic to the Atlas, from Tangier to Mogador, and then away through the fertile province of Soos, one of the chief features of Morocco is the series of wide alluvial treeless plains, often apparently as flat as a table, but here and there cut up by winding rivers and crossed by low ridges. The fertility of these districts is remarkable, but owing to the misgovernment of the country, which renders native property so insecure, only a small portion is cultivated. It is on the untilled slopes which border these plains that the Arab encampments are to be found—circles or ovals of low, goat-hair tents, each covering a large area in proportion to its height. As the traveller approaches them he is greeted by a chorus of barking, which soon brings out some swarthy form—in the daytime usually that of a woman, for the men will be away with the flocks or cattle, ploughing, sowing, or reaping. Unless they are travelling or fighting, here ends the chapter of their occupations. In the evenings they stuff themselves to repletion, if they can afford it, with a wholesome dish of prepared barley or wheat meal, seldom accompanied with meat; then, after a gossip round the crackling fire, or, on state occasions, three cups of syrupy green tea apiece, they roll themselves up in their long blankets and sleep on the ground. The first blush of dawn sees them stirring, and soon all is life and excitement. The men go off to their various labors, as do many of the stronger women, while the remainder attend to their scanty household duties, later on basking in the sun. But the moment the stranger arrives the scene changes, and the incessant din of dogs, hags, and babies commences, to which the visitor is doomed till late at night, with the addition then of neighs and brays. Outside the circle of tents is a ring of thorny bushes, cut and piled in such a manner that their interwoven branches prove an effective barrier, and at night the only space left free for an entrance is closed in the same manner. The roofs only of the tents are of cloth; the sides, about three feet high, are formed of bundles of thistles stood on end, or of any brushwood the locality affords. Inside, the leaves of the palmetto serve for plush, being supplemented by a mat or two. The furniture consists perhaps of a rude hand-loom, a hand-mill, and three

OUTSIDE THE WALLS OF FEZ.

stones in a hole for a fireplace. Around the sides are tethered donkeys or calves, while fowls and dogs have the run of the establishment. Dirt is the prevailing feature.

It never seemed to me that these poor folk enjoyed life, but rather that they took things sadly. How could it be otherwise? No security of life and property tempts them to make a show of wealth; on the contrary, they bury what little they may save, if any, and lead lives of misery, for fear of tempting the authorities. Their work is hard; their comforts are few. The wild wind howls through their humble dwellings, and the rain splashes in at the door. In sickness, for lack of medical skill, they lie and perish. In health, their only pleasures are animal. Their women, once they are past the prime of life, which means soon after thirty with this desert race, go unveiled, and work often harder than the men, carrying burdens, binding sheaves, or even perhaps helping a donkey to haul a plough. Female features are never so jealously guarded here as in towns. Yet these are a jolly, simple, good-natured folk. Often have I spent a merry evening round the fire with them, squatted on a bit of matting, telling of the wonders of "That Country"—the name which alternates in their vocabulary with "Nazarene Country" as descriptive of all the world but Morocco and such portions of North Africa or Arabia as they may have heard of. Many an honest laugh have we enjoyed over their wordy tales, or perchance some witty sally, but in my heart I have pitied these poor down-trodden people in their ignorance and want. Home they have not. When the pasture in Shechem is short, they remove to Dothan; next month they may be somewhere else. But they are always ready to share their scanty portion with the wayfarer, wherever they are.

Though there are other dwellers in the country, who perforce must go unmentioned in so brief a sketch, we must seek the mingled people we call Moors in the cities they have founded—at the busy mart and in the seat of office. Cloaked and turbaned, they glide about in slippered feet, the women shod in red, the men in bright yellow. But for their exceedingly substantial build, the Moorish women in the street might pass for ghosts, for their costume is, with this one exception, white. A long and heavy blanket of coarse homespun effectually conceals every feature but the eyes, which are touched up with antimony on the lids, and, as a rule, are sufficiently expressive. Sometimes a wide-brimmed straw hat, its edges supported by adjustable cords from the crown, is jauntily clapped on; but here ends the plate of Moorish out-door fashions. In-doors all is color, light, and glitter. Where cash is plentiful nothing is spared to make the home a paradise—in Muslim eyes; yet all is forbidden to male outsiders. But in matters of color and flowing robes the men are not far behind, and they make up abroad for any lack at home. I think no garment is more artistic and no drapery more graceful than that in which the wealthy Moor takes his daily airing, either on foot or muleback.

Beneath a gauzelike woollen toga—relic of ancient art—glimpses of luscious hues are caught—crimson and purple, deep greens and "afternoon-sun color,"* salmons and pale clear blues. A dark blue cloak, when it is cold, negligently but gracefully thrown across the shoulders, or a blue-green prayer-carpet folded beneath the arm, helps to set off the whole.

Side by side with this picture of ease and comfort, cheek by jowl, wanders the tattered negro whose eyes have been put out—a punishment now very rare. His sightless orbs follow appealingly the guidance of a little child, as one after another of the passers-by is importuned in vain. "May God bring it"—the alms —is a refusal far more conclusive than an excuse or negative, and the appeal is made to another. The narrow winding streets, ill-paved, and ofttimes ankle-deep in mud, are crowded with men and beasts; the ever-changing scene is a kaleidoscope of Eastern fancy: Ali Baba and the Forty Thieves, Bluebeard, Aladdin, and the Grand Vizier all pass the corner in succession. Donkeys bearing loaded panniers of garden produce or rubbish are followed by stately officials on barrel-bodied mules, and in the coast towns a good sprinkling of European costumes, worn by foreigners and Jews, add fresh variety.

* The native name for a rich orange.

Chez lui our friend of the flowing garments is a king, with slaves to wait upon him, wives to obey him, and servants to fear his wrath. His every-day reception-room is the lobby of his stables, where he sits behind the door in rather shabby garments attending to business matters, unless he is a merchant or shopkeeper, when his store serves as office instead. Those whom he wishes to honor are asked inside the house, after the order has been shouted to his women folk to "make a road." Pausing to allow this to be accomplished, a scuffle of feet is heard, and a moment after the deserted court is entered, with no reminder of its recent occupants but the swing of the curtain in the doorway, where a dainty finger holds it back to feed inherent curiosity. Dinner may then be served, or the traditional three glasses of tea, but only a slave lass or two will be seen, as they silently do the serving, after respectfully kissing the hands of the guests. No, the Moor has no home life—no family unity—not half so much as the Arab or Berber in tent or hut. It is seldom that the wife eats with the husband, and the children with the father never. Lust reigns supreme in the lives of both sexes, and no other relationships than it allows between them are dreamed of. Morals in practice they have none, though their theories are perfect enough to deceive many into thinking

A HIGH-CLASS MOORISH HOUSE.

Islam a model system. The grand idea of their lives is to live like beasts in this world, and to trust to Mohammed and good deeds to secure their admission to a hereafter where all sin shall be lawful.

Of intellectual pleasures, occupations which should raise their social tone and feed the mind, the Moors know nothing. What study some few of them do is so bewildering in its complexity and uselessness that they gain little by it, and reading for information's sake is rare. Their evenings thus hang heavily, and if not passed in a state of lethargy from overeating, idle gossip is their only amusement. Chess and draughts are sometimes seen, but are not general. In business the Moor is keen and parsimonious, though, as results show, a poor match for the sons of Israel, who swarm on every hand. At first suspicious, if well treated he treats well, and becomes a steady if perhaps self-seeking friend.

But list! what is that weird, low sound which strikes upon our ear and interrupts our musings? It is the call to prayer. For the fifth time to-day that cry is sounding—a warning to the faithful that the hour for evening devotions has come. See! yonder Moor has heard it too, and is already spreading his felt cloth on the ground for the performance of his nightly orisons. Standing Meccawards and bowing to the ground, he goes through the set of forms known throughout the Mohammedan world. The majority satisfy their consciences by working off the whole five sets at once. But that cry! I hear it still; as one voice fails, another carries on the strain, in ever-varying cadence, as each repeats it to the four quarters of the heavens.

It was yet early in the morning when the first cry burst upon the stilly air; the sun had not then risen o'er the hill-tops, nor had his first soft rays dispelled the shadows of the night. Only the rustling of the wind was heard as it died

ARAB BOY AND GIRL, TOWN.
After a photograph by G. W. Wilson.

among the tree-tops—that wind which was a gale last night. The hurried tread of the night guard going on his last—perhaps his only—round before his return home, had awakened me from my dreaming slumbers, and I was just about to doze away into that sweetest of sleeps, the morning nap, when that distant cry broke forth. Pitched in a high clear key, the Muslim confession of faith was heard: "La iláha il' Al - lah ; wa Mohammed er-rasool Al-l-a-h!" Could ever bell send thrill like that? I wot not.

A Moorish "college" is a simple affair —no seats; no desks; a few books. For beginners, boards about the size of foolscap, whitened on both sides with clay, take the place of book, paper, and slate. On these the various lessons, from the alphabet to the Koran, are plainly written in large black letters. A switch or two, a sand-box in lieu of blotter, and a book or two complete the paraphernalia. The dominie squats on the ground, tailor fashion, as do his pupils before him. They, from ten to thirty in number, imitate him as he repeats the lesson in a sonorous singsong voice, accompanying the words by a rocking to and fro, which sometimes enables them to keep time. A sharp application of the switch to bare pate or shoulder is wonderfully effective in recalling wandering attention, and really lazy boys are speedily expelled. Girls, as a rule, get no schooling at all.

On the admission of a pupil the parents pay some small sum, varying according to their means; and every Wednesday, which is a half-holiday, a payment is made of from half a cent to five cents. New moons and feast-days are made occasions for the giving of larger sums, as are also holidays, which last ten days in the case of the greater festivals. Thursdays are whole holidays, and no work is done on Friday mornings, that day being the Mohammedan Sabbath, or at least "meeting-day," as it is called.

After learning the letters and figures, the youngsters set about committing the Koran to memory. When the first chapter is mastered—the one which with them corresponds to the "Pater Noster" of Christendom—it is customary for them to be paraded round the town on horseback with ear-splitting music, and sometimes charitably disposed persons make small presents to the young students by way of encouragement. After the first chapter the last is learned, then the last but one, and so on backwards to the second, as, with the exception of the first, the longest chapters are at the beginning.

Though reading and a little writing are taught at the same time, all the scholars do not arrive at the pitch of perfection necessary to indite a respectable letter, so that there is plenty of employment for the numerous scribes and notaries who make a profession of this art. These sit in a little box-shop, with their appliances before them—reed pens, ink, paper, and sand, with a ruling-board with strings across at regular intervals, on which the paper to be lined is pressed. They usually possess also a knife and scissors, with a

case to hold them all. In writing, they place the paper on the left knee, or upon a pad or book in the left hand. The plebs who cannot read or write, and all who wish to make declarations or arguments, appear with their statements before two of these—there are usually four in a shop —and after it has been written out and read over to the deponent, it is signed by two of the notaries. Such a document is the only one recognized by Moorish law. Individual signatures, except of high officials, are worthless, and even then the signature of the local judge (kadi) is necessary to legalize the others. These signatures are nicknamed by the natives "beetles," being absolutely undecipherable scrawls, crossed and recrossed till they are almost a blot. Naturally this system, like so many others in Morocco, is open to serious abuses, as notaries often make more by twisting a statement to suit a client behind the scenes than ever a simple fee could amount to.

Even to the visitor unacquainted with the language the sight of the Arab bard and his quaint attentive audience on some erstwhile bustling market, towards the close of the afternoon, is a source of never-failing attraction, and full of interest to the student of human nature. After a long trudge from their homes, and a weary haggling over the most worthless of "coppers" during the heat of the day, the poor folk are all the better for the quiet resting-time, with something to distract their minds, and fill them with thoughts for the homeward way and the week to come. Here have been fanned and fed all the great religious and political movements which have from time to time convulsed the empire, and here the pulse of the country throbs. In the cities men lead a different life, and though their inhabitants enjoy tales as much as anybody, it is on these market-places that the wandering troubadour gathers his largest crowds.

Like public performers everywhere, a story-teller of note always goes about accompanied by regular assistants, who act as summoners to his entertainments and chorus to his songs. They usually consist of a player on the native banjo, another who keeps time on a tambourine, and a third who beats a kind of earthenware one-sided drum with his fingers. Less pretentious "professors" are content with the manipulation of a tambourine or

THE SULTAN ON HIS WAY TO PRAYERS AT THE MOSQUE.

two-stringed banjo for themselves, and to many this style has a peculiar charm of its own. Each pause, however slight, is marked by two or three beats on the tightly stretched string, or twangs with a palmetto-leaf plectrum, loud or soft, according to the subject of the discourse at that point. The dress of this .class, the one most frequently met with, is usually of the plainest if not of the scantiest: a tattered brown jelláb (a hooded round woollen cloak), and a camel's-hair cord round the wrinkled and shaven skull, are the garments which strike the eye. Waving bare arms and sinewy legs, with a wild, keen featured face lit up by flashing eyes, complete the picture.

This is the man of whom to learn of love and fighting, fair women and hair-

MOSQUE TOWER OF A DESERTED TOWN.

breadth escapes, the whole on the model of the *Thousand and One Nights*, of which versions more or less recognizable may now and again be heard from his lips. Commencing with plenty of tam-

bourine and a few suggestive hints of what is to follow, he gathers around him a motley audience, the first-comers squatting in a circle, and later arrivals standing behind. Gradually their excitement is aroused, and as their interest grows, the realistic semi-acting of the performer rivets every eye upon him. Suddenly his wild gesticulations cease at the most entrancing point. One step more for liberty, one blow, and the charming prize would be in the possession of her adorer. Now is the time to "cash up." With a pious reference to "our lord Mohammed — the prayers of God be on him, and peace!"— and an invocation of the local saint, an appeal is made to the pockets of the faithful, "for the sake of Mûlàï Âbd el Káder" —our lord Slave-of-the-Able. Aroused from a trance, the eager listeners instinctively commence to feel in their pockets for the balance after the day's bargaining. One by one throws down his hard-earned coppers—one or two—and turns away with a long-drawn breath to untether his beasts and begin the journey home.

One of the features of Moorish society, whether Arab or Berber, or of the mixed races of the town, is the numerous class of individuals who have succeeded in establishing a reputation for sanctity. This is far larger than is generally imagined, for their calling is, on the whole, a profitable one, and well suited to indolent natures. To be considered a saint it is sufficient either to be or to act as a madman, whose thoughts are believed to be so much occupied with heavenly matters that mundane interests have no hold upon him. Of course this quaint fancy opens a wide door for imposture, and as it would be impious to interfere with such worthies unless they were actually dangerous to society, the most remarkable performances are tolerated. I have myself met a naked man in the streets of Fez, "remarkably" holy in the popular mind. Once when dining with the governor of an important place, a really loathsome personage entered without the slightest ceremony, unopposed by the servants, and squatted at the side of the dish into which we two were plunging our hands. Needless to say that when his fist went in, ours came out to await the next course, while on the removal of the dish our visitor finished it and departed. He had spoken no word beyond the customary greetings. As I saw with relief the last of his rags and tatters at the door, I asked what it all meant. "He is a saint," was the curt but conclusive reply.

The majority of these individuals claim hereditary sanctity, many tracing back their pedigree to Mohammed himself, though of the thousands who for this reason are dubbed nobles (shereefs) only a small proportion are actually what one may call saints. The tombs of the original saints of a line are jealously guarded by their heirs, who make a good thing out of the offerings of those who visit them as pilgrims. Every sort of supernatural power for assisting mortal man in his troubles is ascribed to these "seyyids," as they are called, and no supplicant comes to their shrines empty-handed. One has some bodily infirmity, and another believes himself bewitched. One wants to find hidden treasure, and another yearns for offspring. There are stones and old guns on which would-be mothers sit for hours in faith. One seeks a husband and another a divorce. Some saints are patrons of particular callings, and the medicinal value of certain hot mineral springs is ascribed to the workings of defunct celebrities of this stamp belowground. Their shrines are sanctuaries, including often whole streets in their vicinity, where evil-doers of every sort are safe from the clutches of the law. At the mosque of Mulai Edrees at Fez hang boards which may be carried away by refugees in search of pardon or composition, which shall entitle them for a limited time to equal protection to that afforded by the limits of the shrine itself. These sanctuaries are forbidden to all but Muslims, under pain of death or "resignation" to the teachings of Mohammed. However, success in disguise in other parts of the country led me to explore some of the holiest in Fez and elsewhere, as the only one or two Europeans who had ventured inside had left such scanty descriptions. On an occasion I went through the motions of evening prayers in the mosque referred to, perspiring freely, though cool outwardly, and busy with mental notes.

The ends of the streets approaching the sanctuary of Mulai Edrees II. at Fez are crossed by chains or bars to keep out four-footed animals and warn off Jews

A MOORISH SCHOOL-BOY.

or Christians. They are the only decently paved ones in the whole of the metropolis, and the shops in them, chiefly devoted to the sale of native candles, relics, and sweetmeats, are better than usual. One end of the street, past the chief door, is prettily arched in colored plaster, and the door itself is very elegant in pink and gold carving, the design including the Muslim creed. Inside is first a carpeted room surrounded by mattresses, like an ordinary native sitting-room, with the walls plain whitewashed, a sort of antechamber. Beyond this is another similar apartment, and then the tomb in the third room, but the direct way is barred, and a side door is used. The tomb resembles a large chest of casket shape, about four feet high, covered with rich gold-embroidered cloth. Round the edge were eighteen gilt censers, and round the top fourteen more, with a tall one in the centre, all reputed to be gold. The walls were covered with gold-braided

CHIEF MOSQUE OF TANGIER.

into paradise is assured. The body of the mosque attached to this tomb is very pretty, being completely ornamented with the local cut tiles, as used in the Alhambra. The main tint is blue, which, intermingled with white, looks very cool and inviting.

The mosque of the Karueein, reputed to be the largest in Africa, is close by, but it is not grand. Only one court, reminding one of that of the Lions at Granada, is at all beautiful. As near as I could calculate, the number of pillars is about 416, but they are not marble, as often erroneously stated, with the exception of twenty-eight in the court mentioned. I visited it several times, and was greatly struck with the appearance of those many aisles, divided by the square matting-covered pillars and whitewashed horseshoe arches, but it comes nowhere near the mosque of Cordova for beauty.

Another class of forbidden buildings my curiosity has tempted me into was the steam baths, but I am thoroughly disgusted with them, they are so poor and dirty, with few conveniences. Being very cheap, they are patronized by every class, men at one hour, women at another.

One section of the inhabitants of Morocco—by no means the least important—has still to be glanced at: these are the ubiquitous persecuted and persecuting Jews. Everywhere that money changes hands and there is business to be done they are to be found. In the towns, and among the thatched huts of the plains, even in the Berber villages on the slopes of the Atlas, they have their colonies. With the exception of a few of the ports where European rule in past centuries has destroyed the boundaries, they are obliged to live in their own quarters, and in most instances are only permitted to cross the town barefooted and on foot, never to ride a horse. In the Atlas they live, as it were, in separate villages adjoining or close to those belonging to the Berbers, and sometimes even larger than they. Always clad in black or dark-colored cloaks, with hideous black skull-caps or blue cotton handkerchiefs with white spots on their heads, they are conspicuous everywhere. They address the Moors with a villanous cringing look, which makes the sons of Ishmael savage,

hangings, and the ceiling exquisitely carved and painted in arabesque designs. There were very many lanterns and gilt and glass chandeliers suspended from the roof, the principal one, a monster, being in the centre. There were about eighty gilt glass lamps, and thirty-five plain ones, like huge tumblers of oil with floating wicks. There was one Moorish lantern about eight feet high, and a large gilt candlestick with eighteen lights, some six feet high. Among other ornaments were two large "grandfather" clocks, and three large gilt round ones, some bearing London makers' names. At the left end of the sarcophagus, looking from the mosque, is a richly ornamented alms-chest. In front of the tomb is the pulpit of the imam, who thus, while facing Mecca, also faces the shrine. It is believed that Gabriel is wont to visit this holy spot from time to time in human garb, and that if any visitor has had the good luck to touch the hem of his garment, his entry

for they know it is only feigned. The Moors treat the Jews like dogs, and cordial hatred exists on both sides. So they live, together yet divided; the Jew indispensable but despised, bullied but thriving. He only wins at law when richer than his opponent; of justice there is scant pretence. He dares not lift his hand against a Moor, however illtreated, but he has his revenge by sucking his life's blood by means of usury. Showed no mercy, he shows none, and once in his clutches, the Moor is fortunate to escape with his life.

The whole round of the system is this: Government officials, only nominally paid, prey each upon the one below him, till the local sheiks recoup themselves by preying on the people. A sudden demand for cash is made upon an official or private individual; some trumpery charge is brought up against him, and he has the alternative of paying or being thrust into a dungeon in irons, and being stripped of his possessions. Recourse is had to the Jewish money-lender—Europeans are also employed in this trade—and a notarial document is drawn up stating that he has received double the amount actually lent to him, the price in advance of such and such nature produced to be delivered in six months' time or the cash returned. If this is not then forth-coming, he must either give a new bond for double the sum, or fall again into the hands of his superior. This goes on till the debt is as much as he is worth, when he goes to prison after all, has his property seized, and maybe dies there. This picture is one of every day in Morocco.

I am thankful to say that the influence of European Jews is making itself felt in the chief towns through excellent schools supported from London and Paris, which are turning out quite another class of highly respectable citizens. While the Moors fear the advancing tide of civilization, the town Jews court it, and in them centres one of the chief prospects of the country's welfare.

The greatest obstacle to progress in Morocco is the blind prejudice of ignorance. It is hard for them to realize that their presumed hereditary foes can wish them well, and it is suspicion rather than hostility which induces them to crawl within their shell and desire to be left alone. Too often are they shown by subsequent events what good ground they have had for suspicion. It is a pleasure for me to be able to state that during all my intercourse with them I have never received the least insult, but have been well repaid in my own coin. What more is to be expected?

GROUP OF MOUNTAIN JEWS.

BEHIND THE PINK WALLS OF THE FORBIDDEN CITY OF PEKING

IN one of those pregnant sentences with which Lord Salisbury occasionally relieves the decorous tedium of debates in the gilded chamber of the House of Lords at Westminster, the British Prime Minister, replying to the leader of the Opposition on the China question, indicated the great unknown quantity which baffles every calculation of Western diplomacy at Peking. "If the noble lord," he remarked, with an undisguised touch of irony, "wants to know what is the destiny impending over China, I will ask him to reveal to me what is going on in a certain palace in Peking, and perhaps in a certain island within that palace. The future of China does not lie in our hands. It lies in the hands of the governing power of China."

Breached and battered like the Great Wall which the rulers of China erected hundreds of years ago against the forays of Central-Asian hordes, the adamantine wall of self-isolation which sheltered them for centuries against all contact with "the outer barbarians" has given way in every direction before the aggressive impact of Western energy. Not only have the Chinese within the last half-century tasted the bitterness of defeat in three foreign wars, but they have had to witness in sullen helplessness the gradual invasion of their country by all those subtle forces of modern civilization which are the irresistible forerunners of foreign ascendency and dominion wherever they come in contact either with absolute barbarism, as in Africa, or with effete mediævalism, as in Asia. The foreign locomotive shrieks at the gates of Peking; foreign steamers plough their way for a thousand miles up the Yang-tse; foreign engineers are busy sinking shafts into the bowels of the earth, without the slightest compunction for the mysterious *Fung-shui* whom their operations may disturb; gigantic factories equipped with all the appliances of modern industry are springing up in the foreign settlements, each of which forms an *imperium in*

imperio; the foreign missionary and the foreign merchant enforce with increasing energy their treaty rights to circulate their spiritual and their material wares far away in the interior of the country; the very revenues of the state are being mortgaged one after another to foreign creditors, and every foreign loan means a tightening of foreign control over some new branch of the administration; the whole territory of the empire is being carved out into foreign "spheres of influence" and "spheres of interest," and its chief strategic positions "leased" to foreign powers under a new diplomatic formula which barely pretends to disguise the reality of annexation; the Tsung-li-Yamen serves chiefly as a buffer to receive and deaden the shock of diplomatic conflicts between the foreign powers within the gates of Peking; even the Emperor and his masterful guardian, the Empress Dowager, have been fain to receive in public audience, and on a footing of outward equality, foreign princes and ambassadors who but a few years ago were only grudgingly admitted into the hall of imperial tributaries in the outer precincts of the Forbidden City.

Yet of the mysterious forces generated within the pink walls of the Forbidden City, of the "governing power" to which Lord Salisbury referred, and which still holds, to some extent at least, in its hands the future of China, the outside world is as profoundly ignorant to-day as it was five or fifty or five hundred years ago. Weather-beaten and battered by storms from within and from without, the huge, unwieldy, disjointed empire still lives and moves, and has a being of its own, and from the hidden recesses of the imperial palace there still flows to the remotest Yamens of far-away provinces a steady, if attenuated, tide of enduring vitality. But who among foreigners has ever succeeded in tracing that tide back to its true fountain-head?

The traveller can pass nowadays unmolested through any one of the sixteen

THE PRESENT EMPEROR, KWANG SHU, AS A CHILD.

gateways which at regular intervals pierce the long line of grim gray walls that conceal behind their counterfeit battlements the gaudy splendor and unspeakable squalor of Peking. He can wander at his leisure over the stretches of waste sand and cultivated fields which within the walled enclosure of that huge parallelogram mark the gradual decay of its former grandeur and the shrinkage of its population; or he can thread his way through the crowded streets of the few populous quarters in which the life of the capital is now concentrated, and watch the bewildering flow of ceaseless traffic surging in and out of the Chun-man Gate under the inner wall which divides the Chinese from the Tartar city. If he follow the stream of swift Sedan chairs, in which ladies of rank and mandarins of high degree are borne behind closely drawn curtains by relays of panting, shouting bearers, he will find himself outside yet another walled quadrangle, about seven miles in circuit. Into this

enclosure, again, he can penetrate unhindered, for though it is called the *Huang-cheng*, the Imperial City, and though it contains all the public offices and the residences of the highest officials, and of many of the princes of the blood and other imperial clansmen, it is as it were but the outer court of the Emperor's own residence. Here, just as in all the other quarters of the capital, everything—to borrow Lord Curzon's suggestive description—is "public and indecent." But in the heart of this enclosure there rises a last and innermost enclosure where "everything is clandestine, veiled, and sealed." It is the *Hsu-ching-cheng*, the Pink Forbidden City, the hidden sanctuary into which none but the privileged few can penetrate, and then only at rare and stated intervals. Shortly after midnight the gates are opened every night to admit the highest officials and dignitaries of the state, who, prostrate before the throne, report in the sacred presence on the progress of affairs in their respective departments, and, having taken the imperial commands, leave the palace again before sunrise. Very rarely in the earlier years of foreign intercourse, but of late more frequently, the representatives of the powers at Peking are hustled in through the serried ranks of court eunuchs and imperial clansmen to deliver formal messages of courtesy to the Son of Heaven in person in one of the outlying halls of the palace. Nor has the Emperor himself ever left the precincts of the Forbidden City, except to offer up on the great festival days the customary sacrifices at the imperial temples, or to pay ceremonial visits to the Dowager Empress at her own court in the Summer Palace. Not a single male adult of whatsoever rank or age is allowed to reside in this sacred city of yellow-tiled palaces and pleasure-gardens where the Emperor dwells alone, *kwa-jin*, "the one man" amongst a horde of some ten thousand women and eunuchs. Manifold are the titles used in addressing the imperial person — *Tien-hwang*, "celestial august one"; *Shing-ti*, "sacred sovereign"; *Wan-sui-yeh*, "sire of ten thousand years"; etc., etc.; but the truest of them all, though perhaps not in the sense originally contemplated by his ancestors, is the one by which the Emperor designates himself—*Kwa-kuin*, "the solitary prince." For what prince more solitary than the unhappy youth who, still nominally reigning on the dragon throne, the lord of life and death over 400,000,000 souls, yet cannot call his very soul his own? Not for the first time in Chinese history there looms behind the throne one of those mysterious, masterful types of Asiatic womanhood who, bursting asunder, by the subtle craft of their uncultured intellect and by the fierceness of their passions, all the trammels which Oriental custom and tradition impose upon their sex, get such a grip of power, when they have once been fortunate enough to seize it, as male rulers seldom acquire even in the most autocratic states.

Of the tortuous and blood-stained paths by which the Dowager Empress has reached her present position of unchallenged supremacy we cannot track the whole intricate course. Only the distant echo of the tragedies enacted behind that girdle of pink walls ever reaches the outer world. But we can mark at least the most important stages of her strange career.

When the Emperor Hsien Fung, who had fled from Peking in 1860 at the approach of the Anglo-French expedition, died in the following year at Jehol, he was succeeded by a son barely six years old, borne to him by one of his concubines. Worn out by debauchery, and surrounded by greedy courtiers whose only thought was to retain for themselves the control of the empire, Hsien Fung had been induced on his death-bed to appoint from amongst his favorites a council of eight, which was to form a Board of Regency during his son's minority. But Hsien Fung's brother, Prince Kung, a man of character and ability, who had been brought into close contact with foreigners during the recent peace negotiations, had measured the new dangers which threatened the empire from without, and he clearly foresaw the disastrous consequences which would ensue if the supreme power fell permanently into the hands of a knot of profligate and reactionary officials. He entered into communication with Hsien Fung's widow, and in accordance with his recommendations she succeeded in escaping from Jehol with the young Emperor and his mother. By a bold *coup de main* the whole Board of Regency, which had hastened to follow in pursuit of the fugitives to Peking, was summarily arrested, and the two leading members, both imperial princes, were merely allowed to commit suicide as an alternative to being executed, together with their less-favored colleagues, in the public market-place. The young Emperor was duly proclaimed under the title of Tung Chi and the Regency was committed during his minority to the widow of the defunct Emperor, conjointly with the mother of the reigning one. The senior Regent, who, as the principal wife of Hsien Fung, was already the Empress Tsu An, was styled the Dowager Empress and Empress of the Eastern Palace. The junior Regent, though only an imperial concubine, was raised, as mother of the Emperor, to the rank of Empress, and under the name of Empress Tsu Tsi was styled the Empress Mother and Empress of the Western Palace. The moving spirit in this bold and, on the whole, justifiable *coup d'état* was unquestionably Prince Kung, but though the part played in it by the two Empresses, and especially by the Empress Tsu Tsi, was doubtless rather passive than active, the lesson which it taught was at any rate not lost

THE EMPRESS MOTHER TSU TSI, NOW EMPRESS DOWAGER, AFTER A CHINESE PORTRAIT.

THE EMPEROR KWANG SHU AT FOURTEEN.

upon the latter. For it is by similar methods she has succeeded in retaining for forty years, with brief intermissions, the increasing power which accident then placed in her resolute hands.

The Chinese artist whose portrait of her we reproduce would presumably in any case have been too much of a courtier not to lend his imperial mistress every charm demanded by the æsthetic canons of Chinese art, but there seems to be very little doubt that, according to Chinese standards, the Empress Tsu Tsi had considerable personal beauty, and that, like Catherine the Great, to whom she has sometimes been rather superficially compared, she never hesitated in the earlier stages of her career to make her beauty subserve her ambition, nor in its later stages to make the ambition of her favorites minister to the satisfaction of her own passions. Whilst cautiously strengthening and extending her influence as co-Regent, she was sufficiently — prudent during her first Regency never to excite unduly the jealousy of her senior partner. In 1872 the Emperor Tung Chi was solemnly married to Ah Lu-Teh, a Manchu lady, who forthwith assumed the rank of Empress, and in 1873 the two Regents formally handed over to the Emperor the reins of power. Their retirement, however, was destined to be of short duration. In the following year rumors got abroad that his Majesty's health was causing great anxiety, and on the 18th of December, 1874, an edict was published requesting the Dowager Empresses to resume control of the government. Within four weeks from that date Tung Chi "ascended upon the dragon to be a guest on high." His widow was left pregnant, but though, had a male child been born, Tung Chi's posthumous son would have been the rightful heir to the empire, the Dowagers determined not to await the event. They hastened, on the contrary, to proclaim a successor to the throne, and to depart, in doing so, not only from the traditions of the dynasty, but from the most sacred principles of the one religious rite cherished by the whole nation, *viz.*, the rite of ancestral worship. To the due performance of that necessary rite, equally incumbent upon the highest and the lowest, upon the richest and the poorest, it is deemed absolutely necessary that the heir should belong to a younger generation than the deceased. In defiance of this rule, the Dowager Empresses selected a son of Prince Chun, brother to the Emperor Hsien Fung, and proclaimed him Emperor under the title of Kwang Shu, or *Illustrious Succession*. The new Emperor was therefore first cousin to Tung Chi, and as such he was not, strictly speaking, qualified to perform the usual rites before his predecessor's tablets. Indeed, one of the censors committed suicide in the imperial presence as a public protest against this violation of the sacred law, on the first occasion when Kwang Shu visited for that purpose the temple of his ancestors. But though the Dowager Empresses and their advisers cannot possibly have overlooked the gravity of that drawback, there was another consideration which far outweighed it in their ambitious estimation. Kwang Shu was only three years old, and his accession meant the undisputed continuance of their regency for another long term of years. The Empress Ah Lu-Teh, it is true, was still with child, and unpleasant questions might have arisen had she lived to bear a son. But she sickened and died—of grief, it was

officially stated, for the death of her imperial spouse.

For the second time a successful palace *coup d'état* had placed in the Empress Tsu Tsi's hands a full share of the supreme power, and as years passed by during the second regency that share grew more and more predominant until, in 1881, at a moment when there was considerable friction between the two august ladies, the senior Regent was carried off by sudden illness, alleged to have been failure of the heart. How that failure exactly occurred the surviving Regent and her confidants could probably alone explain. From that moment, however, until the Japanese war the Empress Dowager, as Tsu Tsi was now styled *par excellence*, was supreme. Prince Kung still remained nominally at the head of affairs, but his influence was gradually being overshadowed by that of Li Hung-Chang, who, since his appointment as Viceroy of the home province of Chih-li in 1870, had risen steadily in the favor and confidence of Tsu Tsi. In July, 1884, the trouble which had arisen with France over the Tongking question gave the Dowager Empress a not unwelcome opportunity of dispensing with Prince Kung's services. The veteran statesman was dismissed from all his offices, and he retired for a period of eleven years to the tranquil obscurity of a Buddhist monastery. Li Hung-Chang, however, as a Chinaman, could not succeed to a position which under the Manchu dynasty had always been reserved for a Manchu. Again the Empress Dowager did not hesitate to depart from every precedent. Though a father cannot, according to Chinese custom, serve under his son, the reigning Emperor's father, Prince Chun, was appointed to serve under him as First Minister of the state. But the Empress Dowager's judgment would seem on this occasion to have been at fault. Prince Chun soon showed himself dissatisfied with the dummy part assigned to him, and as the young Emperor was growing in years, the authority his father acquired over him, and the use to which he put it, began to cause considerable alarm in the Empress Tsu Tsi's suspicious mind. The return of the Marquis Tseng from a prolonged sojourn in Europe, as minister in London, materially added to the anxieties of Li Hung-Chang and his imperial mistress, for his liberal ideas and large European experience were at once enlisted by Prince

Chun in support of a bold and relatively enlightened policy, which might not have permanently arrested the decay of the empire, but which would certainly have clipped the old Empress's claws.

Once more fortune came to the assistance of the Dowager Empress. In 1890 the Marquis Tseng died prematurely in the prime of life, and a few months later, in January, 1891, a not less opportune illness removed Prince Chun. Once more the old Empress's power was absolute, and though she nominally retired when the Emperor Kwang Shu attained his majority, it remained absolute until the disastrous war with Japan. That war was essentially the Empress's war. Though it was in some measure the outcome of Li Hung-Chang's short-sighted policy, which in Korea, as a few years previously in Tongking, had arrogantly maintained the rights of Chinese suzerainty whilst shirking its corresponding obligations, the old Viceroy was dimly conscious of the inadequacy of China's military and naval resources. At the last moment his mind misgave him, and he implored his mistress to avoid the hazard of a final rupture. But the Dowager Empress was bent upon chastising "the insolent pigmies," as the Japanese were disdainfully called. She was to celebrate in the forth-coming autumn, on a scale of unprecedented magnificence, the sixtieth anniversary of her birth. The whole empire had been laid under contribution to defray the costs of this celebration. Caravans loaded with the more or less spontaneous offerings of a grateful people were already on their way to Peking from the most remote provinces. A new road was being built from the Forbidden City to the Empress's own residence, near the Summer Palace, for the imperial procession to pass over, and every house and shop along the road, and the very city gates and walls, were being rejuvenated and decorated in view of the auspicious occasion. All that was needed to complete the apotheosis of her reign were the trophies of victory in a foreign war, and she was determined to have them. But for the first time fortune played her false. Instead of the intoxicating draught she had dreamed of, she had to drain almost to the very dregs the bitter cup of humiliation. As Hsien Fung's concubine she had fled with the court from Peking at the approach of the British and French armies in 1860, and now, after more than thirty years of power and pleasure and glory, she had once more to pack up and make preparations for flight at the approach of another despised invader. The conclusion of an armistice ultimately arrested the Japanese advance and averted the necessity of actual flight; but how bitter must have been the proud old woman's feelings when the imperial edict announcing the restoration of peace pleaded, in extenuation of the humiliating terms on which it had been obtained, the filial piety of the Emperor towards the Dowager Empress —"the venerable lady who, if hostilities were renewed and Peking threatened by the Japanese, would have had to seek refuge in flight, and have been exposed once more to the hardships of a long and arduous journey."

Her pride was wounded to the quick, her power shaken, her prestige impaired, and not alone her own power and prestige, but those of her devoted henchman Li Hung-Chang, who, as Warden of the Frontier and Guardian of the Capital, was, according to the Chinese theory of responsibility, primarily answerable for the disasters of the war. There were stormy scenes within the palace, and angry recriminations between the old Dowager and the young Emperor. Two of the censors audaciously memorialized the throne, imploring the sovereign to save the empire from the evils of "petticoat government," and the mild reproof their exhortations elicited showed them to have been not altogether unwelcome. There were signs of ferment in the provinces, signs of discord even amongst the highest officials of the capital, who were gradually ranging themselves into two opposite factions— the Emperor's party and the Empress's party. The Emperor himself was, however, still an almost unknown quantity. He was believed to be a youth endowed with considerable intelligence, of a kindly but somewhat melancholy disposition, whom a natural infirmity had saved from the gross temptations which beset an Oriental prince brought up in the corrupt atmosphere of the harem, impulsive and irresolute, and subject to violent fits of childish petulance. The first of the two photographs we have obtained from private sources in China represents the Emperor Kwang Shu as a child shortly after his accession to the throne; the second represents him about the period of his marriage, which took place in 1889, and, as was to have been expected, has produced no issue. The foreign diplomatists who when received in audience have been privileged to see the Son of Heaven seated on his throne, and even to exchange with him a few words of formal salutation, agree in describing his appearance as by no means unprepossessing. His small oval face and delicate features lack virility, and there is a hunted look, as it were, of fright and suffering in his dreamy eyes, but a bright and pleasant smile occasionally plays about the mobile lips. Prince Henry of Prussia was allowed last year to converse with him on a footing of greater intimacy than had hitherto been accorded to any foreigner. Kwang Shu's demeanor was at first painfully timid and embarrassed, but after he had overcome his nervousness he appeared genuinely to enjoy the novel experience, and his simplicity of manner and unaffected courtesy made a very favorable impression upon his distinguished visitor.

That the young Emperor realized in some measure the dangers which beset his empire on every side after the Japanese war had disclosed its hidden weakness there seems to be no reason to doubt, but few people believed that a youth reared in such an atmosphere of ignorance and corruption could possibly possess either the judgment or the strength of purpose necessary to cope with so desperate a situation. Moreover, however excellent might be his own intentions, where was he to look for enlightened advisers to put them into practical shape, or for patriotic officials to carry them into execution? Where was he to find, amongst the effete bureaucracy which lived by sucking dry the life-blood of the empire, either the moral or the material support required for enforcing, mainly at the expense of that very class, the vigorous and sweeping reforms which could alone arrest the fatal progress of decay? For a couple of years, indeed, the struggle between "the Emperor's party" and "the Empress's party," which was known to be going on with fluctuating vicissitudes in the councils of the capital, seemed to be little more than a petty squabble between rival factions over the flesh-pots of China. Then suddenly the outside world was aroused by a succession of almost revolutionary edicts, such as had never

before been issued under the Vermilion Pencil, to the fact that a new spirit was moving over the stagnant waters of the Chinese Empire.

While foreign observers had been for the most part absorbed in the conflict of international ambitions and the jealous competition of rival concession-hunters, which had turned Peking into the cockpit of modern diplomacy, the awakening of the younger generation amongst the gentry and officialdom of China had passed almost unnoticed. Under the sanction of a few honest and enlightened viceroys and high officials, and with the enthusiastic co-operation of a small but active body of young *literati*, there had suddenly grown up, especially in the great provincial centres of middle and southern China, a deliberate movement in favor of Western knowledge and Western ideas.

One of the most striking indications of this movement was a large and growing demand for the translations of foreign works and similar publications in the Chinese language, which "the Society for the Diffusion of Christian and General Knowledge amongst the Chinese" has done so much to popularize.* The sale of the society's works, for instance, rose from $817 in 1893 to $12,146 in 1897 and $18,457 in 1898, and the demand in these last years far outran the supply. The books issued by the society do not deal, it should be noted, exclusively or even chiefly with religious questions. On the contrary, the majority, and those especially which have enjoyed the widest circulation, deal with questions of history, of political economy, of social science and general education. Perhaps the most popular of the whole series have been Mackenzie's *XIXth Century, The Outline of History of Thirty-one Nations, The History of the Japanese War, The Relation of Education to National Progress, Reform Papers by Seventeen Foreigners,* and *The Review of the Times*—a monthly publication. In the course of three years (1895–8) the number of native newspapers, most of them edited and written by natives, rose from 19 to 70; and almost every one of these papers was a new wit-

* Those who may be induced to take a closer interest in the Chinese reform movement should consult the "Eleventh Annual Report" of that excellent society (with which the writer of this article has, however, no personal connection), published at the *North China Herald* office, Shanghai, October, 1898.

ness in the cause of progress and reform. At the same time considerable sums were subscribed by the Chinese themselves in various provinces for the opening of schools where their children could acquire Western learning and Western languages. Fifteen hundred young men of good family applied to enter the new Peking University, under Dr. Martin's presidency. Reform societies, often more or less openly sanctioned by the local authorities, were founded in the provincial centres, and rapidly spread into the more remote townships. The *literati* in many places began to court the society of foreigners, and to solicit the advice of missionaries and consuls as to the regeneration of the country. Perhaps the most striking incident in the whole movement, until it ultimately reached Peking and invaded the sacred precincts of the Forbidden City, was the rapid conversion of the great central province of Hoonan from a hot-bed of anti-foreign fanaticism into a centre of progressive activity.

It was not till early in 1898 that the reform wave beat up against the pink walls of the imperial residence, and its vivifying waters seemed for a time to have penetrated into its most sluggish recesses. At the beginning of last year it was reported that a few ardent reformers had been summoned by the Emperor to important offices in the capital in order to assist him with their advice in the reforms which he was already contemplating. A short time afterwards the Emperor sent for a large number of foreign books, which he studied under the guidance of his new advisers. Chief amongst these was a Cantonese, Kang Yu-Wei, about forty years of age, whose liberal ideas, coupled with a profound knowledge of the time-honored classics of Chinese literature, had earned for him the appellation of the "Modern Sage." He had been appointed a secretary of the Tsung-li-Yamen, and had gained the Emperor's ear by his courageous and enlightened patriotism no less than by his scholarly accomplishments. Of the rest of that small band of fervid reformers the most distinguished perhaps were Liang Chi-Chao, also a Cantonese, and a disciple of Kang Yu-Wei, and the first editor of the chief organ of the party, the *Chinese Progress*; Lin Shio, a native of Fo-kien, and a descendant of the notorious Commis-

sioner Lin of Canton fame; Su Chih-Ching, one of the readers at the Hanlin College at Peking, the *alma mater* of Chinese orthodoxy; and his son Su In-Chi, also a member of the Hanlin, and Chancellor of Education for the province of Hoonan. These and their fellow-workers did not probably all belong to quite the same school of thought, but they all strove for a common purpose, and behind them there undoubtedly stood some of the most powerful dignitaries of the state, such as Chang Yin-Huan, who was member both of the Grand Council and of the Tsung-li-Yamen, and who had represented his sovereign in London as special ambassador at Queen Victoria's jubilee in 1897; Chang Chi-Tung, the Viceroy of the middle Yang-tse, and the veteran rival of Li Hung-Chang; and Weng Tung-Ho, the Emperor's tutor, and the leader of the so-called "Emperor's party."

With generous impulsiveness the young sovereign responded to the eager teachings of his new councillors. Edict after edict appeared under the imperial sign-manual, heralding, as it seemed, a revolution as sweeping and as far-reaching as that which had transformed the face of Japan just thirty years before. One edict abolished the fossilized system of examination for the public service which for centuries had made the classical essay the supreme and only test of efficiency for every branch of the administration. Others established a university for the study of Western science in Peking, and a board of translation for the publication of books of Western learning in the vernacular. Another exhorted the young Manchus, *i. e.*, the scions of the ruling race, to travel abroad and study foreign languages and customs. Another decree emphasized the duty of tolerance towards Christianity and of protection for Christians, which had already been so often proclaimed in theory and evaded in practice. Another recommended the conversion of a number of temples into schools of Western education; and finally, not only was the abolition of all useless offices decreed both in the capital and in the provincial administrations, but an edict was reported to be in course of preparation doing away with the pig-tail, and substituting European for native dress. To the Western, and especially to the Anglo-Saxon mind, accustomed to the mature and orderly progress of evolution, such drastic measures may well have appeared dangerously crude and hasty. The case of Japan can of course be quoted in favor of the radical treatment advocated by Kang Yu-Wei and his associates, and they are believed to have enjoyed the benefit of the Marquis Ito's advice and experience, that distinguished statesman, who had himself played so conspicuous a part in the regeneration of Japan, having paid a prolonged visit to Peking just when the reform movement was at its height. But the Japanese reformers had had at their back not only a large and influential class imbued with traditions of patriotism and unselfishness which were almost unknown in China, but also a powerful reserve of physical force. The Chinese reformers had barely begun to leaven the ignorant and corrupt mass of the bureaucracy. Their revolutionary measures were bound not only to provoke the bitter hostility of all those who had a vested interest in ancient abuses, but also to alarm the old-fashioned prejudices of many of the more respectable conservatives. However much faith they had in the triumph of the moral forces they were setting in motion, they should at any rate have realized that fair play could only be secured for those moral forces by mustering in their defence a reserve of physical force not altogether disproportionate to that which would inevitably be arrayed against them. In this respect they unquestionably displayed the most culpable lack of forethought. It was not till the eleventh hour that they attempted to take the most elementary precautions for the protection of the imperial person, though they had made the Emperor the standard-bearer of their cause.

A catastrophe was in these circumstances inevitable. The old Empress had bided her time, resolute, vindictive, implacable, but cool-headed as ever. For three years she had played a waiting game, living patiently in semi-retirement, but from time to time showing her hand sufficiently to reassure her adherents and prove that she was still a power in the land, watching events and guiding them, but careful not to precipitate them. Now her opportunity had come. The predominance of the Chinese element in the Emperor's new *entourage* had aroused the arrogant spirit and racial hatred of the six thousand Manchu princes and imperial clansmen who live by levying blackmail on their celestial kinsman. The two thousand bloated eunuchs who batten on the corruption of the palace were in almost open revolt against the interlopers who talked, "not wisely, but too well," of sweeping out the Augean stables of the Forbidden City; the priests who trembled for their temples and their perquisites; the old-fashioned *literati* whose intellectual ascendency was bound up with the ancient methods of learning; the mandarins of every "button," whose greed of power means greed of wealth; the high officials who plunder whole provinces, and the Yamen runners who are content to steal a few copper "cash"—all were in a ferment of alarm and discontent, all watched eagerly for a sign from the Summer Palace, where the same angry passions were surging in the breast of a shrivelled and painted old woman. But it was not upon the like of them that she relied. She knew what the reformers had forgotten, that a brigade of soldiers, even of Chinese soldiers, would suffice to overawe the whole population of Peking, mandarins and eunuchs, priests and populace, and it was with the army she had laid her plans. What was to become of the army? What was, above all, to become of its officers when the reformers handed it over—and hand it over they would, as sure as fate—to the "foreign devils," to be trained and drilled and turned into food for cannon, according to "barbarian" custom? Under the Empress's orders a large force had been moved up to the neighborhood of Peking and carefully plied with promises and threats. When the reformers woke up too late to these dangers and sent out an emissary to parley with the general in command, the latter listened to their overtures just long enough to learn their secret intentions, and then hurried off to his imperial mistress to inform her that a scheme was on foot for seizing her sacred person and conveying her to a safe place of confinement in the interior of the country. Exactly what happened then has never yet become known. It is believed that the Emperor, warned of an imminent *coup de main*, attempted to escape from the palace, intending to seek refuge at one of the foreign legations, but was discovered and forcibly restrained. What is known is that his last spontaneous act was to send a pathetic note to Kang Yu-Wei urging him to fly without delay.

Then the curtain falls upon the drama of the reforming Emperor. The epilogue is such as might be expected in an Oriental country. An imperial edict restored the regency of the Empress Dowager. Shortly afterwards an ominous announcement appeared in the Peking *Gazette*, that the Emperor was seriously ill, and for a time he was thought to be actually dead. But a significant warning from Sir Claude MacDonald to the Tsungli-Yamen, that his death would create a disastrous impression in Western countries, probably did more to promote his recovery than the prescriptions of all the Chinese doctors who had been ostentatiously summoned by imperial edict to his bedside. Kang Yu-Wei and a few of the leading reformers succeeded in making their escape. But six of their less fortunate associates were executed in the market-place at Peking. They met their fate, according to all accounts, with a heroism worthy of their cause. Many others were exiled, degraded, imprisoned. Edict succeeded edict annulling all the Emperor's reforming edicts. The reform societies were dissolved and proscribed, the organs of the reform party suppressed, their schools closed, officials suspected of sympathy with them dismissed or frightened into abject submission, while honors and promotions were showered on the anti-foreign party. A new era of reaction had set in, of which the end cannot yet be foretold.

Once more the old Empress had triumphed, and for the third time within four decades a successful palace conspiracy had restored her supremacy; but even in the cup of triumph there must have been a dash of bitterness. She had had to rely almost exclusively upon the Manchus for the success of her bold schemes, and just as the reform movement had been essentially a Chinese movement, so the reactionary revolution had been essentially a reassertion of Manchu supremacy over the Chinese. She is too shrewd a woman not to have realized the danger of arraying Manchus against Chinese, and of relying on mere force to maintain the ascendency of a ruling race long since intellectually and morally degenerate. Nor were the Manchus slow to exact from her the price of their support. Li Hung-Chang, the oldest and most devoted of her Chinese henchmen, had been one of the moving spirits of the *coup d'état*, but he had, none the less, to be sacrificed, at least temporarily, to Manchu jealousy; and the Empress was fain to send him into honorable exile, to superintend in his old age the hopeless task of damming up the Yellow River. Again, though foreign diplomacy, absorbed in its own rivalries, had held aloof, in some cases perhaps with deplorable apathy, from the life-and-death struggle that had been going on within the Forbidden City, the Empress can hardly have failed to note that Russia and her faithful handmaid France alone expressed approval of the new régime. It has, indeed, been stated that an explicit agreement exists between the Empress and Russia for the maintenance of the dynasty under her supreme control; but even if that be so, the price she must have had, or may yet have, to pay for such an agreement may well cause her some secret heart-burning. And so long as the young Emperor still lives, can she feel absolutely safe that the past is irrevocably buried in "that island within the palace" to which Lord Salisbury so mysteriously alluded? Though his spirit may be cowed and crushed, though he may have submissively accepted his fate and resigned himself once more to such childish amusements as the training of goats and monkeys, it may be gathered, from the precautions that were taken throughout the winter to keep the ice constantly broken on the ornamental water which surrounds his island prison, that, though his life may be but a living death, it still constitutes a restraint if not a danger to the old Empress's usurping power. Nor can she permanently set back the clock of progress. Whatever the issue may be for the unfortunate Kwang Shu or for his masterful old kinswoman, the traces of the reform movement can never be wholly obliterated. Tan Sze-Tung, one of its noblest protomartyrs, loudly proclaimed, as he was led forth to execution, that for every head cut off that day a thousand would arise to carry on the work of reform. The seed thus fertilized by the blood of fearless apostles must yet bear fruit amongst the teeming millions of a race endued with unconquerable vitality, though its earliest blossom has been ruthlessly plucked from the Dragon Throne.

FROM HOME TO THRONE IN BELGIUM

IT rebukes our national vainglory that nine out of ten average Belgians, on meeting an American, break the ice of first acquaintance by speaking sociably and familiarly of Brazil, the Argentine Republic, Venezuela, Paraguay — of all the South American republics, in fact —but not of the United States, concerning which less is known in Belgium, notwithstanding our fond imaginings that the scream of our eagle rings round the globe. Our great country not only recedes into relative unimportance in the geographical perspective of our foreign friends, but they sometimes saddle our colder civilization with the sins of warm-blooded, more reckless South Americans, whose lavish living, debts, gambling, mixed blood, and ethnic type are indiscriminately ascribed to every denizen of the Western hemisphere. Even Parisians make few distinctions between our northern and southern continents, familiar though the French are with Uncle Sam's dollars, and dependent on his trade.

In our vernacular the word American means a Yankee, or a Westerner, or a Southerner, a viking, a master and statesman, who discovers continents, dominates the realms of invention and intellectual development, hews primeval forests, spans continents with railways, creates colossal fortunes, makes laws, and fights for principle. To many French and Belgians, however, the name American rather implies an olive-skinned creature, passionate, luxurious, often tricky, always spendthrift, possibly immoral, half Spanish, half Indian, and wholly degenerate — a being embodying all that to us is intensely, disagreeably alien. He is supposed to have his front teeth filled with diamonds instead of gold, to divorce eight wives, and to shoot whoever opposes his abducting a ninth. Only the grotesque, the eccentric, the abnormal, is published about him in the press. The women of our race are frequently conceived of either as mushroom heiresses, the spawn of mining-camps, or as sybarites or adventurers; when not tattooed, then enamelled and painted; selfish and languid, and venal if not corrupt. For those Anglo-Saxon qualities which we pride ourselves on displaying—our practical virtues, our culture and independence — "ces Anglaises," with whom we are confused, get all the praise.

Even our financial credit suffers from this lack of discrimination between the two Americas. Belgian capitalists having lost heavily in Argentine securities, the soundest six-per-cent. investments in prosperous United States bonds and stocks are classed with other hybrid monetary schemes hatched south of the equator. Wherever the foreign pocket was depleted by such ventures, a grudge against us and our institutions is felt, not lessened by the passage of the "Mack-in-lee Bill." For each Belgian tourist, pioneer, or business exploiter who has visited New York and Boston, ten have seen Rio or Montevideo, have planted coffee in Guatemala, or mined in Peru. Even my letters posted from Brussels, and addressed to Washington and New York, U. S. A., went sometimes to the United States of Colombia, unless plainly marked "L'Amérique du Nord." The educated classes, happily, understand our civilization. Portaels the artist told me more of the American Indian than I ever heard outside of an anthropological society.

The shock of finding my country dwindling, from the ordinary European point of view, into an insignificant territory, instead of covering the foreground of the universe, made me reflect that the Belgians' close connection with and accurate knowledge of other nations than ours betokens a commercial reach and activity which we as a people might well copy. Moreover, their familiarity with regions to us ill-defined inspires sincere respect. The map of Africa, revised and corrected to date, with its latest determined and intricate boundaries, hangs in every library and counting-room; and Belgian children are better posted about the distant Congo and its resources than are our Eastern public-school pupils concerning sister States like Dakota or Utah.

And educated Belgians are such polyglots! Not for nothing do these famous linguists come of mixed Flemish and Walloon stock, allied through blood and tradition with France, through philologic roots and customs with Germany, and long bound captive by the tyranny and armies of Spain. Russians find no lan-

IN CHURCH, GHENT.

guage difficult after mastering their own; and next to them in facile speech rank the Dutch, who nearly all possess three vernaculars besides their native idiom— English, German, and French. Pushing the Hollanders close in fluent command of foreign languages are Cæsar's old foes and final subjects, the Belgians, in comparison with whose inheritance from Babel we Americans seem tongue-tied dolts. Due to many causes is this enviable lingual gift: first, to the prevalence of two distinct national languages among the peasantry, Flemish and Walloon, both being often spoken by the agricultural workers and by the cultured classes as well. With the latter, however, French is the universal medium, as it is the organ of the court, of trade and commerce, and of most schools. Laws and placards are written and instruction is given both in Flemish and French. The geographical position of the little kingdom, squared by France, Germany, Holland, and the North Sea, makes the acquisition of foreign idi-

oms almost compulsory. One Sunday I journeyed sight-seeing from Verviers in Belgium to Aix-la-Chapelle in Germany, then to Maestricht in Holland, and back to Brussels, challenged by customs officials of three nations in one day.

An over-crowded population, too, with its attendant keen struggle for existence, whets the people's faculties. My acquaintances in Belgium speak English, French, German, and Flemish or Walloon, as the locality of their birth favors; and not a few ambitious students add Italian and Spanish to their list, besides reading and writing two or three ancient or other modern languages. While under the escort of a man of this cosmopolitan type, able to converse in six tongues and write three more, I met a London cockney, who somehow had managed to become teacher of English at a night school. Observing, after a few civilities, that I was not native to the heath, this mighty Briton, by way of being amiable and ingratiating, remarked, " You'll learn Henglish yet, mum—never fear, mum—hif you'll honly keep hon speaking, mum. I quite hunderstand you now, mum!"

On that occasion my guide of varied accomplishments combined, as business men abroad often do, the rôles of country gentleman, manufacturer, bank president, school trustee, and —broadening the gulf between his kind and the typical American "boss"—he holds the more important position of alderman. In every city the aldermen and mayor, or burgomaster, are of high social repute, elected to office because of special fitness for the branch of public affairs they are chosen to manage. Said one, with horror and shame, "We hear that in America aldermen are sometimes—thieves!" The first "alderman of public instruction" to whom I presented my credentials in a Brussels commune proved to be a barrister of note, author of several well-known law treatises. In another commune the alderman of public instruction is professor at the normal school, progressive and public-spirited. The alderman responsible for the Ghent schools fills also the chair of political economy at the university, keeps in touch with the methods of other nations, reads the reports of the United States Department of Labor, and, much to my surprise, identified me at once from having seen my name in one of those volumes. The faculty of the university at Liège has more than one representative in the "college" of aldermen—a suggestive title, losing none of its dignity when applied to the body of brilliant men who administer civic affairs with scrupulous fidelity on broad wise lines.

Life away from the Belgian capital is

THE CHÂTEAU OF WALZIN.
A typical château, in the Walloon country.

full of interest to a stranger and student of social customs, however dull its round to those who year after year have only a provincial outlook. Great landed estates still survive, noble châteaux, stately ceremonial—an aristocracy so rigidly orthodox and exclusive as to make one credit a story told of the duchess who was recently entreated to invite to her daughter's wedding a Hebrew family in favor even with royalty: "In three hundred years, perhaps, the A——s may receive the R——s, not now." To other social strata, however, my observations were confined — to the duties, pursuits, and surroundings of professional men, officials, manufacturers, teachers, artists, university people, and to the life of the working classes.

Hospitality in Belgium is a rite, not perfunctory nor self-seeking, but spontaneous and effervescing, resembling the cordial expansiveness that marks our Southern customs. New-Englanders, so it is hinted—though my own experience falsifies the implication—invite a stranger to their house only when they can get something out of him; English attentions to transatlanticans savor either of patronage or servility; the French rarely, under any circumstances, take new-comers into the inner circle; the Spaniards never do, though offering home and worldly goods with facile lip-service. But the Belgians are by nature social and hospitable, combining the vivacity and quick wit of the Latin races with a sturdy energy and holdfastness born of their fighting Flemish ancestry. So many gestures and lively movements do they make that at table glasses for wine and water are never grouped at the side of the plate, as with us, but are put in a line beyond the plate, out of harm's way. For water? A slip of the pen, water being deemed good for laundry and toilet purposes alone. One young woman in Ghent declared that the taste of this beverage was unknown to her; and I envied her the bliss of ignorance after drinking the nauseous liquid of that city. Wine is everywhere served at breakfast and dinner—of better quality than the French use, connoisseurs claim, Belgian wine-cellars being more commodious and suitable than the apartment-house life of France admits. Old wines, in bottles thick with dust, and handled with respect due their rare contents, were brought out in honor of the American guest. Beer and coffee besides are provided, with frequent potations of tea between meals, at four and ten o'clock P.M., and always at eight o'clock, on the assembling of an evening company—gentlemen, however, forswearing the afternoon cup to which their English cousins are so addicted.

About half past eleven in the morning all the business men, who sallied forth from seven to nine o'clock after taking coffee and rolls, stroll home, and luncheon or breakfast is served about twelve or one o'clock. This meal proceeds in courses, with a change of plates at each service, but not a change of knives and forks. These implements must be used through successive courses, however dissimilar, resting betweenwhiles on glass or silver holders, placed beside each cover. The holders, alas! I often forgot to employ, sending my knife and fork out on my plate, to the maid's confusion and my own dismay. An English woman, long resident in Brussels, invited me to dinner with the cheering assurance: "We are English, not Belgian, in our ways. We change the knives and forks." Indeed, in native households fashionable and magnificently appointed entertainment, British plum puddings, roasts, and dainties, fell to my lot as often as the strictly Belgian menu of soup, soup-meat with carrots, then veal, potatoes, and chiccory, or else

tender shoots of hops, finished off with a salad and a Léopold—a cake worthily named for royalty. Meats and the fruits to which we are accustomed are dear in Belgium, but Yankee products grace many tables. "I don't know what we should do without your beef-extracts for sauces, and your California tinned fruits," observed my hostess at a charming breakfast near a great iron establishment. "Feel at home," said another lady, pleasantly; "here is some *manse pea*." As her pronunciation and the dish itself—a so-called mince pie—resembled nothing familiar to my ear or vision, I was baffled for the moment as to the nature of her kind intentions.

The almost universal formula of welcome in the provinces is, "Will mademoiselle take something?" puzzling me at first as to whether I might be allowed to run off with the fascinating old Delft and Dresden ornaments, or was merely ex-

THE KITCHEN OF A PROSPEROUS HOUSEHOLD.

THE INTERIOR OF A PEASANT HOUSE.

dressed himself yet." Which alarming statement proved too true, as I soon discovered when an apparition appeared on the threshold, unwashed, uncombed, with overcoat and neck-handkerchief by no means concealing the unmistakable loose night robe beneath. So suggestive was the spectacle that, declining the unembarrassed entreaties of monsieur's spouse. "Pray take something, mademoiselle," I despatched my inquiries and fled.

Back of reception and dining rooms most Belgian homes have a charming living-apartment, with tiled floor and rugs, partly enclosed by glass, banked with palms and growing plants, and furnished with a piano, lounges, easy-chairs, and little tables for books, tea or coffee, and wine. Bedchambers are usually uncarpeted and daintily clean, containing for married couples two single beds, two wardrobes, and two dressing-cases—this double outfit either for hygienic purposes and comfort, or because connubial loyalty shrinks from the test of sharing toilet accommodations. The interiors of many dwellings are rich in precious old china and works of art, bewildering carved cabinets, hand-wrought iron and brasses, with modern additions enough to give grace and a homelike look. National relics and antiquities are preserved or copied with reverent affection. The drawing-room of the lamented Emile de Laveleye contains a noble old Belgian chimney-piece and mantel with a Swedish text above—"To the hearth of a friend is never far." Before the fire in a silk-lined basket lay a tiny dog, the pet and companion of de Laveleye, and almost the last object of which he spoke. My admi-

pected to quaff the syrups and light wines produced on all occasions. If I visited a weaving-school at eight in the morning, when all the men were yet in that startling home undress which prevails in some households before the formal *déjeuner*, the wife of the weaving-master would press me, "Prenez quelque chose, je vous en prie, mademoiselle." I called early one day on a secretary at Charleroi, with whom I had business, hearing that he was about to leave town. He was out on the street. "But he can't have gone far," protested his son, "for he hasn't

ration of this spacious and beautiful house was great and unconcealed—so rich, yet so refined, every ornament and picture embodying a thought; each room devoted to a special study or a separate art. "Yes," rejoined his youngest daughter, sadly, "I often laughed and said to papa, 'You glory in democracy, you decry luxury, and you live in a palace!'"

Such charming surroundings, exquisite cleanliness, and gracious hospitality imply excellent domestic service. The Walloons are the best servants, energetic and tireless, but the Flemish yield to no other race in faithfulness. The maids adore copper and brass utensils, and are never happier than when scrubbing and polishing the fire-dogs in the library, or pots and pans of the kitchen array, often assisted on Saturday cleaning-days by the mistress herself, in gloves and apron, dusting and burnishing her treasures. In country establishments under-housemaids earn fifteen francs a month, upper-housemaids thirty, and cooks from twenty-five to forty francs. A larger staff is employed than in America. Maids-of-all-work in Brussels, where but one is kept, receive from fifteen to thirty francs, and live on the premises. Changes are infrequent, and devoted domestics follow the family fortunes a lifetime. In the delightful home which was truly mine in Brussels the cook has been twenty-five years with her mistress, manages the housekeeping in part, and is almost a member of the family, never forgotten on ceremonial occasions or fêtes. Whether for coffee before an early

morning train, or the nightly hot-water bottle in bed, or mulled wine for colds, or refreshments in the salon at 11 P.M., or ushering out the Queen's maid of honor, Fannie is unfailing and unflagging. It is etiquette abroad to ring for a servant to open the door for each departing guest. Fees are not obligatory, as in England, though they are usually given. Most cooks also market, and receive from the dealers a percentage on all purchases they make for the household. An American resident in Brussels assured me that, what with coffees and beers, her servants expect and demand meals and collations

ON THE WAY TO MARKET.

nine times a day—"always nibbling," said she.

In provincial Belgium living costs less than in United States towns, equal comfort considered. The agricultural peasantry fare more miserably than any American people except our poorest tenement-dwellers in cities. Field-laborers' houses are squalid, their food mean, consisting chiefly of soup, a vegetable, and brown bread, with sour wine or beer, meat being too dear to be much used in the dietary. Even the numerous well-to-do middle class expend far less than those of the same trade or calling here, whose daughters must go to college or drive a stylish cart, whether or not the family employs a servant. In Belgium a servant is indispensable; but the unprogressive "petite bourgeoisie," content to dwell in their ancestral homes without modern improvements, are also independent enough to disregard in dress and belongings the changes of fashion, and not to join the scramble for social honors. Sons follow the trade of their father. A young man does well if he begins a commercial life in a first-class establishment at $6 a month, and the chance to rise to a position paying from $1000 to $1500 a year. Type-writing machines are abhorred as supplanting human labor. I received hundreds of business letters from commercial and manufacturing firms in Belgium, teachers, schools, private employers, and public functionaries, only one letter of this whole number being type-written. This communication came from the head of the Bell Telephone Company, at their great factory in Antwerp. Belgium being the most densely peopled country of Europe, competition is keen, and men work a lifetime for pay which only beginners in the United States would accept. Even lucky fellows who, as the French say, "have arrived," earn little compared with our big salaries, and their services may be secured for secondary or outside work at small compensation—which, in fact, is the secret of the economical administration of the large and efficient schools of art and industry. Specialists in every line, artists, architects, chemists, literary and professional men, poorly paid according to American standards, are willing to undertake extra classes or night teaching to secure the additional income. Remuneration from legitimate art being small, it is gladly eked out by other employment.

which, in public value, in time becomes the greater work. Not many of the craft, if artists only, flourish in Belgium from the monetary stand-point. Gloomy critics declare that all native painters and sculptors, except a few who have moved to Paris, are living beyond their means, on the hope of future sales. On the other hand, Mlle. Beernaert, who has had the honor—rarely accorded women—of being decorated by government for distinguished ability in art, has bought her beautiful home and studio, with treasures of antiques and bric-à-brac, from money earned in Belgium by her brush. She prides herself on keeping her style free from French influence, and on following the national type, or creating her own type, as her townswoman Madame Ronner has done with her famous and delightful cats.

In most of the provincial cities—which, by-the-way, contain marvels of architectural, plastic, and pictorial art—at small, comfortable inns, a sitting-room and a chamber with fair *table d'hôte* meals may be had for $1 a day. A premium is put on wine-drinking by a higher charge for food with which no wine is ordered—a considerable item, I found. In Ghent, at a first-rate hotel, the market-day dinner, always the best of the week, costs 75 cents—"oysters and everything," said the waiter, urging me not to miss it. I did not miss it, martyrizing myself from one to three o'clock with coppery bivalves and fourteen courses, but capitally entertained by the assembled company and their lively toasts and gestures—officers, lawyers, merchants, brokers, priests, and neighborhood gentry, including fashionable women. That night I paid only four francs for an excellent seat at the theatre where the Coquelins were playing. Musical advantages also are good and cheap in provincial Belgium, and musical standards are high. Prime donne of worldwide fame were trained and first became celebrated at the Théâtre de la Monnaie in Brussels.

Private schools for girls are as yet more showy or practical than classical in their curricula, teaching housekeeping and domestic economy admirably along with the regular course. The only young girl I met, not in a university, who was studying Latin was learning it from her small brother of nine years, a pupil at the Athénée. A school once famous persists for generations. The Heger-Parent insti-

THE MARKET-DAY DINNER.

tution, which Charlotte Brontë attended, bears the same name on the door-plate as when the lonely English girl walked its garden paths, and other English girl students still weave romances under its ancient gables.

At the capital expenses and rents are dearer. With a house to let at Brussels nothing is included except the bare walls; neither mantels, chandeliers, grates, range, tubs, nor bath. A bath outside once a week for every male member of the family is reckoned as part of the monthly outlay; but females, even of the buxom type Rubens painted, are considered too frail to risk their lives by bathing "the altogether." Every chimney smokes more or less, and modern window construction with weights is unknown. In rooms with fires the temperature is rarely over 62°— a condition we might emulate, as well as the convenient foreign fashion that requires strangers to make the first call. Whoever intends to receive needs several servants, and a house with wide hallway and entrance. Cabs, cheap as they appear, are yet "gnawers of the purse-strings"—*rongeurs des bourses*. In the long-run, a Brussels establishment involves the same expenditure for a style of living equally good as in American cities of equal population. The secret of so-called Continental cheapness is that one exists as a hermit, without social ties, or resides in apartments which would be scorned at home.

The best shops in Brussels are the smallest—dealing in elegant fabrics, however; for the capital is gay, and court costumes are in demand. Crowned heads of many countries buy whole trousseaux here. The fine underwear of Brussels is justly noted, and supplies the best French trade. Fans, gloves, jewels, are made in perfection, and the lace and antiquary shops are the most seductive in the world. Everywhere crops out the commercial instinct, one secret of Belgium's greatness, manifesting itself in studied politeness to intending purchasers—politeness at the expense of truth often, so anxious are the merchants to please. The shopkeeper lies are not ugly, spiteful, and tricky, but ingenious and naïve; and one is amused rather than angry at the transparent excuses for not keeping appointments, or for adding a few francs more to the bill than the price agreed upon. Time is of no value, apparently; for my bootmaker's messenger made twenty-six trips to the house concerning four pairs of shoes and slippers I ordered.

The leisure class, people who live on incomes or *rentes*—and they alone constitute high society—walk for an hour or two every morning between ten and one o'clock about the boulevards, along the Avenue Louise to the park—men with dogs, women with dogs, children with dogs and nurses. It is not uncommon to meet the royal family out for exercise, the ladies fresh, fair, and simply dressed;

the men magnificent of stature, gracious and dignified. The burgomaster walks; members of the Chamber of Deputies take a constitutional before the session begins; women, army officers, and men of fashion promenade alone and in groups. These last as frequently ride, and the clatter of equestrians and cavalrymen in gay uniforms resounds at all hours. For long distances trams are resorted to. The car is divided into two compartments, the fare in the uncushioned end being only half as dear. This second-class division is patronized by the peasantry and by workers, who are thus spared the mortification of intruding bundles and packs, mortared or sooty shoes and soiled garments, among well-dressed passengers. But, useful though the trams are, they are unfashionable.

Special delivery for letters was adopted in Belgium long before the convenience was established here. No special stamp is required. Twenty-five centimes (five cents) in postage, instead of fifteen centimes, is put on a letter, the word "exprès" is written, and the missive is mailed in a box for that purpose on the tram. At a station where the car stops a messenger takes the epistle and delivers it to post-office or house, so that a letter written in Ghent after two o'clock is often in the hands of the person addressed at Brussels by five the same afternoon.

The Belgians are shocked at our want of politeness and ceremony, and charge that Americans do not take time even to salute each other on the street. So elaborate and formal are foreign manners that our most punctilious deportment seems in comparison almost brusque. At breakfast and on saying good-night, one must shake hands all round; and merely to bow to an acquaintance who happens to be in the salon calling when one enters for a single moment is a breach of etiquette, since more cordial and special greeting is expected. No matter how engrossed you may be in writing or casting up accounts, a child coming with a message to some one else in the room insists on shaking hands with you, both on entering and leaving—a courtesy distracting to busy workers. Men, however hurried, shake hands invariably, clinging to each other's fists as if life and repute depended on contact of palm with palm. A distinguished alderman, who presented me to a brother official in the Hôtel de Ville at Liège, shook hands with this colleague at parting, claiming to be pressed for time, but paused at the door for further talk, then recrossed the room, grasped his friend's hand again, "Au revoir, mon cher," and turned to go. More words, then another effusive good-by and handclasp. This time the door closed on my alderman, but only for a second. His head reappeared, then his body, and flinging a few sentences at monsieur at the desk, who was about to

A SIGNAL-WOMAN AT A RAILWAY CROSSING.

give my business attention, the alderman followed his voice and traversed
the room a fourth time solely to shake
hands again—"Adieu, mon collègue,
adieu!"

It would be deemed extremely rude
were two college students to meet
on the street without twice shaking hands, and saying, each in turn,
"Mes compliments à madame votre
mère." Women of extreme fashion
courtesy backwards without offering
the hand. Bowing is another serious
and important ceremony, performed
by clicking the heels together and
bending the torso suddenly as if it
were hinged. One afternoon three
very agreeable men escorted me to
divers schools, museums, and functions, and our progress was snail-like,
because at each entrance and exit, after
I had passed, these gentlemen stood,
hat in hand, saluting furiously, and
each vowing that precedence was due
the others, until I wanted to throw
out grappling-hooks and drag them
along. Another scene recurs in dizzy
retrospect—the lighted hall of a famous drawing-school which I was
leaving one night, and in the spacious
doorway half the faculty ranged to bid
me good-by, and bowing again and
again, professors, janitor, and even a
friendly policeman on duty, all swaying and swaying and swaying across
the gas-jets, "Adieu, mademoiselle,
adieu!" until from my cab window the
universe seemed toppling.

At New-Year's everybody on "terms"
with anybody sends a visiting or New-
Year's card, showers of little white envel-
opes falling at each door; and such importance is attached to this recognition
that rich people who announce through
the press "the gift of 500 francs to the
poor, with dispensation from exchanging
the cards of the season," are criticised.
"They owe more consideration to their
friends," say the captious. Men call on
every intimate acquaintance, and whole
families pay duty visits even to remote
connections. Indeed, after any momen-
tous event calls are made to impart the
tidings, and for congratulation in return.
A marriage is arranged for mademoiselle:
her mother flutters about announcing the
daughter's settlement in life. A son is
installed in a promising business: at once
madame orders a cab and seeks from all

SECOND-CLASS COMPARTMENT OF A STREET CAR.

her friends the sympathy and bubbling
expansive pleasure in good fortune that
make the charm of social intercourse in
Belgium. Birthdays and anniversaries are
fêted; long terms of service in church,
state, school, or art are celebrated by ju-
bilees, gifts, and poems. The heart cannot wither nor life grow barren, watered
as they are from springs of unceasing
interest and affection. Americans are too
reserved to give or ask such tributes, too
busy with worship of material things to
offer this fine incense to the spiritual life.

Certain conventional protestations common in foreign society must of course be
accepted with pounds, not grains, of allowance. Such signatures as "Your wholly
devoted Charles Steven" from a gentleman to a lady, or "My respectful and
most devoted homage," mean nothing
more than "Yours truly." The greater

warmth implied in "Yours sincerely" has its Belgian equivalent in "Yours with perfect consideration." Delicate shadings exist between "sentiments empressés" at the close of a missive, and "sentiments distingués"—the first being employed to one's dressmaker; the second, to one's friend. It is an affront if all official designations are not given on business letters; and strangers, underrating the importance attached to titles of every description, offend through ignorance, not disrespect. Among men a common and much-sought distinction is the title of engineer (*ingénieur*), borne in walks of life far removed from the pursuits that name represents with us. We democrats cannot understand how decorations from the state are coveted and valued in Europe. The order of Léopold in Belgium, like that of the Legion of Honor in France, is bestowed for services in all lines, its honors being graded from a mere civil list to officers of high rank, named because of long and distinguished service to humanity in diplomacy, letters, art, education, invention, philanthropy, science, jurisprudence, or war. Every man of note wears the tiny red knot in his button-hole.

Wedding invitations are printed upon a double sheet. On the first page the bride's parents bid you to the festivities; on the second, the bridegroom's family bespeak your presence. For these invitations the bridegroom pays. The bride pays for church decorations, beadles with gorgeous uniform and staff, and the wedding mass. Accompanying the bridal couple, and sitting with them in the chancel, are the witnesses — always the grandest acquaintances possessed by the respective families. While the mass proceeds, the contracting parties are enthroned be-

A LACE-MAKER, MECHLIN.

fore the altar in two big chairs,
the bride's veil spread out behind her; and whenever the
couple stand up or kneel, ver-
gers disengage the veil, and
carefully rearrange it after the
genuflections cease. During the
service a collection for the poor
—*la quête*—is taken up by gayly
dressed maids of honor, or under
the ushers' escort, the coins being thrown to beggars at the
church door as the marriage procession departs. After a drive
in the park and posing in bridal
attire for photographs, the wedding breakfast occurs in the
banquet-room of some hotel, the
guests often remaining at table
from six to eight hours. The
wife retains her maiden name,
but hyphens it after her husband's, as Madame Franeau-de
Wevelghem.

Not even funerals in Belgium are lugubrious; for, in spite
of black-bordered death-notices
tacked on walls, gate-posts, telegraph poles, and grocers' windows, and notwithstanding the
solemn garb and mourning
weepers of the *croque-morts*—
municipal officials whose duty
it is to attend and direct all ob-
sequies for the dead—love of

THE BLACK CROSSES OF ASH-WEDNESDAY.

color finds vent in gay artificial wreaths,
often ten feet in circumference, that load
down hearse or pall. In better-class families no women ever follow a corpse to
the grave. A single female servant walks
behind the coffin, bearing crowns and
crosses of tinsel. Priests and male mourners march near the catafalque or hearse,
then empty carriages close the impressive cortége, before which every passer-
by stands uncovered. Death, our universal doom, is the one solemn fact that
commands respect from the Latin races
and their congeners, to whom many of
life's sacraments are often jests. At the
city outskirts the procession halts, the maid
deposits her burden in the nearest vehicle,
the mourners enter other carriages in waiting, and the long line trots off to consign
the dead to a gloomy vault, and an immortality of fadeless bead wreaths. Funerals
among the poor are marked by unseemly
haste in church and at the cemetery; but
when a great personage departs this life

no means are spared to make the occasion memorable. Cathedrals are draped
in black, and pomp, music, and ceremonial
add lustre to a shining name.

At social functions music is the leading
pleasure and pursuit, no evening company
being complete without a symphony or
concerto, in which young women frequently play violin or 'cello parts. Each member of the family usually is proficient on
some instrument, and boys of seven years
old are sometimes allowed to sit up to
dinner to accompany their big sisters on
the violin. Art of all kinds crosses the
warp of existence in a way incomprehen-
sible to gain-chasing Americans. In
January, 1892, the burgomaster of Brussels, wanting money for the poor, conceived the happy thought during a heavy
snow of a "winter salon" in the King's
Park, already fairylike with its crystal-
burdened twigs and delicate snow traceries. All the sculptors of the city were
summoned, with their pupils; the park

THE PALACE OF JUSTICE, BRUSSELS.

day small maids with dolls, and boys with drums or horses, parade the boulevards. To the poor, alms are given, and to the servants, ridiculous gingerbread figures. Our cook received a cock and thirty-nine chickens.

Again, at Christmas every house has its tree, or at least a branch of fir, and a candle or two lighted while hymns are sung to the Christ-Child. All the churches are decorated. Protestants celebrate this festival even more than Catholics, who divide its honors with St. Nicholas's day. New-Year's is the great occasion for all classes—the eagerly expected time when decorations are dispensed by government and addresses are presented to the King; when gifts are exchanged, cards are sent, calls are made, friendships are renewed, feuds are dropped, and a new life is begun.

was turned over to them for a day to decorate, and then opened for charity. Everywhere within were the artists' snow creations—serious, serio-comic, side-splitting. Snow tramps were sleeping on the benches; snow priests lounged and read forbidden literature; snow policemen flirted with snow nursery-maids on secluded seats, while neglected snow babies howled. Punch and Punchinello, ballet-girls and opera-singers, made merry on the frozen ponds with Lohengrin and his swan, Siegfried and Faufner. Icy counterfeits of hostile political celebrities hobnobbed together, and on the King's effigy flamed this mortifying placard, "Moved during the pose!" The entertainment had enormous success; money rained in; and the artist fraternity received no compensation, but gave both time and talent to secure the success of a popular fête, now become an annual event if snow falls heavily.

Indeed, Belgian life is full of fêtes. For days before St. Nicholas's the thoroughfares are thronged, everybody walking out in the street perforce, the sidewalks being so narrow, and on rainy nights umbrellas make a solid phalanx from wall to wall. The saint arrives early on December 6, riding an ass, for which each child provides turnips and hay. If the little one has been good, hay and turnips disappear from the basket, and gifts and toys are left. All that

Not many weeks later comes the carnival—season of mummeries, balls, street processions, and unbridled fun. Most of the young people would give worlds to wear masks and dress in character, but women of the better orders rarely assume disguises or mingle with the fantastic throng. There is no lack of bonbons and flowers thrown from balcony to street and back again, while cries and songs resound at all hours, and groups of grotesque figures cut antics as they play. The festivities continue several days. At Binche and a few other Belgian towns the carnival celebration wears unchanged its mediæval character. On Ash-Wednesday, however, all this abandon of gayety is checked; men, women, and children go to church in sombre garments, and leave the edifice with a heavy black cross stamped on their foreheads, which is worn for twenty-four hours.

St. Valentine is duly worshipped abroad, and the absurd little portfolios of the stolid postmen bulge unusually that day with amatory verse and comic cuts. Six weeks later the shop windows are full of *poissons d'avril*, the cold-blooded fish being made the scapegoat for practical jokes and April idiocies under many forms—papier-maché fish; chocolate, gingerbread, and ice fish; dainty porcelain and silver fish. All the world sends fish to friends. A month later are ushered in the May festivals, religious and secular, musical and social; and through the year one gay event succeeds another, life and its aims being summed up in the injunction that at parting takes the place of our God bless you!—"Amusez-vous bien." One never sneezes, however, that some devout soul does not cry, "Que Dieu vous bénisse!"

When the question was mooted of an exhibit of woman's work for the World's Fair at Chicago, most Belgian men of prominence said, sugaring their disapproval of the "new woman": "We have nothing to show as the distinctive product of your sex. Our ladies do not follow careers, professions, and trades, like you wonderful Americans. They are essentially homestayers and housekeepers." Notwithstanding such discouragement, Belgian women made a fine collection for the exposition without help from the government commission; and adequately to describe the manifold industries and trades pursued by females in the kingdom would require a separate paper. Women of the cultured ranks are clever, progressive, and active in founding and developing, both in cities and villages, those normal, industrial, and housekeeping schools and kindergartens that finally have been engrafted on the state public-school system. Madame Montefiori supports and directs the only lecture course yet in existence for the higher education of the sex. Every "great lady" overlooks and is responsible for from one to five schools, either in her city parish or on her estates. Women are busied with prison reforms—and Belgium has a model prison system—temperance and social purity agitations, charities of all kinds, hospitals, crèches, the care of disabled and delinquent children, and workinggirls' clubs. The burgomaster of Brussels, Monsieur Buls, assured me that he had received from a committee of women invaluable help in his efforts to substitute rational treatment of beggars and the unemployed for the wholesale mistaken charity in vogue, which pauperizes so many Belgian communes.

In prose writing a number of women have achieved distinction, but the first volume of verse published by any Belgian female is from the pen of my friend Madame Sheler. One woman lawyer adorns the land, Mademoiselle Potvin, who has never been allowed to plead a case. A young female doctor of medicine was, indeed, graduated at the Brussels Univer-

THE HÔTEL DE VILLE, LOUVAIN.

sity; getting no practice, a minor position was found for her on the staff of a children's hospital. In this university—"free," as distinguished from those at Liège and Ghent under state control—twenty to thirty girl students stand in all respects on the same footing as men: elective courses, examinations, and diplomas, with even more study-room privileges than the males. In Greek, women sometimes surpass the men, and are distinguished in other branches, taking pharmacy, medicine, and science. These candidates for the higher education, it must be noted, are usually foreigners—Bohemians and Russians in the majority. The native Belgian girl is not emancipated enough for co-education, her life being socially much too guarded. Of late, since communal and normal schools have reached so high a grade of excellence, good families that ten years ago would have employed governesses send their daughters to the public schools, and in rare instances to the trade schools—escorted there and back, however, by mother, brother, or maid. Private masters and home instruction, it is at last conceded, fail to fit for self-support other than at teaching; and self-support in new careers is now considered a possible, although dreaded, factor in the future of girls of social standing. In the railway and postal service women hold clerical positions, but are never trusted with administrative functions; and some Belgian officials could not conceal their surprise that any department of the United States government should send a woman to foreign countries to report on industrial schools and their results. The only similar precedent that I heard of in Belgium was the deputing of a woman teacher of dairy classes to study, for two months, the practical methods used in English dairy schools. With difficulty I convinced certain provincial functionaries there that *I* am no dignitary at all; that at home my position is not unusual, and is strictly subordinate. Notwithstanding my protests, they seemed to expect, on visiting the United States, to find me and other female employees under government enthroned in state, and issuing mandates like any ruler. To myself, from *outre mer*, more courtesy and distinction were accorded than Belgian ladies doing similar work would probably receive; for among the leisure aristocratic class a certain prejudice still prevails against women bread-winners, and for our sex self-maintenance entails not social ostracism exactly, but condonation, as of serious disadvantages to be excused. Downright ostracism follows if any well-born woman starts in trade, or, having resorted to teaching or a semi-professional career, fails to dignify the avocation by signal ability. The average teacher has little prestige merely as a teacher, though the successful teacher or writer may attain an enviable position as a gifted woman.

Middle-class wives assist their husbands in hotel and shop keeping, trade and manufacturing, and manage whole estates; but not many individual employments are open to the sex, and those embarking in untried ventures are liable to criticism or to be tabooed as cranks. To pursue a novel calling in any conservative community presupposes eccentricity; and from such progressives are always expected bizarre ideas, dress, and behavior. A prominent Brussels woman confided to me, in view of my own unusual occupation (collecting statistics): "You have been a great help to us who advocate new fields of industry for girls, because you wear dinner gowns when invited to dinner, because you are conventional and womanly. Henceforth we shall be able to say to all objectors, 'Here is a lady representing the advanced position and work of women who is neither unbalanced, unfeminine, nor ill-bred.'" The speaker evidently agreed with Ruskin, that the reformers were burned, not for their morals, but their manners.

A word about the reigning family, descendants of the ancient Counts of Flanders. When, in 1830, Belgium revolted against being ruled jointly with Holland by the House of Orange, and declared for a constitutional monarchy, its foremost citizen, the Count of Flanders, was chosen King, as Léopold I. His son and successor is Léopold II., who has three married daughters, but no male heir. The crown will fall to the family of a younger brother, the Count of Flanders, who, still in the prime of life, presents the unusual spectacle of a liberal, scholarly man, fitted to rule, yet refusing to be heir-apparent, and transferring the future inheritance under the law to his son. Prince Beaudoin, however, died in 1891, when Prince Albert, the second son, was named heir. He is a noble-looking young man, over six feet tall, like his father and uncle, blond and majestic, and he is being carefully trained for his high station. The ladies of both royal households, by womanly virtues and accomplishments, endear themselves to people who do not hate monarchy on principle. The Queen, an ardent Romanist, is a fine musician and a capital horsewoman. She is also untiring in devotion to the King's unfortunate sister, ex-Empress Carlotta. The Countess of Flanders, mother of the future King — unless the Socialists wax strong enough to abolish kings —is yet young, and one of the most charming and distinguished princesses in Europe. With fewer responsibilities than the Queen, having more time to devote to public movements and reforms, broad in sympathies and ideas, she is a ruling spirit in every undertaking to enlarge the opportunities and better the condition of women, especially of the humblest industrial class. Partly to her initiative are due the housekeeping and cooking schools for the children of workers. Widely read on economic and sociological topics, she feels keen interest in female bread-winners of all types, and wherever practicable starts remunerative industries for the low-paid women toilers of Belgium.

MILK-WOMEN.

Tiny as the kingdom is, compared with former territories of the Dukes of Burgundy and Counts of Flanders, it owns a triple dowry—priceless art treasures from its splendid past, hereditary art aptitudes from its complex ancestry, and enormous material possibilities in Africa. Whether the Congo's undeveloped resources will enrich or ruin the state, time only can determine; but as to Belgium's enlightened and fascinating civilization, and the historic value and importance of its museums and architectural monuments, there cannot be two opinions. Men and women at the theatres, in the shops, on the streets of quaint nomenclature, are the very types that the Van Eycks, Memling, Quentin Matsys, and Rubens immortalize. Every mile of ground boasts some triumph of the builder's skill, or precious national relic, which the government's wise policy preserves or restores lovingly and with a master-touch. Here exist the two most glorious Gothic municipal structures in the world, comparatively unknown to tourists—the Hôtel de Ville at Louvain and the Cloth Hall at Ypres, the latter a superb record of the past greatness of a city of two hundred thousand inhabitants, now dwindled to fifteen thousand, which had no rival as a weaving-mart, and gave its name to the finest damasks— d'Ypres, d'ipre, diaper. As little visited by foreigners are the ruins of the Abbey of Villers or of the Cathedral of St. Bavon. Few earlier or more interesting churches adorn northern Europe than the cathe-

GEORCE WHARTON EDWARDS.

MARKET-DAY AT GHENT—PEASANTS GOSSIPING.

cancy is to be supplied, the judges unite in council and nominate two candidates. Then the council of the commune concerned nominates two more — frequently the same two named by the judges—and finally the King selects the worthiest of the nominees. Rich and successful barristers often refuse to go on the bench, since the income is lower than they earn. *Avocats*, or barristers who plead, wear gown, cap, and scarf with ermine border. The *avoués*, or attorneys, omit the ermine. Ushers and court officers are arrayed in dress-coats and hats with gold bands. The judges wear black gowns and caps, that of the president of the council of judges having a gold band. On great occasions the judges are clad all in red—without wigs, however, unlike the English. The supreme court meets in a grand chamber of the Palais de Justice for formal ceremonies, such as annual opening councils or special sessions ; but causes are heard in an ordinary room.

Capital punishment, although contemplated by the statutes, is at present never carried out, the condemned remaining in prison for life. In the reign of Léopold I. two young men were executed for a crime of which the real culprit afterwards on his death-bed affirmed their innocence. The monarch was so deeply impressed by this that he refused to validate death-warrants, and is said to have exacted from his successor a promise to sign none.

Belgium recognizes no established religion or state church. Protestant denominations are subsidized as the Catholics are, and their ministers also are paid from national funds, although chosen by

dral at Tournai, St. Bartholemé and St. Croix at Liège, St. Sang at Bruges, and the miracle-working Lady of Halle. Everywhere are traces of the Roman occupation, overlaid by marks of successive conquering influences, each imprinted on the architecture and racial type; so that as in narrow ancient quarters, and even among the haunts of the nobility, one hears Spanish names and sees Spanish faces, it seems but yesterday that Philip duped and Alva scowled.

The Belgian judiciary is chosen for integrity and talent, from lower courts or from the provincial bench. When a va-

due form of church law. Numerically the strongest Protestant sect is the Presbyterian, with its synod and general assembly, affiliating with and sending delegates to congresses abroad. The Episcopalians are mostly English residents, who flock to Belgium for business, or to curtail expenses, or for educational advantages. Other free Protestant churches flourish, accepting no state funds, and supporting their own pastors. Unitarianism, too, is rooted in Brussels, and counts strong and influential disciples.

Not only does the government pay the clergy, but in the two state universities of Ghent and Liège it appoints the professors; and while choice in the main is based on fitness, it must be confessed that the Clericals, or Conservatives, when in power, do not always select a shining Liberal or Protestant, while the Liberals in turn sometimes overlook the best qualified Romanists. With the free universities at Louvain and Brussels the politicians cannot meddle.

A Chamber of Deputies and a Senate compose the Belgian Congress, the King having rights of appointment and veto, but, on the whole, less power than the President of the United States. Deputies are elected throughout half the country at one date, throughout the other half two years later, so that every four years the Chamber renews itself, the Senate in the same manner being renewed every eight years. Practically elections controlling popular policy happen but once in four years. As in England, the ministry is responsible. The Premier is Minister of Finance, and may sit as a Deputy also, but he need not. He chooses the other members of the cabinet from the party in power, and they, moreover, need not be, though they usually are, Deputies. The Secretary of War is always an army officer. Belgium has no navy, except her extensive merchant marine. Léopold is King, by fine distinction, not of Belgium by hereditary right, but of the Belgians by choice and deputed power. He is supposed to have no politics. He may and does dismiss any minister who is intractable; generally, however, the cabinet stands or falls together. The ministers live rent free and in good style in apartments in the government buildings, with twenty-five thousand francs a year, the Premier alone receiving fifty thousand. Votes in the Chamber are cast into an urn, as at Paris. The discussions are often conversational, but speakers rise and address the President when making remarks of length or importance.

At present the political atmosphere in Belgium is highly charged, sparks flying whenever questions arise that bear on socialism or the public schools. The sectarian school bill, now opposed by the progressives, reopens grievances dating back to the seventies, before the accession of the Liberals to power. In 1879 the present school system was organized by the Clericals, who previously were accused of managing public education in the interests of the Catholic Church, many of the teachers being priests and nuns, and the *ouvrières*, or workshop schools, being sometimes, it was suspected, an excuse for the exploitation of child labor without adequate instruction in return. When the Liberals came into power in 1880, they made the extension of this common-school system one of the chief features of their administration. Dismissing many clerical teachers, they multiplied advantages and school buildings, adopted the kindergartens, added to the housekeeping schools founded by Mr. Smit and the Prince de Chimay, and already assumed by the Clericals, and also built up normal schools and a higher regents' course for teachers in secondary education. Such changes involved a considerable debt.

Here was a chance for the Conservative party on regaining control in 1884 to make political capital. Raising the cry of extravagance, they began to retrench, closing some of the schools, the normal included—which the city of Brussels assumed, however—and reinstating some of the dislodged clerical teachers, placing others on a waiting pension. So reactionary seemed this policy as to gain from their enemies the name "the ministry of ignorance." But, according to my own observations, the Clerical ministry in power up to 1892 suppressed chiefly the non-essential, and by throwing each commune to some extent on its own resources, fostered greater public interest in education. They certainly did not cripple the industrial and manual-training schools, but increased their number and efficiency. The present fight in Belgium, then, concerns not the relative merits of the two parties, but the question whether religious instruction shall be given—an issue which confronts us in the United States.

The Belgian government controls the railways of the kingdom—except one, the Chemin de Fer Central—and the postal, telegraph, and postal savings system. It loans money in small sums to working-men for the erection of homes; it regulates and inspects the factories, and provides employment in times of great industrial distress; it owns the museums and libraries, cares for the restoration of architectural monuments, and performs other functions so paternal that Americans would call them socialistic.

The Socialists, however, feel that their principles are ignored, that the government is not a true democracy, as intended, but the engine of the favored classes, and all the propitiation offered in the form of suffrage and public schools is not a sop to Cerberus. The Socialist party wants out-and-out recasting of methods and restating of principles. Its organizations are strong, its ideas deeply imbedded in the more intelligent artisans of Brussels and the Walloon districts. The peasantry of Flanders, Ghent excepted, is Catholic, mostly agricultural, although practising in great perfection certain trades, as weaving and lace-making. These Flemish are unorganized, unless by the clergy; and until lately they were terribly illiterate, but illiteracy is being diminished by the common schools. On the other hand, the Ghenters and Walloons—Catholic also—are affiliated with labor organizations; and these intelligent metal and glass workers and coal-miners look for a day of reckoning with society at large. Here have occurred some of the bitterest strikes on record. Here more efforts are made than elsewhere on the Continent to bridge the gap between capital and labor by concessions to the toiler—shorter hours, exclusion of females from mines, and of children under twelve years old from factories, and plans for conciliation and arbitration. Here, too, will the great industrial principles of the age be established, I predict, sooner than anywhere else in Continental Europe.

A beginning was made by three days' riot in 1893, when a practical revolution was wrought in Belgium, mighty but bloodless, and universal manhood suffrage was wrested from Congress. Till then working-men and peasants had been disfranchised by property and educational qualifications. So emphatic was their demand in April, 1893, for the right to vote that a new clause to the constitution was quickly drafted, meeting the approval of both Chambers and the King. With a desperate clutch at power, property-holders and educated men thought to neutralize the single ballot of workers and peasants by allowing the privileged classes additional franchises on fulfilling other requirements besides merely becoming twenty-five years old—a vote on acquiring a stated amount of property; another on taking certain university degrees; another when entering official positions; another at marriage—five possible ballots for one individual. Yet not all these cumulative ballots of the rich and learned nullify the votes of the newly enfranchised peasantry; and while it was believed that conferring universal suffrage would constitute the opportunity of the Liberals and would wreck the Clerical party, the result of the partial elections in 1894 exactly reversed this expectation, the Clericals winning large majorities, the Liberals being nearly wiped out, except in the towns, and the small Socialist group gaining considerably.

The political benefits to the working classes from this radical measure have not as yet been marked; and it is significant that so progressive a step as granting universal suffrage has occasioned reactionary results—the defeat at the polls of the party standing for popular education and human rights by the very peasant vote it helped to create. Instead of holding the over-balance of power, as when the poor and toiling had no voice, the cultured property-owners, notwithstanding five contingent ballots to each, are outnumbered by the ignorant, religiously biassed agricultural and mechanical laborers, who, being Catholic, keep in power the Catholic faction, which originally opposed the people's demands, and was reluctant to grant secular education to the masses. Now how do these Clericals utilize the support of the Roman Catholic peasantry? By undoing to a degree both the achievements of the Liberals and their own; by sectarianizing the schools and re-establishing religious instruction —in fact, by retrograding. Such a swing of the pendulum backward can be but temporary, and often accompanies reforms for which a nation is not ready. This episode, however, may well make us pause before we make a sweeping extension of the suffrage in the United States.

NEPAUL, THE LAND OF
THE GOORKHAS

NEPAUL, geographically, is a region of independent territory, 500 miles by 150, in the heart of the highest Himalaya ranges, protected and shut off from India on the south by the immense malarious Terai forest, and on the north guarded by such hoary sentinels as Yassa, Dhawalaghiri, Mount Everest, 24,000 to 29,000 feet high.

Nepaul proper, in the sense the natives use the word, applies to a little valley 4500 feet above the sea, extending 25 miles by 10; and still more definitely applied refers to the three neighboring cities in this valley, Bhatgaon, Patan, and Khatmandu, named in the order in which they were built, and in which they laid claim to being the capital city of this remarkably isolated province.

The present capital, Khatmandu, is the seat of the Goorkha dynasty, ruling over a people the bravest and most warlike in the East.

We cannot tell our readers here how we worked our way up from Calcutta to Khatmandu, a distance of some 550 miles, the last 100 on foot. Before such a journey could be undertaken it was necessary to obtain the permission of the British Foreign Office in India, the ways of which are as dark as those of the heathen Chinee, and which takes pride in mulish perversity and an autocratic obtuse aversion to any and all Europeans "airing themselves on the Indian frontier." Then, too, we must have obtained the consent of the Nepaulese Court.

When all this red tape had been successfully encountered, we were obliged to lay in a stock of tinned provisions, ammunition for sport of no mean order, the killing of tiger, rhinoceros, and bear; and lastly, it was necessary to provide what proved the most interesting feature of the outfit, our photographing apparatus.*

REIGNING KING, IN GENERAL'S COSTUME.

* The writer was greatly assisted in his photography by Mr. Hoffman, of the celebrated Calcutta firm of Johnston and Hoffman, photographers. This gentleman made two trips up to Khatmandu, and took numerous pictures of the princes and all objects of interest.

Moreover, coolies were to be negotiated for, and our days' marches prearranged. But, as before stated, we cannot here go into all these details, nor give an account of the dangers we encountered, the difficulties we had to surmount, the exasper-

ROYAL PALACE, BHATGAON.

ating, mutinous spirit exhibited by our coolies, the exposures and night alarms we experienced, not to mention attacks of disease and of wild animals, from which we had miraculous escapes.

On a cold morning in November a caravan of about twenty struggling human beings, mostly coolies with burdens on their backs, could have been seen defiling up the precipitous side of Chundragiri, or Moon Mountain. After a hard struggle the top was reached at a point 7186 feet above sea-level. The ground was white with hailstones of the previous night's storm, and deep frost covered the ground, while the sun was shining its brightest. The coolies now sat down to rest, and we who were in advance of them moved along the top of the pass to its further side. Immediately in front of us was a precipice with a perpendicular fall of some 2000 feet into the valley of Nepaul proper. This valley, stretching east and west, struck us as having been in the dim obscure past the bed of a vast lake, whose waters rose and fell against the encircling sides of the world's highest mountains, until they wore for themselves an outlet by what now marks the channel of the sacred shallow stream of Bagmati.

Scattered all about at our feet, and far beyond, lay numerous thickly populated villages, whose inhabitants, after centuries of patient toil and husbandry, had transformed the valley into a beautiful fertile plain. Out of the centre rose, clearly visible to our unaided sight, the houses, palaces, pagodas, and temples of the two older cities already mentioned, and of the present capital city, Khatmandu, from twelve to fifteen miles distant. Around us were cultivated fields, which were carried in terraces a long distance up the mountain-sides. These in turn gave way to the heavy pine forests, which gradually stooped and belittled themselves as they approached the abodes of snow, and finally, having dwarfed themselves into the lowest orders of vegetable life, they altogether retired from before the presence of a perfect sea of crowned heads, culminating in that white-headed, gray-bearded monarch, old Everest himself, 29,000 feet high. This monster, though a hundred miles off, was distinctly visible, his bifurcated cone-shaped head piercing the blue of the sky. Running our eye along the nearer ranges, there confronted us the towering heads and shoulders of many giants flashing their brilliants in the sunlight. Fully one-third of the extensive visible horizon was required to give sufficient elbow-room to this aged royal assembly. Of those nearest us we recognized Gosain Than, 26,000 feet; Yassa, 24,000 feet; Matsiputra, 24,400; and Dhawalaghiri, 26,800 feet high. As we looked upon them from our lofty position in the grand stillness of that magnificent morning we were filled with awe at the sublime spectacle, and ceased to wonder that the Hindoo associates with each one of these tremendous peaks the abode of some one of his deities.

But we must hasten on to Khatmandu. Passing on through its guarded gateway and the narrowest of filthy streets, we reached the British Residency grounds. Here we found shelter in a little house assigned to occasional travellers.

As a matter of duty, as well as inclination, our first call was on the British Resident—an officer appointed to look after British interests in this corner of the earth. He and the doctor as his assistant are the only European residents in Nepaul, which is an exceptional feature of any country so near India, and shows how well the principle of exclusion has been maintained by the Foreign Office at Calcutta.

The British Resident was in India when we called, but the doctor.

who was acting for him, received us most pleasantly, and insisted on our leaving our plain quarters and lodging with him in his two-storied brick house.

Our next object was to call upon the

REIGNING KING, IN COURT DRESS.

PAGODA AND TEMPLE, BHATGAON.

Maharajah. The term Maharajah, though ordinarily meaning King, is used in an exceptional sense in this state, and signifies Prime-Minister. The King himself is called Maharaj Adhiraj. The reigning one is a mere boy of ten years, not troubled much with state affairs. Our host gave us no encouragement about meeting the Prime-Minister; in fact, considering that the latter was an old orthodox Hindoo with strong antipathy for Europeans, our prospect of securing an interview was very gloomy. However, see him we must, as we could not call on any one in the city and could not transact business with any one without making this preliminary official call, and obtaining personally the sanction of his Excellency.

It was while waiting for this that, to avoid loss of time, we took up our camera and went about on photographic excursions. The objects to take were as numerous as they were unique. We would be followed by a gaping crowd, who were more curious than troublesome. At the same time the authorities caused us to be attended by a body-guard (though we thought it quite superfluous), consisting of two men, one, from the Nepaul government, going in front, and the other, from the British Residency guard, following behind.

The city of Khatmandu numbers about 50,000 inhabitants, about one-half of whom are Newars, of Mongolian cast of features, industrious, good-natured people, the original owners of the soil from the earliest prehistoric times down to a century ago, when the Goorkhas invaded their country and dispossessed them. They are the chief traders, agriculturists, and mechanics of Nepaul. They are Buddhists by faith, with a good deal of Hindooism mixed up in their religion. Along with them might be reckoned the Bhooteas, Limbus, Keratis, and Lepchas, though these are more distinctively Buddhists.

On the other hand, under the head of Hindoos come the dominant race of the Goorkhas, reckoned by some from a quarter to one-third of the population, and along with them must be taken the two lower castes of Majars and Gurungs.

The Goorkhas claim to be Rajpoots by descent—i. e., Brahmins par excellence—having been driven out of Rajpootana in central India by the great Mohammedan conquerors when Delhi was in its glory. The princes themselves trace their lineage directly back to the proud royal house of Oodeypore. The Goorkhas are of light complexion. They have regular features, particularly the princes, except when descended from those who have intermarried with natives. Their language is called Parbitya, a modern dialect of Sanscrit, and written in that character, while the

NEWAR WOMEN WEAVING.

language of the Newars is entirely distinct, and written in a different character.

The Goorkhas, although worshipping the same idols and conforming to the same rites and ceremonies as their more southern high-caste brethren, differ from them in that they are willing to eat flesh of several kinds. The killing of a cow, however, is ranked as murder, and punishable with death. Unlike their southern brethren, further, they are of a decidedly diminutive stature, but wiry and strong, not taking kindly to work of any description, being essentially a military race. Brought up as they are in their mountain homes, they have proved themselves, under good generalship, to be of the bravest and toughest sort of soldiers in the East. It is of such metal that the British government likes to recruit its Indian armies, and it is annually supplied with a number of raw levies for this purpose through an understanding with the government of Nepaul.

Nepaul itself has a regular standing army of 15,000 men, drilled and armed (with muzzle-loading guns). Twice this number could be put into the field if necessary. To keep up this army, which is mostly infantry, a small fraction being artillery, every family is obliged to contribute one of its male members. The officers are selected from the nobility, so that as a result of autocratic government there are boy generals and gray-bearded lieutenants. These officers are all dressed in British uniforms, and can be seen every day, often from morning till night, drilling the troops on the parade-ground beside the city wall. These military manœuvres seem to be the one absorbing pastime, as no games or other manly exercises are at all popular with old or young.

The maintenance of so large a standing army, out of all proportion to ordinary needs, is Nepaul's greatest mistake, and can do her nothing but harm. For Nepaul has nothing to fear from India on the south, and with England as a sworn ally, has nothing to fear from Thibet on the north. Were Nepaul to attempt to withstand England, all her own population added to all her troops could oppose no effectual resistance, and history has already shown that though she might fight Thibet alone successfully, yet Thibet backed by China, as she would invariably be, is more than a match for all of Nepaul's combined forces. One cannot help feeling at times that England is doing her best by her bribes and presents of vast stands of arms, together with immense quantities of ammunition, to the states on her Indian frontier, to induce them to turn their attention to the demoralizing pastime of war, and to keep up a ruinous standing army, behind which she can screen herself, and which she can interpose as a buffer against the ever-growing spectre of Russian aggression.

The reigning boy King,[*] already referred to, is the eighth royal master of the Goorkha dynasty who has succeeded to the throne of Nepaul, reckoning from Sri Maharaj Prithwi Narayana Sah, the first of that famous line. The name of " Goorkha" is derived from that of a little town forty miles west of the present capital, Khatmandu. There the founders of this dynasty, a number of high-bred, high-spirited Rajpoot fugitives, who had escaped with their faithful followers from the detested Mogul conquerors of India, obtained shelter, and finding the good-natured, peaceful Newars quite incapable of resisting their presumptuous demands, readily possessed themselves of the government, and occupied Khatmandu (A.D. 1768). Their power kept pace with their increase of territory. The government, like that of all Oriental nations, is an absolute monarchy, the throne passing from father to son, or nearest heir, whose will is supreme. In the course of constant disputes with independent states bordering its territory, Nepaul has often had recourse to arms, resulting, on the whole, in more gain than loss to herself; on the other hand, she has suffered internally from plots, cruel intrigues, and more cruel assassinations, the chief instigators and actors in which have been members of her own royal family.

During the Indian mutiny of 1857[†] and

* The boy King has the short name of " Maharaj Adhiraj Prithwi Bir Bikram Jung, Bahadur Sah Saheb Bahadur Sumshere Jung."

† Nepaul has for generations proved an asylum for many desperate characters, who escape from India in assumed religious garbs. This was notably the case with many during the Indian mutiny in 1857. Among the fugitives came the Nana of Bithoor, of odious fame, commonly known as Nana Sahib. After reaching the Terai forests he was overtaken by a deadlier foe than the British bullet, the ghastly jungle malaria. This information, given by General Kadar Nur Singh, Nepaul's most distinguished officer, and afterward confirmed by other officials, accounts for the failure to ever find trace

A NEPAULESE PRINCESS AND HER SLAVES.

NEWAR WOOD CARVERS AT WORK.

1858 Nepaul had the foresight, under the wise administration of that most able of all her princes, Sir Jung Bahadur, in his capacity as Prime-Minister (though virtually the King), to offer every possible assistance to the British government. In return the British government gave her a goodly addition to her territory, and presented her with large supplies of arms and ammunition, at the same time binding herself to be the firm ally of the Goorkha government, both for offensive and defensive purposes.

Strange as it may seem, slavery exists in Nepaul, though in a somewhat modified form. The slaves, numbering, it is said, 30,000 (though we regard this as rather too high an estimate), are used exclusively for domestic work. Most of them have been slaves for generations, and are not imported from any country outside. Their numbers are augmented at times by fresh additions from free families, who are brought into servitude as a punishment for misdeeds and political crimes. All well-to-do families possess slaves.

of the rebel chief, in spite of the handsome bounty placed on his head. In Khatmandu we saw his widow, Kaku Maharanee, who had for years lived on an allowance from the Nepaul government. She died October 2, 1886.

The princes have great numbers of both sexes, whom they treat, on the whole, with consideration. A woman having a child by her master can claim her freedom. Early marriages are in vogue. The nuptials of the little King were arranged during our visit to Nepaul, with a princess half his age, who belonged to one of the old princely houses in India. The wedding actually took place soon after we came away. Polygamy is allowed and practised by the wealthier classes. A widow, like her southern Brahmin sister, cannot remarry. On the other hand, there are among the Bhooteas and kindred mountain tribes polyandrous families, in which a woman is married to several brothers, the oldest being called father by the first-born, the second brother claiming this appellation from the next child, and so on.

The dress of the Goorkha ladies of rank is very rich, and the materials are of the costliest silks, velvets, and finest muslins, brought all the way by caravan from China, or imported, *via* Calcutta, from European ports. In and about the house they do not wear the long, graceful *sari* of their Indian sisters, but like them have a kind of tight-fitting jacket and a skirt. The Nepaulese skirt, however, is something immense, having folds and pleats which are increased in number according to the wealth and rank of the wearer, and which sometimes require sixty or eighty yards of cloth. Their costume is in no respect European, though they have the same weakness for jewelry as their sisters the world over. The men's dress, except-ing the military uniform, resembles in general that worn by the natives of north-ern India. Of course there are a number of the younger men who have been to

ciency in this as in other necessaries has to be made good by importations on coolies' heads from India. With practically no manufactures, and with mineral and oth-er internal resources undeveloped, Nepaul has little to export except timber from the Terai forest. The bulk of her revenue is derived from this source. But were Nepaul to improve the means of com-munication with India on one side and with Thibet on the other, she would great-ly stimulate the trade which has been

BLOOD-THIRSTY GOD BHAIRUB.

Calcutta and travelled to other places (a few have even been to England); these dress like Europeans.

The inhabitants of Nepaul are principal-ly agriculturists, and the staple crop culti-vated by them is rice. Owing to the fact that the extent of arable land is small as compared with the number of inhab-itants, enough rice cannot be raised to meet local consumption, so that the defi-

carried on between the two countries in a lame, primitive way for ages, and could reap the advantage of her natural posi-tion as connecting link in what has been from time immemorial the most popular and practicable route between the trans-Himalayan countries north and the far south. A railway might be readily con-structed through the valley of the Trisul Gunga and Gunduck, or even down the

ANCIENT SPECIMEN OF WOOD-CARVING.

valley of the Bagmati, to unite with British railways already projected to within one hundred miles of the Nepaul Valley. But such an enterprise cannot be thought of at present without causing a shudder of horror to the whole of Khatmandu.

To the stranger visiting Nepaul, among the most interesting of all objects are the elaborate Nepaulese carvings, which are executed principally in the splendid wood of the sal-tree,* from the Terai forest. Not only the temples and palaces, but also private dwellings, and often the doorways of the meanest hovels even, are loaded with ornamentation in a great variety of designs—peacocks with outspread tails, griffins, snakes, monkeys, birds, fruits and flowers, scores of fantastic beings, giants and pigmies, gods and goddesses, temples, delicate lattice-work and screens—the last-mentioned looking at a distance like gossamer lace that might be marred by the slightest breeze.

* *Shorea robusta*, Roxb., of botanists.

These carvings are too often disfigured, however, by obscene representations. The reason assigned for introducing these objectionable features is some mysterious magical influence they are supposed to exert in warding off evil. The makers of these carvings, who receive but three or four pence per day, are rapidly decreasing in number from lack of patronage, for the public taste has become so degenerated that it craves for the decoration of buildings a style of painting which has more the appearance of gaudy daubs than of anything artistic or attractive. All the Nepaulese carvings are of distinctly Hindoo origin, and remind one of the elaborate ornamentation in the sacred caves of Ellora and Ajuntah and other rock-cut temples which are found over India. At the same time the shape of the buildings, and particularly that of the temples, gives evidence of Buddhistic or, more properly, Chinese influence, for the pagoda form has been adopted, with its tapering core or centre passing through one or more truncated pyramids. These rise gracefully one above the other in contracting tiers, the whole often surmounted by a bright gilded globe, or ending in a carved chatter (umbrella) fringed with prayer bells. Two principal causes can be assigned for the building and preservation of such marvellously picturesque and elaborately ornamented structures in the Nepaul Valley. First, the encouragement this kind of labored artistic adornment received from all classes, beginning with the princes; and secondly, because of the lasting properties of the sal wood, and the nicety with which it received and kept the outlines conveyed to it by patient generations of Newar carvers. When we recollect that some of the most elaborate designs were chiselled out not less than five hundred years ago, and that nothing so delicate or profuse is produced now, we cannot but express regret at the decadence of such beautifully decorative work, and cherish the hope that something will soon be done to rescue this fast-decaying art.

The most striking ornamental work that we came across on one of our photographic excursions was some window-screens in the side of a temple perched upon a hill infested with monkeys. We passed over an unevenly paved walk, worn smooth by the feet of millions of devotees, and mounted a broad flight of stone steps, guarded at the bottom by two large stone griffins and a huge statue of Buddha. The steps became steeper as we ascended, until, reckoning some three hundred and fifty,

we reached the top of the celebrated shrine of Swayambhunatha. It commands a fine view of the city two miles away, the surrounding valley, and the encircling snow-capped mountains.

At the very entrance to the collection of shrines crowded together above is an immense brass thunder-bolt of the god Indra, which is shaped like a huge hourglass, and is laid across a pedestal or platform three feet in height. The latter is plated over with brass sheets covered with animals in bass-relief. Just back of this rises to a height of fifty feet the solid rock of the hill-top, which is cut into a colossal Buddhistic dome or chaitya, and is surmounted by a tapering wooden pagoda running up for another fifty feet. This is capped in turn by a chatter (umbrella), which, reflecting the sunlight from its gilded sides so that it is visible to the whole valley, reminds the traveller of the pagodas raised by pious hands on every commanding point along the Irrawaddy. This chaitya formed the prominent centre around which a whole pantheon of Hindoo deities in stone and brass, as well as copper bells, Bhootea prayer wheels, and the graves of the dead, were arranged in no ap-

SHRINE AND TOMBS OF SWAYAMBHUNATHA.

CREMATION-GROUND AND SACRED SHRINES OF PASHUPATI.

parent order. Here was a spot where, beneath the shadows of the "abodes of the gods," the world's two greatest sects, forgetting their differences, had clasped hands, where Hindooism and Buddhism had bound together in one volume their Sanscrit shastras* and the writings of Confucius, and where the Mongolian from Pekin and the Malabari from Rameshwaram bent the knee side by side in the same sacred precincts, consecrated alike to Buddha and Siva. On the other hand, the "shades of the ancestors," assuming the forms of monkeys, disported themselves and made light of these hallowed scenes, defiling even the Holy of Holies, taunting the most devout with winks, smirks, and fiend-

* For generations the capital of Nepaul has been the favorite residence of Sadus, Upadyas, Gurus, and Lamas—priests and preachers of the Hindoo and Buddhist faith. Hence the place became a regular depository for numerous religious manuscripts and historical records. Mr. Brian Houghton Hodgson and other scholars have accomplished an important work in unearthing, collecting, and translating many of these old Sanscrit and other ancient manuscripts. An interesting and catalogued collection is that of Dr. Daniel Wright (late Nepaul Residency surgeon), at the Cambridge University library, England.

ish grimaces. Then, as if it was all a good joke, they would add injury to insult by daring on the sly to snatch with their sacrilegious paws the votive offerings out of the very hands of the sin-stricken penitents, would impudently retire with their booty, and sit down to eat it at their leisure, perched up beside the nostrils of the gods themselves, and wiping their whiskers on the divine heads! What was most surprising, no one seemed to take notice of them or resent their conduct, and great was the astonishment manifested by the monkeys when we went at them for trying to upset our camera, and especially when an old red-faced one, who must have once been a thorough scoundrel of a Hindoo, thought of appropriating our camera cloth!

Very different from Swayambhunatha stands at the base of a high mountain the neighboring shrine of Balaji—purely Hindoo—where the god Siva, or the Destroyer, lies upon the petals of an open lotus flower, with the venomous cobra di capello entwined around his colossal body from head to foot. The whole is carved out of rock, and is placed, as though floating, in a tank of water. This and other larger tanks adjoining are full of tame fish. Luxuriantly shady trees surround and arch above them, making a fitting bower for the god. There were many devotees in this secluded spot, most of them women. We found them making offerings of rice and flowers in connection with their morning devotions. They chanted their prayers in low monotones, their voices in unison with the sound of the water flowing and falling out of many carved stone spouts.

We were meditating over the picturesqueness of this scene when a trembling devotee came up and pointed out to us reddish spots on the large stone slabs surrounding the Balaji tanks—blood stains, we thought, from recent sacrifices of animals. The devotee, however, assured us that no animals were ever sacrificed here, and that these stains were drops of blood which had rained down from heaven in the last week's storm. He added, with bated breath, that this was a very bad omen; it portended an early calamity, such as had happened before in Nepaul history after this same omen had been given. We smiled incredulously, turned away from our superstitious informant, and dismissed his remark from our thoughts, little dreaming of what we were so soon to experience.

The most sacred of all Nepaul's shrines is Holy Pashupati—purely Hindoo—three miles to the east of Khatmandu city. It is crowded thick with temples, and with bathing and burning ghats (descents to the river). Its rows of stone steps leading down to the sacred waters of the Bagmati are covered with early morning bathers and devout worshippers, who face the sun and mumble over their *munthra thunthras*. Here every February come

wending their way from the most distant cities of India a procession of weary pilgrims, numbering as many as twenty-five thousand. Without waiting for any special movement of the waters, but only for the time of full moon, they have a dip in the sanctifying Bagmati. Hither too the dead and dying are hurried, and laid where their feet will be washed by the sacred stream, to insure for their souls a safe and rapid passage into the realms of bliss. This ceremony over, the body (sometimes even while the fluttering spirit hesitates to wing its long flight*) is made over to the flames of the funeral pile. Here also, we were told, was a spot where the forlorn widow used to commit suttee by casting herself upon the burning pyre of her dead husband.

We had now been at Khatmandu ten days, when the long-wished-for word came that General Runoodeep Singh, the Maharajah of Nepaul, would be pleased to see us on the following day. Accordingly, at the appointed hour, we called at the palace, and after passing several sentries with loaded muskets and drawn swords, were

* I am here reminded of an incident told me by the Residency surgeon. The young wife of a well-to-do Hindoo was struck down by cholera. Our friend the doctor was called, and under his care she rallied, and bade fair to recover. What was his surprise to be told, two or three days after, that the woman was being carried at that very moment to the Pashupati burning ghat! He mounted his horse and rushed down to the place. Here he found his poor patient still alive, but laid out so that her feet touched the flowing stream, while beside her the wood was being arranged, and the cremation ceremonies were under way. The doctor expostulated with the husband and relatives, and urged them to desist at once from their murderous intentions. They were finally prevailed upon to stay proceedings, and to take the poor woman home. She survived only three days. But for her rough exposure to premature cremation she might have entirely recovered.

NARAYAN HITTI, THE PALACE OF THE MAHARAJAH, AND RAJ. GURU'S TEMPLE.

GENERAL RUNOODEEP SINGH, THE ASSASSINATED PRIME-MINISTER.

from all accounts he was not at all equal in abilities or liberal ideas to his brother and predecessor, the late Sir Jung Bahadur. Our call, growing less formal the longer it was extended beyond all regulation limits, proved most interesting. Seated as we were next to the Maharajah, we wished to converse with him directly, and for this purpose we should have had recourse to the Hindostanee language as our medium of communication ; but the nephew of the Maharajah, General Khudgo Sham Shere Jung, who had been educated at Devotion College, Calcutta, wished to air his English, and insisted on our addressing our remarks through him to his uncle. The latter, however, getting warmed up with the conversation, dispensed with his interpreter, and plied us directly with all sorts of questions about England and America, the latest inventions, and the reason for our coming to Nepaul. At length we started to take our leave, and asked permission to visit in the city, and call on any of his subjects. Our requests were no sooner made than granted, and then, as if to delay our departure, the Maharajah showed us about the palace, and finally recognized our farewell salaams by presenting with the regular tokens of Oriental courtesy in connection with calling. They were "pan suparee," or bits of the areca-nut done up in a spicy leaf with lime, the whole covered with silver-foil, and ready for putting into the mouth. We were sprinkled with rose-water, our handkerchiefs scented with oil of sandal-wood, and we were graciously invited to call again. Little did we think, as we passed out of the palace, what an awful calamity awaited our royal host

ushered into the audience hall. It was a long room, fitted up with mirrors, chandeliers, and English furniture generally. The Maharajah was seated on a chair in the centre of a semicircle composed of a dozen of his most distinguished officers, the majority of whom were in military uniform, and all resplendent in their jewelled attire.

The Maharajah looked like a man of sixty with a decided will of his own. He had sharp eyes and a firm lip, but to judge

hardly a week from that date, and what bloody scenes were to be enacted so shortly within the apartments we had just visited.

It was late Sunday night (the Sunday following our visit at the palace) that, seated around a cheery fire at the house of our host the doctor, we began discussing Bogle's and Manning's trips up into Thibet, and with what superhuman efforts they had finally reached its capital, Lassa. Clement Markham's intensely interesting into the room and whispered, audibly, "Hulla hai!" meaning "There's a massacre!" We went outside, and could hear the ominous low din of some great confusion, and of bodies of troops as if in motion. Then came the sharp piercing calls (reveille) of the bugle, followed by the rattle of musketry and the deep booming of cannon.

The scenes of violence, passion, and cruelty enacted that night will never be known. Though the doctor despatched

THE PRESENT PRIME-MINISTER, GENERAL BHIR SHAM SHERE JUNG.

narrative of these trips sets off in an unfavorable light the present apathy, if not positive opposition, of England's Indian government in regard to all private commercial efforts for opening up connections with the countries on India's frontier. It was while we were thus engaged that the faithful old Jemadar, or chief officer of the Resident's body-guard (consisting of eighty Sepoys, natives of India), burst spies to find out the meaning of the uproar, long before they returned, our quiet quarters had become a house of refuge for those who a few minutes before had been reckoned among the highest in the land, and whose very nod was sufficient to call whole regiments into action. Among the first to come was General Kadar Nur Singh. I had met him at my interview with the Maharajah, dressed in full uniform; now

GENERAL YADHA PRATAP JUNG.

refugees, who, with their followers, took up a good portion of the doctor's house, confirmed the report that the Maharajah had been assassinated in his own palace by General Khudgo Sham Shere Jung, the nephew already referred to as our over-zealous interpreter at the palace. They reported other violent deaths —among them those of General Yadha Pratap Jung and his father, the latter acting as chief of the Nepaulese army. Thus in a few words is portrayed what has again and again been repeated in the course of Nepaul's history.

It was days before the political atmosphere in Nepaul became cleared. The party in the ascendant at the palace appointed General Bhir Sham Shere Jung, own brother of the assassin, as the new Maharajah, to take his turn at Nepaul's political wheel of fortune, while all the principal refugees at the Residency were safely deported, through the intervention of British influence, out of Nepaul territory into India.

he was barely covered with a thin suit of under-garments as he rushed up breathless, and begged to be sheltered from impending death. Close on his heels came, in a sad plight, General Dhoje Nur Singh, the adopted son of the Maharajah, and his little boy with him. They were not at first recognized, their appearance being wofully changed from that presented when we had last seen them at the palace, decked in royal robes and ablaze with precious stones. The brothers General Padum Jung and General Rungbir Jung, sons of the late General Jung Bahadur, followed in hot haste. Last of all, after many hair-breadth escapes, appeared one of the Queens, called Jetta Maharanee, the second wife of the Maharajah. These

And we who had been detained unwilling spectators of the above tragical scenes, laboring under a load of indebtedness to our hospitable host, Dr. Gimlette, and appreciating the kindnesses received from the most obliging of British Residents, Colonel Berkeley, were at length permitted to start out on our return journey.

AT THE COURT OF THE KING
OF KINGS

N the day of my arrival in the capital of Abyssinia I had not much time, even had I possessed the desire, to do anything in the way of sight-seeing. Late at night, just as we were making preparations to turn in, a message was despatched from the palace announcing that his Majesty would receive Captain Harrington, the British Resident, at half past eight the next morning, when I was to be presented to the Negus. Accordingly, early next day I put on my war-paint and sallied forth. I felt very foolish in donning evening clothes and a felt hat at 7 A.M., and must have cut a very ridiculous figure riding a mule through the busy parts of the city *en route* to the palace in these garments; but as the Abyssinians saw nothing laughable about me, it did not matter much. On entering the outer stockade of the palace we crossed an untidy, rough, stony court, where a large, square-looking building was in process of construction. On the other side of this we were met by Monsieur Ilg, the King's secret adviser, who conducted us up a flight of stone stairs into the presence of his Imperial Majesty King Menelek II., K.C.M.G., Negus Negasti, Emperor of Ethiopia, King of Kings.

Having been introduced by Harrington and shaken hands with the monarch, I retired a few paces, but only to advance again very shortly, and after a second hand-shake to depart. Such a brief meeting scarcely allowed me to form a fair judgment of the King. Squatting as he was when we entered, I should have taken him to be quite a small man, whereas he stands five feet ten inches high. Though by no means handsome, there is yet a very taking and frank look about his features; or perhaps I should more correctly say an open look. Shahzad Mir, my Indian surveyor, summed his appearance up in these words: "I saw a very little man and a very big mouth."

The following morning it was announced that the King, who is, among other things, styled Janhoi, intended starting that same day for the province of Tigré, and as we were not quite prepared to leave so suddenly, we agreed, at any rate, to see him off for the wars, and follow on as soon as we conveniently could. Contrary to my expectation, his departure from the palace was entirely without ceremony, and considering the importance of the occasion, there were but few people about. The King was evidently bent on getting away as quietly as possible; for on leaving the palace, instead of coming boldly forward into the open, as he might have done, he kept close by the stockade. He was preceded by a motley crowd of soldiers, both mounted and on foot. A similar force followed in his rear, some leading his extra ponies, gaily decorated with red cloth and silver-colored trappings. We rode alongside of the King for some short distance through a struggling mob, through which men with long canes forcibly made a lane for us. We were able to go at a sufficient pace to compel those on foot to break into a double. The scene was a remarkable one; everybody seemed to be in somebody else's way, and one and all shouted, wrangled, argued, and pushed. Away on the outskirts of the moving crowds stood a line of beggars calling loudly on their King —"Janhoi! Janhoi! Janhoi!" My curiosity was soon satisfied, and I was glad when Harrington gave the signal to bid adieu to Menelek and turn our horses' heads homewards.

Two days later we were following the King's steps.

There was no mistaking the road, which took us over the hills in a northeast direction, for numbers of soldiers and their servants were flocking to the same point, whilst a few who had accompanied the King might be seen returning for the purpose of taking the more direct, though rougher, road and along them. Early in the afternoon we sighted the mighty camp of Janhoi and his followers. At first glimpse it looked as though snow had fallen on the plains and hill-sides, but on closer approach the snow proved to be an enormous collection of tents, which so bewildered us that we despaired of ever finding the space allotted to us for our camp. Fortunately M. Ilg kindly met us and conducted us to a camping-ground close to the tents of the Emperor himself. As the day advanced, more soldiers continued to pour into camp, and more tents sprang up in every direction.

The following day, being Sunday, was duly observed, for the army remained halted, and we had the honor of breakfasting with Menelek himself at 10 A.M. As might be expected, there were crowds of attendants round and about the King's quarters. We passed under an awning, and then entered a very fine circular tent, where we found the Negus seated on a low cushioned sofa ornamented with two wings, or arm-rests. Placed in front of him was a large decorated basket holding a pile of thin round pieces of

KING
MENELEK'S PALACE

rejoining him later at Barumeida. As we proceeded at our leisure, we noticed there were two routes, an upper and a lower one, both clearly indicated by the continuous throng of people moving bread, called injerras, from which he occasionally ate. In front of this was a long row of baskets covered with cloth, and holding bread and little dishes of spices. On either side, seated on the ground, were the governors of the provinces, the generals, and other grandees. Amidst this select company stood attendants dangling before their noses yards of raw, quivering meat, which had been cut from the animals the moment after their throats had been cut. From these appetizing joints the guests themselves, armed with long thin knives, cut off pieces, each according to his taste, which they forthwith proceeded to devour with great gusto. By the side of each guest stood a decanter of tej—the great Abyssinian drink—which was always refilled as soon as emptied.

I was surprised at the silence which pervaded the gathering; occasionally Janhoi would make a remark, otherwise there was very little talking, all being bent on eating and drinking — an operation over which they in no way hurried themselves. This semi-barbarous feast, strange to say, was brought to a most unexpected and incongruous end, for glasses were handed round and then filled with champagne, and were emptied with evident gusto; and I was glad to find this little touch of the civilized world so congenial to their tastes, and I thought

to myself it was indeed civilization washing away barbarism. When the King himself was about to drink, his own personal attendants drank a few drops out of their own palms before pouring out for the King. Other attendants then hid him from view of the "evil-eye" by spreading out their shammas in front. Yet it would seem that this custom is falling into disuse, for the King drank his coffee openly, like a European. Besides the distinguished guests who were breakfasting, other officials of importance stood in groups near or about the King. Nobody smoked, for as yet the Abyssinians have not learned the pleasure and benefit to be derived from this sociable practice.

The absence of this habit is due to the edict of King John, who absolutely forbade smoking. Menelek, however, neither forbids nor encourages it, and one will occasionally meet an Abyssinian who does smoke. Before very long smoking will probably be fashionable. As for Ilg, Captain Ciccadicola, the Italian Resident, Captain Harrington, and myself, we sat at a long narrow table at right angles to the King, and were amply and properly regaled; for besides

ABYSSINIANS PARTAKING OF THEIR FAVORITE FOOD RAW MEAT

WITH MENELEK'S ARMY. FIRING A SALUTE IN HONOR OF THE QUEEN'S
MESSAGE FROM A PHONOGRAPH

prodigious piles of injerras and dabo (thick bread), we partook of excellent soup, omelets, and endless courses of meat prepared in various ways. It was perhaps for this reason that we declined the last item of the menu—a lump of raw, quivering meat—although it was an offer from Janhoi himself.

Whilst enjoying our coffee and champagne, Monsieur Legarde, the representative of France, put in an appearance at the party. As the day advanced, the tent grew proportionately hot and stuffy, so that after the remnants of food had been taken away it was with a great feeling of relief that we suddenly found a large portion of the canvas removed, admitting a flow of fresh air, and disclosing many more baskets of injerras placed here and there upon the ground. At the same moment a blast from a long wooden instrument summoned the various regimental commanders to come and be fed, and in response each approached in order of rank.

Some of the seniors were serious-looking old fellows enough; but no matter —whoever they were, down they all at once squatted, tightly packing themselves round the baskets, entirely regardless of elbow-room, and I wondered how ever the attendants managed to stand in their midst and hold up their loads of raw meat. These enormous pieces of flesh gradually grew less and less, as the officers continued to cut and slice till the bare bone alone remained. After this function great numbers of soldiers in their turn were fed outside; but I had really had sufficient enlightenment in Abyssinian diet for one day, and actually dreamed of raw meat that night. The King himself is a restricted feeder, showing even in this respect ideas far in advance of his subjects. Sometimes he even forgets all about breakfast until the afternoon, whereas one of the chief considerations of an ordinary Abyssinian is his food. The King generally ends the day at nine o'clock, starting early again at 3 A.M. On the afternoon following the feast we were destined to enjoy for a second time the honor of visiting the King, for Harrington had brought a message for him from her Majesty Queen Victoria, which she herself had spoken into a phonograph.

As we entered the tent, nearly half of which had been opened, we found the King seated as usual, whilst around him stood a number of dignitaries. Captain Harrington and his sowars, with drawn and carried swords, took their places immediately opposite the monarch. A table was then arranged in front of the King, and on this the phonograph was placed. With the exception of the gurgling sound produced by the instrument, dead silence pervaded the tent. The Negus was highly gratified with the message, even standing up that he might the more distinctly catch the words, for he was much struck with their clearness and firmness. He listened to the Queen's gracious words time after time, and readily consented to my attempting to photograph the scene. During this time a grand salute of eleven guns was being fired to celebrate the occasion. I stepped outside to try and take a picture of this event also, and found soldiers running about in every direction, anxious to learn why guns were being fired on the Sabbath. The phonograph was then carried off to the private quarters of Queen Taitu, who was equally charmed with the message, demanding several times a repetition of the Queen's words. It was a wonder to me that this particular cylinder was not completely worn out. The Queen, although understanding no English at all, was nevertheless easily able to recognize the mention of her own name.

One day I watched from the neighborhood of the royal tent the approach of Queen Taitu and her suite; she was preceded by a large escort of armed mounted soldiers, and immediately around her rode officers and ladies—the whole making a brilliant patch of color under the bright sunshine. The Queen's procession, as viewed from the royal hill, seemed endless. The Queen herself, who was thickly veiled, rode a brown mule, and was protected from the sun's rays by an enormous scarlet umbrella. As she rode past, close to where we stood, we showed our respect, not after the fashion of her own subjects, by stripping ourselves to the waists, but by saluting. Her Majesty's arrival at the royal hill was the signal for my departure.

Menelek, in spite of some faults, has achieved wonders for the well-being of his country. He is far in advance of any previous Abyssinian monarch, and under his peaceful reign the population and prosperity of the Abyssinians have undoubtedly increased. He differs essentially from his predecessor, King John, and has thoroughly won the love of his countrymen. King John was a great warrior, and being a man of fine physique and an athlete, was esteemed by the people. His decision, whether rightly or wrongly given, was law, and though anxious to be just—for he loved his country—he would take advice from none. Menelek, on the other hand, has not the physical or athletic powers of King John. He is of heavier build, and more given to thought and deliberation; yet he is far in advance of his predecessor, for he takes counsel from those about him, and is always mindful of those below him. It is said that at the time of the "pest," some ten years ago, when the people were in dire distress by reason of their losses, Menelek formed a big camp, and setting the example to his people with his own hand, and assisted by his soldiers, tilled the soil, and in due time handed to the sufferers the fruits of their labor—an example that encouraged others to do likewise. I was told that for three whole years he ate no beef; for he argued, "Why should I enjoy plenty while my people are in want?" I doubt if any European ruler has denied himself to the same extent for a similar cause! Yet Menelek is regarded by many as a barbarian. The severity of the "pest" is felt at the present day, for the price of a cow is from twenty-five to forty dollars, whereas its former value was from two to four dollars—animals then being so cheap that the hide was sometimes sold on the live beast, as the owner was too lazy to slay and to skin it. Every day, excepting Sunday, which, as I have said before, is strictly observed, is a market-day at the capital, but by far the largest is on Saturdays, when from early morning villagers coming from all quarters may be seen driving their donkeys or mules laden with goods for sale. One of the most interesting corners of the market is where the ponies are gathered together and their points exhibited along the open sward. There is a very fair supply of ponies, some hundreds appearing in the market, and were there only Englishmen in the country, measures would be taken to introduce fresh blood and improve the present class. With but little training, many ponies as it is will very soon make polo-ponies, for

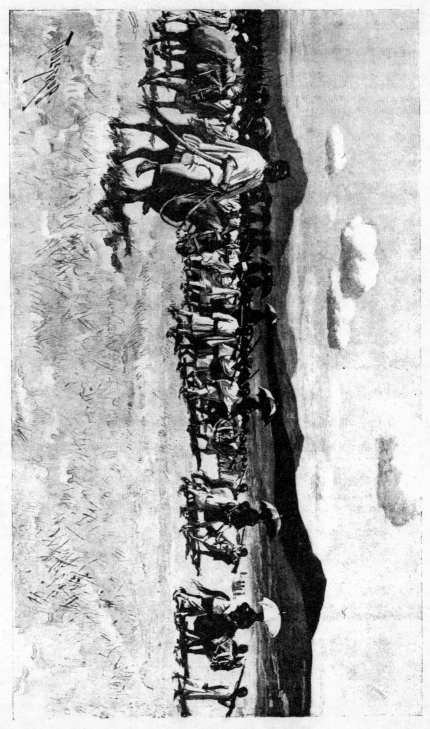

QUEEN TAITU OF ABYSSINIA, AND HER GUARD AND FOLLOWERS

none of them have any fear of the stick, being daily accustomed to the frantic waving of the Abyssinian spears. Few can jump, though most of them take to it willingly enough; but this is not always the case, for on one occasion my latest purchase, in a fit of obstinacy, refused to jump, and knocked down half a mud wall round one of the wattle huts. "Oh,"

women who throng the market, for many of them are excessively pretty. In spite of the big market, the money in circulation is sufficiently awkward to deter most Europeans from buying. A quarter of a dollar is represented by an amole, which is a stick of salt measuring nearly a foot in length. If chipped, however, five or even six of these go to a dollar. Car-

RESIDENCE OF MONSIEUR LEGARDE

cried out the old lady who occupied the place, "it's all very well; if you take a fall, you have the money to pay somebody to nurse you, but I have no one to pay for the nursing of my wall." Next to the ponies the wood-sellers take up their position in the market, and one cannot help being filled with commiseration for these men on comparing the amount of their work and their pay, for they have to bring the "turbs," or long pieces of wood, in to market from a distance of fifteen miles. Close by are the sellers of honey, wax, and butter, the last averaging a dollar for eight pounds. Next are the sellers of various sorts of grain. This is principally barley and teff, but I have also noticed wheat, pease, beans, oats, rice, and linseed. There are also for sale silver trinkets, cloth, beads, cartridge-belts, files, skins, leather straps (machanya), saddles, inferior knives, various articles made of iron, hardware, and so forth, and, lastly, fowls, sheep and cattle. One is much struck by the appearance of the

tridges are employed for smaller sums than this. Adjoining the market-place is the custom-house, where ivory and coffee and piles of Gras rifles are most conspicuous. Mules and donkeys, of which a few months ago large numbers were seen in the market, are now no longer for sale, owing to an edict of the King restricting the price. I was therefore compelled to undertake several two-day trips to search for them.

One day I informed my Abyssinians that I intended paying a visit to the hill called Yerrer, situated west of Adis Ababa, but they did all they could to dissuade me from such a trip, saying that a "Shaitan" dwelt there, and that for this reason they dare not go. This strange bit of news was quite enough to rouse my curiosity, and I made inquiries regarding the Shaitan, and was told the following legend:

Somewhere on this hill there is a cave guarded by the Shaitan, which penetrates so far into the bowels of the earth that nobody has ever been able to reach its limits, where the Gallas, when invaded, were accustomed to conceal their cattle. According to popular belief, in time to come there will at some period emerge from this cave a king whose name will be Theodore, and an abuna (bishop) called Zahai (Sun). These will rule from Yerrer to Gondar. The army of this King Theodore will be composed of Shangkallas.* East of Yerrer all will be prosperous, but towards the west King Menelek and his army will be annihilated. During the reign of this new king a small piece of land will satis fy the wants of thousands of people, and the milk from one cow will be sufficient for thirty men; prosperity will reign throughout, and all will love God, and will strive for paradise and obtain it.

Early the next morning I set out to visit this cave, to try and find out the truth of the legend from the guardian himself. After a pleasant ride of seven or eight miles over grassy, undulating ground, we reached Akaki-a, the clearflowing stream on the opposite bank of which were a number of caves, inhabited by people and their cattle. These caves were all connected by mysterious back passages, and although providing good shelter from sun and rain, still have this drawback—that on emerging from any one of them one stands a very good chance of stepping into space. There are said to be great stores of grass inside these caverns. After another couple of hours' ride we halted by a rivulet for breakfast and to rest the animals. My Abyssinians again took the opportunity of repeating their belief that none who ascended Yerrer would come down alive. Disregarding their assertions, I moved on again at noon, through fields of oats, pease, beans, and linseed, steering for the northeast side of the hill, where a collec-

AT ADIS ABBABA;
SAINT GEORGE'S CHURCH

tion of small villages was situated. Here the present of a "salt" (amole) gained the friendship of one of the inhabitants, who agreed to act as guide and take me to the summit of the mountain and show me the Shaitan's cave. We walked and climbed hard for an hour or so, and were well repaid for our exertions, for I was enabled to take bearings to all my other points. On the return journey, after taking a somewhat indirect route, we climbed with loaded rifles along a precipitous hillside, thick with undergrowth, till quite suddenly we came upon the entrance to the mysterious place. Here lay a quantity of bones, the hoof of a pony, the jawbone of a donkey, porcupine quills, and other tokens of the Shaitan's greed, but all our efforts by shouting and hurling sticks and stones.

* Abyssinians in general call everybody with a black skin a Shangkalla, no matter whether he is a Galla, Turkana Soudanese, or other.

failed to disturb the guardian. To penetrate into the cave was by no means an
inviting task, as it entailed for the first
few yards a crawl, literally *ventre à terre*,
in thick slimy mud, and I preferred to
go off and shoot a couple of gazelles for
supper instead of grovelling in slush. At
daybreak we climbed again to explore

MARKET-DAY, ADIS ABBABA

more caves and renew our search for
Shaitan. Some were most awkwardly
placed, and as we crept along, hanging to
the tufts of grass and hardy plants, my
boots were far from giving me a sound
footing, and my men were equally persistent in warning me that if I did slip, I
should in truth be launched into eternity,
as if the danger of my position was not
sufficiently brought home to me without
frequent reminders. Search as we might,
all was in vain. We therefore returned
down the eastern side, in order to see
some famous ruins of a building said
to have been erected by Cadros (King
Theodore). The outer walls had originally been of circular shape, and inside
them there had been a square building,
where the remains of massive pillars and
the ruins of steps leading up to the interior
could be distinguished. The whole had
been built of slabs of sandstone. Some
of them were of immense size (as much
as twenty feet long), and the sight naturally made me pause and wonder how on
earth men contrived to carry and place
them.

Another excursion I made was to the
famous mount of Zaquala, which has been
described as a kind of Abyssinian Lourdes,

or Pool of Siloam. There is a legend
connected with Zaquala. There is a lake
at the very summit, from the centre of
which a dim light, it is said, used to be
seen shining through the dead of night,
but which latterly, owing to so many sin-
ners visiting the spot, had disappeared.
It is also said that on this mysterious hill
there are two big stones
lying close together.
No sinner is allowed
to pass between them
until he confesses his
faults; but should any-
body whose soul is per-
fect attempt the pas-
sage, he will pass
through without harm.
The lake, too, has mar-
vellous properties, for
all who bathe in its
waters not only cleanse
their bodies, but their
souls also. There is no
end to the legends con-
nected with this priest-
ridden spot. I set out
for the same mountain
with half a dozen Abys-
sinians, taking a fairly good track through
grass, at times over steep and rocky paths.
The climb was enlivened on the way by
a successful stalk after a gazelle, and rewarded at the summit by finding there a
lake of wonderful beauty. It lay silent
at the bottom of a natural hollow; the
hills rose up on every side for some
six hundred feet, and here and there
were thickly wooded. Around the lake
grew turf and shady bushes, and there
was an air of sanctity about the place.
As we stood cooling in the breeze and
gazing on the sombre water, I broke silence by saying that we would first visit
the two holy stones, which our guide
pointed out close by. They certainly
were rather awkward, but majestic. I
was the first to try to get through. When
half-way I stopped short, pulled a long
face, and shouted. The men were at their
wits' end, until my laughter spoiled the
joke, which they all thought tremendous
fun.

We next inspected a rounded rock
standing alone on the grass by the
water's edge. It was actually sweating
in the sun, this being due to the practice
of certain Gallas, who, in order to propitiate the spirit of the stone, deposit a

RUSSIAN REPRESENTATIVE, VLASSOF, AND HIS ESCORT

small dab of ghi on its surface. We then saw, hidden in the midst of cotton and juniper trees, a couple of churches, close to one of which dwelt a "fakir." This holy man had spent his entire lifetime wrapt in meditation, wanting neither money nor food, and living entirely on the grass. He was so concealed by thick bushes that I could not catch a sight of him, though I distinctly heard his mumblings.

Whilst enjoying our luncheon, three priests passed by, who, on hearing that I was Ingliz, expressed a wish to show me a third church, where men came to worship. This sacred spot consisted of three holes in the midst of some rocks, large enough to hold worshippers. There was nothing remarkable in their appearance, but the fact of men electing to bow down in such a place struck me as distinctly odd. The priests told me the depth of the lake was beyond measure, but I had no means of verifying the statement. Its height above the sea-level

was about 9000 feet, water boiling at a temperature of 195.8.°

One day Harrington and I rode out to the forest of Managaska, fifteen miles distant, where some of the best timber is procured, Riding over pleasant grassland, with occasional gullies and rivulets, we eventually reached the abode of the King of the Forest, who happens to be a Greek. Greeks will somehow or other ferret out the least frequented spots on earth and there eke out an existence. Around his circular wattle hut — the home of this particular Greek—a space had been cleared, and the views over the tops of endless cotton-trees were magnificent. He was happy enough with his Abyssinian wife and female slave, drawing sixty dollars a month from the royal treasury, and as we reclined on carpets sipping Turkish coffee beneath a shady tree, hot and tired from our long ride, I for a moment, but only for the moment, envied the little Greek, as he related his battles with the countless panthers, and stalks over the hills after game. The spot well deserves a visit by reason of its beauty, not to mention the hospitality of the Greek.

Amidst my preparations the days slipped by at an alarming rate, and had there been more English people at the capital I might have never wished to quit it. Some of our mornings were spent hunting the "Jack," but the royal pack (the dogs were being trained by Harrington for the King) at first were scarcely accustomed to our ways, and the day generally ended by our chasing the "Jack" with spears and without hounds. Others were employed in visiting our Russian, French, or Italian neighbors, or in a chat with those most hospitable and charming people M. and Mme. Ilg.

In Abyssinia there are as good a climate and as good sport as one could possibly wish to have, but there is a dearth of Englishmen.

The Russian Residency is distinguished by a "tame" ostrich which guards the portals. On entering the enclosure the first time I was taken quite unawares by the "pet" rushing furiously at me and my pony. Had I been able I should have fled straight away, but an irate ostrich, of all animals, gives no time to think of flight, and I mechanically slashed out right and left with my stick, while my attendant aided by throwing stones from a safe distance.

While in the midst of the excitement, Mme. Vlassof appeared on the veranda of the house and called out, in a great state of mind: "Do nothing! do nothing!" This advice, however, I was rude enough to disregard, but retiring and defending, I eventually made good my retreat to where she stood, when the ostrich, more obedient to Mme. Vlassof's voice than I had been, desisted from further attack. In order to guard against any further encounter I promised to arm myself with a sharp sword, hoping that my threat would cause the bird to be tied up if its life were valued.

Sunday, the 18th December, was my last day in Adis Abbaba, and was largely taken up in making final calls on my many good and hospitable friends. Finally I bade good-by to Captain Harrington, the last European I should see for many months, and started on my long journey through unknown Abyssinia, with the hope of eventually joining the Sirdar at Khartoum.

RUSSIAN RESIDENCE AT ADIS ABBABA, SHOWING
M. LEGARDE AND M. AND MME. VLASSOF

THE SONS OF THE STEPPE

MOUNTED KHIVAN AND BOKHARIOT.

THE region with whose inhabitants we have now to do lies between the Irtish and the Oxus, and descends from the parallel of London to the mountains of the Pamir: an area amounting to one-twentieth only of the Russian Empire, but larger than any two of the other states of Europe. Roughly speaking, we may call it Russian Turkistan, with the provinces added of Akmollinsk and Semipalatinsk, which two were formerly part of western Siberia. The surface is of the most varied character. After the Himalayas it contains some of the highest mountains in the world. It possesses, too, enormous plains, fruitful valleys, and barren wastes, as well as sandy, brackish, and marshy tracts. More than half the soil is desert; nearly all the remainder is pastured by nomads, and the portion under cultivation is only about two per cent. of the whole.

The climate of this region is as varied as its surface; for in the north it is sometimes as cold as in Greenland, whilst in the south, in July, the heat equals that of the Cape Verde Islands, which are nearer the equator by 1700 miles. In fact, there is

A KIRGHESE OF THE ADAEF TRIBE.

a difference of as much as 122° Fahrenheit between the temperature of the hottest and coldest days. Dryness is the peculiar characteristic of the climate. Rain in the summer, except in the mountain districts, is an exceedingly rare phenomenon.

One result of this want of humidity in the Turkistan mountains, valleys, and plains is the gradual drying up of the soil during the present geological period, as testified to by the basins of the Syr-Daria and Oxus rivers, wherein are seen old river-beds partially filled up, while numerous rivers that of old were tributaries of some principal stream now stop half-way and lose themselves in the sands. Small lakes have evaporated by hundreds and by thousands, leaving behind only beds of salt. Great lakes like the Balkash, the Aral, and the Caspian have shrunk; others have disappeared.

By reason of this desiccation a large portion of the country has been transformed into Steppe, not only in the lowlands, but also in the mountains, where a depression in the surface is often a Steppe, with vegetation singularly limited both as to the number of species and their period of growth. The climate, in fact, in such cases, is scarcely more favorable to vegetation than in the arctic regions, so that the natives of Siberia, of whom I wrote in a former paper, have this point in common with the children of the Steppe, that the yearly development of plants is limited in both regions to about three months;

in the north by the snow of winter, and in Turkistan by the drought of summer.

The people of Russian Turkistan are of two races, the Caucasian and the Mongolian. The Caucasian has two branches, the Aryan and the Semitic, which latter comprises the Arabs and Jews. The Aryan has also two branches, namely, the Iranians, called Tajiks (descended from the aborigines of Bactriana and Sogdiana), and the Iranians proper, that is, the Persians, Afghans, Hindus, and Gypsies. Again, the Mongolian race is divided into two branches, the Turko-Tatar peoples of the Altai Mountains, and the pure Mongols. To the first belong such as the Kazaks, Kara-Kirghese, Uzbegs, Turkomans, Tatars; and to the second belong the Kalmuks, Chinese, Sibos, and some others.

The Sarts, Taranchis, and Kuramas are a mixture of several races, but may be numbered among the Turkish stock, since Sarts and Taranchis in type and language resemble the Uzbegs, whilst the Kuramas resemble the Kirghese. Another people, called the Dungans, serve to connect the Turkish and Mongol races, but in type they resemble more closely the Turks. In fact, the Turk peoples predominate in Turkistan. The Kirghese are the most numerous; then come the Sarts; after which the relative numbers of the peoples are supposed to range in the following order—Uzbegs, Tajiks, Kuramas, Kipchaks, Russians, Kara-Kalpaks, Taranchis, Kalmuks, Manchus, Dungans, Tatars, Turkomans, Persians, Hindus, Jews, and Gypsies.

Passing now to classifications of the population, we find Muhammadanism is the belief of the mass of the people in Russian Turkistan. The Christians come next in number; then the pagans; and last of all the Jews. A noticeable feature of the Turkistan population is that the male sex far outnumber the female, whereas in Europe the preponderance is of females over males. This abnormality in Turkistan is not accounted for by the existence of Russian troops, for among the natives is seen the same thing.

The Kirghese, who frequent the plains (or more accurately the Kazaks, as they are called, to distinguish them from the Kara-Kirghese, who live in the hills), are not only the most numerous of the people of Turkistan, but they wander over the largest territory. I first caught sight of their tents from the Governor's house at Omsk, on the Irtish, and after driving south and west for more than 1500 miles had scarcely left them behind till I got south of Tashkend, after which I met them again north of Khiva.

The Kirghese are divided into the Little, Middle, and Great Hordes, each of which is subdivided into races, the races into tribes, the tribes into clans, and these into *auls*, or groups of tents, each living in independence. Their number I compute at two and a quarter millions. The Kirghese are fairly strong, but clumsy, with slouching gait on foot, though bold riders. Their sense of sight is so keenly developed that they can see small objects at seven miles' distance. In character the Kirghese is unsophisticated, honorable, and brave, until he sees the chance of gain, and then he is prone to thieving. They are also revengeful. The men work hard only when necessity presses, domestic labors being invariably left to the women. They prefer idleness to work, and having food and raiment, are perfectly content.

Their raiment resembles that of other natives of Central Asia. Nowadays those that are at all well off have shirts; but the poor continue to wear next the skin their *chapan*, as they call it, or *khalat*, closely resembling a loose dressing-gown, over which as many other like garments are worn as the weather requires. Commonly the *khalat* is made of cotton or *armiachina*—that is, a mixture of cotton and silk—but for the rich it is made of silk of gaudy colors in staring patterns, or sometimes even of velvet. I remember seeing a man "at church" in the great mosque at Bokhara clad from head to foot in a crimson velvet robe. These garments for grandees are sometimes embroidered with gold and silver; others again are of fur, one I bought in Bokhara being lined with jackals' skins. Trousers both for men and women are of buff or reddish leather, immensely wide and baggy, but found to be so suitable to the climate that the Turkistan soldiers wear them. The shaven head of the Kirghese is first covered by a skull-cap called a *tibetei*, and over this on certain occasions the men wear tall steeple-crowned hats with brims turning up in two horns, made of felt or velvet embroidered with gold. These, however, are for gala-days. An equally striking hat I saw in use among

A KIRGHESE BRIDE.

the Adaef Kirghese, who wander in the vicinity of the Sea of Aral, made of sheepskin, something in the shape of a baby's hood, the flaps covering the shoulders. It was by no means elegant in appearance, but a great protection from the wind of the Steppe to a man perched for days and nights on the hump of a camel. The foot-coverings are slippers in summer and leather boots in winter, for both sexes, those for women being colored, and often embroidered.

A Kirghese is proudest, however, of his girdle, often richly covered with silver, and from which hang bags and wallets for money, powder, bullets, knife, and tinder-box, or flint and steel, but not a tobacco pouch, the Central Asian represent-

ative for this being a small gourd, which serves for a snuff bottle. Finger-rings I saw among them of silver, and in the Ili Valley I bought from the thumb of a native an archer's ring of jade.

The women dress much like the men, except that the under-garment resembles a close-fitting shirt. Above this they wear a *khalat*. The poor women swathe their heads with calico, forming a compound turban and bib, but the rich wear sometimes a square head-dress of huge proportions enveloped in a white veil, or again an embroidered cap from which falls a kerchief of silk. The hair is plaited in small braids, and adorned with coins and tinkling ornaments. To these may or may not be added necklaces, bracelets, etc., but

TARANCHI MARKET AT KULDJA.

there is one thing rarely omitted from female costume, which is a silver amulet hanging on the breast, in the form of a kernel, cylinder, or triangle, containing Muhammadan writing or perhaps prayers, and given by the husband at the time of marriage.

The various circumstances connected with marriage among the Kirghese remind one strongly of patriarchal times. Fifteen is the marriageable age, and preliminaries are commenced by the parents of the bridegroom sending a deputation of match-makers to the parents of the bride, offering presents, and among them a dish specially prepared for the occasion of liver and mutton fat, which signifies that they mean matrimony. After this the compliment is returned by presents and a similar dish sent by the girl's parents to those of the bridegroom. The bride's father then summons a meeting of kinsmen to consider the *kalim*, or gross amount to be paid for the bride. The *kalim* may consist of forty, sixty, or one hundred sheep, or from nine to forty-seven head of cattle, besides which *kalim* the bridegroom has to give at least two presents of camels, horses, cows, fire-arms, or *khalats*. These

things decided, the bride's father sends to the bridegroom's *aul* for the *kalim* and one of the presents, after which the bridegroom takes the other present and goes to see the bride for the first time. Not that he can easily change his mind when things have gone thus far, for the delivery of his present virtually seals the marriage contract, and he is so firmly betrothed that should he die before the time of marriage, the intended wife has to go home to his parents, and be taken for the wife of the next son. *Vice versa*, if during the period of betrothal the girl should die, her parents are bound to give instead their next daughter, or in default of one to return the *kalim* and pay a fine.

When the period of betrothal is at an end, the bridegroom goes to the *aul* of his bride, who is given up by her parents, with a dowry of a tent, a camel or riding-horse, cattle, and a bride's head-dress, besides a bed, crockery, and a trunk of wearing apparel. On the wedding night the mullah, or priest, places the bride and bridegroom in the midst of a tent, puts before them a covered cup of water, and begins the prayers. Then he asks the contracting parties if it is with their full consent they engage themselves to be married, and three times gives them the water to drink. Mullahs sometimes put in the water vessel an arrow with a tuft of hair tied thereto from the mane of the bride's horse, or one of her ribbons; others dip therein a paper of written prayers. The happy completion of a marriage is followed among the Kirghese by feasting and games, and then the newly married depart to the bridegroom's *aul*, with the camels carrying the trousseau, and the portion of his wealth which a father gives to each of his daughters on her marriage.

The Ili Valley is a continuation of the Steppe, southeast of Lake Balkash, running in the shape of a wedge between the Ala-Tau and Thian-Shan mountains, the base of the triangle being open to the Steppe. It is the most accessible depression by which the great plateau of Central Asia may be reached from the Turkistan plains. Hence the district about Kuldja has served as a resting-place for the vast hordes whose migrations, conquests, and defeats have formed so important a chapter in the history of Asia. Thus the Ili Valley has become a half-way house between the Turanian races of Central Asia and the Mongol races of China. Here meet the settled Mussulman, Taranchi, and Dungan, with the Buddhist Sibo, Manchu, and Chinese, as well as the nomad Muhammadan Kirghese and the lamaist Kalmuk.

The most numerous of the Ili populations are the Taranchis, so called from their occupation as agriculturists, or millet sowers, *taran* meaning millet. Long contact with the Chinese has modified some of their Turkish customs, for, except the mullahs, the men do not wear turbans, but fur caps, whilst women and girls adorn their heads with low cylindrical hats having conical tops. I saw ordinary patterns displayed in large numbers costing 20s. each, but wives of sultans have their caps adorned with jewels, sometimes to the value of over £100. Now and then one sees among the women a pleasant face, but they are all browned, being accustomed from childhood to work in the fields—a striking contrast to their Muhammadan sisters further west, who

GLACIER OF THE KORA.

remain shut up in the house. The males shave their heads, and one of our curious sights in the bazar was a baby boy squalling under this operation. Married women braid their hair in two, maidens in three, long plaits, and both blacken their eyebrows, but do not paint. Most of the Taranchis speak Chinese, but their own tongue is eastern Turki.

The Taranchi bazar in Kuldja has shops somewhat more roomy than those of Central Asia generally, and the street is not covered from rain or sun. It is paved with small stones, and enlivened by mounted horsemen, as well as bullocks laden with brushwood, timber, and fruit.

In this bazar I bought my first Central Asian grapes and nectarines. Apricots ripen at Kuldja in the beginning of July, and we were too late for them; but we found some late peaches that ripen early in August, flat in form, about an inch and a half in diameter and half an inch in thickness. They tasted fairly well, but there was little flesh on the stone. Vegetables and fruit in this bazar were abundant, large melons selling for 5 farthings each, the best apples—good-looking but tasteless pippins—at the same price, and the peaches just alluded to for 4½d. a dozen. These prices for local produce were not exceptional, for eggs cost from 5d. to 8d. a hundred, and fowls from 1¼d. to 2½d. each. Before the advent of the Russians, chickens cost only a halfpenny each. Manufactured goods from Europe, however, were dear, and even Russian tea cost from 2s. to 6s. per pound. Throughout the Kuldja emporiums there is ceaseless movement, bustle, and noise, for the venders of wares scream out to the purchasers, and amongst the inevitables are sheep and dogs, as well as crowds of children, some half naked and others wholly so, chasing one another about and increasing the general hubbub of the restless scene.

When I was in the Ili Valley the numerous peoples mentioned above were under Russian rule, but Kuldja has since been given back to the Chinese, so that many of the races just mentioned do not properly fall within the scope of this paper, but there are still on Russian soil a number of Taranchis who have preferred to remain under the government of the Tsar rather than return to that of their Asiatic rulers.

On leaving the Ili Valley I drove across the plains and came in sight of the northernmost range of the Thian-Shan Mountains, the home of the Kara-Kirghese. The Thian-Shan mountain system is the grandest on the northern slope of the Asiatic Continent, whether regard be had to its area or its length, the height of its crests, the abundance of its snows, or the massiveness of its glaciers. Up to thirty years ago science knew nothing of this vast mountain mass, which now is found to be 1660 miles long, with its highest peaks rising everywhere above the snow line. The average height of these dominant peaks varies from 16,000 to 18,000 feet, and some of them exceed 21,000. The entire mass is estimated as twenty-five times larger than the Swiss Alps, and as forming a protuberance upon the earth's surface considerably larger than all the mountains of Europe put together. The total superficies would cover as much country as the whole of France and Spain.

Almost throughout the dominant range and in certain of its spurs, as in the mountains about the head waters of the Kora, there are glaciers, the number of which is computed to be not less than 8000. Snow bridges also in the Thian-Shan are often met with, much below the glaciers, namely, at 5000 feet or lower. These sometimes attain to a mile and a third in length, and one hundred feet in thickness. They are produced by avalanches, and therefore the snow in them is mixed with rubble brought down together with the snow from the surrounding crags.

The Kara-Kirghese are essentially a nation of shepherds and breeders of cattle, and think it a "come-down" in life when compelled to resort to settled occupations. They are not so rich as their brethren in the plains. Very few own as many as 2000 horses or 3000 sheep. Also they have fewer camels; but, on the other hand, possess an excellent breed of oxen for traversing the mountains. Their cows are large, but do not yield much milk. Yaks are kept by them instead. Their cattle-breeding claims far less labor than agriculture, but is exposed to great risks. For the support of a nomad family for a year are required eleven head of large and ten of small cattle, and to provide hay for the winter consumption even of this number exceeds the working power of one household.

I was much interested to see some of the Kirghese on the march. Their wanderings are thus conducted. When the pasture in a neighborhood is eaten, one or

INTERIOR OF A FAMILY TENT.

two of the young men are sent to select a suitable spot for another encampment, and to clean out the wells. This done, the women pack the tents and the men form the cattle in droves. The camp is ready and starts before dawn, the good women of the family riding in front. I met one old lady in this honorable position, mounted astride a bullock and looking anything but graceful. After her came the other women, variously mounted on the top of carpets, teakettles, tents, etc., the whole being made to wear, as far as possible, a festive aspect. The length of a stage is from 13 to 17 miles, and the *aul* traverses about 25 miles in 24 hours.

On arriving at the place of encampment it is the office of the wife to put up the tent. I chanced to see a woman begin to do so, and would not stir from the spot till I had witnessed the whole operation. The principal parts of a *kibitka*, or tent, are large pieces of felt to cover a frame-work that consists of lintel and side posts for a door, and pieces of trellis-work surmounted by poles that meet in the centre. On this trellis-work are suspended arms, clothes, bags, basins, harness, and cooking utensils. Not that there is a large variety, however, of the last, for most of the cooking is done in a large open saucepan that stands on a tripod over a fire in the middle of the tent. Crockery-ware is not abundant, being of hazardous carriage, and metal goods are not cheap, so that leather has to do duty not only for making bottles (specially those for carrying *koumiss*), but also pails, some of which are furnished with a spout. I met with no small saucepans or teakettles of English shape, their place being supplied by *kurgans*, or water-ewers, somewhat resembling a coffee-pot. Round the walls of the tent are piled boxes, saddles, rugs, and bales of carpet, against which the occupants lean, the head of the household sitting opposite the door, and in front of him the wife in attendance.

I was honored with an invitation to dine in one of these tents, the dishes being

WELLS IN THE "HUNGRY STEPPE."

put before us according to our rank. I heard nothing of grace before meat, but I never saw anything to exceed the alacrity with which the dishes were cleared. Hands were knives and fingers were forks, the meat being torn from the bones as by the teeth of hungry dogs. It is considered polite for a Kirghese superior to take a handful of pieces of meat and stuff them into the mouth of an inferior guest, an elegancy I saw practised on another, but from which, mercifully, I myself was excused.

Leaving the Kazaks of the plains, the Kara-Kirghese of the mountains, and the Chinese races of the Ili Valley, I went further south among the Iranian and Uzbeg populations in the Zarafshan Valley, and visited the cities of Samarkand, Bokhara, and Khiva. Our route thither from the northern crest of the Thian-Shan lay across the "Hungry Steppe." Traces of old canals are here and there visible, showing that certain parts were formerly cultivated, but with these exceptions we know from the accounts of Chinese travellers of more than 1200 years ago that this Steppe was much the same then as now. Not far west of Murza-Rabat the traveller leaves behind him the Steppe and enters the most fertile oasis under Russian rule in Central Asia, namely, the valley of the gold-strewing Zarafshan. The valley is full of ethnological interest,

its peoples being at least eight in number, namely, Tajiks, Uzbegs, Persians, Jews, Hindus, Bohemians, Afghans, and Arabs. The Tajiks are the aboriginal inhabitants of the country.

The upper end of the valley, about the sources of the Zarafshan, is called Kohistan, and here live many of the mountain Tajiks, who are called *Galtchas*. They, in common with the inhabitants of Karategin, Darwaz, Shignan, and some other parts of the Pamir, speak dialects of Persian, and seem to have been driven to the mountains of Central Asia as were the Britons into Wales.

The Galtchas are allowed by the Russians almost to govern themselves. Each village has its elder, who bends to the decision of the majority. They are divided into two classes—the mullahs, or educated, and the poor. When sick they have recourse to medicaments and exorcism, as is to some extent the case with others of the Central Asian tribes. When a man dies his body is wrapped in a mat, placed in a small narrow trench, and covered with branches and earth. On returning from the burial a feast is given, and the family goes into mourning, but the widow may marry again after seventy days. Morality is said to stand high among the Galtchas, the adulterer being turned out of his house, and his goods confiscated. Polygamy is permitted, but the Galtchas seldom have

MOSQUE AT KHIVA.

more than one wife. Slavery appears never to have existed among them.

Very different is it in this last respect with the Tajiks and Persians of the plains, for the latter are descended from captives taken in Merv, and brought hither for slaves by the Emir of Bokhara in the middle of the last century. The Tajiks form by far the largest portion of the population of Samarkand, and represent the industrial class. They weave and knit, do blacksmith's and coppersmith's work, tanning, carpentering, joining, and turning, also boot-making, harness and saddle making, as well as dyeing, pottery, and needle-work. Their products, however, are very inferior to those made in Europe, the implements in use in the factories being of the most primitive and unsatisfactory kind. The Tajiks weave both silk and cotton, but rarely hair or wool, except in the mountains. Among their products are striped glazed materials of cotton, of which a workman can weave about nine yards a day. For this he receives two and a half pence wages, though some weavers can earn as much as sixpence a day.

The sights in Bokhara led me to think of a visit to one of the kings of Israel.

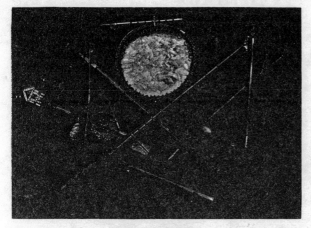

MUSICAL INSTRUMENTS.

and he is expected to be amused by dancing boys called *batchas* and musicians. The musical instruments of Central Asia are somewhat limited in number. One I saw at Bokhara resembled a guitar, forty-six inches long, with a sounding-board nine inches by four. It might be played with a bow or with the thumb. Another instrument resembled the flageolet, and had something of the hautboy sound, or between that and the bagpipe. Singing is frequently accompanied by men beating tambourines before a charcoal fire in a brazier, over which from time to time they hold their instruments to tighten the parchment. The *batchas* allow their hair to grow long like that of girls, and dress in long flowing robes and wide trousers. Their performance interested me to see once, but when repeated again and again it became exceedingly tedious. The musicians on occasions of dancing sit upon a piece of felt or carpet, dressed in their tall sheep-skin hats, which give the Uzbegs a somewhat ferocious appearance.

The cities had walls great and high, the gates of which were closed by night. Mounted embassies in gorgeous clothing and harness were sent to meet and conduct me from town to town, as well as to lodge, feed, and serve me as the Emir's guest.

This barbaric splendor became less observable as we approached the khanate of Khiva, where Persian influence is somewhat more marked than in Bokhara. Speaking generally, however, it may be noticed that such remains of architectural beauty as exist throughout Central Asia are all of Persian origin. The monuments of Samarkand are notable examples of this, and so was the Kashi work, or inlaying of colored tiles.

In Khiva itself the building most revered by the natives is the Mosque of Hazreti Pehlivan-Ata, the patron saint of the city. It has a large dome about sixty feet high, surmounted by a gilt ball, and covered with green tiles. The building is of kiln-burnt bricks. I approached the interior through a darkened passage, where the tombs of former khans were exceedingly dusty and dilapidated. From beneath the cupola was obtained rather a pretty view of the tiles with which it is lined, and varied with blue tracery interwoven with verses from the Koran. This dome, owing to its construction, is said to have peculiar acoustic properties, to which the Khivans attach superstitious importance.

The Uzbeg women are jealously kept out of sight of a male stranger, even though he may be a distinguished guest,

AN UZBEG MUSICIAN.

ATHENS

THE PIRÆUS.

ATHENS.

THE Athens of classic times, where centred the glory of Greece, has, at the mouths and pens of all, her meed of praise. The Athens of to-day, the capital of the realm of George I., King of the Greeks, is an object of interest not simply as "the heir of fame," but for what she actually is, and for what she is likely to become in the near future. Not only the antiquarian and the classical scholar, but the artist, the student of politics, the pleasure-seeking tourist, and the observer of men and manners, will be richly repaid if he takes the pleasant voyage of two or three days from Naples to Athens, even if he go no farther to the east.

Three cities the world honors as the sources of the religion, the law, and the "fair humanities" that have made us what we are: Jerusalem, the mother of Christianity ; Rome, the stern mistress who taught the world state-craft and respect for law; and Athens, in whose pure atmosphere the love of knowledge and the love of beauty first gave a perfect form to art, philosophy, and literature. Rome, with her insatiate thirst of conquest, drew into her own later history that of the Christian Church, as she had imitated and borrowed from the literature, art, and philosophy of Athens. And from the Christian fervor that Rome had thus drawn from Jerusalem, working upon that love of perfect forms of beauty which Athens had taught her, came the greatest latter-day glory of Rome—that art of idealistic painting which made her again the mistress and the teacher of the world.

Yet it is not chiefly for what Greece has done through her influence on these rude Roman conquerors whom she took captive, that the world is indebted to Athens. All the nations of Europe have at their best epochs gone directly to her for instruction. Greek literature has influenced the development of all the literature the polite scholar thinks deserving of his study. Greek constitutions have served as models or as warnings to every statesman and to every student of politics. The central ideas of the constitutional governments now foremost in the world are popular elections; magistrates the servants of the law, but responsible to the people; two legislative bodies, one popular, the other conservative; and local autonomy in local affairs. All these are Greek principles, borrowed from Greek history. And even now we are not beyond learning from the history of Athens. The conditions of Athenian society, the aims and habits of thought of the citizen of Athens in the days of her glory, were in many ways strikingly like those of America to-day. Webster, in the maturity of his power, after reading again the funeral oration of Pericles over the soldiers slain in the war with Sparta, cried out, as he closed the book, "Is this Athens, and an Athenian orator? or is it an American, speaking to citizens of the United States?" Athens saw the rise of "bosses" and "henchmen" in her degenerate days. Her thoughtful citizens lamented the substitution of blind obedience to a "working" demagogue for intelligent allegiance to the patriotic statesman who voiced in his speeches and embodied in law the en-

GENERAL VIEW OF THE ACROPOLIS.

lightened public sentiment he had helped to create. Even the notorious maxim whose influence has cursed American politics for the last fifty years, "To the victors belong the spoils," is a translation from the pages of Xenophon.

In the natural sciences, the Greeks made so many shrewd guesses that science in its greatest strides has seemed but to follow the line of Greek conjectures. Philolaus maintained, twenty centuries before Galileo, that the sun was a globe in the centre of the system, and that the earth and the other planets revolved about it, the earth's own motion on its axis causing day and night and the apparent motion of the stars. Cuvier's work of classification in zoology is in part anticipated, in the *History of Animals*, by Aristotle. Geology was prophesied when Xenophanes inferred, from fossils, extinct races of animals and great changes in the earth's crust. All the world knows how progress in chemistry and physics has followed the revival of Democritus's happy "atomic theory."

Yet it is in the realm of ideas rather than of material science that the glory of Greece and Athens lies. It is because Socrates and Plato made intensely real that distinction between right and wrong which the sophists were attempting to discard and deny; it is because her great

poets set forth so nobly the same commanding force of moral law, however clearly they may have depicted the failures of Greeks to comply with its requirements; and because all this is done in literary forms that are as perfect and as harmoniously proportioned as are her statues and her temples—it is by this perfection of thought in perfect forms that Athens has held her sway over the minds of men. The reign of political law among the nations may have been the lesson of Rome to the world. The recognition of a natural moral law in philosophy, and the reign of harmony, self-restraint, and measured proportion as the basis of beauty in art and in literature, the world owes to Athens. And in architecture (if we except the Gothic—grand by its aspiring lawlessness), in plastic art, in philosophy, oratory, and poetry, the world measures all its later work by a reference to the perfect standard of the Attic ideals.

It has been too much the fashion to speak of the Athens of to-day as having little left to her save these glorious memories of the past. We have been told that the race type has utterly changed, that the language has degenerated almost beyond recognition, that the old customs and traditions are utterly dead. The lectures of Felton, the discoveries of Schliemann, turning all eyes once more toward Greece, and the interesting articles lately published in the *Philhellenic Review*, in London, have done much to remove from the English-speaking public this false impression. Greece is assuming every month a more prominent place in the consideration of those who are troubled by the Eastern Question. And this awakened interest in Greece will lend interest, it is hoped, to an article which, omitting all attempts at detailed description of her wonderful ruins, and her museums so rich in statuary of the best period of art, untouched by the restorer's chisel, shall simply record some of the impressions of a recent stay of two months at Athens.

The traveller approaching Athens from the east changes steamers at Syra, in the heart of the Cyclades, and after a night voyage finds himself coasting Ægina at dawn, and at sunrise anchored in the Piræus, the port of Athens. The harbor presents a busy, thriving aspect. At the close of the revolution in 1830, there were but half a dozen fishermen's huts where now stands a rapidly growing town of twenty or thirty thousand inhabitants.

The idea of entering Athens by railroad is repellent to any lover of her past.

Who would be carried by steam into the presence of that altar-rock to which lovers of the beautiful in all ages have looked for inspiration? Who would lose the delight of the first long look as the Acropolis rises into sight above the roofs of Piræus, or make shorter the keen pleasure of each new identification of hill and plain and stream and ruins before you with the strangely familiar yet unreal image you have formed from maps and books?

We drove slowly up the carriage road, which follows the line of the northern long wall. The railroad (the only passenger line in Greece) follows the line of the south or "middle long wall," thirty rods to the right. In classic times, thronging crowds of laborers, merchants, and travellers filled the space between the rows of closely crowded dwellings which on either side lined these old walls. Now there are not half a dozen houses between Athens and Piræus. The old substructions of the long walls of solid masonry twelve feet thick are still to be seen in many places, and have been used as the bed of the carriage road and the railway.

Half way to Athens we halt at a little

THE BYZANTINE CHURCH.

KING GEORGE.

derful rock draw your eyes irresistibly to themselves; but the Greek Church and the Middle Ages claim your attention as the street divides, passing on either side the little Byzantine church which fills the roadway. Then through a street like the modern parts of Paris, the sharp gray cone of Lycabettus towering before you on the left, close over the city, you drive on toward the park and the royal palace, which close the vista.

Our hotel, the Angleterre, faced the palace, a broad park intervening. It was St. George's Day, and the custom of the Greek Church keeps the birthday festival not on the anniversary of one's birth, but on the saint's day of the patron saint whose name was given the child when christened. So on St. George's Day were to be observed the ceremonies appropriate to the birthday festival of "George, King of the Greeks." The city was astir. The crowd wore, for the most part, the dress and the quick, nervous aspect of a New York crowd. Here and there you saw the Albanian costume, adopted by the Greeks as the national dress for lack of any other more distinctively their own. Blue, close-fitting breeches; white or blue stockings and gaiters; low shoes of red leather with pointed, tasselled, upturned toes, and no heels; a short black jacket, sometimes blue, cut away, and richly embroidered, worn over a red waistcoat, and a white, embroidered shirt with open sleeves; colored garters at the knee, and a red girdle supporting an immense leathern pouch, from which protrude pistols and a knife or two; on the head a pointed red flannel cap, like a prolonged Turkish fez, falling over upon the side, and ending in a silk tassel. The most remarkable feature of the costume remains to be described. From thirty to sixty yards of white linen about thirty inches wide are gathered in a very thickly pleated skirt, which is

way-side cabaret to water the horses. The supply of water which bubbles from a fountain here is brought in pipes underground beneath the bed of the Ilissus (always dry in summer now) from the famous fountain of Callirrhoë, close under the substructions of the Temple of Zeus Olympias. The sign of the little hostelry was two rival chieftains in ancient armor, lance and shield in hand, painted life-size in most startling colors. Over one was inscribed in Greek capitals ΑΧΙΛΛΕΥΣ (Achilleus).

Driving east up Hermes Street, the main thoroughfare of the city, we pass the Temple of Theseus, best preserved of Grecian temples, at a little distance on our right; and at the corner of Æolus Street, which crosses Hermes at right angles, we catch a glimpse of the old octagonal Tower of the Winds to the south, close under the northern slope of the Acropolis. The ruins on that most won-

starched, and worn over the breeches. This is the fustanella; and where this habit is kept scrupulously clean (which is seldom the case with the class of citizens who most affect it), it is strikingly picturesque. The profusion of skirt necessarily gives to its wearer, in Western eyes, a certain feminine air, which no amount of bushy beard, no fierceness of demeanor, no profusely displayed fire-arms, can quite counteract. Yet as the National Corps came marching down the square, thus uniformed, their brawny limbs and determined faces, and the gleaming colors of their dress, gave them an air not unlike that of the Scotch Highlanders. In Megara and Eleusis, as in many other parts of the interior, the inhabitants, especially the women, adhere invariably to their characteristic and high-colored local costumes, many of which are most picturesque in color and in detail.

Several of the women in the crowd before us, and a few of the ladies in the Greek ministers' carriages, wore the national red cap; and several others, who were dressed in Parisian style, had retained the very pretty Thessalian head-dress —a little golden crown or tiara supporting a light veil thrown back from the face.

As the crowd beneath us grew denser, uniformed policemen kept clear a way for the procession. Small, dark-eyed boys, with the preternaturally intelligent look that marks the Athenian boy, sold to the crowd odes and ballads in honor of the day, written in Greek that would have seemed hardly strange to the eyes of a contemporary of Plato, or to St. Paul himself, at Athens.

A squad of cavalry first came down the broad drive from the palace. Except the uniformly fine-looking officers, who spend extravagant sums for horses of showy action, they were very poorly mounted; but they sat their sorry beasts right well.

Fifty carriages followed, every nation represented at Athens sending its diplomatic servants to congratulate the king, and to attend him on his progress to a special birthday service in the metropolitan cathedral. A little cheer greeted the appearance of each national representative, except in case of the Turks, whose red fezes were met with a significant silence. The Duke of Connaught, then at Athens with his bride, occupied a seat in the king's own carriage, and a prominent

place was assigned to the English Minister. English is the court language at Athens. Indeed, King George's close relationship with the Princess of Wales— she is his sister—has given to his reign something of the character of an English protectorate. For this reason, the Greeks took all the more to heart the action of Lord Beaconsfield—his "nasty trick,"

A GREEK BRIGAND.

they called it, with a broad pronunciation of the Englishman's opprobrious epithet —in bidding Greece refrain when she might have wrested from Turkey by force of arms, during the war with Russia, concessions of territory which all the world feels should be hers. But Beaconsfield assured Greece that she "had a future," and bade her trust it, and refrain from war. When peace was restored, in his secret and public negotiations he utterly ignored the claims of Greece. Indignation at this treatment ran high at Athens a year ago. The crowd in general was less demonstrative than an American or an English crowd on a like occasion; but the greetings to the king were said to be less enthusiastic than they would have been had not the presence of the Duke of Connaught and the English officers with him reminded the Athenians afresh of their keen disappointment at England's failure

PART OF THE MODERN CITY.

to maintain their cause against the Turk. During my stay at Athens, the appearance in the street of the white pith helmet so commonly associated with Englishmen in the East called out expressions of aversion from passers-by, which were very unpleasant. The name of American, however, insures one who is properly introduced the kindest attentions in Athens. American aid and sympathy during their revolution have always been held in grateful remembrance; and the labors at Athens of American missionaries in churches and in schools, and the character of the American representatives at Athens, have confirmed this kindly feeling.

The success of Greek scholars who have made a home for themselves in America, too, is keenly enjoyed by their countrymen. At a reception at the house of Professor Philip Joannes, of the university, several elderly scholars were present who had known Professor Sophocles, of Harvard, and who remembered with delight President Felton's stay at Athens; while others among the younger men inquired warmly after Dr. Timayenis, who is now doing so much in New York to make modern Greek more familiar to the eyes and ears of Americans.

Athens numbers not far from 70,000 inhabitants. Its principal streets are paved, and lighted by gas. Its architecture, in the better parts of the city, and in the common buildings designed for business purposes and dwellings, is not unlike the modern part of any European town. In 1832, when Dr. Hill, the venerable American missionary, who still resides at Athens, took up his abode there, he was obliged to live for some months in a ruined tower, as there was literally not a house standing in Athens. The city is entirely of modern growth. It lies almost exclusively to the north and east of the Acropolis. The old city lay chiefly to the south and west of this hill, and in Roman times extended northward and eastward.

Stone and brick are the building materials. There is no supply of wood for building purposes. Even roots and fagots for fuel are fabulously dear. In the poorer quarters of the city, and especially close under the Acropolis, there are rows of stone hovels, many of them but one story high, dark, noisome, and dirty. These huts are constantly encroaching upon the vacant land on the slopes of the rocky citadel. This land is the property of the government, and no one has a right to build upon it. But there is at Athens either a law or a prescriptive right which prevents the removal or destruction of a home once built and occupied. Taking advantage of this, a couple newly married notify their friends, material is quietly got in the open air, and prepare their frugal meal—as you see how pathetically these little houses seem to cling like suppliants about the knees of the marble-crowned, world-famous Rock of Athens—it takes little fancy to imagine that these homes of

QUEEN OLGA.

together, and on the appointed night, as silently as may be, the simple house is erected, between dark and dawn, the hands of scores of friends making light work; and, with such household goods as they can boast, the young householders take possession at once. Then from the sacred home altar they safely answer the questions of the officers of the law, should any notice be taken of their trespass. As you gaze down upon these simple homes from the Acropolis in the earliest dawn of a summer morning, and see the inmates, roused from a night's rest (often passed beneath the open sky, on the flat roof or beside the humble door), light a little fire the poor have crept for protection beneath the mighty shadow of the stronghold of liberty in Athens's glorious past.

Probably the dwellings of the people, in the days when her grandest temples rose, were little more than shelter from sun and rain—far better represented by these poorer dwellings than by the Parisian streets which make up so large a part of Athens now. The outer walls of the finer houses are built of undressed stone, which is plastered over, and often painted. Light yellows and blues and pinks are sometimes chosen for this purpose, but white is the prevailing color. The roofs are for the most part flat. Along their edges rows of the fan-shaped antefixæ of classic architecture are often placed. Wealthy citizens sometimes build isolated houses with fronts and entrances of the classic orders, the Ionic and Corinthian orders having the preference, for private dwellings. The balcony is indispensable. Often this is half filled with house plants; and many a visitor to Athens, in his sultry morning walks, has learned to avoid the tempting shadows beneath the balconies because of the dropping of superfluous water from these projecting flower gardens after their morning shower-bath.

The finer public buildings are of dressed stone or marble, and several of them would do credit to any city of Europe or America. The patriotism of Greek merchants who win wealth in foreign lands is every year finding expression in handsome gifts or bequests to adorn the city of their love. Thus the Varvakion, the boys' high school of Athens, was erected by Barbakes as a gift to the city; while Arsakes, another wealthy Athenian, twenty years ago erected the Arsakion, or girls' high school. The fine building to which the Polytechnic School and Museum have just been removed, and where the treasures from Schliemann's excavations are on exhibition, is the gift of two wealthy Epirotes who are doing business in Germany, and who feel that they best honor all Greece in honoring Athens. By far the most noteworthy building of modern Athens—another gift of patriotic private wealth—is the Academy, still in process of construction. It is designed for the use of a society of scholars and artists and men of letters, not yet formed, but to be modelled after the Academy and the Institute of France. It is constructed of Pentelic marble, and, with the quarries of Pentelicus close at hand, it has already cost more than $1,500,000. In many of its proportions it is modelled after the Parthenon. The tympanum of the principal front has received a colossal group of statuary—a reproduction, as far as is possible, of "The Birth of Minerva," which adorned the eastern front of the great temple on the Acropolis. The work is wonderfully well done. From this building one may form some conception of the splendor of the great Athenian temples of sparkling Pentelic marble in this brilliant Athenian sunshine, before time and exposure had dimmed the sparkling, crystalline purity which this marble shows when newly quarried. Twice, on clear days, I made a serious attempt to study the details of exterior ornament on the Academy, and could not endure the sight, it was so dazzlingly, blindingly white! My third and successful visit I was forced to make on a cloudy day.

The Academy is of especial interest, because in its decoration the architect is trying the effect of those brilliant blues and scarlets in the moulding of the soffits, and along the cornice, and on the capitals of the columns, of which we find so many traces in the Parthenon. However our modern taste may rebel at the idea of painted statues and temples of marble, there can be no doubt that Athenians of the best age of art used these colors, and found the effect pleasing to an eye and an æsthetic taste as highly developed as any age has ever known. And while few who are destitute of a strain of Eastern love of color in their blood at first admire color thus applied—while we Occidentals have always loved to associate the pure white of the marble with perfect ideal beauty of form—yet no one who has not seen it can intelligently condemn the effect of cólor thus used in this brilliant sunshine, and in a climate where purples and blues and reds and yellows are so rich and so plentiful as here in Grecian seas and sunsets, and on Grecian mountain ranges. Nature riots in rich effects of color here in the Ægean.

The first funeral procession which we met in Athens showed the peculiarities of the Greek custom at their best. On an open bier, resting on the shoulders of six young men, lay the body of a beautiful girl of sixteen, dressed in light blue and white, her face and arms exposed, her head garlanded with flowers, and flowers filling her hands, and lying in knots and clusters on her breast. So she was borne through the clear, sweet morning sunshine that flooded the streets of her native city, to her grave beyond its limits, under the shadow of Mount Hymettus.

Delegeorges, ex-Prime Minister, in the quickly succeeding changes of Greek party government several times at the head of the cabinet, and as often the leader of the opposition, died during our stay at Athens. He was a man whose stanch integrity and democratic love of simplicity had endeared him to the people. He was buried on the day after his death—the rule at Athens.

Dense crowds of men and boys thronged the streets near his house, from which the procession was to start. There were no services at his home, but acquaintances passed in to view the remains, and to offer sympathy to the family, who, as a rule, do not accompany the procession to the church or the grave. Every man who entered the house put on a white lace scarf over the right shoulder and under the left arm, the badge of mourning. Many bearded priests of the Greek Church mingled with the crowd. Their luxuriant hair is never cut, but is twisted into a roll, and knotted on the back of the head like a woman's. They wear a tall, cylindrical hat, brimless below, but with a round flat crown which projects laterally an inch or two. The dignitaries of the Church were resplendent in gold-embroidered robes of white, purple, and scarlet.

The coffin was of blue satin. The body, dressed in plain black as in life,

BISHOP OF THE GREEK CHURCH.

the low shoes tied with white ribbon, was brought out and placed on the open bier. As is the custom at Athens, the upper half of the coffin, for its entire length, had been removed with the lid, and was carried in advance of the bier. On it was worked, in white, a cross and a crown. A glass cover was placed over the body. Flowers in profusion lay about the form of the dead statesman.

Two red banners—one with a formal sacred painting, in the Byzantine style, of the Annunciation, and of Mary and the Child; the other representing, in archaic figures, the Crucifixion and the Resurrection—were borne before the coffin. Then followed the clergy and prominent citizens, while the brass band played a slow-moving dirge. Leaving the crowded streets, I went by a shorter way to the cathedral, where the mention of my na-

tionality passed me through the closed doors, and secured me an excellent place—seats there were none, save for bishops and king.

First enter the sacred banners, and the men with the lid of the coffin; then priests with lanterns, censers, tapers, and banners; then the coffin is carried in, and placed on a black catafalque in the choir. The king, with a few attendants, has taken his place just to the left of the Patriarch's throne, which is on the south of the choir. King George is rather tall, erect, well-formed, fair-haired, with a blonde mustache, and pleasantly regular features. He wears the dark blue uniform of a major, and a light blue short cloak with crimson lining, while a wide light blue scarf crosses his breast from the right shoulder.

Young men press forward to the coffin

with garlands of flowers. They are delegates from the university and the schools. The Patriarch takes his seat, two bishops on either hand, venerable, white-bearded men. The loud shrill chant of the priests, men's voices singing in unison, begins the service. Two singers who are not priests intone most of the service, the priests and bishops over against them answering antiphonally. The music has that weird shaking of the voice within a range of four or five notes which recalls Arabian music. Indeed, the Greeks of to-day, in their church chants and in their street ballads, have no music which does not seem to have been borrowed from Asia. Nothing you see or hear at Athens is more unlike Europe and America than the singing.

The service finished, the king goes out first, after him the priests and the coffin. The procession resumes its slow march through the principal streets. Two hours later, as I stood on the Acropolis, I could see the crowd still standing about the open grave among the cypresses beyond the Ilissus, listening to panegyrics delivered in succession by four ex-prime ministers, the rivals and friends of the dead statesman. For several days the newspapers of Athens were filled with eulogies of Delegeorges. Many of them were very eloquent. I had the curiosity to count in one of these articles the words which I could not readily trace to a root used in classic Greek. There were but eleven such words in an article of two columns, so truly is the Greek of to-day *Greek* and not Slavonic.

As to weddings, outside of Sparta, where women have still, as in classic times, more freedom and greater privileges than anywhere else in Greece, the general principle is, at every stage of the proceeding, a heavy discount upon the woman. When a girl is born, the sex is often concealed from the mother as long as possible, lest disappointment kill her outright. "Only a girl," is the despondent answer of the father to inquiring friends. A man is said to be "terribly poor," because with small property he has half a dozen daughters, whom he must, if possible, get married. Matches are usually arranged by the parents or relatives of the contracting parties. Usually the first advances come from the friends of the girl, who try to dispose of her here and there with as small a *dot* as possible. On the other hand, the young man waits to be courted. Even if he be really in love, he is taught to interpose objections and to seem reluctant, that thus he may secure the offer of a larger marriage portion. Often the bride and groom have never seen each other more than once or twice when they meet at the altar.

The student finds again and again delightful illustrations of the Greek classics in Athenian customs and habits of to-day.

Thucydides gives us a vivid description of the half-playful way in which the Athenian soldiers, forced by stress of weather to land in the harbor off the island of Sphacteria (the modern Navarino), set to work, at Demosthenes's request, to fortify the point. He tells us that soldiers, bending over and clasping their hands low on their backs, took, in the receptacle thus formed, loads of mud for mortar, and of stone, which they carried up the hill to the wall. In Nikodemus Street, in Athens, I saw long lines of laborers carrying stones in precisely this same manner four or five rods, and up a narrow staging, to the masons at work on the walls of a new house. Some few of them wore a thick pad to protect the back, but most of them simply bent down, clasped their hands low on their hips behind, and were loaded by other laborers with three or four huge rough stones. The loose earth from the excavation was carried out in baskets strapped on the shoulders.

On a saint's day, in the vacant space close under the north wall of the Acropolis, we came upon a scene which was replete with suggestions of the Homeric sacrificial feast. A group of rather rough-looking men were roasting whole a sheep which they had just killed. At a little distance the grass, crimsoned with gore, showed where the victim's "head had been drawn back, while the sharp knife took away his strength." The pelt, just removed, lay close by. The carcass was spitted from the mouth straight through the body, one end of the spit resting on a huge stone, the other end in a forked stake driven for the purpose. A fire was burning under its whole length, and the master of ceremonies slowly turned it on the spit. A hastily improvised sausage had been made by stuffing some of the finely chopped liver, heart, etc., into the larger intestines; and we saw this broiling sausage, looking not at all unsavory, tasted by the cook as we stood watching

GREAT THEATRE OF DIONYSIUS.

the Homeric scene. Here was a suggestion that the process so often baldly translated "tasting the entrails" may have
been a rather savory sampling of tidbits,
after all. To make the picture completely Homeric, certain impatient youths had
cut up small pieces of the raw meat, had
"pierced them through with little spits,"
had "roasted them carefully," and were
"drawing them off the coals" as we came
upon the ground. But candor compels
the admission that priestly fillets and salted barley and pempobola nowhere appeared.

After the Acropolis and the Pnyx, perhaps no place at Athens has a deeper
charm from its associations than has the
Academy of Plato. We visited its site
one beautiful morning about the middle
of May. From my note-book I venture
to copy the description of our visit.

We walk two miles northwest from
the Acropolis to the olive groves that still
mark the place. The wheat harvest is
just finishing. Men are reaping with
toothed sickles. One or two poorly dressed women are gleaning in the corners of
the fields. Other women follow the reap-
ers, binding the sheaves. The olive-trees
are in blossom. In this warm climate,
wheat and barley ripen well under the

shade of these trees, and are commonly
sown in the orchards. We walk across
fields of wheat stubble, then over meadow-land, gay with yellow, blue, and red
flowers. We count twenty-three varieties of blossoming flowers, all brilliant of
hue. Then through groves of pomegran-
ates, with their great, solid, deep red blossoms, and on through vineyards, where
the blood red of the poppies contrasts beautifully with the tender green of the low-
trimmed vines. Large swallows skim
the fields in every direction, twittering
musically, reminding us of Anacreon's
love for this bird, still so common even
in the streets of Athens, and so well
loved by the people. Other birds sing
constantly in the groves. The tetix
chirps shrilly in the grass. Little brown
and green lizards dart here and there on
the low earth walls which separate the
fields. Immense old olive-trees, with
gnarled and knotted trunks hollow at
heart, remind us of those near Jerusalem.
Fig-trees send out branches which are an
intricate net-work of thick, clumsy shoots,
bending now this way, then that, at the
sharpest possible angle, regardless of all
laws of symmetry. Lovely cloud shadows rest on Salamis, and float up the
slopes of Mounts Ægaleos, Corydallus,

and Parnes. The mountains of Argolis are as blue as is the bay that lies rippling between them and us. To the southeast, above the thickly clustering roofs of the modern city, rises the steep, altar-like rock of the Acropolis, still crowned with the ruins of the Parthenon and the Erechtheum. Thus enthroned above the modern city, the citadel, with its matchless ruins, seems constantly to assert its undying

MARBLE THRONE IN THE DIONYSIAC THEATRE.

right to be regarded as Athens, to the utter oblivion of all which the nineteenth century has built below them. Across this same lovely landscape, to those temples, then perfect, and rearing their snowy splendor against the purple-gray background of Hymettus, in the pauses of their conversation were lifted the eyes of that group of earnest, clear-souled thinkers who talked with Plato in these very olive groves, on the banks of the Cephissus—the men whose calm, enthusiastic search for truth has rendered so illustrious these Academic shades that, through all ages, in all lands, the lovers of wisdom and of art have been fain to borrow from their groves the name "Academy."

The literature and history of Greece become doubly delightful to one who has seen all Attica and half of Greece from the summit of Mount Pentelicus, who has followed Pausanias and Leake and Curtius over all the boundaries of old Athens, who has read the plays of Æschylus and Sophocles and Aristophanes sitting in the old Dionysiac Theatre, on the very seats where sat the quick-eyed, keen enthusiasts for art who witnessed the first triumphs of these dramatists at that bright spring festival to which thronged all the intellect and fashion of young Europe; or, best of all, has ascended, morning, noon, and night, day after day, that airy Acropolis that presides over the modern city like the embodied memory of her glorious past. On this Acropolis the visitor shall learn, as only he who waits long and often there can learn, the soul-satisfying beauty of the ruins of the Parthenon, perfect in decay, mellowed to richest cream tint, the golden gift of this Southern sun, softened by time, and revealing in their exquisite proportions possibilities of harmony of which he had never before conceived, as the rays of the setting sun stream past these fluted columns, half filling the flutings with lines of shadow, and painting on other columns the graceful curves of this building, where curves took the place of rigid lines, and Plato's own "music of mathematics," and not the plumb-line, was the presiding genius as the temple rose.

There is a marvellous æsthetic exaltation in the effect produced on one by this perfect Greek architecture in the transparent, exhilarating atmosphere of Athens. Well might Aristophanes exclaim, "O thou, our Athens, violet-wreathed, brilliant, most enviable city !" Well might Euripides speak of the Athenians as "ever treading, with light and measured grace, through a clear, transparent air."

The last night of my stay at Athens was spent upon the Acropolis. The fascinating charm the perfect moonlight cast around me there was too strong to be broken. As I lay and gazed at the Parthenon, the strong, abiding beauty, the restful strength, of the Doric architecture took possession of me—a new revelation of harmony and delight. One could *feel* these mighty yet graceful columns bearing easily, yet bearing firmly and forever, and with the grace of conscious beauty and strength, the immense weight laid upon them. The perfect proportions of

THE PARTHENON.

the architecture seemed to me to throb in unison, and audibly to hymn themselves. It is but a half-step from such seen symmetry and harmony to harmonies audible and heard symphonies. Surely these architects were more than builders. They were musicians; and, like the other great tone-masters, they send the key-notes and sub-tones of harmony thrilling through you in presence of their work, until you feel new meaning in the coldly perfect phrase, "Architecture is frozen music."

Spare, nervous, thin of face, restless-eyed, quick and energetic of speech, is the modern Athenian. The groups of men who seat themselves toward evening at the little tables which fill the streets before the principal cafés, as they talk politics over their little cups of black coffee or their glasses of water and wine, gesticulate with that energy of action in conversation which marks the passionate son of the South. Often the Athenian carries in his hand a string of beads, not for religious purposes, but that he may relieve himself of excessive electricity by shifting them through his fingers as he bargains and talks—a safety-valve and a re-assuring process akin to the Yankee's whittling. He is keenly sensitive to every word you utter, quick to take your meaning, and polite as a Frenchman in ready deference to your expressed opinion; but none the less he holds firmly to his own belief unless you have convinced his reason. This he may not tell you. He may leave you to infer that you have won him over ; and thus he has sometimes laid himself open to the charge of duplicity and deceit where he meant only to be credited with politeness.

The modern Greek has the Russian readiness in acquiring languages, and the German's patience in investigation, if some slight results can be seen as he works. But, like the hungry Yankee who gave up the attempt to earn a promised dinner by beating on the end of a log with the head of his axe, in his literary and antiquarian work the Athenian "must see the chips fly." Partly to this desire for immediate results, partly to the necessity of self-support, but still more to the utter lack of means and money for prosecuting researches and excavations, and publishing results, at government expense, is due the fact that the Germans have come to be regarded as better authorities upon the sites, the antiquities, and the history of Greece than are the Greeks themselves.

AN ATHENIAN GIRL.

Even a short residence at Athens, and the most superficial acquaintance with her university and its professors, will serve to convince one that many a German reputation has been built largely upon work done by Greeks, and that Athens does not lack for Greek scholars and antiquarians who, with such support in money and facilities for publication as the Germans receive, would soon become world-famous authorities, as they now are acknowledged masters in their departments, among those who know them. There is, unfortunately, a spirit of personal rivalry and petty jealousy among Athenian scholars, which has had a disastrous effect in preventing any united effort to present to the world connected results of Greek investigations.

With a university where fifteen hun-

dred students are instructed by an able faculty of sixty professors, with a high school for boys and another for girls, with a constantly improving system of primary schools, practically free, so that three-fourths of her children between the ages of five and sixteen are in school, Athens seems to be in no danger of undervaluing education. Pallas Atrutone, the Unwearied Power of Intellect, is still devoutly worshipped in the city over which preside the beauteous ruins of her matchless temple.

Many of the charges which have been brought against the good faith of the modern Greek, I believe to be purely the result of ignorant prejudice. Others may be traced to dishonest and defeated rivals in trade. The proverb sometimes heard in the Levant, "It takes two Jews to cheat a Turk, two Turks to cheat an Armenian, two Armenians to cheat a Greek," is not intended to be strictly complimentary to the honesty of the modern Greek. But in the East no trader ever asks the price for his goods which he expects to receive. Every bargain is presumed to be the result of a gradual approach of buyer and seller, who set out from the most widely separated limits, and make alternate concessions, until, after much arguing and gesticulation, with intervals of quiet smoking, common ground is reached at last, and the bargain is concluded. In no way could you so surely make a Levantine merchant miserable as by paying him all he at first demands. I have seen more of deliberate overcharging and barefaced dishonesty attempted in a day at Paris than I saw in two months while in Greece.

Of the glory of ancient Athens, of the world's great debt to Greece, every modern Athenian is keenly conscious. Memories of her glorious past have always been cherished religiously, kept alive during centuries of oppression.

Athens suffers from an excess of intellectual activity. The city is overstocked with brains. Its hands are idle. Greece has no great manufactories; it has no system of roads. Among the many failures of King Otho's reign, perhaps none was more injurious than his failure to provide any means of ready intercommunication between the provinces of Greece. Of course the topography of Greece—her mountain ranges and deep-reaching gulfs and bays—renders the task of road-building a difficult one. But national unity and material prosperity can not come without good roads. To-day, all Greece has but five miles of railroad, and hardly more than fifty miles of good carriage roads. Finding no outlet in the development of the country's material resources, all the energy of the marvellously active Greek mind has been turned to trade, to study, and to politics; and chiefly to politics, always a passion with the Athenian. With a territory but three-fifths as great as that of New York, with a population of nearly two millions, with universal suffrage, and with a monarchy so limited that the government is in reality a democracy in the administration of its internal affairs, the Greek nation of to-day devotes ten times too much energy to governing itself. This concentration of force within narrow limits begets heat at Athens. Un-

der such pressure, the political friction is something enormous. Athens supports from thirty to forty newspapers. Political clubs are more numerous than in classic days, and as influential. Every man of prominence has his newspaper, his club of personal followers, his petty party. When the death of Delegeorges, ex-Prime Minister, was announced on the street to a group of Athenian gentlemen with whom I was talking, the first remark was, "Ah, now Kurie So-and-So" (naming a politician of little influence) "will form a party, will he not?" Room for one more aspirant to office, with his organized clique of followers, was the argument.

Salaries for public services are of course pitifully low. Criticism of all official acts, and of every measure advocated by the government, is bitter and ceaseless. This spirit of criticism is not merely a healthful concern for the public welfare; it is the constant effort to induce a public, ever prone to change its political leaders, so to clamor as to put the "ins" out, and to give to other men a chance at what must be for them too a brief tenure of power. Acrimonious attacks upon men and motives abound. The newspapers give room to angry opponents for virulent personal diatribes against political rivals. The irrepressible life and mental activity of the nation preys upon itself.

Give Greece a mission; let her hope for that influence in the re-adjustment of power after Turkey's approaching dissolution (if the chronic "sick man" is indeed soon to die) which justly belongs to her as the most intelligent, the most enterprising, the most highly civilized race of the Levant; extend her boundaries, as we hope the great powers will soon do; give but a gleam of distant hope to such enthusiastic patriots as joined the club some time since organized at Athens by Makrakes, a shrewd political and religious agitator, which professes for its object to place Prince Constantine, King George's oldest son, on the throne of all Greece at Constantinople—and the truly great qualities of this wonderful race, which were proved to be still hers by the gallant, unflinching heroism displayed in her struggle for independence, but which have suffered a temporary eclipse since that struggle closed, will once more be displayed to a world which has so often been inspired by the words and deeds of the Greeks of ancient times.

MY DISCOVERIES IN TIBET

THE GOVERNOR'S PALACE AT SHIGATSE

Victorian Memorial Medal, R.G.S., and the Karl Ritter Medal, Berlin Geographical Society

OF Lake Manasarowar, on whose shores we spent a month after my discovery of the two-thousand-mile-long chain of mountains (described in the August number of this Magazine) a book could be written. The eight monasteries alone would take up several chapters. But the briefest account will have to suffice for the present. Neither shall I have time to recount some of our many dangerous adventures on this journey round about Rakastal (Tibetan: Lagang Tso). Perpetual southwest storms rage on this lake, whose depths vary like its coasts, and it was on this account that I was only able to carry out three soundings, each full of danger. A truly picturesque journey was the one we made to a rock island popping out of the lake. We had a fair wind out there, and started for the lee shore, but had I known what a sea there was off the island I should never have gone there with the boat. On landing we all three

took a refreshing bath, as the boat was literally thrown up on the rocky edge of the shore. It was out of the question to attempt to get back to the camp, and we had to pass the chilly night as best we could without extra clothing or provisions.

One of my most remarkable experiences of this journey, which was already so full of experiences and adventures, was our wandering round the holy Kailas, or Kang Rimpoche, as the Tibetans call that mountain. The Hindus are convinced that Siva lives in his paradise on the top of it, and only occasionally do the gods descend to the banks of the Manasarowar to adopt the form of a white swan and to swim across its silvery depths. Kailas is regarded as especially holy by the Tibetans, being reputed to be the domicile of "the higher gods, placed starlike beyond the realms of space." From the Kham mountains on the extreme east, from Naktsong and Amdo, from the black tents which like spots on the hide of a panther spread out in the desolate valleys of Tibet, and from Ladak in the far western mountains, thousands of pilgrims come yearly on foot and, deeply meditating, slowly wander the four miles round this the holiest of all the mountains of the earth. I too wandered round Kang Rimpoche by the pilgrim's route. I saw their dusky train, of all ages and sexes, men with wives and children, old people who, before they died, were desirous of winning this last favor, tatterdemalions, cutthroats who had some sin to do penance for, priests and nomads, a perpetual multicolored stream of people passing along the gravel-strewn road leading to the realms of eternal light and consolation far beyond the valley of death. Often the old folks' hope is deceived, death coming to claim them before their goal is attained. I saw one old man who had recently terminated his earthly wanderings and whose body lay stiff and cold between granite blocks by the wayside. All the religious duties, all the superstitious hocus-pocus the pilgrims have to go through, I will not touch upon now. That must be a new chapter, full of mysticism; nor will I describe the temples, which, like precious stones set in a ring, are studded along the pilgrims' path round the mountain. I can well understand that the Tibetans considered Kang Rimpoche as a holy sanctuary, for in its very shape the mountain bears a striking likeness to a *tjorten,* one of those monuments round the temples which have been erected to the memory of deceased Great Lamas, and it also recalls the Tashi Lama's tomb in Tashi Lhumpo, covered with silver, gold, and jewels.

It took us three days to do the four miles round the mountain. Personally I rode most of the way, but my four men from Ladaki, who are also lamaists, went on foot and fulfilled to the letter an orthodox pilgrim's duties. Once we passed two young lamas from Kham on the road. They did not walk like ordinary pilgrims, but literally measured off the distance with their own bodies. Lying down full length on the ground, they would join their hands over their heads and read a prayer, then make a mark on the road, arise, join their hands together

again over their heads, and muttering a prayer, take a few steps forward to the mark, to fall full length once again and repeat the entire ceremony all the way round the mountain. Performed in this manner by "prostration" the journey took twenty days. The two lamas we saw had only done about half the distance, and they contemplated doing the whole journey twice. *One* such journey is worth thirty ordinary journeys on foot. I asked them what they expected to gain by it, and they replied that after death they would sit in the seats of the gods of Kang Rimpoche and in their presence for eternity. They had spent a whole year on the journey from Kham, and their home was situated several months' journey beyond Lhasa. One of them was to return there after having completed his duty as pilgrim. The other—he was barely twenty years old—was to pass the remainder of his earthly life in a dark grotto on the banks of the Upper Tsangpo.

Few forms of self-mortification are of such value as this life spent in the dark, this absolute separation from the world, from one's fellow men and the light of the sun. In Linga-gunpa I obtained much valuable information regarding this curious custom. In the prayer grotto at that place—a little stone hut at the foot of a cliff—was then a lama who had already been immured for three years. No one knew him, no one knew whence he came nor what his name was, and even were one to know his name it was forbidden to mention it before human beings. But they told me that the day he went into the grotto he was followed in most solemn procession by all the red monks of the monastery, and when all the ceremonies prescribed in the holy books had been gone through, the narrow entrance into the grotto had been closed up again. We were standing outside it. I asked the head lama whether he could hear us talk. He replied, "Oh no, he can neither hear nor see; he is sunk night and day in profound meditation." "How do you know that he is alive?" "The food [*tsamba*] which is passed in to him once a day through an underground passage is eaten up by the morning; but should we find the dish untouched one morning, then we should understand that he had died." A stream flows through

LADAK CHIEFS WHO ACCOMPANIED US IN NORTHERN TIBET

the cave in the daytime; by this means he gets water.

How wonderful! For days and weeks I could not drive the picture of this lama out of my mind. Never to hear a human voice, never get a glimpse of the sun, never to see the difference between night and day, only to know of the approach of winter by the lowering of the temperature. I pictured to myself the day when he was entombed in the cave. He sat there alone and watched them fill up the opening with blocks of stone—the light growing continually less, till finally only a tiny little hole was left. Through this he took his last farewell of the sun, and when that too was finally closed up he remained in complete and utter darkness. Since that time three years had now elapsed. In another temple, like Linga absolutely unknown by Europeans, a lama had lived immured in this manner for sixty-nine years! And I heard of many other similar experiences full of enchanting mysticism. Their idea is as follows: What is a short earthly life in the dark to an eternity in the broad light? The sojourn in the dark is only a preparation for that which is to follow. Cut off from the outer world and its temptations, never for a moment disturbed by the outer light, alone the year through, the meditating lama seeks for the answer to the riddle of life—and of death. When he first goes into the dark he knows that he will never leave the grotto until his shrivelled body is carried out by other monks—perhaps a new generation, those who followed him in silent procession to his cave being long since dead. And during all these years, even though it be a man's whole lifetime, no one may visit him but death. To the outer world he is dead, dead from the moment he is entombed in the cave. For his friends and acquaintances he exists no more. And yet he is still alive in there—had not one man survived for sixty-nine years? He longs to be delivered from life, but still must sit and wait, for decade after decade, it may be, until at last death comes and stretches forth both hands to him and leads him out of the dark amid "a burst of psalm from the eternal choir."

Like all lamas, from the Tashi Lama downwards, the recluse must die in a sitting position. But as he is alone and will probably become senseless before the actual moment of death, a small wooden frame is introduced into the cave at the same time as himself, into which he can creep so soon as he feels death approaching. This will prevent him from falling forwards or to one side, and he will be found in the same holy position in which Buddha is depicted in all the thousands upon thousands of portraits of him we find scattered throughout the temples of Tibet. How should I who have come here to study the geography of the land have either time or ability to attempt to fathom the mysteries of Lamaism or to solve the maze of their highly complicated religious teaching? I should certainly have been incapable of succeeding in any way whatsoever, and leave the science of religion without a shade of jealousy to those who are learned in its mysteries. But at all events I have visited and described thirty-one temples in Tibet—described the different halls of their temples and holies of holies, their most important idols; and what is quite new, have hundreds of sketches of interiors and exteriors of these temples. I have collected material for a most detailed account of the daily life of the lamas, their studies, their classes, their daily services in the temples, and their feasts. Everywhere I was received with friendly hospitality; even in a nunnery no opposition was offered to my visit. All through Tibet the life of these monks

has appealed to me and filled me with delight beyond anything I can say. Everything is so picturesque, so unusual, and so rich in color. Why does not some painter come out here instead of sitting at home painting cows and farmyards?

But the most delightful thing in all Tibet is the church music. Fresh young voices, softened by thick dark draperies along the front of an open gallery, pour forth their wonderful hymns, full of peace and love and longing. Betweenwhiles you hear the rumbling thunder of the bassoon and the rhythmical clash of the cymbals, then the flutes with their shrill melodies, and the rolling drums which echo through the high halls of the temples. But the singing is by far the most beautiful—it carries one up and away from the troubles of this earth.

Perhaps what I saw of greatest interest was in Tashi Lhumpo—the great feasts; the doctors' disputations in the presence of the Tashi Lama; processions of hundreds of nuns, who, bareheaded and with their hair cut short like men, would go in a long procession up to the holy Labrang to receive the Tashi Lama's blessing; the dance of devils, and all those other dances which are danced, to keep off evil spirits; the daily lessons when the Kandjut's massive writings were read in a sort of singing tone by masses of lamas in gold mantles, sitting on divans between red columns and hanging, many-

OUR COOLIES AWAITING THE START ACROSS THE ICE

LADAKIES CROSSING THE ICE ON A SOUNDING EXPEDITION

hued temple banners, while the gilded gods, faintly lit up by oil lamps, looked down smiling upon them.

These monasteries and their life are very much alike all over Tibet, and for that matter all over the rest of the world of the Lamaists—and yet how unlike one another are these different temples! I never tired of them, as I always found something new. Lagang has undoubtedly the finest temple hall. One steps in out of the dazzling sunlight and has only to rest a moment in order to get accustomed to the dark. From a lofty opening in the roof the daylight creeps in, faint and pale. From between a double row of columns hangs a perfect forest of temple banners, sacrificial ribbons, and other draperies. On the sides are the drums and other instruments, and against the walls are red and gold bookshelves, carved and varnished, bearing the gigantic volumes of Kandjut and other holy books. Against the far wall, facing the entrance, is the place for the portrait of the gods, and on long narrow tables set out in front of them are the sacrificial offerings, prepared in brass dishes burnished until they shine like the reddest gold. Between them burn oil lamps, vainly endeavoring to conquer the gloom, and from the burning sticks of incense pale blue spirals of smoke mount towards the roof and vanish in a thin cloud of vapor. In the hall there prevails a mystic twilight,—everything is so full of an overpowering mystery, all is so still, so quiet,

that one hardly dares to whisper; I could sit there on a divan by the hour and just dream away the time. How often while there did I not think of Uspenski Sabor in Moscow?—and in reality Lamaism is the Catholicism of Buddhism. From time to time the monks creep around, barefoot, bareheaded, and wearing their red Roman togas: they fill the sacrificial dishes with water and *tsamba*, they snuff the smoking wicks of the butter lamps and put the incense sticks straight, and have a thousand and one things to do in the service of the gods. Silently they draw near to us, and, using a peacock's feather, sprinkle with holy water out of a silver vessel those of my men from Ladak who are with me.

This is only a slight hint of all the wonderful things we saw in Tibetan temples, a few rough notes from memory, for I cannot manage to turn over my journal; nor can I speak of the wonderful cloister town of Tashi-gembe with all its temples and halls, filled with gold, and silver gods, and its hall of knights with its old armaments, breastplates, masks, halberds, and battle-axes hanging in tasteful array on the columns. Neither have I time to describe a magnificent mass we attended for the repose of the soul of a head lama of the first magnitude, a *rimpoche*, eighty years of age, who duly died in a sitting posture with burning lights in his hand.

All these strange pictures rush through

LADAKIES ASSEMBLING FOR THEIR EVENING MEAL

my memory in a whirl of variegated color, a carnival of masks and gold-embroidered clothes, rolling drums and playing flutes, clashing cymbals and red and gold banners on high poles, novices bearing on their shoulders long brass-bound copper bassoons, and innumerable lamas, the priesthood of Tibet, in their red dress, offering their greetings and their service to the gods. Tibet is essentially a religious land. There is no end to the temples, which are generally built on the top of some picturesque mountain, from whose rocky sides their stone walls painted in white and red would seem to have sprung, and from whose roof one can always enjoy the most perfect view over the valleys, rivers, and lakes which lie spread out beneath, as though one were looking down on a map.

It is as I have said—sanctuaries are to be found everywhere, on every pass; even the smallest tracks have their *kla*, a pyramid of stones surrounded by several of smaller size. In these posts are planted, and strings running from the one to the other bear a host of smaller banners, each covered with the holiest of prayer inscriptions: "*on mane padme hum.*" On the cliffs of the roadside red and white cubical *tjortens* have been erected, all covered with rags, *kada-ko*, and other sacrificial offerings. Moreover, one often finds hewn in the polished face of the granite cliffs, worn smooth by the wind and the weather, huge statues of Buddha, and on the smooth rock one sees in giant letters the eternal formula, "*on mane padme hum,*" the six syllables each of which contains an ocean of deep, unfathomable meaning, and which collectively open the way to a higher and happier form of existence. We ride past *mane-ringmos* nearly daily—those stone walls parallel with the road, often one hundred metres long and densely covered with figures, in which with inimitable and untiring patience has been wrought the wonder-working formula, "*on mane pad-me hum.*" These *manes* are often picturesque in the highest degree. At either end is a small cubical tower with a niche, in the dimness of which the wayfarer may see a small figure of a god, frequently a work of great artistic workmanship. On these innumerable altars are often also laid out masses of yak skulls and skulls of wild sheep and antelopes. On the horns and the sun-bleached skull of the yak you will see engraven the eternal formula, and the letters filled in with red or one of the other sacred colors. On every house-top in the towns and villages a perfect forest of small poles with strings of banners are arranged, and as the banners are of the brightest and loudest of colors they remind one of carnival confetti.

At every point where highways cross the Tsangpo and other rivers and where ferries supply the caravans such flag-poles and heaps of *kla* are set up.

In each caravan at least one of the men and probably several have praying-sticks in their hands. With the help of a weight it is wound round the handle of the axle and stuffed full of strips of paper, on each of which the holy formula is printed thousands upon thousands of times. The whole day long, no matter how long the journey may last, the faithful whirls his praying-machine and at the same time mumbles in a singsong voice, *" on mane padme hum."*

On leaving Shigatse we were followed by an escort of Chinese and Tibetans. The former carried with them a portable temple with an altar table for the gods and a narrow table for dishes, lamps, and incense-burners. The interior of their temple tent was really very decorative, with its golden gods gleaming through the haze of smoke—the lamps shaded by steam. And in the evening they sang, the voices accompanied by drums and cymbals.

Thus into the Tibetan's life is woven a succession of religious duties. When he rides past a heap of sacrificial stones he adds a stone to it; when he passes a *mane* stone he never forgets to leave it on the right-hand side, otherwise he cannot have its prayers in his favor; when he passes one of the holy mountains he does not neglect to fall flat and touch the ground with his forehead, and when he is loading up his yak he mumbles his eternal *" on mane padme hum."* These words ring in my ears continual-ly; I hear them when I lie down to rest and when I get up, and not even in the most desolate country can I get free from them; for even my men from Ladak sing them. They belong to Tibet, these words; I cannot imagine the barren plains without them; they are as closely associated with the country as is the hum of bees with a beehive—as the roar of the west wind and the daily storms.

The spiritual meaning and the object of all these flagpoles, stone heaps, etc., is really to keep the powers of evil at bay, to render the journey over a high pass lucky, to protect the traveller crossing a river from drowning, to keep

AN IMPROVISED SLEIGH USED IN CROSSING LAKE NGANGTSE-TSO

RIDERS COSTUMED FOR THE NEW-YEAR'S GAMES AT SHIGATSE

the evil spirits of the air from your dwelling, and in the desert to protect the wayfarer from robbers and attack by wolves. They therefore play the same rôle in the open air as the four spiritual kings in the temple. For it must be mentioned that there is not a temple in Tibet the walls of whose outer halls are not decorated with paintings of these four potentates, often executed with great skill and in screaming Oriental colors. They are armed with clubs, swords, and other weapons, while their faces are contorted in the most diabolical and terrifying manner; their hair is a perfect forest of red serpents, and sheets of flame burst from their sides; the object being to frighten away evil spirits, who would otherwise find their way into the halls of the temple and disturb the peace of the gods.

It would be most interesting to insert into a map of the whole Lamaistic world the great highroads used by pilgrims on their journeys. In the far north one would find numerous ways meeting—like the spokes of a wheel—in the temple of Da-Kuren Majdaris in Urga. But the radii would be even denser around the most famous of all the lama sanctuaries,

Lhasa. They are somewhat scarcer round Tashi Lhumpo, for but few people yield the palm of sanctity to the Tashi Lama when there is question of his brother, the Dalai Lama. We should find many ways meeting in Kang Rimpoche—the holy Kailas,—and between these stars of first magnitude the map would show a number of minor stars, from the heart of each and all of which comes a call to the faithful—a call in some measure akin to the warning in Isaiah (xxxiii, 20): "Look upon Zion, the city of our solemnities: thine eyes shall see Jerusalem. . . ."

From the tent encampments of the Kalmuks on the Volga, from the land of the Tunguses in the north, from the river valleys of the Buriats in East Siberia, from the Mongolian grass steppes, from the regions of the Himalayas: Ladak, Nepal, Sikkim, and Bhutan, and from the countries on the borders of Sechuan and Yunnan—from all the unknown world of Lamaism the whole year round pilgrims are coming to the holy places of Tibet. And throughout half Asia one hears in a sort of undercurrent to the life and wanderings of men the eternal "*on mane padme hum*"—a phrase of a greater frequency than any *Pater noster* or *Ave Maria*.

But Lamaism, like Catholicism, has also its shady side. I will not refer to that now. Peter's pence flourish in Tashi Lhumpo as well as in Rome, and it is well not to travel without money or gifts. Priests dole out holiness for coin, and the rich dwell in the choicest rooms of the cloisters. Many temples are rich, owning large properties and herds.

High up in Chang-tang we met the first lamas of the brotherhood of wandering monks, who throughout their lives wander from end to end of the Lamaist world, not only in Tibet, but far out into foreign lands, living the while on alms. Sometimes they collected together in groups and performed religious dances and songs in front of my tent, with rattles, gongs, wands, and minstrelsy. Sometimes we even met wandering nuns soliciting alms. They traverse incredible distances on foot and beg their way from tent to tent. In those districts of Tibet lying fairly low on either side of the great rivers, where the land is cultivated and gardens surround the villages, one can often see women, alone or in pairs, going about amongst the houses, showing a large painting, supported on poles, about whose religious subject they sing, not infrequently in clear, resonant voices.

And finally let me mention yet another group of faithful and even more egoistical servants of the religion. I refer to the hermits, those holy men who are independent of all temples or cloisters, and spend their lives in lonely grottos, living on the alms given to them by neighboring nomads. I saw one such grotto on a perpendicular cliff over one hundred and sixty feet from the ground. A pitch-black path led sheer up to it inside the mountain. The hermit had already lived there three years without seeing a fellow human being, but his cave was open towards the valley and the sun streamed into it. He was considered very holy, and two brothers and two nuns from Nepal considered it a great honor to live in a cave beneath his and attend to his material wants. Both women were remarkable for their wild picturesque beauty, but the moment mention was made of a photographic

camera they vanished into the dim heart of the mountain. I only managed to see the hermit through a crack in the floor of his cave and heard him mumbling his lengthy prayers. What an extraordinary world of superstition and bigotry! Volumes have been written about it ever since the time when the Capuchin and Jesuit monks first visited Tibet. For the future I shall only describe what I saw with my own eyes— things of which I possess some few proofs, apart from my memory.

In Diri-pu-gunpa, due north of the summit of Kailas from which the peculiar Tetrahedron showed itself like a white spectre between two dark granite cliffs, I broke off to seek for the source of the Indus. But I first had to go down and see how the caravan was getting on, for we had also political difficulties to wrestle with, and I wished to be sure that the men were not getting up to some fatal mischief.

I managed to obtain permission from the authorities in Barkha to make a détour to the north with five men and six horses. It proved a most remarkable flying trip, at once instructive and adventurous in the highest degree, and through an absolutely unknown land. And one night we camped beside the spot where the source of the Indus flows out of the mountain, a spot called by the Tibetans Singi-kabap—*i. e.*, "the mouth out of which the Indus comes forth." This spot is holy in their eyes: piles of stones and cairns are erected there; on a stone platform a well-carved idol was placed, and I was heathen enough to take it with me. To augment the good fortune of that day my huntsman Tundup shot an *Ovis ammon,* with great twisted horns, quite near the source of the Indus.

Perhaps you can picture to yourselves with what feelings of deep gratitude and joy I stood here and watched the source of the Indus flow out from the bosom of the mountain. I stood and watched this unpretentious brook tumbling down the valleys, and thought of the various vicissitudes it would experience before finally in a perpetual crescendo of song it ended by rushing out in a burst of music between cliffs into the ocean, where the steamers in Karachi are lying, loading and unloading their goods. I thought of its restless journey through Tibet, through Ladak and Baltistan, past Skardu, where apricot trees grow on the banks and hang over the water, through Dardistan and Kuhistan, past Peshawar, and over the plains of the western Punjab, to lose itself finally in the salt ocean, the Nirvana and eternal resting-place of all rivers. I stood and wondered over Alexander of Macedonia, who, crossing the Indus twenty-two hundred years ago, had a distant notion where its source was to be found, and I rejoiced in the consciousness of being the first European to set foot at the source of the Indus. In spite of all the difficulties which highly placed personages attempted to put in my way, even higher powers had accorded me the triumph of discovering the source of both the Brahmaputra and the Indus, the origin of both these world-famous rivers, which like the nippers of a crab enclose the mightiest chain of mountains in the world, the Himalayas. Their initial streams are fed by the heavens, and their mighty masses of water pour down in torrents to the lowlands, bringing life and nourishment to half a hundred million children of men. Up here the temples stand silent and white on its shores, in India pagodas and mosques reflect themselves in her waters; up here in Tibet wolves, antelopes, and wild sheep roam along both rivers, down there in the lowlands the eyes of the tiger and leopard glisten like red-hot coal within the jungle that lies on their border. I fancied myself standing and listening to the lapping of the waters of time, to the murmurings of countless human destinies and innumerable generations, which were born, which lived, and which died on the banks of these rivers; and not without pride, although in humble gratitude, I realized I was the first white man to set foot on the source of the Indus and Brahmaputra since the day Noah came out of the ark.

From the source of the Indus I continued my journey northeast right up to the thirty-second degree of latitude through quite unknown country and without any official escort whatsoever. Even had they looked for us we should not have been easy to find, for it is about a five days' march through trackless country

between the villages of tents. A quantity of interesting information was collected here as to the cotton trade carried on with Indians and Ladaks. Finally I turned west-southwest direct to Gartok, which was reached on September 26, and where I found all well with the head caravan. It was half a year to a day of my leaving Shigatse.

The map I constructed during the expedition up to the present time includes 765 sheets, nearly every one representing hitherto unknown land. Notes take up 4900 pages, 60 astronomical points have been ascertained, 990 specimens of mineral have been collected, and many hundred drawings of panoramas made; for at every camping-place and even often between camps I drew in everything to be seen in the landscape in order to be able to give a faithful picture of its general character. As material for illustration I have further several hundred photographs and over five hundred pen drawings. A meteorological journal has been kept without a break from the beginning, and observations taken three times a day. Although this journey has not lasted two years, its geographical results are richer and more important than those obtained during the whole of my last journey (1899-1902), and are richer than those accruing from any other journey hitherto taken in Tibet. In Tibet proper I have now spent fifteen months, although the British government attempted to prevent my entering the country and obliged me to make that long northerly détour, whilst the Chinese and Tibetan governments did their utmost to drive me out.

Our minister in Tokio, Mr. Wallenberg, during his visit to Peking, did everything he could at the cost of much time and trouble to persuade the leading men of China to give me liberty in Tibet, but both he and the Japanese legation in Peking, who most amiably attempted to speak on my behalf, were met with an absolute refusal. In a word, during all my career I never found myself in such a political imbroglio, and the most wonderful part is that everything went off as well as it did.

Finally, to add a few words about the earth's surface in Tibet, I will say that the material we have now in our possession affords a sufficiently clear and concise exposition of the orographical constitution of the country, with its five great mountain chains: Kwen-lun, Arkatagh, Kara-korum, Nin-Chen Tangla, and the Himalayas, together with the innumerable smaller, more or less broken chains between them, a world of mountain roads, to a great extent running west and east, with a strong divergence in the latter direction. With the assistance of all the calculations of height collected, we could easily discover the average height of the plateaux and of the mountain passes. I ascertained the exact height of all passes, lakes, river fords, and camps during my journeys by boiling-thermometers and three aneroids. It is of especial interest to note the enormous rise of the ground north of the Brahmaputra, where one first expected a comparatively flat plateau. Further, having found the sources of all the great rivers, we could draw out the boundaries of the central district having no outlet to the ocean, and calculate its area.

The source of the Hwang-ho was discovered by Prjevalski, the northern arm of the Yangtse-Kiang by Wellby, and the southern by Rockhill; the sources of the Indo-Chinese rivers are also known, although parts of their courses (the Yangtse-Kiang's and the middle Brahmaputra's in particular) have never been thoroughly explored. The geologists of the future will find in this part of the world a perfect Eldorado of the most magnificent, most difficult, and most alluring problems.

As regards the political point of view Tibet is marching towards a new epoch. Things looked black for a while when the English forced their way into the country three years ago, but of that exploit hardly an echo is to be heard today. The Chinese dragon has fixed his claws on the country with a greater energy than ever before in the two or three hundred years during which the lamas have recognized the Son of Heaven as their protector.

Not so long ago China paid the second third of the war indemnity to England, and after the last has been paid (1908),* the English will have

* The last portion of the indemnity has now been paid, and the Chumbi valley evacuated by the British troops.

to clear out of the Chumbi valley, which really from a geographical point of view belongs to India. Afterwards it will cost several decades and millions of pounds to regain the prestige which is now totally lost in Tibet. The Chinese have reaped all the advantages of Younghusband's mission, and a future "mission" of the same sort will come to mean, not a military promenade across the Himalayas, but war with China.

For me personally the policy of the Liberal cabinet in London has been of great advantage. Though an attempt was made to hinder my journey, I have maintained my position for fifteen months in Tibet. For a time, indeed, the authorities were kind enough to close the whole frontier of India and Tibet in order to give me a unique opportunity to collect all the valuable discoveries I have now made.

Unconsciously and for no conceivable reason I was protected from every sort of competition, and what that means to an "explorer" in an unknown land it is impossible to tell. My friends in India were prevented by loyalty to their home government from doing what they would have wished to further my plans, but I know that their keenest sympathy follows me on my journey. And yet it would not astonish me if there were those amongst the younger generation of Englishmen in India, who long to distinguish themselves and go out to meet strange destinies and adventures, who complain bitterly that *they*, for purely political reasons, are shut out from Tibet, whilst *I*, a Swede, can wander round the country, free as any young wild ass.

But enough for this time. Winter is waiting outside my tent with a temperature that already sinks to 24.8 degrees. Merchants from Lhasa, who were here for the yearly market, are breaking up their homes daily, and one hears their horses' bells jingling in the cold air.

The two Garpons, or Viceroys of western Tibet, will presently betake themselves to warmer climes, and the nomads are scattering to the four quarters of the globe. Wild geese are seeking a more hospitable neighborhood.

Gartok is becoming a desert, and I and my fellows are also ready to break up camp.